THE BEING OF
THE BEAUTIFUL

THE BEING OF THE BEAUTIFUL

Plato's Theaetetus, Sophist, and Statesman

Translated and with Commentary by

Seth Benardete

The University of Chicago Press • Chicago and London

The University of Chicago Press, Chicago 60637
The University of Chicago Press, Ltd., London
© 1984 by The University of Chicago
All rights reserved. Published 1984
Paperback edition 2006
Printed in the United States of America
15 14 13 12 11 10 09 08 07 06   2 3 4 5

ISBN-13: 978-0-226-67038-6 (paper)
ISBN-10: 0-226-67038-4 (paper)

Library of Congress Cataloging-in-Publication Data

Plato.
    The being of the beautiful.

    Bibliography: p.
    Includes index.
    1. Plato. Theaetetus.   2. Plato. Sophistes.
3. Plato. Politicus.   4. Knowledge, Theory of—Early
works to 1800.   5. Logic—Early works to 1800.
6. Meaning (Philosophy)—Early works to 1800.
7. Political science—Early works to 1800.   I. Benardete,
Seth.   II. Title.
B358.B46   1984   184   83-18318

For Arnaldo Momigliano

Contents

Acknowledgments

I began work on this book while holding a fellowship from the National Endowment for the Humanities in 1972. I am grateful as well to both New York University and the Department of Philosophy in the Graduate Faculty of the New School for Social Research—to the former for allowing me and to the latter for offering me the opportunity to teach courses on single works of Plato and Aristotle for most of the last eighteen years at the New School. Among the students and friends who have read the whole or parts of this book and suggested many improvements: Allan Bloom, Ronna Burger, Michael Davis, Richard Kennington, Jacob Stern, and Stewart Umphrey. I am particularly indebted to Paulette Mancuso for the great care she took in getting the manuscript ready for the press.

*Plato says: One is not even one, two is
one hardly.*

Theopompus fr. 15K

Introduction

A bibliography of Platonic studies for the years 1958–75 lists 3,326 items; of these 102 are indexed as dealing with the *Theaetetus*, 118 with the *Sophist*, and 21 with the *Statesman*. Since the difficulties of the *Statesman* (cf. 284C), as to its plan and intention, are not less than either of the other two dialogues, the disparity in the number of items can only have resulted from the assumption that epistemology and metaphysics, with which the *Theaetetus* and the *Sophist* in some sense deal, can be cleanly separated from political philosophy. It is the purpose of this book to show that such a separation, however plausible it may appear to be, is wholly mistaken for Plato in general and for these dialogues in particular.

The book is arranged as follows. A justification for the kind of translation given here opens up into a broad consideration of the reasons for presenting these three dialogues together, from which it is concluded that Plato's perplexity before the beautiful, which the *Hippias Major* articulates, would be the best introduction to them. A brief guide to the translations precedes them; the dialogues follow, each with its own notes and commentary. The commentaries of course are not entirely self-contained but link each dialogue with the other two in a connected interpretation.

I

Of the three Platonic dialogues that are here translated, the title of the first one is a proper name and does not need to be translated, but simply transcribed. The titles of the other two do need to be translated and yet can only be translated misleadingly. *Sophist* cannot be bettered as a translation of *Sophistês*, nor *Statesman* of *Politikos*, but in the former case the translation carries with it the pejorative meaning that Plato more than anyone else gave it. Hence the translation anticipates the original, for the word *sophistês,* though it can mean something as disparaging as "wise guy," can also mean someone wise simply and be applied to those as respectable as Zeus and the seven wise men of Greece. In the case of the *Politikos* the difficulties increase, for if "statesman" is decomposed, neither part fits the original, in which there is neither state nor man. *Politikos* could more literally be rendered "politician," if its disparaging tone were not as prominent as in "sophist." If the word were to be translated strictly, it would need to be double-barreled: the *politikos* is both the political being and he who is skilled in political things. Since, then, perfect accuracy is precluded in either case, one falls back on the usual translation and issues a warning that both "sophist" and "statesman" are to be taken more neutrally than either appears to be.

The two principles of translation, which have just been illustrated, do not consist with one another. One is the principle of all imitative art: that the translation appear to let the original shine through and leave no tell-tale sign of its own unoriginality. The second principle is that everything in the original be rendered as it is in the original, for the sake of keeping the original at its proper distance. The inevitable conflict, therefore, between the idiomatic and the literal cannot except speciously be resolved. The verb *sumpheromai* means either "move together" or "agree," but the perfect translation "concur" obliterates the double meaning while containing both. In the case of Plato, however, this conflict does not have to be resolved perfectly in order to show how Plato himself practiced in his writing these two same principles of translation. It was a necessary consequence of his showing philosophy in the city.

Plato has Socrates call philosophy "dialectics." The word is derived from the active and the middle of a verb whose nominal cognate is the word for speech (*logos*), and whereas the middle *dialegesthai* is the ordinary word for "to converse," its far less common active *dialegein* means "to separate and divide."[1] The twofold character of all speaking as both communication and separation is, as Heraclitus was the first to point out, as ultimately inconsistent as the two principles of translation. What Plato, however, managed to do was to bring such a surface consistency between the speech of dialogue and the speech of thinking that he could represent simultaneously both the indispensable agreement between philosophy and nonphilosophy and the partial dissolution of that agreement in the ascent from opinion toward knowledge. Signs of this ascent are the sudden appearances of the literal in the context of the idiomatic no less than of the idiomatic in the context of the literal.

The double aspect of speech is an inseparable difference. In the following exchange from the *Sophist,* Plato points to this without calling any attention to it. "It's unreasonable (*alogon*)," the stranger says, or "it makes no sense to fail to divide the art of hunting"; and Theaetetus replies, "Speak (*lege*) at what point." *Alogon* means literally "without speech," either in the sense of speechless—in modern Greek it is the name for a horse—or in that of something's incapacity to be stated in a speech; but it is only the juxtaposition of the cognate "speak" that reveals speech as essentially both an activity of dividing and of sharing, of *dialegein* and *dialegesthai.* That the distinction the stranger then makes perplexes Theaetetus—he doubts whether one of them is—shows in turn the inevitable interference that the practice of both leads to. To follow the *logos* means to abandon communication for division (cf. *Sophist* 267D). Theaetetus, in this case, expresses his doubt by using the dual—"Why certainly, if, that is, both of the pair are." The dual, which designates a couple or a pair of things (e.g., the eyes or the ears), was already vanishing from Attic in Plato's time except for stereotyped phrases, and Plato seems to have revived it in order to stress the fact that there is no division unless there is a prior combination, which the division articulates but does not cancel (cf. *Epinomis* 978C–D). Plato therefore tends to use the dual both for the two speakers in a dialogue and for whatever is subject to discussion and hence division. This usage is so important that in this translation I have inserted "pair" or "paired," at the cost of some awkwardness, whenever at least one dual occurs in a sentence.

In these three dialogues, moreover, Plato connects the duality of speech with a word that at the peak of the *Sophist* designates the solution to the problem of nonbeing. In Greek, "other" is either *allo* or *heteron*. It is *heteron* if one is speaking of either one of a pair; it is *allo* if it is something else that has no other relation to that from which it is different except that it is different. The mutual relation that *heteron* implies often leads to its duplication, so that when the stranger remarks that both angler and sophist appear to him as a pair of hunters, Theaetetus says: "Of what hunting is the other? For we stated the other." Theaetetus' first "other" is the sophist, the second the angler. But the primacy of the angler, which is implied by the sophist being the other, is lost as soon as the sophist is said to be the other from which the angler is other. In order to bring this out as plainly as possible, *heteron* is always translated as "other"—"another" and "an other" are used to keep a pair of others apart—and *allo* never is, however convenient it would have been to do so. In most cases, it will be clear at a glance why "something other" is not "anything else" and vice versa, but not always, and the reader may feel that a distinction without a difference is being perpetrated. This cannot be helped if the translator is not always to decide on what does and what does not make a difference.

Perhaps the most obvious example of Plato's making words do double duty is *atekhnôs*. Literally, it is an adverb meaning "artlessly" (cf. *Sophist* 225C), but in everyday usage it means "simply." And yet in Plato it is always or almost always both simultaneously. In the *Ion,* the rhapsode Ion wants to learn from Socrates why he pays no attention to any poet except Homer and cannot contribute anything, "but I simply (*atekhnôs*) doze." Socrates' immediate answer is that he has no capacity to speak about Homer by art and knowledge (*Ion* 532C). The difficulty of translating *atekhnôs* has been finessed by always putting its literal meaning in parenthesis. In the case of *ontôs,* which literally means "beingly" and colloquially "really"—that it is colloquial is shown by its almost total absence from Aristotle—one has to decide on a translation and stick to it. The one adopted here, "in (its, his) being," is an awkward solution, for it sacrifices casualness for excessive precision, but that seemed better than "really," which fails, just as "concur" did, by camouflaging its own rightness.

The way in which the casual gets transformed into something strict is best illustrated by two words that in the third person singular are used to convey some degree of assent. *Eoike* literally means "it resembles" and, by extension, "it seems likely," and *phainetai* "it appears." But though both seem to be used interchangeably, one soon notices that they tend to come in pairs, and if the interlocutor first says *eoike, phainetai* will often be his next reply. This peculiarity would seem to be a sign of Plato's indulgence in variety for its own sake were it not that in the *Sophist,* the stranger's puzzlement before the sophist results from his distinction between two arts, one of which is derived from *eoike* and the other from *phainetai.* Indeed, the problem itself is precipitated by Theaetetus' saying *eoiken* (236D), even though the stranger, while still calling his attention to the problem, does not call his attention to the peculiar appropriateness to the problem of what Theaetetus said. The stranger contrasts Theaetetus' *eoiken* with his own *ontôs,* which occurs both before and after Theaetetus' reply.

Pantapasin men oun is an emphatic form of assent, and though it resists a literal translation it could be translated inconsistently by any number of seeming equivalents. Theaetetus tends to use it after hearing a summary of the previous argument (*Sophist* 221C; 223B; 231E), and at no time does the stranger express any disapproval of it (cf. *Sophist* 233D; 253E). But when young Socrates uses it in exactly the same way (*Statesman* 267C), the stranger pulls him up short and wants to know whether what they have done is truly *pantapasi,* totally, accomplished. In this case, Plato has given us a clue to follow up on every occasion where *pantapasi* occurs, and it is easy enough for the translator to conform with Plato's stricture and oblige the reader. As it is obvious that Plato could not always act in this way as our guide, it is as tempting to be careless when there is no explicit indication as it seems to be foolish to base an entire translation on such little things as *pantapasi* and *eoiken* no doubt are. The translator indeed looks foolish even in his own eyes if he does not succumb to the idiomatic and translates strictly even when he does not know why he should do so. Only the wish and hope that the reader will come to understand more than he himself does can keep the translator to the straight and narrow, and it is with this wish and hope that these translations are offered.

There is one word—*to kalon* (the beautiful)—that more than any other bridges the gap between the general problem of translating and the particular problem of translating Greek. That Athens seems to have been as passionately devoted to the beautiful as Jerusalem to the just, that Plato speaks of the nature of each kind as its *eidos,* and that *eidos* on occasion means by itself beauty of form, might lead one to infer that Plato identified the beautiful with the being of the beings because he mistook the spirit of the people to whom he belonged for the essence of things.[2] The beautiful, however, is not Plato's highest principle; that is the good or the *idea* of the good, and it is beyond being. The structure of Socratic ignorance thus culminates in the problematic relation between the beautiful, or the being of the beings, and the good, or that without which there can be no being or beings. If Plato had not first reasoned his way to the beautiful and had simply been the mouthpiece of Greekness, that relation could not have become problematic, and it could not have become problematic in a comprehensive manner unless Plato had begun by considering the common opinions men have of it that are embodied in everyday usages. The *Theaetetus, Sophist,* and *Statesman* are linked together both linguistically and thematically by the beautiful. An introduction to them therefore fulfills its task if it can indicate how the beautiful forms such a link and justifies an examination of Plato's examination of the beautiful in the *Hippias Major.*

II

One's first impression of any Platonic dialogue is that it is complete in itself, but on closer inspection it usually shows a connection with one other dialogue with which it forms a pair. The *Republic* and the *Laws* or the *Symposium* and the *Phaedrus* are two of many such pairs. The

Phaedrus and the *Gorgias*, moreover, cannot be thought of together without bringing in their train another pair, the *Symposium* and the *Protagoras*, which must in turn be coupled. The longest series of dialogues, however, is connected in order of time through an external event, the trial and death of Socrates: *Theaetetus, Euthyphro, Sophist, Statesman, Apology of Socrates, Crito,* and *Phaedo.* Within these seven dialogues, the *Theaetetus, Sophist,* and *Statesman* form their own group, for not only does the cast of characters remain the same (with the exception of the stranger), but they are the only dialogues that explicitly refer to one another. Socrates ends the *Theaetetus* with the suggestion that Theodorus and the rest gather tomorrow at the same place, and the *Statesman* begins with Socrates' expression of gratitude for his acquaintance with Theaetetus and the stranger. The *Sophist* and the *Statesman,* moreover, are the most obvious pair among all the dialogues, for the peculiar way in which they both proceed detaches them from all other dialogues and attaches them to each other.

Long before I had even started on this study, my teacher, the late Leo Strauss, had stated with incomparable clarity the chief theme of these dialogues:

> To articulate the problem of cosmology means to answer the question of what philosophy is or what a philosopher is. Plato refrained from entrusting the thematic discussion of this question to Socrates. He entrusted it to a stranger from Elea. But even that stranger did not discuss explicitly what a philosopher is. He discussed explicitly two kinds of men which are easily mistaken for the philosopher, the sophist and the statesman: by understanding both sophistry (in its highest as well as in its lower meaning) and statesmanship, one will understand what philosophy is. Philosophy strives for knowledge of the whole. The whole is the totality of the parts. The whole eludes us but we know parts: we possess partial knowledge of parts. The knowledge which we possess is characterized by a fundamental dualism which has never been overcome. At one pole we find knowledge of homogeneity: above all in arithmetic, but also in the other branches of mathematics, and derivatively in all productive arts or crafts. At the opposite pole we find knowledge of heterogeneity, and in particular of heterogeneous ends; the highest form of this kind of knowledge is the art of the statesman and of the educator. The latter kind of knowledge is superior to the former for this reason. As knowledge of the ends of human life, it is knowledge of what makes human life complete or whole; it is therefore knowledge of a whole. Knowledge of the ends of man implies knowledge of the human soul; and the human soul is the only part of the whole which is open to the whole and therefore more akin to the whole than anything else is. But this knowledge—the political art in the

highest sense—is not knowledge of *the* whole. It seems that knowledge of the whole would have to combine somehow political knowledge in the highest sense with knowledge of homogeneity. And this combination is not at our disposal. Men are therefore constantly tempted to force the issue by imposing unity on the phenomena, by absolutizing either knowledge of homogeneity or knowledge of ends. Men are constantly attracted and deluded by two opposite charms: the charm of competence which is engendered by mathematics and everything akin to mathematics, and the charm of humble awe, which is engendered by meditation on the human soul and its experiences. Philosophy is characterized by the gentle, if firm, refusal to succumb to either charm. It is the highest form of the mating of courage and moderation. In spite of its highness or nobility, it could appear as Sisyphean or ugly, when one contrasts its achievement with its goal. Yet it is necessarily accompanied, sustained and elevated by *erôs*. It is graced by nature's grace.[3]

Strauss's summary of the *Sophist* and *Statesman* points at once to the following difficulty. Why does Plato entrust the discussion of what philosophy is to a total stranger and not to Socrates? Whatever answer can be given to this question must involve both the general circumstances in which the discussion takes place (the forthcoming trial of Socrates) and the particular situation (Socrates' conversation with Theaetetus the day before). Up on charges of corruption and impiety, Socrates sets out to do what he has always been doing and which distinguishes him from everyone else, the induction of Socratic ignorance. He certainly succeeds in exhausting Theaetetus, but he also seems to exhaust himself. The impression we have of Socrates' impotence before his own perplexities is strengthened by the sense that Theaetetus, who is Socrates' look-alike, is put through the same kind of obstacle course that Parmenides, who was then almost as old as Socrates is now, had inflicted on the young Socrates some fifty years before. In all that time Socrates has made no progress. The philosopher inherits and passes on doubt.

Socrates begins his examination of Theaetetus by casting into doubt the competence of Theodorus, who is Theaetetus' teacher, to decide that Theaetetus is hardly less ugly than Socrates. That resentment seems to dictate such a question is apparently confirmed by Socrates' continual jabbing at Theodorus until he too submits to the ordeal of Socratic refutation and confesses his ignorance. Socrates indeed does not gain satisfaction until he can state that Theaetetus' answer proves that Theodorus was wholly mistaken: Theaetetus is beautiful and Socrates hardly less so. In the face of the evidence, Socrates follows the argument. He idealizes. The perception of ugliness yields to knowledge of beauty while the two beauties who have brought about this surrender are mired in ignorance. This absurdity, which revindicates behind their backs Theodorus' original assertion, cannot but make us lose sight of the truly astonishing thing, that the action of the *Theaetetus* puts beauty and truth in some antagonistic relation to one another. It is the same relation that Parmenides had hinted at to young Socrates when, in contrast to Socrates' "ideas" like the just, the beautiful, and the good, he had asked after the *eidos* of hair, mud, and dirt.[4] Socrates, then, some fifty years later, takes the same stand and thereby shows that he has learned nothing.

Socrates' proven failure to get anywhere in the *Theaetetus* and, by implication, in his whole life would seem to lead to the consequence that Plato turns his back on Socrates and appeals to a Parmenidean stranger to deliver his own reproof of Socrates' way and a restatement of the true task of philosophy. However deficient the stranger's own way may be, it certainly does not look like Socrates'. It looks scientific. It looks as if Plato practices his own irony within Socrates' "customary irony" when Socrates suggests that the stranger has come as a god to punish him for his incompetence.[5] The difference, then, between the *Theaetetus,* on the one hand, and the *Sophist* and the *Statesman,* on the other, could be explained by Plato's proclaiming his liberation from the numbness of Socratic doubt and his recourse to the fruitful methodology of a refined Parmenideanism. The very form of the *Theaetetus* seems to confirm this. Although the conversation Socrates had with Theaetetus and Theodorus occurred right before his trial, its publication, we are told in the dialogue itself, was delayed for many years after Socrates' death, as if Plato wished to make clear that his rejection of Socrates had nothing to do with Athens' prior condemnation. This conclusion, however, is not entirely satisfactory, for Plato has Socrates imply that not the stranger but Socrates himself will be the chief speaker in the projected dialogue to be entitled *Philosopher.*[6] The last laugh will be Socrates', and it will be all the more telling for being silent.

The interpretation of these three dialogues has as its aim to offer a way of keeping one's balance in reading Plato, once one recognizes how every thread that seems to lead out of the maze of compound Socratic and Platonic irony snaps whenever one tries to rely on it. Now, however, one has to go back and ask what makes the issue of Theaetetus' ugliness the proper way to set up the problem of knowledge. As Parmenides' question to young Socrates indicates, the link between them—the all-too-human character of the first question and the more-than-human answer to the second—is supplied by Socrates' turning to the human things and *a fortiori* his denial of the feasibility of philosophy's goal, knowledge of the whole. The beautiful, however, is not just accidentally brought together with the Socratic turn but essentially belongs to it. Their essential connection is this. Socrates' turn to the human things was a wresting away from the poets of the beautiful and an establishing of it as the philosophic question. The *Symposium* and the *Phaedrus* may be said to prove this without arguing for it, for in the former the beautiful is stated to be the culmination of philosophy's quest, and in both the beautiful seems to emerge as the sole means available to philosophy in its quest.

That the *Theaetetus, Sophist,* and *Statesman* may supply the full support of those twin visions rests on the way in which the beautiful keeps recurring as decisive for their joint argument. Besides the issue of Theaetetus' ugliness, with which Socrates begins, and which is no less than the issue of Socrates' way, there is one moment at the start of the *Sophist* and one at the end of the *Statesman* in which the intervention of the beautiful determines the poles of the discussion.[7] The stranger distinguishes between the health and the beauty of soul and' assigns to Socrates' art of purification by cross-examination the task of making the soul beautiful. Much to our surprise, however, this assignment involves a split between moral health, with which Socrates has nothing to do, and intellectual beauty that solely consists in Socratic ignorance. But at the end of the *Statesman,* the stranger corrects himself and argues that the presumably moral virtues of moderation and courage involve an opposition of kinds within the beautiful itself which the statesman's art knows how to mix together without diluting either of them.

Therefore, the inseparability of the moral and the intellectual in light of the beautiful seems to be reaffirmed, but apparently with the loss of some distinctness. The discovery in any case of Socrates the philosopher shows Socrates the sophist and Socrates the statesman to be the beautifier. This very designation, however, seems to implicate Socrates in the spurious trade of the cosmetician. The stranger, accordingly, raises the problem of nonbeing through a perplexing distinction between two arts of image making, only one of which is concerned with the beautiful, and to which he hesitates to assign sophistry. He thus seems compelled to distinguish between true beauty and false beauty; what he does instead is to detect in the not beautiful the key to not being. The being of not being is first stated as the being of the not beautiful. Hair, mud, and dirt *are* no less than the beautiful. The beautiful is not a privileged being. How that conclusion can consist with the duality of the health and beauty of soul, on the one hand, and the duality of the beautiful in the health of soul, on the other, can be said to be the theme of the *Theaetetus, Sophist,* and *States-*

man. It cannot, however, be approached at all before the beautiful itself is examined. These three dialogues need the *Hippias Major.*

III

The *Hippias Major* readily divides into seven parts: (1) Progress and its chief obstacle, the law (281a1–286c2); (2) 286c3–289d5, (3) 289d6–291c5, and (4) 291c6–293b9, Hippias' three attempts at a definition of the beautiful; (5) 293b10–294e10, (6) 295a1–297d9, (7) 297d10–304e9, Socrates' three attempts. Each part is more evidently a unity than the whole of which they are the parts. The dialogue thus seems to exemplify Hippias' criticism of the logic chopping of Socrates and his friends, who cannot, according to Hippias, grasp the wholes of things, and particularly the beautiful, which by nature is a big and indivisible body of being (301b2–7).[8] The conspicuous incoherence of the *Hippias Major* is enhanced by its absurdity, which, again according to Hippias, signifies its ugliness, for he believes that the laughable and the ugly are equivalent, while the beautiful, like the sacred, is laughter proof and cannot be debunked (288b1–3, d1–3, 294a5). Hippias himself, however, contributes to the dialogue's absurdity hardly less than Socrates does, and so the dialogue vindicates Hippias' principles while holding him up to ridicule. We are confronted, then, with a typically Platonic riddle: the way to an understanding of the beautiful seemingly violates every possible canon of the beautiful. On the face of it, the know-it-all Hippias and Socrates at his most perplexed constitute the pair least likely to discover anything together. Indeed, their one point of agreement is tacit. Neither mentions the charm or attractiveness of the beautiful. The beautiful is not lovely. The word for sexual intercourse occurs, but not *erôs* or any of its cognates.

That Hippias and Socrates are virtually irreconcilable shows up in the difference in kind between the three definitions each offers. Hippias offers a being as the beautiful (virgin, gold, man); Socrates, a sign by means of which the beautiful can be recognized (the seemly, the useful, the pleasant). One or more counterexamples prove the inadequacy of Hippias' definitions, but when the counterexample of beautiful practices, customs, and laws threatens Socrates' last definition, Socrates shunts it aside and proves the inconsistency of the definition in itself. The one example Socrates always uses to test Hippias' definitions is God; the one example which always occurs either in the course of the argument about Socrates' definitions or among the things Socrates cites as evidence for them is law. The beautiful, apparently, must be the impossible combination of a substance and a rule, for no matter what being is preeminently beautiful and from which one can best derive the rule, it becomes, on the discovery of the rule, merely an illustration of it. Are we to conclude, then, that the beautiful as a being is not to be sought? Socrates, however, still asks after being (*ousia*) while he discusses the possibility of correcting his last definition (302c5), which, he shows, fails ontologically, and not because it cannot detect infallibly the presence of something beautiful. A nominal definition may easily cover everything beautiful, whether it be by nature, art, or law (295d7–8), but it cannot distinguish between the genuine and the spurious, and Socrates rejects the seemly as the beautiful for its inability to account for more than seeming. Inasmuch as Socrates chooses to speak with Hippias alone and willingly keeps up the discussion long after Hippias seems to have lost all interest in it, Socrates must somehow need Hippias and what he represents in order to complement his own way. Could this complement be Hippias' dumb vision of the beautiful as a being?

Progress
. (281a1–286c2)

Since the dialogue's first words are "Hippias the beautiful and wise," and since the dialogue itself goes from the issue of wisdom to that of beauty, we are invited to consider wisdom and beauty together even when they are not expressly linked. Hippias, for example, consistently identifies the laughably contemptible with ignorance (282a3, 288b2, 290a1) and implies, accordingly, that the nonlaughably admirable is knowledge. Socrates, though he seems at the beginning to allow that the moderns might be wiser than the ancients, realizes at the end the truth of the proverb (i.e., a bit of ancient wisdom) "the beautiful things are difficult" and thereby denies any progress in wisdom, at least when it comes to knowledge of the beautiful. The beautiful seems to be the touchstone of progress (cf. 282d6). If the laughable is the ugliness of ignorance, the fact that Bias would, if resurrected, provoke laughter in comparison with the sophists, is a sign that there has been progress. But if Hippias proves to be no less laughable, perhaps ugliness has nothing to do with the lack of wisdom. The phrase "beautiful and wise" seems to be the modern version of the traditional term for a gentleman, "beautiful and good," in which "wise" replaces "good" while "beautiful" seems to remain the same. Hippias says that the new education he offers makes his pupils better, but his speech about beautiful practices and laws is cast in the form of a question which Achilles' son Neoptolemus put to the oldest of heroes, Nestor. This speech, Hippias believes, is as likely to be praised in innovative Athens as it was in Sparta.

According to Hippias, the art of the sophists has been as progressive as the other arts, and Bias would be as ludicrous today as the sculptors say Daedalus would if he now made the sort of statues from which he got his name. Socrates chooses to exemplify progress in the arts with an art whose chief concern is to represent the beautiful in a fiction that will pass for reality, and he chooses a mythical figure to represent the inferiority of ancient sculptors. Hippias is prudent enough not to discount in public the myth of ancient wisdom, but he seems not to notice the true bearing of Socrates' example. Could not Daedalus have known as much as Phidias about the beautiful while falling short of him in the means to realize it? Or does inadequate knowledge necessarily accompany inadequate technique? If know-how and knowledge are inseparable, the wise men of old were, on the one hand, more backward than Daedalus, since they did not go public, and on the other, more knowledgeable, since they knew enough to be ashamed of going public. To go public, however, means at first to engage in politics, and if politics stands to wisdom as statuary to knowledge of the beautiful, the wisdom needed must be the knowledge which political philosophy supplies. But Socrates discovered political philosophy and abstained from politics.

There has, then, been progress in wisdom without any comparable progress in technique. If such progress cannot be precluded in the future, the sophists would have entered politics too soon. But if politics is more refractory than stone or metal and resists any refinement in technique, Socrates' myth of the Beautiful City in the *Republic* would be the limit of its realization. Let it be granted that Phidias' Athena Parthenos is more beautiful than any statue of Daedalus; is it more beautiful than Homer's way of indicating in speech the beauty of Helen?[9] Even if Athena Parthenos is not less beautiful, the expansion of the materials in which the beautiful can now be displayed would not imply the inferiority of Homer's knowledge, but it might now be easier to grasp the beautiful. Helen's beauty must be inferred from the effect she has on the Trojan elders; Athena's beauty is immediately visible. Progress in wisdom, then, might likewise mean its popularization, with a consequent loss in precision. Hippias the sophist distinguishes between the meaning of law according to precise speech and its customary meaning among the many (284e1–5); Hippias the ambassador has no intention of teaching that distinction to the Spartans or to any other people.

The dissimulation of wisdom is consistent with wisdom. The dissimulation of beauty seems to be self-contradictory, for the beautiful, if it is considered in light of the ugly or shameful (*aiskhron*), seems to be that which one would not be ashamed of displaying before anyone.

Hippias' boastfulness, however, is not beautiful. The beautiful thus seems to be that which, because it calls forth praise, does not need to praise itself, but the boastful does not necessarily consist in the indecency of self-praise, or even in the claim to be able to do what others can and one cannot do. The truly boastful is to present the impossible as possible, and the difference between it and the beautiful might be that the beautiful in its representation declares its own impossibility or at least is supremely indifferent to it.[10] Progress in wisdom, then, could mean the realization of the impossibility of wisdom, as the replacement of "wisdom" by "love of wisdom" suggests. And the beautiful things would not be difficult, as the ancients thought, but impossible to know. Morality too seems always to have been an "ideal."

In the second book of the *Republic*, Socrates puts justice in the most beautiful class of goods, along with seeing, thinking, and hearing, but Glaucon and Adimantus argue that injustice is naturally pleasant and justice compulsorily praised. The private good is publicly indefensible, the public good privately abhorred, and the beautiful, which seems to unify the pleasant and the praiseworthy, cannot be anything but a fiction. Hippias infers from the pleasure the Spartans took in his free speeches and the praise they gave him that, were it not for the law, he, if anyone, would have been amply paid for his teaching. None of the elements, however, which make up Hippias' wisdom, and which remind us of the course of study Socrates proposes for the guardians of Kallipolis—astronomy, geometry, logistics, and music—ever delighted the Spartans or elicited their praise. Instead, Hippias was compelled to learn mythology, or, as he prefers to call it, archaeology—the genealogies of men and heroes and the ancient foundings of cities. Hippias parodies together the compulsory descent of the philosopher into the cave and the noble lie. Socrates once compared him to the Heracles whom Odysseus saw in Hades, for Heracles himself takes his pleasure among the gods.[11]

Virgin
(286c3–289d5)

Hippias knows what the beautiful is, but it is a small part of his polymathy and almost valueless. Knowledge of the beautiful is not beautiful, for it does not pay (cf. 282d2). Hippias does not offer a course in "kalology," for though not just anyone can say what the beautiful is, everyone will at once testify as soon as they hear it that Hippias' definition is correct (288a3–5, 289e4, 291e8–292a1). The beautiful, it seems, is noncontroversial: Achaeans and Trojans fought over Helen and not about her. The beautiful immediately compels agreement and therefore remains hidden as to how it compels agreement. The beautiful enchants. It is paradigmatic of the separation between "that it is" and "what it is"; it is an open mystery. Socrates too must have thought that it was not a difficult thing to know, for otherwise he would not have got angry with himself for not being able to answer the question. He likewise must have experienced its compelling power, for otherwise he could have resolved not to praise or blame any longer. But Hippias himself, as well as his words and thought, had just made him speak of the beautiful.

The public character of the beautiful is manifest in its connection with praise. The beautiful demands that one speak out about it. It is not, like many other goods, something one keeps to oneself. The beautiful is so eminently shareable that it seems incapable of being possessed, let alone consumed. Socrates, at any rate, could not tell Diotima what one got once one had it.[12] The beautiful always seems to keep its distance, and this elusiveness can easily be mistaken for its illusiveness. The public, speech-provoking, nonexclusive, and distance-keeping character of the beautiful seems to entitle it to be called the ground or the core of all intersubjectivity. When Hippias proposes to go off into isolation and examine the beautiful by himself, Socrates beseeches him by the gods to find it in front of himself, or, if he wants, to join with him in the search (295a7–b3). Does the beautiful, like justice, vanish when one is alone and the sun has set?[13]

For the rest of the dialogue, Hippias and Socrates are never alone for very long. Socrates puts the question itself, as well as several of the arguments, in the mouth of someone about whom we know at first nothing except that his only concern is with the truth (288d4–5), but who finally turns out to be the son of Sophroniscus (298b11). In a dialogue about the beautiful, Socrates splits himself between a Socrates (Socrates$_1$) with whom Hippias is willing to converse and a Socrates (Socrates$_2$) whose tastelessness allows him to speak of a beautiful pot of beautiful pea soup (cf. 291a3–4). The Socrates who Alcibiades found disturbing because he talked of pack-asses, blacksmiths, shoemakers, and tanners and who Callicles thought shameless for speaking of the life of pathics is presented to Hippias through another Socrates who tries to imitate him and become what he is (287a3, b5).[14] Socrates first doubles himself and then fuses into his double. In this way, that which cannot decently be said is decently said, and that which ought to be hidden becomes manifest in and through an illusion (293a2–6).

Once Socrates$_1$ has set up this condition, Socrates$_2$ gets Hippias to agree that the beautiful by means of which all beautiful things are beautiful is a being. A question about a causal being gets posed in the element of poetic production. Socrates₁ tries to get as his own predicate what another is as subject, but this other as subject is himself. Socrates₂ is the true Socrates, who is the cause of the predicability of himself for Socrates₁. What looks like the adoption by Socrates₁ of Socrates₂ in an imitation is in truth the re-presentation of Socrates₂ as Socrates₂ in another who is as another an illusion. The duality of Socrates₂ as predicate—Socrates is Socrates₂ and a picture of Socrates₂— is the inversion of the truth, for Socrates₁ is a picture of Socrates₂, not as a being which assumes the image of another, but as an image which assumes the being of that of which it is an image. The predicate is real, the subject unreal. Could the beautiful possibly be of this sort? The beautiful would then have to show itself as other than itself as subject while showing itself as predicate. It would be itself as primarily for us a deficient mode of itself—an other which in working on itself as other would make itself known as itself in another. The beautiful would thus be an efficient cause of a certain kind—the poet, whose making of a fiction would lead us to say that it is the poet—for though we do not say that the housebuilder is the house, we do say that this piece of music is pure Mozart. Aristotle remarks that when the pre-Socratics first raised the problem of the beautiful, they mistook what is in truth the problem of formal/final cause for the problem of efficient cause. This cause they called love, which the Muses told Hesiod was the most beautiful of the gods.[15]

Hippias' answer, "A beautiful virgin is beautiful," begins to make a little sense when he becomes indignant at Socrates₂' question, "What about a beautiful pot? Isn't it, after all, beautiful?" Only someone uneducated, he says, has the face to name worthless names in an august matter. Hippias objects to the name and not the thing. "A beautiful virgin is beautiful" is not a complete sentence: the predicate must be supplemented with an infinitive—"to name," "to speak of," "to write about," or the like—whereas a beautiful pot, however beautiful, can never find a place in educated speech. The ugly is the unmentionable. Socrates₂ had tried to forestall Hippias' objection by citing a god as his witness: if a god can praise a beautiful mare, it cannot be less fit for speech than a beautiful virgin. Hippias' insistence on decency in speech might tempt us to look at his first answer in the same light and take "beautiful virgin" as the symbol of decency and the equivalent of innocence. The beautiful would thus be that which banishes our experience and restores our belief in the unambiguously moral.[16] Hippias, however, agrees so readily to the replacement of virgin in his formula by mare or lyre that he must be understood literally. Hippias says *parthenos kalê kalon*. The adjective is feminine, the predicate neuter; and, according to Hippias, *kalon* is the same whether it has or does not have the article. Hippias says that a beautiful virgin is the beautiful, and he means that whatever is beautiful is the beautiful.

The beautiful is the concrete universal; it is synecdochical. Hippias thus expresses in an extreme way the experience of the lover which Socrates states more moderately in the myth of the *Phaedrus:* of the hyperuranian beings beauty alone is privileged to shine most vividly for us through sight, the most vivid of the senses (250c8–e1). If one does not automatically ascribe the lover's experience to a delusion, the problem it points to is this. If the definition of the beautiful does not specify the being to which it refers, the being which is beautiful seems to be irrelevant to its being beautiful; it becomes nothing more than matter which receives the impress of the beautiful more or less perfectly. But a beautiful filly seems to be beautiful as a filly, and the fact that it is a filly does not signify the degree of its recalcitrance to its being the beautiful itself. $Socrates_1$, in his explication of $Socrates_2$' example of the beautiful pot, lays down criteria for its being beautiful which are solely applicable to pots. It would be absurd to say that "smooth" and "round" equally hold for a beautiful virgin.[17] But if the beautiful is thus class bound, the beautiful is either a wholly equivocal term or double—with a single, comprehensive sense that lays down the minimal condition without which nothing can be beautiful, and with a mulitple precise sense that each kind of being in its own way must satisfy. The inquiry into the second possibility underlies the discussion for the rest of the dialogue.

In the *Hippias Major,* two quotations from Heraclitus occur. The first is used by $Socrates_1$ to defend Hippias, the second by $Socrates_2$ to refute him. That opposites as opposites are in harmony is of course a hallmark of Heraclitus' teaching. On the basis of Heraclitus' saying "The most beautiful of monkeys is ugly in comparison with the human genus," Hippias' own remark, that though a beautiful pot may be beautiful it does not deserve to be judged beautiful in comparison with a filly and a virgin, is revised to read "The most beautiful of pots is ugly in comparison with the genus of virgins." Through Heraclitus the superlative is introduced and the comparative bypassed. Indeed, the comparative does not enter the discussion until Socrates and Hippias are well into Hippias' second definition (291b3). The Heraclitus-Hippias thesis seems to imply that the ugliest man is more beautiful than the most beautiful monkey. Socrates is ugly only because he is a man; if he were a Silenus, he might pass for handsome. If one mistakes the class to which a being belongs, one's judgment will be unsound. He was a good speaker, Thucydides says, for a Spartan. If one judges a pot or a monkey to be beautiful, one must somehow be then unaware of the class of virgins or fillies. Anything beautiful, in calling attention to itself, must suppress our awareness of everything else that is beautiful. The beautiful blocks out the horizon within which comparison is possible; it suppresses the other. One loves this individual and no other. This kind of suppression first came up in connection not with the beautiful, but with wisdom. Despite progress in wisdom, Bias is still thought to be wise, for he would have to be resurrected before he would become ridiculous. The beautiful has now been shown to function in the same way as time. It establishes a manifold of class perspectives, no two of which can be comprehended together without one of them instantly becoming ugly.

The second quotation from Heraclitus brings wisdom and beauty together: "The wisest of men compared to a god will come to light (*phaneitai*) (as) a monkey in wisdom, beauty, and all other things." In order to express the absence of wisdom in the wisest of men Heraclitus reassigns him to another class. But since the reassignment of the wisest man cannot be done unless one has previously identified the class to which he does not in truth belong, "appearance" is necessarily involved. The same principle would hold for the beautiful. To say that something is beautiful is to shift it out of its own class and identify it with either beauty itself or some stand-in for it (e.g., "as pretty as a picture"). Predication of beauty is in the literal sense metaphor. Whatever is beautiful must at least look as if it is something else and be pretending to deny its inclusion in the class to which it ostensibly belongs. Homer's Priam says of Hector: "He was (*eske*) a god among men, nor did he seem (*eoikei*) to be the son of a mortal man, but of a god."[18] The beautiful thus has the structure of an indeterminate dyad: anything beautiful jumps its class and at the same time remains a member of the class it jumps. This unresolvable duality indicates why the beautiful and image making are inseparable. The Athena Parthenos of Phidias refutes Hippias' second definition.

Gold
(289d6–291c5)

Since the mere juxtaposition of something beautiful of one class with another class has had the power to drain that something of its beauty, Socrates$_2$ proposes that the beautiful itself is a species (*eidos*) which when present in or added to all other things orders or adorns them and makes them appear beautiful. The beautiful cannot be something that belongs to the class which it enhances; rather, everything beautiful must borrow its beauty from the beautiful other. The beauty of anything, therefore, is now no less an appearance than its ugliness was before, for, it seems, as soon as more than one kind of being is considered, whether conjunctively or disjunctively, there is appearance. The beings are real in their apartness and illusory in their togetherness: the whole is inferior in being to its parts. Socrates$_2$' proposal also seems to imply that the beautiful is unrestricted in its power. Is there any kind of being that can resist the beautiful? Hesiod says Pandora was a beautiful evil, and Sallust has Catiline speak of a most beautiful crime.[19] And, conversely, is there any kind of being that automatically admits the beautiful in all its members? Flowers seem to be such a kind: their health is the same as their beauty. The ease, in any case, with which they admit the beautiful seems to be due to their being visible representations of life without mind. Were it not for things like flowers, mind, in fact, would be a plausible answer to Socrates$_2$' question. And if one recalls Heraclitus' ambiguously worded saying and that Socrates made Anaxagoras the last of the wise men of old, his indifference to money the proof of their collective folly, it seems that mind would have been the best possible answer ancient wisdom could give.[20] It would not perhaps have been Socrates' own answer, for only a teleological physics could account for the beauty of things like flowers, but the truth about final cause always eluded Socrates.[21]

Formally speaking, "gold" does satisfy several requirements of the beautiful: it exists by itself, can be added to other things, and is highly manifest. If, moreover, beautiful is to the beautiful as golden is to gold, the beautiful is *pros hen* with two possible ways open to it of accounting for the manifold of beautiful things. The nonliteral way would be that things which appear beautiful constitute an insubstantial class of likenesses to gold. Hippias, however, chooses the literal way: things that otherwise appear ugly appear beautiful as soon as they are overlaid with gold. This way is surely disappointing, especially if one considers that the gods have already been introduced as the standard of beauty, but the link between gods and gold is supplied by ancient poetry. Homer restricts the adjective "golden" almost exclusively to the gods and things of the gods. We read of golden Aphrodite and the horses of Zeus with golden manes. If "golden" is the way of saying "beautiful and divine," gold itself would have to be the beautiful itself and the true substance of God. Progress in wisdom would thus consist in discovering the truth behind the poetic imagination of the ancients.[22] Thucydides' Pericles speaks of the gods only once, when he mentions the gold of "the goddess herself" (i.e., Phidias' image of Athena Parthenos), which in being the monetary reserve of Athens, has been decreed to be inviolable except in the greatest need.[23] Athena is now in fact the last hope of Athens. Progress, then, means literalization, for the beautiful is the poeticization of self-interest, that is, its concealment under the cover of the dazzling. This, too, sounds like a parody of Socrates, who brought philosophy down from heaven and into the marketplace. It is Socrates₁, after all, who without any appeal to Socrates₂ suggests that the beautiful is the useful.

That Phidias' Athena is an image and an image of an invisible being does not enter into the argument which Socrates₁ arranges between Socrates₂ and Hippias. The only mention of likeness is of Phidias' having matched as closely as possible stone and ivory. Socrates₂ can thus argue as if Phidias' intention was to make Athena as beautiful as he could, and he did not have to trade off perfect beauty, which might have entailed an all-gold statue, against likeness.[24] Ivory, however, out of which Athena's face, feet, and hands are made, does seem to be a concession to likeness, while her gold peplos is not an image of anything. But if ivory were chosen on the grounds of a simile like "her skin was as white as ivory," perhaps the ivory too, no less than the gold, is to be taken literally, and we are wrong to speak of Phidias' Athena as an image.

Although Socrates₂' counterexample is effective against Hippias' second definition, it seems to undermine his argument against Hippias' first definition, for then the gods were used to show up the ugliness of a beautiful virign, but now the virgin among the gods seems to be nothing but an image of a beautiful virgin among men. Or does Athena Parthenos show up the ugliness of girls because she is ivory and gold while they, however beautiful, can only be likened to her ivory skin and gold dress? Aristotle remarks that a human being cannot be beautiful unless he is tall as well. "Tall and beautiful" is almost a fixed expression in Greek literature.[25] Phidias' Athena was tall with a vengeance; she was a colossus, and no human being could be compared with her. Indeed, if *per impossibile* a beautiful virgin were of such a size, would she not be grotesque? She would, in any case, look to us misproportioned, since the upper half of her body would appear smaller than it is.[26] If, in fact, Athena Parthenos is nothing but the gigantic image of a human virgin, it is the label she has—the goddess Athena—that cancels out the possibility of our regarding her as a *lusus naturae*. Athena the Virgin is beautiful by a nominal class shift. Without further reflection, therefore, it is impossible to say whether Athena's statue is beautiful because it images what is beautiful or because it is a beautiful image of what is beautiful, ugly, or neither. Plato supplies the proper context for our thinking through this question in the *Sophist*.

Hippias always seems to miss the point of Socrates₂' counter-examples; but it is suprising that he can so much distract Socrates₂ that he too fails to make his point. The self-evident conclusion, how-ever, that if ivory is also beautiful, gold cannot be that which makes all things beautiful, is not self-evident. Hippias' argument, which per-haps Hippias himself would not be capable of formulating, is this. Gold is the beautiful itself, and ivory is beautiful only because it is worth ounce for ounce some fraction of gold. Gold is the unit measure of everything beautiful; so no matter how much a block of ivory cost, its beauty would always be less than gold's, for it would not be the standard of its own worth. The beautiful itself as gold stands to beau-tiful things which are not gold as one to numbers. In terms of its beauty, then, no other substance but gold is a substance; as beautiful, every other substance can only be called "golden." But unlike the "golden" of the ancient poets, "golden" has acquired an exact nu-merical meaning. An argument such as this lies behind Socrates$_2$,' shifting from ivory to stone and from stone to figwood, for the stone of Athena's pupils cannot be measured against gold, and figwood was proverbially worthless. Stone thus forces Hippias to go off the gold standard and introduce a different kind of measure, the seemly or fitting. The fitting is the core of Hippias' first generalization: "What-ever is fitting to each, this makes each beautiful." The beautiful is now a verb (*prepei*), which connects an unspecified subject with an un-specified complement. It is the *kosmos* of beautiful and nonbeautiful kinds together.

Despite Hippias' generalization, which no longer speaks of gold, Socrates$_2$ persists in demoting gold until Hippias agrees that, in at least one case, a figwood ladle is more beautiful than a gold one. Socrates$_2$ goes Aristophanes one better in rubbing Hippias in the muck of the beautiful (cf. 291a8). Socrates$_1$ even gets him to utter the word "figwood," though, he admits, it does not fit Hippias, inasmuch as he is "beautifully dressed, beautifully shod, and with a reputation for wisdom among all the Greeks." Indeed, the word "pot" occurs in all of Aristophanes' extant comedies except the *Clouds*, the most decent and wisest of them; and in the *Knights*, when a sausage seller and Cleon the Paphlagonian compete for the favor of Demos, the per-sonified people of Athens, by offering him various delicacies, the following exchange occurs (1168–76):

SAUSAGE SELLER: And I offer you pieces of bread sopped in soup
    By the goddess with her ivory hand.
DEMOS: I never realized, my lady, what a long finger you have!
CLEON: And I offer you a beautiful green pea soup—
    Pallas the Pylos-fighter stirred it.[27]

SAUSAGE SELLER: O Demos! The goddess plainly cares for you.
    And now she extends a pot full of soup over you.[28]
DEMOS: Of course she does. Do you believe this city
    Would still be inhabited unless she plainly
    Was wont to extend her pot over us?

Socrates$_2$ is Plato's version of the sausage seller; he is used to reveal that Hippias' wisdom, which assumes the identity of the private and the public, ultimately rests on an Aristophanic impossibility, that the *demos* be a single animated being, or, more prosaically, that the city be one household. Hippias' indignation, therefore, is misplaced, for his beautiful dress and reputation for wisdom make him the equivalent of Athena Parthenos, who did not disdain to dip her ivory finger in the lowly fare of her people. His indignation, on the other hand, is appropriate, for it is unseemly to speak of Athena and pea soup together. Their juxtaposition, however, fits because it does not fit. The appropriateness of the inappropriate is a principle of the comic, and Socrates' serious suggestion is that only the laughable can resolve the tension between the species bound and the transgeneric beautiful, for it alone can compensate for the suppression of the species-bound beautiful in a *kosmos*. An ordered universe must be funny. Nothing in the *Timaeus* militates against this suggestion.

Socrates$_2$ supplies the example of the figwood ladle, but it is Socrates$_1$ who explains to Hippias why the figwood ladle is more fitting. Socrates$_1$ is the indispensable go-between for the riff-raff Socrates$_2$ and the beautiful Hippias. He is the constantly shifting variable that makes the dialogue possible. He thus succeeds in getting Hippias to acknowledge at last the force of Socrates$_2$' question. Hippias sees that the beautiful must be that which never will come to light anywhere as ugly for anyone. The relativizing of the beautiful through the fitting makes Hippias recognize the need for the beautiful itself. The figwood ladle does its job regardless of how crudely it is made, and the gold ladle cannot do the job regardless of its finish and design. Socrates does not consider the case of a well-made gold ladle stirring some exquisite broth in a gold pot of great beauty. The pleasure of such a sight might more than make up for whatever loss in piquancy the soup might suffer from the absence of figwood flavoring. These considerations, however, are irrelevant since Socrates only argues for the greater beauty of figwood under a given set of conditions. The comparative brings along with it the conditional. A figwood ladle is more beautiful if and only if one recognizes that gold has been rejected. The possible becomes the background against which the beautiful is judged. Socrates$_2$' two examples are artifacts; natural beings do not lend themselves so easily to arguments that distinguish between better and worse possibilities. "If," Socrates₁ says, "I declare the beautiful to be gold, it will come to light, it seems to me, that gold is no more beautiful than figwood." Not only, then, does the more beautiful depend on a rejected possibility, it depends on the prior affirmation of the beauty of something which seems to be unconditionally beautiful. The class-jumping of the beautiful thus reappears in the realm of the more beautiful. The rejected possibility of the seemingly beautiful itself must somehow be preserved if that which surpasses it is to come to light. The disenchantment of figwood requires the copresence, however ghostly, of the enchantment of gold. Only here in the dialogue does the dual occur, the dual of ladle (290e5, 291c2).

Man
(291c6–293b9)

Hippias stakes his knowledge on this third definition; if anyone can contradict it, Socrates is to say that Hippias does not understand anything. Hippias believes that his definition passes the test of the natural (everywhere and always) and the test of consensus (it will appear as such to everyone). The beautiful, then, must be some part of the perceptual field, as it is for Socrates' third definition; but Hippias' definition is wholly conventional: "I say that always, for everyone, and everywhere it is most beautiful for a man (*anêr*), being wealthy, being healthy, being honored by the Greeks, having come to old age, having beautifully arranged the burial of his own dead parents, to be buried beautifully and magnificently by his own offspring." Beauty in the highest degree consists of seven elements. If one or more is missing, the beautiful is still present, but it wholly vanishes if one is not buried, for all the rest are means to that end.

Hippias' definition is negatively determined. The ugliest of all things is to be a woman, poor, sick, without honor, die young, fail to bury one's parents, and to have no descendants to bury oneself. Hippias seems to maintain that the beautiful makes the universality of the natural coincide with the particularity of the lawful, but such a coincidence seems to be impossible if one distinguishes, as Hippias does, between the lawful of precise speech and the lawful of usage, and between the truth of progress and the praise of the ancients.

The beautiful, therefore, must be invariant with respect to truth and falsehood, progress and decline, for it is either that which is truly believed to be the case or that which must be declared to be the case everywhere and always. The beautiful is that prejudice which is ineradicable by nature. Hippias identifies it with the beauty of burial.

The root of the beautiful is the fear of death, for the beautiful is whatever conceals our mortality. The very phrasing of Hippias' definition shows up the concealment: three present participles (being wealthy, being healthy, being honored) are put in asyndeton with two aorist participles (having come to old age, having buried) and one aorist passive infinitive (to be buried). The phrasing thus gives the illusion of a whole while the definition in fact is episodic; its apparent completeness is the finality of the grave.[29]

If Socrates had simply wanted to refute Hippias, he could have cited the custom of the Persians or some other tribe who do not bury their dead, but Socrates drops the condition of "everywhere" and keeps "always." His question now is "What is the beautiful which is beautiful for all and always?" Hippias insists that his answer still holds: "I know well, Socrates, that for all this is beautiful, that which I said, and will be thought so." Socrates' "for all" means "for all things"— stone, wood, man, god, every action, and every course of study— Hippias' "for all" means "for all men" (293a11–b4). The beautiful is a wholly human phenomenon, and this is either because death is in a sense uniquely human, or because the ugly is the shameful, and only men can be ashamed. Socrates$_2$ does not examine Hippias' premise; he refutes him on the grounds of his added phrase "and will be thought so." The belief in gods and demigods guarantees that Hippias' premise will not be granted, and Hippias cannot question that belief, for the beautiful, as he understands it, is the impossible secularization of the sacred. He needs the divine sanction of burial even though he must dispense with the gods. Hippias is compelled to accept in Athens the mythology he was compelled to learn in Sparta. Even if there were neither gods nor heroes, there would still be cities, for which a premature and patriotic death would remain noble.

Does Hippias envision, then, a world without war, and for this reason put his assertion of universal consensus in the future tense? Not even this fantastic hope would save him, for nonbeing lurks in the definition itself: the man who has fulfilled the first six of Hippias' conditions is not that which his offspring bury. The dead cannot be patient of anything unless there are beautiful gods, but there cannot be beautiful gods if to be buried is the beautiful. If, however, it is impossible that Heracles bury Zeus,[30] could Hippias not have argued that the gods are not beautiful but good? Just as we say that Homer was a good poet of two beautiful poems, and Socrates$_2$ implies that Phidias was a good craftsman of a beautiful statue, the gods could be good makers of beautiful things, the chief of which is the holiness of burial. The beautiful is the holy. Hippias, then, who believes in the progress of wisdom, would thus find himself praising sincerely the wisdom of the ancients. When Socrates₂ first mentions the burial of the gods, Hippias euphemistically exclaims, "Go to heaven! (*ball' es makarian*)," but what he really means is, "May you go unburied!" The expression he has in mind (*ball' es korakas*), but which it is not becoming for him to say, often occurs in comedy, where it seems to have lost its original force and to mean no more than "Drop dead!"

The Seemly
(293b10–294e10)

The beautiful has so far come to light as something that is both complete in itself and a pointer beyond itself. Three ways, or perhaps even *the* three ways, in which the beautiful has this double character are explored in the three definitions of Socrates. Each definition in turn forces Socrates and Hippias to recognize an opposition within a pair of terms that the beautiful, it seems, should but cannot resolve. The three pairs are appearing and being, beautiful and good, and aural and visual pleasures. The beautiful, then, looks as if it is the impossible togetherness of the necessarily apart. Deceptiveness belongs to the beautiful in truth; it is the necessary consequence of its privileged position as the unique being which discloses itself in perception. The nature of the seemly, which Socrates₁ and Hippias are to examine, "lest we be deceived in some way," proves to be a kind of deception with regard to the beautiful. Hippias' example forces Socrates to draw that conclusion: "Whenever someone puts on clothes or shoes that are fitting (*harmottonta*), even if he is laughable, he appears more beautiful." Without the example, it would be possible to understand the alternative Hippias chooses as follows. The beautiful as the seemly or conspicuous (*prepon*) makes things come to light as beautiful because they are beautiful but do not in the absence of the seemly appear to be so. The art of the seemly in this sense the Eleatic stranger calls phantastics. It presents the beautiful by correcting for perspectival distortion in light of the beautiful, but if the beautiful is already known, phantastics could at best duplicate the beautiful.

We might wonder, then, whether it is not the beings themselves which are ever beautiful, but the beautiful, like light, is still that which discloses them to us. So while the good causes the beings to be knowable, the beautiful would cause them to be known. The beautiful would be neither a substantive nor an adjective but a verb.[31] The beautiful would be the proof rather than the theorem; it would be dialectics, of which Socrates was always a lover and than which, he thought, there could be none more beautiful.[32] The beauty of things would thus be due to the manner of their disclosure. The beautiful would, on the one hand, be elusive as long as the beings were not fully disclosed, and, on the other, vanish once they were fully disclosed.

Hippias' example suggests that one should distinguish between "forcing" and "permitting" (cf. 294b7). Either the seemly does its utmost to suppress whatever something is—"even if he is laughable"—against its grain or it follows the lead of that which it enhances and brings out what is there but hidden. But even in this case there might be a forcing, inasmuch as it might be in the nature of something to be hidden. The difference between our seeing something with the naked eye and through a microscope indicates the difficulty. Microscopic magnification of an otherwise invisible thing is contrary to its being, but it cannot be made known unless it appears as what it is not. Even though it undergoes no alteration of its proportions under the microscope, its magnification involves a deception that is inseparable from our knowledge of it. The Platonic equivalent to microscopic magnification is the Platonic dialogue itself, in which the very selection and examination of one question apart from all other questions magnifies that question perforce (cf. 286e3–5). Only a single discussion of the whole and all its parts would not involve magnification. But if this is impossible, appearance cannot but be part and parcel of our knowledge and therefore of our nonknowledge of any part.

To label the whole "the good" or "the *idea* of the good" means that that which is necessarily a question of the greatest importance for us, and thus involves the highest degree of incorrigible distortion, is in fact in agreement with the nonperspectivally great. The beautiful, however, might belong to the parts of the whole as long as they are severally subject to inquiry and are therefore magnified. Socrates, however, now connects the big and the beautiful with the argument that what holds for all big things—that they are big regardless of whether they show themselves as such or not—must hold for all beautiful things. All big things, Socrates says, are big by the excess or the outstanding, but all beautiful things are outstanding too, especially if they show in themselves a class shift. The beautiful, then, would be that part of the big which suspends the continuum of magnitude; it would be the eidetic big. The big and the beautiful, however, cannot consist together except in an illusion. The colossal Athena Parthenos of Phidias proves it, and this was the example from which Socrates$_2$ originally elicited the identification of the beautiful and the seemly. That the beautiful is a part of the big and yet cannot be part of the big would thus be a proof of its indeterminate dyadic structure. The beautiful is the impossible union of the eidetic and dimensionality.

Hippias proposes that the seemly by its presence makes things both be and appear beautiful. Socrates interprets this proposal as saying that it is impossible for things truly (*tôi onti*) beautiful not to appear to be (*phainesthai einai*) beautiful. Beautiful things declare in their appearance that they are beautiful. Appearance conveys the message of being. Beautiful customs and practices, therefore, should be opined to be beautiful and always appear as such to all, but instead, as Hippias agrees, they are unknown, and there is the greatest possible strife and battle about them, both privately for individuals and publicly for cities. Hippias fails to notice that beauty would not be controversial unless it disclosed itself. The limit to the concealedness of the beautiful is the universal disagreement about what it is. No one disputes *that* it is. Contentiousness is a kind of agreement, and the beautiful, even if it is the ground of intersubjectivity, does not entail harmony. Indeed, the political struggle about the beautiful seems to point to more than a formal agreement that it is. The patriotic death, or stubborn resistance in a nonselfish cause, seems to call forth universal admiration. But Hippias, who knows nothing of the beauty of defeat (cf. 304a6– b3), might be an exception: his last definition seemed to deny any nobility to Antigone. If courage on the battlefield, then, is the proper starting point for the examination of the beautiful, it would also raise once more the issue of progress. "Good" (*agathos*) originally meant "brave" (cf. 289e7, 290e4).

The Useful
(295a1–297d9)

The transition from the seemly to the useful is remarkable. After Hippias agrees that the seemly, in his opinion, is thought to make things appear (*phainesthai*) beautiful, the dialogue continues as follows:

> SOCRATES: Oh my! The beautiful has fled from us, Hippias, and goes away, (so that) we do not know what on earth it is, since the seemly has come to light (*ephanê on*) as something other than beautiful.
> HIPPIAS: Yes, by Zeus, Socrates, very strangely, in my opinion.
> SOCRATES: Well, comrade, let us not yet let go of it, for I still have some hope that what the beautiful is will become manifest (*ekphanêsesthai*).
> HIPPIAS: Of course, Socrates, for it is not difficult to find. I know well that if I went into isolation for a while and examined it by myself, I could tell it to you with more precision than total precision.
> SOCRATES: Don't talk big, Hippias. You see how much trouble it has given us. (I'm afraid) that in its anger at us it will run

away still more. But I'm talking nonsense. I believe you shall find it easily once you are alone. But, by the gods, find it in front of me, or, if you want, just as now, continue searching for it with me. If we find it, it will be most beautiful; if not, I shall, I believe, be content with my lot (*tykhê*), and you, once you go away, will easily find it.

The Q.E.D. of the proof that the seemly is not the beautiful combines *phainesthai* with the participle of *einai;* in such a combination, which has not occurred before, *phainesthai* no longer means "to appear," but "to be evident." That which supplies nothing but "show" has shown itself to be nothing but "show." Both Socrates and Hippias express surprise at this, Hippias by swearing by Zeus, Socrates by personifying the beautiful. In that part of the dialogue in which the gods are no longer cited as examples of the beautiful, the beautiful assumes the aspects of divinity. Indeed, were it not for the possibility of its getting angry, the beautiful now satisfies the two "types" to which, in Socrates' "theology," the gods must conform: it never deceives us with appearances, and, as the second of Socrates' definitions turns out to mean, it is solely the cause of good.[33] Socrates further implies that the beautiful had been present; but then while it was present, it must have made something truly beautiful. Was the beautiful behind the proof that opened their eyes to the specious beauty of the seemly? However this may be, the beautiful as the seemly is the first definition that was not ridiculed. For the first time Hippias and Socrates were alone. Socrates did not rely on Socrates₂ for his own arguments, Hippias no longer had to be indignant at Socrates₂' shamelessness. Socrates ceased to be provocative; Hippias ceased to be boastful. Does Hippias' participation in the search—his admission that he is perplexed—signify that the beautiful was present and give Socrates some hope that it will not elude them?[34] Hippias at once dashes that hope; he ridicules Socrates' tentativeness and says that he knows that given a little time alone he could find the beautiful by himself. In his reply, Socrates does not remark on Hippias' claim that his answer will be of greater precision than total precision; instead, he fully animates the beautiful. Socrates implies perhaps that the gods, as ordinarily understood, are nothing but hyperbolic impossibilities, and the beautiful could never be as divorced from appearance as the argument seems to entail. He did not exactly say, after all, that the seemly was not the beautiful; he said that it was apparent that the seemly was something other than beautiful.

Socrates admits that he is talking nonsense; despite the willful elusiveness of the beautiful, Hippias will find it easily on his own. However, Socrates beseeches Hippias, in the name of the gods, to find it face to face with him, or at least to continue their joint search. He refuses to see any difference between Hippias' finding the beautiful alone, finding it in front of Socrates, and finding it together with Socrates. Soliloquy, monologue, and dialogue are the same;[35] but only its discovery in a dialogue would be most beautiful. The beautiful on the occasion of its manifestation will not show its causal power unless a common inquiry makes it manifest. The contemplation of the beautiful will not reveal by itself that it is a cause;[36] and the reasoning, which would show that, will have to be a reasoning between two if it is to illustrate its causality at the same time. Socrates knows the effect of the beautiful without knowing the beautiful. His anticipated experience of it is his guide to the way of its discovery. It is therefore almost inevitable that he should at once restrict the beautiful to the beautiful "for us," and soon afterward identify it with power (295e9).

Anything is beautiful to the extent that it has the power to make or produce something. The altogether ugly, then, would be wholly passive, and the altogether beautiful could never be affected but would have the greatest power to affect. This implication overlooks the usefulness of passivity, without which every power is good for nothing. If we allow the passive to be a kind of power, the impossible or total nonbeing would be the ugly itself. Even this allowance, however, is inadequate, for it overlooks the possible usefulness of the impossible: Parmenides showed that one has to think about nonbeing in order to realize the impossibility of thinking nonbeing. The ugly, then, is the useless impossible. The beautiful thus acquires a range that is beyond being, but within that range it seems impossible to pinpoint the most beautiful, for the understanding would have to give very high marks to nonbeing.

The relation between the useful and the possible is obscure. Socrates says that one human body is beautiful if it is as a whole geared to running, another if it is geared to wrestling; he implies that since the requirements of wrestling cannot consist with those of running, no one body can be beautiful in both respects. Homer had indicated their apparent inconsistency by uniting them in Achilles and separating them in Telamonian and Oilean Ajax. Achilles was the most beautiful Achaean who came to Troy; no one could beat him in either running or hand-to-hand combat. But Telamonian Ajax, who was the second best warrior, was built like a fortress, and Oilean Ajax, who was almost Achilles' equal in speed, was slight.[37] Achilles was a miracle. But Odysseus, at the funeral games in honor of Patroclus, when Achilles did not compete, outran Oilean Ajax with the help of Athena and wrestled Telamonian Ajax to a draw by guile.[38] That wisdom duplicates the miraculous would no doubt be an absurd interpretation of Homer's meaning, but no one would argue that the beauty of Homer is the same as the beauty of Achilles.

The beautiful seems to be power partly because it confers power on its perceiver. A beautiful lyre shows its capacity in such a way that it looks as if there is no impediment to its perfect operation. The beautiful lyre "practically plays itself"; the beautiful hammer cannot possibly fail to drive the nail straight; the beautiful tool makes everything look easy. As automatic instrumentality, the beautiful looks alive; indeed, it might seem to be the externalized will. But the beautiful draws to itself, without any awareness on our part, our own projects and intentions and thus confirms that we have the capacity to achieve them. Its moral neutrality, therefore, does not pose a problem for us: we know that our intentions are good. Socrates, however, sees the consequence of the argument is that, in general, beautiful things have the power to do evil, and in particular, wisdom is nothing but omnicompetence. The argument is framed on either side by the verb "to want." Before the argument, Socrates says that he would want his argument to proceed beautifully (296b3); after the argument, he asks Hippias whether this was "what our soul wanted to say, that the beautiful is that which is useful for and capable of producing some good" (296d8). Socrates thus supplies a possible corrective of the argument: power is powerlessness unless its possessor exercises it rationally.[39] The beautiful, then, would be not-mindless power. If, moreover, the big was a condition for the beautiful and the beautiful was defined as power on a large scale rationally employed, the beautiful could be that which suspends our usual understanding of good and evil. What Homer has Helen say to Hector of herself and Paris both terrifies and consoles: "Zeus set upon us an evil fate, so that we might be the subject of song for human beings who will come after."[40]

Socrates further assumes that the good is inert; it is not good for anything. Rather, the beautiful is good for the good. The good, then, must be the ultimate good for which all beautiful things are means. Socrates, therefore, does not mean by the beautiful that which is the cause of everything beautiful; the beautiful is only the collective name for the manifold of beautiful things. But if the beautiful is good for the good, how does he prove that the beautiful is not good? Socrates himself deepens the mystery by indicating what the connection is between beautiful things and the good. "We are in earnest (*spoudazomen*)," he says, "about prudence and all other beautiful things because their product and offspring are the object of earnestness (*spoudaston*), the good." Our concern for the good makes us concerned for the beautiful; the good is the cause of our interest in the beautiful.

So whereas the beautiful causes the good, the beautiful is beautiful only because of the good.

The good as final cause links the beautiful as efficient cause with the good as effect, but whereas the good, apparently, does not disclose the beautiful as the means for its realization, the beautiful does disclose itself as a means. Indeed, the self-disclosure of the beautiful is so complete that it does not stop at indicating its power to do good but becomes manifest as that which does good (296d9, 297a4). The beautiful not only initiates, it seems to be self-initiating. The beautiful, then, in being complete in itself and still pointing beyond itself, is that which gives us the almost ineradicable illusion of the identity of efficient and final causation. The beautiful is the soul in its self-forgetfulness. If the qualification of rationality can correct the defect in the definition of the beautiful as power, and soul without self-knowledge lurks in the conclusion of the beautiful as the cause of good, the two arguments together point to the problem of the relation between mind and soul. Is their problematic unity at the root of the difficulty about the beautiful?

The Pleasant
(297d10–304e9)

The beautiful, Socrates finally suggests, consists of aural and visual pleasures. Sight and hearing are the two most public of the senses. The "this" I see or hear is the "this" you see or hear, but I cannot touch this spot (taste this wine or smell this perfume) without my withholding it at once from the public domain and precluding the possibility of your sensing it simultaneously, if ever. But if sight and hearing thus stand apart from the other senses, they do not thereby stand together; autopsy and hearsay could not be more different. Socrates' examples of visually or aurally beautiful things are these: human beings, embroideries (*poikilmata*), paintings (*zôgraphêmata*), fabricated figures (*plasmata*), sounds, music, speeches, and mythologies. Socrates' list points immediately to three other peculiarities of sights and sounds. They are the only sensibilia which are covered by genuine arts. Of these arts most are imitative, and, as the parallel placement of *plasmata* and mythologies indicates, the beautiful things which delight us on seeing or hearing them are very likely to be lies. The very openness of visual and aural phenomena allows for the most concealment. If sight and hearing were not the most epistemic of the senses, they would not be so liable to deception, and particularly to deliberate deception.

These characteristics, however, still do not put sight and hearing any closer together. The first sign of their inner connectedness is given by the language of Socrates' examples. *Plasmata* means "fabrications," and it is no less applicable to the fictions of speech than to the images of the sculptor. *Zôgraphêmata* likewise is not restricted to paintings (Socrates uses the word for "names" insofar as they are imitations of things), and the Athenian stranger speaks of the *poikilmata* of musical rhythms.[41] The ambiguity of the terms points to the transposability of the visible into the audible and the audible into the visible. A picture can be described, and a speech can be pictured. Much, if not all, of poetry would be impossible if this were not the case, and model making is sometimes indispensable for the understanding. Socrates introduced his third definition with the imperative "See!" (297e5), but he meant "Listen!" (cf. 300e2).[42]

If "beautiful" were a compendious word and equivalent to either "pleasant sight" or "pleasant sound," the phrase "beautiful sight" or "beautiful sound" would be strangely redundant. The redundancy is eliminable if "pleasant" and "beautiful" are the same, but if they are not, one would have to conclude that in the course of time the original meaning of "beautiful" had been forgotten. "Beautiful sight/sound" would be like "consensus of opinion," and what began as a compound subject, "I am delighted to see/hear," would become a predicate, so that the sentence, "I am delighted to see/hear so beautiful a thing," would be without the speaker's awareness the same as, "I am delighted to see/hear a thing so pleasant to my sight/hearing" (cf. 299a3). The "analyticity" of the latter sentence implies that it would be impossible to take no pleasure in beautiful things, and some sincerity in moral matters—one would at least be pleased on seeing or hearing praiseworthy things—would be automatic. This absurd consequence would not follow if Socrates were proposing to replace morality with a refined hedonism, or, as he later calls the aurally and the visually pleasant, beautiful pleasures.

Socrates at once brings up morality in the form of beautiful practices and laws and asks whether it is plausible that they fall under the definition. The implausibility consists not only in the law thus becoming no different from a fairy tale, but in a practice ceasing to be beautiful for its practitioner even if it gives him pleasure. The beauty of morality would only come to light for its auditors or spectators; the moral man himself would have to hear himself praised or see his own actions before he could possibly pass judgment on his own morality. Morality, then, would be beautiful by reflection.[43] Hippias suggests that Socrates$_2$ might not notice the difficulty that beautiful practices and laws cause the definition. Hippias, of course, does not know who the son of Sophroniscus is; he therefore does not realize that while Socrates₁' words—"No, by the dog, Hippias, it won't pass him unnoticed, not him before whom I am ashamed to talk nonsense and pretend to say something while saying nothing"—seem to confirm the need for the presence of others if the moral is to be beautiful, they in fact disprove it. And yet Socrates' shame before himself is presented as shame before another (cf. 304d5); so it still might be the case that at least virtual distance, or the imagining of another's perspective, is indispensable for the beautiful.

As soon as Socrates proposes paradoxically that the problem of the law be put aside and not be allowed out in the open (*eis meson*)—as if the law could be anywhere else than in the open—Socrates₂ reenters the discussion. For the first and only time he addresses Socrates₁ and Hippias together. His questioning leads Socrates₁ to replace tacitly the original statement, "It is pleasant to hear/see the beautiful," with its supposed equivalent, "It is beautiful to hear/see the pleasant." The replacement allows Socrates₁ to admit that everyone insists that it is most pleasant to engage in sexual intercourse but most shameful/ugly to be seen to do so,[44] whereas, according to Socrates' first formulation, men should deny that it is pleasant to see oneself or others engaged in sexual intercourse. Socrates₂ understands that Socrates₁ and Hippias would be ashamed to say that sexual pleasure is beautiful, but their shame, while it fully agrees with the human consensus, is possibly inconsistent with their own definition of the beautiful. Indeed, it is not clear that all human beings would cite this example as a refutation of their definition: Socrates₂ replaces Socrates₁' "human beings" by the "many" (cf. 284e2–4). As possible witnesses for Socrates₁ and Hippias, Socrates₂ is thinking not so much of those tribes whose laws do not prohibit the seeing of sexual acts as of the poets and painters whose representations of sexual acts are not necessarily thought to be ugly.

Socrates₂ particularly has in mind, I believe, a passage in the *Odyssey*, where Odysseus listens with pleasure to the beautiful story of how Hephaestus caught Ares and Aphrodite in bed together. When Hephaestus summoned Zeus and the other gods to see "laughable and unseemly deeds," Poseidon, Hermes, and Apollo came, but the goddesses stayed home out of shame. "Unquenchable laughter then arose among the blessed gods as they beheld the contrivances of Hephaestus." Apollo asked Hermes whether he would be willing, bound in strong chains, to sleep in bed by the side of golden Aphrodite, and Hermes replied, "Would this could only be, lord Apollo; let there be thrice as many bonds, and let the gods and all the goddesses behold it—even so would I sleep by the side of golden Aphrodite" (VIII.266–269). The gods, who cannot be beautiful according to Socrates' definition, make possible the beautiful representation of what the many believe to be ugly, and which in fact might be ugly if they were not gods, and gods who are only visible and audible by art. Not only, then, does this exemplify the suspension by the beautiful of the moral and the coming to light of the beautiful through a class shift, but the example itself has a direct bearing on the final theme of the dialogue. Hippias asserts that if each of two human beings is beautiful they must be beautiful together, but he apparently agrees with the many that in sexual intercourse two human beings are ugly. Surely Hippias, of all people, would not take Aristophanes literally, and believe that in intercourse two bodies are no longer two but one.

Once Socrates$_2$ gets Socrates$_1$ and Hippias to agree that differences of intensity and duration cannot distinguish one pleasure from another insofar as they are both pleasures—he fails to consider whether the presence or absence of pain would make a difference—he puts to them the following question: "Then isn't it because of something else than because they are pleasures that you preferred these pleasures to the others, seeing something of the sort in both, because they have something different from the others, by gazing at which you declare that they are beautiful?" Socrates$_2$ uses the familiar language of the "ideas" to ask Socrates$_1$ and Hippias about that which belongs exclusively to aural and visual pleasures. But in this case, the language seems to be unfortunate, since, we should say, Socrates$_2$ has used the language of sight metaphorically in a question about sight literally understood. Whatever it is that Socrates$_1$ and Hippias see is expressable in a speech, and what they see and look at apart from everything else is the cause of the beauty of aural and visual pleasures.

Their vision is a vision of a cause, which as such is indistinguishable from the conclusion of their reasoning, for in the most literal way Socrates$_2$ is asking them to put one and one together. Although the beautiful, by definition, must be either audible or visible, the cause of that which makes them beautiful cannot be either audible or visible. But the cause must be at least translatable into the audible, and perhaps it might lend itself to a visible model as well. If the visual and aural fields have each a number of distinct characteristics—A, E, I, ... and α, ϵ, η, ... respectively—there must be some common factor, e.g., $\aleph$, which is neither visible nor audible, that affects all the elements of either series that make up on any occasion the perception of the beautiful. When the visual elements A and E are beautiful, they are each, as it were, indexed by $\aleph$, which then acts as their bond, just as it does when the aural elements α and ϵ are beautiful. This bond, though it must be in itself imperceptible, does not have to remain inaudible or invisible when it is at work as the cause of the beautiful sight or sound. It could be like a consonant which loses its natural silence as soon as it is put together with a vowel. What could this common factor be which is both aesthetic and noetic except number?

"It appears (*phainetai*) to me," Socrates says, "that that which I neither undergo to be nor am, and you are not either, it is possible for both of us to undergo; and other things, which we both undergo to be, neither of us is." Socrates seems to make no distinction between affect (*pathos*) and being (*ousia*); what he is, what he undergoes, and what he undergoes to be are treated as equivalent (cf. 301b8). The equivalence reminds us how, in the discussion of the seemly, the distinction between appearing and being was first made doubtful with the expression "appears to be" and then cancelled with the expression "evidently is" (294c5, e9). To be reminded of that discussion, more-over, is to be reminded that the seemly involved at least two things whose togetherness made the whole to which they both belonged appear beautiful, even though one of them was ugly by itself. Hippias, however, had then gone along with the common opinion that the seemly does not have the power to make things be beautiful. He therefore is not now inconsistent when he denies the possibility that he and Socrates could be something together which they are not apart. Any affect that only holds of things collectively must be an appearance. Hippias, however, must also repudiate his own contribution, that the beautiful virgin is beautiful only as long as the race of the gods is not compared with her. The dialogue has thus come full circle: from Hippias' concession that two beautiful things of different classes can-not be beautiful together to Hippias' assertion that two beautiful things cannot but be beautiful together. Hippias' concession depended on Socrates$_2$' citation of the beautiful gods, his assertion depends on the nonarithmetical character of the beautiful, and it occurs in that part of the dialogue in which the gods either cannot be beautiful or are no longer examples of the beautiful. Numbers, it seems, replace the gods as that in light of which the beautiful is to be understood.

Although Hippias at first seems to challenge Socrates to conceive of anything which is not the same collectively and distributively, he at once makes it clear that only human things (*ta en anthrôpois*) are to be considered. Socrates emphatically agrees. Numbers, it seems, are not among the human things. But does Socrates wish to imply that every human whole, like friendship or the city, is not a genuine whole, and the elements which make up such a whole do not truly undergo anything together? Numbers only illustrate the difference between whole and part; they do not constitute the entire range of that phe-nomenon. Hippias and Socrates both speak of wholes (288e7, 295c8, 301b2), but only Socrates ever speaks of a part (299b3).

It is easy to solve Socrates' riddle; it is difficult to understand the solution. Hippias would say that the words "both" and "each" in the sentence "Hippias and Socrates are both two, but each is one" belong to the sentence and not to the beings "Hippias" and "Socrates." One might also remark that "both" does not entail "two": we can say, "Each board is ten feet long," or, "Both boards are ten feet long." It is Hippias and not Socrates who first supplements the word "both" with the word "together" (301b8). In order to extract "two" from "both," one has to stand back, as it were, from the sentence in which "both" occurs and interpret it as an injunction to carry out an operation on the elements which, in anticipation of that operation, it has put together. Socrates had therefore spoken of his vision as a presentation in front of his soul. Unless the speech about "both" and "each" is put at a distance from the speaker, "two" and "one" will never come to light. The speaker has to hear what he is saying if "one" and "two" are not going to elude him. Hippias nevers hears what he says; Socrates always does, for there dwells in the same place with him someone who is closest to him in kind (304d3–4). The single Socrates is necessarily two, for *dialegesthai* is spoken *dianoeisthai*.[45] "Shall I exhibit to you in speech," he asks Hippias, "what we were thinking about them (i.e., us)?" Throughout the discussion of the beautiful, Socrates has represented dianoetic thinking eikastically. Reflection has been shown in the form of poetic reproduction. This fact is a riddle, for it seems to bring together the evident opposition of the beautiful and number upon which both Socrates and Hippias agree.

The digression on number opens up another possibility about the beautiful: that it too might hold for things together but not apart. In order to lead up to this possibility, Socrates rehearses the argument about aural and visual pleasures. The rehearsal, though it seems not to advance the argument, serves to show how untypical Hippias' example of "I" and "you" was. If whatever is pleasant through sight and hearing is beautiful, one can conclude only that both pleasures are beautiful but not each. The strict conclusion seems unsound. Does our hearing of the actors in a play contribute a pleasure that is necessarily distinct and distinguishable from the pleasure we have in seeing them perform? Inasmuch as *ex hypothesi* these two senses are working together, we cannot, it seems, properly speak of each pleasure or both pleasures. Socrates' formula applies to the speech but not to the experience. His first example of what holds collectively and distributively for himself and Hippias—if each is strong, both are strong—suggests at first an inversion that would not hold: if each is weak, are they necessarily weak together? Hippias, however, might argue that their combined strength, if it qualified as strong, was a continuous magnitude that could not be called a "both." It acts as one and not two.

Socrates seems to be guilty of bad arithmetic when, in order to prove that thousands and thousands of cases had presented (*prophainesthai*) themselves to him, he cites those in which both are even but each is odd or each even, and when each is irrational (*arrêton*), their sum (*ta synamphotera*) is sometimes rational and sometimes irrational. But we must think geometrically: if the length of one leg of a right-angle triangle is $2 - \sqrt{2}$ and the other $2 + \sqrt{2}$, then their sum is rational.[46] As parts of a geometric figure, these linear magnitudes do not vanish once they are summed, and "both" and "each" are meaningful. It would thus be clear why Socrates spoke of his *prophainomena,* and one could speculate as to whether he was not thinking of arithmetic and geometry as the arts of the aurally and visually beautiful respectively. Hippias, at any rate, does not question Socrates' examples, and he frees them both of a larger search by agreeing that it would be a case of great irrationality (*pollê alogia*) if both were beautiful and each not, or each beautiful and not both.

Hippias does not notice that Socrates' very language suggests that one replace the older term for irrational (*arrêton*) with the modern one (*alogon*). Could Socrates, then, be implying that the irrationality of his supposition does not preclude its having a rationale? And that Hippias and Socrates are each "irrational" apart but "rational" together? Arithmetically speaking, there is no difference between our saying, "Hippias is one, Socrates is one, but both are two," and Socrates' telling Hippias, "I am one, you are one, but we are two." But nonarithmetically there is all the difference in the world. Whereas "Socrates" is an independent one, Socrates as "I" is a one that is already bound up with another, namely, Hippias as "you," even prior to his counting of themselves. "Socrates" is an *hekastos* (each), "I" is an *hekateros* (either one of two). "Socrates is one" is complete in itself; "I am one" contains latent within it "You are one, but we are two." "We" is not like "both," for whereas "both" does not "follow" each, "we" does "follow" "I." "We" is both what "I" and "you" are together but not separately, and what "I," which each of us is, is separately but not together. "We" is thus the plainest example of the impossible togetherness of the necessarily apart. It was the example supplied by Hippias, who keeps only to the human things and ignores both gods and numbers.

The range of the beautiful, as Plato displays it in the *Hippias Major,* comprehends in a remarkable manner all the themes of the *Theaetetus, Sophist,* and *Statesman* and therefore justifies the view that the beautiful marks not only critical points in these dialogues but also permeates them. It thus offers a way to understand the ugliest man in Athens, who in turning toward hair, mud, and dirt, did not turn away from the beautiful. The double meaning of Socratic dialectics is the double of the beautiful.

Notes

1. Xenophon *Memorabilia* IV.v.12–vi.1.
2. Cf. M. Heidegger, *Hegel und die Griechen* in *Wegmarken* (Frankfurt, 1967), p. 262.
3. L. Strauss, *What Is Political Philosophy?* (Glencoe, Ill., 1959), pp. 39–40.
4. *Parmenides* 130B–D.
5. *Sophist* 216B.
6. *Statesman* 258A.
7. *Sophist* 226B–230D; *Statesman* 306A–309B.
8. *Protagoras* 337e2–338a8; *Hippias Minor* 369b8–c2.
9. *Iliad* III.146–160.
10. *Republic* 472d4–8.
11. *Protagoras* 315b9; *Odyssey* XI.601–14.
12. *Symposium* 204d8–11.
13. *Cratylus* 413b3–c1.
14. *Symposium* 221e1–222a1; *Gorgias* 494e3–8.
15. *Metaphysics* 984b11–29.
16. *Sophist* 234c2–e6.
17. *Philebus* 51c1–d10.
18. *Iliad* XXIV.258–59.
19. *Theogony* 585; *Catalina* 20.3.
20. *Philebus* 28c2–8.
21. *Phaedo* 99c3–d3.
22. *Phaedrus* 229c6–e4.
23. Thucydides II.13.5; cf. L. Strauss, *Interpretation* 4 (1974): 2.
24. *Republic* 420c4–d5.
25. Sappho fr. 111 LP; Herodotus I.60.4.
26. *Sophist* 235e5–236a3.
27. The verb is from the word for "ladle."
28. This means "extends her protection," with a pun on hand (*kheira*) and pot (*khutran*).
29. *Laws* 632c1–4.
30. Aristophanes *Birds* 1642–45.
31. *Cratylus* 416b6–d11.
32. *Philebus* 16b5–7; *Phaedrus* 266b3–5.
33. *Republic* 380c6–9, 382e8–11.
34. *Laches* 194a1–5.
35. *Sophist* 217d8–e3; *Gorgias* 505d8–e3.
36. *Republic* 516b4–c2.
37. *Iliad* II.528; XIII.321–25; XIV.520–22.
38. *Iliad* XXIII.724–25, 770.
39. *Gorgias* 467c5–468e5.
40. *Iliad* VI.357–58.

41. *Republic* 588b10–e2; Xenophanes fr. 1, 22; *Cratylus* 430b3;
Laws 812e2; cf. d4.

42. Socrates perhaps hints at transposability on another occasion.
Socrates $_2$ asks, "Is that which is
pleasant through sight pleasant
through sight and hearing, or is
that which is pleasant through
hearing pleasant through sight?"
Socrates$_1$ replies, "In no way
would that which is through one
be through both—for we think
that this is what you mean"
(299c4–8). Socrates$_1$' doubt as to
Socrates$_2$' meaning indicates that
Socrates$_2$' question could be
read as saying that whatever is
pleasant through sight is also
pleasant through hearing if it is
beautiful.

43. Aristotle *EN* 1095b22–28.

44. *Philebus* 65e9–66a3.

45. *Theaetetus* 189e4–190a2.

46. I owe this suggestion to Diego
Benardete.

Guide for the Reader

The numbers and letters in the margins of the dialogues refer to the pages and sections of Stephanus' edition of Plato. In the commentaries, and in the notes, the references are to Burnet's edition which numbers each line within each letter section.

Parentheses in the translation give: (1) the transcription of the Greek word, for example, account (*logos*); (2) the literal or alternative meaning of the word, for example, "simply" (artlessly); or (3) an omission in the Greek which English cannot dispense with and which seems important, for example, Perception (is) knowledge. In some cases, therefore, (art) could be (science).

The following rules are adhered to as strictly as possible. Hyphenated words that are not standard in English represent compound words, for example, "animal-hunting" is used for *zôiothêrikê*. Contracted forms imply that the Greek lacks something, uncontracted that it is present in the Greek and is to receive some emphasis. For example, "that's so" means that "is" does not occur, "that is so" means that it does. "We've" means that the Greek omits the pronoun, "we have" that it does not, and "we are" that the pronoun is present though possibly not the verb.

To on is always translated as "that which is," *ta mê onta* "the things which are not," and when necessary they are put in single quotes. But in order not to lose sight of their participial form in Greek, the commentary speaks of being and nonbeings. "Being" in the translation is always for *ousia*. *Genesis* is either "becoming" or "coming-to-be." *Gignesthai* is "become," "come to be," "prove to be," "occur," "happen," or "arise."

Eidos is always translated "species" and *genos*, "genus," for the first is cognate with the verb "see" and the second with "become." The distinction has nothing to do with Aristotle's betwen species and genus. *Idea,* which is almost equivalent to *eidos* but rarer (particularly in the plural) and which suggests a whole that is not subject to division, is always "look," with its transcription in parenthesis. "Kind" never translates a Greek substantive but is used either for the indefinite pronoun or to complete the sense in English. "Things" also does not translate for the most part any Greek substantive; when it does, it is *pragmata,* which is always put afterward in parenthesis. *Pragmata* are things with which we deal and are of concern to us.

The phrase "simply true" translates *alêthinos* and is used to distinguish it from *alêthês* ("true"); *alêthinos* implies that something is genuine. "Proper part" is for *morion,* "part" for *meros.*

Although consistency has been aimed at, it has not always been possible to achieve it. The most important variations are these. The three verbs for know, *gignôskô* (know by acquaintance), *oida* (the perfect of "see"), and *epistamai* (connected by Plato with "supervise," "be in charge," *epistatô, ephistamai*) have not always been kept distinct. But "know how to" never translates either of the first two; the aorist of *gignôskô* is "come to know," the present almost always "recognize" or "be familiar with" but sometimes "cognize." The first two, moreover, are used with a personal object more frequently than *epistamai* is, and, in the latter half of the *Theaetetus,* in those sentences in which *gignôskô* and *oida* both occur, the participial form will be the former and the finite the latter (with the exception of 203D). *Agnoô,* which is mostly translated "be ignorant," can also at times be "fail to recognize," or "fail to understand." "Knowledge" or "science" is always for *epistêmê,* "cognition" for *gnôsis,* and "intelligence" and "intelligent" for *phronêsis* and *phronimos* respectively, though "prudence"/"prudent" and even "wisdom"/"wise" might on occasion have seemed more appropriate.

The verb *dokô* is translated in several ways. When it occurs without a personal pronoun, it is translated "seem," "resolve," or "decide." If it is with a pronoun, it is usually either "impression" or "opinion." "Impression" is used when the context suggests that it is an opinion of the moment, "opinion" when it seems to be longstanding. The reader is free to judge each case differently. The noun *doxa* is "opinion," "impression," or "reputation." Parenthetical "it seems," or "it seems that," always translates *eoiken,* which is otherwise "resembles." In replies it is always, "it seems likely." The cognate noun *eikôn* is "semblance," whereas *eidôlon* is "image."

The verbal system for "speak" is complex in Greek, and "speak," "mean," "say," "talk," "mention," "remark," and "state" are all used to convey different tenses, aspects, and nuances. *Logos,* however, is as far as possible always "speech" and never, for instance, "argument."

"To say something" (*legein ti*) means to say something significant or to make sense, and "to say nothing" (*legein ouden*) means to make no sense, as does the adjective *alogon*. Only when the context calls for a literal translation is the idiomatic sacrificed, but it should of course always be kept in mind.

THEAETETUS

Theaetetus

EUCLIDES

TERPSION[1]

EUCLIDES: Just now, Terpsion, or a long time ago from the country?

TERPSION: Fairly long. And I was in fact looking for you throughout the marketplace and was surprised that I couldn't find you.

EUCLIDES: That's because I wasn't anywhere in the city.

TERPSION: Well, where then?

EUCLIDES: On going down to the harbor I met Theaetetus as he was being carried out of Corinth from the army camp to Athens.[2]

TERPSION: Alive or dead?

EUCLIDES: Alive, barely. He's in a bad way also from some wounds, *B* but the outbreak of the illness in the army affects him more.

TERPSION: Don't you mean dysentery?

EUCLIDES: Yes.

TERPSION: What a man you say's in danger.

EUCLIDES: Beautiful and good, Terpsion, and, you know, I was listening even now to some people highly praising his conduct in the battle.

TERPSION: Well, there's nothing strange in that, but far more surprising if he were not of that sort. But how come he refused to *C* take lodgings here in Megara?

EUCLIDES: He was pressing for home, though I begged and advised him, but he wasn't willing. And then, when I sent him on his way, on my way back I recalled with amazement how prophetically Socrates had spoken about him as well as different things. My impression is that Socrates met him shortly before his death when

Theaetetus was a lad, and on the basis of his association and conversation with him expressed great admiration for his nature. And when I came to Athens he narrated to me the speeches of

D   his conversation with him—they're well worth hearing—and he said there was every necessity that he become renowned if he reached maturity.

TERPSION: Yes, and he did, it seems, tell the truth. But what were the speeches? Could you be their narrator?

143   EUCLIDES: No, by Zeus, not at any rate straight off from memory, but I did write down reminders just as soon as I returned home, and later, in recalling it at my leisure, I proceeded to write them up. And as often as I returned to Athens, I questioned Socrates repeatedly about whatever I hadn't remembered, and then on my return here I made corrections. So pretty nearly the entire speech has been written by me.

TERPSION: True. I've heard you mention it before, and though you know I always intended to urge you to show it, I've delayed doing so up till now. Well, what prevents us from going through it now? As for myself, I really need a rest in any case, since I've come from the country.

B   EUCLIDES: But of course, I myself escorted Theaetetus up to Erineos;[3] so I wouldn't take a rest without pleasure. Well, let's go, and while we're resting, the boy will read.

TERPSION: A good suggestion (What you say's right).

EUCLIDES: Here's the book, Terpsion. And I wrote the speech down on these terms, not with Socrates narrating them to me as he did, but with Socrates conversing with those with whom he said he conversed. He said they were the geometer Theodorus and Theaetetus. In order that the narrations between the speeches

C   might not cause trouble (*pragmata*) in the writing, whenever either Socrates spoke about himself, for example, "And I said" or "And I spoke," or in turn about whoever answered, "He consented" or "He refused to agree," it's for these reasons that I removed things of this sort and wrote it as if he were conversing with them.

TERPSION: And there's nothing wayward in that, Euclides.

EUCLIDES: Well, boy, take the book and read.[4]

SOCRATES

THEODORUS

THEAETETUS[5]

SOCRATES: If I were to care, Theodorus, more for those in Cyrene, I *D* would be asking you about the state of affairs there and whether any of the young there make geometry or something else of philosophy their concern. But as it is I don't, for I'm less a friend to those there than to these here, and I'm more desirous of knowing who of our young are expected to prove good and able. Now I myself examine this on my own, to the extent that I can, and I ask everyone else with whom I see the young are willing to associate. Now it's not the smallest number who consort with you, *E* and it's just that they do so, for you deserve it on account of geometry as well as for everything else. So if you did meet anyone worth speaking of, I would hear about it with pleasure.

THEODORUS: As a matter of fact, Socrates, it's certainly worth it for me to tell and for you to hear about the sort of lad of your fellow citizens I met. And if he were beautiful, I'd be afraid to speak of him with intensity, should anyone in fact get the impression that I'm desirous of him. But as it is—please don't get annoyed with me—he is not beautiful, but he resembles you in the snubness of his nose and the bulging of his eyes, but he has them less than you do. I'm speaking fearlessly. Know well, of all whom I've ever *144* met—and I've consorted with very many—I'm aware of no one yet whose nature is as wonderfully good. For to be as good a learner as he is, in a way that's hard for anyone else to match, and yet to be exceptionally gentle, and on top of this to be manly beyond anyone whatsoever, I would have suspected that it doesn't occur and I don't see it occurring, for those who are as sharp as he is, quick witted, and with good memories are for the most part also quickly inclined to bursts of anger, and in darting about *B* they're swept along like unballasted ships, and they grow up rather more manic than more manly, whereas those in turn who are more grave face up to their lessons somewhat sluggishly and are full of forgetfulness. But he goes so smoothly, so unfalteringly, and so effectively to his lessons and investigations, and all with so much gentleness, just as a stream of olive-oil flows without a sound, as for it to be a cause of wonder that someone of his age behaves in this way.

SOCRATES: You report well. But which citizen is his father?

I.5

THEODORUS: Though I've heard the name, I don't remember. But as a matter of fact, of those here approaching us, he's the one in the

C middle. He as well as some of his comrades were just now oiling themselves in the course outside, and it's my impression that with the oiling over they're coming here. But do consider whether you recognize him.

SOCRATES: I recognize him. He is the son of Euphronius from Sunium, a man, my friend, who's very much of the sort you describe him to be, otherwise well thought of and moreover who left, you know, a great deal of property. But I don't know the name of the lad.

D THEODORUS: Theaetetus, Socrates, is his name. But it's my impression that some guardians of his have wasted the property, though all the same, Socrates, he's of an amazing liberality when it comes to money.

SOCRATES: How grand a nobleman you speak of. Please urge him to sit alongside me here.

THEODORUS: It shall be done. Theaetetus, come over here to Socrates.

SOCRATES: Yes, please do, Theaetetus, so that I too may examine

E myself as to what sort of face I have. Theodorus says I have one similar to yours. Still, if each of the pair of us had a lyre and he said they had been similarly tuned, would we straight off trust him, or would we go on to examine whether he's speaking as one who is skilled in music?

THEAETETUS: We would go on to examine.

SOCRATES: Isn't it the case that if we found him to be of that sort we would be persuaded, but if unmusical, we would distrust him?

THEAETETUS: True.

SOCRATES: Yes, and now, I suspect, if our concern was at all for the

145 similarity of faces, we would have to examine whether he speaks as one who is a skilled draftsman or not.

THEAETETUS: That's my opinion.

SOCRATES: Is Theodorus really then a skilled painter?

THEAETETUS: No, not as far as I know.

SOCRATES: And not skilled in geometry either?

THEAETETUS: There's really no doubt that he is, Socrates.

SOCRATES: As well as skilled in astronomy, logistics, music, and everything connected with education?

THEAETETUS: That's my opinion at least.

SOCRATES: So whereas, in something of the body, if in praising or blaming us in some respect, he says we are similar, it's scarcely worthwhile to pay him any mind—

THEAETETUS: Perhaps not.

B SOCRATES: But what if he should praise the soul of either one of us in point of virtue and wisdom? Isn't it then worthwhile for him who hears it to be eager to examine the one praised, and for the latter as eagerly to display himself?

THEAETETUS: Yes, of course, Socrates.

SOCRATES: Well then, it's time, my dear Theaetetus, for you to display and for me to examine, since, know well, though Theodorus has praised many to my face, strangers as well as fellow townsmen, he did not yet praise anyone as he did you just now.

THEAETETUS: That would be all to the good, Socrates, but look and   C
see whether he was not speaking in jest.

SOCRATES: This is not Theodorus' way. But don't back out of what has been agreed upon by pretending that he was speaking in jest, in order that he may not be compelled actually to bear witness— no one will in any case denounce him for false evidence—but stand by your agreement with confidence.

THEAETETUS: Well, I must do it, if that's your opinion.

SOCRATES: So tell me. You're surely learning from Theodorus something of geometry?

THEAETETUS: Yes I am.

SOCRATES: And of that which pertains to astronomy, harmony, and   D
calculations?

THEAETETUS: Yes, and I'm certainly eager.

SOCRATES: Why, I am too, my boy, from him and everyone else who I suspect has a professional competence in any of these things. But still and all, though everything else about them I have down to a fair degree, there's a small point about which I'm perplexed that has to be examined with you and these here. Tell me. To learn, isn't it to become wiser in whatever one learns?

THEAETETUS: Of course.

SOCRATES: Yes, and the wise, I suspect, (are) wise by wisdom.

THEAETETUS: Yes.

SOCRATES: And this doesn't differ at all, does it, from knowledge   E
(science)?

THEAETETUS: What sort of thing?

SOCRATES: Wisdom. Or isn't it in just those things in which they (are) knowledgeable that they (are) wise?

THEAETETUS: Why certainly.

SOCRATES: So knowledge and wisdom (are) the same?[6]

THEAETETUS: Yes.

SOCRATES: Well, this is the very point about which I'm perplexed, and I'm incapable of grasping it adequately by myself, whatever knowledge is. Can we really say it? What do you all say? Who would   146
be the first of us to speak? The one who makes a mistake, and

whoever at any time makes a mistake, will, as children playing ball say, take his seat, an ass; but whoever prevails without a mistake, he'll be our king and enjoin us to answer whatever he wants.[7] Why are you all silent? It surely can't be, Theodorus, that in my love of speeches I am being boorish, eager as I am to make us converse and become friends and mutually agreeable?[8]

B THEODORUS: Not in the least, Socrates, nothing of the sort would be boorish, but urge any of the lads to answer you. I am unused to conversation of this sort, and I'm not of an age to get used to it either. But it would be fitting for these here, and they would improve much more, for youth truly is open to improvement in everything. But, just as you began, don't let go of Theaetetus but ask away.

SOCRATES: Do you hear, Theaetetus, what Theodorus is saying? He's

C not one, I suspect, that you'll be willing to disobey, and it's not sanctioned either for a younger to disobey a wise man who enjoins things of this sort. But in a good and noble fashion speak out. Knowledge is what in your opinion?

THEAETETUS: Well, I must, Socrates, since you all urge it, for if I do make any mistake, you'll all in any case correct it.

SOCRATES: Yes of course, if, that is, we can.

THEAETETUS: Well, then, it's my opinion that whatever one might learn from Theodorus are sciences (knowledges)—geometry and those

D you just now went through and, in turn, shoemaking and the arts of the rest of the craftsmen—all and each of them, are nothing else than knowledge.

SOCRATES: That's noble and lavish, my dear, when you're asked for one, you offer many and complex instead of simple.

THEAETETUS: Just how do you mean this, Socrates?

SOCRATES: Perhaps it's nothing, but what I suspect, however, I'll point out. Whenever you say leathermaking, you're not pointing out anything else, are you, than a knowledge of the making of shoes?

THEAETETUS: Nothing else.

E SOCRATES: And what about when you say carpentry? Are you pointing out anything else than a knowledge of the making of wooden utensils?

THEAETETUS: Just this.

SOCRATES: Isn't it that in the case of both, of whatever each of the two is a knowledge, this is what you are determining?

THEAETETUS: Yes.

SOCRATES: Yes, but the question, Theaetetus, was not this, of what things there's knowledge, nor how many sciences there are either, for we didn't ask because we wanted to count them but to get to know knowledge whatever it itself is. Or am I making no sense?

THEAETETUS: Yes, that's right of course.

SOCRATES: Then examine this as well. If someone should ask us about *147* something trifling and ready at hand, for example, about mud (clay) whatever it is, if we should answer him that there's the mud of potters, the mud of furnace makers, and the mud of brickmakers, wouldn't we be ridiculous?

THEAETETUS: Perhaps.

SOCRATES: First of all, for one thing, because we surely must believe that the questioner understands our answer whenever we say mud, regardless of whether we add that of dollmakers or of all the rest of *B* the craftsmen whatsoever. Or do you believe that someone understands some name of something if he doesn't know what it is?

THEAETETUS: In no way.

SOCRATES: So whoever does not know science does not understand the science of shoes either.

THEAETETUS: No, he doesn't.

SOCRATES: So whoever's ignorant of science does not understand the leatherworking (science), or any different art either?

THEAETETUS: That is so.

SOCRATES: So the answer to the question "What is science?" is laughable, whenever one answers with the name of some art, for though one's not been asked this, one answers with the science of something. *C*

THEAETETUS: It seems likely.

SOCRATES: And in the second place, though it surely must be possible to answer trivially and briefly, one goes round on an endless road. For example, in the case of the question of mud, it's surely trivial and simple to say that should earth be kneaded with a liquid there would be mud and to dismiss whatever it is of.

THEAETETUS: Yes, Socrates, it now appears easy in this way. And you're probably asking the sort of thing that recently occurred also to ourselves as we were conversing, I mean myself and your homonym here, Socrates. *D*

SOCRATES: What sort of thing, exactly, Theaetetus?

THEAETETUS: Theodorus here was giving us some proof (drawing) about powers (roots), about the three-foot (line) and the five-foot (line)—that they're not commensurable in length (*mêkos*) with the one-foot (line)—and in this way he went on choosing each (line) one by one up to the seventeen-foot (line), where for some reason or other he got stuck.[9] Then something of the following sort occurred to us, since the powers (roots) appeared infinite in mul-

titude, to attempt to gather them together into one, by whatever
E   we'll address all these powers (roots).

SOCRATES: And did you really find something of the sort?

THEAETETUS: My impression is that we did, but you too examine it.

SOCRATES: Speak.

THEAETETUS: We took all of number in two, and the number that has
the power of coming to be by the multiplication of an equal by
an equal we made a semblance of its figure to a square and addressed it as a square and equal-sided number.

SOCRATES: That's really good.

THEAETETUS: Then again, the number between this—of which there
148   is the three, the five, and every one which does not have the power
of coming to be by the multiplication of an equal by an equal, but
its becoming is either by the multiplication of a greater number
by a less, or a less by a greater, and a larger and a less side always
comprehend it—we made a semblance of it in turn to the oblong
figure and called it an oblong number.

SOCRATES: Most beautifully. But what next?

THEAETETUS: All lines that make a square of the equal-sided and plane
number, we determined as length (*mêkos*), and all that make a
square of the other-lengthed number, we determined them as
B   powers (roots), on the grounds that they are not commensurable
in length with the former lines but with the planes of which they
are the powers. And something else of the sort about solids (cubes).

SOCRATES: That's really the best that human beings can do, boys. So
my impression is that Theodorus will not be found guilty of false
evidence.

THEAETETUS: And yet, Socrates, as to what you're asking about knowledge, I wouldn't be capable of answering it as I did about length
(rational root) and power (root), even though it's my impression
that you are seeking for something of the same sort, and so once
more Theodorus appears false.

C   SOCRATES: But what of this? Suppose he had said in praising you for
running that he had not met any youngster who was so skilled in
running, and then in running the course, you had been defeated
by the fastest at his peak, do you believe he would have praised
any less truly?[10]

THEAETETUS: No, I don't.

SOCRATES: But knowledge, as I was speaking of it just now—do you
believe that to find out about it is something small, and it's not a
job for the all-round tip-top?

THEAETETUS: Yes, by Zeus, I do, it's certainly for the topmost.

SOCRATES: Well, then, be confident about yourself and believe that

Theodorus is making sense, and be eager in every way both about   *D*
everything else as well as about knowledge to grasp a speech as
to whatever in fact it is.

THEAETETUS: As far as eagerness goes, Socrates, it will come to light.

SOCRATES: Come then—you just now led the way beautifully—in imitation of your answer about powers (roots), just as then you comprehended them, though they were many, in one species, so now
try to address the many sciences too with one speech.

THEAETETUS: But know well, Socrates, it's often that I tried to make   *E*
an examination of it, in hearing the questions that are reported
as coming from you. But for all of that, I am myself incapable of
either persuading myself that I say anything adequately or hearing
some one else speaking in just the way you urge, and I'm incapable
as well of getting rid of my concern with it.

SOCRATES: The reason is, my dear Theaetetus, that you're suffering
labor pains, on account of your not being empty but pregnant.

THEAETETUS: I don't know, Socrates, what, however, I've experienced
I say.

SOCRATES: And then, you most ridiculous fellow, you've not heard   *149*
that I am the son of a midwife, very noble and farouche,
Phaenarete?[11]

THEAETETUS: Yes, I've heard it before now.

SOCRATES: And you've not heard as well that I practice the same art?

THEAETETUS: In no way.

SOCRATES: Well, know well that's the case. Don't, however, denounce
me before the rest. They have not been aware, comrade, that I
have this art, and so, because they do not know, they don't say
this about me, but they say I'm most strange and make human
beings perplexed.[12] Have you heard this too?

THEAETETUS: Yes I have.   *B*

SOCRATES: Am I then to tell you the cause?

THEAETETUS: Yes, of course.

SOCRATES: Do reflect, then, about that which in its entirety characterizes midwives, and you'll more easily understand what I want to
say. You know surely that none of them is still conceiving and
giving birth when she acts as midwife to anyone else, but it's those
who by that time are incapable of giving birth.

THEAETETUS: Yes, of course.

SOCRATES: And they do say that Artemis is the cause of this, because
unallied her lot has lain with lying-in.[13] Now she does not after   *C*
all grant the barren to be midwives, because human nature is too
weak to grasp an art of whatever it is inexperienced, and so, in

honor of their similarity to herself, she charged those who do not bear on account of their age.

THEAETETUS: It's likely.

SOCRATES: Then isn't the following as likely as it is necessary,[14] that those who are pregnant and those who are not are recognized by the midwives rather than by anyone else?

THEAETETUS: Certainly.

D SOCRATES: And, what's more, the midwives by giving drugs and singing incantations are capable of arousing labor-pains or, if they want, of making them milder, and getting those who are having a hard time of it to give birth, and if it's decided to abort at an early stage,[15] they abort.

THEAETETUS: That is so.

SOCRATES: Have you further perceived this, that the following thing is theirs—they also are the most uncanny go-betweens, since they are all-wise when it comes to getting to know what sort of woman must be with what sort of man to give birth to the best possible children?

THEAETETUS: I don't know that at all.

E SOCRATES: Well, know that they take greater pride in this than in the cutting of the umbilical cord. Reflect. Do you believe that the care and harvesting of the fruits from the earth and the recognition, in turn, of what sort of plant and seed must be cast into what sort of earth are of the same or a different art?

THEAETETUS: No, but of the same.

SOCRATES: And into woman, my dear, do you believe there's a different art of something of this sort, and a different one of harvesting?

THEAETETUS: It's unlikely at any rate.

150 SOCRATES: Yes it is. But on account of the unjust and artless bringing together of man and woman—its name is pimping—the midwives, because they are august, shun even the art of go-between, in fear that they may fall into the former charge on account of it, since it's surely suitable for only those who are in their being midwives also to act as go-betweens correctly.[16]

THEAETETUS: It appears so.

SOCRATES: Well, then, that which characterizes midwives is of this extent, but it's less than my own action, for it's not the case that
B sometimes women give birth to images and sometimes to the simply true, and that it's not easy to gain recognition of the difference. For if it were the case, it would be the greatest and most beautiful work for midwives to discriminate whatever's true and whatever's not. Or don't you believe it?

THEAETETUS: Yes I do.

SOCRATES: Yes, but to my art of midwifery everything else belongs just as it does to them, and it differs as much by the fact that it midwifes men and not women as by the fact that it examines their souls in giving birth and not their bodies. But this is the greatest thing in our art, to be capable of assaying in every way whether   C
the thought of the young is giving birth to an image and a lie or something fruitful and true. Since this too belongs to me as it does to midwives, I am sterile of wisdom, and that for which many before now reproached me—that I ask everyone else but I myself don't declare anything about anything because I don't have anything wise—this reproach of theirs is true. The cause of this is the following. The god compels me to midwife and prevented me from generating. Now I myself therefore am obviously hardly wise at all, and I have not had a discovery of this sort as an   D
offspring of my soul. But whoever associate with me, some appear at first as even very foolish, but all—whomever the god allows— as the association advances, make an amazing lot of progress. It's their own opinion and everyone else's too. And this too is as plain as day, that they never learnt anything from me, but they on their own from themselves found and gave birth to many beautiful things. Now of the midwifery the god and I (are) responsible, and it's plain in the following way. Many before now who failed to   E
recognize this and held themselves responsible and despised me, either on their own or persuaded by someone else departed earlier than they should have. And after their departure, they aborted the rest on account of a poor association, and in bringing up badly the things that I midwifed, they lost them, and made more of false things and images than of the truth, and finally they got to be of the opinion (and everyone else was too) that they were fools.   151
Aristides the son of Lysimachus has been one of them, and there have been very many different ones too, and whenever they come back, begging for my association and doing amazing things, the *daimonion* that comes to me checks me from associating with some and allows me to associate with some, and it's these who once more improve.[17] And whoever associate with me undergo this same thing as women in giving birth do. They suffer labor-pains and are filled with perplexity for nights and days far more than women are, and my art is capable of arousing this kind of labor-   B
pain and putting it to rest. Now this is the way it is for these. But sometimes, if I somehow get the impression, Theaetetus, that they're not pregnant, in recognition of the fact that they don't need me, I very kindly act as go-between and, with allowance made for a god's help, guess very adequately by whose association

they would be benefited. And many of them I gave in marriage to Prodicus, and many to different wise and divinely-speaking men.[18] Now I lengthened this out for you, my excellent fellow, for the sake of the following. I suspect that you, just as you yourself believe, are pregnant with something within and are suffering from labor pains. Therefore apply yourself to me as to the son

C of a midwife and myself skilled in midwifery too, and whatever I ask be eager to answer in just the way you can. And if, after all, on examining something of whatever you say, I believe it an image and not true, and then take it out and throw it away, don't be angrily savage as those who give birth for the first time are about their children. Many before now—my wonderful fellow!—have got so disposed toward me as to be simply (artlessly) ready to bite, whenever I remove any nonsense of theirs, and they don't believe I'm doing this out of goodwill. They are far from knowing that

D no god is ill-disposed to human beings, and I don't do anything of the sort either out of ill-will, but it's in no way sanctioned for me to make a concession to falsehood and wipe out truth. Accordingly, once more from the beginning, Theaetetus, try to say whatever is knowledge, and never say you can't, for if a god's willing and you're manly, you'll be able.

THEAETETUS: Well, Socrates, when you're encouraging me in this fashion, it's shameful not in every way to be eager to say whatever

E one has. My opinion is then that whoever knows something perceives that which he knows, and as it now appears, knowledge is nothing else than perception.

SOCRATES: That's good and noble, my boy. One ought to speak in this way when one makes a declaration. But come, let's examine it in common, whether it's in fact fruitful or a wind-egg.[19] Perception, you say, (is) knowledge?

THEAETETUS: Yes.

SOCRATES: Well, you've probably not spoken a trivial speech about

152 knowledge, but the one Protagoras too used to say. He's said these same things in a somewhat different way. He says somewhere, "Of all things (*khrêmata*) (a) human being is the measure, of the things which are, that (how) they are, and of the things which are not, that (how) they are not."[20] Surely you've read it?

THEAETETUS: I've read it, and often.

SOCRATES: Isn't this more or less the sense of what he says, that of whatever sort things severally appear to me, that's the sort they are for me, and of whatever sort to you, they're of that sort in turn for you, and you and I (are) human being?

THEAETETUS: Indeed, he is speaking in this way.

SOCRATES: Well, it's likely you know for a wise man not to talk non- *B*
sense, so let's follow him up. Isn't it sometimes the case when the
same wind's blowing one of us is cold and one not? And one is
slightly cold and one intensely?

THEAETETUS: Indeed so.

SOCRATES: Are we to say that at that time the wind itself in itself is
cold or not cold? Or are we to obey Protagoras that it's cold for
whoever's cold and not for whoever's not?

THEAETETUS: It seems likely.

SOCRATES: Doesn't it then appear thus to each of the two?

THEAETETUS: Yes.

SOCRATES: Yes, but this "appear" is "perceive"?

THEAETETUS: Yes it is.

SOCRATES: So appearance and perception (are) the same in hot things *C*
and everything of the sort. For whatever sort each perceives, it's
that sort that they probably are for each.[21]

THEAETETUS: It seems likely.

SOCRATES: So perception is, after all, always of that which is, and it's
without falsehood inasmuch as it is knowledge.

THEAETETUS: It appears so.

SOCRATES: Was Protagoras really then, by the Graces, someone all-
wise, and did he make this an enigma for us, the vast refuse-heap,
but was he telling the truth as if it were a forbidden secret to his
pupils?

THEAETETUS: How exactly are you saying this, Socrates? *D*

SOCRATES: I shall speak actually a not trivial speech. It says, "After
all, nothing is one alone by itself, and you would not address
anything correctly or of any sort whatsoever, but if you address
it as big, it will also appear small, and if heavy, light, and all things
in this way, on the grounds that nothing is one, neither something
nor of any sort whatsoever. But all things—it's those we say are
the things which are (not addressing them correctly)—come to be
from locomotion and motion and mutual mixing; for nothing
ever is, but (everything) always becomes." And about this let all *E*
the wise in succession except Parmenides converge,[22] Protagoras
and Heraclitus, and Empedocles, as well as the tip-top poets of
each kind of poetry, Epicharmus of comedy and Homer of tragedy.[23] Homer with the line "Ocean and mother Tethys, the becoming (*genesis*) of gods"[24] has said that everything is the offspring
of flowing and motion. Or doesn't he seem to mean this?

THEAETETUS: Yes, to me he does.

SOCRATES: Who, then, would still be capable, should he dispute against *153* so large an army and so great a general as Homer, of not proving himself to be ridiculous?

THEAETETUS: It's not easy, Socrates.

SOCRATES: No, it isn't, Theaetetus. Since, actually, the following kinds of things are adequate signs for the speech that says that motion supplies that which seems to be and the fact of becoming, and rest the fact of nonbeing and perishing. For the hot and fire— it's that which both generates and manages everything else—is itself generated from locomotion and rubbing, and these are a pair of motions. Or aren't these the comings-into-being of fire?

B   THEAETETUS: Yes, they are indeed.

SOCRATES: And what's more, the genus of animals gets born out of these same things?

THEAETETUS: Of course.

SOCRATES: And what of this? Doesn't the condition of bodies get destroyed by quiet and idleness, but get preserved for the most part by exercises and motion?

THEAETETUS: Yes.

SOCRATES: And doesn't the condition in the soul acquire learnings by learning and practice, which are motions, and get saved and become better, but by quiet, which is lack of practice and folly, it does not learn anything at all and forgets whatever it does learn?

C

THEAETETUS: Indeed it does.

SOCRATES: So the good is motion both in terms of soul and in terms of body, and the (bad) the contrary?

THEAETETUS: It seems likely.

SOCRATES: Am I then further to tell you of occasions of windlessness and calm seas and everything of the sort, that quiet conditions rot and destroy, but the other things preserve? And am I to add to them as their summit the golden chain, by which Homer means nothing else than the sun, and he makes plain that as long as the sun and its orbiting are in motion, all things are and are preserved both among gods and human beings, but if this should stop as if it were bound, all things (*khrêmata*) would be corrupted, and, as the saying goes, everything would become topsy-turvy?[25]

D

THEAETETUS: Well, Socrates, my opinion is that he's making plain just those things you mean.

SOCRATES: Make then the following kind of supposition, my excellent fellow. First, in connection with the eyes, that which you call white color—don't appoint it to be itself as something other outside your eyes any more than in your eyes or any place for it at all, for otherwise it would surely be in order and abiding and not be becoming in becoming.

E

THEAETETUS: Well, how?

SOCRATES: Let's follow the speech of the moment, and set down nothing alone by itself as being one. And in this way black and white and any color whatsoever will come to light for us as having come to be from the application (*prosbolê*) of the eyes onto the suitable local motion (*phora*), and precisely that which we say each color to be will be neither that which applies (strikes against) nor that to which there is application (struck against), but something in between that has become private (peculiar) for each. Or would you insist that what sort each color appears to you, it's that sort for a dog and any animal whatsoever? *154*

THEAETETUS: No, by Zeus, I wouldn't.

SOCRATES: And what of this? Does anything at all appear similar to a different human being and you? Do you have (know) this strongly, or is it much more the case that not even for you yourself (is there) the same thing, on account of the fact that you yourself are never in a condition similar to yourself?

THEAETETUS: I'm rather of this opinion than of that.

SOCRATES: Isn't it the case, then, that if that against which we're mea- *B* suring ourselves or which we're touching were great or white or hot, it would never, in its fall on something else, have come to be something else, if, that is, it itself does not at all alter. And if, in turn, that which is doing the measuring against or the touching were each of these things, it would not have become, if itself were not affected in any way, different when a different thing approached it or underwent something. Since as it is now, my dear, we're being compelled somehow or other to say without qualms amazing and laughable things, as Protagoras would say and everyone who tries to say the same as he does.

THEAETETUS: How do you mean it exactly, and what sort of things?

SOCRATES: Take a small paradigm, and you'll know everything I want. *C* We say surely that six dice, if you apply four to them, are more than the four and one and a half times as much, and if you apply twelve, they're less and half as much, and it's insupportable to speak in a different way. Or will you put up with it?

THEAETETUS: No, I won't.

SOCRATES: What then? If Protagoras or someone else asks you, "Theaetetus, is it possible that anything become bigger or more in a different way than by increase?" what will you answer?

THEAETETUS: Well, Socrates, if I answer in light of the present question *D* that which is my opinion, I'll answer that it's impossible, but if in light of the former, being on guard lest I say contrary things, I'll answer that it's possible.

SOCRATES: Gosh, that's good, by Hera, my dear, and divine. But, it seems, if you answer that it is possible, something Euripidean will result, for our tongue will be irrefutable, but our mind (*phrên*) not free from refutation.[26]

THEAETETUS: True.

SOCRATES: Then if you and I were dreadfully canny and wise, having scrutinized all the things of our minds (*phrenes*), we would then for the future be testing one another out of a superabundant

E   store and, engaged in sophistic fashion in a battle of this sort, we would proceed to strike and ring the speeches of one against the speeches of the other. But as it is, because we're laymen, we'll want to observe them in relation to themselves, as to whatever they are which we're thinking, whether in our view they are consonant with each other or not in any way whatever.

THEAETETUS: Yes, of course I would want this.

SOCRATES: And I would too no less. And since this is so, shall we do anything else than calmly go back over the examination, on the

155   grounds that we're very much at our leisure, without feeling peevish, but truly scrutinize ourselves as to whatever these hallucinations in us are?[27] The first of which we'll say in our reexamination is, I suspect, that nothing would ever become greater or less, either in bulk or number, as long as it is equal to itself. Isn't this so?

THEAETETUS: Yes.

SOCRATES: Yes, and a second: To whatever there should be neither addition nor subtraction, this never either increases or decreases but is always equal.

THEAETETUS: Yes, certainly.

B   SOCRATES: And isn't there a third too: Whatever was not before, this is incapable of being later without having come to be and becoming?

THEAETETUS: Yes, it seems so anyhow.

SOCRATES: It's precisely these three agreements, I suspect, that fight against themselves in our soul whenever we speak of the agreement about the dice or whenever we say that I, in being the size I am, without increasing or undergoing the contrary, am within a year now taller than you the youngster but later smaller, though

C   nothing of my bulk has been removed but when you increased. For I am later what I was not before without having come to be, for without becoming it's impossible to come to be, and if I lose nothing of my bulk I would never be becoming less. And there are moreover thousands upon thousands of things in this state, provided we shall accept this case. Surely you're following, Theaetetus; it's my impression at any rate that you're not inexperienced in things of this sort.

THEAETETUS: Yes indeed, by the gods, Socrates, I wonder exceedingly as to why (what) in the world these things are, and sometimes in looking at them I truly get dizzy.

SOCRATES: The reason is, my dear, that, apparently, Theodorus' guess about your nature is not a bad one, for this experience is very much a philosopher's, that of wondering. For nothing else is the beginning (principle) of philosophy than this, and, seemingly, whoever's genealogy it was, that Iris was the offspring of Thaumas (Wonder), it's not a bad one.[28] But do you understand by now why these things are of this sort on the basis of which we say that Protagoras speaks, or not yet? *D*

THEAETETUS: Not yet, in my opinion.

SOCRATES: Then you'll be grateful to me if I join with you in ferreting out the hidden-away truth of the thought of a renowned man, or rather, of renowned men. *E*

THEAETETUS: Of course I'll be grateful, and not a little either.

SOCRATES: Take a look around then and make sure no one of the uninitiated can overhear. They are those who believe that nothing else is except whatever they are capable of getting a tight grip on with their hands, but actions, becomings, and everything invisible they don't accept as in the class (part) of being.

THEAETETUS: Why, it's of stiff and repellent human beings, Socrates, that you're speaking. *156*

SOCRATES: The reason, my boy, is that they are without the Muses to a large degree, but the rest are far cleverer, whose mysteries I'm about to tell you. Their principle (beginning), from which everything is attached—even what we were just now speaking of—is this: the all was motion and there (is) nothing else beyond this, but there (are) two species of motion, and each of the two (is) infinite in multitude, and one (is) with a power to affect (make) and one with a power to be affected. And out of the association and rubbing of these against one another, there come to be offspring, infinite in multitude but twins (double)—that which (is) perceived and that which (is) perception—which (the latter) (is) always falling out together with and (is) getting generated with that which (is) perceived. Now the perceptions have for us the following sorts of names: sights and hearings and smellings and freezings and burnings and, yes, pleasures certainly and pains and desires and fears (are) their designations and different ones as well, the nameless of which (are) without limit, and the named very many. And the perceived genus in turn (is) cogenerated with each of these, omnifarious colors with omnifarious sights, and likewise sounds with hearings, and all the rest of the things per- *B*

C

ceived which come to be congeners with all the rest of the perceptions.[29] Now what exactly, in light of the former assertions,
does this myth of ours want, Theaetetus? Do you have it in mind?

THEAETETUS: Hardly, Socrates.

SOCRATES: Well, look and see whether it may be here brought to
completion in some sense. It just wants to say that all these are in
motion, as we're saying, and speed and slowness are in their motion. Now everything slow conceives its motion in the same and
D relative to the things consorting with it and precisely in this way
generates, and the things precisely so generated are faster, for
they are born(e) and their motion is by nature in bearing (moving
locally).[30] Whenever, then, an eye and something else of the things
commensurate with it consort and generate the whiteness and
perception cognate with it, which would never have come to be
if each of the two of them had come to anything else, it's precisely
at that time when they are being born(e) between—the sight from
E the side of the eyes and the whiteness from the side of that which
(is) giving birth along with sight to the color—that the eye, lo
and behold, becomes full of sight and precisely at that time sees
and becomes not sight but an eye seeing. And that which cogenerated the color gets filled all round with whiteness and becomes
in turn not whiteness but white, whether it (is) wood or stone or
whatever thing (khrêma) turns out to get colored with a color
(khrôma) of this sort. And for all the rest in precisely this way, stiff
157 and hot and everything, it must be supposed in the same way,
nothing is itself by itself—it's what we were saying even then—
but in the association with one another, all things become and
become of all sorts from the motion, since actually it's impossible
in any single case to think fixedly, as they say, on that which affects
(makes) as being something and that which gets affected as being
by itself separately. For there's neither anything affecting before
it comes together with that which (gets) affected, nor anything
affected before it comes together with that which affects, and so
that which comes together with something and affects, if it falls
in turn on something else, comes to light as being affected. Consequently, on the basis of all this, just as we were saying at the
beginning, there is to be nothing that is one itself by itself, but
B always to become for something, and "be" must be removed from
everywhere—not that we've not been often compelled even now
by habituation and lack of knowledge to use it. But, as is the speech
of the wise, one must make no concessions: to be is neither a something nor of something nor of me nor this nor that nor any different
name that makes for stoppage, but one must make utterances

in accordance with nature—becomings and makings and perishings and alterings—since if one stops something in one's speech, whoever does (makes) it is easily refutable. One must also speak in this way piecemeal (part by part) and about many things collected together; it's to this aggregate that they lay down for themselves the names human being and stone and each animal and species. Are you C then of the opinion, Theaetetus, that these things are pleasing to you, and would you enjoy the taste of them as satisfying?

THEAETETUS: I do not know, Socrates, for I'm not even capable of understanding how it is with you, whether you're speaking your very own opinions or you're testing me.

SOCRATES: You don't remember, my dear, that it's I who neither know nor adopt (produce) anything of the sort as mine, for I am incapable of generating them. But I midwife you and for the sake of this I sing incantations and serve up for you to get a taste of the several wise things until I may help to lead out into the light D your very own opinion. And then, when it is led out, I'll go ahead and examine whether it will show up as a wind-egg or fruitful. But be confident and persistent, and in good and manly fashion answer whatever appears to you about whatever I ask.

THEAETETUS: Ask then.

SOCRATES: Well, say once more whether it satisfies you that there not be anything, but good and beautiful and everything we were just now going through (be) always becoming.

THEAETETUS: Well, to me at least, when I listen to you explicating it in this way, it surprisingly appears to make sense, and one has to suppose it to be in just the way you've gone through it.

SOCRATES: Then let's not leave out anything that's missing from it. E What's missing is the stuff about dreams and illnesses—madness as well as everything else—and everything said to be a mishearing or misseeing or any different misperceiving. You know surely that, in all these cases, it seems to be widely agreed upon that the speech which we were just now going through gets refuted, since it's as certain as can be that false perceptions come to be for us 158 here. And far from it being the case that the things appearing to each also are these things, but, wholly the contrary, none of the things which appears is.

THEAETETUS: What you say, Socrates, is most true.

SOCRATES: Then precisely what speech, my boy, is left for him who's laying down perception as knowledge, and that the things appearing to each also are these things for him to whom they appear?

THEAETETUS: Well, I, Socrates, am reluctant to say that I don't know what I'm to say, because you just now rebuked me when I said it, B since truly to this extent I would be incapable of disputing that the crazy or the dreamers are not opining false things, whenever some of them believe they are gods and some feathered and they're thinking of themselves in their sleep as flying.

SOCRATES: Then you really don't have in mind the following sort of disputation about them, and especially about dreaming and waking?

THEAETETUS: What sort?

SOCRATES: That which I suspect you've often heard from questioners—what evidence could one have to prove, if someone should ask now on these terms at the present moment, whether we're *C* asleep and dreaming everything we're thinking, or we're awake and conversing with one another while awake.

THEAETETUS: That's it, Socrates, it is perplexing as to what evidence one must use for showing it, for all the same things follow in parallel as if they were correlative. For just as there's nothing to prevent that what we've now conversed about also be dreamt as (seem) a conversation with one another in sleep, so whenever in a dream what we dream we're explaining (what we seem to be explaining) are dreams, the similarity of these to those is strange.

SOCRATES: You do see, then, that it's not the possibility of disputation *D* which is difficult, when it's even open to dispute as to whether it is in waking or in dreaming, and when indeed the time we spend in sleeping is equal to that when we're awake. In each of the two times, our soul insists that whatever its opinions are at the moment cannot be more certainly true, so for an equal time we say these things are the things which are, and for an equal time those, and we insist with a similar vehemence in each time.

THEAETETUS: That's altogether so.

SOCRATES: Doesn't, then, the same speech hold as well for bouts of illness and fits of madness, except for the time, which isn't equal?

THEAETETUS: Right.

SOCRATES: What then? Will the truth be determined by the length and brevity of the time?

E THEAETETUS: But that would be laughable in many ways.

SOCRATES: Well, do you have anything else that's a clear pointer as to which sorts of these opinions (are) true?

THEAETETUS: No, not in my opinion.

SOCRATES: Well, in that case, listen to me as to what sort of things they would say about them, those who determine that the opinions at any moment are true for him who is of that opinion. I suspect that they speak, by questioning, in this way: "Theaetetus, whatever is altogether other, will it have in any respect any power the same as the other? And let's not suppose that our question is about that which is in some respect the same and in some respect other, but suppose it wholly other."

THEAETETUS: Well, then it's impossible for it to have anything the same *159* either in power or in anything else whatsoever, whenever it is utterly other.

SOCRATES: Isn't it then necessary to agree that something of the sort is also dissimilar?

THEAETETUS: Yes, that's my opinion at least.

SOCRATES: So if it turns out that something is becoming similar or dissimilar to something, either to itself or to something else, shall we say that in becoming similar, it's becoming the same, and in becoming dissimilar, other?

THEAETETUS: It's a necessity.

SOCRATES: Weren't we saying before that the things which affect are many and infinite, and likewise too the things that are affected?

THEAETETUS: Yes.

SOCRATES: And further that if something else mingles with something else, it will not generate the same things but others if it then mingles with something else?

THEAETETUS: Yes of course. *B*

SOCRATES: Let's speak then from now on of me and you and everything else in accordance with the same speech, Socrates healthy and, in turn, Socrates sick. Are we to say that this is similar to that or dissimilar?

THEAETETUS: Do you mean the sick Socrates, this as a whole, is similar or dissimilar to that as a whole, the healthy Socrates?

SOCRATES: You've got it most beautifully. That's the very thing I mean.

THEAETETUS: Surely dissimilar then.

SOCRATES: So he's other too in just the way in which he's dissimilar.

THEAETETUS: It's a necessity.

SOCRATES: And you'll speak similarly of his sleeping and everything *C* we just now went through?

THEAETETUS: Yes, I will.

SOCRATES: Then for each of the things whose nature is to affect something, will anything else be the case than that whenever it gets a healthy Socrates, it will use me as other, and whenever sick, as an other?

THEAETETUS: Why of course it won't.

SOCRATES: And so I, the affected, and that, the affecting, will generate others in each of the two cases?

THEAETETUS: Why certainly.

SOCRATES: Whenever, being healthy, I drink wine, it appears to me pleasant and sweet?

THEAETETUS: Yes.

SOCRATES: The reason is that, precisely on the basis of what has been previously agreed upon, that which affects and that which is af-

D   fected generate a sweetness and a perception, both being born(e) together. And the perception, being from the side of that which is affected, renders the tongue perceiving, and the sweetness born(e) about it from the side of the wine makes the wine both be and appear sweet to the healthy tongue.

THEAETETUS: Yes, of course. The prior things had been agreed upon by us in this way.

SOCRATES: But whenever it gets me being ill, is anything else the case than that first of all in truth it does not take the same me. That's precisely because it approaches a dissimilar.

THEAETETUS: Yes.

E SOCRATES: The Socrates of this sort and the drinking of the wine generate, when paired, other things, about the tongue a perception of bitterness, and about the wine a bitterness coming to be and being born(e), and the wine is not bitterness but bitter, and I'm not perception but perceiving.

THEAETETUS: Yes, certainly.

SOCRATES: And just as I shall never become in just this way if I'm perceiving anything else—for a different perception is of the dif-

160 ferent, and it makes the perceiver a different sort and different—so that which affects me shall never generate the same and become of the same sort if it comes together with a different thing. For if it generates a different thing from a different thing, it will become a different sort.

THEAETETUS: That is so.

SOCRATES: Nor again shall I become of the same sort as myself anymore than that will become of the same sort as itself.

THEAETETUS: No indeed.

SOCRATES: Yes, and it's just as much a necessity that I become of something (perceiving something) whenever I become perceiving—for it's impossible to become perceiving and perceiving noth-

B ing—as for that to become for someone whenever it becomes sweet or bitter or anything of the sort. For it's impossible to become sweet and sweet for no one.

THEAETETUS: That's altogether so.

SOCRATES: Then I believe the only thing thing left is for us to be for one another if we are, or if we become, to become for one another, since necessity binds our being together and it binds it to nothing

else of all the rest, not even to ourselves, so it's only left that it has become bound with one another. Consequently, regardless of whether it's for being or becoming, if someone gives a name to something, he must state that it is or becomes for someone (something) or of something or relative to something. But neither he himself must say that there's something in itself which is or becomes, nor must he accept it from anyone else who says it, as the C
speech we've gone through indicates.

THEAETETUS: That's altogether so, Socrates.

SOCRATES: Isn't it the case, then, that it's precisely inasmuch as that which is affecting me is for me and not for anyone else, that I in fact perceive it and anyone else does not?

THEAETETUS: Of course.

SOCRATES: My perception's after all true for me—for it is of my being on every occasion—and I (am) the judge according to Protagoras of the things which are for me that (how) they are, and of the things which are not that (how) they are not.

THEAETETUS: It seems likely.

SOCRATES: How, then, if I am without falsehood and do not stumble D
in my thought, would I not be a knower of the things which are or become of which I'm the perceiver?

THEAETETUS: In no way is it possible that you're not.

SOCRATES: So after all, it has been said by you very beautifully that knowledge is not anything else than perception, and there has been a coincidence to the same point of the assertion, according to Homer and Heraclitus and the entire tribe of this sort, that all things are in motion like streams; of the assertion, according to Protagoras the most wise, that (a) human being is the measure of all things (*khrêmata*); and of the assertion, according to Theaetetus, E
that since these things are so, knowledge comes to be perception. Is it really so, Theaetetus? Are we to say this is yours, a newborn child as it were, and mine the delivery? Or how do you say?

THEAETETUS: It's a necessity in just this way, Socrates.

SOCRATES: Well this, it seems, we have at last generated with difficulty, whatever in fact it is. But after its birth, on its name-day, it truly has to be run around in a circle by the speech, as we examine it, lest, without our being aware of it, that which is coming to be be unworthy of rearing but be a wind-egg and a falsehood.[31] Or do 161
you believe that in any case, regardless, you must rear that which is your own just because it is yours and you must not expose it, or will you in fact put up with seeing its being tested, and will you not be vehemently distressed if someone slips it away from you though you are giving birth for the first time?

THEODORUS: Theaetetus will put up with it, Socrates, for he's not in any way peevish. But by the gods speak, and say in turn in what respect it's not in this way.

SOCRATES: You are simply (artlessly) a lover of speeches, Theodorus—yes, you are—and good, because you suspect that I am a kind of sack of speeches. And I would with ease take one out and say, "On the other hand, these things are not in this way." But you don't understand that which is happening (coming to be), that not one of the speeches comes out of me but always from whoever is conversing with me. And I, I know nothing of a superior kind, except a little bit, as much as to take a speech from another who's wise and accept it in a measured way. And now I'll try to take it from him here and not at all speak myself.

THEODORUS: What you say's more beautiful, Socrates. And do it in this way.

SOCRATES: Do you know, then, Theodorus, what I wonder at (admire) in your comrade Protagoras?

THEODORUS: What sort of thing?

SOCRATES: All the rest of what he has said pleases me a lot, that that which is the opinion of each this also is for each. But I've been in a state of wonder at the beginning of his speech, that he did not say in beginning his Truth, "Pig is the measure of all things (*khrêmata*)" or "Dog-faced baboon," or anything else of those with perception that's stranger, in order that he could have begun to speak to us in a magnificent and very contemptuous way, by showing that though we admired him as if he were a god for his widsom, he is, after all, not at all better in point of intelligence than a tadpole, let alone than anyone else of human beings. Or how are we to speak, Theodorus? For if it will be true to each whatever each opines through perception, and if neither someone else will discriminate the experience of someone else better nor will another be more competent to examine the opinion of an other whether it's correct or false, but as it has been said many times, each one alone by himself will opine his own things, and all these (are) correct and true, however can it be, comrade, that Protagoras (is) wise, so as actually to claim for himself that he justly deserves to be the teacher—with great wages—of everyone else, and we (are) more foolish and have to frequent his school, since each of us is the measure for himself of his own wisdom? How are we to deny that Protagoras says these as a wooer of the public? As for myself and that which characterizes my own art, the maieutic—I keep silent about it and all the laughter we incur—but I suspect that the entire business of conversation is also open to ridicule.

I.26

For to examine and try to refute the appearances and opinions of one another, when those of each are correct—isn't that a long *162* and immense piece of nonsense, if the Truth of Protagoras (is) true and she did not make her utterances in jest out of the inner sanctum of the book?

THEODORUS: Socrates, the man's a friend, as you just now said. I wouldn't choose then through an agreement of my own for Protagoras to be refuted, any more than I would choose to resist you against my opinion. So take Theaetetus back. He appeared in any case just now to comply with you harmoniously.

SOCRATES: Would you really, Theodorus, should you go to Sparta, to *B* the palaestras there, would you claim it as your right, on observing everyone else naked, and some in poor shape, not to display in turn your looks (species) by stripping alongside them?

THEODORUS: Well, what's your impression, if they were going to leave it up to me and obey me (be persuaded by me)? Just as in the present case I suspect I'll persuade you to allow me to observe and not to drag me, stiff as I already am, to the stripping-place, and to wrestle against the younger and more supple.

SOCRATES: Well, if that's to your liking, Theodorus, it's no skin off my nose, as the proverbialists say.[32] Then I have to go back to the *C* wise Theaetetus. Do say, Theaetetus, first in regard to what we just now went through, aren't you really surprised if so suddenly you'll show up as in no way worse in point of wisdom than anyone whatsoever of human beings or maybe gods? Or do you believe the Protagorean measure is spoken less pertinently for gods than for human beings?

THEAETETUS: No, by Zeus, I don't. And as to what you're asking, I'm very surprised. For while we were going through in what way they were saying that of whatever opinion each is, this also is for him *D* whose opinion it is, it appeared to me to be very well said. But now it has quickly changed around to the contrary.

SOCRATES: That's because you are young, my dear boy. You therefore comply too keenly with demagogery and are persuaded. For Protagoras or someone else on his behalf will say in reply to this: "Noble children and elders, you're sitting down together and making a public speech, and you bring gods into the middle, though I except them from my speaking and writing, that they are or *E* that they are not, and you say just what the many would welcome hearing—'It's just dreadful if each human being will not differ at all in point of wisdom from any kind of cattle whatever. But you don't speak any demonstration and necessity of any kind, but you employ the likely, which if Theodorus or anyone else of the ge-

163

ometers should be willing to use in geometry, he wouldn't even be worth a single pip.[33] So you and Theodorus consider whether you'll accept speeches about matters of so great an importance that are spoken by way of plausibility and likelihoods (semblances)."[34]

THEAETETUS: But it's not just, Socrates, as either you or we would say.

SOCRATES: Then it has to be examined in a different way, it seems, as is your speech and the speech of Theodorus.

THEAETETUS: Yes, of course, in a different way.

SOCRATES: Let's then examine in the following way whether knowledge and perception are after all the same or other, for surely our entire speech was tending toward this point, and for its sake we set in motion these many strange things. Isn't that so?

THEAETETUS: That's altogether so.

B SOCRATES: Shall we really then agree that whatever we perceive by seeing or by hearing, all these we also at the same time know? For example, before we understand the language of the barbarians, shall we either deny that we hear whenever they speak or assert that we hear and know what they're saying? And if in turn we do not know letters but we're looking at them, shall we insist that we don't see them or we know them if we see them?

THEAETETUS: Yes, Socrates, we'll say we know that very thing of them which we see and hear. For we see and know, we'll say, the shape and color of the letters, and we hear and at the same time know

C the sharpness and flatness of the sounds. But what the letter-experts and the interpreters teach about them, we neither perceive by seeing or hearing nor know.

SOCRATES: That's excellent, Theaetetus, and it's not worthwhile to dispute with you on these points, in order that you may grow. But look! Here's something else on the attack, and consider at what point we'll repel it.

THEAETETUS: What sort of thing exactly?

D SOCRATES: It's of the following sort. If someone should ask, "Is it possible, in the case of whatever one should become a knower, while still having a memory of this very thing and keeping it safe, not to know this very thing which one remembers at the moment when one remembers it?" I'm being long-winded, it seems, in wanting to ask whether someone if he gets to know (learn) something does not know it when he remembers it.

THEAETETUS: But how could that be, Socrates? What you're saying would be a monster.[35]

SOCRATES: I am uttering nonsense, you mean? But consider. Don't you say seeing's perceiving and sight perception?

THEAETETUS: Yes, I do.

SOCRATES: Isn't it the case then that, according to the speech of the   *E*
moment, whoever saw something has become a knower of that
which he saw?

THEAETETUS: Yes.

SOCRATES: And what of this? Now memory, don't you say it's something?

THEAETETUS: Yes.

SOCRATES: Of nothing or something?

THEAETETUS: Of something, doubtless.

SOCRATES: Isn't it of whatever one learnt and whatever one perceived,
of some sorts of things like this?

THEAETETUS: Why certainly.

SOCRATES: Then precisely that which one saw, one surely remembers
sometimes?

THEAETETUS: One remembers.

SOCRATES: Even with one's eyes shut? Or if he does this he forgets?

THEAETETUS: But it's dreadful, Socrates, to assert that.

SOCRATES: Yes, but we must, however, if we're to save the former   *164*
speech, and if not, it's lost and gone.

THEAETETUS: I too, by Zeus, suspect it, yet I don't quite adequately
understand. Say in what respect.

SOCRATES: In the following. Whoever sees, we say, has become a knower
of that which he sees, for sight and perception and knowledge
have been agreed to be the same.

THEAETETUS: Certainly.

SOCRATES: Yes, but whoever sees and has become a knower of what
he was seeing, if he shuts his eyes, he remembers but does not
see it. Isn't that so?

THEAETETUS: Yes.

SOCRATES: Yes, but "he doesn't see" is "he doesn't know," if "he sees"   *B*
is also "he knows."

THEAETETUS: True.

SOCRATES: So it turns out, of whatever someone becomes a knower,
that though he's still remembering, he doesn't know, since he
doesn't see. And we said it would be a monster should that prove
to be the case.

THEAETETUS: What you say is most true.

SOCRATES: So it appears that something impossible results if one says
knowledge and perception are the same.

THEAETETUS: It seems likely.

SOCRATES: So one must say each of the two (is) different.

THEAETETUS: Probably.

SOCRATES: What then would knowledge be? We have to speak again   *C* from the beginning, it seems. But, Theaetetus, what in the world are we about to do?

THEAETETUS: About what?

SOCRATES: It appears to me that we jumped away from the speech and just like an ignoble cock we're crowing before we've won.

THEAETETUS: How's that exactly?

SOCRATES: We seem in the contentious way of contradiction to have gained an agreement in light of agreements about words (names) *D* and to be satisfied with our prevailing over the speech by something of the sort. And though we say we're not competitors but philosophers, we are, without our being aware of it, doing the same things as those dreadful men.

THEAETETUS: I don't yet understand how you're speaking.

SOCRATES: Well, I shall try to make plain about them just exactly what I have in mind. We asked whether someone doesn't know something if once he's learnt it he remembers, and we proved that whoever saw it and shut his eyes was remembering and not seeing, and we then proved that he did not know at the same time he was remembering, but this was impossible. And it was precisely in this way that the Protagorean myth got lost and perished, as well as your own at the same time, that knowledge and perception are the same.

E THEAETETUS: It appears so.

SOCRATES: It wouldn't have, I suspect, my dear, if the father of the other myth were still alive, but he would now be defending it in lots of ways. But as it is, we're casting reproaches on a lone orphan, for not even its guardians, whom Protagoras left behind—and Theodorus here is one of them—are willing to take the field; but, more to the point, we'll probably have to go to its assistance ourselves for the sake of the just.

THEODORUS: That's because it's not I, Socrates, but rather Callias the *165* son of Hipponicus who's the guardian of his things,[36] but we for some reason or another inclined rather early away from bare speeches and toward geometry. Still and all, we'll be grateful to you if you do assist it.

SOCRATES: You speak beautifully, Theodorus. Consider then my assistance, such as it is. If one should not pay attention to words, on whose terms for the most part we've got accustomed to affirm or deny, one would agree to more dreadful things than those just now. As to what the terms are, am I to tell you or Theaetetus?

B THEODORUS: No, rather in common, but let the younger answer, for if he makes a slip he'll cut a less disgraceful figure.

SOCRATES: Then I speak the most dreadful question, and it is, I suspect, something of the following sort. "Is it possible for the same person in knowing something not to know this which he knows?"

THEODORUS: Then what shall we answer, Theaetetus?

THEAETETUS: Impossible, surely, I suspect.

SOCRATES: No, not, that is, if you're to set down seeing as knowing. For how will you handle an inescapable question, when you're stuck, as the saying goes, in a well and an unflappable man asks, once he's covered your other eye with his hand, whether you see the cloak with the covered eye? *C*

THEAETETUS: I suspect that I'll deny that I see with this one of course but I'll affirm, however, that I do with the other.

SOCRATES: Then aren't you seeing and not seeing the same thing at the same time?

THEAETETUS: Yes, this is somehow the case.

SOCRATES: I'm not at all ordering this, he'll say, nor did I ask as to the how, but only whether what you know this you also do not know, and it's now evident that you're seeing what you do not see. And you've in fact agreed that seeing's knowing and not seeing not knowing. Then on the basis of this, figure out what's the result for you.

THEAETETUS: Well, I figure that it's the contrary to what I just laid *D* down.

SOCRATES: Yes, and perhaps—my wonderful fellow!—you would have experienced several more of the sort if someone went on to ask you whether it is possible to know sharply, and is it possible bluntly, and to know close at hand but not far away, and to know intensely the same thing and slightly. There are thousands of different things with which—had a light-armed mercenary in speeches asked them as he lay in ambush, when you set down knowledge and perception as the same, and with an assault on hearing, smelling, and perceptions of that sort—he would now be pressing his refutative attack and not let up before in amazement at his much *E* prayed-for wisdom you had been hobbled by him, and exactly where he had worsted you and bound you hand and foot, he would then be holding you for as big a ransom as you and he decided on. Now perhaps you would say, what kind of speech will Protagoras speak as an auxiliary to his own? Are we to try to say?

THEAETETUS: Yes of course.

SOCRATES: There are not only all these things—as many as we say in defending him—but, I suspect, he'll come and engage in close combat (with that mercenary) out of contempt for us and say: *166* "Here's that good Socrates of yours! He's responsible for a mere child getting a fright, when he was asked whether it was possible for the same person to remember and at the same time not know the same thing, and in his fright denied it on account of his incapacity to see ahead, and thus in his speeches showed up poor little me as a laugh. But, most slovenly Socrates, this is the way it is: whenever you're examining any of my things through questioning, if the one to whom the question is put slips up in answering it in just the sort of terms that I would answer, then I

B am refuted, but if the terms are different, then the one to whom the question is put is alone refuted. For instance, is it your impression that anyone will concede to you that a memory of what one experienced, if it is present to one, is an experience of just the sort that it was when he experienced it, if he is no longer experiencing it? Far from it. Or is your impression that he will, in turn, be reluctant to agree that it's possible for the same person to know and not to know the same thing? Or if he is frightened of this, that he'll ever grant that whoever is getting to be dissimilar is the same as the one who he is before he is getting to be dissimilar? And, if he'll really have to take precautions against the spoils of the chase of each other's words, he'll prefer to grant that someone is he but not *hes*, and, what's more, these *hes* keep on

C becoming infinite, provided that dissimilarity keeps on becoming? But," he'll say, "You blessed innocent!—Approach what I'm saying in a nobler and grander way, if you're capable, and prove straight out that to each of us there do not come to be private (peculiar) perceptions, or that though they do come to be private, it would not any the more follow that that which appears becomes for him alone, or—if 'be' has to be the name used—is for just him to whom it appears. But in speaking—of all things!—of swine and dog-faced baboons, not only are you yourself a swine, but you're convincing also your auditors to do this against my writings. There's

D nothing beautiful in doing (making) that. I assert the truth is as I've written: each of us is the measure of the things which are and are not, and another differs from an other in thousands of things by this very fact, that to one different things are and appear, and to one different. And I'm far from denying that wisdom and a wise man are, but I'm saying that he's the very one who's wise, whoever by inducing a change makes appear and be good things for anyone of us to whom they appear and are bad. So don't prosecute again the speech by my phrasing, but learn with still

E greater clarity in the following way what I'm saying. Recall the sort of thing that was being said in the previous remarks, that whatever he eats appears and is bitter to whoever is ill, but to whoever is healthy the contrary is and appears. Now one must

not make either of these the wiser—for it's not at all possible— *167*
nor deliver the accusation that the ill (is) a fool because he opines
those sorts of things, and the healthy (is) wise because he opines
different sorts of things, but one has to change the former to the
other things, for the other condition (is) better. And this holds as
well in education—one has to effect a change from another condition to the better. But the physician effects a change by drugs,
the sophist by speeches. Since it's not at all the case that one makes
someone who's opining false things later opine true things, for
it's impossible to opine either the things which are not or different
things beyond whatever one experiences, but these things (are)
always true. But, I suspect, whoever is opining by a poor condition *B*
of soul things akin to itself, a good condition makes him opine
other things of the sort. It's these that some out of inexperience
call the apparitions that are true, but I call the others better than
the others, but in no way truer. And I'm far from saying, my dear
Socrates, that the wise (are) frogs, but I am saying they're physicians in terms of bodies and farmers in terms of plants, for I
assert that they too make good and healthy perceptions and truths
be in plants in place of poor perceptions,[37] whenever any of them *C*
is ill. But it's wise and good public speakers who make cities be
of the opinion that the good things in place of the poor things
are just. Since no matter what sorts of things these are that are
just and beautiful in the opinion of each city, these also are for
it as long as it holds them to be so, but the wise makes good things
be for it and be so in its opinion in place of the several poor things
it has. And in accordance with the same speech, the sophist too,
if he's capable in this way of tutoring those who are being edu- *D*
cated, (is) wise and deserves a lot of money in the eyes of the
educated. And so others are wiser than others and no one opines
false things, and you have to put up with being a measure, whether
you want to or not, for it's in these terms that this speech gets
saved. If you can dispute it from the beginning, then go ahead
and range a counterspeech against it and dispute it; or if you want
to do it through questions, do it through questions, for this in no
case must be avoided, but anyone of sense must pursue it most
of all. Act (make), however, in this way; don't be unjust in your
questioning. For it makes little sense to claim to care for virtue *E*
and then to go ahead and continually be unjust in speeches. And
to be unjust in a situation of this sort is to fail to separate, whenever
one's engagements are of this kind, competition and conversation,
and in the former be playful and trip up one's opponent to the
extent that one is capable of it, but in conversation be in earnest

168

and put one's interlocutor on his feet again, pointing out to him only the slip-ups in which he had been led astray by himself and his former associations. For if you act (make) in this way, those who spend their time with you will blame themselves for their own confusion and perplexity, and they won't blame you, and they'll pursue you and love you; they'll hate themselves and flee from themselves into philosophy in order that, once they've become different, they may be rid of who they were before. But if, just as the many do, you do the contrary of this, the contrary will befall you and instead of as philosophers you'll reveal your as-

B

sociates as loathers of this business (*pragma*) whenever they become older. If you obey me then—and this was stated even before—if not in a spirit of enmity or contention, but with gracious condescension in thought, you will truly examine what we're saying, in declaring that all things are in motion, and that which is the opinion of each, this also is for a private person and a city. And on this basis, you'll go on to examine whether knowledge and perception (are) the same or maybe different, but not as you're doing it now on the basis of the habitual usage of words and

C

phrases: it's these that the many, by dragging and pulling in any which way, make the occasion for mutual perplexities of all sorts.

I offer this, Theodorus, to your comrade by way of assistance to the best of my capacity, a small bit from a small store. But if he were still alive himself, he would have gone to the assistance of his own things in a more magnificent way.

THEODORUS: You're joking, Socrates. You've assisted the man in a very lively way.

SOCRATES: It's good of you to say so, comrade. Tell me. You surely noticed that when Protagoras was speaking just now and reproaching us because in conducting our speeches before a mere

D

child we competed against his own things by means of the boy's fear, and in his calling off in disparagement any kind of charming whimsy, while setting off the measure of all things with august majesty, he urged us to be in earnest about his own speech?

THEODORUS: Of course I noticed it, Socrates.

SOCRATES: What then? Do you urge obedience to him?

THEODORUS: Yes, exactly.

SOCRATES: Do you see then that all these here are mere children except for you? So if we'll obey the man, then it's you and I who must,

E

in asking and answering one another, prove to be in earnest about his speech, in order that he cannot bring this charge at least, that in being playful before lads we examined his speech.

THEODORUS: But what of it? See here. Wouldn't Theaetetus better follow an examination of a speech than many who have long beards?

SOCRATES: Well, not at all better than you at least, Theodorus. So don't suppose that I must defend your dead comrade in every way and *169* you in none. But come—my excellent fellow!—do follow just a little way, up to this very point, when we know whether you, after all, must be the measure of geometrical theorems (drawings) or all are as competent for themselves as you are in astronomy and everything else in which you are charged with excelling.

THEODORUS: It's not easy, Socrates, to sit beside you and not give an account (*logos*), and I was just now distracted into uttering nonsense when I said that you'd leave it up to me not to strip and wouldn't use compulsion as the Spartans do. But my impression is that you tend rather toward Sciron, for Spartans order one *B* either to go away or to strip, but my impression is that your act is rather on the model of Antaeus, for you don't release anyone who approaches before you compel him to strip and go to the mat in speeches.[38]

SOCRATES: Yes, Theodorus, it's an excellent semblance that you made of my disease; I am however more stubborn than they. Thousands of Heracleses and Theseuses, mighty in speaking, have before now met and thrashed me roundly, but I none the less do not stand aside and withdraw—it's to that extent that a dreadful love of exercise in *C* matters of this kind has slipped into me. So don't you begrudge a drubbing and a benefit of yourself and me at once.

THEODORUS: I no longer speak of resisting, but lead wherever you want, for I must in any case be refuted and endure whatever fate you spin out for me in these matters.[39] I'll not, however, be able to submit myself to you beyond what you propose.

SOCRATES: Well, it's enough even to go so far. Now please watch the following sort of thing very closely, lest at some point we slip unawares into conducting a childish species of speeches, and *D* someone once more reproach us for it.

THEODORUS: Well, I'll try of course, to the extent that I'm able.

SOCRATES: Well, then, let's get our grip back on this at just the same point as before, and let's see whether we were correctly or incorrectly annoyed when we faulted that speech that was making each one self-sufficient in point of intelligence. And Protagoras did concede to us that some are superior when it comes to the better and worse, and it's these he granted were the wise. Isn't that so?

THEODORUS: Yes.

SOCRATES: Now if he were present and was making the agreement himself, and it was not we who had in taking the field conceded *E* it on his behalf, there would now be no need to take it up again and confirm it; but as it is, someone might cancel our authority to make an agreement on his behalf. It's for this reason that it's more beautiful to come to an agreement of greater clarity about this very point, for it's not just a slight variance whether it's in this or a different way.

THEODORUS: What you say is true.

SOCRATES: Let's not then through different (speeches) but on the basis

170   of his speech gain the agreement as briefly as possible.

THEODORUS: How?

SOCRATES: In this way. He surely says that whatever is the opinion for each, this also is for him whose opinion it is?

THEODORUS: Yes, he says so indeed.

SOCRATES: Then aren't we too speaking, Protagoras, the opinions of (a) human being, or rather of all human beings, and we assert that there's no one who's not convinced that he's wiser than everyone else in some things but in some things different people are wiser than he is. And in the greatest dangers, whenever they are foundering on campaigns, in illnesses, or at sea, their relation to

B   the rulers on these several occasions is as to gods, in the expectation that they're their saviors, and they don't differ by anything else than by the fact that they know. And all human affairs surely are as full of people seeking teachers and rulers of themselves, of the rest of the animals, and their occupations, as they are of those who believe in turn that they're competent to teach and competent to rule? And in all these matters what else shall we say than that human beings themselves are convinced that wisdom and folly are at home among them?

THEODORUS: Nothing else.

SOCRATES: They're convinced that wisdom (is) true thought and folly false opinion?

C THEODORUS: Why certainly.

SOCRATES: How then shall we handle the speech, Protagoras? Are we to assert that human beings always opine what is true, or at times true and at times false? For it surely turns out on the basis of both that they don't always opine what is true but both. Consider, Theodorus, whether anyone of Protagoras' circle or you yourself would be willing to insist that no other is convinced that an other is foolish and opines what is false.

THEODORUS: Well, it's unbelievable, Socrates.

D SOCRATES: And yet the speech that says (a) human being (is) the measure of all things (*khrêmata*) has come to the point of submitting to this necessity.

THEODORUS: How's that exactly?

SOCRATES: Whenever you judge something by yourself and declare in front of me an opinion about something, then in accordance with his speech let this be true for you. But is it not possible for all the rest of us to come to be judges of your judgment, or are we always deciding that you opine what's true? Or don't thousands battle you on each occasion with counteropinions, convinced that you judge and believe what is false?

THEODORUS: Yes, by Zeus, Socrates, it's indeed thousands, Homer says, *E* and it's they who give me all the trouble (*pragmata*) that I have from human beings.[40]

SOCRATES: What then? Do you want us to say that you at that time are opining what is true for yourself and false for the thousands?

THEODORUS: It seems on the basis of the speech at least to be a necessity.

SOCRATES: And what of Protagoras himself? Isn't it a necessity that if not even he were to believe that (a) human being was the measure, or the many either—just as they don't at all believe it—this truth *171* which he wrote is strictly for no one? And if he were to believe it, and the multitude do not share his belief, you know that first of all, to the extent that more are of the opinion that it's not than that it is, to that extent it is not more than it is.

THEODORUS: It's a necessity, provided, that is, it will be and will not be in accordance with each opinion.

SOCRATES: Yes, and, in the second place, this is the cleverest thing about it. He surely concedes that the belief of those who have a counteropinion to his own about his own belief—in which they're convinced that he's speaking what is false (lying)—is true, since he agrees that everyone opines the things which are.

THEODORUS: Yes, of course.

SOCRATES: Would he then concede his own is false if he agrees that *B* the belief of those convinced he's speaking falsely (lying) is true?

THEODORUS: It's a necessity.

SOCRATES: Yes, but everyone else does not concede that they themselves are speaking falsely?

THEODORUS: Indeed they don't.

SOCRATES: Yes, but he's agreeing that this opinion too is true on the basis of what he has written?

THEODORUS: It appears so.

SOCRATES: So will there be after all a dispute from all who take their start from Protagoras, or rather won't there be an agreement at least by him, whenever he concedes to the one contradicting him that he's opining what is true, and at that time Protagoras himself *C* will also concede that neither a dog nor the chance human being is a measure about even one thing which he does not understand (learn)? Isn't that so?

THEODORUS: Just so.

SOCRATES: Isn't it the case then that since it's disputed by all, the Truth of Protagoras would not be true for anyone, neither anyone else nor himself?

THEODORUS: We're running down my comrade too much, Socrates.

SOCRATES: Well, you know, my friend, it's not plain whether we're not in fact running right past the right, for it's likely that he, since he is older, be wiser than us. And if he should for instance pop up here on the spot and just up to his neck, he would, as is likely, once he charged me with talking a lot of nonsense and you with agreeing, slip down out of sight and be off and running. But I suppose it's a necessity for us to deal with ourselves as the sort we are, and to say whatever are our own opinions on each and every occasion. And so, now in this particular case, are we to assert that anyone whatsoever would agree to this at least, the fact of another being wiser than an other and similarly more foolish?

D

THEODORUS: It's my opinion at any rate.

SOCRATES: Are we also to say that the speech would especially take its stand in the region we outlined when we were going to the assistance of Protagoras, that the many things in which, in whatever way one's opinion is, it's in that way that they are for each—hot things, dry things, sweet things, all things of this cast? But if it's anywhere that he'll concede that in some things someone differs from someone else, he would be willing to say it's about the healthy and the sick things that not every mere woman and child, let alone every beast, is competent to cure itself, because it recognizes what is healthy for itself, but it's exactly here if anywhere that someone differs from someone else.

E

THEODORUS: I'm of the opinion, at least, that this is the way it is.

SOCRATES: Isn't it the case about political things too, that though for beautiful and ugly things, just and unjust, and holy and not, of whatsoever sort they are that each city in its belief lays down for itself as lawful, these also are in truth for each, and in these things neither layman than layman nor city than city is in any way wiser? Still, in the case of laying down for itself things that are to its own advantage or not to its own advantage, it's here, if anywhere, that he'll agree again that adviser differs from adviser and another opinion of a city from an other in light of truth. And he would scarcely have the nerve to assert that whatever a city lays down for itself in the belief they're to its advantage, it's as certain as can be that these things will be to its advantage. But it's in the former

172

B

case, I mean in the just and unjust, holy and unholy things, that they're willing to insist that none of them is by nature with a being of its own, but the opinion resolved on in common, this becomes true at that time, whenever it's resolved on and for as long a time as it's so resolved. And everyone who does not altogether speak the speech of Protagoras,[41] leads wisdom in one way or another to this. But a greater speech, Theodorus, from a lesser speech is *C* overtaking us.

THEODORUS: Aren't we at leisure, Socrates?

SOCRATES: It appears we are. And though I often realized it at other times of course—you extraordinary being![42]—it's striking now as well how likely it is that those who passed much time in the practices of philosophy show up as laughable public speakers when they enter the courts.[43]

THEODORUS: How exactly do you mean that?

SOCRATES: It's probable that those who since youth knock about courts and places of the sort are, in comparison with those who have been reared in philosophy and that sort of engagement, like domestics in comparison to free. *D*

THEODORUS: In what respect exactly?

SOCRATES: In the sense that they always have available that which you said—leisure—and they conduct their talks in peace and at their leisure. And just as we at the present moment are now taking for a third time a speech in exchange for a speech, so they do too, if the speech that comes along pleases them more than that which lies in front of them, just as it did us. And it's of no concern to them whether they talk at length or briefly, if only they hit upon 'that which is'. But *they* are always speaking in the press of busi- *E* ness—water in its flow is bearing down on them[44]—and there's no room to have their talks about whatever they desire, but the plaintiff stands over them holding necessity and an outline that is read alongside as they speak and outside of which they must not speak.[45] And their speeches are always about a fellow-slave before a seated master, who holds some kind of suit (justice) in his hand, and the contests are never indifferent, but he's always *173* the case in point, and the course is often in fact about his life (soul): as a result of all this, they become sharp and shrewd, knowing how to cozen their master in speech and beguile him in deed, but they become small and not upright in their souls, for their enslavement since their youth on has deprived them of the possibility of growth, straightness, and liberality. It compels them to do crooked things, imposing on their still tender souls great dangers and fears which they're incapable of supporting with the just

and true, and so turning at once to the lie and mutual injustice
B   they often get bent and stunted, and from lads they end up as
men with nothing healthy and sound in their thought. They have
become, they believe, dreadfully uncanny and wise. And here you
have the sort that they are, Theodorus. But as for those of our
chorus, do you want us to go through it or dismiss it and turn
once more to the speech, in order that we may not in fact abuse
too much in excess the freedom and possibility of exchanging
speeches that we were just now speaking of?

C   THEODORUS: In no way, Socrates, but let's go through it. You've made
a very good point, that we who are choristers in this sort of thing
are not subservient to the speeches, but the speeches are as it were
our domestics, and each of them waits around to be completed
whenever we decide. No judge and no observer supervises us as
he does poets to rebuke and rule.

SOCRATES: Let's speak then, since, it seems, you're of the opinion that
we are to, about those at the top—for why should one speak of
those who spend their time in philosophy so poorly?—it's surely
these who since their youth, first of all, don't know the way to the
D   marketplace, or where's a court, councilhouse, or anything else
that's a common assembly of the city. And laws and decrees, spoken or written, they neither see nor hear, and the serious business
of clubs for gaining office, and meetings, banquets, and revelries
with flute girls—it doesn't even occur to them to do them in their
dreams. And whether someone has been well-born or base-born
in the city, or whether someone has incurred some evil from his
ancestors, on the men's or women's side—he's less aware of it than
E   of the proverbial pitchers of the sea.[46] And he doesn't even know
that he does not know all these things, for he's not abstaining
from them for the sake of good repute, but in truth his body
alone is situated in the city and resides there, but his thought,
convinced that all these things are small and nothing, dishonors
them in every way and flies, as Pindar puts it, "deep down under
the earth"[47] and geometricizes the planes, "and above heaven"
174   star gazing, and in exploring everywhere every nature of each
whole of the things which are and letting itself down to not one
of the things nearby.

THEODORUS: How do you mean this, Socrates?

SOCRATES: Just like Thales, Theodorus, while star gazing and looking
up he fell in a well, and some gracefully witty Thracian servant
girl is said to have made a jest at his expense—that in his eagerness
to know the things in heaven he was unaware of the things in
front of him and at his feet. The same jest suffices for all those

who engage in philosophy. For someone of this sort has truly *B*
become unaware of his neighbor next-door, not only as to what
he's doing but almost to the point of not knowing whether he is
a human being or some different nursling. But what (a) human
being is and in what respect it's suitable for a nature of that sort
to act or be acted on that's different from all the rest—he seeks
that, and all his trouble (*pragmata*) is in exploring it. Surely you
understand, Theodorus, or don't you?

THEODORUS: Yes I do, and what you say is true.

SOCRATES: It's precisely for this reason, my friend, that whoever is of
this sort in associating with each in private and in public, just as *C*
I was saying at the beginning, whenever he's compelled in a court
or anywhere else to converse about the things at his feet and things
before his eyes, he gives not only Thracian girls but the rest of
the crowd a laugh, falling into wells and every kind of perplexity
by inexperience, and his lack of deportment is dreadful as he
gives the impression of plain silliness. For just as on occasions of
abuse he has nothing peculiar to revile anyone with, because he
knows of no evil of anyone from his failure to have practiced it
(and so in his perplexity he's evidently laughable), so no less on *D*
occasions of praise and the boastings of everyone else when he's
not in any feigned way but truly and openly laughing, he seems
to be nonsensical. For when a tyrant or a king is praised, he's
convinced he's hearing that one of the herdsmen is deemed to be
happy—a swineherd, for example, a shepherd, or some cowherd—for milking a lot of cattle. But he holds that they are grazing
and milking a more peevish and conspiratorial animal than the
herdsmen are, but it's necessary that a ruler of this sort become
by lack of leisure no less boorish and uneducated than the herdsmen, with his wall cast around him as a sheepfold on a mountain. *E*
And whenever he hears of someone in possession of ten thousand
acres of land or still more—"Oh! he possesses an amazing quantity"—his impression is that he's hearing of a very small amount,
accustomed as he is to look at the entire earth. And when people
harp on families—"How grand and noble so-and-so is; he can
show seven wealthy ancestors"—he's convinced the praise is from
those whose sight is altogether dim and limited, who are incapable,
by lack of education, of looking over all eternity and calculating
that each and every one has had countless thousands of grand- *175*
fathers and ancestors, and anyone whatsoever has had among
them many thousands of rich men and beggars, kings and slaves,
barbarians and Greeks. But for those who make themselves august
in a recitation of twenty-five ancestors and refer themselves to

B   Heracles the son of Amphitryon, their petty calculation seems strange to him; and because whoever was the twenty-fifth further back from Amphitryon was the sort he was as chance befell him, and the fiftieth further back from him no less, he laughs when they're incapable of calculation and release from the vanity of a foolish soul. And on all these occasions whoever is of this sort is laughed at by the many, since he seems to be partly arrogant and partly ignorant of the things at his feet and is perplexed in particular.

THEODORUS: You altogether speak, Socrates, of the way it happens.

SOCRATES: Yes, but whenever he himself gets to drag someone up,
C   my friend, and he's responsible for someone being willing to leave off from "How am I wronging you, or you me?" and turns to the examination of justice itself and injustice, what each of the pair (is) and in what respect they differ from everything or each other, or from "Whether a king's happy in possession of mickle gold,"[48] and turns to an examination of kingship and of human happiness and misery in general, of what sort the pair is and in what way it's suitable for the nature of (a) human being to acquire one and
D   avoid one of the pair—whenever that one who's small in his soul and shrewd and a shyster has to give an account (logos) of all these things, then he pays back the converse. Hung up on high he's dizzy and looking from high above he's in dismay by his unfamiliarity, he's perplexed and stutters, and he does not give Thracian girls a laugh, or anyone else who's uneducated either—for they don't perceive it—but all those who have been reared in a fashion contrary to slaves. So here you have the way of each of the two, Theodorus: the way of him who has been truly nurtured
E   in freedom and leisure—he's the one you call a philosopher—it's no matter of indignation for him to seem to be naive and nothing, whenever he falls into slavish services (it's as if he does not know how to pack up bedding or flavor a relish or fawning speeches); and the way of him in turn, who's capable of serving in all things of this sort keenly and sharply, but who doesn't know how to arrange his cloak on the right in a free man's way or for that
176 matter get a harmony of speeches and hymn correctly a life of gods and happy men.

THEODORUS: If you should persuade everyone, Socrates, of what you're saying as you did me, peace would be more widespread and evils less among human beings.

SOCRATES: But it's not possible for the evils either to perish, Theodorus—it's a necessity that there always be something contrary to the good—or for them to be established among gods, but of ne-

cessity they haunt mortal nature and this region here; it's for this
reason that one ought to try to flee from here to there as soon as
possible. Flight (is) assimilation to a god as far as possible, and   B
assimilation (is) to become just and holy with intelligence. But as
a matter of fact, it's hardly at all easy—my excellent fellow!—to
persuade that it's not after all for the sake of which the many say
one should avoid wickedness and pursue virtue, that it's for this
sake that one must practice virtue and not vice, in order that, of
all things, one may seem to be good and not bad. For all this is,
as the saying goes, the drivel of old women, as it appears to me.
But let's tell the truth as follows. A god (is) in no way unjust in   C
any respect, but he's the most just that it's possible to be, and there
is nothing more similar to him than whoever of us becomes in
turn as just as possible. It's in his dealing with this that there's the
truly dreadful uncanniness of a man or his nothingness and un-
manliness, for the cognition of this (is) wisdom and simply true
virtue, and its ignorance folly and manifest vice, and all the rest
of seeming uncanniness and wisdom that occur in the practice of
political power (is) vulgar, and what occurs in the arts common.
As for whoever, then, is doing an injustice and saying or doing   D
unholy things, it's best by far in his case not to make the concession
that he is uncanny by his criminal willingness to stop at nothing,
for they glory in the reproach and believe they're hearing that
they're not utter nonsense, merely burdens of the earth,[49] but that
they're men as they ought to be in a city—those who will get
themselves to safety. So one must tell the truth, that they are by
so much more the sort they suspect they're not because they don't
suspect it, for they're ignorant of the penalty for injustice, and
it's what they least ought to be ignorant of. For it's not what it is
in their opinion, beatings and executions—people who do no injustice undergo them on occasion—but it's what's impossible to
avoid.   E
THEODORUS: What exactly do you mean?
SOCRATES: Paradigms stand in 'that which is', my friend, of the divine
    which is most happy and of the godless which is most miserable,
    and they don't see that this is the way it is, but by their folly and
    extreme foolishness they unawares make themselves similar to the 177
    latter on account of their unjust actions, and make themselves
    dissimilar to the former. So they pay the penalty for exactly this
    by living the life that resembles that to which they make themselves
    similar. And if we say that unless they get rid of their uncanniness,
    even when they're dead that region clear of the bad won't receive
    them, but it's here they'll always have their own similarity of a

way of life; bad in association with bad, they'll listen to this as altogether the talk of some mindless people, uncanny and criminally willing to stop at nothing as they are.

THEODORUS: Indeed they will, Socrates.

B SOCRATES: I know it, be sure, comrade. There's one thing, however, that has befallen them. Whenever they have to give and receive in private an account (*logos*) of the things they blame, and they're willing in a manly fashion to put up with it for a long time and not to take flight in an unmanly way, then strangely—you extraordinary being!—they end up as not being satisfied with themselves about what they're saying, and that rhetorical (art) of theirs somehow or other shrinks up, so as for them to seem to be no different from children. Now let's stand apart and withdraw from

C these things—they were in fact said as by-products—for if we don't, always more will keep on flowing in and choke up the speech with which we began, and let's go to the previous remarks, if you're of that opinion too.

THEODORUS: As for me, Socrates, things of this sort are less unpleasant to listen to, for they're easier for someone of my age to follow. If, however, it's been resolved on, let's go back.

SOCRATES: Weren't we then at some point hereabouts of the speech, in which, we claimed, those who speak of that sweeping being,[50] and whatever is the opinion of each on any occasion also is for him whose opinion it is, are willing in everything else to insist upon this and not least in the case of the just things, that it's as

D certain as can be that whatever a city lays down for itself, once the city has got an opinion about them, these also are just for the city which laid them down for as long as they are laid down. But about the good things, there is no one still so manly as to have the nerve to fight it out that whatever a city lays down for itself in the belief they're beneficial, then these things also are, for as long a time as they are laid down, beneficial—unless one should give it the name, but it would surely be a jest in light of what we're saying. Or isn't it?

THEODORUS: Certainly.

E SOCRATES: The reason is that he is not to say the name but to observe the matter (*pragma*) that is named.

THEODORUS: Don't let him then.

SOCRATES: But whatever a city names this, surely it's aiming at that in its legislation, and all the laws, to the extent that it believes and is capable, it lays down for itself as beneficially as possible. Or does the city legislate by looking at anything else?

178 THEODORUS: In no way.

SOCRATES: Does it really then also always hit upon it, or doesn't each often fail too?

THEODORUS: I suspect there's failure too.

SOCRATES: Well, it's still more the case that everyone would agree to these same things from the following viewpoint, should one ask about the species in its entirety in which the beneficial also happens to be. And that surely is in fact about future time. For whenever we legislate for ourselves, we're laying down the laws on the grounds that they will be beneficial in later time, and this we would correctly speak of as "future."

THEODORUS: Certainly.   *B*

SOCRATES: Come then, let's ask in just this way Protagoras or anyone else of those who say the same things as he does. "Of all things (a) human being is the measure," as you all assert, Protagoras— of white things, heavy things, light things, everything of the sort without exception—for with his own tribunal for them in himself, believing they're the sort as he experiences them, he believes they're true for him and are the things which are. Isn't that so?

THEODORUS: That's so.

SOCRATES: Shall we really assert, then, Protagoras, that he does have   *C*
the tribunal in himself also for the things that will be, and whatever sort he believes they will be, these things also become to him who conceived the belief? For example, a feverish heat. Whenever some layman believes he'll get a fever and this hotness will be, and another, but a physician, holds the counterbelief, in accordance with the opinion of which of the two are we to assert how the future will turn out? Or will it be in accordance with the opinion of both, and he won't be hot for the physician and won't be feverish, while to himself there'll be both?

THEODORUS: In that case it would be laughable.

SOCRATES: Well, I suspect in regard to the future sweetness and dry-
ness of wine, the opinion of the farmer is authoritative and not   *D*
that of the lyre-player.

THEODORUS: Why certainly.

SOCRATES: Nor, in turn, about what will be out of tune and in tune, would a trainer's opinion prove to be better than a musician's, since later, too, the trainer himself will be of the opinion that it is in tune.

THEODORUS: In no way.

SOCRATES: And isn't it also the case for the future feaster, whoever's not an expert cook, when a banquet is being got ready, his judg-ment is less authoritative than the relish-maker's about the future pleasure. Let's not yet fight it out with the speech about the pleas-   *E* ant that is now or has been for him, but about that which will in the future be for each and be the opinion of each—is he himself his own best judge? Or you, Protagoras? Would your anticipatory opinion prove to be better, at least in the case of what will be persuasive in speeches for each of us in court, or any layman's whatsoever?

THEODORUS: Yes, indeed, Socrates, it was in exactly this that he used to promise to surpass everyone.

179 SOCRATES: Yes, by Zeus, my good man,[51] or else no one would converse with him and offer him a lot of money, if he were not persuading his associates that neither a soothsayer nor anyone else would better judge that which will be and will seem than he himself.

THEODORUS: Most true.

SOCRATES: Isn't it the case, then, that both acts of legislation and the beneficial are concerned with the future, and everyone would agree that it is often a necessity for a city in legislating for itself to fail to hit upon the most beneficial?

THEODORUS: Yes indeed.

SOCRATES: So it will be stated by us in a measured way before your
B teacher that it's a necessity for him to agree that someone is wiser than someone else, and that whoever is of that sort is the measure, and there is no necessity whatsoever for me the nonknower to become the measure, as the speech on his behalf was just now compelling me to be of that sort, whether I was wanting to or not.

THEODORUS: It's my impression, Socrates, that the speech particularly gets convicted in the former way (though it's also convicted in this), in which it makes the opinions of everyone else authoritative, and these opinions believe, evidently, that his speeches are in no way true.

C SOCRATES: There're many different ways, Theodorus, in which a conviction of the sort might be gained against the view that every opinion of everyone is true. But in regard to the experience each has in the present, out of which the perceptions and the opinions in conformity with these perceptions come to be, it's harder to gain the point that they're not true. But perhaps I'm making no sense, for maybe they are unconvictable, and those who assert they are as plain as day and are sciences would perhaps be saying the things which are, and the speech of Theaetetus here has not been way off the mark when he set down perception and knowl-
D edge as the same. We have to approach it more closely, then, as the speech on behalf of Protagoras prescribed, and give this sweeping being a sharp tap and see whether it rings sound or

hollow. Now, whichever way it is, there has been a battle about it, not a trivial one, and it has involved not a few.

THEODORUS: It's far from being trivial, but it's been very much on the increase around Ionia, for the comrades of Heraclitus are the very vigorous choral leaders of this speech.

SOCRATES: That's all the more reason, my dear Theodorus, you see, to examine it, and from the beginning, just as they themselves *E* present it.

THEODORUS: That's altogether so. About these Heraclitean opinions, Socrates, or, as you say, Homeric and still more ancient, it's no more possible to converse with all who pretend to be experienced with them—the members of the Ephesian circle—than with those driven to madness by the gadfly. They simply (artlessly), in accordance with their own writings, sweep along. And as for the possibility of staying by a speech and question, and quietly an-   *180* swering and asking in turn, there is less than nothing in them of that, or rather even nothing does not surpass these men when it comes to the small degree of quietness in them.[52] But if you ask any of them anything, they send off shots as if they were drawing up enigmatic shaftlets from a quiver, and if you seek to get an account (*logos*) of this, as to what he has said, you'll be struck by another freshly altered name.[53] And you'll never get anywhere with any one of them, any more than they themselves will with one another, but they take very good care to permit nothing to be stable either in speech or in their own souls, convinced as they *B* are, in my opinion, that that is to be stationary. And they are wholly at war against that, and as far as they are capable, they throw it out from everywhere.

SOCRATES: Perhaps, Theodorus, you've seen the men fighting, but you've not been with them when they are at peace, for they are not your comrades. But, I suspect, they point out things of this sort (i.e., the stable things) to their pupils at their leisure, whomever they want to make similar to themselves.

THEODORUS: What do you mean, pupils? You extraordinary being! *C* For this sort there's not another who becomes the pupil of an other, but they grow up spontaneously, from whatever source each of them happens to get a god in him, and the other is convinced that the other knows nothing. Now from these, as I was going to say, you would never get an account (*logos*) regardless of whether they're willing or unwilling. But we must take it off their hands and examine it by ourselves as if it were a problem.[54]

SOCRATES: And there's a measure of sense in what you say. And as for the problem, have we taken on anything else than this—from *D* the ancients who were concealing it from the many with poetry,[55] it was that the becoming (*genesis*) of everything else happens to be streams, Oceanus and Tethys, and nothing is at rest, and from those later who, because they were wiser, were revealing it openly, in order that even the shoemakers, once they heard it, may understand their wisdom and stop believing in their foolishness that some of the things which are are at rest and some in motion, but once they understand that everything is in motion they may honor them? But I almost forgot, Theodorus, that different people, on

E the other hand, declared the contrary to this—"As the sort that is immoveable, there is 'to be' as the name for the all"[56]—and all the different things that the Melissuses and Parmenideses in opposing all of them insist on, that all things are one and it is at rest in itself without a place in which it moves. How shall we handle all of these, Theodorus? For in advancing little by little, we have, without being aware of it, fallen into the middle of both, and

181 unless we somehow manage to defend ourselves and escape, we'll pay the penalty, as those do in gymnasia who play at tug-of-war, whenever they are seized by both sides and dragged in contrary directions.[57] Now I'm of the opinion that we must examine the others first, toward whom we started out, the streamers. And if it's evident they're making sense, we'll drag ourselves off with them, and try to avoid the others, but if the arresters of the whole seem to be saying truer things,[58] we'll flee over to them and away

B from those who set the immoveable things in motion.[59] And if it's evident that there's no measure of sense in what both are saying, we'll be laughable, convinced that we're making sense though we're nobodies, and have repudiated in the scrutiny very ancient and all-wise men.[60] See, then, Theodorus, whether it's profitable to advance into so great a danger.

THEODORUS: Rather it's unendurable, Socrates, not to examine thoroughly what each of the two groups of men is saying.

SOCRATES: If you of all people are that eager, we must make the

C examination. Now it's my impression that the start of our examination is about motion—what sort of thing are they saying after all, those who assert that all things are in motion? I want to say the following sort of thing. Do they say there's some one species of motion, or, as it appears to me, two? Don't, however, let it only be my opinion, but you too share in it, in order that we may, if in fact we have to, suffer in common. Tell me. Do you call it motion whenever something changes from place to place or even when it's revolving in the same?

THEODORUS: Yes I do.

SOCRATES: Well, then, let this be one species. But whenever it is in the   *D*
same but grows old, or becomes black from white or stiff from
soft, or alters in any different alteration, isn't it worthwhile to
declare it another species of motion?

THEODORUS: It's necessary rather.

SOCRATES: I mean, then, by the two species of motion this pair, alteration and locomotion.

THEODORUS: And it's right to say so.

SOCRATES: Well, then, now that we made this kind of division, let's
converse with those who assert that all things are in motion, and
let's ask: Do you assert that everything's in motion in both ways,   *E*
moving locally and altering, or some move in both ways, and some
in one of the two?

THEODORUS: But, by Zeus, I for one cannot say. But I suspect they
would say in both ways.

SOCRATES: Yes, for if not, comrade, it will be evident that for them
things are both in motion and at rest, and it will be no more
correct to say that all things are in motion than that all things are
at rest.

THEODORUS: What you say is most true.

SOCRATES: Then, since they must be in motion, and nonmotion must
not be in anything, it's all things without exception that are always   *182*
in motion with every kind of motion.

THEODORUS: It's a necessity.

SOCRATES: Please examine the following point of theirs. In the case
of the becoming of hotness, or of whiteness, or of anything whatsoever, weren't we saying that they assert somehow in this way,
that each of these is born(e) along with a perception between that
which affects and is affected, and that which is affected becomes
capable of perceiving (it does not become perception), and that
which affects becomes a certain sort (it does not become sortness)?
Perhaps "sortness" appears an odd name, and you don't understand it when spoken of collectively.[61] Listen, then, part by part.   *B*
That which affects is neither hotness nor whiteness, but it becomes
hot and white—and so for all the rest. You surely remember we
were speaking in this way previously, that as nothing is itself one
by itself, so neither is that which affects or is affected, but from
both of them becoming mutually together, the perceptions and
the things perceived come to be and give birth to some as certain
sorts and some as perceiving?

THEODORUS: Of course I remember.

SOCRATES: Now let's dismiss everything else, whether they speak in a   *C*
different way or in this way. But for the sake of which we're

speaking, let's only guard this, and ask: All things are in motion and flow, as you say? Don't they?

THEODORUS: Yes.

SOCRATES: In respect, then, to both the motions we divided, they move locally and they alter?

THEODORUS: Yes, of course, provided that it's in the strict sense they are to move completely.

SOCRATES: Now if there was only local motion but not alteration, we could surely say what sort of things are the things that move locally in their flow. Or how are we saying?

THEODORUS: It's in this way.

D SOCRATES: But since not even this abides, that it's the white that's flowing which flows, but it changes, so as for there to be a flowing even of just this, of whiteness, and a change into a different color, in order that it may not in this way be convicted of loitering, is it ever possible to address it as some color so as really to be addressing it correctly?

THEODORUS: But what possibility is there, Socrates? Or for that matter anything else of the things of this sort, if it's always slipping out and away while one's speaking and precisely because it's flowing?[62]

SOCRATES: And what are we to say about any sort of perception what-
E ever, for example, of seeing or hearing? Does it ever abide in just seeing or hearing?

THEODORUS: It ought not, at any rate, if all things are in motion.

SOCRATES: So one must address it no more as seeing than as not-seeing, nor any different perception either rather than not, since all things in all ways are in motion.

THEODORUS: Indeed one must not.

SOCRATES: And yet perception (is) knowledge, as Theaetetus and I said.

THEODORUS: That was so.

SOCRATES: So on being asked what knowledge is, we no more answered after all about knowledge than about nonknowledge.

183 THEODORUS: It seems that's what you did.

SOCRATES: The correction of our answer would turn out to be for us a beauty if, in order that that answer may appear, of all things, correct, we should be eager to prove that all things are in motion. For this is what comes to light, it seems, if all things are in motion—every answer, about whatever one answers, is similarly correct. Or if you want, in order that we may not put a stop to them in the speech, every answer becomes correct[63]—to say "This is so" and "This is not so."

THEODORUS: What you say's correct.

SOCRATES: Yes, Theodorus, except that I did say "so" and "not so."
But one must not even say "so," for "so" would no longer be in *B*
motion, nor in turn "not so," for not even this is a motion. But
those who speak this speech must set down some different language, since now at least they don't have the words for their own
hypothesis, unless, after all, "not even so" would most particularly
fit them, since it is spoken without a limit.

THEODORUS: This is at any rate a dialect they're most at home with.[64]

SOCRATES: Are we then quit of your comrade, Theodorus, and do we
not as yet concede to him that every man is the measure of all *C*
things (*khrêmata*), unless someone is intelligent? And we'll not concede knowledge (is) perception, at least in terms of the quest for
all things to be in motion, unless Theaetetus here has something
different to say?

THEODORUS: What you've said is excellent, Socrates. For with this
brought to an end, I too must be quit of answering you, in accordance with the contract that specified it as the completion of
Protagoras' speech.

THEAETETUS: Don't, Theodorus, not before you and Socrates go *D*
through those who assert in turn that the all is at rest, as you just
now proposed.

THEODORUS: So young, Theaetetus, and you teach your elders to be
unjust and violate agreements? But get yourself ready to give
Socrates an account (*logos*) of that which remains.

THEAETETUS: Yes, if, that is, he wants to. I would have listened in any
case with the greatest pleasure about those whom I'm speaking
of.

THEODORUS: "Horsemen to the plain" is your challenge to Socrates in
inviting him to speeches.[65] Ask and you'll hear.

SOCRATES: But, Theodorus, it's my impression that I'll not obey Theaetetus, at least about what he's urging. *E*

THEODORUS: Why exactly won't you obey him?

SOCRATES: Although I'm ashamed before Melissus and everyone else,
who speak of the all as one at rest, lest our investigation be vulgar
and common, I'm less ashamed before them than before Parmenides who is one. Parmenides appears to me at once, in the
saying of Homer, "as awesome to me as uncanny."[66] In fact, I
once got together with the man when I was very young and he
very old, and he appeared to me to have some altogether grand *184*
and noble depth.[67] So I'm afraid that we'll fail as much to understand what he was saying as we'll fall far short of what he
thought when he spoke, and—this is the greatest thing—that for
whose sake the speech has started out, about knowledge, whatever

it is, that that will prove to be unexamined under the press of the speeches that are bursting in like revellers, if anyone will obey them. And this is all the more the case now, since the speech we now awaken makes it impossible to handle by its immensity, regardless of what one will do. For if one will examine it incidentally, it would undergo what it does not deserve, and if one will do it adequately, it will by its lengthening wipe out the issue of knowledge. We must do neither, but we must try by means of the

B   maieutic art to deliver Theaetetus from whatever he's pregnant with in regard to knowledge.

THEODORUS: Well, if it's so resolved, we must do it in this way.

SOCRATES: Well, then, Theaetetus, go on and examine still further this much of the following sort about what has been said. You answered that knowledge (was) perception. Didn't you?

THEAETETUS: Yes.

SOCRATES: If then someone should ask you as follows, "By what does (a) human being see the white and black things, and by what does he hear the high and low notes?" You would, I suspect, say, "By eyes and ears."

THEAETETUS: Yes, I would.

C SOCRATES: To be accommodating when it comes to words and phrases and fail to examine them with precision is in many cases not an ignoble trait, but rather, the contrary to it is illiberal. But sometimes it is necessary, just as now it's necessary to get a handle on the answer you give, in what way it's not correct. Consider. Which answer's more correct? By which we see, this is eyes, or through which we see; and by which we hear, ears, or through which we hear?

THEAETETUS: It's my opinion, Socrates that it's rather through which we perceive each several thing than by which.

D SOCRATES: That's because it's surely dreadful, my boy, if many kinds of perceptions sit in us as if in wooden horses, but all these do not strain together toward some single look (*idea*), regardless of whether it's soul or whatever one must call it, by which we perceive through these as if they're tools all the perceived and perceptible things.

THEAETETUS: Well, it's my impression that it's more in the latter way than in the former.

SOCRATES: It's for the following reason, you see, that I'm being such a stickler for precision with you about them—is it by some same kind of thing of ourselves that we attain through eyes white and black things, and through the rest, in turn, some other things?

E And will you be able, on being questioned, to refer all things of the sort to the body? But perhaps it's better for you to speak and answer the question yourself rather than for me to meddle on your behalf. Tell me. Hot things, stiff things, light things, and sweet things—those through which you perceive them, do you set them down severally as belonging to the body? Or is it to something else?

THEAETETUS: Nothing else.

SOCRATES: Will you also be willing to agree that those things which you perceive through another power, it is impossible to perceive   *185* them through a different power? For example, what through hearing, through sight, or what through sight, through hearing?

THEAETETUS: Of course I'll be willing.

SOCRATES: Then if you think something about both, you would not have any more through the other tool than through the other a perception of both.

THEAETETUS: Indeed I wouldn't.

SOCRATES: So about sound and about color, first, do you think this very thing about both, that both of the pair are?

THEAETETUS: Yes, I do.

SOCRATES: And each of the two (is) other than each of the two, but the same as itself?

THEAETETUS: Why certainly.   *B*

SOCRATES: And that both of the pair (are) two, and each of the two one?

THEAETETUS: This too.

SOCRATES: And you are further capable of examining whether as a pair they (are) similar or dissimilar to one another?

THEAETETUS: Perhaps.

SOCRATES: So through what do you think all these things about the pair? For it's possible neither through hearing nor through sight to grasp the common thing about them. And there's still this as a piece of evidence for what we're saying. If it should be possible to conduct an examination as to whether both of the pair are salty or not, you know you'll be able to say by what you'll examine it, and this appears as neither sight nor hearing but something else.   *C*

THEAETETUS: Of course it does, it's the power through the tongue.

SOCRATES: What you say is beautiful. But the power through what exactly makes clear to you that which is common in all things as well as that which is common in these, by which you apply the name "is" and "is not," and what we were just now asking about them? What sort of tools will you assign all these through which the perceiving element of us perceives each thing severally?

THEAETETUS: You mean being and to be not and similarity and dis-

D similarity and "the same" and other[68] and, further, one and the rest of number about them. It's plain that you're asking about both even and odd as well, and everything else that follows them, through which of the things of the body do we perceive them by means of the soul.

SOCRATES: You're following exceedingly well, Theaetetus, and these are the very things I'm asking about.

THEAETETUS: But, by Zeus, Socrates, I for one could not say, except that I'm just of the opinion that there's no private (peculiar) tool of that sort at all for these things as there is for those, but

E the soul itself through itself, it appears to me, examines the common things about all of them.

SOCRATES: It's because you *are* beautiful, Theaetetus, and not, as Theodorus was saying, ugly. For whoever speaks beautifully (is) beautiful and good. And besides being beautiful you did me a favor and freed me from a very large speech, if it appears to you that the soul itself through itself examines some things, and some things through the powers of the body. For this, which was my opinion too, I wanted it to get to be your opinion as well.

186 THEAETETUS: Well, it does appear to be so.

SOCRATES: In which of the two do you place being? This most particularly follows along in all cases.

THEAETETUS: Well, I place it in those things which the soul by itself aims at (desires).[69]

SOCRATES: And the similar too and the dissimilar and "the same" and other?

THEAETETUS: Yes.

SOCRATES: And what of this? Beautiful and ugly, good and bad?

THEAETETUS: It's my opinion that it's the being of these things in their mutual relations which the soul most especially examines, calcu-

B lating in itself the past and the present things relative to the future.

SOCRATES: Hold it. Whereas one will perceive the stiffness of the stiff

190 through one's touch, and the softness of the soft likewise—

THEAETETUS: Yes.

SOCRATES: Still, their being, and that the pair of them is, and their contrariety to one another, and the being in turn of the contrariety—does the soul itself go back over them and compare them with each other and try to judge them for us?

THEAETETUS: Yes, of course.

SOCRATES: Aren't there some things that are just there by nature to

C be perceived for human beings and beasts as soon as they are born—and these are all the experiences that stretch to the soul through the body? But the calculations about these things in regard to being and benefit come about, to whomever they do come about, with difficulty and in much time through a lot of trouble (*pragmata*) and education?

THEAETETUS: That's altogether so.

SOCRATES: Is it possible, then, for him to hit upon truth if he does not even hit upon being?

THEAETETUS: Impossible.

SOCRATES: But if one will fail to hit upon the truth of anything, will one ever be a knower of this?

THEAETETUS: But how could that be, Socrates? *D*

SOCRATES: So in the experiences, after all, there is no knowledge, but there is in reasoning about them; for in this case, it seems, it's possible to touch upon being and truth, but in that case it's impossible.

THEAETETUS: It appears so.

SOCRATES: Do you really then call this and that the same, though the pair of them has so many differences?

THEAETETUS: It's certainly not just, at any rate.

SOCRATES: What name then do you give to that, to seeing, hearing, smelling, feeling cold, feeling hot?

THEAETETUS: I for one name it perceiving. What else?

SOCRATES: So you call it in its entirety perception? *E*

THEAETETUS: It's a necessity.

SOCRATES: For which, we say, there is no share in the possibility of touching on truth, for it cannot on being either.

THEAETETUS: It cannot indeed.

SOCRATES: And so it has no share in knowledge either?

THEAETETUS: No, it doesn't.

SOCRATES: So perception and knowledge, Theaetetus, would never after all be the same.

THEAETETUS: It appears not, Socrates. And it has moreover now become most manifest that knowledge is different from perception.

SOCRATES: Well, it certainly wasn't at all for this purpose that we began *187* conversing, in order that we may find whatever knowledge is not, but what it is. But still and all, we've advanced so far at least, so altogether not to seek it in perception but in that name, whatever the soul has, whenever it alone by itself deals with the things which are.

THEAETETUS: Well, this is called, Socrates, as I believe, to opine.

SOCRATES: Yes, it's right for you to believe it. But wipe out everything before, and now, once more from the beginning, look and see *B* whether you can spy out any better, since you've come so far. And say again whatever is knowledge.

THEAETETUS: Now it's impossible, Socrates, to say it's every kind of opinion, since there is also false opinion, but it's probable that true opinion is knowledge, and let this be stated as my answer, for if it appears to us as we go on not to be so, we'll try, just as we did now, to say something else.

SOCRATES: Yes, that's really the way you must speak Theaetetus, eagerly
C rather than as at first when you hesitated to answer. For if we act in this way, it's one or the other of a pair of things that will follow, either we'll find that toward which we're going, or we'll less believe we know what we in no way know. And for all of that, a wage of this sort is not to be despised. And now in particular what do you assert? When there is of opinion a pair of looks (*ideai*), and one is of the simply true, and one is of the other false, are you defining true opinion as knowledge?

THEAETETUS: Yes I am, for this now appears to me so.

SOCRATES: Is it then still worth it to resume once more about opinion—

THEAETETUS: What sort of thing exactly are you speaking of?

D SOCRATES: It's something that in a sense disquiets me now and often at different times has done so, so as to have got me into a lot of perplexity before myself and before everyone else, when I'm not able to say whatever is this experience we have and in what manner it comes to be in us.

THEAETETUS: What sort of thing exactly?

SOCRATES: The fact of someone opining false things. So I'm considering and I'm still even now in doubt whether we're to let it go, or are we to go on to examine it in a somewhat different way than a little while ago.

THEAETETUS: Why not, Socrates, provided that it appears we should in any sense whatsoever? For just now you and Theodorus were making a good point about leisure—there's nothing urgent in matters of this sort.

SOCRATES: You rightly recalled it, for perhaps it's not inopportune to
E track it, as it were, once more, for it's surely a better thing to accomplish a little well than a lot inadequately.

THEAETETUS: Why certainly.

SOCRATES: How then? What exactly are we saying? We do assert on several occasions there's false opinion, and someone of us is opining false things, and one, in turn, true things, and all on the grounds that it is this way by nature.

THEAETETUS: Yes, we do indeed assert it.

188 SOCRATES: In the case of all things and individually, doesn't this hold for us, either to know or not to know? I dismiss for the moment

learning and forgetting on the grounds that they are between them, for nothing is pertinent there for our speech.

THEAETETUS: Well, Socrates, there's nothing left in the case of each except to know or not to know.

SOCRATES: Isn't it a necessity now that whoever opines, opines either something of the things which he knows or does not know?

THEAETETUS: It's a necessity.

SOCRATES: And yet it's just impossible, if one knows, not to know the same thing, or if one does not know, to know.   *B*

THEAETETUS: Of course.

SOCRATES: Is it the case then that whoever is opining the false believes these things not to be those things which he knows, but some other things of those which he knows, and though he knows both he is in turn ignorant of both?

THEAETETUS: But it's impossible, Socrates.

SOCRATES: Well, does he then believe that whatever he does not know are some other things of whatever he does not know, and this is possible, for him who knows neither Theaetetus nor Socrates to take into his thought that Socrates (is) Theaetetus or Theaetetus Socrates?

THEAETETUS: But how could that be?   *C*

SOCRATES: Well, it's surely not the case that whatever one knows, one believes they are what one does not know, nor in turn whatever one does not know, what one knows.

THEAETETUS: It will be a monster.

SOCRATES: How then would one still come to opine false things? For outside of these, it's surely impossible to opine, inasmuch as either we know or we don't know all things, and in these cases it nowhere appears possible to come to opine false things.

THEAETETUS: Most true.

SOCRATES: Are we then not to examine what we're looking for along these lines by proceeding in terms of knowing and not knowing,   *D* but in terms of being and not?

THEAETETUS: How do you mean?

SOCRATES: Maybe it's this simple, that whoever is opining the things which are not about anything whatsoever cannot possibly not opine false things, regardless of whatever different conditions may hold for the state of his thought.

THEAETETUS: Yes, it's likely, Socrates.

SOCRATES: How then? What shall we say, Theaetetus, if someone quizzes us, "But is that which is being said possible for anyone whatsoever, and will any human being opine that which is not, whether about any of the things which are or itself by itself?" And then we shall

say, it seems, in reply to this, "Yes, whenever in believing he does
E   not believe what is true." Or how shall we speak?

THEAETETUS: In this way.

SOCRATES: Is there something of this sort also anywhere else?

THEAETETUS: What sort of thing?

SOCRATES: Can someone see something but see nothing?

THEAETETUS: But how?

SOCRATES: But if he sees some one thing at least, he sees something
of the things which are. Or do you believe that the one is ever
among the things which are not?

THEAETETUS: No, I don't.

SOCRATES: So whoever sees some one thing at least, sees something
which is.

THEAETETUS: It appears so.

189 SOCRATES: And so whoever hears something, hears some one thing at
least and hears something which is.

THEAETETUS: Yes.

SOCRATES: And besides, whoever touches something, touches some
one thing at least and which is, since (it is) one?

THEAETETUS: This too.

SOCRATES: Then whoever opines, doesn't he opine some one thing at
least?

THEAETETUS: It's a necessity.

SOCRATES: But whoever's opining some one thing, isn't he opining
something which is?

THEAETETUS: I concede it.

SOCRATES: So whoever opines that which is not, opines after all nothing
(not even one thing).

THEAETETUS: It appears he does not.

SOCRATES: But whoever then opines nothing is altogether not opining
at all.

THEAETETUS: Plainly, it seems.

B SOCRATES: So it's not possible after all to opine that which is not, either
about the things which are or itself by itself.

THEAETETUS: It appears not.

SOCRATES: So to opine what is false is something else than to opine
the things which are not.

THEAETETUS: It's something else, it seems.

SOCRATES: So neither in this way nor as we were examining it a little
while ago is there false opinion in us.

THEAETETUS: No, there isn't in fact.

SOCRATES: Well, do we then address it with this name when it comes
to be in the following way?

1.58

THEAETETUS: How?

SOCRATES: It's by being a certain kind of else-opining that we claim there is false opinion. It's whenever someone makes an exchange C in his thought of some one of the things which are for something else of the things which are and says it is that. For in this way he's always opining that which is, but it's another instead of an other, and in mistaking that which he was aiming at, he would be justly spoken of as opining false things.

THEAETETUS: It's my opinion that you've now spoken most correctly. For whenever anyone opines (something as) ugly instead of (as) beautiful or beautiful instead of ugly, then truly he's opining false things.

SOCRATES: It's plain, Theaetetus, you despise me and do not fear me.

THEAETETUS: Why exactly?

SOCRATES: You're of the opinion, I suspect, that I would not attack D your "truly false," and ask whether slowly swift is possible or heavily light, or it's possible for anything else that's a contrary to become contrary to itself, not in accordance with its own nature, but in accordance with the nature of its contrary. Now as for this, I let it go, so that you may not have gained confidence to no purpose. But it's satisfactory, you say, to opine what is false is to else-opine?

THEAETETUS: It satisfies me at any rate.

SOCRATES: So it is possible, according to your opinion, to set down in one's thought something other as an other and not as that (i.e., other)?

THEAETETUS: Of course it is possible.

SOCRATES: Then whenever the thought of someone does this, isn't it E also a necessity that it by itself think either both or the other?

THEAETETUS: Yes, it's a necessity, and either together or in turn.

SOCRATES: Most beautiful! But do you call thinking just what I do?[70]

THEAETETUS: What do you call it?

SOCRATES: A speech which the soul by itself goes through before itself about whatever it is examining. As one who does not know, of course, I'm declaring it to you. Soul thinking looks to me as nothing else than conversing, itself asking and answering itself, and affirming and denying. But whenever it has come to a determi- *190* nation, regardless of whether its sally was on the slow or keen side, and then asserts the same thing and does not stand apart in doubt, we set this down as its opinion. Consequently, I for one call opining speaking, and opinion a stated speech; it's not, however, before someone else any more than it's with sound, but in silence before oneself. But what of you?

THEAETETUS: I too.

SOCRATES: So whenever someone opines the other as an other, he then asserts before himself, it seems, the other is an other.

B THEAETETUS: Why certainly.

SOCRATES: Then go ahead and recall whether you ever said before yourself, "It's as certain as can be, you see, the beautiful is ugly," or, "The unjust is just." Or even, and this is the chief point, consider whether you ever did try to persuade yourself, "It's as certain as can be, the other is an other." Or it's wholly the contrary, that not even asleep did you ever yet get the nerve to say before yourself, "It's altogether so after all, the odd is even," or anything else of the sort.

THEAETETUS: What you say is true.

C SOCRATES: But do you believe that anyone else, whether healthy or crazy, had the nerve to speak before himself in all seriousness in persuading himself that it's a necessity for the ox to be a horse or the two one?

THEAETETUS: No, by Zeus, I do not.

SOCRATES: Then if to speak before oneself is to opine, no one, in speaking and opining both, would come to say and opine, in touching on both with his soul, "The other is an other." Now you too must disregard my wording, for I mean it in the following

D way: no one opines that the ugly (is) beautiful or anything else of the sort.

THEAETETUS: Well, Socrates, I disregard it, and it's my opinion that it is as you say.

SOCRATES: So it's impossible in opining both to opine the other as an other.

THEAETETUS: It seems likely.

SOCRATES: And further, if it's only the other one's opining and in no way the other, one will never opine the other to be an other.

THEAETETUS: What you say is true, for otherwise he would be compelled to touch on that which he is not opining.

SOCRATES: So there's no room, after all, in opining either both or the

E other to else-opine. Consequently, if one will define to other-opine as false opinion, one would not be making any sense, and that's because it's evident that neither in this way nor in terms of the former is there false opinion in us.

THEAETETUS: It seems likely that there's not.

SOCRATES: But, Theaetetus, if it will be evident that it is not, we'll be compelled to agree to many strange things.

THEAETETUS: What sorts of things exactly?

SOCRATES: I shan't tell you before I try to examine it in every way, for I would be ashamed on our behalf, in the perplexity in which we are, if we're compelled to agree to the sorts of things I'm *191* speaking of. But if we find a way out and get ourselves free of it, it's then that we'll speak about everyone else as if they're suffering from it, while we stand free and clear of ridicule. But if we turn out to be perplexed in every way, then, I suspect, in all humility we'll hand ourselves over to the speech to be trampled on like the seasick and be handled in whatever way it wants. So listen to the kind of way out I still find for our inquiry.

THEAETETUS: Just speak.

SOCRATES: I'll deny we agreed correctly when we agreed that it's impossible to opine what one does not know to be what one knows and to be deceived, but it's possible in a sense. *B*

THEAETETUS: Do you mean what I even then suspected, when we said it to be of this sort, that sometimes I, being familiar with Socrates, but seeing someone else from a distance with whom I'm not familiar, came to believe he was Socrates whom I know? For in a situation of that sort, there occurs the sort of thing you say.

SOCRATES: Didn't we stand apart and withdraw from it because what we know was making us, though we know, not to know?

THEAETETUS: That's altogether so.

SOCRATES: Then let's not set it down in this way but as follows. Perhaps one will make us some concession, and perhaps one will resist, *C* but in the sort of situation in which we're caught, it's a necessity to twist around every speech and put it to the torture. Consider, then, whether I'm making sense. Is it possible not to know something earlier and understand (learn) it later?

THEAETETUS: Of course it is.

SOCRATES: And at a later time another and another.

THEAETETUS: Why of course.

SOCRATES: Then please set down for talking's sake a wax block in our souls, larger for someone and less for someone else, of purer wax for someone and more fouled for someone else, and stiffer for some and more liquid for some, and for some it's of a measured consistency. *D*

THEAETETUS: I'm setting it down.

SOCRATES: Well, then, let's say it is a gift of Memory, the mother of the Muses, and whatever we want to remember of the things we see, hear, or we ourselves think of, by submitting it to our perceptions and thoughts, we strike off into this, as if we were putting in the seals of signet-rings. And whatever gets impressed, let's say

that we remember and know as long as its image is in it, but
whatever is wiped off or cannot get impressed, that we forget and
do not know.

THEAETETUS: So be it.

SOCRATES: Then observe whether in the following sort of way whoever
knows them and is examining any of the things he see or hears,
might after all opine what is false.

THEAETETUS: In what sort of way exactly?

SOCRATES: In the belief that what he knows are sometimes what he
knows and sometimes what he does not. Our prior agreement
that this was impossible was not beautifully agreed on.

THEAETETUS: But now, how do you say it is?

SOCRATES: We must make a reckoning of them as follows, by determining from principle that (1) whatever one merely knows, if one
gets a memorial of it in the soul, but is not perceiving it, it's
impossible to believe it's something other of what one knows, if
one has an impress of this too but does not perceive it; and (2)
it's impossible to believe that just what one knows is whatever one
does not know and does not have a seal of either; and (3) whatever
one does know, whatever else one does not know; and (4) whatever
one does not know, what one knows; and (5) what one just perceives, it's impossible to believe it's some other of what one perceives; and (6) what one perceives, it's something of what one does
not perceive; and (7) whatever one does not perceive, it's of what
one does not perceive; and (8) whatever one does not perceive,
of what one perceives. And still further, (9) what one knows and
perceives and has the seal of in conformity with the perception,
to believe it's some other of what one knows and perceives and
has the seal of that too in conformity with the perception, that's
still more impossible, if possible, than the former cases. And (10)
what one knows and perceives having the memorial of it correctly,
it's impossible to believe it's what one knows; and (11) what one
knows and perceives having it on the same terms, what one perceives; and (12) what else one does not know and perceive, what
one does not know and perceive; and (13) what one does not
know and perceive, what one does not know; and (14) what one
does not know and perceive, what one does not perceive.[71] It's in
the impossibility of anyone opining what is false in these cases
that all of them go beyond anything. So it's left in the following
sort of cases, if there's anywhere else at all, that something of the
sort must occur.

THEAETETUS: In what cases exactly? Maybe I'll get some better understanding from them, for up to now I'm not following.

SOCRATES: In those cases in which one knows, it's possible to believe them some other things of which one knows and perceives; or of what one does not know but perceives; or of what one knows and perceives, of what else one knows and perceives.   *D*

THEAETETUS: But now I'm left much further behind than before.

SOCRATES: Then hear them all over again as follows. If I know Theodorus and remember in myself the sort he is, and Theaetetus likewise, don't I sometimes see them and sometimes not, and touch them at times and sometimes not, and hear them or gain some different perception of them, and sometimes I have no perception of you all, but I remember you no less and I myself know you in myself?

THEAETETUS: Yes, of course.   *E*

SOCRATES: Well, understand, then, that's the first of the things I want to make clear, that it is possible not to perceive what one knows and it is possible to perceive.

THEAETETUS: True.

SOCRATES: And whatever one does not know, it is often possible not to perceive it at all, and it's often possible only to perceive it?

THEAETETUS: This too is possible.

SOCRATES: See then whether you are now following somewhat better.   *193* If Socrates is familiar with Theodorus and Theaetetus, but sees neither of the two, and there is present to him no different perception about them, he would never come to opine in himself, "Theaetetus is Theodorus." Am I making any sense or not?

THEAETETUS: Yes it's true.

SOCRATES: Well, this was the first of those I was speaking of.

THEAETETUS: Yes, it was.

SOCRATES: Then the second case is when in being familiar with him (you) and unfamiliar with you (him), and on perceiving neither, I would never come to believe that the one I know is the one I don't know.

THEAETETUS: Right.

SOCRATES: And the third case is if I should be unfamiliar with either   *B* and not be perceiving either, I would not come to believe the one I do not know to be some other of the ones I do not know. And suppose that you've heard once more in order all the rest of the previous cases, in which I shall never opine what is false about you and Theodorus, neither being familiar with nor being ignorant of both, nor being familiar with one and with one not, and about perceptions—it's on the same terms, if after all you follow.

THEAETETUS: I follow.

SOCRATES: To opine the false things, then, is left only for this kind of situation: Whenever in being familiar with you and Theodorus,

C and having in that waxen thing the ring-seals, as it were, of both of you, I see you both from a distance and not adequately, and in assigning the proper seal of each of the two to its proper sight, I'm eager to set it in and fit it to its own trace, in order that recognition may occur. And then, of all things, I mistake them, and like those who put their shoes on backwards, I exchange them and apply the sight of each to the seal of the other. Or it's even like the experiences of sight in mirrors, when the sight exchanges its flow from right to left;[72] this is when other-opining and to

D opine what is false result.

THEAETETUS: Yes, it does seem likely, Socrates. The experience of opinion—how amazingly you speak of it.

SOCRATES: Well, there's still further the case when, in being familiar with both, one I perceive (in addition to knowing) and one I don't, but I do not have cognition of the other in conformity with its perception—this is the way I was speaking of it before, when you couldn't understand me.

THEAETETUS: Indeed, I could not.

E SOCRATES: Well, I meant this, if in being familiar with and perceiving the other, one has the cognition of him in conformity with his perception, one will never believe that he is some other with whom one's familiar and perceives, and of whom, too, one has one's cognition in conformity with his perception. Wasn't this agreed on?

THEAETETUS: Yes.

SOCRATES: But what is now said was surely at least left open. It's the

194 case in which we assert false opinion occurs when being familiar with both and seeing both or having some different perception of both, one does not have the pair of seals in conformity with the perception of each, but like the shooting of a poor bowman, one deviates from the mark and mistakes it—it is precisely this that has in fact been named falsehood.

THEAETETUS: Yes, it's likely enough.

SOCRATES: And so further, whenever perception of one of a pair of seals is present and one is not, and one adjusts the seal of the absent perception to the present perception, in this way thought is wholly deceived. And in a word: about whatever one does not

B know and never perceived, it is not possible, it seems, either to be deceived (speak falsely) or for there to be false opinion, if we are now saying anything sound. But about what we know and are perceiving, it's in these very cases that opinion whirls and twists about and becomes true and false—true if it brings together its own impressions and (fresh) impresses straightforwardly and in a direct line, but false if it's crosswise and crooked.

THEAETETUS: Isn't it said beautifully, Socrates?

SOCRATES: Well, once you hear this, you'll say it all the more. Now to opine what is true (is) beautiful, and to speak falsely (be deceived) ugly.　C

THEAETETUS: Of course.

SOCRATES: They assert, then, that these conditions arise from the following. Whenever the wax in someone's soul is deep, extensive, smooth, and kneaded in a measured way, the things that are proceeding through perceptions, in putting their seals into that feature of the soul which Homer, in hinting at its similarity to wax (*kêros*), said was heart (*kear*),[73] it's then that the seals for them come to be pure in the wax and with adequate depth prove to be　D long lasting. And people of this sort first of all learn easily and secondly have good memories, and so it's not they who interchange the seals of their perceptions, but they opine what is true. For inasmuch as their seals are plain and have plenty of room, they distribute them quickly to their own several casts,[74] and it's these casts which get called the things which are, and it's these people who get called wise. Or aren't you of this opinion?

THEAETETUS: Yes, I am, overwhelmingly.

SOCRATES: So whenever the heart of someone is shaggy—it's that which　E the all-wise poet praised[75]—or whenever it's as dirty as dung and its wax is impure, or it's excessively liquid or stiff, if theirs is liquid they learn easily but prove to be forgetful, and if theirs is stiff, it's the reverse. But whoever have a shaggy, rough, and somewhat stony heart, full of either earth or dung mixed in, they obtain casts without clarity; and theirs are without clarity too who have their casts stiff, for there is no depth to them; and theirs are without clarity too who have them liquid, for they quickly become　195 dim by being confounded. And if, besides all this, they have been made to fall in a heap together on top of one another by the narrowness of the room, if the 'soullet' of anyone is small, the casts are with still less clarity than the former. All these then prove to be the sort who opine what is false, for whenever they see, hear, or think of anything, in their incapacity to assign quickly each to each, they are too slow, and, in distributing what does not belong, they missee, mishear, and misthink most of the time. And it's these who get called fools, and they're said to be deceived about the things which are.

THEAETETUS: What you say, Socrates, couldn't be more correct.　B

SOCRATES: Are we to say then that, after all, false opinions are in us?

THEAETETUS: Yes, exactly.

SOCRATES: And true too?

THEAETETUS: True too.

SOCRATES: Do we believe, then, that we have by now adequately agreed upon this, that it's as certain as can be that both of this pair of opinions are?

THEAETETUS: Yes, overwhelmingly.

SOCRATES: In all probability, Theaetetus, a chatterbox of a man is truly a dreadful and unpleasant thing.

THEAETETUS: What of it? What's the point of your remark?

C SOCRATES: It's because I'm distressed at my own incapacity to learn easily and at what's truly just chattering. For what different name would anyone give it, when someone drags his speeches up and down, and by his own dullness is incapable of being convinced, and finds it hard to get free from each speech?

THEAETETUS: But why is it you who's distressed?

SOCRATES: I'm not only distressed but I'm afraid as well as to what answer I'll give if someone asks me, "Socrates, you have found false opinion, have you, and it's neither in one's perceptions relative to one another nor in one's thoughts but in the conjunction

D of perception with thought?" I shall affirm it, I suspect, and preen myself on the grounds that we've found something beautiful.

THEAETETUS: I, at least, am of the opinion, Socrates, that what has now been proved is not ugly.

SOCRATES: "Aren't you saying then," he says, "that, on the one hand, the human being we only think of but do not see, we would never come to believe him to be a horse, which, in turn, we neither see nor touch but only think of and perceive nothing else about it?" I suspect I'll say I'm saying this.

THEAETETUS: Yes, and correctly too.

E SOCRATES: "What then?" he says. "The eleven which one only thinks of and does nothing else about, would one never come to believe, on the basis of this speech, to be twelve, which in turn one only thinks of?" Come now, you answer.

THEAETETUS: Well, I'll answer that though, while seeing or touching, someone might come to believe the eleven to be twelve, but that which he has only in his thought, he would never on this condition come to opine this about it.

SOCRATES: What then? Do you believe that anyone has ever alone in himself proposed to examine five and seven—and I don't mean

196 seven and five human beings or anything of the sort, but five and seven themselves, which we say are there as memorials in the block

and in which case it is impossible to opine what is false—did any human being ever yet examine them by themselves and in speaking before himself and asking how many they are, did one of them say, and believe it, they are eleven, and someone else they're twelve, or does everyone say and believe they are twelve?

THEAETETUS: No, by Zeus. But of course there are many who say and *B* believe they're eleven. Yes, and if one examines in the case of a larger number, one is more liable to make a slip, for I suspect you're speaking of every number.

SOCRATES: Your suspicion's correct. And reflect. Does anything else then happen than the belief that the eleven in the block is the twelve itself?

THEAETETUS: It seems likely at any rate.

SOCRATES: Isn't there then a recurrence to the first speeches? Whoever experiences this believes that which he knows to be another of the things which he knows. And we said this was impossible, and it was due to this that we were making it a necessity for there to *C* be no false opinion, in order that it might not be a necessity for the same person in knowing the same things not to know them at the same time.

THEAETETUS: Most true.

SOCRATES: Then one must show that to opine what is false is anything else whatever than an interchange of thought with perception, for if it were, we would never be deceived in the thoughts by themselves. But as it is, either, you see, false opinion is not, or it's possible not to know what one knows. And which of these do you choose?

THEAETETUS: You're proposing a choice that has no way out, Socrates.

SOCRATES: Well, it's certainly probable that the speech won't allow *D* both. Still and all—one has to have the nerve for everything— what if we should try to be shameless?

THEAETETUS: How?

SOCRATES: By our willingness to say what sort of thing it is to know.

THEAETETUS: And why's this shameless?

SOCRATES: It seems that you don't realize that the entire speech has been for us from the beginning a search of knowledge on the grounds that we do not know whatever it is.

THEAETETUS: No, I realize it.

SOCRATES: And then doesn't it seem shameless if we don't know knowledge to declare what sort of thing it is to know? But as a matter of fact, Theaetetus, we've been infected for a long time now by *E* our conversing impurely, for we've said thousands of times "We recognize" and "We don't recognize," and "We know" and "We don't know," as though we somehow understand one another while still being ignorant of knowledge. And if you want, even now at the very moment we've used again "to be ignorant" and "to understand," as though it were suitable to use them if we're deprived of knowledge.

THEAETETUS: But, Socrates, in what manner will you converse if you abstain from them?

197　SOCRATES: In none, for I am who I am. But what if I were a contradictor? Suppose that sort of man were now here, he would claim that he abstains from them and he would rebuke us vehemently for what I am saying. Since we're no good, then, do you want me to have the nerve to say what sort of thing it is to know? It appears to me there would be some advantage to it.

THEAETETUS: Well, in that case, by Zeus, be nervy. And if you don't abstain from them you'll be much forgiven.

SOCRATES: Have you heard what they're now saying it is to know?

THEAETETUS: Perhaps. I don't, however, remember at the moment.

B　SOCRATES: They surely say it is a having of knowledge.

THEAETETUS: True.

SOCRATES: Well, let us change it a little and say it's a possession of knowledge.

THEAETETUS: How exactly will you say this differs from that?

SOCRATES: Perhaps in none. But still listen to what the difference seems to be and join in confirming it.

THEAETETUS: If I can.

SOCRATES: Well, to have appears to me not to be the same as to possess. For example, if someone buys a cloak and becomes its owner but does not wear it, we would deny he has it but he still possesses it.

THEAETETUS: Yes, correctly.

C　SOCRATES: Look then and see whether it's possible in this way to possess knowledge and not have it. But it's just as if someone should hunt down wild birds, doves or anything else, and having arranged a dovecote for them bring them up at home—we would surely say that though in some way he always has them, and precisely because he possesses them—Isn't that so?—

THEAETETUS: Yes.

SOCRATES: Still, in a different way he has none of them. But since he's got them under his thumb in his home enclosure, a capacity has
D　accrued to him in regard to them, to seize and hold them whenever he wants to, once he's hunted down whichever one he wishes on any occasion, and again to let it go, and it is possible for him to do this as often as he's of that opinion.

THEAETETUS: That is so.

SOCRATES: Once more then, just as when before we were working up in souls some kind of wax mold—I don't quite know what—so now once again let's make in each soul a kind of dovecote of all sorts of birds. Some are in herds apart from the rest, some in small groups, and some are alone and fly through all of them in whatever way they happen to.

THEAETETUS: Let it have been so made. But what follows from it?   E

SOCRATES: We have to say that this vessel when we're children is empty, and instead of the birds, we have to think knowledges (sciences). And whatever knowledge one acquires and confines in the enclosure, one has to say that he has learned or found the matter (*pragma*) of which this was the knowledge, and this is to know.

THEAETETUS: Let it be.

SOCRATES: Then the fact of hunting down once more whichever of   198
the knowledges one wants, and once one has seized it to hold it and again let go, consider what names it needs, the same as when one was first gaining the possession of them or other. You'll understand with greater clarity what I'm saying from this position. You say there's an arithmetical art?

THEAETETUS: Yes.

SOCRATES: Then suppose this to be a hunting of the knowledges of every even and odd (number).

THEAETETUS: I'm supposing it.

SOCRATES: It's precisely by this art, I suspect, that both he himself has the knowledges of the numbers under his thumb and, in trans-   B
mitting them, transmits them to someone else.

THEAETETUS: Yes.

SOCRATES: And transmitting is that which we call to teach, and receiving to learn, and having, by the fact of possessing in that dovecote, to know.

THEAETETUS: Yes, of course.

SOCRATES: Now pay close attention to that which follows from it. If one is perfectly an arithmetician, does one know anything else than all numbers? For he has knowledges of all numbers in his soul?

THEAETETUS: Why certainly.

SOCRATES: Would someone of this sort ever number anything, by   C
himself and before himself, either the numbers themselves or anything else of the things outside that have number?

THEAETETUS: Of course.

SOCRATES: But to number, shall we set it down to be anything else than the examination of how great a number there happens to be?

THEAETETUS: Just so.

SOCRATES: So it's evident that the one who we've agreed knows every number is examining as though he does not know that which he knows. You surely hear of disputes of this sort.

THEAETETUS: Yes, I do.

D SOCRATES: Then we, in making our semblance to the possession and hunting of doves, will say that the hunting was twofold, one before the possession for the sake of possession, and one by the possessor for the sake of seizing and having in his hands what he has possessed for some time. It's in this way that for him there were knowledges for some time of the things he once learned and he knew them, and it is possible to learn to know these same things once more by taking up the knowledge of each and holding it, a knowledge he possessed for some time, but which was not ready at hand for his thought?

THEAETETUS: True.

E SOCRATES: It was precisely this I was just now asking about, as to how one must use the names in speaking about them, whenever the arithmetician goes to number, or the skilled reader to read something, and say, "After all, in a situation of this sort he knows and yet goes once more to learn from himself what he knows?"

THEAETETUS: Well, it's strange, Socrates.

SOCRATES: Well, are we to say that it's what he does not know he'll read and number, though we've granted him to know every letter

199 and every number?

THEAETETUS: But this too makes no sense.

SOCRATES: Do you want us to say, then, that we don't care about the names, in whatever way any one enjoys dragging and tugging at 'to know' and 'to learn'? But since we've determined that the fact of possessing the knowledge is some other thing, and the fact of having it is another, we say it is impossible not to possess whatever one possesses, and so it never turns out that one does not know

B what one knows, and yet it is possible to seize a false opinion about it? For it's possible not to have the knowledge of this, but another instead of that, whenever in hunting on some occasion some knowledge somewhere, while they're all flying about, one misses and seizes another instead of an other, it's just at that time that one comes to believe the eleven is twelve—when one seizes the knowledge of the eleven in oneself instead of the knowledge of the twelve, as if it were a ring-dove instead of a dove.[76]

THEAETETUS: That indeed makes sense.

SOCRATES: Yes, but whenever one seizes what one is trying to seize, is it then that there's no falsehood and one is opining the things

which are? And is it precisely in this way that there is true and   C
false opinion, and nothing at which we were distressed before
proves to be a stumbling-block? Perhaps you'll agree with me. Or
what will you do?

THEAETETUS: Just so.

SOCRATES: That's because we've got rid of "They don't know what
they know." For it turns out that it's no longer the case anywhere
that we do not possess what we possess either when we're deceived
about something or not. It's my impression, however, that a different, more dreadful experience is coming to light alongside this
one.

THEAETETUS: What sort is it?

SOCRATES: It's whether the interchange of knowledges will ever prove
to be false opinion.

THEAETETUS: How's that exactly?

SOCRATES: First, the fact that in having a knowledge of something,   D
one is ignorant of this very thing, not by ignorance but by one's
own knowledge. Second, to opine another as this and this as the
other, how isn't it a lot of nonsense, if with the presence of knowledge the soul comes to know nothing and be ignorant of everything? On the basis of this speech, nothing stands in the way of
the presence of ignorance making one know something and blindness making one see, if knowledge in fact will ever make someone
ignorant.

THEAETETUS: The reason is perhaps, Socrates, that we were not putting   E
the birds in beautifully when we put in only knowledges, but we
should also have put in nonknowledges and have them fly about
together with them in the soul. And the hunter sometimes seizes
knowledge and sometimes seizes nonknowledge, and by nonknowledge he opines what is false and by knowledge what is true
about the same thing.

SOCRATES: It's really not easy, Theaetetus, not to praise you. Do, however, examine once more what you said. Let it be as you say.
Whoever then seizes the nonknowledge will opine, you say, what
is false. Isn't that so?   200

THEAETETUS: Yes.

SOCRATES: He surely won't be convinced at any rate that he's opining
what is false.

THEAETETUS: How could he?

SOCRATES: But rather what is true, and his state will be as if he knew
those things about what he has been deceived.

THEAETETUS: Why certainly.

SOCRATES: So he'll believe he has hunted and has knowledge and not nonknowledge.

THEAETETUS: Plainly.

SOCRATES: Then we went a long way around and are back once more with the first perplexity. For that skilled refuter will laugh and say, "Is it the case, your excellencies, that someone who knows

B both, knowledge and nonknowledge, believes that the one he knows is some other of what he knows? Or is it that in knowing neither of the pair, he opines that the one he does not know is another of what he does not know? Or one he knows and one he doesn't, and he opines the one he knows to be the one he doesn't know? Or the one he doesn't know, he's convinced it's the one he does know? Or will you tell me once more that there are in turn knowledges of the knowledges and nonknowledges, which their pos-

C sessor confined in some other ridiculous dovecotes or wax molds and knows as long as he possesses them even if he does not have them ready at hand in his soul? If it's in this way, won't you all be compelled to run around to the same point thousands of times and get nowhere?" What answer shall we give in reply to this, Theaetetus?

THEAETETUS: But, by Zeus, I for one don't know what we should say.

SOCRATES: Doesn't the speech really then, my boy, rebuke us beauti- fully and point out that we do not correctly seek for false opinion

D prior to knowledge and let knowledge go? The fact is that it's impossible to come to know it before one grasps knowledge ad- equately as to whatever it is.

THEAETETUS: It's a necessity, Socrates, at the moment to believe it to be as you say it is.

SOCRATES: What then will one say once more from the beginning knowledge is? We'll surely not give up yet in weariness?

THEAETETUS: Not in the least, unless, that is, you are giving the order.

SOCRATES: Speak then. What could we most of all say it was and least contradict ourselves?

E THEAETETUS: Just what we were trying to say before Socrates, for I at any rate don't have anything else.

SOCRATES: What sort of thing?

THEAETETUS: That true opinion is knowledge. To opine what is true surely is at any rate infallible, and everything that comes to be as a result of it becomes beautiful and good.

SOCRATES: The river-guide, Theaetetus, said, "It will show up by it-

201 self."[77] So if we go and look for it, perhaps it too might turn up at our feet and show what is sought. But if we stay here, nothing will be plain.

THEAETETUS: You're right to say so. Well, let's go and consider it.

SOCRATES: This does in fact require a brief inquiry. A whole art indicates to you that it is not knowledge.

THEAETETUS: How exactly? And what's this art?

SOCRATES: It's the art of the greatest people in point of wisdom. It's those they call public speakers and advocates.[78] They surely persuade and don't teach by their own art, but they make one opine whatever they want. Or do you believe there are any teachers so uncanny that, in cases where people were robbed of money or *B* experienced some different act of violence, they're capable of teaching adequately, with the clock running, any who were not present on these occasions the truth of what happened?

THEAETETUS: No, I don't believe it, in no way, but persuade, yes.

SOCRATES: And by "persuade," don't you mean to make opine?

THEAETETUS: Why certainly.

SOCRATES: Then whenever jurors are justly persuaded about whatever it's only possible to know if one sees it, but not in a different way, in deciding on these things at that time by hearsay, and in their *C* acceptance of a true opinion, don't they decide without knowledge, though they've been persuaded rightly if they judged well?

THEAETETUS: That's altogether so.

SOCRATES: A tip-top juror, then, my dear, if in the courts true opinion and knowledge were the same, would never opine rightly without knowledge. But as it is, it seems that each of the two is something different.

THEAETETUS: Yes, Socrates, it's what I heard someone say it was but forgot, but now I have it in mind. He said that true opinion with *D* speech was knowledge, but true opinion without speech was outside of knowledge, and of whatever there is not a speech, these things are not knowable—that's just the word he used[79]—and whatever admit of speech are knowable.[80]

SOCRATES: You're really speaking beautifully. But tell at just what point he was dividing these knowable and not knowable things. Maybe you and I have heard it along the same lines.

THEAETETUS: Well, I don't know whether I'll find it out myself; should another speak, however, I suspect I would follow.

SOCRATES: Hear, then, a dream in exchange for a dream. I dreamt *E* that I heard some people say that the first things were just like elements (letters), out of which we and everything else are composed, and they do not admit of speech; that it's only possible to give a name to each thing alone by itself, but it's impossible to address it any differently, either that (how) it is or that (how) it is not. For in that case one would be applying being or nonbeing *202*

I.73

to it, and one should apply nothing to it if one will speak of it as that thing alone, since none of those must be applied at all—"it," "that," "each," "alone"[81]—and 'this' and many different ones of the same sort neither. For these expressions in running around get applied to everything, being other than the things to which they're applied. But it should be the case, if it were possible for it to be spoken of and have its own proper speech, for it to be spoken of without all these different things, but as it is, it's im-

B   possible for any one of the first things to get stated in speech. For there is nothing else for it except only to get named—for it only has a name—but just as the things that are then composed out of these things are composed by their plaiting, so too their names, once they're plaited together, become a speech. For the plaiting of names is the being of speech—that it's in exactly this way that the elements, though they are without speech and unknowable, are still perceptible, but the syllables are knowable, speakable, and opinable by true opinion. And that, in short, whenever anyone

C   gets the true opinion of anything without speech, his soul tells the truth about it but does not know, for whoever is incapable of giving and receiving an account (speech) is without knowledge of this very fact. But if he gets in addition a speech, he becomes capable in all these respects and is in a perfect condition relative to knowledge. Is it in this way that you've heard the dream or in a different way?

THEAETETUS: No, it's altogether in this way.

SOCRATES: Are you then satisfied and do you set it down for yourself in this way—true opinion with speech is knowledge?

THEAETETUS: Yes, utterly.

D   SOCRATES: Is it really so, Theaetetus, that on this day and in this way we now have grasped what many of the wise sought for a long time and grew old before finding?

THEAETETUS: I, at any rate, Socrates, am of the opinion that the present statement is said beautifully.

SOCRATES: Yes, and it's likely that so far this is just the way it is, for what would knowledge still in fact be, apart from (the) speech and correct opinion? There is, however, one of the things stated which displeases me.

THEAETETUS: What sort exactly?

SOCRATES: It's the point that seems to be most cleverly said, that the elements (are) unknowable, but the genus of the syllables (is)

E   knowable.

THEAETETUS: Isn't that right?

SOCRATES: One has to know. There are paradigms of the speech that we hold like hostages and that he was using when he said all this.

THEAETETUS: What sort exactly?

SOCRATES: The elements and syllables of letters. Or do you believe that he gave a glance anywhere else when the one who spoke said those things which we're saying?

THEAETETUS: No, but at these.

SOCRATES: Let's take them up and put them to the torture—but, rather, *203* let's do it to ourselves—was it in this way or not that we learned letters? Come. First: The syllables admit of (have) speech, but the elements are without speech?

THEAETETUS: Perhaps.

SOCRATES: Yes, of course, rather, and it appears so to me too. Should anyone, at any rate, ask for the first syllable of Socrates in just this way—"Theaetetus, speak what is SO?"—what will you answer?

THEAETETUS: That it's sigma and omega.[82]

SOCRATES: Don't you then have this as a speech of the syllable?

THEAETETUS: Yes, I do.

SOCRATES: Then come, speak in this way too the speech of the sigma. *B*

THEAETETES: But how will one say the elements of the element? The reason is, Socrates, that the sigma belongs to the voiceless. It's only a sound; it's like when the tongue hisses. And of the beta in turn and most of the elements as well there's neither voice nor sound. The saying therefore holds good that they're without speech, since the most vivid of them are the very seven that only have voice and no speech whatever.[83]

SOCRATES: Then it's this, comrade, that we've put right in the case of knowledge.

THEAETETUS: It appears that we have.

SOCRATES: But what of this? That the element is not knowable, but *C* the syllable is—have we accepted that correctly?

THEAETETUS: It's likely at least.

SOCRATES: Come then. Do we mean by the syllable both elements, or if there are more than two, all of them, or some single look (*idea*) that has come to be when they are put together?

THEAETETUS: It's my impression that we mean all of them.

SOCRATES: Look then at the pair, sigma and omega. The first syllable of my name is both. Whoever knows it, does he know them both?

THEAETETUS: Why certainly. *D*

SOCRATES: So he knows the sigma and the omega.

THEAETETUS: Yes.

SOCRATES: And what of this? Is he ignorant of each of the two, and in knowing neither knows both?

THEAETETUS: But that's dreadful, Socrates, and makes no sense (without speech).

SOCRATES: But yet it's the case that if there's a necessity to know each of the two if one will know both, there's every necessity for whoever's going to know a syllable to know first its elements. And in this way the beautiful speech of ours will have run away and be gone.

E THEAETETUS: Yes, and very suddenly too.

SOCRATES: That's because we're not guarding it beautifully. We should not have, perhaps, set down the syllable as the elements, but some single species that has come to be out of them, with its own single look (*idea*) and other than the elements.

THEAETETUS: Yes, of course. And perhaps it might rather be in this way than in that.

SOCRATES: We ought to consider it and not betray in so unmanly a fashion a great and august speech.

THEAETETUS: No, indeed we ought not.

204 SOCRATES: Let it be then as we now claim it is: the syllable comes to be one look (*idea*) out of those several elements that fit together, and it similarly holds no less in letters than in everything else.

THEAETETUS: Yes, of course.

SOCRATES: Then there must be no parts of it.

THEAETETUS: Why's that exactly?

SOCRATES: Because of whatever there are parts, it's a necessity that all the parts be the whole. Or are you saying that the whole too that has come to be out of its parts is some single species other than all its parts?

THEAETETUS: Yes, I am.

B SOCRATES: Are you then calling the all and the whole the same or each of the two other?

THEAETETUS: I don't have anything with clarity, but because you urge me to answer eagerly, I risk it and say, other.

SOCRATES: Well, your eagerness, Theaetetus, is right, and we must examine whether your answer is too.

THEAETETUS: Yes, we certainly must.

SOCRATES: The whole, then, would differ from the all, as is the present speech?

THEAETETUS: Yes.

SOCRATES: And what of this then? Is it possible that all the things and the all differ? For example, whenever we say one, two, three, four, five, six, and we say twice three or thrice two, or four and two, or three and two and one—in all these cases are we saying the same or other?

C

THEAETETUS: The same.

SOCRATES: Is it anything else than six?

THEAETETUS: None else.

SOCRATES: Haven't we then said in each of these kinds of speaking all six?

THEAETETUS: Yes.

SOCRATES: But is there no one all that we're saying in saying them all?

THEAETETUS: It's a necessity.

SOCRATES: Is it anything else than the six?

THEAETETUS: None else.

SOCRATES: So it's the same, then, that we address as the all and all of D them in at least all those things that are out of number?

THEAETETUS: It appears so.

SOCRATES: Let's then speak as follows about them. The number of the plethron (100 feet) and the plethron are the same. Aren't they?

THEAETETUS: Yes.

SOCRATES: And the number of the stade (600 feet) likewise?

THEAETETUS: Yes.

SOCRATES: And further, the number of the army and the army, and similarly for all things of the sort? For all the number is all that each of them is?

THEAETETUS: Yes.

SOCRATES: And the number of several things isn't anything else, is it, E than parts?

THEAETETUS: None else.

SOCRATES: So however many parts it has, it would be out of parts?

THEAETETUS: It appears so.

SOCRATES: Yes, and it's been agreed upon that also all the parts are the all, provided that all the number will be the all.

THEAETETUS: Just so.

SOCRATES: So the whole, then, is not out of parts, for otherwise it would be an all in being all the parts.

THEAETETUS: It seems likely that it's not.

SOCRATES: But is a part which is just what it is, of anything else whatever than of the whole?

THEAETETUS: Yes, of the all.

SOCRATES: You're fighting in a manly way at least, Theaetetus. But 205 isn't the all, whenever nothing is absent, this very thing, all?

THEAETETUS: It's a necessity.

SOCRATES: But won't a whole be this same thing, from whatever nothing in any way stands apart? But from whatever there is a standing apart, it is neither a whole nor an all, and that is the same result for both of them at once out of the same?[84]

THEAETETUS: I'm now of the opinion that an all and a whole do not differ.

SOCRATES: Weren't we saying, then, that of whatever there are parts, the whole and all will be all the parts?

THEAETETUS: Certainly.

B SOCRATES: Once more then—it's just that which I was trying to get at—if the syllable is not the elements, isn't it a necessity for it not to have the elements as its own parts, or if it is the same as them, it's a necessity that it be as knowable as they are?

THEAETETUS: Just so.

SOCRATES: Didn't we then set it down as other than them in order that this might not occur?

THEAETETUS: Yes.

SOCRATES: And what of this? If the elements are not parts of a syllable, can you speak of some different things which, though they are parts of a syllable, are not, however, its elements?

THEAETETUS: In no way, for should I concede, Socrates, that there are some proper parts of it, it's surely laughable to dismiss the elements and go to different things.

C SOCRATES: Then according to the present speech, Theaetetus, a syllable must be some single look (*idea*) altogether indivisible into parts.

THEAETETUS: It seems likely.

SOCRATES: Do you remember, then, my dear, that a little while ago we welcomed the assertion, in the conviction that it was a good point, that speech is not of the first things out of which everything else is composed—inasmuch as each of them, itself by itself, was noncomposite—and it wasn't right to speak about it by applying even 'to be' to it, or 'this' either, on the grounds that they are other and spoken of as not their own but alien to them, and it was this cause precisely that made it be without speech and unknowable?

THEAETETUS: I remember.

D SOCRATES: Is there really, then, anything else than this that's the cause of its being single-specied and not divisible into parts? I for one don't see anything else.

THEAETETUS: It really does appear that there isn't.

SOCRATES: Hasn't the syllable then fallen into the same species as that, if it does not have parts and is a single look (*idea*)?

THEAETETUS: That's altogether so.

SOCRATES: So if the syllable is many elements and some kind of whole, and these are its parts, then the syllables are as knowable and sayable as the elements, since all the parts came to light as the same as the whole.

THEAETETUS: Yes indeed.   E

SOCRATES: Yes, but if it's one and without parts, a syllable no less than an element is in the same way without speech and unknowable, for the same cause will make them be of the same sort.

THEAETETUS: I cannot speak differently.

SOCRATES: So let's not accept this, whoever says a syllable's knowable and speakable, but for an element it's the contrary.

THEAETETUS: Let's not, provided we're to obey the speech.

SOCRATES: And what of this in turn? Wouldn't you rather accept, on   206
the basis of what you yourself know about your own learning of letters, someone's saying the contrary?

THEAETETUS: What sort of thing?

SOCRATES: That you continued to do nothing else in learning than to try to recognize the elements distinctly in sight and in hearing, each one itself by itself, in order that their placement when being spoken and written might not perturb you.

THEAETETUS: What you say is most true.

SOCRATES: And in the lyre-player's studio, to have learned perfectly, was it anything else than the capacity to attend to each note, of   B
what sort of chord it was? It's these that everyone would agree are spoken of as the elements of music?

THEAETETUS: Nothing else.

SOCRATES: So, after all, in the case of the elements and syllables we ourselves have experience of, if one has to transfer the evidence from them to everything else, we'll say that, in point of grasping each lesson perfectly, the genus of the elements admits of a knowledge more vivid and authoritative than that of the syllable. And if anyone says a syllable is by nature knowable and an element unknowable, we'll be convinced that, willingly or unwillingly, he's being playful.

THEAETETUS: Yes, utterly.

SOCRATES: Well, my impression is that still different proofs of this   C
would also come to light. But let them not make us forget to look at that which lies before us—whatever is meant exactly by saying that if a speech is added to true opinion, the most complete and perfect knowledge is the result.

THEAETETUS: We must indeed look at it.

SOCRATES: Come then. Whatever does it want 'speech' to signify for us? It's my impression that it's saying some one of three things.

THEAETETUS: Which exactly?

SOCRATES: The first would be that speech is that which makes one's   D

I.79

own thought evident through sound with words and phrases, just as if it were into a mirror or water one was striking off one's opinion into the stream through one's mouth. Or isn't it your impression that speech is of this sort?

THEAETETUS: Yes, it is. We say, at any rate, that whoever's doing it is speaking.

SOCRATES: Isn't it the case, then, that everyone, whoever's not dumb or mute at the start is capable of doing (making) this at least, regardless of whether it's more quickly or more slowly—the indication of what his opinion is about each thing? And in this way

E as many as opine something rightly, all will evidently have it with speech, and in no case will right opinion any longer prove to be apart from knowledge?

THEAETETUS: True.

SOCRATES: Well, let's not too readily issue a condemnation, to the effect that whoever declared knowledge to be what we're now examining has made no sense at all. For perhaps the speaker was not saying this, but rather that it's the capacity, when asked what each thing

207 (is), to give the answer back to the questioner through the elements.

THEAETETUS: What are you saying, Socrates? Give an example.

SOCRATES: It's just as Hesiod in fact speaks about a wagon, "But the timbers of a wagon are one hundred."[85] I for one would not have the capacity to tell them, and I suspect that you wouldn't either, but we would be content should we be asked what a wagon is, if we could say, "Wheels, axle, carriage-body, rails, yoke."

THEAETETUS: Yes, of course.

SOCRATES: Yes, but he would perhaps believe us to be ridiculous, just as if we were asked about your name and answered syllable by

B syllable. Because, though in this case we're opining and speaking rightly what we're speaking, we believe we're skilled in letters and know (have) and speak in a letter-skilled way the speech of Theaetetus' name. But the fact is, he'd believe, it is impossible to say anything scientifically (knowledgeably) before one goes through each through its elements from end to end with true opinion, and this surely was stated also in the previous remarks.

THEAETETUS: Yes, it was stated.

SOCRATES: Well, then, is it in this way too that he'd believe we have a right opinion about a wagon? But that whoever has the capacity

C to explicate its being through those hundred things of it, by his addition of this, has added speech to his true opinion, and has become, instead of an opiner, artfully competent and a knower of a wagon's being, because he has gone through the whole through its elements from end to end?

THEAETETUS: Isn't it your impression that it's good, Socrates?

SOCRATES: Tell me whether it's yours, comrade, and whether you accept the procedure through elements to be speech about each thing, while the procedure which is syllable by syllable or is in terms of something greater still is not-speech (*alogia*), in order that we may go on to examine it.   *D*

THEAETETUS: Well, I very much accept it.

SOCRATES: Are you, in accepting it, convinced that anyone whatever is a knower of anything whatever, when he's of the opinion that the same thing belongs at times to the same thing and at times to another, or whenever he opines that another belongs at times to the same thing and at times an other?

THEAETETUS: No, by Zeus, I do not.

SOCRATES: Is it, then, that you don't remember that you and everyone else does this when you start to learn the letters?

THEAETETUS: Are you saying that in the case of the same syllable, we   *E* believe another letter belongs at times to it and at times an other, and we put the .same letter at times into the appropriate syllable and at times into a different syllable?

SOCRATES: That's what I'm saying.

THEAETETUS: Well, by Zeus, I'm not one to forget it, and I'm convinced as well that those whose condition is this do not know as yet.

SOCRATES: What then? Whenever on an occasion of this sort, someone in writing "Theaetetus" believes he must write theta and epsilon and writes it, and then, in turn, in trying to write "Theodorus," believes he must write tau and epsilon and writes it, shall we claim   *208* that he knows the first syllable of your names?

THEAETETUS: But we just now agreed that whoever's condition is this does not know as yet.

SOCRATES: Does anything then stand in the way of the same person being in this condition also in regard to the second, third, and fourth syllable?

THEAETETUS: No, nothing.

SOCRATES: Won't he then, at that time, in keeping to the procedure through elements write "Theaetetus" with right opinion, whenever he writes it in succession?

THEAETETUS: That's plainly so.

SOCRATES: Though he's still without knowledge but opines what is   *B* right, as we claim?

THEAETETUS: Yes.

SOCRATES: Even though he has speech with right opinion, for while he was writing, he was maintaining his way through the elements, and it's this which we agreed was speech.

THEAETETUS: True.

SOCRATES: So there is after all, comrade, right opinion with speech, which one must not yet call knowledge.

THEAETETUS: Probably.

SOCRATES: Then, it seems, we grew rich just on a dream, in our belief
C that we had the truest speech of knowledge. Or are we not yet to issue an accusation? For perhaps one will not define it as this, but as the remaining species of the three, just one of which, we said, he will set down as speech, whoever defines knowledge to be right opinion with speech.

THEAETETUS: You recalled it rightly, for there's still one left. One was the image, as it were, of thought in sound, and one was just stated, a going to the whole through elements. But what exactly are you saying is the third?

SOCRATES: It's just what the many would say, to have some sign to say by means of which that which is asked about differs from all things.

THEAETETUS: What speech of what do you have to tell me by way of an example?

D SOCRATES: For example, if you want, in the case of the sun, I suspect this would be enough for you to accept it: "It is the most brilliant of the things that go around the earth across the sky."

THEAETETUS: Yes, of course.

SOCRATES: Take it, then, for the sake of which it has been spoken. It is exactly what we were just now saying it is: "If you take the difference of each thing by which it differs from everything else, you'll take, as some say, a speech; but as long as you touch on anything in common, the speech will be for you about those things, whichever they are, of which the commonness is."

E THEAETETUS: I understand. And it's my impression that it's beautiful to call something of the sort a speech.

SOCRATES: But whoever with right opinion takes in addition the difference from all the rest of anything whatever of the things which are will have become a knower of that of which he was previously an opiner.

THEAETETUS: Yes indeed, we say that.

SOCRATES: Now all of a sudden, Theaetetus, I don't understand anything at all, not even a little, since I've got too near to what is being said, just as if it were a shadowpainting. For as long as I stood way off from it, it appeared to me that something was being said.

THEAETETUS: How and why is that?

209 SOCRATES: I'll point it out if I can. If I for one have a right opinion

about you and take in addition the speech about you, that's exactly when I know you, but if not, I only opine.

THEAETETUS: Yes.

SOCRATES: Yes, but the interpretation of your difference was agreed to be a speech.

THEAETETUS: Just so.

SOCRATES: Then when I was only opining, whatever else I was doing, I was touching in my thought on not one of those things by which you differ from everything else.

THEAETETUS: It seems likely that you weren't.

SOCRATES: So I was thinking something of the common things, none of which you have any more than anyone else.

THEAETETUS: It's a necessity.   *B*

SOCRATES: Come then, by Zeus. However in a situation of this sort was I opining you rather than anyone else whatsoever? Set me down as thinking, "Here is Theaetetus, whoever is a human being and has a nose and eyes and mouth and so on for each of his limbs." Is it possible that this thought will make me think Theaetetus rather than Theodorus, or the most remote of the proverbial Mysians?[86]

THEAETETUS: How could it?

SOCRATES: But if I think not only the one who has a nose and eyes, but also the snub-nosed and exophthalmic, shall I any the more   *C* opine you rather than myself or all who are of this sort?

THEAETETUS: Not at all.

SOCRATES: But, I suspect, Theaetetus will not be opined in me before this snubness of yours lays down a memorial in me that stamps its difference from all the rest of the snubnesses I have seen, and in this way for all the rest of the things out of which you are— which will remind me—if in fact I meet you tomorrow and make me opine rightly about you.

THEAETETUS: Most true.

SOCRATES: So right opinion too would be about the difference of each   *D* thing.

THEAETETUS: It appears so at least.

SOCRATES: Then the fact of taking a speech in addition to right opinion would still be what? For if, on the one hand, it tells one to opine in addition in what way something differs from everything else, the injunction proves to be very ridiculous.

THEAETETUS: How?

SOCRATES: Of those things of which we have right opinion, by which they differ from everything else, it urges us to take in addition a right opinion of these things by which they differ from everything else. And if this is the case, compared to this injunction, the proverbial twirling of a baton, a pestle, or whatever names it goes by,[87] would be as nothing in point of nonsense. And this injunction would more justly be called the exhortation of a blind man. For to command us to take in addition those things which we have, in order that we may understand (learn) what we're opining, does resemble in a very grand manner a man who is wholly in the dark.

THEAETETUS: Then say what you just now put as if it were a question.[88]

SOCRATES: If to take a speech in addition, my boy, urges us to come to know but not just to opine the difference, what a pleasantry the most beautiful speech of all about knowledge would be! For to come to know is surely to take knowledge, isn't it?

THEAETETUS: Yes.

SOCRATES: Then, it seems, if the speech is asked what knowledge is, it will answer, "Right opinion with knowledge of difference," for according to it, this would be the supplementary taking of a speech.

THEAETETUS: It seems likely.

SOCRATES: And it's really altogether naive, when we are seeking knowledge, for the speech to state it to be right opinion with knowledge, whether of difference or anything whatever. So knowledge, Theaetetus, would not, after all, be perception, true opinion, or a speech that's getting added to true opinion.

THEAETETUS: It seems unlikely.

SOCRATES: Are we then still pregnant with something, and still suffering labor-pains, my dear, about knowledge, or have we given birth to everything?

THEAETETUS: Yes, by Zeus, and I for one have said even more on account of you than all I used to have in myself.

SOCRATES: Doesn't our maieutic art then declare all these to have been born as wind-eggs and unworthy of nurture?

THEAETETUS: That's altogether so.

SOCRATES: Well, then, if you try to become pregnant, Theaetetus, with different things after this, and you do become so, you'll be full of better things on account of the present review. And if you're empty, you'll be less hard on your associates and tamer, believing in a moderate way that you don't know what you don't know. My art is only capable of so much and no more, and I don't know anything at all which everyone else does, all those who are and have been great and amazing men. But my mother and I have obtained from a god as our lot this midwifery, she of women, and I of the young and noble and all the beautiful. Now, however, I have to go to the porch of the king and meet the indictment of Meletus which he's drawn up against me. But at dawn, Theodorus, let's come back here to meet.

Theaetetus Commentary

I. MEGARIANS
(142a1–143c7)

All Platonic dialogues are written, but only the *Theaetetus* presents most of itself as written. Its author is not Plato. The voice is the voice of Plato, but the hand is the hand of Euclides. We owe, however, its publication to Plato. A short dialogue of his own between Euclides and Terpsion makes Euclides' work known to us. Euclides seems to think, in any case, that without the kind of explanation he gives Terpsion, which Plato himself never thought necessary for his own dialogues, his writing is defective. The dialogue, then, has two authors, Plato and Euclides. The Platonic part seems superfluous. Its absence would leave us with a nonnarrated dialogue as complete in itself as *Euthyphro* or *Laws*. We would not then know Euclides' "principles of composition," nor that Theaetetus later distinguished himself in battle. But neither the change from narration to drama nor the sufferings of a mathematician can remotely bear on Socrates' penultimate question, What is knowledge? Plato thought otherwise.

The structure of the *Theaetetus* most resembles that of the *Protagoras*. There Socrates meets a comrade with whom he discusses the beauty of Alcibiades and the greater beauty of Protagoras, and on the comrade's prompting he reports the conversation he just had with Protagoras. His talk with the comrade is over after twenty-one exchanges. Here Euclides meets his friend Terpsion to whom he reports Theaetetus' dying, and on Terpsion's prompting he has a slave read to them both the conversation he has written up that Socrates once had with Theaetetus and Theodorus. His talk with Terpsion lasts for twenty-one exchanges. The *Protagoras* discusses for much of its length the problematic unity of virtue, and it ends with Socrates' suggestion that, if the good is the pleasant, what we need is a science of hedonistic measurement. The *Theaetetus* poses the problem of the unity of knowledge. For much of its length, Socrates explores with two mathematicians the Protagorean thesis that if knowledge is perception, man is the measure of all things. Protagoras determines the course of the *Theaetetus*, absent though he is and represented only by lukewarm adherents, as much as he determines the course of the *Protagoras*.

In both dialogues, Socrates is the narrator. In the *Protagoras* he reports almost directly to us; in the *Theaetetus* he reported to Euclides, who then took the trouble to eliminate Socrates as the source of his dialogue. He is less faithful to what he had heard than either the *Symposium*'s Apollodorus or the *Parmenides*' Cephalus, both of whom usually keep themselves distinct from the several voices of their informants. Euclides, in contrast, in eliminating Socrates, also eliminates himself. Confronted with the minor difficulty of separating "He (Socrates) said that he (Socrates) said" from "He (Socrates) said that he (Theaetetus or Theodorus) said," Euclides took the easy way out. He tells Terpsion that he dropped Socrates' "I said" and Theaetetus' "He agreed," or "He did not agree;" but he seems to be unaware that, for all the care he took to get his transcription exactly right, he was forced to find verbal equivalents for what might have been just a nod or shake of the head. As a Megarian, Euclides recognizes nothing but speech;[1] for all we know, Theaetetus might have reluctantly agreed to something or Theodorus fidgeted in annoyance.

The two advantages that narration has over drama—in giving us not only the sweat of Thrasymachus or the blush of Charmides, but also Socrates' understanding of what his interlocutors had in mind in saying what they did and what his own intentions were—all this vanishes in Euclides' representation. In a dialogue about knowledge, the body in its manifestations of what the soul harbors seems to be suppressed along with the silent thinking of the mind. Indeed, the dialogue's most obvious defect seems to consist in its failure to consider knowledge in its relation to learning, intention, and understanding. Socrates does distinguish between understanding what Parmenides said and what Parmenides' speech intended, but the very context in which he makes the remark prevents it from affecting the discussion. Only the explicit and utterable are admitted by Euclides or acknowledged by Theaetetus and Theodorus. The verbatim account of Euclides would thus echo the literalness of Theaetetus and Theodorus.

Euclides' manner of writing does not preclude the possibility that within its limitations ways could be found to express both bodily movements and silent intentions, but it would surely require that Euclides be as skilled as Plato. Rather than to attribute to Euclides so large a talent, we could suppose that either Socrates said nothing about anyone's expressions or intentions and refrained from all interpretation, or Socrates himself, knowing the pedantry of Euclides (Socrates chose him, after all, as the most suitable recorder of this dialogue), smuggled into the speeches all that he suspected Euclides would have otherwise omitted. We should then have in Euclides' writing virtually a writing of Socrates, his own testament, as it were, of his perplexity. In light of the question it raises, the *Theaetetus* is more comprehensively sceptical than any other so-called sceptical dialogue. As the first of the seven dialogues that present the last days of Socrates, it lies at the opposite pole from the last of them, which in its assertion of the soul's immortality appears to be the most dogmatic. Plato has fittingly assigned to a Megarian the apparent scepticism in Socratic philosophy, and to the Pythagoraean Phaedo its equally apparent dogmatism.

The time at which Socrates' conversation with Theaetetus and Theodorus occurred is not the time during which we must imagine ourselves to be reading the *Theaetetus*. We read it while the dying Theaetetus is being carried from Megara to Athens; it occurred just prior to Socrates' meeting with Euthyphro and his subsequent hearing of the indictment against him at the stoa of the King Archon. We are reading it not because it pertains, in Euclides' opinion, to the trial and death of Socrates, but because Euclides recalls with wonder Socrates' divination that Theaetetus was fated, if he lived, to become renowned. We can well wonder at Euclides' wonder. It would not have required a Socrates to make so easy a prediction. Theodorus divines as well as Socrates Theaetetus' potentiality. Euclides, however, again as a good Megarian, would have to deny the existence of potentiality,[2] and hence the confirmation of Socrates' total confidence in Theaetetus' future could hardly seem to him to be less than a miracle. Now that Theaetetus is almost dead, he can safely bring to light, without fear of any Solonian doubt, the evidence from which Socrates inferred the future. We ourselves, however, must not connect the dialogue with the pathetic but philosophically trivial occasion of Theaetetus' dying, but with the far from trivial death of Socrates. We must turn away from the military and patriotic death of Theaetetus to the judicially criminal death of Socrates. Behind the memorial to a mathematician lurks his apparent look-alike, the philosopher.

In calling our attention to the dialogue as written, and the almost Thucydidean effort Euclides spent on translating his notes into a complete record, Plato rehearses on the level of historiography the problem with which the dialogue deals. Does the recording of what happened stand to what happened as the knowledge of what is stands to what is? Euclides presents what has happened as if it were happening now; he has suppressed the difference of time and place. Should, then, the knowledge of what is likewise present what is? But how can knowledge avoid a representation of what is? Is knowledge to eliminate its own speeches? Knowledge would then be nothing but immediate, and all reasoning would prove suspect. If, however, we are not to imitate Euclides but set the knowledge of what is apart from what is, how can this apartness consist with its title to be knowledge? We seem forced to choose between an immediacy that is unavailable and a mediacy that is uneliminable. The distortion Euclides was compelled to introduce into his writing, which thus only looks as if we are overhearing the speeches of Socrates, Theaetetus, and Theodorus, is more incorrigible but less serious than the abstraction he might have made from Socrates' account.

Euclides gives the speeches by themselves, the raw material from which we might be able to recover the several intentions and degrees of understanding of the speakers. Our discovery of their intentions and understanding would bring us to the action, the deeds, which animate the speeches, and we should then know their causes. If interpretation of the *Theaetetus* or any other Platonic dialogue precisely consists in this, can we suppose it to be the model to serve us for getting out of the dilemma with which the problem of knowledge confronts us? Can "the weakness of speeches" be circumvented through a comparable effort to discover the deeds, the beings, apart from which but of which the speeches of knowledge are? To chart the concealment and the revelation, which are inseparable from the kind of imitation Plato employs, could itself be the proper beginning for resolving the perplexity with which Socrates and Theaetetus end.

II. Looks and Likeness
(143d1–146c6)

The Euclidean part of the dialogue begins with Socrates asking Theodorus whether he has met among the Athenian young who care for geometry or some other kind of philosophy any who are likely to prove proficient. Socrates' greater love of Athenians does not fully explain why he asks such a question now. If Socrates were not old, and Meletus' indictment did not threaten him, we could suppose that Theodorus is to act as Socrates' talent scout. No one would say that Socrates, in divining the coming of the Eleatic stranger in the *Sophist*, anticipates the need to have at hand the proper interlocutor for the discussion of the sophist. Is Socrates, then, looking for his own successor—someone who will continue philosophy in Athens after him?

But Socrates already knows Plato, and the circumstances now are not like those before Plato's birth in the *Charmides*, where on Socrates' return from Potidaea (the prelude to the Peloponnesian War), he asks, in his concern for philosophy in Athens, whether anyone in his absence has come to be outstanding in wisdom, beauty, or both.

Theaetetus turns out to be among all the young men that Plato ever has Socrates converse with the most prominent within the field of philosophy. Theaetetus and Theodorus are the only "scientists"—the only theoretical men—that we meet in argument with Socrates. Both perhaps become a little less naive as a result of this one encounter, but neither turns fully to philosophy. Theodorus has already rejected it as "bare speeches," and Theaetetus merely pursued, as far as we know, the same inquiries he had already begun before he met Socrates. Socrates surely did not succeed in getting the best out of Theaetetus, for he thanks Theodorus for his acquaintance with Theaetetus only after he has listened to the stranger's conversation with him.[3] Was Socrates not competent to examine mathematicians? That he later proposes to question young Socrates implies no such disability.[4] Perhaps his relative failure with Theaetetus is indispensable for the stranger's success. The *Sophist* offers us a unique "control" for checking up on how much Theaetetus learned from Socrates. If Theaetetus had proved to be of another sort—someone for whom Socrates could have been of decisive help—would Socrates have tried to stay alive by conducting a different defense? Does Theaetetus' becoming as barren as Socrates himself determine Socrates' suicidal defense?

Theodorus praises Theaetetus at some length without once mentioning his name. This unnamed Athenian had had the discernment to associate voluntarily with Theodorus; he had chosen not to associate with Socrates, despite his interest in the questions he knew that Socrates raised. The dizziness these questions induce in him is no hindrance to his learning all he can from Theodorus. Socratic philosophy is, to say the least, not indispensable for making great discoveries in mathematics, and mathematicians themselves seem to be wholly immune to philosophy if neither Theodorus nor Theaetetus sees any difficulty in accepting the view that knowledge is perception. In the face of both Socratic and Protagorean doubts, they are serenely confident in their own competence. Science and scientists look on as neutrals at the conflicts within philosophy. Theodorus, however, cannot praise Theaetetus without defending himself against the possible charge that his appraisal is not altogether dispassionate. He is more afraid that he might be thought to be in love with Theaetetus than he is concerned with the consequences for his discipline of "bare speeches." He is certainly less afraid to offend Socrates than to be

thought Theaetetus' partisan. Paederasty is far worse a charge than
lack of urbanity. In the only Platonic dialogue Plato did not write,
Socrates is told to his face that he is ugly. Since Theaetetus looks
almost as repulsive as Socrates, Theodorus assumes either that no
one could possible love Theaetetus or Socrates—Alcibiades notwith-
standing—or that Theaetetus' ugliness protects him against the charge.
He thinks he has adequately forestalled the accusation that he has
corrupted Theaetetus.

Theaetetus has all the qualities except gracefulness that Socrates
lists as prerequisites for potential philosophers.[5] He is outstanding in
docility, gentleness, and manliness. He seems to be already the perfect
offspring of the union between moderation and courage that the
Eleatic stranger later suggests the stateman's art must effect. Socrates,
however, tells Theaetetus at the end that the conversation at least has
gentled him even more, so that in his moderation he does not believe
he knows what he does not know. Socrates was apparently unable to
enhance Theaetetus' natural gentleness without sacrificing his manliness. Theodorus, on the other hand, believes it is less difficult to
combine gentleness with manliness than either or both of them with
docility. The gentle are stupid, the quick-witted mad; or, since the
quick-witted are impatient and prone to anger, while the more easy-
going are sluggish and forgetful, Theodorus implies that the just are
likely to be stupid and the smart unjust. Theodorus uses two images
to convey to Socrates how remarkable Theaetetus is. The first likens
him to a ballasted ship. Wind and waves are the medium through
which the learner must go, and as these elements are naturally in a
turbulent state, if one does not counteract them with one's own weight-
iness, they are apt to carry one away. The medium of knowledge, one
would say, does not by itself lead to knowledge. The second image
likens Theaetetus to a silently flowing stream of olive oil. The medium
of knowledge would be the learner himself. Nothing outside him
resists the way he slowly takes. Theodorus' two images do not exactly
agree with one another. His competence in mathematics does not
support him in his attempt at poetry.

Socrates seems to be rather obtuse if he cannot figure out from
Theodorus' speech that the son of Euphronius is meant. How many
Athenians could there be who look like a youthful Silenus? A surer
way of identifying him would be for Theodorus to tell Socrates his
father's name. Theodorus does not remember the name; he appeals
instead to sight: Theaetetus is the one in the middle of an odd number
of freshly oiled young men who are approaching them. Socrates then
recognizes him. He is far from being as unique as Theodorus thinks.
His father was just like him. Theodorus then gives Theaetetus' name;

he adds that Theaetetus' guardians are thought to have dissipated the large estate of his father, but Theaetetus is still marvelously liberal. Socrates is finally impressed: "How grand a nobleman you speak of." Socrates throughout shows himself as rather parochial and more concerned with superficial things like genealogy, names, and money than with Theodorus' enthusiastic analysis of Theaetetus' soul. But from the point of view of knowledge, does "son of the Athenian Euphronius" less surely identify Theaetetus than Theodorus' speech? At a distance, Theodorus could mistake Theaetetus for Socrates; Socrates could never confuse them. If we ask what is knowledge, we must ask whether, as well as how, knowledge of resemblance, knowledge of soul, knowledge of body, and knowledge of names form a unity. To answer that each is due to perception and memory does not do away with the manifest differences among them.

Socrates has Theodorus call Theaetetus over so that he can examine what kind of face he himself has. Has Socrates never looked in a mirror? Theaetetus, after all, is not as exopthalmic as he is, but because he is not looking at his own face, the love of his own will not interfere with his deciding whether he is ugly. Socrates is far too urbane, of course, to tell Theaetetus that his teacher finds him ugly. He does not initially raise the problem of knowledge because of Theodorus' praise of Theaetetus, but because Theodorus had invoked a standard (beauty) in asserting the likeness of Socrates and Theaetetus. He wants to know how Theodorus' praise and blame fit with his discernment of likeness; that is, he questions Theodorus' competence not only to assert that Theaetetus is ugly if he is not a painter but to make likenesses of Theaetetus' soul if he is not a poet.

Socrates gives a single example. If Theodorus had said that Socrates and Theaetetus had each a lyre that was likewise tuned, they would only trust him if he were skilled in music; otherwise, they would examine whether he was so skilled, and if not, they would distrust him. Theaetetus takes the arts so much for granted that he does not ask how without being an expert oneself, in which case trust in another expert would be superfluous, they could proceed to examine Theodorus' competence in music. Theodorus is now teaching Theaetetus advanced music. Socrates, in any case, distinguishes between trust and knowledge, and thereby demolishes in advance Theaetetus' later proposal that knowledge is true opinion. Socrates, furthermore, in having Theaetetus deny that Theodorus is a painter but allowing him to be a geometrician, seems to distinguish between the kind of proportional beauty a mathematician could know, of which a tuned lyre would be an example, from the beauty of the human face, to which Theodorus' mathematics gives no access. He implies that the knowledge of human beauty falls as much outside the knowledge of proportion as does the knowledge of the differences of rank among the statesman, philosopher, and sophist. Euclides calls the dying, sick, and wounded Theaetetus beautiful and good.

After having gently instructed Theaetetus that neither should mind if a nonexpert like Theodorus calls them ugly, Socrates turns to Theodorus' praise of Theaetetus' soul. Not what uninformed opinion says but only the view of experts counts. There is an extraordinary lack of parallelism between the model Socrates has set up for testing competence in the arts and the way he now proposes to handle the praise of Theaetetus' soul. It is no longer a question of resemblance but of Theaetetus' difference from almost everyone else, and Socrates does not even stop to ask whether Theodorus is an expert in souls. Theaetetus and Socrates can dismiss Theodorus' opinion about their ugliness even if they were interested in such a question, but whoever hears the praise of another in point of virtue and wisdom should at once be as eager to examine the praised as the praised should be eager to exhibit himself. They have no time to look for other experts. Either there are no other experts whom they could trust, Socrates sets himself up as the expert in souls, or they can join together in examining Theaetetus' soul without either of them being an expert. Regardless of whether Theodorus is an amateur or an expert, Socrates proposes that they test his praise themselves. He proposes that what at best could be only trust be replaced by knowledge.

Although Theaetetus agrees with Socrates in principle, he shies away from displaying himself. He fears that Theodorus spoke in jest. Socrates assures him that this is not Theodorus' way. With these few words, Socrates tells us more about Theodorus than Theodorus' highly wrought speech tells us about Theaetetus. Socrates then goes on to say that Theaetetus' pretence, as if he too must know that Theodorus is always in earnest, could only force Theodorus to swear to the sincerity of his praise. Not to be playful means not to be liable to the charge of perjury. Socrates' own playfulness, on the other hand, of which Theodorus is occasionally aware, would point to Meletus' indictment, that Socrates does not believe in the gods in which the city believes. However this may be, Theodorus finds nothing funny when Socrates soon after consults him as the expert on urbanity.

Nothing could be more abrupt than the way in which Socrates shifts from the question whether Theodorus correctly praised Theaetetus to his own small perplexity, What is knowledge? Theaetetus' self-knowledge and Socrates' knowledge of Theaetetus are presumably to be gained through an inquiry into knowledge itself. The problem of knowledge seems to come up only as a means to these ends. It is unclear whether Socrates has chosen the most direct route. It turns out, in any case, that Theaetetus' self-knowledge is paradoxically independent of his knowing what knowledge is. But what makes this shift even more surprising is that Socrates first asks that all the others present join with Theaetetus in examining the new question, and then, in the face of Theaetetus' silence, asks whether anyone else would speak first. And yet only Theaetetus could have served to discover Theaetetus' excellence. The new question, far from being connected with Theodorus' praise of Theaetetus, seems to postpone its examination indefinitely. If Euclides had preserved Socrates' narration, perhaps we would have learned that Socrates' *daimonion* checked him in midcourse and ordered him to stop talking exclusively to Theaetetus. Theaetetus does in fact remain the main interlocutor only because Socrates calls it his sacred duty to obey the wise Theodorus, and not because he has just agreed with Socrates that he should reveal himself. But whatever might explain Socrates' shifting from Theaetetus to the others, we would still have to explain the juxtaposition of the questions. The problem of the knowledge of souls somehow makes the problem of knowledge peculiarly acute, for the lack of acknowledged experts in knowledge of souls would necessarily make it impossible for Socrates and Theaetetus, no matter what they discovered about Theaetetus' soul, to decide whether it was deserving of praise or blame. Knowledge becomes a problem as soon as Theodorus speaks without authority. Even this literal-minded mathematician had to speak in riddling images when he praised a fellow mathematician's soul.

III. MUD
(146c7–147c6)

Theaetetus agrees to two propositions that seem incompatible even before he ventures his first answer. If in learning geometry one becomes wiser in geometry, and in learning astronomy wiser in astronomy, but the wise are wise by wisdom, what could this unqualified wisdom be that renders the wise wise? It cannot be the wisdom of astronomy that makes the geometer wise, to say nothing of the wise shoemaker. That Theaetetus singles out shoemaking among the arts, seems to indicate that he has heard something of Socrates' ways, and perhaps that he wishes to ingratiate himself with him. If he had not added the crafts, his answer could have been more readily generalized. Knowledge is nothing but mathematical knowledge, and therefore to know is to count and measure, or less strictly, there can be no knowledge where there is not the numerable. Since, however, Theaetetus does add the productive arts, we should have to say that for him there is no knowledge apart from the arts and sciences. Socrates' recognition of Theaetetus is not knowledge.

Socrates offers his usual objection to any manifold. Theaetetus has given a many when asked for a one, and a complex for a simple. The alternative—that which is one and simple—is not the only possible answer. Knowledge could be a one that is complex, in the way that mud is, or a simple that is a many, which would nicely characterize the set of all the mathematical sciences. Socrates wants Theaetetus to tell him neither the kinds nor the number of sciences, just as the Eleatic stranger in the *Sophist* wants the philosophers to tell him neither the kinds nor the number of beings. Socrates opposes counting to knowing, but he thereby implies that Theaetetus had tacitly asserted their equivalence. In the strict sense, one only knows in the various arts and sciences that which one counts.[6]

Socrates clarifies his question by an example. He chooses something homely and ready-at-hand. He does not ask a physicist's question, like what is water or what is earth; he asks what is mud (*pêlos*). The example reverberates for us because we recall that Parmenides once asked Socrates, when he was of about the same age as Theaetetus is now, whether he thought there was an *eidos* of water apart from all the water we see, and that on Socrates' replying that he was perplexed as to what he should say, Parmenides had pressed him with the same question about very homely and contemptible things—hair, mud, and dirt. These are, Socrates said, just what we see them to be; but he then confessed that he was troubled. Perhaps they too had the same sort of *eidê* as he was certain just, beautiful, and good had. Parmenides then remarked that Socrates' youth made him too subservient to the opinions of human beings; if philosophy really took hold of him he would no longer despise such things.[7]

The way in which morality once gripped Socrates corresponds in Theaetetus' case to the hold the established arts and sciences exert on him. All the results of science as true opinion, he will say, are beautiful and good (200e5–6). Socrates tries to be as much a liberator for Theaetetus as Parmenides once was for him. He shows Theaetetus that he has restricted knowledge to the arts and sciences, for whereas Socrates' definition of *pêlos* applies equally to mud or clay, Theaetetus' answer would have been solely in terms of *pêlos* as an ingredient in the arts of the potter, dollmaker, and brickmaker. Socrates' definition is, though prescientific, more comprehensive than the enumeration of the clays used in several arts. But the scientific answer is not as absurd as Socrates makes it out to be. It tells us that *pêlos* is that out of which pots, dolls, and bricks are made, and that if one then wants to know what is the clay of the potter, one should consult the potter, who could say exactly what constituent elements, and in what proportions, are needed to make this or that kind of pot. The scientific answer may be fragmentary, but it does give one numbers.

It is never easy with Platonic examples to discriminate between their illustrating the way in which a question is to be answered and their serving as a guide to the answer itself. If knowledge is like mud, and mud is just that out of which it is formed, then knowledge too would be nothing but its origins, and perception would be a very plausible answer. But since mud cannot be defined without specifying how its constituents are put together, knowledge in turn could only arise if its ingredients were mixed together in some way. Knowledge perhaps requires both a passive and an active element. The discovery of its material and efficient causes would then tell us what knowledge unqualifiedly is, while the various sciences would be due to the shapes we impose on its unformed bulk—the uses to which we put knowledge. The difficulty such a picture of knowledge confronts us with is that, in showing us only that without which there can be no knowledge, it sanctions our mixing its ingredients in whatever way we wish. Pure earth is not mud, nor is pure liquid, but the range of their mixture within which there is mud does not legitimately admit of any differentiation. We should be involved in a vicious circle if we appealed to what we made out of earth and liquid for our needs as the proof that we had correctly handled the mud with which we began. The transformation from prescientific knowledge (mud) to the sciences (bricks, dolls, and pots) would thus be legitimated through that which lies outside knowledge itself.

Socrates tried to convince Theaetetus of the absurdity of his answer with two very different arguments. He draws a parallel between the impossibility of understanding the name of something without knowing what the something is and that of understanding the knowledge of shoemaking without knowing what knowledge is. If "to know what something is" is taken strictly, it is certainly possible to understand the name of something, namely, that to which it refers, without knowing what it is. So Theaetetus' answer tells us to what knowledge applies and to what, by implication, it does not. If, however, "to know what it is" is taken loosely, so that it is a matter of identification, then the name of something could not be understood without such knowledge. Socrates, however, seems to compare knowledge first with the name of something, and then to turn around and compare it with the something of which the name is. But this confusion is meant to reveal the hidden redundancy in the arts themselves (e.g., the science of astronomy), by means of which they deluded Theaetetus into believing that what they jointly assume they severally show. Socrates' second argument contrasts the interminable circumlocution that a listing of all the different clays would involve with the trivial and short answer that could be given. He thereby implies that the way of enumeration in the absence of any shortcut might have to be taken. The dichotomies of the *Sophist* and *Statesman* certainly look as if epistemic roundabouts were all that was available.

IV. SURDS
(147c7–148b4)

Theaetetus discerns a resemblance in what he and young Socrates had recently discussed to the question Socrates has asked them. The resemblance seems to consist in the nonenumerability of surds, despite which they found a single expression to comprehend them all, and the practically nonenumerable arts and sciences, for the division of all numbers into two cannot be comparable to the unity of knowledge. The question of knowledge would seem more nearly to correspond to asking what is number. But since, in fact, Theaetetus' now-rejected definition of knowledge already looks like Euclid's definition of number—a multitude composed of ones—the mathematical equivalent to what is knowledge is not what is number but what is one. The starting point for Theaetetus and young Socrates was Theodorus' demonstration that the square root of the three-foot line was incommensurable, and the same held for certain magnitudes up to seventeen feet. They, however, looked at the infinite multiplicity of surds, and tried to gather them into one. They first divided all numbers into two. Those numbers which could be produced by a number multiplied by itself they likened in figure to a square and called them square and equilateral numbers. So self-evident are these numbers that Theaetetus does not mention a single one. Those numbers, however, which lie between the square numbers, among which are three and five, and for which no number exists that when multiplied by itself will produce them but a greater and a lesser side always comprehends them, they likened to oblong figures and called them oblong numbers. They then said that length (*mêkos*) is the name for all lines that form as a square an equal-sided and plane number, and surds those lines which form an oblong as a square. These two kinds of lines are not commensurable in their lengths but in their squares.

It is necessary to go over again what Theaetetus and young Socrates did, for which Socrates suitably praises them, in order to see how remarkable and perplexing their procedure was. They first dropped Theodorus' talk of lines of so many feet and considered numbers by themselves, but they were compelled to turn back to geometry in order to obtain likenesses of the two kinds of numbers. Magnitude vanishes as a first-order phenomenon only to reappear as the source of images. The status, however, of the square as an image is not the same for the two kinds of numbers. The square for square numbers is an image that in no way interferes with our returning to the pure-number equivalent of the side of the square. The image for the square root of four is dispensable as far as comprehending the class of all such numbers goes. But the image of the square becomes necessary as soon as one tries to translate the negative determination of all numbers without integral square roots, in which guise they are merely other than square numbers, into a positive determination. The image of the square then acts as the standard without which their class as that of incommensurables cannot be comprehended at all. The oblong image of the number three has to be replaced by the image of a square of equal area. This second image is commensurable with the image of four as a square, but one can no longer dispense with the image and still speak of three's root. The construction which has brought it to light is inseparable from it. The root of a pure number is not a number, and yet, though it only exists in the image of an image of a pure number, it has the power to generate the pure number.

Socrates sets Theaetetus no easy task if he expects him to imitate all this in the case of knowledge. Should he say that there are two kinds of knowledge, one "rational," the other "irrational," which are not comparable with one another because of their different "roots," but a single speech can still comprehend them if one gives to each a similar image, even though only one of them needs the image in order to be understood? Socrates, at any rate, presents the knowledge he himself has in a very elaborate likeness and thus implicitly asks Theaetetus to find a definition of knowledge equally adequate for both the many sciences he has acknowledged and Socrates' singular maieutics. This twoness of knowledge turns out to dominate the three dialogues *Theaetetus, Sophist,* and *Statesman;* it was first intimated in Socrates' denying Theodorus' competence to pronounce on his own and Theaetetus' ugliness.

V. BIRTH
(148b5–151d6)

Theaetetus has now confirmed the truthfulness of Theodorus' praise, but since he cannot speak about knowledge as he had about roots, Theodorus is, though sincere, evidently a liar. Theaetetus assumes that only if he could answer any question of this type would the praise be warranted. Socrates encourages him through a likeness. Theodorus' praise was relative. He did not mean that Theaetetus had reached the peak of virtue and wisdom, but only that if compared with his contemporaries he was outstanding. Socrates' encouragement is disturbing. If the problem of knowledge will defeat Theaetetus, as it is bound to do if Theaetetus is outclassed by it, why should Socrates run Theaetetus against the strongest possible competition? It will no doubt stretch him to the utmost, but will it not just as much discourage him? Theaetetus does not seem to be in need of humiliation. Must he jump all at once from a mathematical youth to philosophic maturity? In the *Sophist*, the Eleatic stranger seems to be more successful with Theaetetus because he leads up to the problem of being in easy stages. Socrates, however, perhaps rushes Theaetetus because he is aware that he has not enough time left to go more slowly. His imminent trial forces the pace.

Theaetetus' perplexity is not new; ever since he has heard of Socrates' questions, they have resisted his own and other's efforts to answer them, but unlike Theodorus he has been unable to get rid of his concern. Theaetetus, then, is not a beginner; Socrates has caught him just before his total immersion in mathematical studies would have made him oblivious of these questions. "The reason is, my dear Theaetetus, that you're suffering labor pains, not on account of your being empty but pregnant." Theaetetus is neither pregnant without being in labor, nor in labor with a false pregnancy. "I don't know, Socrates, what, however, I've experienced I say." Theaetetus distinguishes between his immediate knowledge of his own experience, which he does not call knowledge, and his ignorance of its cause. He identifies knowledge with knowledge of causes, but as his identifying of knowledge with perception indicates, he is unaware that he has done so. Indeed, I should venture to say that Theaetetus and Theodorus are of all the interlocutors in Platonic dialogues least aware of how what they themselves say or do bears on what they are discussing.

Theaetetus' confession of ignorance can be interpreted not only as containing within it a definition of knowledge, which by its very containment illustrates how one knows when one does not know, but it also is open to another interpretation. Theaetetus' ignorance might not be about the truth or falsity of Socrates' account of the cause of his perplexity, but rather about the very meaning of Socrates' words— *ôdineis* (you are in labor), *kenos* (empty), *enkymôn* (pregnant). Socrates had spoken them without the qualification of an "as it were" or "to speak metaphorically." He had spoken as if poetry were prose; for had he so qualified them and admitted them to be elements of an image, the distinction he later draws on its basis between phantoms and truth would itself be grounded in a phantom, and knowledge of cause would be nothing more than a fiction. This is one puzzle around which much of the *Theaetetus, Sophist,* and *Statesman* turn. There is another.

Theaetetus presents himself as someone who does not know. He knows that he does not know. He thus seems to have achieved already the level of Socratic ignorance, for his modesty is such that we can readily imagine his drawing up a list of everything he does not know. But Socratic ignorance cannot be as easy as putting anything in the form "What is ———?" Socratic ignorance must consist in knowledge of the structure of such ignorance. It must be ignorance that has been fully informed by knowledge. And yet this informing cannot be due to a methodology that would predetermine what was a permissible answer; rather, the informing must be due to the recognition that something "out there" is perplexing. The Socratic question has to be encountered; it can neither be posited nor generated from a preestablished scepticism. It must be an object of wonder. The disclosure of a Socratic question as such thus hovers between a being's self-disclosure and a thinker's self-knowledge. This peculiar doubleness of a Socratic question is what allows Socrates to move from his initial question, the nature of Theaetetus' nature, to its extension, the nature of knowledge.

Theaetetus has heard that Socrates' mother was a midwife, but he has not heard that Socrates practices the same art. Instead he has heard that Socrates is most strange and makes human beings perplexed. Theaetetus, like all the nonknowers, does not know that Socrates' ability to perplex him is due to an art. He therefore did not have to take it into account when he defined knowledge. What others report about Socrates' effect and Theaetetus himself experiences has its cause in an art. The cause of the cause of Theaetetus' experience is Socrates' art. This is a secret Socrates asks Theaetetus to keep, and we are only let in on it at the moment of Theaetetus' death. The more secret part of the secret is that Socrates has the art of the go-between, which he can only reveal by informing Theaetetus that midwives, who up to this time have been as successful as Socrates in concealing it, are also marriage-brokers. Socrates is far less careful of his mother's reputation than of his own.

Since Socrates assures Theaetetus that his art and that of midwives exactly correspond, with the exception of two obvious differences, he seems to entitle us to deduce all we can from the correspondence. Midwives are women who are past the child-bearing age: Socrates was once fertile but is no longer. If, however, human nature were not too weak to obtain an art without experience, Artemis would have given midwifery to the barren: Socrates did not need experience to be the artful midwife of men's souls. Socrates has an a priori knowledge. The contradiction seems inescapable; Socrates, amazingly enough, evades it. Many, he tells Theaetetus, get so angry at him, when he removes their folly, that they are ready to bite him, for they do not believe he acts with good will, "being far from knowing that no god is ill-disposed to human beings." Socrates is a god. It would be no wonder that he urged Theaetetus to keep his secret just before he was to go on trial for impiety. Admittedly, one is inclined to shy away from such madness and fall back on Socrates' claim to be barren in wisdom, which would altogether destroy the point of his account. The barrenness of midwives is not an element in their art, but without it they could not act as justly toward their patients. Nothing of their own interferes with their care for others, but if Socrates had ever had his own offspring, he would still be their partisan, for he never could have tested them, let alone have become later the touchstone of others. He cannot be critical if he is productive, nor maintain his justice unless he is barren, and he cannot be barren unless he is a god. He could only have answered Meletus' indictment of his injustice in corrupting the young by agreeing with the indictment of his impiety. If forced to choose between Socrates' injustice and Socrates' madness, we should choose his injustice: In the *Sophist*, Socrates himself suggests that the Eleatic stranger has come to punish him.

The serious suggestion in all this apparent playfulness is that experience and knowledge are incompatible: Theaetetus had the experience of perplexity; Socrates knows its cause. Socrates seems to assume that thoughts are like crimes and unlike diseases, for whereas doctors should, in addition to learning their art, come into contact with the worst bodies, themselves suffer all the diseases, and be not very healthy by nature, judges who had consorted with wicked souls and themselves committed every kind of crime would keenly detect the crimes of others but out of a base suspicion misconstrue the character of the good.[8] And just as we prefer the judge who does not call upon his own experience in condemning the unjust, so we must choose Socrates, who solely by his art aborts the false. Experience and knowledge could only coincide if no experience produced falsehood, for one cannot oneself cure the infection of a self-generated falsehood. Self-knowledge is impossible. To say, therefore, as Theaetetus does, that knowledge is perception, is to follow Socrates' reasoning insofar as it inspires a fear of ineradicable error, but to deny Socrates his art. It seems plausible to do so, for as he proceeds, Socrates speaks as much of his guesswork as of his art.

Midwives take less pride in delivering babies than in knowing what kind of woman in intercourse with what kind of man would bear the best possible children. True midwives know what in the *Statesman* the Eleatic stranger assigns to political science and that which Socrates once posited as the art indispensable for preserving the best city: with the guardians' forgetting of the "nuptial number," the city starts its decline. Socrates does not have this presumably mathematical art, nor is his art in any way political. His art, to be truly effective, needs to be supplemented by the art of go-betweens, who can bring about the birth of the best souls by nature; in the absence of their art, Socrates can only work on what chance has brought forth. Go-betweens can only practice their art in the best city, for everywhere else it would entail the contravention of the law against adultery. It would seem, moreover, indistinguishable from unjust and artless pimping, since it would have to persuade wherever mutual desire was absent, and dissuade wherever it was incorrectly present. Socrates, then, in labeling his whole art maieutics, conceals that part of it which he elsewhere calls erotics.

At this point the resources of Socrates' image break down, for whereas the barrenness of midwives prevents them from ever considering themselves the proper mothers of the best children—Phaenarete became a midwife after the birth of Socrates—nothing prevents Socrates from considering himself the best father of wisdom. He gave out in marriage many young men, who were fertile but not pregnant, to Prodicus and other wise men, whose acceptance of money apparently condemns them to the charge of prostitution,[9] but his silence about young men whom he made pregnant seems to imply that he is not only barren but sterile as well. The birth of wisdom requires a male principle and a female and fertile soul, for falsehood is an unfertilized egg. But in the case of those who improved under his own care, Socrates speaks as if their souls were both: "They on their own from themselves found and gave birth to many beautiful things." If Socrates' questions solely induce his patients' labor pains, they either impregnate themselves or are impregnated by others, but if his questions are also the seed he plants in the soul of the young, then his art is not restricted to delivery and diagnostics. Socrates would be a father through his art of questioning. His art of questioning, however, is not wisdom, any more than is his knowledge of souls. Neither is the offspring of his soul. Socrates opposes his barren soul to his infallible art. They are as incompatible with one another as experience and knowledge. Wisdom, then, as that truth which one's own soul brings forth, is not the same as knowledge. The perplexity Socrates has now set for Theaetetus, in the course of encouraging him in his perplexity, could not be greater: the soul's experiences interfere with knowledge;

knowledge cannot become wisdom without the soul's experiences; only wisdom can tell us the truth about the arts and sciences.

If women ever gave birth to phantom children, it would be the greatest and noblest task of midwives to distinguish them from genuine children. Socrates enlarges *per impossibile* the domain of midwifery, so that he can continue to employ the language of midwifery where it has no counterpart in midwifery. He has shown that the art of the go-between and the art of the midwife are the same art, but he cannot show that an art which cannot exist belongs to maieutics in either the ordinary or true sense of the term. He therefore cannot establish on the basis of an image he has falsified the essential unity of his diagnostics and his maieutics. That Socrates can spot the pregnant and ease or intensify their birth pangs does not entail that he can tell the true from the false, unless such an art is the same as his art of discriminating between good and bad fathers and mothers. If true midwives know who should mate with whom in order to produce the best children, they must know how to tell apart good children from bad, and if they know when to abort, they must know when the fetus is unworthy of coming to term. If, then, the art of midwives completely corresponds to Socrates' art, we are forced to conclude that as bad children are children as much as good children are, so the false offspring of soul are truly as much offspring as true offspring are. Such a conclusion, however, would undercut Socrates' equation of phantoms with falsehoods. It would thereby prompt us to ask from the start how false opinion is possible. Its possibility, at any rate, is shown by the Eleatic stranger in the *Sophist* to depend on the understanding of phantoms and images.

The obstacles Socrates puts in the way of Theaetetus are not all of a "theoretical" kind; his speech lays far greater stress on his failures, of whom he names one, than on his successes. Some young men he sent away to others if he thought them virgins; all the rest, some of whom appeared at first to be stupid, improved, "whomever the god allowed," that is, some did not improve. Some of those who did improve stayed, and many, however, who did not know that Socrates and the god were the cause of their improvement—the others apparently did know—went away sooner than they should have. All of those who left too soon became stupid; many of them then carried on in an amazing way and begged to be let back in. Most of these the *daimonion* rejected; the rest improved once more. There are altogether twelve groups of young men distributed into six pairs. Four groups are outright failures, a fifth is given a second chance. The number of evidently gifted successes is very small, but Socrates nowhere says that they gave birth to the truth. They could have discovered many beautiful things that were false, and Socrates could have checked their perplexities without their having discovered the truth. Socrates would be a straightforward Protagorean if a true speech, recognized as such by Socrates, did not become Socrates' wisdom too. Socrates, then, holds out to Theaetetus the very faintest of hopes: ugly though he is, he just might have beautiful offspring.

VI. MEASURE
(151d7–157a7)

If philosophy begins in wonder, it must draw the distinction between opinion and knowledge, for wonder is the recognition of the disparity between our clarity about the "that" of things and the obscurity of the "why" of things. To assert that knowledge is perception is to renounce the starting point of philosophy. Socrates calls Protagoras' thesis enigmatic because he seems to be saying that each of us knows the beings, whereas in fact he means that there are no beings to be known. The truth is neither that the truth is already known to each of us nor that the truth eludes us, but rather that there is nothing there to elude us. Theaetetus' wonder, even more than his mathematics, contradicts his answer. His soul's experiences, to which he himself testifies, do not come to light in his answer. Socrates therefore can at once conclude that he took his answer from a book. Protagoras' book is the father of Theaetetus' phantom offspring.

Socrates has just said that he himself is the measure of truth and falsehood: "It's in no way sanctioned for me to make a concession to falsehood and to wipe out truth." If Socrates is a man and is such a measure by virtue of being so, then Protagoras' thesis is its legitimate generalization: "Man is the measure of all things, of the beings that (or how) they are, and of the nonbeings that (or how) they are not." Theaetetus, as Socrates interprets him, could not have more completely denied Socrates' maieutics. Maieutics is a way of saying that thinking is not in any sense a kind of making. The Protagoras, however, whom Socrates resurrects to defend himself, will hold that wisdom is nothing but a making. And so Protagoras, in both forms of his argument, has Socrates the midwife as his chief antagonist. The counterevidence to Protagoras' Truth is the maieutical conversation Socrates now has with Theaetetus. Its possibility, which is nothing but the possibility of philosophy itself, is the issue between them. Only if we confront continually the dialogue's maieutic action with its speeches, can we hope to enter into its argument.

Just prior to Socrates' account of his maieutics, Theaetetus had asserted that in confessing his ignorance he merely stated what he had experienced, and after hearing Socrates' account of his maieutics, he asserts that knowledge is perception. Socrates' account seems to have had the effect on Theaetetus of bringing about an equation between his experience of perplexity and the sign of knowledge. Socrates' account has guaranteed the genuineness of his experience, and it is very easy to move from the genuineness of the experience to its truthfulness. Socrates' account has at least had the effect of making Theaetetus forget the characterization of knowledge implicit in his first answer—that the knowable is the countable and the measurable.

Consider what has happened. A mathematician began with a mathematician's answer; then, a single counterexample was presented to him, which, no matter how peculiar, could still account for his own experience. Theaetetus abandoned the science of number for perception, but perception colored by the Socratic science of the soul's experiences. His own example of the experience of truly opining falsely is opining the ugly instead of the beautiful or the beautiful instead of the ugly (189c5–7), and in the *Sophist* he agrees with the stranger's distinction between the perception they have of moral vice and the knowledge they have of every soul's unwillingness to be ignorant (228b4, c7).

Theaetetus says that knowledge is perception. But literally he says, "As it now appears, knowledge is nothing else than perception." Socrates then yokes the terms together: "Perception, you say, (is) knowledge." He inserts between perception and knowledge Theaetetus' own assertion of their sameness. He thus brings out that their sameness depends on a bond which Theaetetus has expressed and yet concealed from himself. This express and hidden bond, which can do double duty for both "knowing" and "being," is "appearing" (*phantasia*). Since "to be" seems to be very different from "to be for me," it looks much easier to tell knowledge apart from perception than to make a distinction between "to appear" and "to appear to me." Now that appearing, however, is made to serve both for what we know (being) and our knowing (perceiving), a distinction within perception itself must collapse. "I see" and "I appear to see"—whether the latter refers to dreaming or waking makes no difference—must be the same. But to banish doubt from perception is to banish negation. How can men be the measure of nonbeings, that is, of nonappearings? When we say, "I do not sense the cold," are we saying the same as "I do not sense"? For if they are the same, nonperception is as much knowledge as perception is, and ignorance is knowledge, and if they are not the same, I should in the second case be sensing my non-sensing and therefore not be sensing my non-sensing. This difficulty, to which Socrates barely alludes, shows that Protagoras "spoke in the language of men," and a new formulation is necessary, in which the distinction between the beings and the nonbeings can yield to their union, "becomings."

Protagoras' Truth did not declare the truth; he spoke enigmatically to the human refuse heap, to which Theaetetus and Socrates belong, and told the truth in secret to his pupils. Although in deed there is nothing but appearance, there is still in speech a difference between the appearance of truth telling and truth telling. The immanifest resists every effort to get rid of it. Protagoras covered up that on which the two best poets and all the wise except Parmenides concur. Socrates tears away the veil from Protagoras' Truth only to replace it with a veiled speech of Homer: "Both Oceanus and mother Tethys, the *genesis* of gods." This says, according to Socrates, that all things are the offspring of flowing and motion, whereas it seems to say that the gods have their origin in a male and a female god, who did not themselves become. Even if one replaces "gods" with "all things" and "Oceanus" with "water," Homer would still be saying that the principle of everything is a something, permanent, comprehensive, that gives its own character to everything. The interpretation of Theaetetus needs the interpretation of Protagoras, which in turn needs the interpretation of Homer. We are now three removes from our beginning. Neither the first of the poets nor the last of the wise said what they meant; only now with Socrates can the truth be brought entirely into the light. Just after Socrates has told Theaetetus the secret of his own wisdom, he tells him the secret of the wise.

The truth is that not even one thing is; the manifest signs of this truth are of two sorts. Fire shows that motion supplies what is thought to be and becoming, while rest supplies nonbeing and perishing, and learning shows that motion is good and rest bad. We do not need the dysenteric Theaetetus, dying on his way to Athens, to know that the signs hardly suffice as signs of the second-order truths, let alone of the truth that nothing is. Socrates therefore has to go from signs, no number of which would ever add up to a proof, to an example taken from the thesis itself, which does not admit of being refuted. The example does not prove the thesis; it merely asks whether we are so convinced of our ordinary understanding that we can say confidently that this alternative is false. The thesis only needs an indirect proof: we have to disprove the thesis. Its internal consistency will be enough if it can show up our own inconsistency. Our own inconsistency lies in the way we speak when we count and measure, on the one hand, and the hallucinations of becoming, on the other. We easily abandon in our uncertainty the possibility of asserting either the sameness of another's perceptions with our own or our own sameness over time.

But we lay down for ourselves conditions for becoming, which support the way we usually speak of our perceptions, and yet contradict our protomathematical speeches. These speeches fully conform with the denial that any one thing is by itself, and cannot be squared with our account of becoming, which has surreptitiously borrowed the language of being.

The application (*prospherein*) of four dice to six, which results in our saying that six is more than four, is exactly like the Homeric-Protagorean thesis, which says that the application (*prosballein*) of the eyes to a suitable motion (*phora*) is white. White has no more a place in or outside the eyes than the ratio 3:2 has any other "place" than that between six dice and four. The obstacle, then, to our accepting the Homeric-Protagorean thesis is not as we might suppose our mathematics, but our "axioms" of becoming. To relativize our perceptions is to bring them into line with relative numbers and measures, which we find intolerable to treat in any other way. We say, however, that nothing can become greater or less either in bulk or in number, as long as it is equal to itself, for a deeply rooted illusion is always at work in us separating what is an indivisible one into two beings. The incidence of A on B, we say, can only lead to an alteration of A if A changes. But what eludes us in this "self-evident" proposition is that A and B in their coincidence are not two but one. If something were warm in itself, it would not alter in contact with another unless it itself changed, but this "itself in itself" is what the thesis denies and what Theaetetus cannot defend. When the measurer comes alongside what is to be measured, the measure obtained is not due to either the measurer or the measured in their apartness. So if "big" is the resultant reading, it does not belong to either of them but to both as one. And, likewise, if the eye and a suitable motion come together, the white seen is not due to a change in the eye or in the motion but to their union, in which the joint alteration of the eye and the motion is not a change in the eye or in the motion.

The illusion counter to this, however, would be ineradicable if it were not for our speeches about number and measure; for though Theaetetus changes in himself (increases), and thus becomes taller than Socrates, Socrates has not then changed and yet has become shorter than Theaetetus. We can save ourselves from this absurdity if we cut loose alteration from change, motion, and becoming as we understand them and allow "otherness" to be in itself. We can then say that the short Socrates solely exists as the "product" of Socrates and Theaetetus and is inseparable from that product. The short Socrates is an instantaneous other, and the instantaneous other is not what we call the result of becoming, but of what the wise call motion.

Motion must be grasped as the source of a between without place and a now without time. Only mathematics suggests a way in which this could be done, for our hallucinations of becoming are too powerful to yield to any other kind of argument.

That Theaetetus does not hide his opinion about becoming, which yet contradicts what he must agree to about number, elicits Socrates' praise. It is divine of him to have acknowledged his double standard, for he could have refused to admit the hallucinations of becoming and thus have solved at a stroke the apparent impossibility of reconciling them with either his mathematics or his thesis. Theaetetus does not suspect that his mathematics (knowledge) and his thesis (perception) are to come together in the mysteries into which Socrates is about to initiate him; all he now divines is that he could only be consistent at the expense of his soul. He could have been doctrinaire in speech with impunity if he had kept to himself his hallucinations. Without any compulsion, then, Theaetetus owns up to the contradiction which forced him to wonder.

Wonder, says Socrates, is the unique source of philosophy, and Theaetetus' wonder appears to show that Theodorus did not make a bad guess about his nature, even as he who said that Iris was Thaumas' offspring seems not to have made a bad genealogy. Iris or Rainbow, which one admires and wonders at—a set of colors without an apparent body—comes from Thaumas or "Wonder." Between one's own wonder and the source of wonder stands an apparition. The wonderful induces in the wonderer its own cause. Iris, according to Hesiod, is the daughter of Thaumas and Electra or "Shining," and Thaumas, in turn, is the son of Pontus (the brother of Oceanus and Tethys), and Electra the daughter of Oceanus and Tethys. The genealogist would then be saying, if we follow Socrates' way of interpreting Homer, that the ultimate source of everything, which is motion, is the beginning of philosophy. Theaetetus' nature has experienced a pathos grounded in the nature of things. His nature is the nature of nature. Theaetetus is motion: Theodorus had likened him to the silent flowing of olive oil.

Socrates explains, or rather points to an explanation of, Theaetetus' perplexity in terms that do not fit his former explanation of it in terms of his own art. Theaetetus' soul was pregnant, and Socrates' art had—at a distance—induced in it labor pains, which it was equally capable of easing as it brought his thoughts to birth. But now he implies that Theaetetus' wonder has its source in Theaetetus' own nature, a nature which has no need of any art to generate both an understanding of itself and perplexity before itself. Motion both perplexes and informs Theaetetus, who is motion, that there is nothing but motion. Motion like Oceanus moves in a circle. Wherever it is in its moving there is wonder and wisdom. The conjunction, therefore, of Socrates and Theaetetus is not, as Socrates implies, a togetherness in which both are two and yet each is one, but an indivisible one that simply does not allow Socrates to be the midwife and Theaetetus the mother. Socrates' detachment from his involvement is an illusion. His conjunction with Theaetetus alters each of them in such a way that whatever they agree to solely exists as the result of their conjunction and has the same truth as the assertion that six is more because it is more than four. That knowledge is not perception only holds for this being together (*synousia*) of Socrates and Theaetetus, his double. Socrates has so unfolded Theaetetus' thesis that it becomes simultaneously an examination of Theaetetus' soul, as Theodorus understands it, and of the possibility of his conversation with Theaetetus. To question Theodorus' competence is to question Theaetetus' thesis that has now confirmed Theodorus' competence and denied Socrates' art of questioning. Theodorus is guilty of perjury only if Socrates can establish the twoness of Theaetetus and himself in their union. He must show that "both" is not "one."

Theaetetus does not yet understand his own thesis; he will be very grateful if Socrates joins with him in searching out the truth hidden away in the thought of famous men. The uninitiated, however, must not overhear them; they believe nothing else is except what they can get their hands on fully. They are, according to Theaetetus, hard and repellent human beings. They have no mysteries, for they deny the invisible and the changeable, dragging everything to earth, as the Eleatic stranger says, out of heaven and the invisible, and defining body and being as the same.[10] Theaetetus applies to the partisans of earth and body the attributes of earth and body. Just after Socrates has hinted at the congruence between Theaetetus and his thesis, Theaetetus declares on his own that the same holds for those without music. They too say what they are. If Theaetetus represents "the streamers," and the Parmenideans "the arresters of the whole," what is Socrates? If he is altogether barren of wisdom, he can have nothing to say. Or does he too say what he is—nothing? The nonbeing of Socrates would seem to illustrate perfectly the Homeric-Protagorean thesis that nothing is by itself, and his conversation with Theaetetus, its complementary thesis that whatever is, is only relative to itself. Without his diagnostics, Socrates' maieutics would look as if it were in agreement with Protagorean wisdom.

Socrates splits his account of the mysteries into two parts; the first he calls the myth, the second that which the myth means. The meaning of the myth differs from the myth in one obvious respect: Socrates drops all mention of differences in power and replaces it with differences in speed. Power must be a mythical element because it entails a distinction within a continuum between itself and being-at-work. But there can be no potentiality where there is no being. To read back from a perception and a perceived, which are one, a dual power of agent and patient, would be to distinguish agent and patient prior to their conjunction, but "neither is there any agent before it meets together with the patient, nor a patient before it meets together with the agent." Eyesight is not the patient and whiteness the agent. Eyesight, a motion generated by agent and patient motions, becomes a seeing at the moment it falls together with whiteness, another motion generated by the same agent and patient motions that generated eyesight. The being-at-work of eyesight and whiteness does not depend mutually on light but only on each other. Seeing occurs in total darkness.

If, however, the meaning of the myth is that there is no potentiality, why must the myth speak in terms of power, when it would seem to be sufficient to speak of the double motion of perceptions and their congeners? Sights and colors are twins; they look as though they must be identical twins, for otherwise a distinction could be made between what each is in itself (agent or patient) and what they are together. As identical twins, they would necessarily be commensurate with one another, and though it would be a mistake to label one of them sight and another color, they would still be motions whose abiding character was optical. Neither identical twin within the range of sights and colors could then ever jump its own class and generate a sound, and the class of sights and colors would thus be a constituent and primitive class of the whole.

But the whole is nothing but motion; it is not infinitely many classes of aesthetic motions, each of which is distinct from the start. The twins, therefore, of each aesthetic class must have nonaesthetic sources, roots, or powers that generate them without being the same as they are. The nonaesthetic sources split into two classes, neither of which has any member that belongs exclusively to it, though at any moment their aesthetic product must be due to an agent working on a patient power. The difficulty, then, in Socrates' account can be formulated as follows. A sight and a color must be in their conjunction identical twins; apart from their conjunction, each must be nonidentical and yet generated by the same principles that are different at the time of generation and yet not permanently different. Sameness (the color seen) must come from difference (sight and color), and this difference in turn from another difference (agent and patient) that is always altering.

Socrates' language suggests that he is imitating the way in which

Theaetetus and young Socrates had found a universal definition of surds. To the two classes of number, each of which comprehends infinitely many numbers, there would correspond the two classes of motion, one of which has the power to act and the other to be acted upon. Theaetetus had then made a geometric likeness of each class of numbers, square and oblong, in which numbers were translated into magnitudes (plane numbers). Socrates now does the same when he replaces power with speed, which easily lends itself to linear representation. So if the agent and the patient are considered in their linearity, then an agent acting on a patient motion (for example, four on three) will be representable as one line at right angles to the other, for Socrates says that agent and patient motions conceive their motion in the same and in contact with another (fig. 1).

Their contact will always generate a larger (faster) number (twelve), which as the product of two numbers is representable as a plane area. Let us then say that the two possible oblong figures so generated, either 4 × 3 or 3 × 4 (cf. 148a2), show the impossibility of fixing the difference between individual agent and patient motions, though in either case one number must be acting on the passive other. The two oblongs can stand for the difference between, for example, the motion from the eye and the motion from whiteness (fig. 2). We could then further suppose that the two oblongs can only come into contact with one another if they rearrange themselves into squares of equal areas, and then their simultaneous motion toward one another (at the speed twelve) will, if they are properly aligned, generate a solid representable as a cube with an irrational side of $2 \sqrt{3}$ (fig. 3).

The cube root of its volume is now the single, nonaesthetic root of

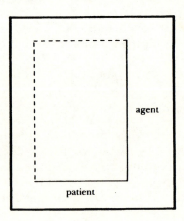

agent

patient

Figure 1

I.110

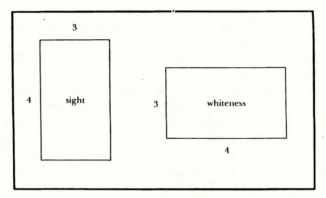

Figure 2

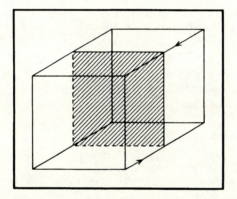

Figure 3

the identical twins, whiteness and sight, and the planes, as insubstantial as a rainbow, moving between and from the opposite faces of the cube, will be indifferently either whiteness or sight. The white seen will be a between without place. It therefore will solely be able to exist in this "solid," for its root would disappear with its dismantling, and motions (four and three) would be left that were no longer congruent coauthors of this unique perception perceived.

The significance these diagrams have lies less in their being a faithful picture—motion is to color as number is to its imaged square—than in their possibly uncovering the premises of the myth and its interpretation. Socrates had indicated that the illusions of becoming could be removed through reflection on our speeches about number and measure. The contact of six dice with four was not a becoming, any more than the contact between two powers can lead to the becoming of a faster motion, for otherwise the faster would not remain between them. The becoming and power of Socrates' account are not natural but mathematical, the becoming and power which Theaetetus spoke of in defining surds. There are no bodies for Theaetetus. Natural becoming has been replaced by mathematical metaphors, which are nothing but the mathematician's own practice—his own constructions and imagings—ascribed to his theorems.[11] Man is thus the measure of all things, for becoming is his own kind of image making, and perception his commensuration with it.

The coincidence of the Homeric-Heraclitean thesis that all things are moving like streams, a passive motion, with the Protagorean thesis that man is the measure of all things, an agent motion, generates the offspring that knowledge is perception. Between Homer of the inner mystery and Protagoras of its outer veil there comes to be Theaetetus, a product of both without being either. A mathematician generates a mathematical "physiology" which comes to be between the motion of all and the measure of man. Theaetetus' thesis duplicates in its twin roots the origin of everything. The thesis passes the test of explaining itself as it explains everything else. Theaetetus has read off, as it were, from himself his own self: the union of his mathematics and his moving soul. All knowledge is, in a non-Socratic sense, self-knowledge.

VII. DREAMS
(157a7–162b7)

In summarizing these mysteries, Socrates says that we are compelled by habit and ignorance to speak of being, but utterances according to nature would only be in terms of change. He admits that the mysteries merely outline a program that has not yet been carried out. The first step in such a revision of language would be to replace true and false with pleasure and displeasure, for it seems plausible to restrict the pleasant to my pleasure and the unpleasant to my displeasure. Theaetetus, in fact, had rejected the view that being is body because he found its proponents hard and repellent. Accordingly, Socrates asks Theaetetus whether he thinks the mysteries are pleasant, and would he taste them as satisfying. To our amazement, Theaetetus answers, "I do not know, Socrates." He had used almost the same expression before, when Socrates had told him the cause of his perplexity. Theaetetus had then known his own experience but not its cause; now he does not even know his own experience. Just when Theaetetus should have become transparent to himself he becomes opaque. Theaetetus' ignorance of his own experience does not refute but rather strengthens his thesis, for he confesses to it out of habit and ignorance. If he could figure out Socrates' own opinion, he would know what his own taste should be. Theaetetus is a natural-born follower; it is the detrimental side of his smoothly flowing nature. He will not defend his own thesis to the death but abandon it on the slightest show of a counterargument. Theaetetus is a "pushover"; the one time he challenges Socrates he speaks against his own thesis. Theaetetus' inborn deference, then, which makes him balk at being as wise as any god, needs to be mixed somehow with a stiffening element. The dialogue's success or failure depends on whether Socrates ever manages to stop the flow of Theaetetus.

The proposed revision of language is not free of difficulties, for we speak of mishearing, misseeing, and misperceiving, as though our senses then are false, and especially so when we can connect our errors with our bodily or psychic states. The illusions of dreams, madness, and other illnesses are the accepted way of refuting the equation of being with appearing. These illusions, in which everyone agrees the distinction between to be and to appear vanishes, are the model for doing away with the distinction in all other cases. The community of the waking, healthy sane has to be assimilated to the privacy of the dreaming, sick, or mad. But the departures from the standard cannot just become in turn the standard, for then the new standard will label the old as illusions, and when we are awake, healthy, and sane, our senses will play us false. It is therefore necessary for the conflicting evidence from dreaming and waking, illness and health, madness and sanity to be resolved through a transposition of each into a language between and neutral to each.

Theaetetus himself seems to supply the clue to such a transposition. He neutralized through an image the difference betwen integral and irrational square roots. The irrationals (*aloga*) obtained a *logos* that belied their name. They are on the continuum of the straight line incommensurable with the integers, but in their squares commensurable. So if the perceptions of the dreamer do not square with those of the waking, in a suitable translation of both, each could be made to look like the other without there being any need for the translation to favor either. Theaetetus, however, does not at first recognize the way out; he is struck by the obviousness of false opinion in two cases—the madmen who believe they are gods, and the dreamers who believe they are winged and think of themselves as flying in their sleep. Theaetetus, one might say, wishes to restrict his thesis to the waking sane, for whom there is partial but not total mistaking. He draws the line at self-ignorance: what appears to someone is for someone if and only if someone is a human being and knows himself to be such. He assumes he knows what a human being is (cf. 152a8–9), and on that certain ground he proposed a complete relativism. His thesis, which in modern terms would be the subjectivity of all objectivity, seems to depend on the total objectivity of subjectivity itself.

Theaetetus had hesitated to say that the dreamer, in believing himself to be a bird, is a bird, for not even the dreamer goes in the morning to the pyramids because he dreamt he flew to Egypt;[12] but Socrates looks away from the dreamer's own belief and action to the dream itself and asks whether there would be any discernible difference between Socrates' and Theaetetus' being asleep and dreaming everything they are now thinking through (*dianoeisthai*), and their conversing (*dialegesthai*) with one another while awake. Socrates could be in Theaetetus' dream or Theaetetus in Socrates', and whatever one of them then dreams by himself would not alter if they were two and wide awake. The convertibility of a separate two, though together, into a one with an illusory other exemplifies the thesis of Theaetetus. If the resemblance Socrates and Theaetetus bear to one another concealed an identity, as would be the case if either dreamt the other, the speeches of one would be the speeches of the other, and each would be testing his own offspring. The dreaming of the individual Socrates-Theaetetus would generate a phantom offspring, as immune from the charge of falsity as it is closed to the possibility of its being true. There would then be no light into which it could be brought (157d1), but its instantaneous self-generation would allow for its instantaneous self-destruction in the ever-fleeting contact of the same with the same.

Theaetetus accepts the complete transposability of a shared conversation into a private communion, despite the consequence (but perhaps because of it) that Socrates would not then have the maieutic art and still be barren of wisdom. The equivalence of either transposition, in fact, has been inserted into the very form the dialogue itself has. Euclides had taken a narration, in which Socrates reported Theaetetus' speeches as well as his own, and put it back into direct discourse. Euclides believes that the direct discourse he has restored has not altered in its moving in and out of Socrates' narration. His indifference to the difference is the same as equating the talk you and I are having with the talk you and I have after the talk one of us dreamt has been converted into the talk you and I are having. The mutual bonding of the speakers—two agents—in the first conversation gets established in the second by one of them. One of them becomes the other's patient. But to restore the first conversation as simply speeches seems to suppress the mutual bonding of the speakers and to be indistinguishable from one's talking to oneself—a single complex of agent and patient. Thinking (*dianoeisthai*), however, is conversing (*dialegesthai*) when the soul asks itself and answers, affirms or denies. A conversation, whether open or not, would thus seem to be invariant, no matter how often quotation marks were put around it and struck out again. Is thinking, then, a kind of dreaming, and does the soul, as though it was a double agent, in asking itself a question, consistently delude itself? Perhaps the soul can be awake even in its silent self-questioning, and it does not always need the confirmation of publicity. Is there a daylight for the soul, in whose illumination thinking is possible? Without such daylight, incoherence and self-contradiction would be as much a hallucination as are, according to the thesis of Theaetetus, the hallucinations of becoming.

Theaetetus agrees that the truth cannot be time-bound. To assert just once that one is a god could be unqualifiedly true, while to assert all the rest of one's life that one is a human being would be false. The proponents of Theaetetus' thesis do not intend this; instead, they propose to preserve the truth of every instant and eliminate time. The thesis, which seems to be about motion, is a doctrine of atomicity. There is nothing but the other. Every nonidentity is an other, for each must be taken as a whole. "Socrates sick" is not a being plus an accident but an inseparable unit—a simple complex like mud—in which neither Socrates nor sickness has any priority, temporal or otherwise. Socrates does not get well while being sick or get sick while being well. He alters without changing. There is no being or becoming because everything always stands in need of another to be or to become. If numbers were beings, every number would be a ratio. Two would be twice. Being, then, is the mutual bonding together of whatever two are indispensable for each other.

That we speak of two as two and not one is the flaw in the language of habit; it is at the root of all our hallucinations of becoming. The origin of this habitual language is wholly mysterious, for the revised language seems to be parasitic on it and derivative from what it wants to deny. We are compelled to speak of two when there is only one, but this compulsion is inexplicable if there is only one. The necessity that binds two nonbeings together into being is a necessity of fact. The fact or being is contingent, but the character of every fact is necessary. Knowledge is not of the facts but of the necessary character of the facts whatever they are. The being of any being is known before any being is sensed, but every being is sensed and thereby known. Knowledge is sense at the same time that it is knowledge of the un-sensed and nonexistent causes of sense. The between of Theaetetus' thesis, like the between which Theaetetus himself is, is a phantom. Theaetetus has not given birth.

The dialogue up to this point, just before Theaetetus begins to abandon his own offspring, has been carried through on the assumption that Theodorus understands Theaetetus' soul correctly. Just as the thesis of Theaetetus entails that his soul be of the sort Theodorus says it is, so his soul if it is of this sort entails the thesis he proposes. Socrates has gone the midwives one better. He has figured out, with the clue Theodorus supplied, who the parents of Theaetetus' offspring must be. The figurative poetry of Homer has mated with the literal prose of Protagoras to produce a ghostly image (*eidôlon*), which Homer called the soul that he likened to a dream. Theaetetus has to wake up. But Socrates has so vividly presented this dream, which originally had been Theaetetus' own, that Theodorus cannot but find it amazing when Socrates asks Theaetetus if he can bear to expose it. Theodorus is shocked to learn that the baby he sponsored is to be killed. He does not realize that if Theaetetus can put up with setting his thesis aside even though it is his own, which Theodorus' knowledge of Theaetetus' soul assures him he will do, the thesis is already refuted, since Theaetetus would then be affirming his authorship while denying its truth. This is the only way to kill a ghost.

Theodorus can live his own life if he is safe from the opinions of others. Protagorean scepticism guarantees his neutrality in philosophy. But Protagoras only guarantees it because his authority is godlike; if he is a human being, he can have no authority. The thesis holds for every sentient being. Men alone do not know that they know. The pig is not blind to its knowledge; men need to be enlightened. Protagoras must be either a beast or a god if he knows what no other man knows. If men do not heed Protagoras, they are ignorant; once they do, he is ignorant. Protagoras can be wise only as long as he is not an authority. He therefore cannot help Theodorus to keep his distance from philosophy. Socrates offers Theodorus a way out: Protagoras' Truth spoke in jest from the inner sanctum of his book. Theodorus refuses to take this way out; he can no more conceive of Protagoras' playfulness than of his own. He prefers that Protagoras contradict himself than that he lack seriousness, but he wants to conceal from others his acknowledgment of the self-contradiction. If he is himself not the instrument of the refutation, he has kept his friendship with Protagoras intact and not argued against his own opinion.

Theodorus is another Hippolytus. He reserves for himself the right to be insincere. He is unwittingly playful, but if no one can publicly charge him with it, he does not mind. Theodorus craves respectability. He has hitherto obtained it through the Protagorean version of the thoughtless saying "You have your opinion, I have mine." Protagoras can still be of help to Theodorus in any city in which the neutrality of the spectator is respected. Theodorus is perfectly safe from self-exposure in Athens, but Socrates asks whether he could get away with it in Sparta, where the spectators are compelled to strip themselves naked if they wish to look at the nakedness of others. If Theodorus could not persuade the Spartans to make an exception in his case, he would not stay, but he believes he can persuade the present company to leave him alone. Theodorus can always find a place congenial to his studies; unlike Socrates, he is neither bound to Athens nor in need of others. He regards himself as completely free. For Socrates to get Theodorus to examine the conditions of his freedom would entail the denial of his freedom as he understands it. But to concede him a privileged position would turn him into another god, whose wisdom is not open to question. Socrates will have to use just the right mixture of compulsion and blandishment to persuade Theodorus to give up the advantages of dreaming.

VIII. Protagoras Revised
(162b8–171e9)

Theaetetus' offspring has two parents, neither of which is exactly the same in their union as each is apart from it. Socrates therefore examines each of them separately—the Protagorean doctrine with Theodorus, the Homeric-Heraclitean doctrine again with Theodorus, and Theaetetus' with Theaetetus. He had already made the transition to Protagoras himself as other than Theaetetus' Protagoras when he spoke of his own infallibility in thought if knowledge is perception (160d1). From then on, Socrates blurs the difference between perception and opinion. This blurring, of which Theaetetus is unaware, sponsors his countering Theaetetus' physiology with lexical arguments, in which the words men use are treated as if their meanings are as plain as perceptions, and one neither had to ask, for example, whether memory was a perception, nor had to refrain from all talk of knowing as other than something lexically distinct from perceiving. Socrates himself points out the unfair advantage he takes right at the beginning. He asks Theaetetus whether he is not amazed to be suddenly as wise as any man or god, but this is to invoke the opinion that the gods are, and are wise, whereas Protagoras in Theaetetus' version should hold that not only do men not know that they know, but men believe they know what they do not know. Theaetetus, however, does not distinguish between primary hearing, through which this or that sound is known, and hearsay, through which the gods are known to be.

Protagoras, or his spokesman, gets out of the difficulty in another way. Socrates disregards Protagoras' express denial of knowing whether the gods are or are not, and since he only knows what he knows, Socrates cannot question him as if he accepted the opinion of others as his own. Protagoras demands that they refute him with demonstrative necessity, without demagogery or images. He demands a much higher standard for falsification than verification of the Protagorean measure. Protagoras did not give a proof; he only made an assertion, for what proof could he have given which would not have contradicted his measure? Before one adopts his measure as one's own, whatever man says that he is a god seems mad. Though one might persuade him that he is not a god, one could still be puzzled as to how one could prove it to him; but after one has adopted the measure, one would simply leave to everyone his beliefs, and proof of the sort Protagoras asks for would be meaningless. Socrates lets Protagoras appeal to an opinion Theaetetus and Theodorus share about mathematical proof right after Socrates has had him reject a common opinion about the gods. It is unclear why one is superior to the other: Theaetetus' definition of surds was no worse for its use of images.

The first of Socrates' lexical arguments is to ask whether in our ignorance of a foreign language or of the letters in our own, we are to deny that we hear or see if we do not know what the barbarians or the letters say or mean. Theaetetus does not observe that the difference in what the literate and illiterate know when they look at letters is not at issue, but whether there is knowledge when there is perception. Theaetetus grants that as a matter of course and distinguishes instead between primary perception, by means of which the illiterate knows the shape and color of the letters, and that which he denies is perception at all, by means of which the literate knows how to read. Theaetetus jumps beyond perception all too easily, for perception is for the literate still a means to knowledge even if it is not knowledge itself. Protagoras, moreover, could have turned Socrates' argument right around and said that the literate sees one thing and the illiterate another, and they do not differ any more than "Socrates sick" does from "Socrates healthy."

Socrates lets Theaetetus have his own way now, just as in the next two arguments he does not correct Theaetetus' errors, because he wishes to show Theodorus that Theaetetus' nature is not what Theodorus said it was. The spurious arguments for which Theaetetus falls are not demonstrative refutations of Protagoras' doctrine; they are demonstrations of Theodorus' misunderstanding of Theaetetus' soul. Theaetetus' pliability is not due to his liquid nature but to the incompatibility of his nature with his phantom offspring. The first hint of Theaetetus' true nature emerges in his hasty ascription of the knowledge of letters or a language to a nonaesthetic source. He thus misses something important: without the knowledge of a language we do not even hear its sounds distinctly. We cannot sort out the taps of Morse code unless we know what they stand for. So even if, as Theaetetus would have it, we do not perceive the meaning of a language, this knowledge still gives us access to what we do perceive. Perhaps Theaetetus' own science, mathematics, is the highest of these types of knowledge.

Theaetetus assumes that the way of demonstration itself is empty of knowledge. Since it does not assert that this or that being is, it should be applicable to any proposition. He therefore does not realize that Protagoras denies the principle of noncontradiction without which no demonstration is possible. Accordingly, Socrates can impose on Theaetetus the minimal conditions for demonstration without his meeting any objection. These minimal conditions are embedded in language. Socrates asks whether it is possible, of whatever one gets knowledge, if one still has a memory of that very thing (*auto touto*) and preserves it for oneself, not to know that very thing (*auto touto*) which one remembers when one remembers. Once one accepts this *auto touto* everything else follows, and Theaetetus, if his heart were in his thesis, should deny that a memory of something can ever be the same as its perception. That Theaetetus does not rely on his thesis shows how little his thesis is his own. But it shows something more, for when Protagoras is made to speak in its terms he must deny the very existence of memory. Protagoras would not grant that the memory someone has of what he experienced is an experience of the same sort as that which he had but is no longer experiencing. The memory would seem to be, not a memory of the experience, but of that which one had experienced, for one no longer has the experience; but the memory cannot be of the something directly unless it is a perception. If, however, the memory is the experience of an experience, the second experience must be present. But if the experience is present, there could not be a memory of it but just another experience, for which we have no name. Protagoras thus gives an example of what a thorough-going revision of language would involve: memory would vanish along with time. Protagoras cannot handle the presence of the absent, in which memory's peculiarity consists. The other, if not wholly other, must elude him (cf. 165c1, 3).

Socrates learned from Theodorus Theaetetus' name (*onoma*) and that as an orphan his guardians squandered his substance (*ousia*). Socrates now says that Protagoras' speech is an orphan, which they treat unphilosophically—they defeat it with words (*onomata*)—in the absence of guardians who are willing to defend it. He seems to imply that the substance or being of the speech Protagoras fathered has been left intact. He can draw this far-fetched analogy because being has been defined as property (cf. 172b4–5). Like property, there is no being by itself, but only if it is someone's being. And since it disappears if it is not someone's, Socrates will, for the sake of the just, impart being to what is not. He resurrects Protagoras, but the resurrected Protagoras—again according to the doctrine—is not the same Protagoras. He has been made better. Socrates does to the old Protagoras precisely that which the new Protagoras says is the mark of wisdom—to be able to change bad into good perceptions. The consequence of Socrates' justice is his wisdom. He is no longer barren. The mutual binding together of the dead Protagoras and the barren Socrates has produced a being that Socrates apparently cannot question, for he would then have to submit, not to the death of his first-born, but to his own. The new Protagoras-Socrates intensifies the dispute between sophistry and philosophy, for with its breakup goes the last possibility of reconciling philosophy with the city.

Protagoras' speech is in four parts: (1) Socrates' verbal quibbling and how it can be answered; (2) the restatement of the thesis, still in terms of truth; (3) the explanation of the revised thesis, now in terms of the good; (4) how Socrates should justly behave. Protagoras gets out of the lexical arguments by reaffirming the most radical atomicity. He who knows is not the same as he who does not know, for there is no same which both of them know. There is no simultaneity. Protagoras, however, cannot dissolve the knower and the known into disconnected points when he maintains the possibility of wisdom. Wisdom requires that there are states or conditions (hexeis) which persist over time. Knowledge and wisdom are not the same. Knowledge, which Protagoras mentions only once, is of the Heraclitean flux; wisdom works within the horizon of ineradicable illusion, where the non-knowers live and the same has its place. This is best exemplified not by man's or even the pig's horizon, but by the plants', to which Protagoras attributes perceptions; when he refers to men he speaks of their opinions. The wise do not touch the illusory ground of men's opinions; they are effective only if they leave this ground alone. Protagoras speaks so carefully that it is impossible to tell whether the wise in changing opinions make the apparent and the real bad get changed into the apparent and the real good, or the apparent and the real bad get replaced by the apparent and the real good. Protagoras seems to imply that this distinction is false: the change of state can be interpreted either way indifferently. If Socrates is accused of making the weaker argument the stronger, the weaker is then weaker but only comes to appear stronger. But perhaps the weaker is and appears weaker, and then is and appears stronger. It makes no sense to ask whether it is the same argument.

In recalling Socrates' example of his drinking wine when sick and healthy, Protagoras speaks instead of eating food. The doctor changes by means of drugs the patient's opinion of a food's bitterness; he knows of its bitterness from the patient. Protagoras does not explain how the doctor would know of the patient's illness if the patient told him that the food tasted pleasant. The sophist's drugs are speeches; what, then, is the soul's food? Protagoras indicates what it is only in passing. He cites the case of cities. The just and the beautiful, or the moral, is for cities what truth is for individuals; it is whatever the city says it is. But the good is not of the same order as the moral. Each city believes the moral to be good. The sick and the healthy city believe they know what the moral is; but the sick city believes the bad is moral, the healthy city the good. The moral is the ineradicable illusion of the city; it is the way in which it sees the condition it is in. It never sees its own condition apart from the moral. The good speaker makes the city akin to his own condition; his own condition consists in the power to bring about this kinship. To be good or healthy means to be an agent-power, to be bad or sick means to be a patient-power. A city that can resist its own assimilation to another city is a healthy city, and the city in the best condition can feed on every other city.

The same holds for the soul. The soul is healthy when it assimilates other souls to itself—the teacher surrounds himself with his own duplicates—and the soul is sick when it cannot resist such absorption. Protagoras had himself proved to be quite dead. He could not change for long either Theodorus or Theaetetus into himself; but he now tempts Socrates with the hope of almost infinite power. All he must do is point out the errors of his disciples which are due to themselves and their former associations and refrain from perplexing them anew (cf. 146c5–6, 167e7). If he conceals his own doubts, he can make everyone into his own kind of philosopher, and no one will ever hate him. Philosophy means love of Socrates. At the very end of Socrates' life, Protagoras proposes a radical alteration of Socrates' stance to his art and the city. Protagoras counsels badly even in death.

Wisdom is power. He is wise who can make someone or something into his own image. The wise need the unwise or sick. The city does not become wise when it becomes healthy, for it never ceases to be patient of the wise speaker. Protagoras therefore must admit a difference between apparent and real health—a difference, admittedly, the healthy patient can never draw (this is what keeps him a patient) but without which the wise could not alter another unless he himself altered. All but the wise live in the element of the derivative. The derivative is stamped as such by the identity of being and appearing, the nonderivative by their separation and its power to cause their identity for others. To be is to be an agent-power, not to be is to be a patient-power. Nonbeing somehow is. The resurrected Protagoras still contradicts himself.

Socrates apologizes to Theodorus for the inadequacy of his aid to Protagoras. Theodorus is as innocently rude as ever; he says that Socrates is being playful in deprecating his vigorous aid. He implies that Protagoras' abuse of Socrates is fair comment and, in particular, that it is unjust to be playful. Theodorus is serious; if he engaged in the investigation, Protagoras could not complain that Socrates, in talking with a child (*paidion*), was being playful (*paizein*), for Theodorus would not let Socrates get away with it. Theodorus is so serious that he takes Socrates' pun literally, as if Socrates meant that Theodorus was qualified simply because he had a long beard, not because he was serious. His seriousness in this case is reinforced by the topic: they are to consider whether Theodorus is the measure in mathematical theorems or whether all are as competent as he is in astronomy and everything else in which he is charged with superiority. Protagoras has apparently accounted for the arts that are concerned with human goods but not for those that look to the truth. If mathematics were good for men, in the Protagorean sense, it would be like medicine; but if it is bad for them, in the same sense, like poison, Theodorus would have to prove that it is good without thereby affecting its status as being true. He would have to say why men should acquire this knowledge if it is not wisdom and lacks all power, and he would have to do this while showing that there is knowledge and his theorems are knowledge.

Theodorus' self-interest therefore not only reinforces his seriousness, it seems to compel him to abandon the dead Protagoras in order that he can maintain his self-interest. The discussion seems tainted from the start. If truth is only manifest if one keeps one's distance from it, and one can only discover the truth if it is close to one's heart (cf. 165d4), then the concern with its goodness, which one's own self-interest demands, will preclude the seeing of the truth, since disinterested concern with the truth is a contradiction. Theodorus can remain the spectator he was (cf. 177c5), but then there was no falsehood, or he can now become a participant, but then there will be no truth. He can have unfalsifiability without the good, or unverifiability with it. Theodorus' seriousness, which blinds him to the possible vanity in his competence, seems to be an indispensable but self-defeating ingredient in the examination of Protagoras' measure.

Theodorus is justifiably very annoyed with Socrates; he can find no more fitting images for Socrates than those of two mythical criminals. He had foolishly assumed that Socrates was at least as respectable as the Spartans, who leave one the choice of going away. Theodorus no longer speaks of his being a spectator, for he senses that he now must fight for his very life (cf. 165e1–4). He has hitherto lived under no necessity. Socrates has so stepped up the pressure on him that he speaks of Socrates as one of the Fates who weave a destiny he must endure. Theodorus wants to be wholly passive, stripped by Socrates, beaten to the ground, and then released. He does not believe he is another Theseus or Heracles who can defeat Socrates; he does not even wish to try. Theodorus, though nothing but serious, cannot take Socrates' challenge seriously. His dedication to geometry, to which he has fled as a refuge from the unreality of speeches, prevents him from listening to what he himself says. The extravagance of his language— Socrates is a merciless killer—covers up his indifference to the question Socrates has posed. The word that best characterizes Theodorus is *pôs:* "For some reason or other (*pôs*) we inclined rather soon away from bare speeches to geometry." He refuses to come to grips with this *pôs*. Socrates is just the reverse. He glories in Theodorus' charge of his supreme criminality. Theodorus has made a most excellent likeness of his disease (cf. 148b3). He is not healthy with the power of the wise, as Protagoras had urged him to be, nor has he ever been cured by the speeches of his opponents, so as to get the semblance of health without its reality. His disease looks like injustice because it does not allow any room for consent. His disease is his strength; it is his "awesome love (*erôs*) of naked exercise in these things." If Theodorus will not begrudge him this mutual drubbing and rubbing, he will benefit both himself and Socrates. The good comes to be from a motion (cf. 153b5–7), initiated by an incurable disease which aims at beauty. Socrates could not have put more succinctly the differences between himself and Theodorus on the one hand, and himself and Protagoras on the other.

The shift from the playful or childish form of conversation, which Socrates and Theaetetus had, to the manly contest that is about to begin, seems to be a shift from innocence to experience, in which mathematics will yield to the problem of good and evil. The two contestants, however, are very unequal in their understanding of this matter; it is therefore safer to say that Theodorus stands to the problem of good and evil as Theaetetus stood to his own experience, the cause of which he did not know. Theaetetus, to be sure, has experienced evil, but the loss of his inheritance did not bother him, since he is in spite of it still generous; but Theodorus is troubled by his experience, the cause of which he does not know. Theodorus is not pregnant with any child from which he can be delivered, but Socrates does deliver him, at least in part, from his moral indignation. Socrates asks whether his own indignation was justified in his censuring the argument that made each self-sufficient in point of understanding or prudence. Theodorus had not shared his indignation when Socrates deduced that if Protagoras was right, his own maieutics was ridiculous. But Socrates draws Theodorus' attention—he would never have noticed it himself—to the equal applicability of Protagoras' measure to his own mathematics. The mathematician and the midwife must join together in order to defend themselves from Protagoras' ridicule. It is this ridiculous alliance of the knowledge of number with the knowledge of soul that makes the discussion serious.

Socrates and Theodorus agree to examine the problem of opinion by itself, independent of both Theaetetus' equation of perception and knowledge and Protagoras' concession that in matters of better and worse some men are superior to others, and these are wise. They ask Protagoras whether everyone is convinced that he is wiser than others in some things, and others wiser than he is in other things. No one takes anyone else as wiser than himself in everything, nor does anyone believe that he himself is wiser than everyone else. Socrates replaces Protagoras' assertion that whatever each opines is true for him who opines it with a much deeper observation: all men are convinced that all men opine truly and falsely. What all men share is not the Protagorean view but a conviction about the character of human opining as such. This universal conviction is not subject to doubt; men are proof against enlightenment in this regard by any Protagorean wise man. This is not like any other opinion because men always act on it. In the greatest dangers, in which there is the greatest need and the greatest fear, men seek for saviors in the belief that others are wiser than themselves, and in the expectation that their rulers will save them, they behave toward them as if they were gods. Socrates surely overstates his case. The saviors sought for are not always those who men believe surpass themselves in knowledge. Greater strength or daring is all that is sometimes needed, and those who need it believe they themselves know how it is best to be used. Socrates' exaggeration, moreover, would imply that all men are convinced that the sole title to rule is knowledge; neither Protagoras nor the many would agree. Socrates may be pointing to his own peculiar strength, the knowledge of his own ignorance, which is neither a saving wisdom for others nor yet wisdom's lack as false opinion. Socrates' knowledge of ignorance has no place in the domain of human convictions.

Theodorus conceded that it would be unbelievable if there was someone who was not convinced of the false opinion of another. Any one can always be paired with another who is convinced of his lack of wisdom. No one, therefore, is ever thought to be wise in anything by everybody. Socrates chooses as his example Theodorus. He asks him whether thousands upon thousands (*myrioi*) on each occasion battle against his opinion with their own, convinced that he discriminates and believes falsely. One would suppose that Theodorus of all people, who does nothing but mathematics, would object to this unscientific and hyperbolic *myrioi* (cf. 196e2). Socrates, however, has touched a raw nerve: "Yes, by Zeus, Socrates, 'truly *myrioi*' (*mala myrioi*) indeed, Homer says, since they give me all the trouble that can possibly come from men." In a comical way, and with what must be the shortest and least poetical of quotations, Theodorus assures Socrates that he is not exaggerating at all. Theodorus refers to a line in the *Odyssey*, where Telemachus is telling his father, whom he has not recognized, that in the absence of Odysseus truly thousands of hostile suitors dwell in his house. Theodorus cannot bear ridicule, but he cannot help sounding ridiculous when he expresses his indignation at the ridicule he must suffer. We recall how careful he was to avoid the imputation that he praised Theaetetus because he was in love with him, and yet we also noticed that Theodorus prides himself on his freedom and that the attraction Protagoras had for him consisted in his doctrine that apparently guaranteed his right to be left alone. Socrates will soon tell him that he cannot help but appear ridiculous, and he now shows him that Protagoras' wisdom is as subject to doubt as his own. Its popular character is an illusion (cf. 161e4).

Protagoras wrote a book in which this sentence appeared: "Man is the measure of all things, of the beings that (or how) they are, and of the nonbeings that (or how) they are not." Now that Protagoras is dead, we can surely imagine that no one utters it; indeed, the sentence cannot be spoken, as it is written, by anyone, though as written it has a certain plausibility. As a written sentence it does not belong to anyone, but if it is adopted and someone utters it, the sentence alters. The sentence as written is in the indicative mood, but as soon as it is read it becomes an imperative (cf. 170d6), for it commands the reader to replace "man" with "I." "Man" is a dummy word that conceals an injunction. If the injunction is carried out, it becomes once more indicative, and the speaker can then assent to it or not. The sentence does not supply the conviction as to its truth, but the speaker's own conviction prior to his utterance determines its truth or falsity. The written sentence could be true, and yet no one might believe it, but the sentence says that whatever one believes is true. So everyone in saying the sentence is false is telling the truth and denying the truth of the truth, but it is only the sentence in the book that says that everyone's denial is true. One does not have to know that the sentence is false, one only has to suppose it to be false for it to be false. But it cannot be merely because it is one's own opinion that an opinion is true, nor merely because no one holds a certain opinion that it is false.

That the invalidation of Protagoras' sentence only follows at once when a human being reads the sentence, identifies himself as a human being, and obeys the injunction, can readily be seen if we replace human being with any other sentient being in the sentence. He might be thought a fool if someone wrote that pig or crane is the measure of all things, but the sentence would not be invalid in itself. Theaetetus drew the line at self-ignorance when Socrates mentioned dreams and madness as the ordinary counterexamples to Protagoras' doctrine. And it now is evident that the ground of his qualms were wholly in accord with the self-contradiction in his doctrine. Protagoras appealed to Theaetetus because both had forgotten themselves in taking themselves for granted.

Socrates did not examine Protagoras' measure while Protagoras was still alive but only after his death. If to be dead is to be without life or soul and thus to be like something written down, a self-contradiction would in this sense be dead, for that it is a self-contradiction becomes manifest as soon as it returns to life in its being spoken. To give it life is to destroy it. Protagoras' measure thus encapsulates the pre-Socratic failure to understand soul, for this failure is the same as their inability to account for themselves. Self-contradiction is grounded in ignorance of soul; and it would be no accident that Plato has Socrates formulate the principle of noncontradiction in the context of a discussion of soul.[13] Theodorus never speaks of Protagoras as dead; he does not use the past tense of him until he has been cured of his infatuation (178e7). The half-life Protagoras leads in Theodorus' imagination, and which Socrates has fostered by twice calling Theodorus Protagoras emerges in Socrates' picturing him as he pops out of the ground up to his neck and, after much abuse of Socrates' folly, slips below and is gone. Protagoras is likely to be wiser than themselves, Socrates tells Theodorus, because he is older. Protagoras' written sentence is the most extreme parody of the law, which necessarily asserts that it is superior to the wise man on the spot. Protagoras' measure parodies this because it insists, like the law, on its own wisdom while enjoining each of us to think of ourselves as the wise man on the spot. Protagoras' Truth straddles the timeless and the now in an impossible way. She lacks prudence.

IX. THALES
(172a1–177c5)

Socrates has now fully justified the liberty he took in revising Protagoras. He does not, however, repeat exactly what he had had Protagoras say in his own defense. For one thing, he adds to the lawful things that the city lays down for itself, about which there can be no dispute, the holy and the unholy, which Protagoras, in accordance with his exclusion of the gods from his speaking and writing, had not mentioned. For another, he interprets Protagoras' good as the useful and therefore speaks of the superiority of a city's opinion in point of truth, whereas Protagoras had divorced wisdom from truth. The parallelism Socrates draws between the recalcitrance to verifiability of the individual's opinion about hot, dry, and sweet, and the susceptibility to verification of the individual's health or illness, on the one hand, and the same recalcitrance of the city's opinion about the noble, just, and holy, and the same susceptibility of the city's advantage or disadvantage, on the other—this parallelism is more apparent than real. In the private sphere, health has a much higher rank than hot, dry, and sweet, but in the political, the advantageous as such is not asserted to be higher than the holy, the just, and the noble. Further, the individual's perception of the hot, dry, and sweet is thought to be symptomatic of his health or illness, whereas it is not as obvious that the city's opinion about the noble, just, and holy are signs of its health or illness. The city could have on its books one set of opinions and yet transgress them, but it is impossible for the individual to contravene the perceptions he has. The truth of a perception, moreover, is not the same as its correctness, for no one concludes from the wine's bitterness when he is sick that the wine is bitter. But the city never ceases to identify its own opinion as true with its correctness.

The parallelism has forced the differences between perception and opinion to be wholly blurred. The senses are thought to work independently of one another, and it seems not to be inevitable that if the individual tastes the wine as sweet he must feel it to be cool. That what the city lays down as holy should in no way determine its opinion about the just, nor its opinion about the just its opinion about the noble—this is not at all self-evident. No one pays attention to diverse perceptions of the same "hot," since everyone assumes that, since heat is a continuous magnitude, anyone who does not feel hot now can be made to feel hot later. But is the just a continuous magnitude of the same kind, and is there anything like the "luke-just"? If to pay one's taxes is luke-just, it would be because it is clearly to the advantage of everyone to do so, but if to rescue a drowning man is more just, the just would cease to be in the same sense to one's own advantage. One would therefore have to distinguish between the just which all cities lay down as just and the just about which cities disagree, but this distinction is meaningless for perceptions. There is no praise or blame attached to perceptions in themselves, but there is to opinions and the actions in accord with them.

A limited Protagoreanism must confuse perception and opinion for the following reason. Its proponents look at the city from the outside, from which vantage point it is obvious that the city holds opinions and that these opinions differ from the opinions of other cities and from its own former and future opinions. They therefore conclude that the lawful is as private to each city as perceptions are to the individual. But though a Theaetetus will not insist that as each color appears to him so it does for every or any other human being, each city will insist, to the point of war and beyond, that the just is what it says it is for every other city. Had these Protagoreans paid sufficient attention to the difference between the city's perspective and their own, they would have gone on to distinguish between the individual's perceptions as they are by nature and as they are in opinion—for which the white of one healthy man is the same as another's—and again between the noble, just, and holy as they possibly are by nature and as they are in opinion. But Protagoreans cannot do so, for they deny that there are such things by nature, a denial that no more follows of itself from the variety of political opinions than does the consensus about perception entail automatically that their doctrine is false. On the basis of their understanding of nature, they infer that the individual's perceptions as given by nature are of the same order as positings of the city. The city, they then should say, must be acting in accordance with nature in believing its own opinions to be true. But they do not draw this conclusion; rather, they project the subjectivity of the city's opinions, which they observe from the outside, and the truth of the city's opinions, upon which the city itself insists, back onto the individual's perceptions—an individual who neither observes their subjectivity nor proclaims their truth. This projection is inadvertent on their part, since they do not see where they themselves are standing. They would only sink more deeply into incoherence if they replied that the intersubjective agreement about perceptions corresponds to the agreement among fellow citizens about morality and religion. For the first is a universal agreement constant over time and place, and the second is not. It is to the credit of Socrates' Protagoras that he never mentioned nature or confused truth with wisdom.

Socrates has brought Theodorus to the point where he is trapped in the middle of a three-sided conflict within himself: (1) the necessity to accept the opinion of the many and abandon the measure of Protagoras, whose attraction for him was its assertion that his opinion was no worse than that of the many; (2) his indignation at the many for setting themselves up as his judges; (3) his subservience to the opinion of the many, whose ridicule he fears. A modified Protagoreanism still seems possible, in which competence is neither arbitrary nor in the control of the many. Theodorus, however, does not have any such competence, for it has been confined to those arts which everyone would agree are the causes of human goods. Theodorus' competence, in terms of its lack of obvious usefulness, has much more the status which the new doctrine of Protagoras has ascribed to the city's opinions about the noble, just, and holy. Neither the city nor this doctrine has any place for him. Socrates must give him a place from which he can look down on his tormentors. The starting point, therefore, is the kind of activity to which Socrates and Theodorus in their different ways are devoted.

Socrates remarks that the denial of being to the just and the holy involves them in a bigger argument than before. "Are we not at leisure, Socrates?" Theodorus asks. With a demonic prescience (cf. 154e8), Theodorus picks the single characteristic which marks off what he does from the business of the city. But is Socrates at leisure? He says in reply, "It looks as if we are." Socrates is thinking of his forthcoming trial, at which he will not speak at leisure but will be forced to follow the rules of the court. Theodorus is entirely oblivious of the import of what Socrates will say, for he knows nothing of the situation Socrates is in, who soon will not just face ridicule—Theodorus' bogey—but capital punishment. Although they have long been friends, Theodorus has no interest in Socrates' fate, not because he does not have some regard for Socrates, but because his fate is not his own and belongs to the here and now to which Theodorus never pays any attention. Theodorus could very well have been the silent auditor to whom Socrates narrated, more than twenty years before, the talk he had on moderation with the future tyrants Charmides and Critias (cf. 155d3–e2); for though the time of the *Charmides* narration is the day after that talk, and the place is still Athens, Socrates' auditor has not heard of the battle at Potidaea which heralded the start of the Peloponnesian War (153b5–6), and Socrates properly omits to tell him what he told his acquaintances about it. What links the midwife and the mathematician is their unpolitical character. The *daimonion's* restraining of Socractes from politics is more than matched by Theodorus' indifference to the worldly.

The leisure of the philosophers consists in their being able to repeat an inquiry and flit from subject to subject. The repeatability of an inquiry—neither does the inquiry alter the being it examines nor the being impose a time limit on its discovery—has the side effect of easily becoming or looking like gossip, which is equally outside the vital concerns of both the teller and the listener. In political life, however, and particularly in the law courts, there is no possibility of our starting all over again, not only because a decision must be made now—whether it be to condemn this man or acquit that one in the face of our ultimate ignorance of what justice is, or to make war or peace on evidence which is necessarily incomplete—but because our deeds and speeches change the conditions for our next deeds and speeches. Time is always running out, and the time is never the same. The water clock of the courtroom is both that which times the length of one's speech and that which characterizes in its flowing the mutual bonding of the speaking and its occasion into a unique moment. The Homeric-Heraclitean thesis, if asserted about the nature of nature, seems an extravagant and metaphorical conceit, but it is the literal truth about political life.

Both the pettifogger as slave and the jury as his master are enslaved in the flow of things, but the pettifogger is twice enslaved, for his own life is often at stake, and he must run just to save it. The low cunning he must practice ties him to his master, and the more he is successful the more he becomes one with him. But the master, since he never has to exercise his wits, remains sunk in the belief in his own sovereignty. Theodorus is delighted by Socrates' picture. After Socrates has compelled him to speak, Socrates tells him he is not compelled to speak. Theodorus picks up the distinction between masters and slaves: he is the master, the speeches are his slaves. Although Socrates pointed to the indifference of our own mistakes to the being we examine, Theodorus stresses the patient waiting of the speeches until we resolve to complete them. The *logos* is not our judge, for there is no necessity to follow the *logos*. Theodorus wants to be the jury, whom Socrates would always flatter with pleasant speeches (cf. 177c3–5). Not in spite but because of his great distance from the city, Theodorus imitates the city.

Socrates' portrait of the tiptop philosophers begins as a portrait of Theodorus and Theaetetus. He begins with what they do not know. Their ignorance is of four kinds. They do not know the way to the marketplace, nor where the courthouse is, or any other common gathering place of the city; they neither see nor hear the so-called unwritten and written laws and decrees; not even in a dream does it occur to them to join a political club or private party; and they are as unaware of the high or low birth of anyone in the city, or of what

I.130

evil befell anyone's maternal or paternal ancestor, as of the number of buckets in the sea. The philosopher's ignorance of the all-too-human things is total, for he does not even know that he does not know them. He therefore cannot inquire into the being of these things, for his thought is convinced—it does not know—of how petty and nonexistent they are. He has turned away from them out of contempt. His understanding of the beautiful and the noble determines his understanding of being. His body remains in the city, but he never asks what body is, for his thought, oriented by geometry and astronomy, never condescends to investigate what is near at hand, but flies everywhere below the earth and above the heavens, inquiring into the nature of each of the beings. Theodorus' question—"How do you mean this, Socrates?"—illustrates what Socrates has just said: Theodorus does not know what he does. The peculiarity of the *Theaetetus* is that, despite its concern with the difference between opinion and knowledge, there is no conversion in it to philosophy from non-philosophy. Theodorus is a professional, and Theaetetus an apprentice; so neither of them has any doubt that there is knowledge, or any awareness of the problem of philosophy's possibility, for after all, Theodorus already is flying.

Thales looked up at the stars and fell into a well. He stumbled into what he thought was the principle of everything, but he did not expect to find out the nature of the stars by looking at what was at his feet. And yet if the ground on which one stands is unseen, one does not know what in the ground makes it possible for one to look up. It is not every kind of ground from which one can take off. The ground must somehow be illuminated prior to one's looking up, for one does not in fact visit the stars. The Thalesian philosopher does not ask this question: if one were on a star, and looked at the earth, would one then be able to understand the ground upon which one formerly stood? One's own place is not simply interchangeable with any other place, for the sameness of the measure from Athens to Thebes and from Thebes to Athens does not entail the sameness of the motion in either direction. This is what the witticism of the Thracian servant girl seems to mean, but Socrates twists it in such a way that he too can apparently be bracketed with Theodorus.

What is before the philosopher and at his feet is not himself but his neighbor, about whom he hardly knows whether he is a human being and what he is doing. But the philosopher asks what is a human being, and what it is peculiarly fitting for human nature to do or suffer. Heaven is to earth as Socratic questioning is to gossip. But is that Socratic questioning? If one knows nothing about one's neighbor, one must take one's own nature as human nature, and one's own activity and experience as the standard. Neither geometry nor astronomy can disclose what is one's own nature, for it seems to be part of being human that one has a neighbor, and his nearness is not susceptible to measure. If the astronomer looked at himself astronomically, he should conclude that he was a bird and not a human being at all.[14] And the geometer could as well be dreaming as awake if to know human nature were the same as to know that the odd is never even (190b6–7). It is Socrates who knows the name, reputation, and wealth of Theaetetus' father and who cares more for potential philosophers in Athens than in Cyrene.[15] But Theodorus, who can only see what is close to him through the most distant prospect, must understand Theaetetus' soul imagistically, for the image is the vehicle for losing sight of what is before one.

The ridicule the philosopher encounters whenever he is compelled to speak of what concerns human beings is matched by the ridicule the pettifogger encounters whenever he is willing to discuss what justice and injustice, human happiness and misery are. The philosopher, however, must laugh hypothetically, for he can never compel the merely clever to rise up to his heights; and even if such a discussion occurred, no one would join him in his laughter, for they would not see what was ridiculous. Yet the philosopher seems compelled to laugh at himself, since his success evidently falls short of his aspirations. Theodorus is unaware of either difficulty. He believes it is possible that Socrates could persuade everyone and the consequence would be more peace and less evil among men. Socrates tells him his wish is impossible; Socrates' speech is not a proposal for legislation. The good cannot be unless there is something contrary to it. It is hard to make out what Socrates means; he cannot, at any rate, be like Theodorus, who does not know of this necessity.

Socrates could mean, it seems, only one of two things. That the good cannot come to be for men unless the bad comes to be along with it seems to be the theme of Plato's *Republic*, but here he speaks of being, not becoming. Or that since the bad haunts mortal nature of necessity, the bad ever attends the good which the philosopher obtains. But this would be a necessity of the contingent, which would not explain how Socrates can speak of the bad as a paradigm at rest in its being,[16] or how the philosopher when dead gets accepted into the region free of evils. Socrates says nothing about the immortality of the soul; he never even speaks of the philosopher's soul. Those of low cunning have a soul, the philosopher has only thought (*dianoia*). Socrates says that the punishment for injustice is misery, but since misery is to be out of sight of the divine, there is no punishment unless the unjust comes to recognize his own blindness, and such blindness is ineradicable. He therefore implies that happiness solely consists in the examination of what happiness is and all other kindred questions;[17] or, more precisely, since it necessarily consists in the examination of the bad as well as of the good, and consequently of one's neighbor and what is at one's feet, its goodness is inseparable from the badness of others. Socrates has moved from a celebration of the free Theodorus, whose inquiry into the nature of every being he calls neither wisdom nor happiness, to a celebration of political philosophy, whose ground is the despised human things and whose guide is the gods. Socrates thus looks even more ridiculous than Theodorus, for without a shred of proof or the shadow of a doubt he proclaims what god is, while saying the philosopher has trouble in finding out what man is. Socrates assigns every virtue to the philosopher except moderation.

X. Sortness
(177c6–183c4)

Socrates separates the discussion of future affects from that of present ones. The first is conducted with the revised Protagoras; the second examines the problem itself, since its Heraclitean proponents are too incoherent, according to Theodorus, to be questioned. The first discussion is reminiscent of the first book of the *Republic,* but with these differences: the just is assumed to be other than good, the good to be the beneficial, and the city to lay down all its laws with a single aim, that they be as beneficial as possible. This has one of three consequences: the just, the noble, and the holy are merely names for the beneficial; these names designate, in the present, degrees and kinds of future benefits; or, whenever the city makes a mistake, its errors are the just, the noble, and the holy. Socrates gives an example of the third possibility in the *Republic,* where he says the most beneficial marriages are sacred (458e4) and therefore marriage between brother and sister is to be permitted in certain cases. For the supposedly sacred prohibition against incest is only sacred because the city has not hit upon the good. Socrates, however, now has his own way because Theodorus is no Thrasymachus and cannot ask for whose benefit in the city does the city legislate. Theodorus is too far away from the city to see the difference between the greed of the brutish shepherd and the peevish rebelliousness of the unenlightened sheep (174d3–e1), which makes it as impossible for the city to acknowledge that it makes a mistake as a whole as for it to agree as a whole that in some instances it had hit upon the good. Would it then suffice to discredit Protagoras' thesis if the rulers would admit that sometimes they make a mistake? For Thrasymachus it would, but not for Clitophon, who is so bold as to maintain that the ruler's opinion about his own advantage is the justice of the stronger and therefore, presumably, that as long as he held this opinion (i.e., does not change the laws), he has not made a mistake.[18]

In order, then, for Socrates' argument to stand as more than *ad Theodorum*, it would be necessary that he consider whether or not the city does have a common good, but this would be to shift from opinion to knowledge and insert at this point the whole *Republic*. That is impossible, since Socrates has already summarized the culmination of the *Republic* (Books V–VII) in his previous speeches about the just, that is, the philosophic, life. Socrates had no need to go through the city to bring Theodorus to philosophy. And since he replaced the movement out of the cave with only an implicit argument about the need to start in the cave, he can ask Theodorus to look at the facts (*pragma*) as if the facts were known. Theodorus' inexperience thus makes it possible for him and Socrates to reach at once an agreement about the city which only political philosophy could establish. Theodorus has no notion of how treacherous an argument based on opinion can be.

The difference between perception and opinion becomes evident as soon as the future is introduced, for whereas there is no perception of the future, an opinion about the future does not differ qua opinion from an opinion about the present. Socrates can then show that the nonexpert's opinion about a future perception is less authoritative than the expert's; but what he does not stress is that the expert's opinion merely anticipates the nonexpert's, and the ultimate authority as to the correctness of the expert's opinion is the nonexpert's perception. The expert knows the same truth as the nonexpert for a longer time (cf. 158e1, 178e8). Art, on this basis, cannot be distinguished from knack or experience, or the spurious from the genuine art, as Socrates' example of cookery indicates. Theodorus has been led from siding with the many against Protagoras to his being shown the unbridgeable gulf between himself and the many, and then to a realliance between himself and the many. The city is the authority, not because it can figure out what is most beneficial for itself, but because it must confirm it as beneficial. The experts know the taste of the city better than the city knows it. Theaetetus had suggested this when Socrates asked him whether the taste of the doctrine satisfied him and he put off answering until he could hear what the expert Socrates would say.

The new revision of the Protagorean thesis is now stronger than ever: the wise know in advance what everyone will hold to be true.

Socrates for this reason ended his speech on the philosopher with a prediction about the afterlife, at which time, apparently, the miserable will know their own misery. Wisdom is ultimately consensus. It solely consists in knowing which turn the endless flow of things will take next. The wise are just one step ahead of the unwise, but the step never remains hidden from the unwise because it is their own step. The wise are those most honored in the cave, who predict which image is going to flash by next: Theodorus is an astronomer. The argument, therefore, against Socratic wisdom is that it can never be confirmed in this way; he cannot tell the many now what the many will later see for themselves. Socrates will suggest that had his trial lasted more than a day he could have won an acquittal, but he does not say that the Athenians would then have seen that the unexamined life is not worth living, for they have already had a lifetime to make up their minds about Socrates' way of life. Theodorus, on the other hand, can console himself; he may at any moment look ridiculous, but in the long run the last laugh will be his. The arts and sciences, no matter how abstruse, are not a standing threat to the city's opinions.

Now that all opinion has to submit to the authority of what at some time will be present opinion, Socrates must show that the grounds for asserting that present opinion is true are groundless. This, I think, he accomplishes, but the paradox of Socratic wisdom becomes all the more vivid. The many are now the authority, but the "physiology," which supports their authority, asserts what the many do not believe, that everything is in motion. They believe that some things are in motion and others at rest, and Socrates shares this belief, but he does not hold that their opinion is authoritative. So we are confronted on the one hand with a doctrine that in elevating the opinion of the many to knowledge undercuts that very elevation and, on the other, with Socrates, who in distinguishing between opinion and knowledge, and again between spurious and genuine happiness, asserts what the many will never accept—and yet he confirms in a way in which the many do not accept what the many do accept—the being of both motion and rest. It is perhaps this duality that allows Socrates to say that the greatest madness is moderation incarnate.

Theodorus claims to be familiar with the proponents of the Homeric-Heraclitean thesis. But as he goes on to describe them, he gets very angry with them, and far from their sharing in a common doctrine, he implies that they have no doctrine at all. When Socrates mildly suggests that when they are at peace and not fighting they do speak coherently and firmly to their pupils (whomever they want to make like themselves), Theodorus becomes even more indignant and denies that any of them has a single pupil. Theodorus believes they

are crazy and inspired; he finds them as unapproachable as Theaetetus had found the uninspired body-people repellent (cf. 156a1),
who do not admit that anything is but what they can get their hands
on. Theodorus' two speeches seem to imitate the incoherence he as-
cribes to the Heracliteans. The literal Theodorus resents the literalness of the Heracliteans. They are what they should be according to
the writings of Heraclitus, for this is not, as Socrates suggested, a
pretence on their part: they are unintelligible by nature and through
nature. Each of them is in the most literal sense an original: neither
the cause of others nor caused by another. Each is his own cause. This
is intolerable to the professional Theodorus, who takes as his model
for rationality the orderly transmission of knowledge from teacher to
pupil. He presents the soul-destroying and *logos*-destroying character
of the doctrine, and yet he does not conclude that this refutes the
doctrine. It would still be true with regard to being, even if one could
not live the doctrine on the level of either speech or soul.

Socrates had conducted his examination of Theaetetus on the assumption that what Theodorus had said imagistically about Theaetetus he had meant literally. This engendered a phantom offspring
in Theaetetus. But Theodorus now seems to believe that if man is not
the measure of all things, motion could still be the nature of all things,
for the Heracliteans prove by their very existence that this is the nature
of all things. Theodorus, however, has a way out of this dilemma; he
proposes that they treat the doctrine as a problem (*problêma*). A problem is the geometer's term for the setting out of a construction. They
are to attempt to construct an argument that will exhibit the behavior
of the Heracliteans, as Theodorus understands their behavior, without introducing soul. Such a construction will be intelligible while
leaving the Heracliteans as phenomenally unintelligible as they were
before. Theodorus looks upon the soul as if it were a problem in
astronomy: given the erratic motion of a planet, construct a model
that will fully describe the motion and yet will not causally explain
the motion.[19] Just as, if the planets were gods, they could do by will
what we show them as doing by design, so too the Heracliteans, each
with a god within him, will preserve their irrationality while displaying
in our model a rational order.

Theodorus is caught in a contradiction. If the souls of the Heracliteans look the way they do because we see them perspectivally (in
the perspective of war, as Socrates says), Theodorus cannot then say
that they look as they are. As an astronomical phenomenon, their
cause cannot be known, but if their cause is known, they cannot be
an astronomical phenomenon. Theodorus thus illustrates in himself
the stumbling of Thales. He looks, without knowing it, through both

ends of a telescope at once; the near becomes distant and the distant near. And so in observing from afar, as he supposes, the enthusiasm of others, he catches it himself. Theodorus' problem, then, cannot be construed on Theodorus' terms, for as Socrates points out, if the Heracliteans say what they are, the Parmenideans too would say what they are, and neither would be the nature of all things. Theodorus and Socrates got so involved with the Heracliteans that they forgot Parmenides, but now they are both trapped in the middle of the Heraclitean-Parmenidean tug-of-war. Not only are they ridiculous in the eyes of the city, they will be equally ridiculous in the eyes of philosophy if they neither take refuge with immobility nor drag themselves to safety in motion. Socrates takes it for granted that the body-people cannot rescue them.

Although the authority of the city has exposed the inadequacy of one version of Protagoras' thesis and has left Socrates as deficient in knowledge as he claims to be, it cannot be invoked again. For though the shoemaker can be neutral and laugh at both camps, on the grounds that one effectively cancels the other, neither Socrates nor Theodorus can withdraw. Even if Theodorus—his eagerness for discussion is feigned (161a7, 181b8)—gets out of the engagement as soon as he justly can and Socrates too slips out of danger in an apparently shameless way, still they both somehow recognize the authority of philosophy. In his sudden recollection of Parmenides, Socrates remembers the problem of being. The ultimate question is not what is knowledge, but what is being; it is not whether knowledge is compatible with becoming, but whether becoming is compatible with being. The exigencies of the dialogue have aligned Protagoras with the Heracliteans, but in his assertion that it is impossible to opine what is not (167a7–8), he is the representative of Parmenides as well. Protagoras will thus be demolished along with Homer and Heraclitus, only to reappear once more with the problem of false opinion. The ever-changing masks of Protagoras in the *Theaetetus* are the evidence for Socrates' last question—the sameness and the difference of sophist, statesman, and philosopher. Behind Theodorus' naive bafflement at the Heracliteans lies the problem of nonbeing.

Theodorus seems already to have admitted what Socrates is going to prove, that the Heracliteans cannot speak without contradiction; but Socrates does not admit the paradox of Theodorus, that their necessary silence is in accordance with the nature of their souls, and so they do not need any speech to show that motion is the nature of all things. Socrates, however, does take advantage of their silence; he has Theodorus agree to what in his former exposition he said they denied. He now speaks of place and of motion from place to place (cf. 153e1–2) and thus introduces two kinds of motion which cut across the former distinction of passive and active motions. Socrates is not being wholly arbitrary, for he has just implied that the denial of place properly belongs to the Parmenideans, whose "the one" is at rest in itself without place (180e4). Protagoras, it seems, in joining for the moment with Heraclitus, imported something of Parmenides, and it was his essential eclecticism that gave the doctrine all its persuasiveness. Socrates, at any rate, now shows the amazing clarity that comes with the discernment of kinds. He disregards the question of cause and effect and looks instead at what is first for us.

Motion had formerly come to light as part of a doctrine; the doctrine determined the distinctions to be made. But Socrates and Theodorus now come to an agreement about motion that is prior to any "theory" about motion. Its priority appears most strikingly in two ways. First, locomotion, in Theaetetus' physiology, only occurred in the "between" of agent and patient, and the *genesis* of *sensibilia* was this locomotion, while alteration was denied, for there was no change in the same; but neither the locomotion they did admit, nor the alteration they did not, was perceptible. Second, Theaetetus' physiology said that there was only motion and yet talked constantly of *genesis* or becoming. But as soon as one looks at locomotion, one does not see there any coming-to-be. Homer had spoken of *genesis,* the moderns of motion, but the distinction Socrates makes shows at once that they are not the same. That he never asks Theodorus whether his classification of motions is complete is the only hint he gives of the difficulty involved in becoming. Socrates therefore does not ask the Heracliteans to explain how the white comes to be out of any possible combination of locomotion and alteration; he grants them a mysterious causality and forces them to look instead at change as it shows itself to us. Socrates is very modest. His distinction resembles more the distinction between odd and even numbers than anything so high-powered as Theaetetus' classification of roots. He does not raise the question, for example, whether alteration could not be a kind of locomotion, in the sense that either something in local motion changes another into something else, or something in the same changes its place and supplants what was there. Locomotion and alteration are more certain in their difference than any hypothesis about their ultimate sameness. Socrates, however, has Theodorus agree to something that is far less certain. He asks him to include rotation in the same as a variety of locomotion. But rotation assumes a perfect body, which will not deviate locally from its axis. It assumes, in short, a mathematical construction, the existence of which could well be doubted. It is not surprising that Theodorus accepts rotation, but it does indicate how difficult this elementary dichotomy of apparent motion is. Socrates, indeed, carefully refrains from saying that any of these motions is; being only occurs in the remark "Let this be one *eidos*."

Socrates does not show that everything is not in motion; he limits himself to showing that, on the basis of total motion, knowledge could not be perception if knowledge means correct naming. The irreducible time lapse between the now of utterance and the now of perception warrants the conclusion that no possible revision of language could satisfy the requirements of the doctrine. Diagrammatically, every perception is of this sort (fig. 4).

The point of intersection of perception and quality is inexpressible, but nothing Socrates says militates against the notion that though unknowable it is always true. It would be true neither to the perceiver nor to the observer: it would be "ideally" true. Its language would be the mathematics of points, neither verifiable nor falsifiable. It order to understand what Socrates is getting at, it is necessary to ask why he replaces what he had called the perceived class (156b7) with what he now calls sortness or quality (*poiotês*), spoken of as a collective (182a9). The word "quality" or "sortness" has its source in two different models; it takes its suffix from that in hotness (*thermotês*) and whiteness (*leukotês*), and its stem from a pun on "making" and "sort" (*to poioun poion ti*). Every sort is not of something (*ti*) but solely its

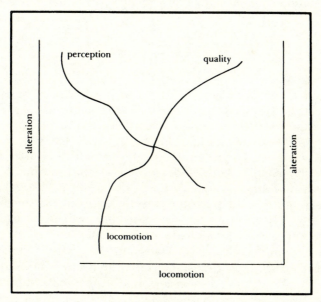

Figure 4

effect, which in turn is not perception but itself perceived, for itself perceived is the cause of it as perceived and not the cause of its becoming perceived.

Sortness is a word that belongs to the proposed revision of language. If color entirely changed, while seeing remained constant, the correct answer to the question "What do you see?" would not be a color but simply color. But since seeing does not abide either but is always changing into another sense, which includes the sensations of pleasure, pain, fear, desire, and countless others that are nameless (156b2–7), the correct answer to the question "What are you experiencing?" is not "I see" or "I am afraid," but simply "I sense." The thesis that knowledge is perception must be taken literally and, if taken literally, is irrefutable, for it does not admit of any articulation whatsoever. Knowledge is of sortness, a collection of an infinite number of names, none of which could ever be used correctly. Sortness is a universal that is never applicable, for its particularization is never perceptible. Socrates puts before us the difference between his own distinction of motion into two kinds and the spurious collection, sortness, which looks as if it separates an *aisthêsis* from an *aisthêton* but which in fact collapses them to such a point that its members vanish along with every kind of perception. We now understand why Socrates, in revealing the mysteries to Theaetetus, distinguished between the myth and its meaning. In the myth he spoke of *eidos* and *genos;* in his interpretation of it, he spoke of *hathroisma* (aggregate) and opposed it to *eidos* (157b8–c2).

XI. HELEN ·
(183c5–187c6)

Socrates has complied to some extent with Theodorus' demand that they treat the Heracliteans problematically, that is, without directing any question to their souls, for their thesis has turned out to be as unsayable as Protagoras'. Theodorus is relieved that he has now fulfilled his contract, and when Theaetetus reminds him that they had proposed to examine Parmenides as well—Theodorus had said, after all, that it would be unbearable not to do so—he is told not to teach his elders, young as he is, to transgress their agreements and be unjust (cf. 162d3). Theodorus is not joking. He has evidently sworn to himself to live up to his obligation but no more, not even if the compulsion is in the argument itself. Unlike Theaetetus, he prefers to be consistent at any price, for nothing must interfere with his freedom. Theodorus applies the standard of exactness found in mathematics to justice,[20] and this twin "idealism," which he takes as more real than "bare speeches," he combines with freedom. He wants to please both the truth and Protagoras, afraid to appear ridiculous and yet oblivious of his own bad manners, accepting of the authority of the city and yet wholly unaware of the city. He is a mixture of whimsicality and indignation. He meticulously draws a circle around himself and then wants to be left alone within that inviolable circle to do whatever he likes. He shuns any compulsion on himself but is not adverse to ordering Theaetetus about—"Get yourself ready to give Socrates an account of that which remains"—or treating the works of reason (speeches) as his own irrational slaves. Theodorus does not want to be the subject of comedy but of tragedy. The fate Socrates has woven for him was not an improvement but a punishment. A mathematician understands himself in the light of poetry. He whom Theodorus calls a philosopher is, according to Socrates, the one who knows how to clothe himself elegantly as a freeman should and hymns correctly the true life of gods and happy men (175d7–176a2). Of the ancient quarrel between poetry and philosophy Theodorus knows nothing.

Theodorus makes a false prediction. He thinks Socrates will do that which would give Theaetetus the most pleasure to hear—examine those who say that the whole is at rest. Socrates cannot resist, he says, the invitation to speak on anything at any time. Socrates refuses either to accommodate Theaetetus or to cover for Theodorus. But it was none other than Socrates who remembered Parmenides and put Theodorus and himself in the middle of a war without neutrals between Motion and Rest. So Theodorus was right after all: speeches do wait around like slaves for us to complete them. In the greatest dangers, Socrates had said, men acknowledge most readily the wisdom of others, and though he spoke of the war and the danger they themselves were in, it was not serious, and they do not have to play the game. The problem of being can wait. But though they are free they are not completely free: Theaetetus is pregnant. Socrates' maieutics must relieve him of his offspring. Theaetetus' soul takes precedence over being. They are to imitate political life, where the pressure of events postpones indefinitely the possibility of reaching full clarity about the foundations of political life. Theaetetus' soul is at stake (cf. 172e7). He must present himself before the infallible tribunal of Socrates' art despite his not even knowing the most important question. This is so urgent a matter that Socrates does not consult Theaetetus as to his pleasure. Socrates' subordination of being to knowledge recalls the way he had stopped speaking of philosophy (cf. 177b7–c5); for if Parmenides first asked the first question in philosophy, then to evade the question "What is philosophy?" is equivalent to the evasion of the question "What is being?" It would seem that the coming of the Eleatic stranger is a godsend.

Having liberated Theodorus from his fear of ridicule before the many, Socrates presents himself as full of fear and shame before the one Parmenides. In order to underline the disparity between Parmenides and himself, he quotes half a verse from Homer: Parmenides is "as awesome to me as uncanny." Helen spoke this line to the aged Priam. Iris, the offspring of Wonder, had arranged their meeting. They met on the walls of Troy, where the aged counselors of Priam had, on seeing Helen, said that her beauty was so awesomely like the goddesses' that the war between Achaeans and Trojans could not arouse their indignation. In reply to Priam's gentle words, Helen had burst out with the wish that death had then pleased her when she followed Priam's son to Troy. The ugliest of men, whom the gods had made barren of wisdom, compares himself to the most beautiful of women, whom the gods punished with barrenness for her crime.[21] Now that Socrates has done with Theodorus, he repudiates Theodorus' competence to judge his looks: there was not a word about the beautiful when he gave his speech in praise of Theodorus as the philosopher.

It seems absurd to say that Socrates is another Helen and the cause of the war between Rest and Motion. In describing that playful war, Socrates distinguishes between the ancients, who through their poetry concealed from the many that nothing was at rest, and the wise moderns who openly declare that everything is in motion, so that even the shoemakers could understand their wisdom and honor them. But the proponents of rest have no ancient counterparts, and though Parmenides also speaks poetically, he apparently has no followers who try to make the many understand their wisdom, let alone honor them.[22] Socrates, however, who will soon be put on trial, seems to have been even worse than Homer's proselytizers. He has surely not tried to impress the shoemaker with his wisdom, for he has none, but he has done nothing else but talk about shoemakers, and he has already admitted to Theaetetus that his practice has caused much hatred. Socrates' Protagoras had urged him to stop inciting enmity for philosophy and start converting, but Socrates defended himself to Theodorus on the grounds that evil was necessarily coterminous with good. He had further indicated that the many can never accept Protagoras' wisdom, nor do they have to concern themselves with the conflict between Motion and Rest.

Socrates has become the greatest threat to philosophy ever since he brought her down to earth and began to consider things like hair, mud, and dirt. Parmenides, indeed, had told him to do so, though he could now very well wonder whether he had understood Parmenides correctly. Socrates here hesitates to justify himself before the tribunal of philosophy. He chooses instead a middle course between the problem of being on the one hand, which is never urgent, and the issue of philosophy's relation to the city on the other, which he himself has brought to a head and which now involves his own life. The compromise between a matter of the greatest urgency and a matter of the greatest importance is Theaetetus' soul, on whose behalf he continues to do what he has always done. It is in this context that Socrates let us infer that he is beautiful.

Socrates' conversation with Theodorus has purified Theaetetus' original answer; that knowledge is perception now stands by itself as Theaetetus' own opinion, without either Homer or Protagoras as its parent. If, Socrates asks, Theaetetus were asked by what or with what a human being sees the white and black, and by what or with what he hears the high and low, he would presumably say by or with eyes and ears. Socrates does not let Theaetetus say by or with sight or hearing.[23] He compels him to say that it is more correct to speak of the eyes and the ears as those through which we see and hear than of the eyes and ears in the instrumental dative without any preposition, but only after Theaetetus has agreed to this does Socrates explain its greater correctness. In poetry, to be sure, the preposition *dia* with the eyes or ears is common, but we do not look on poetry as the model of exactness. Throughout Plato the dative is used alone, even in passages where exactness would seem to be in order.[24] The instrumental dative is neutral with regard to the question of soul or no soul, but the prepositional phrase requires something like soul to complete it. Socrates uses brute force on Theaetetus in order to introduce soul. The dative *ommasi* (with or by the eyes) runs together eye and sight; it is the more correct answer if the eye strictly understood is the seeing eye. But the phrase *dia ommatôn* (through the eyes) entails a distinction between the nonseeing and seeing eye, and once the eye has thus become equivocal, it becomes terrible for the senses to be lodged in us as if we were wooden horses. The more precise answer shows the necessity that the manifold of perceptions jointly pertain or extend to a single whole or class (*idea*). The less precise answer, on the other hand, because it treats the sense organs only in their being-at-work, lets us be content with what seems to be a limited number of beings-at-work. But as soon as we consider touch, we would have to allow it to be infinite in number—each hand, each finger, each patch of skin—and we would perhaps be driven to suppose that the body as a whole in its being-at-work was that with which (or by which) we touch. The body as a perceiving whole raises the question of the cause of its being such a whole, and once again something like soul would have to be invoked. Socrates avoids this more roundabout argument through the nonce distinction he has imposed on Theaetetus. The way in which the manifold of perceptions pertains to a single whole is not simply as their container, but as a cause of the manifold being what it is. The *idea* is that which gives to its members their class character.

No sooner has Socrates extracted from Theaetetus what he wants than he lets him go again. He will no longer meddle in his answers but will let Theaetetus speak for himself. Theaetetus thus becomes free again, but at a price: the argument loses its newly won precision. Socrates asks Theaetetus whether the instruments of perception belong to the body or to something else, and whereas Socrates had suggested that these instruments could be referred to the body, Theaetetus says that they belong exclusively to the body. If they are instruments, they could only be the soul's, and only in their idleness could they be the body's. Socrates then speaks, without explanation, of the power through which we perceive and has Theaetetus' willing assent that one power cannot do the job of another. He implies that all the powers of perception belong to the body (185e7), and that as instruments are to their user, so the five powers are to a single *idea*. Perhaps, however, the powers are like the fingers of the hand, and the hand as a whole is the single *idea*. The mention of soul, indifferent though Socrates declares the name for the *idea* to be, predisposes Theaetetus toward a separation of *idea* from body. He imagines the body to be a wooden horse pierced like a sieve, inside of which an Odysseus sits in control of an unruly host of sensations. Theaetetus rejected the body-people out of hand.

Socrates offers four statements, the first three of which would seem to be always true, and the last suggests wherein error could arise. Theaetetus, in any case, assents to the first three and hesitates over the last. Theaetetus thinks about both sound and color that (1) both of the pair are; (2) each of the two (is) other than each of the two, but the same as itself; (3) both of the pair (are) two, and each of the two one. As Socrates presents it, "two" and "one" are somehow derivative from "both" and "each," "same" and "other," and of these in turn "both" is prior to the rest. The being of sound and color first gets thought with the coupling of them in thought, and it is as a thought couple that what they share gets thought through. The community they are given in thought as a couple precedes the thinking of what is common to them: being, otherness, sameness. It therefore does not follow that without qualification each is the same as itself and other than the other, for Socrates asks whether Theaetetus could not go on to examine whether they are like or unlike one another. Unlike being, sameness, and otherness, the like and the unlike are not "known" instantly, and since nothing forbids one's examination to conclude that color and sound are wholly alike except in the way we perceive them, the three statements are not so much instant knowledge as they are conditions for our thinking. The first part of the dialogue raised the question whether knowledge and perception were the same or other, but as long as they were taken for the same, thought was completely paralyzed, for there was no room for thought in such an equation. It could not think without already knowing, and yet it only had to think for the equation to vanish.

However, Socrates now has led Theaetetus back to what was latent in his very first answer, that there is no knowledge where there is not number. Theaetetus counts color and sound; he cannot count them unless he thinks of their common being. Their common being makes them countable, but does it also make each of them what it is? Does the common being of sound and color stand to sound and color each by itself, as the single *idea* stands to the manifold of perceptions? Soul would then be the common being of all perceptions (like Aristotle's aesthetic soul), and to speak of it as by itself would be as if one spoke of the two of sound and color as simply two. Soul by itself would then be to the soul of perception as two is to two perceived things. Theaetetus, at least, assumes that the soul, which, he says, examines what is common, is the same *idea* by means of which we perceive through the instrumental powers of the body. That which is the common ground of perception is that which examines the common ground of everything perceived, and this common ground is not body, magnitude, motion, or rest, but being. Being is wholly unmysterious to Theaetetus.

If it were possible to find out whether sound and color were both salty, Theaetetus would say that the power through the tongue would be the means to determine it. Socrates asks in this indirect way how one can say of both a sound and a color that they are both intense, or both pleasant or unpleasant, and most of all, how one knows that one cannot taste a color or a sound. The things common to the senses, along with the discrimination among the senses, elude Theaetetus. The phrase "the power through the tongue" is his own; it is his way of combining "through an instrument," "through a power," and "through a sensing." Power could now be the soul's, which would use the tongue as its instrument for this particular job, and the soul would be, as an *idea*, a power. If Theaetetus had listened to his own answer, he would have realized its beauty (185c4), for it not only shows that the tongue cannot by itself discriminate between two tastes, but also that it contains the answer to Socrates' next question. Socrates accepts Theaetetus' "power." The question he asks is, The power through what, that is, the soul through what, makes plain to us that which is common? The answer is, through speeches (*dia logôn*), whose corporeal instruments are the tongue and the ear.[25] Theaetetus, however, hears Socrates' question in terms of Socrates' original formulation and not in terms of his own: Through which of the instruments of the body do we perceive by means of the soul the common?

It appears to Theaetetus that the soul has no proper instrument for the common, but it by itself is its own instrument. And it appears thus to Theaetetus, Socrates says, because he is beautiful. Theaetetus' beauty is a cause; its effect is to open up to him something that would otherwise require a long argument. Beauty is insight; it is the shortcut through an argument. It therefore bypasses the "weakness of speeches" and runs the risk of oversimplification.[26] The beauty of Theaetetus consists as much in his ignoring speeches as the soul's instruments as his hitting upon soul in itself. It is inseparable from Theaetetus' benefaction to Socrates, who does not have to supply a long argument. Socrates, who has cast himself in the role of Helen, tells his look-alike Theaetetus that he is not ugly. Socrates was beautiful because he avoided the problem of being in order to help Theaetetus; Theaetetus is beautiful because he gets hold of the soul by itself without the help of speeches. But their joint evasion has brought them back to being, which more than anything else is common to everything. Parmenides, without Theaetetus' awareness, has slipped into the argument. His beauty seems to have made a confrontation with Parmenides unavoidable. This confrontation takes the form of Theaetetus' own experience of false opinion—that knowledge is not perception—against the Parmenidean contention that false opinion is impossible. That Theaetetus cannot defend his experience against these arguments shows up the weakness in his beauty.

The difficulty to which Theaetetus' insight is exposed immediately becomes plain in the concluding part of the argument. He tells Socrates that in his opinion being is one of the things which the soul alone by itself aims at or desires (*eporegetai*). This is the most extraordinary remark that Theaetetus ever makes. Nothing has prepared us for it, for we should have expected him to say that being is one of the things which the soul by itself examines. It seems as if Theaetetus' newfound beauty has affected his understanding of being, or, better perhaps, that his understanding of being comes to light in his newfound beauty. He says, at any rate, that especially in the case of the beautiful and the ugly, the bad and the good, the soul by itself examines being, "calculating in itself the past and the present things (goods, etc.) relative to the future." Theaetetus remembers the argument in which Socrates got Theodorus to agree that not everyone was equally competent about the future. The gathering point of being and benefit is the future. Being primarily consists in the being of temporal relations, and the science of being is a kind of divination. There is no being in perceptual experiences through the body because there is no experience in them of the future. Theaetetus seems to discern the soul's independence from the body as most evident in its hopes, fears, and desires.

The relationship, then, of these experiences of the soul to perceptual experiences through the body would be being, and the science of their relationship would be that science which comprehends the manifold of arts and sciences into one class. The unity of knowledge is warranted by the unity of soul. Theaetetus' beauty, which Socrates has sparked into shining out by reminding him of his mathematics, has led him away from his own body. Body has disappeared altogether into the experiences we have through it. If truth is ungraspable by means of perception, no perception is true or false, and truth is obtained by reflection on what has neither truth nor being. Theaetetus has fallen back into Protagoreanism. When asked to supply that name which the soul has whenever it alone by itself deals with the beings, of which there has been no mention, Theaetetus does not say "to figure out" (*syllogizesthai*), "to calculate" (*analogizesthai*), or "to think through" (*dianoeisthai*), but "to opine" (*doxazein*), the key word of Socrates' Protagoras (cf. 170b8–9). Theaetetus in his beauty has forgotten *logos* along with body and that ordinary human beings, according to Socrates, believe wisdom to be true thought (*dianoia*).

XII. Parmenides
(187c7–190c4)

For the rest of the dialogue, the recurring example of knowledge is knowledge of Theaetetus, Socrates, and Theodorus, any two of them, but especially of Theaetetus and Socrates. The dialogue thus becomes reflexive and turned back on itself—a conversion to their own doing and being. This conversion is initiated by Socrates, who exhibits to Theaetetus his barrenness of wisdom. What we now witness is no longer Socrates' practice of maieutics on Theaetetus, but Socrates' giving birth *per impossibile*. The proper element of this impossibility is false opinion. Socrates is recalled to himself by Theaetetus' reminder of what he had said about leisure, but since Socrates in fact is pressed for time, it would seem that, if it is now opportune to examine false opinion, his forthcoming trial must bear on the question. At the trial, he asserts that he knows that he knows nothing, which, if translated according to Theaetetus' definition, would apparently run "Socrates has the true opinion that he has no true opinion about anything." Socrates therefore would truly opine that he opines falsely. Even if we exclude Socrates' true opinion from everything he opines falsely, it is absurd for Socrates to hold onto opinions he truly opines to be false (cf. 189e7). If, however, "to know nothing" means "not to have any opinion," Socrates would truly opine that he has no opinion about anything. But this is no less absurd, for Socrates has many opinions, all of which he must hold to be true, and one of which is that the soul deals with some things alone by itself.

Theaetetus, in reminding Socrates of the city, has compelled him to reflect on the meaning of his own ignorance. Socrates' ignorance stands naked before the all-wise philosophers, all of whom, despite their "ontological" disagreements, agree with each other on the impossibility of false opinion. The shift from Theaetetus' second offspring to the problem of Socratic ignorance resembles the shift from Theaetetus' soul to the problem of knowledge, which Socrates had as abruptly introduced at the beginning of the dialogue. But just as the problem of knowledge turned out to be at the root of the question of Theaetetus' soul and Theodorus' competence, so now Theaetetus' offspring points directly to the problem of Socrates' competence. The city and the philosophers together apply the same kind of compulsion to Socrates as Socrates had just applied to Theaetetus. Theaetetus then emerged as beautiful. Will Socrates fare as well?

The *Theaetetus* as a whole thus examines two Socratic characteristics, his midwifery and his knowledge of ignorance, and for the most part each is treated separately. The first is under the surface of the Heraclitean-Protagorean section, insofar as Heraclitus and Protagoras seem to supply the epistemological and physiological basis for the uniqueness of Socrates' art. The second dominates in a more explicit way Socrates' discussion with Theaetetus, once Theodorus has abandoned both Heraclitus and Protagoras, for the question of identity, in terms of which the problem of false opinion is posed, amounts to various attempts to distinguish Socrates from everyone else. In the *Sophist*, it is their apparent failure to discover the *logos* of Socrates that makes Theaetetus and Theodorus ask the stranger almost the same question Socrates asked: How is the philosopher to be told apart from the sophist?

If knowledge were true opinion, Theaetetus would now know (have the true opinion) that this was the case. But if Socrates and Theaetetus will discover that Theaetetus had a true opinion, his true opinion would then have lacked the proof that true opinion was knowledge.

Knowledge as true opinion is indistinguishable from an inspired guess. Theaetetus does not realize that the distinction between true and false opinion cannot be made on the basis of true opinion, for if both are by nature (187e7), that is, prior to any calculation, both are as experiences equal, and neither can do any more than deny the truth of the other. A true opinion affords no access through itself to the validation of its truth. It has precisely the same status as an individual's perception had in Theaetetus' physiology; the soul, simply because it acts by itself when it opines, does not at once become superior to its joint action with the body in perception, for it opines either truly or falsely. To work out a way, then, to tell true opinion from false is already to be beyond true opinion, but Socrates and Theaetetus cannot make this step before they backtrack and examine the true and the false in perception.

Perception had first been tied into a doctrine of motion, but now that they are to consider knowing apart from learning and forgetting, motion must be discarded. The very mention of Parmenides has had its effect. No "physiology" accompanies the three successive arguments Socrates employs to account for false opinion; as arguments, they prove to be so powerful as to destroy its very possibility. But Socrates begins to make some progress when he resorts to images. The two images—of wax and of birds—impart imaginary motion and body into the presentation of soul. Motion and body are more real in these images than they were in Theaetetus' physiology, where body and motion only existed (if at all) as the geometrical imaging of number. A physiology of soul in images seems less illusory than a physiology of illusion. Socrates and Theaetetus end up once more in need of the Eleatic stranger.

In the first argument, Socrates not only speaks of knowledge and ignorance but also of belief (*oiesthai*) and conviction (*hêgeisthai*) and thus implicitly marks off the real state of the knower or nonknower from his own awareness of his state. Such a separation seems not to have any effect on the first two cases, but in the third, in which Theaetetus thinks it monstrous, it is not so obvious that false opinion is impossible. "Surely no one believes," Socrates says, "that what he knows is what he does not know, nor, in turn, what he does not know, what he knows." A businessman knows how to make money; he believes that this knowledge is knowledge of how to manage a city. Closer to home, Theodorus knows mathematics, astronomy, and music; he believes that this knowledge is knowledge of soul. Theaetetus' exclamation of horror at such vanity—how could anyone be so dishonest with himself?—testifies to his innocence and shows the danger of argument if one does not know the way to the marketplace. Theaetetus knows nothing of the spurious extension of itself into which each art and science necessarily lapses if it is not guided by an awareness, which it itself cannot supply, of itself as a part of knowledge. So if one now reconsiders the second case, it too becomes far less certain. "Can anyone be convinced," Socrates asks, "that what he does not know is something else he does not know, and knowing neither Theaetetus nor Socrates to get it into his head that Socrates is Theaetetus or Theaetetus Socrates?" Although Anytus knows neither the sophists, as he himself admits,[27] nor Socrates, as we should say, he certainly believes that Socrates is a sophist. Theaetetus' sincerity, which prevented him from playing the part of Hippolytus, totally blinds him to its possible lack in others. If, however, knowledge is replaced throughout by true opinion, and ignorance by no opinion, then false opinion is impossible, and Theaetetus' definition collapses, for true opinion must vanish along with false opinion. Theaetetus and Socrates have each a stake in establishing false opinion, one in order to maintain his definition, the other in order to distinguish true opinion from knowledge.

The second argument reveals the difference between perceiving and thinking, for the parallel Socrates draws between seeing and opining shows that "nothing" has its proper home in perception. To see nothing in the absence of light is an everyday experience, but the minimal conditon for thinking, inasmuch as it is an activity of the soul by itself, is thinking "at least one." Since being rides in on the coattails of one, thinking must involve the thinking of being. Is the "at least one" of thinking an a priori object of thinking? And if it is, does thinking bring it to light, or is the light which makes possible its being thought prior to thinking? And, finally, if thinking does not furnish its own illumination, does the illumination necessarily cast light on some particular one, as Parmenides seems to believe, or does it merely guarantee the possibility of thinking anything, while the something thought comes in from elsewhere? Furthermore, to look and not to see anything, or to listen for something and not to hear it or anything else, is an equally ordinary experience; it seems impossible to conceive of any kind of thinking that could be an attempt to think and yet think nothing. Thinking is either off or on, in contact or not.[28] One cannot first be thinking and then turn one's thought, as one directs one's gaze, to something. Thinking is a being-at-work without potentiality. Socrates, therefore, has justified through a proof of the impossibility of thinking nothing his seemingly arbitrary assertion that the soul alone by itself deals with the beings.

The third argument proceeds on the basis of the preceding two arguments, and hence completes the number of possibilities for false opinion. It borrows from the first argument "the other" and from the second "being" and considers false opinion as the exchange of one being for another. Two beings would seem to be the minimal condition for false opinion. Is it also the minimal condition for true opinion? Thinking was first presented by Socrates as the thinking of a both; Socrates is now implying that there might be two kinds of thinking, for one of which "two," and for the other "one," would be its minimal condition. However this may be, Socrates' description here of false opinion seems to fit better what occurs when one misunderstands an intention, an example of which is found in the *Republic* (523a10–524c2).

Some things, Socrates tells Glaucon, do not invite the understanding (*noêsis*) to reflection, on the grounds that perception has adequately discriminated among them, whereas other things urgently require reflection, since perception is not acting soundly. "It is plain," Glaucon said, "that you mean things that appear from afar and shadow-paintings." "You have scarcely hit upon what I mean," Socrates said. Glaucon gives examples where perception invites perception to further investigation; he is literally thinking of something else and therefore has a false opinion of what Socrates means. But though he is not in himself opining falsely, still, since he was intending to hit on Socrates' meaning, he has hit on something else than what he wanted. What he wanted, Socrates has given in a speech, and Glaucon believed he had found the being that fitted the speech. It is not, then, the exchange of one being for another that brings about false opinion, but the connecting of a being with a speech to which it does not belong. Diagrammatically, the situation is as follows:

Speech₁ (things not inviting reflection)	Being₁ (the region of trust)
Speech₂ (things inviting reflection)	Being₂ (the contrarieties of beings)
Speech₃ (things not inviting further perception)	Being₃ (the phenomena seen close at hand)
Speech₄ (things inviting further perception)	Being₄ (the phenomena seen from afar)

Glaucon mistakes being₃ for being₁, for he mistakes speech₃ for speech₁, and being₄ for being₂, since he takes speech₄ as speech₂. The minimal condition for this kind of false opining is two beings and one speech, where given the speech, one finds the wrong being of the speech, and in this sense exchanges one being for another. We therefore see how fateful it is for Theaetetus that he overlooked speeches as the soul's instruments.

Theaetetus illustrates the interchange of beings in false opinion with an example of opposites. "Whenever anyone opines what is ugly as what is beautiful, or what is beautiful as what is ugly, then truly he opines falsely." He seems to be thinking of Theodorus, who took him to be ugly, as he has now learned from Socrates, instead of as beautiful, but since without speech the universal and the particular are indistinguishable, Theaetetus misses the fact that to opine is to opine something about something, and on the nonpredicative level mistaking is impossible. Theaetetus, therefore, misunderstands precisely in the way he thinks is impossible. He takes the two of predication for the one of nonpredication and thus persists in treating thinking as if it were perceiving. Socrates pokes fun at Theaetetus' "truly" and complains that Theaetetus does not hold him in the same awe and fear as Socrates holds Parmenides. Theaetetus' "truly" validates his opinion that if someone exchanged the beautiful for the ugly he would be opining falsely. Socrates playfully asks whether this "truly" is compatible with knowledge as true opinion (cf. 189d7). I know or truly opine, Theaetetus says, that Theodorus opines falsely; but that Theodorus opines falsely is the consequence of a definition, and Theaetetus' true opinion is not open to correction but is necessarily true, whereas in true opinion there can be no "knowledge" of necessity. "Theodorus truly opines falsely" means that he takes the beautiful for the ugly without knowing it. One cannot replace the inadvertence expressed in "without knowing it" with "without opining truly." Theaetetus, moreover, fails to observe that to opine the beautiful could be a false opinion without any exchange of the beautiful for the ugly, for someone would, if he believed he had a golden soul, nobly opine falsely. Only if the true were the beautiful, and the false ugly, would it necessarily follow that such opining of the beautiful would involve an exchange with the ugly. Theaetetus takes it for granted that the true is the beautiful (194c1–2; cf. 195d2–5, 200e5–6). He seems to be a duplicate of Socrates when young.

Socrates tries to get Theaetetus to recognize his own speaking and conversing. On account of Theaetetus' self-forgetting, Socrates can only do this if he translates the speaking of Theaetetus to Socrates into his soul's silent conversation with itself. Theaetetus stands before his own speaking as if it were a foreign tongue. If to opine (*doxazein*) and to think (*dianoeisthai*) are the soul's silent versions of to speak (*legein*) and to converse (*dialegesthai*), then one can genuinely opine if and only if one has gone through the thinking that has resulted in a conclusion (*logos*). (To share a *logos* (*homologein*) does not count as the sharing of an opinion unless the reasoning is also shared.) Socrates here interprets the relation of the images of pregnancy and giving birth as that of silent thinking and silent speaking, and maieutics as nothing other than dialectics. This interpretation, however, does away with both Socrates' barrenness and the infallibility of his art. He now does not know, and the soul only phantomlike appears (*indalletai*) in its thinking to be conversing.[29]

The identity Socrates claims between a spoken and a silent questioning and answering equates the self-identity of the soul with two different speakers. But even within the soul there is a difficulty. If the soul asks and then answers itself, the soul must deceive itself in its either denying or assenting to what it already has figured out. The condition for all thinking would be to take the same for the other, and what Theaetetus has just said to be false opinion would be thinking. The impossibility of positing something (*heteron ti*) as another (*heteron*) in one's own thought, would thus be due to the spurious otherness in thinking itself. Mistaking could not occur within a soul which already is both the knower as answerer and the nonknower as questioner (cf. 145e9, 187d2). Meno's paradox flourishes anew, and neither the image of wax nor that of birds can adequately resolve it.

Socrates now points out to Theaetetus that the consequence for his definition of false opinion is somewhat the same as what they formerly concluded from the equation of knowledge and perception. In terms of what one might opine falsely, dreaming cannot be distinguished from waking, sickness from health, or madness from sanity. But there is a difference. With perceiving, one's perceptions varied according to one's condition, but with opining, though the assertions themselves are just as private (to oneself), they are all invariant and held in common, regardless of anyone's condition. It looks at first as if their invariance were that of empty "concepts"—the odd is odd, the ox is an ox, and the two is two—while the noninvariance of perceptions showed richness of content but they were wholly nonconceptual. The problem is then to put together the invariance of empty concepts with the invariance of content-rich experience. This, however, is not the case, for odd, even, ox, horse, two, and one are beings and not concepts. Socrates means something else, and Theaetetus has not been listening closely enough. It is perfectly possible to utter the sentence, "Odd is even," but it is not possible to speak it, if to speak means to draw the conclusion of one's own thinking. The sayable is not the opinable, for speech as it is ordinarily understood is not thought. Speech, properly understood, is always a conclusion and never a premise. A proof, known to the ancients, shows that, if the hypotenuse of an isosceles right triangle is commensurate with its side, the odd would be even. Someone could surely have the opinion, in the non-Socratic sense, that they are commensurable, but he could not have that opinion, in the Socratic sense, for the reasoning which must accompany it as an opinion would cancel it. Socrates' conversation with Theaetetus now illuminates the same point. They prove that to have the opinion, in the strict sense (190e1), that false opinion is heterodoxy or opining the other, is to speak nothing, and therefore it is to opine nothing, which the second argument has shown to be impossible. The dialogue itself is the proof of the definition's alogical character, from which it cannot be separated if its irrationality is to be grasped. Socrates has now vindicated Parmenides. His vindication is twofold. Whether the being which is thought is just what it is and nothing else, or an opinion is genuine only if it is backed up by a proof—in either case mistaking is impossible. Neither Truth nor Opinion admits of falsehood.

XIII. WAX
(190e5–196c3)

Theaetetus has not understood what he has just experienced; he has fallen back into the same condition he was in before Socrates explained to him the cause of his perplexity in the face of Socratic questions. He does not even know the very strange consequences if false opinion will not come to light—that the false opinion they had about false opinion would, despite their proof, cease to be false. Socrates refuses to enlighten him. He is very hard on Theaetetus. His inoculation of Theaetetus against sophistry and the ordinary understanding of Parmenides has not "taken." It can only "take" if Theaetetus rehearses by himself what he has experienced. No one can conduct this internal dialogue for him. Theaetetus would literally have to become Socrates in order for the argument to become manifest to him, for the *logos* remains invisible as long as the speaking is embedded in sounds spoken to another. As the phantom image (*eidôlon*) of thought, it resists every effort to make it transparent in itself (cf. 206d1–6). Speaking out loud has the same apparent reasonableness as the sentence Protagoras wrote in his book, which only collapsed when the reader obeyed its concealed injunction. Euclides, therefore, acted correctly without knowing it when he put Socrates' narration into direct discourse. Theaetetus is in the position of someone who looks at a mathematical proof in a textbook and confesses that he does not "see" it. No one can "see" it for him. Theaetetus is wholly enslaved to the *logos;* he cannot get free of it if he turns away from it as Theodorus did, but only if he understands what the *logos* is. Understanding resists *logos* even though it is a *logos*. If, for example, Socrates' "I have nothing wise" is said ironically, it can be translated as: "Socrates knows nothing which Theaetetus would accept as wisdom." This ipso facto cannot be explained to Theaetetus. But in the meantime, in the face of Theaetetus' incomprehension of the bare *logos*, it is necessary to examine the corporeal counterpart of speech as the image of thought-memory.

Socrates proposes a wax block in our souls for the sake of argument. The wax block is an image which contains images; it is not an image in the way in which the images it receives are images. The original, whether it be a perception or a thought, is not to its image in the wax as the unknown something in the soul is to the wax which is its image. Socrates begins by exchanging one being he does not know for another. The mnemonic image is the product of its original; it cannot do what the original can do. But the wax block is not a product of the unknown, for it is set up to do what the unknown does. The wax is not there merely as a receiver of everything; if it is to count as a source of knowledge, we must be able to submit it to whatever we want recorded, for otherwise retrieval would be hampered if not blocked altogether, and everything we perceived we would know.

The wax has a finite capacity, both as to the number of images it can receive and the degree of subtlety its impressions can have. It requires, moreover, that perceptions and thoughts be interpreted in a certain way, "like the seals or signs on rings." These signs cannot be what the beings themselves are; they are stand-ins for the beings. As stand-ins they can be either arbitrary—like a letter for a sound— or natural signs of the beings, and if they are natural, does their reversal in the wax reproduce something of the originals which they themselves do not have? We do not know, moreover, whether the perceptual or intellectual signs are spoiled by the wax, so that only the first impression can be good, while afterwards every repeated application of the seal blurs the original clarity. Socrates seems to assume that each perception, once it has made its impress, is completely wiped out, just as he had urged Theaetetus, in the case of his thoughts, to wipe out all that had gone before. In the memory, the difference between thoughts and perceptions fades, for now every term like "blunt" or "sharp," with which knowledge, if it were perception, would have to be qualified, admits of a possible meaning.

Now all of these, at which Socrates barely hints, are deductions from the wax block as image; they are inseparable from almost any image that prior to its serving as an image exists in its own right. It is therefore always difficult to "read" any but the simplest image, for one can easily mistake that which only belongs to the stuff of the image and without which the image would cease to be an image and become the thing itself. Of the two images Socrates employs, the wax block, because it seems to be so close to what the soul must do in remembering, is more liable to mislead us than the birds, whose outlandishness and recalcitrance to a one-to-one correspondence make them perhaps more revealing if less easy to read.

Not even Plato's Parmenides, who offers to the young Socrates his way of hypothesis as a way out of the impasse created by the necessity for and the impossibility of the "ideas," can altogether abstain from images and examples. Parmenides' own stance, before he embarks on the illustration of his hypothetical way, requires for its understanding an allusion to a poem of Ibycus that contains an elaborate metaphor. The eighth hypothesis becomes intelligible only when Parmenides cites shadow-paintings and dreams;[30] at which point we cannot but suppose that, had Parmenides been willing to be less austere in the other hypotheses, we should have had much less trouble in following him. What seems casual and adventitious in Parmenides' speech becomes in Plato's Socrates a matter of policy. Examples and images everywhere abound, and whenever Socrates does not bother to connect his own thinking with what his interlocutor understands, the interlocutor has to stop him and ask him for an illustration. One of the longest passages Plato gives of Socrates' sustained thinking is now before us. Socrates lists fourteen cases in which mistaking is impossible and then three in which it is possible. Within the limits of the argument, this is as sound as it is an exhaustive enumeration. Quick as Theaetetus is, he does not follow until Socrates gives an example. Here, Plato seems to be saying, is the way in which Socrates silently spoke to himself: completeness and necessity were the criteria to which he always tried to measure up.

For his not understanding what a *logos* is, Socrates almost punishes Theaetetus with a *logos* he cannot understand. Socrates' account raises several questions. Knowledge as recognition would seem to consist in the ability to report on the congruence between a past impression and a present perception; at best, this can only be true opinion, for one can always be deceived. In order to check on congruence, one would have to compare the impression with the seal. If the seal were replaced in the impression, the impression would become adjusted to the seal; there would always be congruence, and one could not say that here is Socrates, but he looks older. The seal must be "projected" on the impression, or the impression on the seal. The wax block would seem to need both depth for memory and a reflecting surface for projection. If, moreover, the impression is poor, over which one has little or no control, the impression is not congruent with the seal even at the moment of impression; but at that moment, the speech label is put down correctly, and when the seal is withdrawn, the label remains attached to the impression, which is of nothing that one has perceived. If, for example, a seal with three vertices left an impression of four vertices but with the label "triangle," there would be knowledge in some sense. As long as nothing but this seal recurred, there would be recognition, even though the impression itself if read would say "rectangle." Socrates thus fails to consider possible mismatchings of impressions, where "three" is linked with "four" in the wax but is labeled "three," so that "three" is unknown when there is no perception and known when there is. Theaetetus' addition of *logos* to true opinion might be a way of avoiding such errors. There are also possible misreadings of seals—those cases in which what is perceived stands on two levels at once, as, for example, in Theaetetus' distinction between letters in their shape and color and as representations of words. Perhaps all perceptions are double in this way, and knowledge is that which transforms a perception as a possible sign into an actual sign of a being.

The wax block makes one think of all the senses in terms of touch. But if a color becomes in the wax a kind of surface, it would seem that, in the absence of the perception, it would be known in its corrugations and not as a color. We should perhaps suppose that a sound recorded in the wax block would not preserve the sound as sound but a simulacrum of that which made the sound. Though present, it would not then even be known until one "played" the simulacrum with a mental needle, and recognition would only arise if the sound when reheard played the simulacrum without damaging its grooves. We are more likely to remember a speech than the sound of a speech, and we might surmise that something similar happens with sight. We see MAN and read it even if it is now shaped in a way we never saw before.

The reversal, then, of the seal in the block would mean that the present perception undergoes there two transformations. First the wax block simulates at least one cause of every kind of perception without being any one of them; second, it separates the "intention" of the perception from the perception to the same extent that Socrates had distinguished between his understanding what Parmenides said and his following what Parmenides intended. Error, therefore, could arise either on the level of intention, to which Theaetetus now points in his not following Socrates' enumeration (cf. 184a3, 192d2), or on the level of matching impressions in the wax. Socrates speaks exclusively of mismatching and ignores misunderstanding, for misunderstanding, as we have said, cannot be explained.

Socrates has now listed seven possible states of the soul: (1) Knowledge, (2) Ignorance, (3) Perception, (4) No Perception, (5) Knowledge and Perception as True Opinion, (6) Neither Knowledge nor Perception, (7) Mismatching as False Opinion. Since to know is not to mistake something for something else, to know is to identify. Socrates seems to indicate what knowledge as identification involves when he speaks of the poor bowman who hits the wrong target. First of all, there is the distance, whether of time or place, between the would-be knower as bowman and the target as that which is to be known. Next there is the soul as the sight which looks at what is to be known, identifies it as such, and itself will do the knowing. Third, the pair of hands is the power that is to initiate the bringing of the arrow into contact with the target; the hands correspond to thinking, which the soul guides while it itself manages the bow, which are the speeches, and the arrow, which brings what is to know into contact with what is to be known, is knowledge. Knowledge is the bond between soul and being, and truth is the light in which the soul sees that the bond is a bond. This kind of knowledge, however, could not occur unless the target or being had first been singled out, prior to its identification, as something to be known. The being must already have been set up before us. Who or what does this? If the beings were already in place for us, knowledge would necessarily fall to our lot, provided that the soul were at all capable of knowing. The beings, then, must not be in their proper places, and we must sort them out. Error is always possible because we must constantly sort, for we cannot fundamentally alter the confusion in which things are. This sorting-out is what the Eleatic stranger calls dialectical knowledge, in the *Sophist* and the *Statesman*, but Theaetetus, despite his sorting of numbers into two kinds (though he did not call them kinds), does not recognize the necessity for such sorting, for the numbers do not lie in confusion but in order. Had Theaetetus imitated in his answer to the question of knowledge what was latent in the very first step of his division of numbers, he would have hit upon the truth. He missed the mark because the numbers had for him complete clarity and distinctiveness. His knowledge interfered with his recognizing what knowledge is.

Instead of having straightforwardly said what false opinion is, Socrates enumerated all the possible cases of both false and true opinion. If his enumeration is complete, his subsequent assertion of what false opinion is should hold regardless of whether the "physiology" implicit in his image of the wax block were true or not. The image should now be dispensable. Socrates, however, does a very strange thing. After Theaetetus has asked, "Isn't it beautifully spoken, Socrates?" (cf. 195d4), Socrates tells him that when he listens further he will say it is still more beautifully spoken. On the basis of Theaetetus' agreement that to opine the truth is beautiful and to lie or be deceived is ugly, Socrates proceeds to replace the wax as an image with the wax as the literal truth (194e1). The beauty of true opinion requires the beauty of its instrument, just as the ugliness of lying requires a comparably ugly soul. The wax in the soul is that which Homer allusively called the heart. Heart in Homer is a metaphor for wax. However, Homer did not understand his own riddle, for otherwise he would not have praised the shaggy heart, which again is not a metaphor for fierceness, but is literally the condition of the forgetful, whose impressions (*ekmageia*) are indistinct. The word *ekmageion* had formerly denoted the block of wax as an image; it now reappears as the impressions in the heart. Socrates seems to be indulging in a gratuitous beautification of Homer, who had, at any rate, a much higher opinion of lying.

The consequence of this beautification is that Socrates' proof of possible kinds of true and false opinion turns into an assertion of the necessity of the beautiful and ugly, for false opinion is now a necessity for some kinds of souls. Indeed, one could take Theaetetus' vehement assent to the question whether false opinions are "in us" as meaning that no human soul is altogether beautiful (cf. 195b1). Socrates had told Theodorus that the bad could not be banished, for there necessarily must be something contrary to the good. It now appears that the same is true of the beautiful: false opinion is indispensable for knowledge. Socrates and Theaetetus have just found something beautiful—a true opinion, which is beautiful, about false opinion, which is ugly.

Socrates' beautification of himself (*kallôpizomenos*) is, however, spurious. He really is ugly. Socrates presents himself as being as terrible as Parmenides, but disagreeable and not at all an object of respect. He is disagreeable because in his sluggishness he cannot leave any argument alone. He learns slowly, which means, according to his own account, that his heart is hard and probably shaggy. Perhaps, then, the all-wise Homer praised such a heart correctly, but only if the beautiful wax is not good. My ugliness, Socrates seems to be saying, is that of an old woman, and signifies the art I practice. The concern of my art with the ugly—hair, mud, and dirt—is due to the affinity between the ugly and my soul. But we should not forget that Socrates by this same art revealed that Theaetetus was beautiful, and beautiful precisely because he forgot speeches (cf. 157c7, 167b7). Dialectics, then, seems to be the art of properly making use of the ugly and the beautiful.

The question which demolishes the beautiful discovery of Socrates and Theaetetus is a question about questioning. Since the literalization of the wax block has led to its assuming the character of the whole soul insofar as it is cognitive, the soul can no longer think or ask itself questions. The beautiful wax, which is necessary in order to guarantee perfect recognition, precludes thereby the possibility of putting two and two together. The wax stands in the way, not only of our ever making a mistake, but also of our combining anything with anything else. The "and" between five and seven has no place in the impressions of the wax. Plato's Parmenides leads the young Aristoteles to overlook "and" in the second hypothesis.[31]

> PARMENIDES: Is it possible to say "being"?
> ARISTOTELES: It is possible.
> PARMENIDES: And again to say "one"?
> ARISTOTELES: This too.
> PARMENIDES: Isn't then each of the pair said?
> ARISTOTELES: Yes.
> PARMENIDES: And whenever I say "being and (*te kai*) one," aren't both said?
> ARISTOTELES: Certainly.

The command to say both "being" and "one" can be obeyed either by saying "being and one" or by saying "being, one." The both that characterizes one's own performance as a speaker is transferred in the first case to that of which one speaks. To say both is to say "both." The both of the counting (speaking) is applied to the counted, for otherwise there would be no counting. "Five, seven" is not "five and seven." If five and seven were two consonants, and someone was asked to utter both of them, he could not comply with the request unless he inserted a vowel between them. They will not "add up" otherwise. He could, to be sure, give their word equivalents, but this would be as if one answered "five and seven" when asked what $5 + 7$ are. If, however, we imagine *per impossibile* that thought can move the impression of five and seven around, and the impressions of the four numbers are like those in figure 5, then, of course, the comparison of the newly combined twelve with the old eleven and twelve could easily lead to mistaking it for eleven. The wax block would then be working both as memory and the equivalent of perception. Socrates had excluded this originally because the wax had at first a very modest role; only when he had let the wax (now the heart) usurp every cognitive function, in order that true opinion could be wholly beautiful, did it collapse.

The manifold of numbers does look like the manifold of perceived things, but the separate stamps of Theaetetus and Theodorus are not at all like those of five and seven. Theaetetus and Theodorus together are two human beings; five and seven together are not two numbers but twelve. Theaetetus acknowledges the difference when he says that

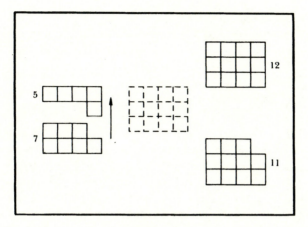

Figure 5

mistaking becomes more common among very large numbers. Again he does not hear what he himself says, for no one has a stamp in his heart of $12^{69} - 1$, even though one might readily make a mistake about it in some calculation.

Theodorus is wholly mistaken about Theaetetus' soul; it is not moderation itself, but in the most exalted state a soul can be in. His soul's exaltation is so dazzling that Theaetetus himself does not know the state he is in but, as he says, sometimes spins around in darkness when he looks at questions of relation. Had Theaetetus understood himself, he would have said that knowledge is intellection (noêsis), the contact of the soul with the beings without mediation or the need for thinking. Knowledge is not knowledge of causes but of beings in themselves.[32] His actual answer intends the same, for not only does perception, especially as Socrates interprets it, have the character of intellection, but the word aisthêsis in the sense of awareness even could serve for noêsis.[33] Nothing, indeed, would have changed if Theaetetus had said that knowledge is intellection. The disappearance of the distinction between what is perceived and what perceives would have recurred on the highest level, and the thesis would have proved to be as inherently contradictory.

Socrates seems to have discerned at once what Theaetetus was—someone on an almost permanent "high" as we say—and he has tried to verify the guess and at the same time bring Theaetetus down to earth. Socrates saw in Theaetetus a look-alike of his younger self, who heard and talked with Parmenides, but with differences. Theaetetus has not yet come to the "ideas," nor has he reflected on the problem of cause. He has altogether bypassed the body, and is more a potential convert of Parmenides than of Socrates. It is therefore not surprising that in the *Sophist* an ex-Parmenidean, the Eleatic stranger, will be able to do more with and for Theaetetus than Socrates can.

XIV. Birds
(196c4–201c7)

Socrates offers Theaetetus the alternative of either denying his experience of false opinion and obeying the argument that knowledge and ignorance of the same thing cannot consist with one another at the same time in the same person, or affirming his experience and denying the argument. Theaetetus says it is no choice at all. Socrates proposes that they act shamelessly and say what sort of thing it is to know. Theaetetus does not know why it is shameless. He has assumed from the start that knowledge is available and that Socrates really knows what it is; he is further unaware of the priority of the question of what something is to that of its quality. Socrates tells him that he seems not to have realized that their very question implied that they knew from the start what it meant to be ignorant, and that they understood one another while saying "we recognize" and "we do not recognize," and "we know" and "we do not know." Their conversation has long been infected with impurity (cf. 194e6); the beautiful heart of wax is worthless as long as they must speak with one another as if they know what not to know what knowledge is means. Socrates here gives casually the strongest argument against the equation of knowledge and perception, for if perception did not both reveal and conceal at the same time, we should never ask questions. Things could not be riddling if we were wholly in the dark, but the fact that we all are very much in the dark, Theaetetus has interpreted as his own occasional spells of vertigo. Socrates says that they must now be shameless and advance in the face of their own ignorance; as good-for-nothings they can get away with it, for that is how such people are expected to behave. They cannot avoid being the subject of comedy.

The distinction between possession and use or having was already implied in the image of the wax block, for there was knowing apart from perception and knowing with perception; and to label the impression by itself knowledge as a possession (prior to its being either recalled in thought or called on to identify a present perception) would seem to be far simpler than for Socrates to indulge in a fancy as grotesque as his birds. Socrates must be after bigger game. How easily he could have adapted the wax block for his ostensible purpose is shown in the conversation Theaetetus and he have.

SOCRATES: Have you heard what they're now saying it is to know?
THEAETETUS: Perhaps. I don't, however, remember at the
    moment.
SOCRATES: They surely say it's a having of knowledge?
THEAETETUS: True.

Theaetetus has an impression he is not using; before he uses it he cannot be certain that he even has it. When he does remember, he is using it, and finds that it conforms with what Socrates says. The small correction Socrates now suggests in the way people speak of knowing is reminiscent of the distinction he forced on Theaetetus between the preposition "through" and the instrumental dative for the eyes and ears, where the prepositional phrase entailed a difference between possession and use, while the dative only acknowledged use. That distinction had enormous consequences; this one looks as if it only peters out in a return to the original perplexity. It is striking, however, that the same inexactitude of terms which then crept in under the cover of compulsory exactness is repeated here.

To buy a cloak and not wear it is like possessing knowledge and not using it. To be without knowledge is to be naked. A bought but unworn cloak would correspond to barbells bought but not used; it would seem not to be like knowledge, which cannot be yours to the exclusion of everyone else's: strictly speaking, a cloak one buys and never wears more resembles a book one buys and never reads—the dialogue Terpsion is hearing now that Euclides has long kept in his drawer. This parallel indeed is not exact. That Euclides wrote it down does not mean he understood it. Socrates, moreover, complicates his presentation by likening knowledge or sciences to wild birds, for whom one has built a cage at home in which one feeds them after their capture. Socrates thus implies that (1) all sciences must be hunted before they can be possessed; (2) when captured, the sciences do not become completely domesticated, that is, clipped of their wings and staked somewhere in the cage; (3) the sciences are alive; (4) they do not naturally move in the element in which we live; (5) their capture requires secrecy and guile, for they are elusive and unwilling to be captured; (6) there is possibly something unnatural about our possession of them, that is, we are not of the same kind as the sciences, for we never fully assimilate them; (7) if the hunter hunts by knowledge, this knowledge cannot be a bird, unless there is among the birds an informer or traitor of the birds, the only bird that is by nature tame; and (8) it is not necessary to hunt the sciences oneself, for one can buy them from a science hunter. Some of these immediate implications Socrates makes use of, others he reinterprets. Although the image is as complex as the wax block, it differs from the wax block in two important respects. First, it can never be so abused as to be understood physiologically; it remains distinct as an image from that of which it is an image, for unlike the wax block all the cages are the same and not a lucky or unlucky gift of a goddess. And second, whereas the wax block implied that knowing was a kind of image making over which we have no control, the birds imply that this is not the case; they are essentially outside the cage of our soul what they are inside it.

In his first application of the image, Socrates introduces another kind of hunting, that which one does when one wants to use a particular science one has. It surely is not the same science one might have used in capturing it originally—there is no need at any rate for the same subtlety—but if it is a science (mnemonics), it is closer at hand than any other science. In his second application, Socrates introduces the notion that the cage in the soul—it is not the whole soul—has all kinds of birds. This cage is not made by us, for it exists when we are children and is then empty. The cage does not contain knowledge of perceived individuals (cf. 186b11–c2); it is a cage peculiar to man as man. Socrates, therefore, can only be speaking of men who have many different kinds of knowledge, for the shoemaker, however vast his experience, has only one bird. Not even Theodorus, but only a polymath like Hippias, would be a suitable candidate for such a description. For even if the arithmetician has a different bird for each number he knows, all his birds would have to flock together. Some birds flock together in herds apart from the others, some are in small groups, while others are one of a kind and fly through all the birds at random. Sciences come in kinds; one never acquires the kind itself but only an individual member of the kind. Two individuals can thus have the same science but not necessarily the same degree of proficiency in that science. But if there are no perfect birds, no science is complete; so perhaps Socrates means that in feeding the birds we make them more complete than they were at the time of capture. Sciences in their wild state are poor specimens.

Their quasi domestication suggests a political setting for the sciences (cf. 174e1–2, 197e4). We could then picture the inhabitants of a city, insofar as each is understood solely as a knower, as the various birds. Those which congregate in flocks would be the artisans, who in taking care of our various needs belong together (e.g., tailor, cleaner, shoemaker, hatter, etc.); those in small groups but not flocks, who are not said to stay apart from the others, would be the judge, the orator, the priest, the poet, and the general; and the isolated birds would be the mathematician, the physiologist, and the dialectician. All the arts keep to themselves "naturally," but not philosophic wisdom. There is no necessity for it to join any group, and it never stays anywhere for long: each art points to wisdom but not for everyone who has the art.[34] In terms of the *Republic* and the *Statesman,* this interpretation of the image makes some sense, but Socrates says the cage is in each soul, and unless the soul is an image of the city, the interpretation breaks down.

Knowledge itself no more exists than bird itself does; knowledge is always knowledge of a thing (*pragma*). The thing which each knowledge knows shows up in the knowledge as the kind of knowledge it is, and the kind of knowledge is the species of the bird. One would thus be inclined to say that arithmetic as a whole is "dove," and the knowledge of each odd and even number is a particular dove. But Socrates speaks of eleven as a ring-dove and twelve as a dove, and even if he had not said so, the knowledge of twelve could never then be shared with anyone. If, on the other hand, knowledge of each number is a species, there would be an infinite number of species, and arithmetic would be an essentially incomplete science. Theaetetus accepts without question that the arithmetician knows all numbers perfectly, and obviously he can say at once about any number whether it is odd or even, and that it is different from any other number. However, if knowledge of twelve means knowledge of all its factors, whether by addition or multiplication, not only could he never mistake seven and five for eleven, but he would have the same knowledge of every number, no matter how large, and that seems to be beyond the capacity of even a Ramanujan. We could then say that Socrates is presenting knowledge, which is always of kinds, as true opinion, which can never be of kinds, and the difference between them is in this way revealed. True opinion is always of individuals; it can never supply the connection between one individual and another, both of which it truly opines.

Socrates, however, does seem to be pointing to a genuine difficulty if knowledge is knowledge of kinds. He replaces our ordinary picture of a science, in which the science ranges over an indeterminate number of individuals, with the apparently more exact picture of any science being as distributive as what is known (cf. 207d3–7).[35] Arithmetic is not meaningfully the science of number, for there is no number which is not either odd or even, and therefore no knowledge which is not knowledge of some odd or even number. Socrates would thus be casting doubt on Theaetetus' dichotomy of all numbers into those with either rational or irrational square roots and instead be praising Theodorus for having proved the irrationality of each magnitude up to seventeen separately. Theaetetus' procedure tells us the character of every irrational square root, but it does not show that 288 is not the square of some integer. We should then be back at the original question as to how one could comprehend all the arts and sciences in a single kind. Such a comprehension now looks as if it could not be knowledge, while a complete enumeration of the sciences is impossible. We have not yet unriddled Socrates' birds.

There is something spurious even about asking how someone can mistake seven plus five for eleven. It is simply due, as we say, to the inattention of the adder, who perhaps also does not know that the sum of any two odd numbers is even. One can, moreover, ask for the sum of two numbers which no one could mistake. How much is 100 and 2? One hundred and two. A language could be devised, it seems, in which the difference between the question and the answer was only that of stress. In Homer, after all, twelve is two and ten (*dyo kai deka*) spoken as one word (*dyokaideka, dyôdeka,* or *dôdeka*). If Socrates wanted to explain error in terms of inattentiveness, his image of the wax block would be far more suitable, for he could have said that the indistinctness of an impression has inattention as its equivalent in the act of looking at an impression. Errors as an occasional event seem incapable of illustration. Lichtenberg's paradox is well-known: illustrate a misprint. To take a ring-dove for a dove illustrates the fact of the mistake but not the mistaking itself, since in our having the ring-dove in hand, one is knowing eleven. If our left hand held the bird of five and the bird of seven, the fact that our right hand held the bird of eleven would not entail that we mistook them. The link between the two hands is not itself a bird.

Socrates' silence about seven and five throughout the bird section shows that arithmetic cannot be the kind of knowledge he has in mind. If the question is how much do seven and five make, they are two facts (*pragmata*), and one would, in hunting for the knowledge of their sum, not have it at home in the cage. If one did have it there, one could have forgotten it (i.e., not attempted to use it), or have done the sum again to check it against the knowledge already possessed. Socrates, moreover, calls Theaetetus' attention to the unsuitability of his image when he has him agree that arithmetic is transmittable. The pupil does not receive the teacher's birds. Does the teacher breed his birds? Does the bird of twelve suddenly materialize inside the pupil's dovecote when he has understood the lesson? The absurdities seem endless.

The distinction between the use and the possession of knowledge has the consequence that one's own knowledge makes one ignorant, so that possibly one's own ignorance could make one know. To be ignorant by knowledge is to know that one knows nothing; to know by ignorance is to know that the unexamined life is not worth living. Neither is false opinion; together they describe Socratic philosophy. If the bird cage is the philosopher's, and especially Socrates', then to say that a science or an art is a living bird means that Socrates always considers each science and art in light of the human soul that possesses it. He never puts anything into his soul in which the soul itself is omitted. The image for the way in which competence about something and the soul show up in any knowledge is a bird, for competence becomes elusive as soon as the question of the soul is raised.

Theodorus was a bird, according to Socrates, who flew above the heavens and below the earth, and if Theaetetus can deliver a wind-egg, he too must be a bird. Socrates has shown that both are the dreamers who, Theaetetus said, believe themselves winged and think they are flying. Theaetetus had the insight that being and benefit were the subject of dialectics, for their conjunction is to be found in soul. Socrates' image of the bird cage, therefore, looked like the city. Only in the city with its urgent questions does the good intrude on competence, and though political urgency cannot perforce reveal that the good and competence are themselves problematic, to be oblivious of the city is tantamount to not even seeing as much as the city does. Theodorus' alliance with Protagoras is meant to show us that. Theaetetus, however, is far more innocent. He has forgotten that he is a human being. He is Euthyphro's nobler twin: he urges the Eleatic stranger to kill his father Parmenides.[36] Socrates juxtaposes the wax and the birds in order to put Theaetetus and himself side by side. Theaetetus' competence, on reflection, becomes knowledge of beautiful fictions; Socrates' competence is just this knowledge of Theaetetus. Knowledge of soul is not knowledge simply; but without knowledge of soul's delusions, each and every knowledge, as the breeding ground of soul's delusions, would be unapproachable. Competence would be an inviolable sanctuary for the expert were it not for knowledge of soul.

A moment's reflection would show that nonknowledge cannot be, as Theaetetus proposes, a bird which flies together with the bird of knowledge in the soul. Who would ever have gone out to hunt for ignorance? If, however, Theaetetus had said that knowledge and nonknowledge looked as if they were one and the same bird outside the cage, and in hunting knowledge, ignorance took its place, he would have hit upon the truth. Nonknowledge is such a good mimic of knowledge that it induces in its possessor the belief that it is knowledge. Nonknowledge is a decoy, but it could not be a decoy unless it had borrowed some of the plumage of knowledge and therefore in a sense is knowledge.

Theaetetus will not acknowledge that unadulterated knowledge is not in front of us (201a1). False opinion would not be in the soul if it were not first outside the soul. Since Theaetetus believes that being never appears as anything other than itself, he is driven to believe that being and appearance are the same. Clarity thus becomes darkness, and sight blindness. Theaetetus is a somnambulistic hunter of knowledge. Anything he puts in the cage must be knowledge because the cage is, after all, the cage of knowledge. Socrates had given hunting a fourfold character: (1) the hunting of the knowledge; (2) its capture and possession; (3) the secondary hunting of the knowledge once possessed; (4) its use. Theaetetus entirely ignored the first step. The fact (*pragma*) one seeks to know is for him entirely unproblematic (cf. 194c6, d6). False opinion, therefore, becomes something "mental," an aberration in the soul as trivial and as mysterious as is the mistaking of eleven for twelve. It is false opinion as the semblance of knowledge that is the true perplexity. Theaetetus needs the Eleatic stranger in order to learn what his semblances of knowledge are, and how they are possible. Socrates can only give him the experience of them.

Socrates assumes that Theaetetus' definition of knowledge as true opinion is done with. If they have not found out what false opinion is, they did not find out what true opinion is either. If they had accounted for false opinion, they would have accounted for true opinion as well, but such an account would have replaced their true opinion with knowledge. Theaetetus, however, does not understand that, even if his definition is true, he is now in the position of a just jury who have been persuaded and not taught. If they remain where they are, Socrates says, nothing is evident. In order to establish that true opinion is knowledge, it would be necessary, according to Theaetetus' own criterion, to enumerate every case of it and show that none of its consequences is ever ugly and bad, but a single counterexample suffices to refute it.

Socrates' counterexample is taken from the city, about which Theaetetus knows nothing. Theaetetus is obviously thinking of mathematics: if someone's answers were always correct, his true opinion would be indistinguishable from knowledge. The teacher gives the pupil problems in order to find out whether he only knows by rote, but no test can be devised that the soul of beautiful wax cannot pass perfectly. But Theaetetus would be hard put to affirm that someone who copied his own test paper, or said whatever he said, really knew the answers. Such dishonesty does not occur to him. He is not Hippolytus. In his innocence, he overlooks mimicry and persuasion, the two elements in which every city lives. Theaetetus is too distant from the city either to see these elements in others or to think of their applicability to himself. He solely becomes wise by wisdom; he learns everything he knows (145c7–d12). The cogency, however, of Socrates' example would seem to be diminished by its appeal to the difference between hearsay and an eyewitness report, for the senses have presumably been disallowed as sources of the truth. Socrates is thinking of his forthcoming trial and Plato of his dialogues. Just as Socrates will not have taught even those who will acquit him that the unexamined life is not worth living, so Plato will have us decide, without any first-hand evidence of either Socrates or philosophy, on Socrates' innocence. The section on false opinion both begins and ends with an allusion to Socrates' trial.

XV. LETTERS
(201c8–206b12)

No sooner has Socrates said that knowledge and true opinion must be different, than Theaetetus, without stopping to acknowledge Socrates' proof, suddenly recalls what he once heard someone say: Knowledge is true opinion with speech (*logos*). Since, however, Socrates' proof consisted of an example in which speech as hearsay was true opinion as opposed to knowledge through eyesight, Theaetetus must mean by speech something else. Theaetetus seems to have finally caught up with Socrates, for Socrates had defined opining (*doxazein*) as a silent speech backed up by reasoning (*dianoeisthai*). Theaetetus therefore would mean by *logos* proof. To have knowledge is to have the proof of a true speech.[37] Theaetetus has just experienced this; he has heard from Socrates a proof of why true opinion cannot be knowledge. This is now known. But Theaetetus knows neither the Socratic source of his definition nor his own experience. He does not know why he just recalled the definition. The seal of his present experience seems to have fitted so perfectly an impressed memory that it has been obliterated in the matching. He is in fact mistaken, for he has put the seal in the wrong impression. What he remembers is not what he just heard but quite a different thesis: Knowledge is of the knowable, and the knowable is that which has or admits of a *logos*, while the unknowable does not. *Logos* here cannot mean proof; it is merely in opposition to name (201d3). Theaetetus is daydreaming. He has put together two things which do not belong together. His present experience has stimulated an old memory which only looks as if it were the same as his present experience. He has remembered an "atomic theory," which the body-people he so much disliked propose. They now have their revenge on his fastidiousness. But Theaetetus has nonetheless made an important advance. For the first time he gives the objects of knowledge along with his definition of knowledge.

The first things are like simple sounds, about which nothing can be said except their conventional names. Each of the first things is a proper noun. Nothing else can be said about them without violating their uniqueness. They are wholly heterogenous; each is its own class, and it cannot be explained why these are the first things and not others. What they have in common is their mode of recognition; they are perceptible. The model the speakers of this dream have in mind is the alphabet. In the Greek alphabet, seven letters are vowels, and these are perceptible by themselves. The other seventeen are consonants, nine of which are not perceptible, while eight are just about perceptible by themselves. If we disregard this last refinement, we can say that the alphabet finds a perceptible representation for the consonants that puts them on a par with the vowels. The name for the long vowel O in Greek is the sound itself ($\hat{o}$), but the name of the consonant S is sigma. The vowel does not need to be represented—think of the nonvocalized scripts of several languages—but the consonant does. The sound $\hat{o}$ gets as its representative Ω; it has not been in any way altered, for the representation is pronounced $\hat{o}$. The sigma, on the other hand, has never been heard by itself but always in conjunction with a vowel. The syllabic sound $s\hat{o}$ gets transmuted through the dropping of $\hat{o}$ and the isolation of what remains as Σ. It is now as perceptible as Ω. The difference between Σ and the sound $s\hat{o}$ is as great as that between the oblong number 12 and its image as a square. The squaring of an irrational (*alogon*) is exactly the same as the alphabetization of a consonant. It is no wonder that Socrates recognized it as Theaetetus' dream.

Knowledge consists in the representation of the unknowable. This representation is arbitrary (the shapes and names of letters) but not entirely. It results from the breaking down of the perceptible into a perceptible and nonperceptible element. This breakdown, in turn, allows for the working out of all possible syllables or compounds. The compounds, all of which are knowable, yield the possible objects of experience. Their elements, however, are divided between possible objects of experience and impossible objects of experience, all of which are unknowable. The impossible objects of experience correspond to the atomists' void. Socrates implies that none of the elements is ever found in isolation; so the simplest of all beings is compounded of two elements, only one of which is even in principle isolatable. *Logos*, whose being (*ousia*) is the weaving together of two names, has its image in the syllable. The syllable, in turn, because it joins a consonant with a vowel, images the conjunction of atom and void in a being. Void and atom, each of which is never apart from the other, are the two principles of being. Being and *logos* are thus interchangeable, for only the rational "is." The being which has a *logos* has it in just the way in which the knower has it. The *logos* the knower gives for showing that his opinion is true is the *logos* by which the being itself is. The proof for the knower is the cause for the being.

Socrates distinguishes between the definition—what could knowledge still be apart from *logos* and right opinion?—and the "physiology." The ingenious part of the physiology displeases him: the unknowability of the letters and the knowability of the class of syllables. Why does he not speak of the class of letters? When Socrates asks Theaetetus for the *logos* of sigma, Theaetetus says: "But how will one say the elements of the element? The reason is, Socrates, that the sigma belongs to the voiceless; it's only a sound. It's like when the tongue hisses. And of the beta in turn and most of the elements as well there's neither voice nor sound. The saying therefore holds good, they're without speech (*aloga*), since the most vivid of them are the very seven that only have voice and no speech whatever." Theaetetus makes a threefold classification; he does not regard this as a *logos*, nor even speak of it as a classification. He divines without comment that an account in terms of efficient cause—the hissing of the tongue—is not a *logos*. To state the class to which an indivisible belongs is not a *logos*. "One" has no *logos;* only the countable has a *logos*. Theaetetus has returned once more to his first answer, but he now is in a bind, since there is obviously knowledge of the countable class of vowels even if not of each vowel separately (cf. 206b7). Theaetetus says that there are seven vowels because there are seven letters for vowels. But that is a convention which is not always true, for there are either only five or ten—five if one disregards the difference between long and short, ten if one introduces that distinction everywhere. Moreover, there are only that many vowels in Greek; the seven conventional vowels belong to a continuum which admits of an uncountable number of vowels. The stops a language puts into one and the same continuum are conventional, and though there is a limit of discrimination for the human ear, there is no real limit in itself. The class of vowels, however, is wholly distinct from that of the consonants. The class is by nature, while every articulation within the class is conventional. Theaetetus does not listen to his own voice. He dreams better than he knows.

The paradigms of the physiology are neither more nor less than the syllables and letters of writing. Everything that is true of writing must hold for the physiology of knowledge. Writing is not an image; it is a sample of the thesis. Socrates and Theaetetus hold this sample like a hostage. A hostage is meant to serve as a guarantor for the good behavior of others: the letters are meant to guarantee that all the beings are knowable and unknowable in the same way. Are letters, then, the best possible hostages? Does everything we know have the same character as our knowledge of letters? The model for prescientific knowledge is illiteracy. That which is the condition for rapid progress in the sciences is the goal of the sciences. The sciences have looked at a social characteristic of themselves in order to determine what science is. Writing is an advance over the beautiful wax block in the soul, for it replaces the private with publicity. The seals of perception are now of science's own devising, limited in number and wholly corrigible should any mistake occur in their combination. *Logos* puts its own stamp on the beings. We know a priori that KPG does not exist.

There are three levels of "reality": the finite atomic letters, the finite molecular syllables, the infinite number of syllabic complexes which most things/names are. Theaetetus is asked for the first syllable of Socrates. He says sigma and *ô;* he does not say *ô* and sigma (cf. 206a8). The *logos* of the syllable must specify the order of the elements as well as the fact that they must be uttered without "and." "And" is the expression of their being bonded which disappears when they are bonded. This "and" is the same as the "and" of the sum of seven and five. "A conjunction makes many one."[38] To say "twelve" is the correct way of saying seven and five together, just as "ΣΩ" is the correct way of saying sigma and *ô* together. If it were true that every even number is the unique sum of two prime numbers, the *logos* of twelve would be seven and five.

Letters and numbers seem to be in competition with one another for being the model of knowledge. The commutability of certain mathematical operations would, if applied to letters, make ΣΩ and ΩΣ fundamentally the same. The perceptible would thus be merely an initial guide to the symmetry of what is. Letters, in contrast, have the advantage of finiteness. Euclid's proof that there is no greatest prime number puts a limit on the intelligibility of what is. Either not everything with a *logos* could be known or if what is, is finite—this could not be known through numbers. Letters, however, no less than numbers seem unable to handle meaning. Theaetetus had distinguished between the illiterate's seeing the shape and color of letters and the literate's reading of them. The reading of them is the reading of them in a *logos:* "Socrates sits." Nothing corresponds in letters to the gap between Socrates and sits. SOCRATESSITS, which is how it would appear when written in Greek, would be a name/thing different from but somewhat alike to SOCRATES. Theaetetus' physiology, which asserted the otherness of "Socrates sick" from "Socrates healthy," reappears in another guise. It is unfortunately no more plausible, for it entails that every complex is in principle infinite and necessarily linked with every other complex. There are no separate names/things. The private atomicity of Theaetetus' physiology now becomes a public atomicity in which all things are together.

Socrates offers Theaetetus the choice of saying that the syllable is all its elements or that when the elements are put together some single whole comes to be. Theaetetus chooses the first possibility; he had formerly agreed that in the case of perceptions there must be some single whole to which they as a manifold pertain (cf. 184d6, 203e6). He therefore tacitly acknowledges that there are two kinds of beings, one of which is most manifest in a number, all of whose parts are the whole number, and another most manifest in soul, whose unity does not consist only in its parts. It is unclear to which kind the syllable belongs. Socrates quickly shows that the syllable cannot be known if its elements are unknown and proposes that they consider the alternative, which he reformulates: "We should not have perhaps set down the syllable as its elements, but some single species that has come to be out of them, with its own single look and other than the elements." The syllable as a single kind with a single look can no longer be known as merely that out of which it comes to be. Material causation does not suffice. The syllable is opposed both to a hybrid like the mule, with its single look but doubleness of kind, and a single kind with a variety of looks like the human face. That it could be a third kind seems doubtful. It seems to be as much a hybrid as the mule—donkey and horse are like consonant and vowel—and as various in looks as the face. If ΣΩ is taken to mean the written letters, there is a wide range of deformation open to it without its losing its recognizability, though there might be a perfect ΣΩ as invisible as the perfect triangle; and if ΣΩ is the sound, it too allows for a range of variations within which one can still hear it as *sô*, to say nothing of the difference between its accentless form Σωκράτησ (nominative) and the effect the accent has on it in Σώκρατεσ (vocative).

If we allow Socrates for the sake of argument to gloss over these difficulties, the new thesis says that there are two kinds of knowledge, of wholes and of parts, and that knowledge of parts does not yield knowledge of wholes. Theaetetus, however, does not notice that Socrates slips in a new consideration when he repeats the thesis: "The syllable comes to be one look out of those several elements that fit together." Knowledge of the syllable must include knowledge of those elements which do not fit together. Knowledge of what is not is part of the knowledge of what is. There is room for nonbeing in knowledge even if not in being. Socrates then shows that the syllable could not have any parts, for the whole is all its parts, but Theaetetus wants to distinguish between whole and all: the single kind that comes to be from all its parts is other than all its parts. Theaetetus' instinct in all its rashness is sound, but not as he understands his answer. Σ and Ω when they are apart from ΣΩ are not parts of ΣΩ.

Socrates asks whether there is any difference in our saying one two three four five six; twice three; thrice two; four and two; or three and two and one. Socrates implies that to speak is to count—to be a teller is to tally—and therefore to ask for a *logos* that does not enumerate is impossible. But if a speech is a summation, it can only be told if it is tellable, that is, articulated into a tellable form, which must be there before it is told. The manifold must already be there as a manifold, for otherwise there is no end to the tale. Socrates gives three ways in which the tale can be told, only one of which—twice three or thrice two—includes the operation as part of its telling. The summation with "and" can be read as either two separate groups (four and two) or three (three and two and one) which are not to be summed. Socrates has reimported the notion of numbers in themselves and disregarded the perceptible character of the syllable, as well as the difference between the consonant Σ and the vowel Ω. In the first telling, moreover, one two three four five six, the teller must not repeat himself but gather up in each successive telling the former tale. The soul of the teller which is invisibly present in the telling does this gathering. The hearer cannot tell whether he means six or twenty-one. Theaetetus is too adept in mathematics to hear what Socrates says in any but a mathematical way. His beautiful speech, in which he recognized the soul as a whole in itself, has run away. He would never have come to recognize it at all, if Socrates had not enslaved him to the illiberality of precise speech.

The difficulty with which Socrates confronts Theaetetus concerning whole and part, is independent of the restriction that the whole be knowable and the part not. That restriction forced Theaetetus to distinguish all and whole in an artificial manner and therefore to overlook the more obvious—that if the parts of six are expressable in more than one way, its parts are not always elements, and when they are all elementary, they are all the same. Five is as much a whole as six, and four as five, and so on; at each summation there is completion, the sign of which is the asyndeton between the numbers of the series. The sound *sô*, on the other hand, determines from the initial hearing the phonetic shape of its every bit, apart from which it is not a syllable.[39] Indeed, one can go further and say that the vocative Socrates as a whole controls the enunciation of its first syllable, but six has no effect on the counting of two. Wholes becomes most manifest as wholes when there is something missing from them (cf. 186a4), but numbers are never caught short. Counting has the double character of always being complete and never being complete. To begin to count is never to stop and already to stop counting. Theaetetus, therefore, cannot avoid agreeing that whole and all are the same, for at any moment the number is a total, and just as in a whole nothing is missing.

What, then, is the problem of whole and part?[40] If Σ and Ω are each a part of the whole speech (*logos*) ΣΩ, and no part can be a part unless it takes part in a whole, then Σ takes its character as a part of the speech from the whole speech ΣΩ, and likewise Ω. Σ and Ω, therefore, have each as its own speech the whole speech; but then each speech of each part doubles again, and an unending duplicity results. The doubleness of part, itself and of the whole, cannot be handled, as Plato's Parmenides says, by the distinction between same and other (146b2–5). Parmenides shows their difference in the two-fold structure of his first hypothesis, the first five sections of which deal in sequence and as if deductively with part-whole, beginning-end, figure, place, motion-rest, while the last five in turn seem to be in the deductive sequence of same-other, like-unlike, equal-unequal, older-younger, being as time. The second section contains no mention of whole and just one of part (140c9), but the first section cannot dispense with same and other. Socrates does not give Theaetetus the proper tools for dealing with the problem of whole and part, which he presents, like all the problems of the dialogue, solely in terms of same and other. He does not give them because Theaetetus does not yet know that being is a problem apart from time.

XVI. Speech
(206c1–208b10)

To ask what is knowledge is to ask what is the most perfect or complete knowledge (cf. 206a10, b9). It is not to ask what kind of knowledge we have or can have. Theaetetus is wholly unaware of the difference between these two questions. Socrates has been trying to make him see that difference. He proposes that they explore what could be meant by *logos* in the definition of the most perfect knowledge as the addition of *logos* to true opinion. Socrates seems to want the *logos* of *logos* (cf. 208b12). If *logos* means proof, he cannot want the proof of proof, but an accounting of proof: What constitutes a proof? We usually say "It does not follow" when there is a gap of some sort in an argument, something which is not explicitly listed but nonetheless assumed to be true, and which if made explicit would at once appear doubtful. To raise to the level of *logos* what is only a silent opinion is to make the opinion known. Socrates opines that *logos* can only mean one of three things according to the present definition of knowledge. He does not prove that there are only three possibilities. After he has shown that *logos* adds nothing to true opinion, he has not shown that knowledge cannot be true opinion with *logos*. But if he is correct in saying that there are only three possibilities, he has shown that knowledge cannot be of such a sort, though he himself has only true opinion without *logos*.

His proof by *logos* yields the knowledge that knowledge is not true opinion with *logos;* but it is not truly knowledge, for he does not know why there cannot be another sense of *logos* which could save the definition. True opinion cannot be known as true opinion unless there already is knowledge. If the meaning of *logos* were self-evidently an either/or proposition, Socrates could have proved conclusively that the definition of knowledge is false. He leaves out of his accounting his own counting. His accounting partakes of all three definitions: he speaks, he goes through the elements of speech, and he seeks to find the difference between true opinion and true opinion with *logos*. His failure to find the difference could be, for all we can know, due to his failure to go through all the elements of speech.

To speak is "to make evident [to another] one's own thought (*dianoia*) through sound with words and phrases, just as if it were into a mirror or water one was striking off one's opinion into the stream through one's mouth." The stream is Heraclitean. It constantly changes its quality and its place; it must be both before one starts and after one stops speaking, for otherwise one would always run the risk of not impressing either the first or the last edge of one's opinion on the stream. One's opinion is in words and phrases; it is a translation of one's thought, which can be revealed in the opinion more or less plainly. The words and phrases appear as sounds; if the words and phrases were the thought, the thought would be like letters on a page of writing, and there would be no difficulty in reading the silent writing aloud, and Socrates could not speak of the difference between Parmenides' thought and its expression. Thought must be truly silent; it cannot be silent while being potentially audible. Silent thought can only be like the consonants, not audible until they are inserted into the variable stream of vocalization. Thought therefore can never become manifest except in the company of that which is not thought. Mistaking, both on the part of the speaker and the listener, can thus easily occur.

Socrates likens the stream of sound to a mirror; he calls our attention to the reversal thought undergoes in becoming audible. The reversal perhaps consists in the denial of the priority which thought has to sound. That which is not thought looms larger than thought in speech. Not to correct for this reversal would be to speak thoughtlessly. If, moreover, speech is the image of thought, as Theaetetus says (and as the example of the mirror implies), the pointing out of speech would consist in making images. The knower par excellence might therefore be the best image-maker: whoever could image his thought in speech with the greatest clarity would know perfectly. Unless, however, one said that he who had false opinion could never image his thought with the greatest clarity, the knower would be indistinguishable from the sophist. But perhaps one could say this: The greatest clarity of an image is the revealing in the image that it is an image. Perhaps Parmenides was not the best image-maker.

Socrates exemplifies elemental knowledge with a quotation from Hesiod. Socrates and Theaetetus know only five pieces of a wagon; Hesiod says there are one hundred. The wheelwright must know the hundred pieces, but the wheelwright's superior—whoever knows what kind of wagon the circumstances require—does not need to know anywhere near that number. Socrates might casually be adding a meaning of *logos,* which either could not have been meant as that which changes true opinion into knowledge or, if meant, leaves his examination of *logos* unfinished. *Logos* in this sense has obviously something to do with wholes, but since whole has been equated with the sum total of parts, such a *logos* could not be part of the definition of knowledge. Socrates can thus survey completely the meanings of *logos* only by omitting any consideration of completeness, and he does this despite the fact that the elemental knowledge of something needs a proof that it has gone through the whole of that something (cf. 207c3–4, 208c6). A proof of this kind cannot be self-evident unless everything we know is what we make. Socrates' example was an artifact, the number of whose parts was known to the poet (maker) Hesiod. The image making implicit in ordinary speech stands right beside a making that illustrates the second definition of *logos.*

Socrates distinguishes between the syllabic and the elemental knowledge of Theaetetus' name, but it seems absurd to say that the syllabic knowledge of his name is inferior. Syllabic knowledge is knowledge of how to pronounce the name as a whole; it knows that it is a proper name, and that its syllables are meaningless separately. There are four perceptible parts to Theaetetus' name (THE-AI-TE-TOS), all of which are in Theaetetus' name exactly what they are in its knowledge; but the elemental knowledge knows nine parts, not one of which is in its knowledge just what it is in Theaetetus' name. "A" is a part of the grammarian's knowledge in a way in which it is not part of the spoken name. Not his scientific knowledge, but his prescientific true opinion tells him that "A" and "I" are one sound. The syllabic knowledge is a part of the elemental knowledge, but the elemental knowledge adds nothing to the syllabic knowledge, which remains as a part what it was by itself. Knowledge therefore is two and not one. As a whole it is true opinion, in its parts a *logos*. *Logos* is the analytical content of true opinion, without which it would know everything possible but nothing actual.

This twoness yields the following paradox. The man with true opinion or prescientific knowledge never makes a mistake (220e4); but the man who is on the way to scientific knowledge can make mistakes. He will at times write Teodorus instead of Theodorus, but the illiterate always says Theodorus. Socrates here points to the difference between knowledge and to know. In knowledge there are no mistakes, but the knower can make mistakes. There are two kinds of mistaking. Either the same is believed to belong to the same and the other, or the other and the other are believed to belong to the same. In terms of letters, whoever mistakes in the first way writes D at the beginning of both THIS and DOES, and whoever mistakes in the second, writes D at the beginning of DOES and T at the beginning of DOZE. Theaetetus, it seems, made the first mistake when he said knowledge was true opinion, and he made the second when he said knowledge was true opinion with *logos,* for this was the same as true opinion.

In writing DIS incorrectly but DOES correctly, one's mistake is to take DOES as a paradigm for THIS. In writing TOZE and DOES, one's mistake is not to take DOES as a paradigm. Knowledge therefore must consist in knowing what paradigm to use in any particular case. Theaetetus' first mistake was due to his believing that all knowledge is immediate—his paradigm was perception. His second mistake was due to his believing that all knowledge is deduction—his paradigm was mathematics. In his first mistake he misread his own soul, in the second he forgot it. The atomists assumed that their paradigm was simple, but if they discerned correctly that letters were the model—the difference between literacy and illiteracy was manifest—then no knowledge of paradigms would seem possible. We should not hit upon, except by luck, which paradigm was to be used when, and for what purpose. If, however, paradigmatic knowledge were possible, and we had obtained it, we would know how to select from the proper paradigm (as D from DOES) just that element which recurred somehow in that which we wished to examine.[41] Plato presents Socrates as the master of paradigmatic knowledge. Its indispensable guide and companion is Socrates' knowledge of soul. The Eleatic stranger tries to instruct Theaetetus and young Socrates in paradigmatic knowledge,[42] but he does not succeed so well in instructing either of them in knowledge of soul. Perfect knowledge, then, is the unity of paradigmatic knowledge and elemental knowledge. But we do not know what could bring about this unity, for elemental knowledge, proceeding as it does on the basis of true opinion, cannot supply a proof of its own completeness; and paradigmatic knowledge, since it looks at one thing to know another, can always be mistaken. Paradigmatic knowledge can inadvertently become image making, elemental knowledge a making.

XVII. Difference
(208b11–210d4)

Socrates has so far considered two possible meanings that "with speech" can have in the definition of knowledge as true opinion with *logos*. The first was speech as the reporting to another of one's own true opinion (intersubjectivity); the second was that speech split up into its parts what was already known as a whole. If, however, the definition of knowledge is true, it must have the same character as any other kind of knowledge. The definition consists of two parts; so *logos* must be the addition of something not already present in true opinion. *Logos,* therefore, must mean a speech which tells what something has which distinguishes it from everything else. Only this characterization of *logos* strictly conforms with the definition of knowledge. The two other meanings are possible and in fact seem to contain glimmerings of the truth, but not for the proposed definition. Only with this meaning can Socrates strictly prove the redundancy of "true opinion with *logos;*" for with the first and second meanings, the would-be knower might not know perfectly, but he knows something which the man with true opinion does not know (cf. 208b8–9). Socrates had to disqualify the deaf and dumb in equating true opinion with public speech (206d9). Theaetetus was really dreaming when he remembered this definition. He meant that knowledge was elemental knowledge, but he said that it was knowledge of difference. He did not express his thought.

Elemental knowledge and knowledge of difference are not incompatible with one another; indeed, the Eleatic stranger combines them in his dichotomies, for he begins with a whole like art or science, articulates the whole into its parts, and ends up with an indivisible form, which is the distinctive *logos* of whatever he is seeking. Whether this combination meets Socrates' separate arguments against each of them can for the moment be left aside, but their juxtaposition does illustrate a perplexity which, Socrates says in the *Phaedo,* put him on the trail of "ideas" (96e6–98b7). Socrates began with a search for causes, why each things becomes, perishes, and is, but he became puzzled by the fact that the causes of the coming to be of two were two and contrary to one another. If a two comes to be when one and one draw near to one another, and their coming together, which consists in their juxtaposition, is the cause of their becoming two, Socrates was amazed that if one splits a one in two the cause of their becoming two should then be this splitting.

Division and addition have the same result. Division is the second meaning of *logos*, and addition the third. Theaetetus' very first definition of knowledge, that knowledge is the arts and sciences, is an additive definition and as such, redundant: Knowledge is knowledge and the knowledge a, b, c, d, etc. (cf. 146d2). Socrates' counterdefinition, in contrast, is divisive. If Socrates had gone on dividing knowledge as if it were mud, he would presumably have comprehended every member of the single class of knowledge, and the result would have been Theaetetus' enumeration of the arts and sciences. His alphabet of knowledge might have been more detailed and complete than Theaetetus', but no better. None of his letters could tell us what a letter is. Both the additive and divisive answers have to fall back on what each of them started with, true opinion. Prescientific knowledge, like mud, is right before us (cf. 147a2, 170b6). It is one. Scientific knowledge is two or more than two, the cause of which multiplicity we do not know. We could well ask, therefore, whether the *Sophist* and the *Statesman,* the two dialogues Plato devotes to answering the *Theaetetus'* question, are two by juxtaposition or by division.

Socrates gives an example of speech as the interpretation of difference: The sun is the most brilliant of things in the sky that go around the earth. The speech of correct opinion would presumably say that the sun was one of the things that go around the earth. Socrates, however, rejects this understanding when he cites his own recognition of Theaetetus. If a correct opinion about Theaetetus will suffice to make Socrates recognize him tomorrow, a correct opinion about the sun will make him recognize it tomorrow. Socrates' exemplary speech, then, is the speech of correct opinion. Whatever else we added to it would not improve our capacity to recognize the sun. Is Socrates belittling astonomy (cf. 145d1–5)? Perhaps, but his speech is not as concise as it might be. As far as recognition goes, "the most brilliant" would suffice,[43] but as Socrates presents it, the sun's difference is embedded in an astronomical speech, which asserts that the sun moves, the earth is round, and something—lightning perhaps—is more brilliant than the sun. Socrates seems to be indicating that true opinion is not as available as Theaetetus has been led to believe.

Socrates' recognition of Theaetetus is equally perplexing as an example. Recognition of Theaetetus through perception would be far more infallible than any speech could possibly be. Theodorus, at any rate, could not make Socrates recognize Theaetetus through his speech. Socrates thus suggests the following distinction. Whoever has an impression of Theaetetus, which a speech about his difference does not accompany, can only recognize Theaetetus when he sees him again, but the knower, who has this speech, can present Theaetetus to himself even in his absence. This speech is what the dialogue itself has conveyed to us. As a speech, it is potentially universal. It does not improve our ability to recognize this Theaetetus, but to recognize all other Theaetetuses, who just because they are before us might be invisible to us. Speech makes for the proper distance (cf. 208e7–10). One would hesitate, however, to call this speech anything more than true opinion. Socrates says it is a very noble blindness to demand to take up those things we have "in order that we might learn or know what we opine." A taking up of this kind is not as idle as Socrates makes it out to be. No one fails to recognize laughter, but a speech that distinguishes it from everything else is not to be despised. Everyone knows what mud is, and Socrates' speech is just the content of true opinion, but as a speech it suddenly becomes capable of being paradigmatic. If the *logos* of mud is taken by itself, it ceases to be a paradigm and sinks to the level of the trivial; and if Plato's presentation of Theaetetus is isolated, as if it were an overelaborate way of remembering Theaetetus, it too becomes no better than the dialogue Euclides thought he wrote.

Socrates, in poking fun at a definition of knowledge which reports what already is present to true opinion, obscures the speech of true opinion. With an "unwonted discursiveness,"[44] Socrates seems to imitate the uninformative lengthening of which he accuses the definition. His first sentence is a fitting conclusion: "Of those things of which we have right opinion, by which they differ from everything else, [the definition] urges us to take in addition a right opinion of those things by which they differ from everything else." But then Socrates begins to waffle on his own: "Compared to this injunction, the twirling of a *skytalê*, a pestle, or whatever name it goes by, would be as nothing in point of nonsense." The proverb Socrates has in mind—the turning round of a pestle—means to go round in circles and accomplish nothing. Socrates seems to have himself gone round in circles in his groping for the right expression. And yet he cannot help saying something new while awkwardly attempting to repeat himself.

A *skytalê* was "at Sparta a staff or baton, used as a cypher for writing dispatches, thus: a strip of leather was rolled slantwise round it, on which the dispatch was written lengthwise, so that when unrolled they were unintelligible: commanders abroad had a staff of like thickness, round which they rolled these papers, and so were able to read the dispatches."[45] We ambush a Spartan messenger; his dispatch is in code. Since we read all the letters, we have a correct opinion about them and would not mistake the dispatch for another, but since we cannot read the dispatch, we do not know the *logos*. The jumble of signs on the dispatch becomes a *logos* as soon as we use the *skytalê*. Socrates has assumed throughout the argument that true opinion is necessarily in order, but he should have asked what puts the manifold of perceptual signs into their proper order. The addition to true opinion which makes for greater knowledge is not *logos,* which is rather the result of the ordering, but the *skytalê* of soul. He himself has called this *skytalê* thinking (*dianoeisthai*). The Eleatic stranger pretends that he knows of an automatic *skytalê*. It is dichotomy.

Socrates has clipped Theaetetus' wings. He has made him as barren as he himself is. He has tried to place Theaetetus on his own ground. It is unclear, however, whether he has handled Theaetetus in the best possible way. Theaetetus has less than a day to understand what he has experienced before the Eleatic stranger puts him through another kind of course in the *Sophist*. The stranger agrees with Socrates that Theaetetus is not as unassuming as Theodorus believes him to be, but he does not deflate Theaetetus by suddenly confronting him with the disparity between the brilliance of his visionary's dream and the semidarkness of Socratic wakefulness; rather, he accepts Theaetetus' assumption that the true beginning is completely known, and they can deduce everything from it. He shows Socrates that if one encourages Theaetetus in this illusion—Socrates had tried to encourage Theaetetus while disillusioning him—Theaetetus can advance much further. The stranger draws up a powerful indictment of Socrates' maieutics; that is, at any rate, the impression everyone has of the *Sophist,* and which Socrates confirms when he thanks Theodorus for his acquaintance with Theaetetus only after he has heard him in conversation with the stranger. In the *Theaetetus,* however, Socrates consoles Theaetetus. At worst, he will be less harsh to his associates— Theodorus is mistaken even on this point—and with a greater tameness will not in his moderation, the only mention of moderation in the dialogue, believe he knows what he does not know. Socrates' art can do no more. He has obtained it from a god to practice on all the noble and beautiful young. And yet despite the impasse they have reached, Socrates only goes away because he must now answer Meletus' indictment; tomorrow at dawn, he tells Theodorus, they should meet again at the same place. Socrates is not easily discouraged. Only here in the Platonic dialogues does Socrates make a definite appointment which he keeps; he does not now say, as he did once, in putting off the importunity of others, that he will meet them "if a god is willing."[46] Socrates seems to divine that the Eleatic stranger is coming.

The *Theaetetus* is the *logos* of Socrates. It is that by means of which Socrates can be recognized and known. He is, however, negatively determined, for he is not anyone Theodorus would call a philosopher. It is in light of this that the two main conclusions of the dialogue have to be understood: the soul and its experiences cannot be the truth of all things, and the soul and its experiences cannot be understood mathematically. The first conclusion is connected with the attempt to separate Socrates' maieutics from Protagoreanism, that is, from the improvement Socrates made in the thesis of Protagoras himself, and the second is connected with Socratic ignorance, whose character resists any attempt to understand it in arithmetical terms. It might seem, however, that these conclusions are a function of the peculiar circumstances of this dialogue and do not pertain to the truth of Socrates in himself. The *Sophist* and the *Statesman* are needed to show that the *Theaetetus*' negative determination of Socrates obtains of necessity for the philosopher simply. This universalization of Socrates as a problem thus brings in its train the problem of being. The discovery through the perplexity of nonbeing of the equal perplexity of being is the *Sophist*'s equivalent to Socratic ignorance. Being, too, is not wholly countable.

Notes

Dialogue

1. Euclides and Terpsion appear without speaking in Plato's *Phaedo* 59C. They belonged to the Megarian school of philosophy of which Euclides was the founder. They denied potentiality and had recourse only to *logos* in rejecting all phenomena.
2. The date of the battle in which Theaetetus was wounded and possibly died afterward was either sometime between 390–387 B.C. or in 369 B.C., when the Athenians and Spartans combined against the Thebans under Epaminondas. The earlier date would seem to condense Theaetetus' achievements into too short an interval.
3. Erineos is on the border between the Megarid and Attica, a distance of some ten miles from Megara. It was on the Cephisus, and Persephone was said to have been snatched by Hades there.
4. In a papyrus fragment of an anonymous commentary on the *Theaetetus*, written sometime in or before the second century A.D., there is the following (3.28–34): "It is reported that there is a different prologue, rather frigid, and consisting of an almost equal number of lines; its beginning is: 'Are you bringing, boy, the speech about Theaetetus?' " Cf. *Anonymer Kommentar zu Platons Theaitet*, Berliner Klassikertexte II, ed. E. Diels and W. Schubart (Berlin, 1905).
5. Theodorus of Cyrene (a Greek colony in Libya) was a younger contemporary of Socrates (b. ca. 460 B.C.). Theaetetus (414–369 B.C.) was most famous for showing that only five regular solids could be constructed; he also analyzed the various kinds of irrationals.
6. Wisdom (*sophia*), whose identity with knowledge is later denied by Socrates' Protagoras (166D), does not occur in either the *Sophist* or the *Statesman*. After 150C it has become tainted: "sham-wisdom" (*doxosophia*) occurs at *Sophist* 231B.
7. Pollux (IX.106) describes the game. A ball was tossed against a wall and the number of bounces before it was caught was counted; the loser was

called the ass, the winner the king, and he could order the loser to do whatever he wanted.

8. "Agreeable" (*prosêgoros*) could also be a mathematical term, "congruent"; cf. *Republic* 546B.

9. For a plausible account of Theodorus' individual proofs and why he got stuck at 17, see W. R. Knorr, *The Evolution of the Euclidean Elements* (Dordrecht-Boston, 1975), pp. 21–96, 170–93.

10. Cf. *Protagoras* 335E-336A.

11. "Noble and farouche" also occurs together at *Republic* 535B. "Farouche" (*blosuros*) is a rare word, whose tone is not exactly known; cf. M. Leumann, *Homerische Wörter* (Basel, 1950), pp. 141–48; P. Chantraine, *Dictionnaire étymologique de la langue grecque* (Paris, 1968–1980), s.v.

12. Cf. *Meno* 79E–80B.

13. Socrates indulges in a series of alliterative puns that this is meant to reproduce: *alokhos ousa tên lokheian eilêkhe*. Alokhos ("unallied") elsewhere means spouse, but Socrates takes it as an alpha-privative formation with the stem cognate with *lokheia* ("lying-in").

14. For the likely and the necessary, see *Symposium* 200A; *Laws* 656A–B.

15. The text is uncertain here, but the sense is not.

16. For Socrates the pimp, see Xenophon *Symposium* iii.10, iv.56–64.

17. Socrates' *daimonion* is referred to by Plato in the following passages: *Apology of Socrates* 31C–D; *Euthydemus* 272E; *Republic* 496C; *Theages* 128B–131; *Phaedrus* 242B–C. The word itself is difficult to translate since, as Socrates indicates in the *Apology* (27B–28A), it could be understood as either the diminutive of *daemôn*, which in turn has no fixed distinction from "god" except that it is usually nameless, or a neuter substantive from the adjective *daimonios*, "that which pertains to the more than human."

18. "Divinely-speaking" (*thespesios*) is a poetic word.

19. "Wind-egg" is an unfertilized egg, which was extended to mean fruitless and vain.

20. This sentence occurred in Protagoras' book *Truth*. Another book, *On Gods*, stated that he did not know whether the gods are and what sort they are; it is alluded to at 162D–E.

21. "Appearance" (*phantasia*) is not a separate faculty as it is in Aristotle, and which it may be at *Sophist* 260C, but merely the substantival equivalent to the verb *phainesthai*. Outside of *Republic* 382E the word occurs only in the *Theaetetus* and *Sophist*.

22. "Converge" is meant to convey the pun on the original meaning of *sumpheromai* "move together" and its extension "agree." The word occurs in the fragment of Heraclitus that the stranger quotes at *Sophist* 242E.

23. Epicharmus (540?–443? B.C.) wrote comedy in Doric. He lived most of his life in Sicily (Megara and Syracuse). The extant fragments contain passages that read like Platonic dialogues, but their genuineness has been doubted.

24. *Iliad* XIV.302. It is spoken by Hera to Zeus with the intent of deceiving him as to her purpose, which she says is to reconcile Oceanus and Tethys but in fact is to seduce Zeus. Cf. also in the same book line 246.

25. The passage alluded to is at the beginning of the eighth book of the *Iliad*, where Zeus threatens all the assembled gods: "Come, gods, try it, in order that you all may know, hang from the sky a golden chain, and all you gods and goddesses attach it, but you would not draw to earth out of the sky Zeus the highest, the wise, not even if you should wear yourselves out with toil. But whenever I should wish to draw it, I would draw it along with earth and sea, and then I would tie the chain around the ridge of Olympus, and everything would be up in the air; it's by so much that I am superior to gods and human beings" (18–27); cf. *Laws* 644E–645A.

26. Euripides *Hippolytus* 612: "The tongue has sworn, the mind (*phrên*) is unsworn." Hippolytus says it to Phaedra's nurse after he threatens to divulge Phaedra's passion though he had sworn unconditionally not to repeat anything he heard from the nurse.

27. "Hallucinations" (*phasmata*) is perhaps a slight overtranslation: *phasma* literally means an appearance or sight, usually sudden, as in "portent."

28. In Hesiod's *Theogony*, Pontus bore Thaumas (237), and Thaumas married Electra who gave birth to Iris (rainbow) and the Harpies (265–68).

29. The use of parentheses around "is" and "are" in this passage is meant to indicate the extent to which the Greek avoids it.

30. *Pheromai*, the middle of *pherô* ("carry"), means to move locally (sometimes translated as "sweep"), but the active can mean to bring to birth (particularly of plants); since the surrounding language suggests a pun, the "e" in borne is put in parenthesis. For the pun see *Republic* 546A.

31. The name-day for Athenian children was called the *Amphidromia* (Runaround). A week or so after birth, a child was carried around the hearth and presented to the family and their guests who witnessed the naming.

32. The proverb literally is "If it's dear to you, it's not even hateful to me."

33. According to the scholium "not worth even a single one" is a term from dicing, where one is the lowest score.

34. *Eikosi* could be the dative plural of either *eikos* (likely) or *eikôn* (semblance).

35. "Monster" (*teras*) is anything put together out of disparate parts, or a prodigy of some kind.

36. Socrates' confrontation with Protagoras took place at Callias' house in Plato's *Protagoras;* it is also the setting of Xenophon's *Symposium.* For the family of Callias and their wealth, see J. K. Davies, *Athenian Propertied Families* (Oxford, 1971), 7826, pp. 254–70.

37. "Truths" seems to be a necessary correction for the manuscript's "true," which involves an impossible placement of a connective. But "truth" is nowhere else in Plato in the plural.

38. Sciron was a robber who waylaid travelers on the road between Megara

and Athens; he forced them to wash his feet, and while they were doing so pushed them off a cliff. He was killed by Theseus. Antaeus was the son of Poseidon and Earth and lived in Libya; since his strength was derived from his contact with the ground, Heracles lifted him into the air and crushed him.

39. The tragic man, Socrates says in the *Phaedo* (115A), would use the word "fate" (*heimarmenê*).

40. *Odyssey* XVI.121. Telemachus tells the disguised Odysseus that he has very many thousands of enemies in his house; at line 236 the revealed Odysseus asks for an accurate count.

41. Another reading is possible which would imply that those who deny natural right are more extreme than the Protagorean position as improved by Socrates, but this seems to be a misunderstanding of pre-Socratic philosophy.

42. *Daimonie* is a not uncommon form of address from Homer onward. In Plato, perhaps because of Socrates' *daimonion*, it is usually spoken with a sense of surprise at the addressee's prescience; cf. *Crito* 44B.

43. "Practices of philosophy" (*philosophiai*). The plural of "philosophy" is rare and does not recur in Plato. Isocrates has it thrice. Wisdom (*sophia*) is plural at 176C.

44. The speakers in court had to speak within a given time, which was measured by a water clock (*clepsydra*).

45. The manuscripts have after "outline" the clause, "which they call an affidavit"; it is usually held to be interpolated.

46. An expression for the uncountable and immeasurable.

47. Pindar fr. 292S. It is not quite clear how much is Pindar's own words; "exploring" could also be his. "Under the earth and the planes" became a proverbial expression for a busybody.

48. "Mickle" translates Madvig's correction (*taü*) for the manuscripts' *t' au* ("and in turn"), which if genuine implies a separate quotation ("and possessing in turn gold") with no connection in the context.

49. Cf. *Iliad* XVIII.104: "I sit by the ships a vain burden of the field." Achilles says it to his mother after the death of Patroclus. Socrates quotes it in *Apology of Socrates* 28D.

50. "Sweeping being" (*pheromenê ousia*) recurs as "sweeping becoming" at *Sophist* 246C.

51. "Yes, by Zeus, my good man" occurs in Aristophanes *Clouds* 1338 as well as elsewhere in his work, but nowhere else in Plato.

52. The text seems not to be sound here, and the clause ("or rather . . .") has been held interpolated, but it's probable that Theodorus' indignation has got ahead of his grammar.

53. Cf. Aristophanes *Clouds* 942–44. Unjust Speech is talking: "And then I'll strike him with my arrows of fresh phraselets and thoughts."

54. A problem (*problêma*) is a mathematical term for the setting out of a construction of a figure.

55. Cf. *Protagoras* 316D.

56. This line is also cited by Simplicius, but it is not known where it fits into the poem; it resembles fr. VIII.38 "(Destiny fettered it) to be whole and immovable; therefore everything (mortals laid down) will be a name," since "whole" (*oulon*) looks like "such" (*hoion*), for which Simplicius apparently read *oion* ("alone").

57. The game is described by Pollus IX.112. Two groups of boys tried to pull over to their own side the members of the other group one by one.

58. "Arresters" (*stasiôtai*) brings out the pun in the word, which otherwise means seditionaries.

59. "To move the unmovable things" is a proverbial expression for a violation of the sacred.

60. The scrutiny (*dokimasia*) was an examination of elected magistrates to determine whether they met certain qualifications for public office.

61. *Poiotês* ("sortness" or "quality") became the standard substantive for the pronoun for "sort" (*poios*), but here it is clearly not meant to imply a substance with a quality.

62. Cf. *Timaeus* 50A–B.

63. Socrates first phrases the conclusion with the verb "be" and then corrects it out of deference to the Heracliteans with "become."

64. "Dialect" (*dialektos*) is the same word translated as "conversation" at 146B.

65. The scholium offers two explanations for the proverb. Either it's an invitation to compete, issued to those who are better than you are, or an invitation to those who want to anyway.

66. *Iliad* III.172. Helen says it to her father-in-law Priam, as the Trojan elders are surveying the marshalled troops of the Achaeans.

67. Such a use of "depth" is not common in prose. Herodotus speaks of "ways deeper than the Thracians" (IV.95.1), and Socrates is said to have remarked that Heraclitus' writings need for their interpretation a Delian diver (Diogenes Laertius II.22); cf. *Laws* 930A.

68. The quotation marks around "the same" are meant to represent the double article of the Greek (*to tauton*); it indicates that "the same" is being used as a universal (sameness). The device recurs at *Sophist* 254E.

69. For the phrase, cf. *Phaedo* 65C.

70. Campbell suggests assigning "And either together or in turn?" to Socrates, "Most beautiful" to Theaetetus, and "But . . . do?" to Socrates.

71. These possibilities can be represented as follows. Let a rectangle and a triangle represent two seals, and when perceived or known in the memory let their lines be solid, and when neither perceived nor known dotted. The first four cases in the block of wax are these, in which error is impossible:

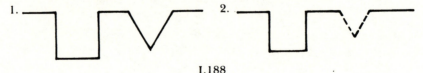

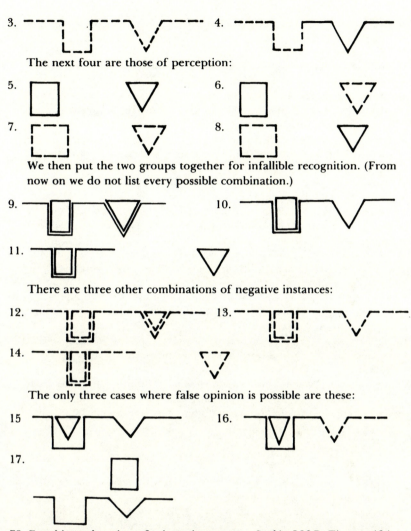

3. 4.

The next four are those of perception:

5. 6.

7. 8.

We then put the two groups together for infallible recognition. (From now on we do not list every possible combination.)

9. 10.

11.

There are three other combinations of negative instances:

12. 13.

14.

The only three cases where false opinion is possible are these:

15 16.

17.

72. For this explanation of mirror images, see *Sophist* 266C; *Timaeus* 46A–C. The shoe exchange sounds like Electra's recognition of Orestes' footprints in Aeschylus' *Choephoroe* 205–10.

73. *Kear* or *kêr* is a poetic word for heart (*kear* among the tragic poets, *kêr* in Homer); cognate with it is the ordinary word for heart (*kardia*).

74. "Casts" (*ekmageia*) is the same word in the plural that had been used for the wax block itself (*ekmageion*).

75. "Shaggy heart" occurs at *Iliad* II.851; XVI.554 of Pylaemenes and Patroclus respectively. Achilles has a shaggy breast at I.189.

76. "Ring-dove" or "woodpigeon" (*phatta*) is a species of wild pigeon.

77. A proverbial expression for those things only known from experience.

78. "Advocates" translates *dikanikoi,* which had previously been rendered "shysters" (175D).
79. "Knowable" (*epistêta*) is being signaled as a new word; the ordinary word would be *gnôsta,* which Socrates uses at 202B and everywhere else.
80. Cf. *Symposium* 202A.
81. All the words in double quotes are to be found in the previous sentences; 'this' is an addition.
82. Omega is not the Greek name for the long O sound; it along with epsilon, upsilon, and omicron had its sound for its name (cf. *Cratylus* 393D).
83. There are seven vowels in the Greek alphabet (alpha, epsilon, eta, iota, omicron, upsilon, omega), eight semivowels (zeta, lambda, mu, nu, rho, sigma, ksi, psi), and nine consonants (beta, gamma, delta, theta, kappa, pi, tau, phi, khi). Semivowels and consonants are sometimes counted together.
84. "The same result" is that "not a whole" is equivalent to "not an all:" "out of the same" is that "whole," as that from which nothing is missing, is equivalent to "all."
85. Hesiod *Works and Days* 455–56: "A man rich in his own opinion talks of putting together a wagon, the fool, he doesn't know, but the timbers of a wagon are one hundred."
86. The Mysians were proverbially the lowest of the low (cf. *Gorgias* 521B); so "most remote" would ordinarily have meant the bottom of the barrel.
87. The proverb "twirling of a pestle" means to do the same thing again and again without accomplishing anything.
88. Theaetetus is probably referring to Socrates' question at 209A.

COMMENTARY

1. Aristocles *De philosophia* VII (Eusebius *Praep. Ev.* XIV.17.1).
2. Aristotle *Metaphysics* 1046b29–1047a7.
3. *Statesman* 257a1–2.
4. *Statesman* 258a3–6.
5. *Republic* 487a2–6
6. *Philebus* 55e1–56a2; *Statesman* 284e11–285b6.
7. *Parmenides* 130c1–e4.
8. *Republic* 408c5–409e3.
9. Xenophon *Memorabilia* I.vi.13.
10. *Sophist* 246a7–b1; *Republic* 509d3.
11. *Republic* 527a6–b2.
12. Aristotle *Metaphysics* 1010b10–11.
13. *Republic* 436a8–437a10.
14. *Timaeus* 91d6–e1.
15. *Laches* 187e6–7; *Apology of Socrates* 30a4; *Sophist* 265a2; *Hippias Major* 304d3.
16. *Parmenides* 132d2.
17. *Apology of Socrates* 38a1–6.
18. *Republic* 340a9–b8.
19. *Republic* 530b6–c1.
20. *Statesman* 257b7–8.
21. *Odyssey* 4.12.
22. *Parmenides* 128a4–e4.
23. *Republic* 507c1–2.

24. *Republic* 352e5–8, 518c5.
25. *Republic* 582d7–14.
26. For this use of *kalon*, see *Gorgias* 454d1–4.
27. *Meno* 92b7–c7.
28. Aristotle, *Metaphysics* 1051b24–25.
29. *Republic* 381e4; *Laws* 959b1.
30. *Parmenides* 136e9, 164d2, 165c7.
31. *Parmenides* 143c4–8.
32. *Republic* 516b9–c2.
33. *Charmides* 159a2; *Republic* 490a8–b7.
34. *Republic* 496b5–6.
35. This sort of nominalism is discussed by Aristotle *Posterior Analytics* 71a30–71b8.
36. *Sophist* 241d1–242a4.
37. *Symposium* 202a5–10.
38. Aristotle *Rhetoric* 1413b32.
39. Aristotle *Metaphysics* 1041b11–33.
40. What follows is an adaptation of the argument at *Parmenides* 142d6–143a3; cf. Aristotle *Physics* 185b11–16.
41. *Republic* 368d1–369a3.
42. *Sophist* 253d1–3.
43. Xenophon *Memorabilia* IV.vii.7.
44. L. Campbell on 209e5. *The Theaetetus of Plato* (Oxford, 1866), p. 209.
45. *A Greek-English Lexicon*, compiled by H. G. Liddell and R. Scott, 7th ed. (Oxford, 1882), s.v.
46. *Laches* 201c4–5.

SOPHIST

Sophist

THEODORUS

SOCRATES

A STRANGER

THEAETETUS

THEODORUS: It's in accordance with yesterday's agreement, Socrates, *216A*
that we ourselves have come in due order; and we're leading him
here, a kind of stranger, who in birth (*genos*) is from Elea, a
comrade of the circle of Parmenides and Zeno, and a man very
much a philosopher.[1]

SOCRATES: Have you really then failed to observe, Theodorus, that in
accordance with Homer's speech it's no stranger you lead but a
kind of god?[2] He asserts that not only do different gods accompany all those human beings who share in a just shame, but that *B*
also, in particular, the god of strangers proves not least to be their
companion and looks down on the acts of outrage and of law-
abidingness of human beings? So perhaps your stranger who attends you might also be one of the Mightier,[3] come to look us
over and refute us who are poor in speeches, and is a kind of
refutative god.

THEODORUS: No, Socrates, this is not the stranger's way.[4] He's more
measured than those whose zeal is devoted to contentiousness.
And the man, in my opinion, is in no way a god; he is, however,
divine, for I address all the philosophers as of this sort. *C*

SOCRATES: And beautifully, my friend. This genus, however, is in all
probability scarcely much easier to discern than that of the god.
For on account of the ignorance of everyone else, these men—

those who not in a fabricated way but in their being are philosophers—certainly show up in all sorts of apparitions and haunt
cities, looking down from on high on the life of those below. And
in the opinion of some they are worth nothing and of some every-

D   thing, and at times they take on the apparitions of statesmen, and
at times of sophists, and there are times when they might give
some the impression that they are altogether crazy. From our
stranger, however, I would with pleasure inquire, if it's to his

217   liking, what those in that region were accustomed to believe and
name these things.

THEODORUS: What sorts of things exactly?

SOCRATES: Sophist, statesman, philosopher.

THEODORUS: But what question in particular do you intend to ask, and
in what sort of perplexity about them are you?

SOCRATES: It's this. Were they accustomed to hold all these one or
two, or, just as their names are three, to divide their genera into
three as well and attach a name to each individually?

THEODORUS: Well, I suspect he's not one to begrudge a discourse on
them. Or just how are we to speak, stranger?

B   STRANGER: In just this way, Theodorus. I'm not one to begrudge it,
and it's not difficult to say it either—they believed them three. It's
no small and easy work, however, to distinguish with clarity whatever they severally are.

THEODORUS: Why, just by chance, Socrates, you touch on speeches
pretty nearly the same as those that we happened to put to him
in questioning him before we came here. And though he claims to
have heard about it adequately and not forgotten it, he was then
giving us the same excuses he just now gave you.

C   SOCRATES: Well, in that case, stranger, don't deny us the very first
favor we ask you, but tell us this much. When you speak about
whatever you want to point out to anyone, is it more your pleasure
usually to go through it by yourself on your own in a long speech,
or through questions, as Parmenides once handled it in my presence when I was young—and he was very old indeed and went
through very beautiful speeches?

D   STRANGER: Well, Socrates, if the interlocutor submits to guidance easily
and painlessly, it's easier in this way, to do it before someone else;
but if that's not the case, by oneself.

SOCRATES: Well, it's possible to select anyone you want of those present,
for everyone will gently comply with you, but if you take me as
your adviser you'll choose one of the young, Theaetetus here, or
anyone of the rest who suits you.

STRANGER: Socrates, in my first association with you now a kind of

shame holds me in its grip—not from conducting the association
in brief exchanges of words but from the drawn-out extension of *E*
a vast speech by myself (or even before another), and putting on
a kind of exhibition. For in truth, the question as now formulated
is not of the size one might expect it to be, but it needs in fact a
very lengthy speech. But, on the other hand, not to gratify you
and everyone else here, especially when you spoke as you did,
appears to me somewhat unbecoming a stranger and savage,[5] since *218*
I altogether welcome at any rate Theaetetus as my interlocutor
on the basis of my own previous conversation with him and your
present recommendation.

THEAETETUS: Act accordingly, stranger, and just as Socrates said, you'll
earn everyone's gratitude.

STRANGER: There's probably no need to speak any longer to this point,
Theaetetus, but from now on after this, it seems the speech would
be directed to you. But if, after all, you get wearied and distressed
by its length, don't blame me for it but these here your own
comrades.

THEAETETUS: Well, I suspect that as I am now I won't get tired, but *B*
if anything of the sort does occur, we'll enlist Socrates here. He
has the same name as Socrates but is my contemporary and fellow
gymnast. It's not unusual for him to work out with me a lot.

STRANGER: That's good, and you'll take your own counsel about it in
private when the speech advances. But in common with me, you
are now to join in the investigation by first beginning, as it appears
to me, from the sophist, seeking and making evident in speech
whatever he is. The reason for this is that as of now you and I *C*
have only a name in common about him, but we might perhaps
have by ourselves in private the work for which we severally call
him. And one must always in regard to anything have gained
together an agreement about the matter (*pragma*) itself through
speeches rather than only about the name apart from speech. The
tribe that we're now intending to seek is not at all the easiest to
comprehend, whatever it is, the sophist; but in all great things
that one has to elaborate beautifully, everyone has held the opinion even from long ago that in these sorts of things one should
practice first on small and easier things before tackling the very *D*
biggest.[6] Now, then, Theaetetus, this is my own advice to the pair
of us, inasmuch as we believe the genus of the sophist to be difficult
and hard to hunt down, to make a practice run of his pursuit in
something else that's easier—unless of course you can from somewhere or other speak of a different and easier way.

THEAETETUS: Well, I can't.

STRANGER: Do you want then in our pursuit to try, in the case of something trivial, to establish it as a paradigm of the greater?

E THEAETETUS: Yes.

STRANGER: What, then, should we set in front of us as easily knowable and small, but that admits of a speech inferior to none of the greater things? For example, angler. Isn't it something knowable to everyone, and it scarcely deserves, does it, a lot of serious attention?

THEAETETUS: That's so.

219 STRANGER: I expect, however, that he admits of a pursuit and a speech that's not unsuitable for us in light of what we want.

THEAETETUS: That would be beautiful.

STRANGER: Come on then. Let's begin it at this point. Tell me. Shall we set him down as an artisan or someone artless, but with a different capacity?

THEAETETUS: He's not in the least artless.

STRANGER: Well, now, (there are) just about two species of all the arts.[7]

THEAETETUS: How?

STRANGER: There's farming and as much treatment that involves all of the mortal body, and, in turn, that which is put together and fabricated—it's that to which we've given the name utensil—and there's the mimetic (art). All of these would most justly be ad-

B dressed with one name.[8]

THEAETETUS: How and with what?

STRANGER: Everything which previously is not but subsequently one leads into being, we surely say of the one who is leading that he makes, and of the thing being led that it is being made.

THEAETETUS: Right.

STRANGER: But all the things we just now went through had their own capacity geared to this.

THEAETETUS: Indeed they had.

STRANGER: So let's then sum them up together and address them as the art of making (poetics).

C THEAETETUS: Let it be.

STRANGER: Next, on the other hand, the whole species of learning, and that of familiarization, and the moneymaking, competitive, and hunting kinds, and since none of these is a handicraft, but in the case of the things which are and have become, they get the better of some of these by speeches and actions, and some they do not give up to those who are bent on getting the better of them—surely on account of this, all the parts together, should they be said to be a kind of art of acquisition, would especially stand out as suitably spoken of.

THEAETETUS: Yes, it would suit them.

STRANGER: So if all the arts together are acquisitive and poetic, into *D*
which are we to put, Theaetetus, the art of angling?

THEAETETUS: It's plain, surely—into the art of acquisition.

STRANGER: But aren't here two species of the acquisitive art? There's
that which is characterized by the exchange of the willing with
the willing through gifts, wages, and sales, while the remainder,
whether it gets the better of anything in terms of deeds or in
terms of speeches, would be a mastery.[9]

THEAETETUS: On the basis of your remarks, at any rate, it does appear
to be so.

STRANGER: And what of this? Is not the art of mastery to be cut in
two?

THEAETETUS: At what point?

STRANGER: By establishing the whole that is open mastery as compe- *E*
tition, and all of it that's concealed as hunting.

THEAETETUS: Yes.

STRANGER: But then to fail to cut in two the art of hunting makes no
sense.

THEAETETUS: Speak then. At what point is it to be done?

STRANGER: By the division of the soulless genus and the ensouled.

THEAETETUS: Why certainly, provided that both of the pair are.

STRANGER: Of course they are. But we must go on and dismiss that *220*
of the soulless things—it is nameless except in the case of some
parts of the diving art and a few different things of the sort—but
that which is a hunting of the ensouled animals, that we must
address as the art of animal-hunting.

THEAETETUS: Let it be.

STRANGER: And wouldn't a double species of the art of animal-hunting
be spoken of justly—one of the pedestrial genus, which has undergone divisions into many species and names, a pedestrial-hunting,
and the other of swimming animal, all an in-liquid-hunting?

THEAETETUS: Certainly.

STRANGER: Now of swimming animal we do see the feathered tribe *B*
and the aqueous?

THEAETETUS: Of course.

STRANGER: And our entire hunting of the feathered genus is surely
said to be a kind of fowling.

THEAETETUS: It's said so indeed.

STRANGER: But of the aqueous, just about the whole of it together's
fishing.

THEAETETUS: Yes.

STRANGER: And what of this? Wouldn't we make a division, in turn, of this kind of hunting into its two greatest parts?

THEAETETUS: Into which?

STRANGER: There's that which does its hunting solely by means of fences and that which does it by striking.

THEAETETUS: What do you mean, and at what point are you dividing each of the two?

C STRANGER: All that confines something for the sake of prevention by surrounding it, that's likely to give it the name of fence.[10]

THEAETETUS: Yes, of course.

STRANGER: Weels, then, nets, meshes, traps, and things of the sort—should one address them with the name of anything else than fences?

THEAETETUS: Nothing else.

STRANGER: So we'll say that this part of capturing a quarry is fence-hunting or something of the sort.

THEAETETUS: Yes.

STRANGER: But that which occurs by means of striking with hooks and
D   tridents is other than this, and we should now address it in one speech as a kind of strike-hunting. Or how could one say it more beautifully, Theaetetus?

THEAETETUS: Let's neglect the name, for this in fact suffices.

STRANGER: Of the art of striking, then, whereas the nocturnal kind, which occurs in the light of fire, happens to be called, I suspect, by the very ones engaged in the hunt 'torching'—

THEAETETUS: Certainly.

STRANGER: Still the diurnal, since even the tridents have hooks on their tips, all of it's hooking.

E THEAETETUS: It's said so indeed.

STRANGER: Well, then, of the hooking kind of the art of striking, whereas that which gets its blow to go from above downwards, on account of the fact that they especially employ tridents in this fashion, has got the name, I suspect, of some kind of trident-spearing—

THEAETETUS: Some at least say so.

STRANGER: Still the remainder is still just about only one species.

THEAETETUS: What sort?

STRANGER: It's characterized by a striking contrary to the former; it occurs by means of a hook, and one hits not just any part of the body of fishes, as one does with tridents, but on each occasion it's
221   around the head and the mouth of the prey, and it's in the opposite direction, an angling downwards up by means of rods and reeds. What name, Theaetetus, shall we say must be said of it?

THEAETETUS: Well, it's my impression that the very thing has now been finished off which we just now had proposed we had to find.

STRANGER: So now, after all, in the case of the art of angling, you and I have come to an agreement not only about the name but we've *B* also seized adequately the speech about the work itself. Of art in its entirety, a half-part of it was acquisitive, and of the acquisitive there was mastery, and of mastery hunting, and of the hunting a hunting of animals, and of hunting of animals an in-liquid-hunting, and of in-liquid-hunting the lower section as a whole was fishing,[11] and of the art of fishing there was striking, and of striking hooking, and of this, that which was involved with a down- *C* ward stroke and angling upwards, since its name was made similar to the action itself, has got designated as the presently sought-for art of angling.[12]

THEAETETUS: Now this at least has altogether adequately been made clear.

STRANGER: Come then. In terms of this paradigm, let's try to find the sophist too, whatever he is.

THEAETETUS: Yes, certainly.

STRANGER: Well, this at any rate was the first inquiry in the case of the angler: Was he to be set down as a layman or with some art?

THEAETETUS: Yes.

STRANGER: And now this one, Theaetetus, shall we set him down as *D* a layman or altogether truly a sophist?

THEAETETUS: In no way a layman, for I understand what you're saying, since with this name at least he utterly fails to be of that sort.

STRANGER: Well, we must set him down, it seems, with some art.

THEAETETUS: What ever is it then?

STRANGER: By the gods! Have we really failed to recognize that there is a kinship of the man with the man?

THEAETETUS: Of whom with whom?

STRANGER: Of the angler with the sophist.

THEAETETUS: At what point?

STRANGER: Both appear to me a pair of hunters.

THEAETETUS: Of what hunting is the other one? We already spoke of *E* the other.

STRANGER: We surely just now made a division in two of the entirety of the pursuit of a quarry, by cutting off a swimming part, and the pedestrial characterized the rest.[13]

THEAETETUS: Yes.

STRANGER: And we went through the former, all that pertained to the swimming kinds of the aqueous, but with the remark that it was many-specied we dismissed the pedestrial unsplit.

222 THEAETETUS: Certainly.

STRANGER: Now, whereas up to this point the sophist and the angler proceed together as a pair away from the art of acquisition—

THEAETETUS: It seems likely that the pair does at least.

STRANGER: Still the pair diverges after the art of hunting animals, one to sea, no doubt, and rivers and lakes, in order to hunt the animals in them—

THEAETETUS: Why certainly.

STRANGER: And one to earth and some other kinds of rivers, unstinting meadows, as it were, of wealth and youth, in order to get the better of the nurslings in them.

B THEAETETUS: How do you mean that?

STRANGER: There proves to be in the case of pedestrial hunting a pair that's somehow its two greatest parts.

THEAETETUS: What sort is each of the two?

STRANGER: One of the tame and one of the savage.

THEAETETUS: Is there really a kind of hunting of the tame?

STRANGER: Yes, provided, that is, (a) human being is a tame animal. But set it down however you please. Either suppose that nothing is tame, or something else is tame, but the human being is savage; or you mean, on the other hand, the human being is tame, but you believe there's no hunting of human beings. Whichever of these remarks you believe to be to your liking, make it this distinction for us.

C THEAETETUS: Well, stranger, just as I believe we are a tame animal, so I say there is a hunting of human beings.

STRANGER: So let's then say that the art of tame-hunting is also twofold.

THEAETETUS: On what terms are we to say it?

STRANGER: By the determination of the piratical, the enslaving, the tyrannical, and all of the martial art as a violent hunting and all of them one—

THEAETETUS: Beautiful.

STRANGER: And by the address of the forensic, public-addressing, and
D associative arts as, in turn, a comprehensive single whole and a certain single art of conviction-producing.

THEAETETUS: Right.

STRANGER: So let's speak of the double genus of the art of conviction-producing.

THEAETETUS: What sort?

STRANGER: One occurs in public, the other in private.

THEAETETUS: Each of the two species does indeed occur.

STRANGER: And isn't it the case that of the art of private-hunting there is the earning of a wage and there is the giving of gifts.

THEAETETUS: I don't understand.

STRANGER: You do not yet, it seems, pay attention to the hunting of lovers.

THEAETETUS: About what?

STRANGER: That they offer the hunted gifts in addition.　　　　　*E*

THEAETETUS: What you say is most true.

STRANGER: Well, then, let this be a species of an erotic art.

THEAETETUS: Certainly.

STRANGER: Yes, but the wage-earning kind, that which makes its association through catering to whims and altogether has made its lure by way of pleasuring and only exacts as the wage for itself *223* sustenance, we all would assert, I suspect, that as flattery it is some kind of art of flavoring (pleasuring)—

THEAETETUS: Of course.

STRANGER: While that which professes to be making its associations for the sake of virtue, and exacts money as a wage, doesn't this genus deserve to be addressed by another name?

THEAETETUS: Of course.

STRANGER: What's this name precisely? Try to say.

THEAETETUS: It's really plain. We've found, in my opinion, the sophist. So if I should say this, I'm convinced I would be calling him by the appropriate name.

STRANGER: It seems, then, that in terms of the present speech, Theae- *B* tetus, the hunting that occurs of the wealthy and prominent young is an art that in engaging in a sale by means of money educates in opinion. It is a wage-earning art that hunts in private, and hunts human beings, a tame-hunting, on dry land, a pedestrial hunting that hunts animals, an art of hunting, of acquisition, and appropriation, which has to be addressed as sophistics, as the present speech falls out for us.[14]

THEAETETUS: That's altogether so.

STRANGER: But let's still look over here as well, for that which is now *C* being sought does not at all share in a trivial art but rather a very complex one. There's, for instance, among the previous remarks, an apparition that suggests that it is some other genus and not that which we now claim it to be.

THEAETETUS: At what point exactly?

STRANGER: There was surely a double species of the acquisitive art, one part with hunting and one with exchanging.[15]

THEAETETUS: There was indeed.

STRANGER: Let's say, then, that of the two species of the art of exchange, one is gift-giving and the other marketing.

THEAETETUS: Let them have been so stated.

STRANGER: And we shall, in turn, assert that the art of marketing cuts itself in two.

D THEAETETUS: At what point?

STRANGER: By its dividing the marketing of those who make their own wares into the art of selling their own (self-selling), and (by its dividing) the exchanging of the works of others into the art of exchange.

THEAETETUS: Certainly.

STRANGER: And what of this? Of the art of exchange isn't there an exchanging in the city, which is just about a half-part of it and is addressed as the retail art?

THEAETETUS: Yes.

STRANGER: But that which makes exchanges from city to city by way of buying and selling is the mercantile art?

THEAETETUS: Why of course.

E STRANGER: But of the mercantile art, haven't we observed that in making its sales through money, one exchanges all that the body and one all that the soul is sustained by and uses?

THEAETETUS: How do you mean this?

STRANGER: Perhaps we fail to recognize that which involves the soul, since we surely understand the other at any rate.

THEAETETUS: Yes.

224 STRANGER: Let's say, then, that when there is a purchase of art on any occasion in one city and it is being conveyed from there to a city elsewhere, and the art is music in its entirety, the art of painting no less than the art of puppetry (conjuring), and many other things of the soul, some of which are conveyed and offered for sale for the sake of entertainment and some in all seriousness— then, should it be said that he who conveys and sells them is a merchant no less than if the selling is of foods and drinks, it would be correctly rendered.

THEAETETUS: What you say is most true.

B STRANGER: Won't you also then address with the same name the one who buys up learnings and exchanges them for money from city to city?

THEAETETUS: Yes, exactly.

STRANGER: Then if one kind of this soul-merchandising would most justly be said to be the art of exhibition, isn't it a necessity to address that which engages in the selling of learnings with a name no less ridiculous than the former but still and all akin to its action?

THEAETETUS: Yes, of course.

STRANGER: Then of this art of the selling-of-learning, one has to ad-
C dress that which involves the learnings of the different arts with

another name, but that which involves the learning of virtue with a different name.

THEAETETUS: Of course.

STRANGER: Well, for that which involves all the rest, 'art-selling' would fit, but for the latter let it be your effort to say the name.

THEAETETUS: But why, if one should say a name different from that which is now being sought—the sophistic genus—how could one not strike a false note?

STRANGER: There's no different name. So come, let's now draw it together and say that that which the art of acquisition, exchange, marketing, merchandising, soul-merchandising characterize as a   *D* selling involved with speeches and learnings of virtue came to light in second place as sophistics.[16]

THEAETETUS: Indeed it did.

STRANGER: Yes, and I suspect that if anyone set himself up on a spot in a city and purchased some and devised on his own some learnings of this same subject and offered them for sale and proposed to make his living from it, you would call him for the third time by a name no different from that which you employed just now.

THEAETETUS: There's no doubt I would.

STRANGER: So in the case of the art of acquisition, that which exchange   *E* and marketing characterize, whether it be retailing or selling of one's own, in both ways, whatever is a selling-of-learning in matters of this sort, you, it appears, will always address it as the sophistic genus.[17]

THEAETETUS: It's a necessity, for one must follow the speech.

STRANGER: Let's still consider whether the genus that is now being pursued does not resemble after all something like the following.

THEAETETUS: What sort of thing exactly?   *225*

STRANGER: A competitive art was for us some part of the art of acquisition.

THEAETETUS: It was indeed.

STRANGER: There's nothing wayward then in dividing it in two.

THEAETETUS: In what sort of terms? Speak.

STRANGER: By our setting down its divisions as the rivalrous kind and the combative.

THEAETETUS: They are.

STRANGER: Well, then, in the case of the art of combat, whereas it's pretty nearly fit and seemly for us to set down as a name for that which involves body against bodies something like the forcible—

THEAETETUS: Yes.

STRANGER: For that which involves speeches against speeches, Theae-

B   tetus, what name is one to give it that's different from the disputative?

THEAETETUS: None.

STRANGER: Yes, but in that which concerns disputations, one has to set down a doublet.

THEAETETUS: At what point?

STRANGER: Whereas to the extent that it occurs by (continuous) lengths of speeches in the face of contrary (and continuous) lengths of speeches, in public, and is concerned with just and unjust things, it's forensic—

THEAETETUS: Yes.

STRANGER: That which, in turn, occurs in private and by questions in the face of answers is chopped into bits, have we got accustomed to call it by a name different from the contradictory?

THEAETETUS: No different.

C STRANGER: And though all of the contradictory that involves disputes about contracts, and is randomly and artlessly engaged in it, must be set down as a species, since the speech has distinctly recognized it as being other, though no one before us gave it a name and it does not now deserve to get one from us either—

THEAETETUS: True, for it has undergone divisions into exceedingly small bits of every sort.

STRANGER: Still the artful kind, which disputes as a whole about just things themselves, unjust things, and about everything else as well, haven't we got accustomed to speak of it in turn as eristic?

THEAETETUS: Of course.

D STRANGER: Now of the eristic there are in fact the money-losing and the money-making kinds.

THEAETETUS: Altogether so.

STRANGER: So let's make a try at giving the name which one must call each of the two.

THEAETETUS: Indeed we must.

STRANGER: Well, it's my opinion that that which neglects its own home affairs on account of the pleasure it takes in a pastime of this sort, and in its speaking is heard without pleasure by many of its auditors, is called in my judgment nothing other than garrulity.

THEAETETUS: Something like that is indeed said.

E STRANGER: Then as for its contrary, the one which makes money out of private disputes, now it's your turn to try to designate it.

THEAETETUS: But how would one not make a mistake if one should say anything other than that that marvel has now come round again for the fourth time as the one we are now pursuing—the sophist?

STRANGER: Then the sophist, as the speech has now in turn revealed, 226
is no different, it seems, from the money-making genus, which
eristic, contradictory, disputative, combative, competitive, and acquisitive arts characterize.[18]

THEAETETUS: Yes, utterly.

STRANGER: You do see, then, that it's truly said that this beast is complex and, as the saying goes, cannot be taken by the other hand.[19]

THEAETETUS: Then we must do it with both.

STRANGER: Indeed we must, and to the best of our ability we have to B
do it in this way, tracking a trail of his of the following sort. Tell
me. We call some things surely by the names in use for domestic
tasks.

THEAETETUS: Yes, many of them, but of the many, which sorts precisely
do you ask about?

STRANGER: The following: we speak of to filter, to sift, to winnow, and
to discern.[20]

THEAETETUS: Why certainly.

STRANGER: And besides them, there's still to card, to spin, to comb,
and we know, do we not, that in the arts there are thousands of
them, all different but of the same sort?

THEAETETUS: What sort of thing about them did you want to make C
plain, and proposed these as paradigms for all of them with what
question in mind?

STRANGER: It has surely been said of all the things mentioned that
they're divisive.

THEAETETUS: Yes.

STRANGER: Well, then, in terms of my speech, we shall claim for it one
name, on the grounds that there is one art in all that deals with
these things.

THEAETETUS: What do we address it as?

STRANGER: The art of discernment (diacritics).

THEAETETUS: Let it be.

STRANGER: Consider, in turn, whether at some point we're capable of
sighting two species of it.

THEAETETUS: It's too quick for the likes of me to do as you charge.

STRANGER: And yet, in just the discernments we've mentioned, there D
was the setting apart of worse from better and similar from similar.

THEAETETUS: Now that it's put this way it's pretty nearly self-evident.

STRANGER: Now, I don't have the name down in general use for the
latter, but where the discernment leaves behind the better and
throws away the worse, I do have it.

THEAETETUS: Say what it is.

STRANGER: All discernment of this sort, as I for one conceive it, is said by everyone to be a kind of purification.

THEAETETUS: It's said so indeed.

E STRANGER: Now wouldn't everyone see at least that the purificatory species is in turn double?

THEAETETUS: Yes, perhaps at their leisure. I, however, don't catch sight of it now.

STRANGER: Well, it's fitting to comprehend with one name the many species of purifications of bodies.

THEAETETUS: What sorts of species and with what sort of name?

STRANGER: There are the insides of the bodies of animals, all that, by
227 being rightly discerned by gymnastics and medicine, get purified, and there are as well their outsides, trivial to speak of no doubt, but all that the art of bathing attends to; and in the case of the soulless bodies, to which the fuller's art and all of cosmetics give their care, by their small divisions these arts have got many and seemingly laughable names.

THEAETETUS: Indeed they have.

STRANGER: They certainly have, Theaetetus. But, as a matter of fact, the pursuit of their speeches does not at all care either less or more for the art of bath-sponging than for the drinking-of-drugs, regardless of whether the purification they do benefits us a lot or
B a little. For this pursuit, for the sake of the acquisition of mind, tries to understand the kinship and the lack of kinship of all arts, and with this in mind honors all of them on an equal basis. It does not believe that in terms of similarity the others are more laughable than the other ones, and it does not hold that the one who shows an art of hunting through the art of generalship is any the more august than the one who does it through the art of lice-killing, but it does hold him to be for the most part more vain. So in the present particular case, the name you asked for, with which we'll address all capacities together that have got as their
C lot to purify body, whether it be ensouled or soulless, it will make no difference to it what sort of name, if spoken, will seem to be the most decent. Let it only have everything bound together that purifies something else apart from the purifications of the soul; for if we understand what it wants, it has just now tried to distinguish the purification of thought from all the rest.

THEAETETUS: Well, I've understood, and I concede that there are two species of purification—the species that deals with the soul is one, and it is apart from that which deals with the body.

STRANGER: That couldn't be more beautiful. And listen to me as to
D what follows next and try again to cut what is said in two.

THEAETETUS: Whatever sort of guidelines you give it, I'll try to join you in the cutting.

STRANGER: We speak of wickedness in soul as something other than virtue?[21]

THEAETETUS: Of course.

STRANGER: And it was further agreed that to leave the other and cast out everything that is anywhere worthless is purification.

THEAETETUS: Indeed it was.

STRANGER: So in the case of soul, to the extent that we find a certain removal of vice, if we say it's purification, we'll be speaking in tune.

THEAETETUS: Indeed we shall.

STRANGER: Two species of vice of soul have to be stated.

THEAETETUS: What sort?

STRANGER: That which comes to be in it like illness in body and that *228* which (comes to be in it) like ugliness.

THEAETETUS: I don't understand.

STRANGER: Perhaps you do not hold illness and sedition as the same?[22]

THEAETETUS: But I don't know in regard to this either how I must answer.

STRANGER: Do you believe that sedition is anything else than the disruption (variance) of the naturally akin that comes to be from some kind of corruption?[23]

THEAETETUS: Nothing else.

STRANGER: But ugliness, is it anything else than the genus of deficient measure that is everywhere deformed?[24]

THEAETETUS: It's not at all anything else. *B*

STRANGER: And what of this? Have we not perceived in soul opinions at variance with desires, anger with pleasures, speech with pains, and all these with each other when people are in a poor and sorry condition?

THEAETETUS: Yes, exactly.

STRANGER: And yet, of necessity, they have all become akin?

THEAETETUS: Of course.

STRANGER: So if we say, after all, that wickedness is a sedition and illness of the soul, we shall speak correctly.

THEAETETUS: Most correctly rather.

STRANGER: But what of this? Everything that has got a share in motion *C* and once it has set for itself some target, tries to hit it, and yet on each impulse it strays off the target and misses it—shall we say that it's affected by a coincidence of mutual proportion, or, contrariwise, by lack of measure?

THEAETETUS: By lack of measure, plainly.

II.17

STRANGER: But yet we further know that every soul is unwillingly ignorant of everything.

THEAETETUS: Exactly.

D STRANGER: But when understanding goes astray, when soul is setting out for truth, ignorance is nothing else than distraction.[25]

THEAETETUS: Yes, of course.

STRANGER: So soul that lacks understanding must be set down as ugly and lacking measure.

THEAETETUS: It seems likely.

STRANGER: There are then, it appears, these two genera of evils in it, that which is called by the many wickedness and is most plainly its illness.

THEAETETUS: Yes.

STRANGER: Yes, but that which they call ignorance they're unwilling to agree that if it only occurs in soul by itself it's vice.[26]

E THEAETETUS: I must utterly concede the point, which when you just now mentioned it I hesitated to decide on, that there are two genera of vice in soul. And while cowardice, lack of self-control, and injustice have all to be believed an illness in us, the experience of extensive and omnifarious ignorance has to be set down as ugliness.[27]

STRANGER: And isn't it the case that in body at least there proves to be a kind of pair of two arts that deals with this pair of two experiences?

THEAETETUS: What is this pair?

229 STRANGER: Gymnastics deals with ugliness, medicine with illness.[28]

THEAETETUS: The pair does appear to.

STRANGER: And it is by nature that the art of chastisement that deals with insolence, injustice, and cowardice is of all arts the one most closely related to Justice.

THEAETETUS: It's likely at any rate, if one is to speak according to human opinion.

STRANGER: But what of this? Could one be more correct than to say that there's nothing else than the art of instruction that deals with all of ignorance?

THEAETETUS: Nothing else.

B STRANGER: Come then. Are we to assert that there's only one genus of the art of instruction or several, but its biggest are somehow two of a pair? Consider.

THEAETETUS: I'm considering.

STRANGER: And it's my impression that we would find it most quickly somewhere around here.

THEAETETUS: Where?

STRANGER: Look and see whether ignorance admits of some kind of cut somewhere along its middle, for if it proves to be double, it's clear that it compels the art of instruction to have two proper parts as well, one for each one of the two of its own.

THEAETETUS: Then what? Is that which is now sought for evident to you somewhere?

STRANGER: Well, at least it's my impression that I see a certain big and C difficult species of ignorance that's distinctly set apart and balances all the rest of its parts.

THEAETETUS: What sort exactly?

STRANGER: That of not knowing something and having the opinion (giving the impression) that one knows it.[29] It's probably through it that all the slips we make in thought occur to everyone.

THEAETETUS: True.

STRANGER: And I suspect that in fact this kind of ignorance alone gets addressed with the name of folly.

THEAETETUS: Certainly.

STRANGER: But then what must we say is the part of the instructional art that gets rid of this?

THEAETETUS: Well, I suspect, stranger, that all the rest are the arts of D instruction in handicrafts, but that this one has got through us the name here of education.[30]

STRANGER: And just about among all Greeks, Theaetetus. But we still have to consider this. Is all of it really now uncuttable, or does it admit of a division that deserves its own name?

THEAETETUS: We must consider it.

STRANGER: Well, it's my impression that this still gets a split somewhere.

THEAETETUS: At what point?

STRANGER: There seems to be for the instructional art in speeches not only E the rougher path but also another proper part of it that's smoother.[31]

THEAETETUS: What sort exactly do you mean by each of the two?

STRANGER: There's a certain old-fashioned and paternal kind, which fathers used to apply specially on their sons, and many still now use it. Whenever in their view their sons make some mistake, they 230 are partly harsh and partly consoling in a softer way—but regardless of this difference one would speak of it in its entirety most rightly as the art of admonition.

THEAETETUS: That is so.

STRANGER: Yes, but, on the other hand, some took their own counsel and seemed to have come to the belief that all folly is unwilling, and that no one who believed he was wise would ever be willing to learn anything of those things in which he believed he was dreadfully clever, and that with a lot of effort the admonitory species of education accomplishes little.[32]

THEAETETUS: Yes, their belief is right.

B STRANGER: Therefore, you see, they set out on a different way for the casting out of this kind of opinion.

THEAETETUS: What way exactly?

STRANGER: They question thoroughly about whatever anyone believes he's saying something while saying nothing. And then, because those questioned wander, they examine their opinions with ease, and once they bring the opinions together into the same place by their speeches, they put them side by side one another, and in so putting them they show that the opinions are simultaneously contrary to themselves about the same things in regard to the same things in the same respects. And those who are being examined,

C on seeing this, are harsh on themselves and grow tame before everyone else, and in just this way they get rid of the great and stiff opinions which encase them, and this is of all riddances the most pleasant to be spoken of and for the one who undergoes it proves the most stable. The reason is, my dear boy, that those who purify them hold the view, just as physicians of bodies have held the view that a body would be incapable of deriving any advantage from the sustenance to be applied before one casts out the internal impediments to it, so it's just the same that they thought about soul, that it will not have the benefit of the learnings to be

D applied before one puts, by way of refutation, the one examined into a state of shame, takes out the opinions that are impediments to the learnings, and shows him forth pure and believing he knows just the things he does know and no more.[33]

THEAETETUS: It's the best at any rate and most moderate of conditions.[34]

STRANGER: It's precisely because of all of this, Theaetetus, that we have to say that refutation is after all the greatest and most authoritative of purifications. And one must hold in turn that whoever's un-

E refuted, even if he is in fact the great king,[35] if he is unpurified in the greatest things, has become uneducated and ugly in those things in which it was fitting for whoever will be in his being happy to be purest and most beautiful.

THEAETETUS: That's altogether so.

231 STRANGER: But what of this? Who shall we say are those who use this art? I for one am afraid to assert that they're sophists.

THEAETETUS: Why's that?

STRANGER: Lest we attach to them too great an honor.

THEAETETUS: But it's still the case that the present remarks do bear a resemblance to someone of the sort.

STRANGER: So, for example, does a wolf to a dog,[36] the most savage to the most tame. But whoever's not to slip up must always and more than anything else keep his guard up when it comes to similarities, for the genus is most slippery. But still and all, let it be, for their boundary-disputes (definitions), I suspect, won't then be about a small matter whenever they (the purifiers) stand guard satisfactorily. *B*

THEAETETUS: It's likely, at any rate, not to be small.

STRANGER: Let there then be of the diacritical art cathartics, and of cathartics let the part that deals with soul be set distinctly apart, and of this part there's the art of instruction, and of the instructional art the art of education, and in the case of the educational art—the refutation that deals with the vain seeming-wisdom (*doxosophia*)—let it be said in the speech that has now come to light sideways to it to be nothing else for us than the sophistics noble and grand in descent.[37]

THEAETETUS: Let it be said. But on account of the fact that he has come to light as so many, I am by now perplexed. Whatever should one say, speaking truly and with conviction, that the sophist in his being is? *C*

STRANGER: That you are perplexed is likely enough. But, you know, we must believe that he too is by now intensely perplexed as to wherever he will still slip through the speech. The proverb's right, it's not easy to escape from all the holds.[38] So we must be now especially keen to set upon him.

THEAETETUS: You speak beautifully.

STRANGER: But first let's step aside and take as it were a breather, and let us calculate before ourselves while we're resting just how many *D* the sophist has appeared to us. It's my impression that he was discovered at first to be a wage-earning hunter of wealthy young men.

THEAETETUS: Yes.

STRANGER: And in second place, a kind of merchant of the learnings of the soul.

THEAETETUS: Certainly.

STRANGER: And did he not show up for a third time as a retailer of these very things?

THEAETETUS: Yes, and a fourth besides—he was for us a self-seller of learnings.

STRANGER: You recalled it rightly. But I shall try to recall the fifth. *E* As a kind of prizefighter involved with speeches, he belonged to the competitive art and set himself distinctly apart with the eristic art.

THEAETETUS: He was indeed.

STRANGER: The sixth was, to be sure, disputable, but all the same we set him down, by way of a concession to him, to be a purifier of soul—of its opinions impedimental to learnings.

THEAETETUS: That's altogether so.

232 STRANGER: Do you then realize that whenever someone comes to light as a knower of many things, but he is addressed with the name of one art, this apparition is not sound, but it's clear that whoever undergoes it in regard to any art is incapable of sighting that feature of the art to which all these learnings look and therefore he addresses the one who has them with many names instead of one?

THEAETETUS: It's probable that this is especially close to the way it naturally is.

B STRANGER: Let it not be us, then, who through idleness undergo it in the search, but let's first take up one of the remarks made about the sophist. There was some one thing that appears to me particularly revealing of him.

THEAETETUS: What sort of thing?

STRANGER: We surely said that he was a contradictor.

THEAETETUS: Yes.

STRANGER: And that he proved to be as well a teacher of this very thing to everyone else.

THEAETETUS: Why certainly.

STRANGER: Let's consider: What is it about, then, that those of this sort in fact claim to make the rest contradictors? Let our examination somehow be from the beginning in this way. Come. Is it

C about the divine things, all that are not evident to the many, that they make them competent to do this?

THEAETETUS: That is, at any rate, certainly said about them.

STRANGER: But what about all that's evident of earth and sky and the things that pertain to things of this sort?

THEAETETUS: To be sure.

STRANGER: And, furthermore, in their private associations, whenever something is said of everything,[39] about becoming and being, we know for a fact that not only are they themselves skilled at contradiction but they make everyone else as capable of it as they themselves are?

THEAETETUS: Altogether so.

D STRANGER: And what, in turn, of laws and all the political things—don't they promise to make them disputatious about these?

THEAETETUS: Yes, for otherwise, if they were not promising this, just about no one would now converse with them.[40]

STRANGER: And there are, further, the things which pertain to all arts as well as to each one individually—what one must say before each craftsman to contradict him[41]—they have surely been made public and laid down in writings for anyone who wants to learn them.

THEAETETUS: You appear to me to have referred to the Protagorean writings on wrestling and all the rest of the arts. *E*

STRANGER: Yes, and they are of many others besides, you blessed innocent![42] But doesn't it seem that what characterizes in general the art of contradiction is its adequate capacity to engage in disputes about everything?

THEAETETUS: It does appear, at any rate, that there's pretty nearly nothing that it leaves out.

STRANGER: By the gods! Do you, my boy, believe this possible? Perhaps you youngsters might see more keenly into it, and we more dimly.[43]

THEAETETUS: What sort is it? What's the special point of your remark? *233* I'm not sure I understand the present question.

STRANGER: It's whether it's possible for any human being to know everything.

THEAETETUS: In that case, stranger, our genus would be blessed.

STRANGER: How ever, then, would anyone who is not himself knowledgeable ever be able to say anything sound in contradicting the knower to his face?

THEAETETUS: In no way.

STRANGER: Whatever, then, could the amazing conjuring trick of the sophistic capacity be?

THEAETETUS: In regard to what exactly?

STRANGER: In whatever way they are capable of inducing in the young *B* the opinion that they alone are the wisest of all in everything. For it's plain that if they neither were contradicting correctly nor were they appearing to the young to do so, and in appearing they were no more on account of the disputation to seem intelligent, then your remark would hold. Hardly anyone would be offering them money and be willing to become their pupil in these very matters.

THEAETETUS: Hardly, in that case.

STRANGER: Yes, but as it is, they are willing?

THEAETETUS: Indeed they are.

STRANGER: The reason is, I suspect, that they themselves seem to be *C* knowledgeable on those very points in which they contradict everyone else.

THEAETETUS: Of course.

STRANGER: And they do this, we say, in everything.

THEAETETUS: Yes.

STRANGER: Then they do appear, after all, to their pupils as wise in everything.

THEAETETUS: Why certainly.

STRANGER: But they are not, for this came to light as impossible.

THEAETETUS: Of course it's impossible.

STRANGER: So the sophist has come to light for us with a certain opinionative science (knowledge) about everything, but he's without truth.

D   THEAETETUS: That's altogether so, and the present remark about them has probably been stated most correctly.

STRANGER: Let's then get a somewhat clearer paradigm for them.

THEAETETUS: What sort precisely?

STRANGER: It's this one. Pay very close attention and try to give me an answer.

THEAETETUS: What sort?

STRANGER: Should anyone say, not that he knows how to say or contradict, but that he knows how to make and do all things (*pragmata*) together by one art—

E   THEAETETUS: What do you mean by all?

STRANGER: You are failing right from the start to understand the beginning of our statement. You don't understand, it seems, 'all-together'.

THEAETETUS: No, indeed I don't.

STRANGER: Well, I mean you and I belong to all and besides us the rest of the animals and trees.

THEAETETUS: How do you mean this?

STRANGER: Should someone say that he will make me and you and all the rest of the plants—[44]

234   THEAETETUS: Just what kind of making do you mean? You'll not say he's any kind of farmer, for you said he was a maker as well of animals.

STRANGER: I say so, and, what's more, of sea and earth and sky and gods and all the rest together; furthermore, he makes each of them quickly and offers them for sale for a very small sum.

THEAETETUS: It's a kind of child's play you mean.

STRANGER: What? Do you mean that we have to hold the craft of whoever says that he knows everything and would teach this to another for little money and in little time to be child's play?

THEAETETUS: No doubt about it.

B   STRANGER: And do you know of any more artful or maybe more charming species of child's play than the imitative?

THEAETETUS: In no way. You've spoken of a very extensive species and just about the most complex and collected it all into one.

STRANGER: Now we're surely familiar with this point, that whoever promises to be capable of making everything by one art, will be able, by producing homonymous imitations of 'the things which are,' by the art of painting and by showing the paintings at a distance, to slip past the foolish among young children the notion that he is most competent to complete in deed (work) whatever he wants to do.

THEAETETUS: Of course.   *C*

STRANGER: But what of this? In the case of speeches, don't we expect there is some different art, by which it is in fact possible by speeches through their ears to enchant the young who stand even still further away from the truth of things (*pragmata*), by showing spoken images of everything so as to make them seem to be truly said and, in addition, the speaker to be the wisest of all in everything?

THEAETETUS: Is there a reason why there couldn't be some different *D*
art of the same sort?

STRANGER: Now the many, Theaetetus, among those who then listened, isn't it a necessity for them, when sufficient time has passed and their age advances and they're compelled to fall in with the things which are near at hand and through experiences to get their hands on the things which are in all their vividness, to change the opinions they then had, so as for the great things to appear small and the easy things difficult, and for all the apparitions in speeches which they had to be totally inverted by the works that come to be present in their actions?   *E*

THEAETETUS: Yes, if I am any judge at my age, but I suspect that I too am one of those who still stand further away.

STRANGER: It's precisely for this reason that all of us here shall try and are now trying to lead you as near as possible without those experiences. But, however that may be, tell me this about the sophist. Is it plain by now that he is one of the enchanters, being *235*
an imitator of the things which are, or are we still in doubt that in everything he seems to be capable of contradicting, in all of that he truly has the sciences (knowledges)?

THEAETETUS: But how could he, stranger? It's pretty nearly plain by now on the basis of what has been said that he is just one of those who share in child's play.[45]

STRANGER: So we have to set him down as a kind of enchanter and imitator.

THEAETETUS: That's of course what we must do.

STRANGER: Let us come, then, now and from this point on have our task to be no let-up on the beast.[46] For we've pretty nearly en- *B* compassed him in the kind of net that's instrumental in dealing with things of this sort in speeches, and so he'll not escape from this at least.

THEAETETUS: What sort is that?

STRANGER: The fact that he is just one of the genus of conjurors.

THEAETETUS: That's my impression too about him.

STRANGER: It's been resolved, then, to divide as quickly as possible the art of image-making, and in our descent, if the sophist straight off awaits us patiently, to seize him on the orders set forth by the

C   royal speech, and on our handing him over to it to declare the catch. But if, after all, he slips in somewhere into the several parts of mimetics, then it's been resolved to follow his trail by always keeping up the dividing of the portion that welcomes him until he is seized. Neither he nor any different genus shall ever on any terms make the boast that it has avoided the pursuit of those capable of pursuing in this way in each individual case and in general.[47]

THEAETETUS: What you say is good, and it must be done along these lines.

STRANGER: Now in terms of the previously traversed way of division,

D   it appears to me that even now I, for one, catch sight of two species of mimetics. But the sought-for look (*idea*), in which of our two it happens to be, it's my impression that as of now I'm not yet capable of understanding it.

THEAETETUS: Well, speak anyhow and divide for us what two paired kinds you mean.

STRANGER: I see in it the eikastic art as one, and this is especially the case whenever in conformity with the proportions of the paradigm

E   in length, width, and depth, and besides this, in giving back the colors appropriate to each, one produces the *genesis* of the imitation.

THEAETETUS: But don't all imitators of anything try to do this?

STRANGER: No, not at any rate all those who somewhere or other mold or paint any of the big works. For should they give back the simply

236   true proportions of the beautiful things, you know that the upper segments would appear smaller than they should and the lower bigger, because the former are seen by us far away and the latter near at hand.

THEAETETUS: Yes, of course.

STRANGER: Don't, then, the craftsmen nowadays dismiss what's true and work at producing in their images not the proportions that are but those that seem beautiful?

THEAETETUS: Altogether so.

STRANGER: So isn't it just to call the other a semblance since it resembles?

THEAETETUS: Yes.

STRANGER: And the part of mimetics that ranges over this and which   B
we spoke of in the previous speech must be called eikastics.

THEAETETUS: It must be called so.

STRANGER: But what of this? That which appears to resemble the
beautiful because the sighting of it is not from a beautiful position,
but if one should get the power to see things of this sort of size
adequately, and it does not resemble that which it declares it
resembles, what do we call it? Isn't it, inasmuch as it appears but
does not resemble, an apparition?

THEAETETUS: Why certainly.

STRANGER: And isn't this part very extensive, both throughout painting   C
and all of mimetics?

THEAETETUS: Of course.

STRANGER: Then wouldn't we address most correctly as phantastics
that art that produces an apparition and not a semblance?

THEAETETUS: Yes, very much.

STRANGER: Well, it was these two paired species of the art of image-
making that I meant, eikastics and phantastics.

THEAETETUS: Right.

STRANGER: Yes, but that which I then was in doubt about, in which
art of the two the sophist is to be set down, I'm not yet capable
even now of observing with clarity. But in his being, the man's
amazing and very difficult to be caught sight of, since even now   D
he has very skillfully and elegantly fled into a species that affords
no way for a definite tracking.

THEAETETUS: It seems likely.

STRANGER: Are you really then giving your consent because you recognize it, or did a kind of swing, now that you have grown accustomed to it by the speech, draw you along, as it were, to a
quick consent?

THEAETETUS: What do you mean, and what's the point of your remark?

STRANGER: You blessed innocent! We're engaged in an altogether
difficult examination, and that's the way it is in its being. For to   E
appear and seem but not to be, and to speak some things but not
true—all these are forever full of perplexity, in former times and
now. What manner of speech there must be to say or to opine
(that) false things in their being are, and in the utterance of this
not get stuck in a contradiction, that's altogether difficult,
Theaetetus.[48]   237

THEAETETUS: Why exactly?

STRANGER: This speech has the nerve to lay down that 'that which is
not' is, for falsehood would not in any different way become that

which is. But Parmenides the great, my boy, beginning when we were boys and right through to the end protested this, speaking as follows on every occasion both in prose and in meter—"For never shall this be forced," he says, "whatever are not to be; but you in searching keep your thought away from this way."[49] There

B is, then, his testimony, and there is certainly (the) speech, which, if it should be put to a fair degree of torture, would as certain as anything make its own confession. So unless it makes any difference to you, let's look first at this very point.

THEAETETUS: I'm at your disposal, however you want me. But the speech, how it will best proceed, go and consider it on your own and then lead me too along this way.

STRANGER: Well, I must do this. Tell me. We surely have the nerve to utter, "that which in no way is"?

THEAETETUS: Of course.

STRANGER: Well, let's not for the sake of contention or child's play,

C but if in all seriousness one of the listeners should on reflection have to give an answer to the question as to where he must apply this name, 'that which is not'—What's our opinion? To what and for what sort of thing would he employ it and show it to his inquirer?

THEAETETUS: Yours is a difficult question and, for the likes of me at least, pretty nearly altogether impossible to say.

STRANGER: Well, but anyway this much is clear at least, that 'that which is not' must not be applied to any of the things which are.

THEAETETUS: Of course.

STRANGER: Isn't it the case, then, that if it's not to be applied to 'that which is', one would not in applying it to 'something' be applying it correctly?

THEAETETUS: How's that exactly?

D STRANGER: This is in fact surely evident to us, that we speak this 'something' on each and every occasion for 'that which is', for to say it alone, naked as it were and isolated from all the things which are, is impossible. Isn't it?

THEAETETUS: Impossible.

STRANGER: Do you consent to this point and consider that it's a necessity for him who is saying something to say at least some one thing?

THEAETETUS: That's so.

STRANGER: For you'll assert that at least 'something' is a sign of one, and 'a pair of somethings' of two, and 'someones' of many.[50]

THEAETETUS: Of course.

STRANGER: It does seem, then, that it's most necessary for him who is *E*
   not saying something to be saying not even one thing.⁵¹

THEAETETUS: Most necessary indeed.

STRANGER: Then one ought not to concede this either, that though a
   speaker of this sort says nothing he does speak, but rather one
   must deny that he's speaking at all, inasmuch as he's trying to
   utter 'that which is not'.

THEAETETUS: The speech would then have at any rate the complete
   and final perplexity.

STRANGER: Don't talk big yet,⁵² you blessed innocent! There is still a *238*
   perplexity, and what's more, the biggest and first of them. It is
   in fact concerned with its very principle.

THEAETETUS: What are you saying? Speak and don't hesitate.

STRANGER: Now to 'that which is', surely, some other of the things
   which are might be added.

THEAETETUS: Of course.

STRANGER: But shall we say it is ever possible that something of the
   things which are be added to 'that which is not'?

THEAETETUS: How could it be?

STRANGER: So we set down all number in its entirety as of the things
   which are.

THEAETETUS: Yes, provided that anything else is to be set down as *B*
   'that which is'.

STRANGER: Then let's not even try to apply either a multitude of
   number or a one to 'that which is not'.

THEAETETUS: It would at any rate not be right for us to try, it seems,
   as the speech asserts.

STRANGER: Then apart from number, how might one either through
   the mouth utter or even by one's thought seize in general the
   things which are not or that which is not?

THEAETETUS: Tell how.

STRANGER: Now whenever we say the things which are not, don't we *C*
   try to apply (add) a multitude of number?

THEAETETUS: Why certainly.

STRANGER: And whenever we say 'that which is not', don't we in turn
   try to apply (add) the one?

THEAETETUS: Yes, most clearly.

STRANGER: And yet we assert that it's neither just nor correct to try
   to fit 'that which is' onto 'that which is not'.

THEAETETUS: What you say is most true.

STRANGER: Do you then understand that it's possible neither to utter
   correctly, nor to say, nor to think 'that which is not' alone by itself,
   but it is unthinkable, unsayable, unutterable, and unspeakable?

II.29

THEAETETUS: That's altogether so.

D STRANGER: Did I really then tell a lie just now when I was saying that I would speak of its biggest perplexity, but the fact is that we can speak of some different and greater perplexity?

THEAETETUS: What exactly?

STRANGER: Why, my wonderful fellow, don't you understand that just in the very things said, 'that which is not' so puts its refuter in a perplexity that, whenever someone tries to refute it, he himself is compelled to contradict himself about it?

THEAETETUS: What do you mean? Speak with still greater clarity.

E STRANGER: There's no need in my case to look for what you call greater clarity, for I laid it down that 'that which is not' must not share in either one or the many, and yet then and now I have spoken of it as one in just this way. For I say 'that which is not'. Do you understand?

THEAETETUS: Yes.

STRANGER: And furthermore I said it to be a little while ago unutterable, unsayable, and unspeakable. Are you following?

THEAETETUS: Of course I'm following.

239 STRANGER: Then in trying to attach 'to be', I was contradicting the previous remarks.

THEAETETUS: You appear to.

STRANGER: And in attaching this, was I not conversing with it as one?

THEAETETUS: Yes.

STRANGER: And furthermore, in speaking of it as unspeakable, unsayable, and unutterable, I was conducting my talk before it as if it were one.

THEAETETUS: Of course.

STRANGER: Yes, but we say one should, if one will speak correctly, distinguish it neither as one nor as many, and not even call it 'it' at all, for it would be addressed even in this manner of address in the species of one.

THEAETETUS: Altogether so.

B STRANGER: Whatever then should one say about poor little me? One would find that I've been defeated for a long time now, no less than at the moment, in the refutation of 'that which is not'. So let's not consider, as I said, the correctness of speech in my speaking about 'that which is not', but come on, let's consider it in yours.

THEAETETUS: What do you mean?

STRANGER: For our sake, come and try in a good and noble fashion, because you are young, and strain to the best of your ability, and by applying neither being nor the one nor a multitude of number to 'that which is not', utter something about it along correct lines.

THEAETETUS: I would in that case have an overwhelmingly strange   *C*
eagerness to try my hand at it, if when I see you undergoing this
sort of thing I myself should try it.

STRANGER: Well, if that's the decision, let's dismiss you and me, and
until we meet with someone who is able to do it, let's say until
then that it's as certain as anything can be that the sophist is a
criminal in the way he has of stopping at nothing, and he has
slipped into a trackless region.

THEAETETUS: It appears very much the case.

STRANGER: It's precisely for this reason that if we'll say he has some
kind of art of phantastics, he'll easily get from this way of using   *D*
speeches a handle on us and twist our speeches back against us,
whenever we call him an imagemaker, by asking whatever in general do we mean by image. You must consider, Theaetetus, what
answer to the question you'll give the youth.

THEAETETUS: It's plain, we'll say, the images in bodies of water and in
mirrors, and further the things that have been painted and
sculpted, and all the rest surely that are other things of the sort.

STRANGER: It's evident, Theaetetus, you've not seen a sophist.   *E*

THEAETETUS: Why's that exactly?

STRANGER: Your impression will be when you do that he has shut his
eyes or does not have them altogether.

THEAETETUS: How's that?

STRANGER: Whenever you offer him your answer in this way, if you
mention something in mirrors or fabrications, he'll laugh at your
speeches, whenever you speak to him as if he were seeing, by
pretending that he's not familiar with either mirrors or bodies of
water or sight altogether, but he'll ask you it only on the basis of   *240*
speeches.[53]

THEAETETUS: What sort of thing?

STRANGER: That which went through all those many things you mentioned, and which, you claimed, deserved to be addressed in every
case with one name, image, on the grounds that it is one. Speak
to this point, then, and defend yourself, and don't yield an inch
to the man.

THEAETETUS: Well, in that case, stranger, what would we say an image
is except, of course, another of the sort that has been made similar
to the simply true?

STRANGER: And by 'another of the sort' you mean what's simply true,
or for what did you say 'of the sort'?   *B*

THEAETETUS: It's in no way simply true, of course, but resembling.

STRANGER: Meaning by the simply true 'that which is' in its being?

THEAETETUS: That's so.

STRANGER: And what of this? Isn't whatever's not simply true contrary to true?

THEAETETUS: Why certainly.

STRANGER: By the resembling, then, you mean, after all, that which is not in its being, if, that is, you'll say it's not simply true.

THEAETETUS: But it still is in a sense.

STRANGER: Though not truly, at any rate, you assert.

THEAETETUS: No indeed, but it's in its being a semblance.

STRANGER: So, not being in its being, it is in its being that which we mean by a semblance.

C THEAETETUS: It's probable that 'that which is not' has got woven in with 'that which is' in a kind of plaiting of this sort. It's very strange too.

STRANGER: Of course it's strange. You do see, at any rate, that even now, through this interchanging, the many-headed sophist has compelled us to agree, albeit not willingly, that 'that which is not' is in a sense.

THEAETETUS: I do indeed see it.

STRANGER: And what of this point? What's the distinct art we're to determine as his that shall enable us to be consonant with ourselves?

THEAETETUS: How is it that you're speaking in this way, and what sort of thing are you so afraid of?

D STRANGER: Whenever we say that it's about the apparition that he does his deceiving, and his art has somehow a capacity to deceive, shall we not then affirm that our soul is then opining false things by his art, or whatever shall we say?

THEAETETUS: This. Is there anything else we might say?

STRANGER: And false opinion, in turn, will be opining the things contrary to the things which are, or how?

THEAETETUS: That's so, the contrary.

STRANGER: Then you mean, after all, that false opinion opines the things which are not?

THEAETETUS: It's a necessity.

E STRANGER: Is that because it opines that 'the things which are not' are not, or that 'the things which are not in any way' are in a sense?

THEAETETUS: Yes, 'the things which are not' must be in a sense, provided, that is, one is ever to lie (speak falsely) even a little bit about anything.

STRANGER: And what of this? Doesn't false opinion opine as well that 'the things which are in every way' are in no way?

THEAETETUS: Yes.

STRANGER: And this too's a falsehood?

THEAETETUS: This too.

STRANGER: And if this is the case, a speech too, I suspect, will be held false on the same terms if it says that 'the things which are' are not and 'the things which are not' are.   *241*

THEAETETUS: Yes, for how else would it prove to be of that sort?

STRANGER: Just about in no way. But the sophist will deny this. Or what possibility is there for anyone sensible to concede this, whenever there has been a further confirmation (as now) of our prior agreements?[54] Do we understand, Theaetetus, what he's saying?

THEAETETUS: Of course we understand. He'll say that we are now contradicting what we just now said, and had the nerve to say (that) false things, in opinions as well as according to speeches, are.[55] He'll say that we are often compelled to attach 'that which *B* is' to 'that which is not', though we came to an agreement just now that this is the most impossible of all.

STRANGER: You recall it correctly. But now's the time to take counsel: What must we do about the sophist? If we track him to his lair and set him down in the art of the lie-makers and enchanters, you do see how readily available and many the objections and perplexities are?

THEAETETUS: They are indeed.

STRANGER: Well, it's just a small part of them that we've gone through, though they are almost unlimited.   *C*

THEAETETUS: If that's the case, it's impossible after all, it seems, to seize the sophist.

STRANGER: Then what? Shall we in that case go soft and now stand aside and withdraw?

THEAETETUS: No, I for one say we shouldn't, if even to a slight degree we can get a hold on the man at any point.

STRANGER: You'll then have forgiveness and, as you now said, be content if at any point even slightly we pull ourselves away from so mighty a speech.[56]

THEAETETUS: Of course I will.

STRANGER: Then I have this still further request to make of you.   *D*

THEAETETUS: What sort is it?

STRANGER: Don't take me to be, as it were, a kind of parricide.

THEAETETUS: Why's that exactly?

STRANGER: It will be necessary for us, in defending ourselves, to put the speech of our father Parmenides to the torture and force it to say that 'that which is not' is in some respect, and again, in turn, 'that which is' is not in some point.

THEAETETUS: It's apparent that something of the sort must be fought out in the speeches.

STRANGER: Of course it's apparent, and, as the saying goes, even to

E   the blind. For if these things submit to neither a refutation nor an agreement, hardly anyone will ever be able to avoid being ridiculous when he's compelled to contradict himself in speaking about false speeches or opinion, whether images, semblances, imitations, or apparitions, either about these things themselves or even about all the arts that deal with them.

THEAETETUS: Most true.

242   STRANGER: Well, it's on account of this that we now must have the nerve to set upon the paternal speech, or dismiss it altogether, if a kind of reluctance keeps us from doing it.

THEAETETUS: Well, let nothing ever keep us from this.

STRANGER: I'll further ask you for a third favor, a small one.

THEAETETUS: Just say it.

STRANGER: Just now in speaking I made the remark somewhere that I have in fact on every occasion renounced through exhaustion the refutation of these things, and it was no less so now.

THEAETETUS: You did make it.

STRANGER: I now fear that remark, that it will ever be your impression on account of it that I'm crazy if I change myself topsy-turvy at
B   every step. For it's thanks to you that we shall set upon refutation of the speech if we do refute it.

THEAETETUS: Well, go to it then, since you can be confident as far as this goes that it shall never be my opinion that you strike any false note if you go to this refutation and demonstration.

STRANGER: Come on then. In the case of a speech fraught with danger what kind of beginning would one make? It's my opinion, my boy, that the most indispensable way for us to turn into is the following.

THEAETETUS: What sort exactly?

STRANGER: To make an investigation first off of those things that now seem to be as plain as day, lest, though being in a sense in a state
C   of confusion about them, we agree easily with one another as if we were in a state of discernment.

THEAETETUS: State with greater clarity what you mean.

STRANGER: It's my opinion that Parmenides and everyone else who has ever started out to make a determination of the things which are, how many they are and of what sort, have conversed with us too good-humoredly.

THEAETETUS: How's that?

STRANGER: Each of them appears to me to narrate to us, as if we were children, a kind of myth: one saying that 'the things which are'
D   (are) three, and sometimes some of them are, in a sense, at war with one another, and sometimes they become friendly and make

arrangements for marriages, births, and the sustenance of their offspring; another says two, liquid and dry or hot and cold, and he has them keep house together and offers them in marriage;[57] and our Eleatic tribe, which had its beginning from Xenophanes and still earlier, on the grounds that all the things so-called are one, proceeds in this way with its own myths. And later some Ionian and Sicilian Muses figured out that it's safest to weave both *E* together and say that 'that which is' is many and one, and it's held together by enmity and friendship. "Differing with itself it always concurs with itself," the more tightly strained of the Muses say; but the softer let them slacken off from this always being their condition, and they say that in turn the all is sometimes one and friendly by Aphrodite, and sometimes it is many and at war with *243* itself on account of some kind of strife.[58] But all these things, whether one of them has spoken them truly or not, it's hard to say, and it's offensive to rebuke renowned men of old with so great a charge as falsehood, but still it cannot occasion resentment to declare that—

THEAETETUS: What?

STRANGER: That they look down upon us the many and despise us to excess, for they don't care whether we're following them as they speak or we fall behind, but they severally get on with their own *B* thing.

THEAETETUS: How do you mean that?

STRANGER: Whenever one of them opens his mouth to speak and says it is, or it has become, or it is becoming many, one, or two, and hot in turn is mixing together with cold, and he lays down in different places disjunctions and conjunctions[59]—by the gods, Theaetetus, do you at all understand what they're saying on each occasion? Now when I was younger, just as whenever anyone spoke of this present perplexity, that which is not, I believed I understood it precisely—but now you see where we are in the perplexity about it—

THEAETETUS: I see. *C*

STRANGER: Well, perhaps, then, with regard to 'that which is' we have no less taken into our soul this same experience, and we say we understand and are not perplexed by it whenever anyone utters it, but that this is not so about the other, though we are in a similar state in respect to both.

THEAETETUS: Perhaps.

STRANGER: And, further, let this same point be stated about everything else that we have spoken of before.

THEAETETUS: Certainly.

D STRANGER: Now about the many, we'll examine them next, if it's so decided, but now we must consider the biggest and first founder.

THEAETETUS: What exactly do you mean? Or it's plain that you're saying we must first make an investigation of 'that which is', whatever it is that those who speak of it believe they're making plain?

STRANGER: Yes, Theaetetus, you're right in step. I mean that we must go on in our pursuit along this trail—ask them just as if they themselves were present as follows: "Come, all of you who declare all things to be hot and cold or any two of the same sort of pairs,

E whatever is this that you utter in the case of both, in saying both and each of the two to be? What are we to suppose about this 'to be' of yours? Is it a third beyond those two? And we're to set down the all as three and no longer two according to you? It's surely not the case that you call the other of the two 'that which is' and still say that both of the two similarly are? In both of the two cases they would pretty nearly be one but not two."

THEAETETUS: What you say is true.

STRANGER: "Well, do you want, after all, to call both as a pair 'that which is'?"

THEAETETUS: Perhaps.

244 STRANGER: "But in this case too, friends," we'll say, "the two would most clearly be spoken of as one."

THEAETETUS: That's a most correct remark.

STRANGER: "Well, then, since we are in a state of perplexity, you go ahead and make them evident to us adequately, whatever you want to indicate whenever you utter 'that which is'. It's plain that you have been familiar with this for a long time, and we used to believe it of ourselves before, but now we are in a state of perplexity. Teach us, then, this very point first, in order that we may not seem to understand the things said on your side, and the

B complete contrary of this prove to be the case." If we say this and make this claim upon them and everyone else who says the all is more than one, it's not possible, is it, my boy, that we'll strike any false note?

THEAETETUS: Not in the least.

STRANGER: And what of this? Mustn't we inquire to the best of our ability of those who speak of the all as one, whatever do they mean by 'that which is'?

THEAETETUS: Of course.

STRANGER: Let them then answer the following. "You surely declare only one to be?" "We do declare," they'll say. Won't they?

THEAETETUS: Yes.

STRANGER: "And what of this? Do you call 'that which is' something?"

THEAETETUS: Yes.

STRANGER: "Is it just what you call one, employing two names for the   C
same, or how?"

THEAETETUS: What's their next answer, stranger?

STRANGER: It's plain, Theaetetus, that whoever lays down this supposition cannot have the easiest time of it to give an answer to
the present question, or to anything else whatsoever either.

THEAETETUS: How's that?

STRANGER: To make it one's own position that nothing (not even one)
is except one and still go on to agree that two names are, is surely
as ridiculous—

THEAETETUS: Of course.

STRANGER: As it would make no sense to accept in general from anyone   D
who says that some name is.

THEAETETUS: In what way?

STRANGER: If he sets down the name as other than the thing (*pragma*),
he's surely speaking of a pair of some two.

THEAETETUS: Yes.

STRANGER: And yet, if he sets down the name as the same as it, he'll
be compelled either to say it's the name of nothing or, if he'll say
it's of something, it will turn out that the name is only a name of
a name and is of nothing else.

THEAETETUS: That's so.

STRANGER: And the one, in turn, being the name of one will also turn
out to be the one of the name.[60]

THEAETETUS: It's a necessity.

STRANGER: And what of this? Shall they say the whole's other than
'that which is one' or the same as this?

THEAETETUS: Of course they'll say, and they do say, it's the same.   E

STRANGER: If then, it is a whole, just as Parmenides says—

"From all quarters like unto the bulk of well-rounded sphere,
And from its midpoint equivalent in every direction, for it must
    not be
Any bigger or any smaller in this direction or in this"[61]—

then, 'that which is' in being of this sort has a middle and extremes,
and if it has these, there's every necessity for it to have parts, or
how?

THEAETETUS: That's so.

STRANGER: And though there's nothing to prevent that which has been   245
partitioned to have the experience (affect) of the one over all its
parts, and in just this way to be that which is an all and one whole—

THEAETETUS: Certainly.

STRANGER: Isn't it really impossible for the one itself to be that which has experienced it?

THEAETETUS: How's that?

STRANGER: Surely it must have been said of the truly one, according to the correct speech, that it's completely without parts.

THEAETETUS: Indeed it must.

B STRANGER: Yes, but that something of the sort is out of many parts will not be consonant with that speech.

THEAETETUS: I understand.

STRANGER: Will 'that which is', if it has the experience (affect) of the one in this way, be one and a whole, or are we to say altogether that 'that which is' is not a whole?

THEAETETUS: You've put forward a hard choice.

STRANGER: That's really most true what you say. For it's no less so if 'that which is' has been affected to be one in a sense, since it will evidently not be the same as the one, and all the things will be strictly more than one—

THEAETETUS: Yes.

C STRANGER: Than if 'that which is' is not a whole on account of the fact of its having been made to be affected by that (i.e., the one), and the whole itself is, since then 'that which is' turns out to fall short of itself.

THEAETETUS: Certainly.

STRANGER: Moreover, according to this speech, 'that which is', in being deprived of itself, will not be 'that which is'.

THEAETETUS: That's so.

STRANGER: And all the things once more become more than one when 'that which is' and the whole have each apart from the other taken a private nature.

THEAETETUS: Yes.

D STRANGER: But if, on the other hand, the whole is not at all, then these same things belong to 'that which is', and in addition to the whole not being, it would never have become 'that which is'.

THEAETETUS: Why exactly?

STRANGER: That which becomes always has become a whole, so that if one does not set down the whole among the things which are, one must address it as being neither being nor becoming.

THEAETETUS: It seems likely that this is altogether the case.

STRANGER: Moreover, the not whole must not be any many whatsoever, for if it is a definite many, whatever that many is, so great a whole must it necessarily be.

THEAETETUS: Yes, utterly.

STRANGER: And it will, accordingly, be evident to whoever says that

'that which is' is only some two or one that thousands upon thou-   E
sands of different points have severally been the recipient of unlimited perplexities.

THEAETETUS: Even the present indications made that pretty nearly
plain. For another gets attached from something else and brings
with it a greater and more difficult aberration in regard to whatever had been one's previous remarks.

STRANGER: Well, anyway, though we've not gone through everyone
who gives a precise speech about 'that which is' and 'that which
is not', still and all let it be enough. But we must now in turn look
at those who speak in a different way, in order that we may from
all sides see that it's no more readily available to say about 'that
which is' whatever it is than about 'that which is not'.   246

THEAETETUS: Then we must advance against these as well.

STRANGER: Well, as a matter of fact, there seems to be among them a
kind of gigantomachy on account of their mutual dispute about
being.

THEAETETUS: How's that?

STRANGER: Some drag everything to earth out of the sky and the
invisible, and simply (artlessly) get their hands on rocks and oaks,[62]
for in clinging to all things of the sort they insist on this: only
that is which affords the possibility of some kind of application   B
and touching, defining body and being as the same, and if anyone
will say of anything else that it is, though it's without body, they
altogether despise him and are unwilling to hear anything else.

THEAETETUS: You've spoken of really dreadful men. I too have met
many of them before now.

STRANGER: It's precisely for this reason that those who dispute with
them defend themselves very cautiously from way up high somewhere from an invisible position and force the simply true being
to be some kinds of intelligible and bodiless species, but *their* bodies
and the truth spoken of by them—they smash them up into little
bits in their speeches and address them, instead of as being, as a   C
kind of sweeping becoming.[63] And in the middle of them both,
Theaetetus, there has always consisted an immense battle about
these things.

THEAETETUS: True.

STRANGER: Let's then get piecemeal from both of this pair of genera
a speech on behalf of the being they set down for themselves.

THEAETETUS: How exactly are we to get it?

STRANGER: From those who set it down among species, it's easier, for
they're tamer; but from those who forcibly drag everything into

body, it's harder, and perhaps it's pretty nearly impossible. But
D   it's my opinion we must act as follows about them.

THEAETETUS: How?

STRANGER: If it were in any way possible, the best thing would be to make them better in deed. But if this is not admissible, let's make them so in speech, by supposing that they would willingly give their answers in a more lawful way than they now do. For an agreement that's reached by the better is surely more authoritative than that from the worse. And we don't care about them, but we're seeking the truth.

E   THEAETETUS: Most correct.

STRANGER: Then order those who have become better to make their answers to you, and you interpret whatever is said on their side.

THEAETETUS: It shall be done.

STRANGER: Let them say whether they assert that mortal animal is something.

THEAETETUS: Of course.

STRANGER: And don't they agree that that's an ensouled body?

THEAETETUS: Certainly.

STRANGER: And they set down soul as one of the things which are.

247   THEAETETUS: Yes.

STRANGER: And what of this? Don't they say there is the just and the unjust, and the intelligent and the unintelligent (senseless) soul?

THEAETETUS: Why certainly.

STRANGER: Well, don't they say that by the having and presence of justice each of them becomes this sort, and the contrary by the contraries?

THEAETETUS: Yes, they consent to this as well.

STRANGER: And they'll further say that that which can be present at or absent from something is in either case something.

THEAETETUS: They do say it rather.

B   STRANGER: If then justice is, and intelligence and the rest of virtue, as well as their contraries, and, in particular, if soul is, in which these things come to be, do they say of any of them that it is visible and touchable, or that all are invisible?

THEAETETUS: Pretty nearly none of them's visible.

STRANGER: But what of things of this sort? Do they say they have a kind of body?

THEAETETUS: On this point they no longer answer altogether on the same terms, but though it's their opinion that the soul itself pos-
C   sesses a kind of body, still as for intelligence and each of the rest that you've asked about, they're ashamed to have the nerve either

to agree that they are none of the things which are, or to insist that they all are bodies.

STRANGER: That's because, Theaetetus, these men of ours have clearly become better, since at least those among them who are sown and autochthonous would not be ashamed before even one of these assertions, but they would strenuously insist that everything whatever they are incapable of squeezing with their hands—"All this," they'd say, "altogether is not."[64]

THEAETETUS: You say pretty nearly the sort of things they think.

STRANGER: Well, then, let's ask them once more, for it's enough if they're willing to concede that something, no matter how small, *D* of the things which are, is bodiless. What they have to state is this. What is that which has proved to be naturally cognate with these things as well as with all those that have body, by looking at which they say that both are? They might perhaps be perplexed. So if they have been affected by something of the sort, consider, if we were to make an offer, whether they would be willing to accept it and agree that 'that which is' is something of the following sort.

THEAETETUS: What sort exactly? Speak, and then perhaps we'll know.

STRANGER: I'm speaking of that which possesses any power whatsoever, whether it be naturally geared to affecting another in any *E* respect whatsoever or to being affected even to the smallest degree by the most trivial thing, even if that only occurs once—all this in its being is. I'm proposing, in short, a definition (boundary-mark): 'The things which are' are not anything else but power.[65]

THEAETETUS: Well, since they on their own at least cannot speak at the moment better than this, they accept it.

STRANGER: Beautiful. At a later time, perhaps, to us as well as to them, it might appear other. Now let this agreement that we have reached *248* with them be on standby here.

THEAETETUS: It's on standby.

STRANGER: Then let's go to the others, the friends of the species, and you interpret for us what's said on their side as well.

THEAETETUS: It shall be done.

STRANGER: Of becoming, and being, on the other hand, you surely make a division and speak separately?[66] Don't you?

THEAETETUS: Yes.

STRANGER: And we, you say, share in becoming through perception by means of body, but through calculation by means of soul in being in its being, which is always, you assert, in the same state in the same respect, but becoming (is) at different times in different states.

THEAETETUS: Indeed we do assert it. *B*

STRANGER: But this sharing, your excellencies, what is it that we're to assert that you speak of in both cases? Is it to be the remark just now made on our side?

THEAETETUS: What sort?

STRANGER: An affection or an affecting (making) that becomes from their mutually coming together out of some kind of power. Now you perhaps, Theaetetus, do not overhear their answer in reply to this, but I perhaps do because of my familiarity.

THEAETETUS: What, then, is the speech they speak?

C STRANGER: They do not concede us the remark just now made to the earthborn about being.

THEAETETUS: What sort?

STRANGER: What we surely set down as an adequate definition (boundary-mark) of the things which are—whenever the power of being affected or affecting (doing) is present to something even to the slightest degree?

THEAETETUS: Yes.

STRANGER: Now in reply to this, they say the following: becoming shares in a power of being affected or affecting. But they deny that the power of either of the two fits with being.

THEAETETUS: Aren't they making sense?

STRANGER: Yes, but to which we must say in reply that we need to
D learn from them with still greater clarity whether they agree besides that the soul cognizes and being is cognized.

THEAETETUS: This much they do say.

STRANGER: But what of this? The fact of cognizing or the fact of being cognized, do you assert it to be an affecting or an affection or both? Or one is an affection, and one is the other? Or altogether neither gets a share in either one of them?

THEAETETUS: It's plain, neither in neither, for otherwise they would be contradicting their previous remarks.

STRANGER: I understand. It's this, if the fact of cognizing will be a
E kind of affecting, it turns out in turn that that which is being cognized is necessarily affected. But, according to this speech, the being that is being cognized by the cognition, to the extent that it is being cognized, to just that extent is in motion on account of its being affected, and it's this, we say, that would not occur in the case of that which is at rest.

THEAETETUS: Right.

STRANGER: But, by Zeus, what of this? Shall we easily be persuaded
249 that motion and life and soul and intelligence are truly not present to that which perfectly is, and it's not even living, not even thinking, but august and pure, without mind, it stands motionless?[67]

THEAETETUS: We would in that case, stranger, be conceding a dreadful speech.

STRANGER: Well, are we to say it's with mind but not life?[68]

THEAETETUS: But how are we to?

STRANGER: But if we're saying both of these are in it, shall we deny that it has them in soul?

THEAETETUS: But in what other way would it have them?

STRANGER: But is it then to have mind and life and soul, and yet, though it is ensouled, to stand altogether motionless?

THEAETETUS: All of this appears to me at least to make no sense.　　*B*

STRANGER: And we must further concede that motion and that which is in motion are things which are.

THEAETETUS: Of course.

STRANGER: And, regardless of this, Theaetetus, it no less turns out that if the things which are, are motionless, there never is mind to anything about anything—

THEAETETUS: Yes, utterly.

STRANGER: Than that if, in turn, we concede that all things are sweeping along and moving, we'll remove by this speech too this same thing from the things which are.

THEAETETUS: How's that?

STRANGER: Is it your opinion that that which is in the same respects and in the same state and about the same thing would ever come to be apart from rest?　　*C*

THEAETETUS: In no way.

STRANGER: And what of this? Without these things, do you see mind ever being or coming to be anywhere at all?

THEAETETUS: Not in the least.

STRANGER: And so one must fight with every speech at one's command against him, whoever, in making science (knowledge) or intelligence or mind disappear, insists upon anything in any respect whatever.

THEAETETUS: Exactly.

STRANGER: For the philosopher, then, who particularly honors these things, there's every necessity, it seems, on account of this, to refuse to accept the all as stationary from those who speak of one or even the many species, and no less, in turn, not even listen to those who set in motion in every way 'that which is'; but, in ac-　*D* cordance with the prayer of children, to say that all that is motionless and in a state of motion are both together 'that which is' and the all.

THEAETETUS: Most true.

STRANGER: What then? Do we appear by now to have fairly comprehended in the speech 'that which is'?

THEAETETUS: Yes, of course.

STRANGER: Oh my, Oh my! Theaetetus. It's just now, in my opinion,
that we'll get to recognize about it the perplexity of its examination.

E THEAETETUS: Once more, what do you mean, and what's the point of
your remark?

STRANGER: You blessed innocent! Don't you realize that now we're in
a most overwhelming ignorance about it, but we appear to ourselves to be making sense?

THEAETETUS: To me at any rate. But at what point we've slipped
unawares into this state, I scarcely understand.

STRANGER: Consider then more clearly whether in our present agreement we would be justly asked the very points that we ourselves
250 were asking those who say the all is hot and cold.

THEAETETUS: What sort of points? Remind me.

STRANGER: Yes, of course. And what's more I'll try to do it by asking
you as I then asked them, in order that together we may advance
somewhat.

THEAETETUS: Right.

STRANGER: So far so good. Don't you speak of motion and rest as most
contrary to one another?

THEAETETUS: Of course.

STRANGER: And you furthermore say that each of the two and both
are in a similar way?

B THEAETETUS: Indeed I do say it.

STRANGER: You mean, then, whenever you concede them to be, that
both and each of the two move?

THEAETETUS: In no way.

STRANGER: Well, in saying that they both are, are you indicating that
they are at rest?

THEAETETUS: How could I?

STRANGER: Then are you, after all, setting down in the soul 'that which
is' as a third something beyond these, on the grounds that both
rest and motion are comprehended by it, and do you take them
together, look at their sharing in being, and thus address both as
being?

C THEAETETUS: It's probable that we truly divine 'that which is' as a third
something, whenever we say motion and rest are.

STRANGER: Then 'that which is' is not motion and rest together as a
both but a certain kind of something other than these.

THEAETETUS: It seems likely.

STRANGER: Then in terms of its own nature, 'that which is' neither stands nor moves.

THEAETETUS: Pretty nearly.

STRANGER: In which direction, then, must he who wants to have some vivid confirmation about it for himself still turn his thought?

THEAETETUS: In which?

STRANGER: Well, I suspect it's no longer easy in any. For if something does not move, how isn't it at rest? Or that which is in no way at D rest, how doesn't it in turn move? But 'that which is' has now come to light for us as outside of both of these. Is this then really possible?

THEAETETUS: No, it's the most impossible of all.

STRANGER: Well, it's just in these matters to recall the following.

THEAETETUS: What sort of thing?

STRANGER: That when the question was put to us as to the name of 'that which is not', to whatever one must apply it, we got stuck in every kind of perplexity. Do you remember?

THEAETETUS: Of course.

STRANGER: Then are we now in any less perplexity about 'that which E is'?

THEAETETUS: In my view, stranger, if it's possible to say it, we appear to be in a more extensive one.

STRANGER: Well, then, let this be set down here as a thoroughly examined perplexity. But inasmuch as 'that which is' and 'that which is not' have equally partaken of perplexity, there's now the expectation that from now on, just as the other of them comes to light, whether more dimly or more clearly, so too the other comes to light. And if, in turn, we're incapable of seeing either of them, 251 then we'll push the speech at least—whatever be the most decent way we can muster—in this way simultaneously through them both.[69]

THEAETETUS: Beautiful.

STRANGER: Let's then say in what manner it is that we address on each occasion this same thing with many names.

THEAETETUS: What exactly, for example? Give a paradigm.

STRANGER: In speaking of a human being, we surely name him many things besides, applying to him colors, figures, sizes, vices and virtues, in all of which and thousands of others we say not only that he is a human being, but also good and infinitely other things. B And with everything else besides in just this way, in accordance with the same speech, we lay down each as one and then again we go on to speak of it as many and with many names.

THEAETETUS: What you say's true.

STRANGER: It's from this vantage point, I suspect, that we've arranged a feast for the young and the late-learners among the old, for it's straight off ready-at-hand for everyone to get a counterhold— "Its just as impossible for the many to be one as the one many." And there's no doubt that they take pleasure in not allowing the speaking of a human being as good, for the good (is) good and

C the human being a human being. You've often met, I suspect, Theaetetus, with those whose zeal is devoted to things of this sort, and sometimes they're rather elderly human beings, and through their poverty in the acquisition of intelligence, they're in a state of wonder before things of the sort, and they suspect besides that this very thing they've found is something entirely wise.

THEAETETUS: They certainly do.

STRANGER: In order, then, for our speech to be addressed to all who

D have ever in their conversation had anything whatever to say about being, let what will now be said in the form of a question be stated before these as well as everyone else with whom we had conversed earlier.

THEAETETUS: What sort of things exactly?

STRANGER: Are we to attach neither being to motion and rest nor anything else to anything else, but on the grounds that they are immiscible and it's impossible for them to partake of one another, are we to set them down in just this way in the speeches we use? Or are we to bring them all together into the same on the grounds that they're capable of sharing in one another? Or some do and

E some don't? Which of these, Theaetetus, shall we say they would choose?

THEAETETUS: Well, I for one cannot on their behalf make an answer in reply to this.

STRANGER: Why then don't you answer one by one and consider the consequences in each case?

THEAETETUS: What you say is beautiful.

STRANGER: Let's suppose that they first say, if you want, that nothing has any capacity for sharing with anything in any respect. Motion and rest, then, won't as a pair share in being in any way?

252 THEAETETUS: Indeed they won't.

STRANGER: And what of this? Will either of them be if it does not share in being as well?

THEAETETUS: It will not be.

STRANGER: So by this agreement everything has been quickly rooted up simultaneously, it seems, whether they set the all in motion, or put a stop to it on the grounds that it's one, or do as all those do who say the things which are by species are always in the same state in the same respect—for all those add 'to be' at least, some by saying that they move in their being, and some by saying they are at rest in their being.

THEAETETUS: Yes, utterly.

STRANGER: And, further, all those who at times put everything to- B gether and at times divide them, regardless of whether they divide, and put together out of them an infinity of things into one and out of one or into elements with a limit, and similarly whether they set this down as alternate becoming, and similarly whether they set it down as always—in all these cases they would be saying nothing if there is no mixing together.

THEAETETUS: Right.

STRANGER: And, further, those who forbid the address of anything, by its sharing in the affection of another, as the other, would themselves be pursuing the speech in the most ridiculous of all ways.

THEAETETUS: How's that? C

STRANGER: They're compelled surely in everything to use 'to be' and 'apart' and 'everything else' and 'by itself' and thousands of others, and because they are powerless to stay away from them and not to join them together in their speeches, they don't need anyone else to refute them; but, as the saying goes, they have the enemy at home ready to oppose them, and they always go around carrying inside them a ventriloquist like the strange Eurycles.[70]

THEAETETUS: What you say is utterly similar and true. D

STRANGER: And what of this—if we allow everything to have the capacity of mutual sharing?

THEAETETUS: Now even I can resolve this.

STRANGER: How?

THEAETETUS: Because motion itself would altogether be at rest, and rest itself, in turn, would once more move, if they should supervene on one another.

STRANGER: But surely this is, by the greatest necessities, impossible, for motion to rest and rest to move?

THEAETETUS: Of course.

STRANGER: So the third alone is left.

THEAETETUS: Yes.

STRANGER: And it's necessary that it be at least some one of these: E either everything or nothing, or some are and some are not willing to mix together.

THEAETETUS: Of course.

STRANGER: And it was two that were found to be impossible.

THEAETETUS: Yes.

STRANGER: So everyone, who wants to answer correctly, will set down the one remainder of the three.

THEAETETUS: Yes, certainly.

253 STRANGER: So when some things are willing to do this and some not, they would have been affected in just about the sort of way letters are, for whereas some of them surely do not fit one another and some do fit together—

THEAETETUS: Of course.

STRANGER: Still the vowels in a different way from everything else have gone through everything as a sort of bond, so as for it to be impossible without some one of them to fit even another of the rest with an other.

THEAETETUS: Yes, indeed.

STRANGER: Does everyone know what sort of letters are capable of sharing with what sort, or does whoever's going to do it adequately need an art?

THEAETETUS: An art.

STRANGER: What sort?

THEAETETUS: Grammatics (the art of reading and writing letters).

B STRANGER: And what of this? Isn't this the case for the sounds of high and low notes? Isn't the musician the one who has the art to recognize the sorts that mix and don't mix together, and the one who does not understand is unmusical?

THEAETETUS: That's so.

STRANGER: And in the case of all the rest of the arts and nonarts, we'll find other things of the sort?

THEAETETUS: Of course.

STRANGER: And what of this? Since we've agreed that the genera too are in the same condition with regard to their mutual mixing, isn't it necessary for him who is going to show correctly which of the genera are consonant with which and which don't receive one C another to proceed through the speeches with a kind of science? And in particular he must know whether there are some that hold them together through all of them, so as for them to be capable of mixing together, and again in the divisions, whether others are causes of the division through wholes?

THEAETETUS: Of course there is a need of a science, and perhaps pretty nearly the greatest.

STRANGER: What then shall we address this as, Theaetetus? Or by Zeus! Did we fall unawares into the science of the free, and is it probable that in looking for the sophist we've first found the philosopher?

THEAETETUS: How do you mean that?

STRANGER: We'll assert, shall we not, that to divide according to genera   *D*
and not to believe either the same another species or if it is other
the same, this is the characteristic of the dialectical science?

THEAETETUS: Yes, we'll assert it.

STRANGER: And whoever is able to do this, perceives adequately one
look (*idea*) stretched in every way through many, though each one
is situated apart, and many (looks) other than one another comprehended on the outside by one (look), and one (look), in turn,
bound together into one through many wholes, and many (looks)
set apart and distinct in every way—and this is to know how to   *E*
discern according to genus, in which way the (genera) are severally
capable of sharing and in which not.[71]

THEAETETUS: That's altogether so.

STRANGER: But the dialectical capacity—you won't give it to anyone
else, I suspect, except to whoever philosophizes purely and justly.

THEAETETUS: How could one give it to anyone else?

STRANGER: We'll find, then, if we seek, both now and later, the philosopher in some sort of region like this, and though he too is
difficult to see vividly, it's in another way than his that the sophist's
difficulty is.   *254*

THEAETETUS: How's that?

STRANGER: One's a fugitive into the darkling of 'that which is not', to
which he attaches himself by a knack, and on account of the
darkness of the region, he's hard to get an understanding of. Isn't
that so?

THEAETETUS: It seems likely.

STRANGER: Yes, but the philosopher, devoted to the look (*idea*) of that
which is always through calculations, it's on account of the brilliance of the place that he's in no way easy to be seen, for the eyes
of the soul of the many are incapable of keeping up a steady gaze   *B*
on the divine.

THEAETETUS: That this is the case is no less likely than that is.

STRANGER: Then we'll soon go on to consider him as well with greater
clarity, if it's still our wish—but about the sophist, it's surely plain
that we must not give up before we observe him adequately.

THEAETETUS: You put it beautifully.

STRANGER: Since, then, it has been agreed upon by us that some of
the genera are willing to share in one another, and some not, and
the range of some is slight and of some extensive, and there's
nothing to prevent some from having a share through everything
in everything, let's follow up on the speech with the next point,   *C*
and examine in the following way—not all the species, in order
that we may not be confused among many, but let's choose some

of the biggest spoken of—first what sort they severally are, next how they are in terms of their capacity of sharing in one another, in order that both that which is and is not, if we're incapable of seizing them with complete clarity, still we may not at least fall short of a speech about them, to the extent that the way of the present examination allows it, which is whether, after all, 'that which is not' gives way at some point and allows us, in saying that

D   it is in its being 'that which is not', to get off scott-free.

THEAETETUS: Well, we must.

STRANGER: But the biggest of the genera that we just now were going through are 'that which is' itself and rest and motion.

THEAETETUS: Yes, the biggest by far.

STRANGER: And we assert besides that the two—a pair—(are) immiscible with one another.

THEAETETUS: Exactly.

STRANGER: But 'that which is' (is) miscible with both, for surely both of the pair are.

THEAETETUS: Of course.

STRANGER: These then become three.

THEAETETUS: Why certainly.

STRANGER: Each of them is other than the two, and itself the same as itself.

E   THEAETETUS: Just so.

STRANGER: But whatever have we meant by "the same" and "the other" with this present remark? Are they themselves a kind of pair of two genera, different from the three, but always of necessity joining with them in a mixture, and on the grounds that our examination is about their being five and not three, we have to consider

255   them? Or are we addressing them without being aware of it, both this "the same" and "the other" as some one of them?[72]

THEAETETUS: Perhaps.

STRANGER: Well, motion and rest at least are neither other nor the same.

THEAETETUS: How's that?

STRANGER: Whatever kind of address we make to motion and rest in common, neither of the pair can be this.

THEAETETUS: Why exactly?

STRANGER: Motion will rest and rest in turn will move, for in the case of both, whichever one of the pair becomes the other, it will compel the other in turn to change into the contrary of its own

B   nature, inasmuch as now it does participate in its contrary.

THEAETETUS: Utterly.

STRANGER: Yet both of the pair participate in the same and the other.

THEAETETUS: Yes.

STRANGER: Let's not say, then, that motion is the same or the other, and let's not say it of rest either.

THEAETETUS: Let's not.

STRANGER: Well, then, must we think of 'that which is' and "the same" as some one?

THEAETETUS: Perhaps.

STRANGER: But if the pair 'that which is' and "the same" indicates nothing different, then in saying in turn once more that motion and rest both are, we shall in this way address both as being the same.   C

THEAETETUS: But that's impossible.

STRANGER: Then it's impossible, after all, for the same and 'that which is' to be one.

THEAETETUS: Pretty nearly.

STRANGER: Are we then to set down "the same" as fourth in addition to the three species?

THEAETETUS: Yes, of course.

STRANGER: And what of this? Must we say "the other" (is) fifth? Or must we think of this and 'that which is' as some two names for one genus?

THEAETETUS: Perhaps.

STRANGER: But you concede, I suspect, that some of 'the things which are' are spoken of by themselves, and some are always spoken of in relation to different things.

THEAETETUS: Why, of course.

STRANGER: Yes, but the other (is) always relative to another, isn't it?   D

THEAETETUS: That's so.

STRANGER: They wouldn't be, if 'that which is' and "the other" were not extensively different. But if the other participated in both of the pair of species, just as 'that which is' does, then at some time or other there would also be some other of the others not in relation to another, but, as it is, it has simply (artlessly) turned out for us that whatever is other is of necessity that which it is as of another.

THEAETETUS: It's just in the way you say.

STRANGER: Then among the species which we choose, the nature of the other must be counted as being the fifth.   E

THEAETETUS: Yes.

STRANGER: And we'll assert besides that it has gone through all of them, for it's not on account of its own nature that each one is different from all the rest, but on account of its participation in the look (*idea*) of the other.

THEAETETUS: Yes, certainly.

STRANGER: Let's then take up the five one by one and speak in their case as follows.

THEAETETUS: How?

STRANGER: First, motion, that it is altogether other than rest. Or how do we speak?

THEAETETUS: In this way.

STRANGER: So it is not rest.

THEAETETUS: In no way.

256 STRANGER: Yes, but it is, on account of its participating in 'that which is'.

THEAETETUS: It is.

STRANGER: Then, again, motion is other than the same.

THEAETETUS: Pretty nearly.

STRANGER: So it is not the same.

THEAETETUS: No, it isn't.

STRANGER: But this motion was still agreed to be the same on account of the fact that everything participates in it.

THEAETETUS: They do indeed.

STRANGER: Then we have to agree and not be distressed that motion is the same and not the same. For we've not spoken in a similar way whenever we say it's the same and not the same; but whenever

B we say it's the same, we speak thus on account of its participation in the same in relation to itself, but whenever we say it's not the same, it's on account of its sharing, in turn, in the other, on account of which it gets to be apart from the same and has become not that but another, and hence once more it is said correctly that it's not the same.

THEAETETUS: Yes, of course.

STRANGER: And wouldn't it be the case, that were motion itself to partake in rest at some point, it would not be at all strange to address it as stationary?

THEAETETUS: Most correctly, provided that we'll concede that some of the genera are willing to mix with one another and some are not.[73]

STRANGER: But we did come to the demonstration of this before the demonstration of the present point, in proving that this is natu-

C rally the case.

THEAETETUS: Of course.

STRANGER: Then let's say once more: Motion is other than the other, just as it was different from the same and from rest.

THEAETETUS: Necessarily.

STRANGER: So it is in a sense not other and other according to the present speech.

THEAETETUS: True.

STRANGER: And what of the next point? Are we to say that it is other than the three, and deny it's other than the fourth, though we *D* agreed they are five, about which and in the region of which we proposed to conduct our examination?

THEAETETUS: How could that be? It's impossible to concede that the number's less than that which just now came to light.

STRANGER: Are we to say then fearlessly and contentiously that motion is after all other than 'that which is'?

THEAETETUS: Most fearlessly rather.

STRANGER: Then motion plainly is in its being 'not that which is' and 'that which is', since it participates in 'that which is.'

THEAETETUS: Most plainly.

STRANGER: So it is after all of necessity, in the case of motion and throughout all the genera, that 'that which is not' be, for in each *E* and every case the nature of the other, in producing each to be other than 'that which is', makes it 'not that which is', and on the same terms we'll in this way speak correctly of all things as 'not the things which are'. And, once more, because they participate in 'that which is', we'll say they are and 'the things which are'.

THEAETETUS: Probably.

STRANGER: So for each of the species, then, 'that which is' is extensive, but 'that which is not' is infinite in multitude.

THEAETETUS: It seems likely.

STRANGER: Then it must be said that 'that which is in itself' too is other *257* than all the rest.

THEAETETUS: It's a necessity.

STRANGER: And so, for us, 'that which is', to the extent that everything else is, to that extent is not, for in not being those it is itself one, and everything else, in turn, unlimited in their number, is not.

THEAETETUS: It's pretty nearly so.

STRANGER: And we must not be distressed by this either, inasmuch as the nature of the genera admit of the possibility of sharing in one another. But if someone does not concede this, let him first persuade our former speeches, and then, on this condition, go on to persuade us next.

THEAETETUS: You've spoken most justly.

STRANGER: Let's take a look at the following point. *B*

THEAETETUS: What sort?

STRANGER: Whenever we say 'that which is not', we're not saying, it seems, something contrary to 'that which is' but only other.

THEAETETUS: How?

STRANGER: For example, whenever we say something (is) not big, do we at that time appear to you to make clear by the expression the small any more than the equal?

THEAETETUS: How could we?

STRANGER: So we'll not concede the point, whenever it's said that a negative indicates a contrary, but only so much, that the prepositioning of "not," general and particular,[74] reveals something of everything else than the names that come after it, or rather than the things (*pragmata*), whatever they are, for which the names uttered after the negative are laid down.

THEAETETUS: That's altogether so.

STRANGER: But let's think our way through the following, if you share my opinion that we should.

THEAETETUS: What sort of thing?

STRANGER: The nature of the other appears to me to have been chopped into bits just as science (knowledge) has.

THEAETETUS: How?

STRANGER: Surely science too is one, but that which ranges as a part over some bit of it, once it is made distinct (isolated), each severally gets a name peculiar to itself. It's for this reason that arts and sciences are spoken of as many.

THEAETETUS: Yes, of course.

STRANGER: And haven't also the proper parts of the nature of the other, though it is one, been affected in this same way?

THEAETETUS: Perhaps. But are we to say in what way exactly?

STRANGER: Is there some proper part of the other set down in opposition to the beautiful?

THEAETETUS: There is.

STRANGER: Shall we say that this is nameless or it has a name?

THEAETETUS: It has, for whatever we utter on each occasion as not beautiful, this is not other than anything else except the nature of the beautiful.

STRANGER: Come on then and tell me the following.

THEAETETUS: What sort of thing?

STRANGER: Hasn't the not beautiful turned out in this way to be, in its isolation, of some one genus of 'the things which are', and, again, in turn, in its opposition, relative to something of 'the things which are'?[75]

THEAETETUS: That's so.

STRANGER: Then it turns out, it seems, that the not beautiful is a certain kind of opposition of 'that which is' relative to 'that which is'.

THEAETETUS: Most correctly.

STRANGER: What then? According to this speech, is the beautiful for us more of the things which are and the not beautiful less?

THEAETETUS: Not at all.

STRANGER: And the not big and the big itself must be said to be *258* similarly?

THEAETETUS: Similarly.

STRANGER: And the not just too must be set down on the same terms as the just, in regard to the fact that the other is not at all more than the other is?

THEAETETUS: Why certainly.

STRANGER: And we'll speak of everything else besides in this way, since the nature of the other is evidently of 'the things which are', and since it is, it's strictly a necessity to set down its proper parts too as things which are no less than anything else.

THEAETETUS: Of course.

STRANGER: Then, it seems, the opposition of a proper part of the nature of the other and of the nature of 'that which is' in their *B* opposition to one another, is, if it's sanctioned to say so, no less being than 'that which is in itself', and it indicates not a contrary to that but only so much, an other than it.[76]

THEAETETUS: Yes, most plainly.

STRANGER: What then is the address we are to make to it?

THEAETETUS: Clearly, this is that very thing, 'that which is not', which we were seeking on account of the sophist.

STRANGER: Isn't it the case, then, just as you said, that it is and falls short in point of being from none of the rest, and one must from now on say with confidence that 'that which is not', is securely with its own nature, just as the big was big and the beautiful was beautiful, and the not big and the not beautiful likewise,[77] so also *C* 'that which is not' in the same way was and is 'that which is not', one species to be counted in among the many things which are? Or do we, Theaetetus, any longer harbor any distrust on this point?

THEAETETUS: None.

STRANGER: Do you know then that we've disobeyed Parmenides to a further extent than his prohibition?[78]

THEAETETUS: Why exactly?

STRANGER: More than just examining what he forbade us to do, we with a still further investigation proved it to him.

THEAETETUS: How?

STRANGER: Because while he says somewhere *D*

"For never shall this be forced, whatever are not to be;
But you keep your thought away from this way of searching"[79]—

THEAETETUS: He does indeed speak thus.

II.55

STRANGER: We not only proved that 'the things which are not' are, but we also declared what is in fact the species of 'that which is not'. Once we had proved that the nature of the other both is and has been chopped into bits to extend over all 'the things which are' in their mutual relations, we had the nerve to say that this very thing is in its being 'that which is not'—a proper part of the nature of the other in its opposition to that which severally is.[80]

THEAETETUS: And it's my impression, stranger, that we've spoken altogether most truly.

STRANGER: Well, then, let no one say of us that we have the nerve to say, in declaring that 'that which is not' is, that it is the contrary of 'that which is'. We have long ago dismissed all talk of any contrary to it, whether it is or is not, admitting of speech or altogether failing of speech (*alogon*). But that which we've now said 'that which is not' to be, either let someone persuade us by a refutation that we're not speaking beautifully, or as long as he's incapable, he too must say as we say, that the genera mix together with one another and the pair of 'that which is' and the other has gone through everything and each other—the other, because it participates in 'that which is', is (on account of its participation), yet it is not, however, that in which it gets to participate but other, and in being other than 'that which is' it is most plainly and of necessity 'that which is not'; and 'that which is', in turn, having partaken of the other, would be other than the different genera, and, in being other than all of them, is not each of them or all the rest together either but only itself, and hence, in turn, 'that which is', indisputably is not in thousands upon thousands of cases, and everything else in this way, individually and all together, is in many different ways, and in many different ways is not.

THEAETETUS: True.

STRANGER: And, further, if someone distrusts these contrarieties, he must examine them himself and say something better than the present remarks. Or if, on the other hand, as though he had understood something difficult, he takes pleasure in dragging the speeches at times to the other things and at times to the others, he has shown his zeal in things that do not deserve much serious attention, as the present speeches assert. For while this is not at all clever and difficult to find, that now is both difficult and beautiful together—[81]

THEAETETUS: What sort of thing?

STRANGER: It's just what has been remarked on previously, to dismiss the former[82] and to be able to follow the things that are said both whenever someone says it to be the same while it is other in a

sense, and whenever someone says it to be other while it is the *D*
same, and show by examination in case by case that it's in that
sense and according to that that either of them has been affected
as the speaker says it has. But to show that "the same" (is) other
in some way no matter what, and "the other" the same, and the
big small, and the similar dissimilar, and in this way to take pleasure in always putting forward the contraries in one's speeches,
this is not a simply true examination, and it shows as well that it
is the fresh offspring of someone who just now is getting his hands
on 'the things which are'.

THEAETETUS: Yes, utterly.

STRANGER: The reason is, my good fellow, that to try to set apart
everything from everything is not only especially jangling, but it *E*
is, in particular, the mark of someone altogether unmusical and
unphilosophic.

THEAETETUS: Why exactly?

STRANGER: To loosen each thing away from everything is the most
complete way to make all speeches disappear, for it's on account
of the weaving together of the species with one another that (the)
speech has come to be for us.

THEAETETUS: True.

STRANGER: Well, consider then how opportunely we were just now *260*
fighting against things of that sort and were compelling there to
be allowance made for the mixing of another with an other.

THEAETETUS: For what purpose exactly?

STRANGER: For the purpose of (the) speech for us being some one of
the genera which are. For should we be deprived of this, the
biggest thing would be that we would be deprived of philosophy.
But still, at the moment we must come to an agreement on whatever speech is, for if we had been denied its being altogether, we
surely would no longer be now able to say anything; and we would *B*
have been so denied if we had conceded that there is no mixing
of anything with anything.

THEAETETUS: That's right of course, but I don't understand why we
must now agree on speech.

STRANGER: Well, perhaps you would most easily understand if you
should follow along this way.

THEAETETUS: Which way?

STRANGER: Well, now that 'that which is not' came to light for us as
being some one genus of everything else, scattered and distributed
across all 'the things which are'—

THEAETETUS: That's so.

STRANGER: Mustn't we then consider next whether it mixes with opinion and speech?

THEAETETUS: Why exactly?

C STRANGER: If it doesn't mix with them, it's necessary that all things be true, but if it does mix, false opinion and speech come to be, for to opine or to say 'the things which are not', this surely is the falsehood that comes to be in thought and speeches.

THEAETETUS: That's so.

STRANGER: Yes, but if there is falsehood there is deception.

THEAETETUS: Yes.

STRANGER: And lo and behold, if there is deception, it's a necessity that then everything be full of images and semblances and appearance.

THEAETETUS: Of course.

D STRANGER: Yes, but we said that the sophist has taken refuge somewhere in this region and has denied altogether that there is ever falsehood, for no one, he says, either thinks or speaks 'that which is not', for 'that which is not' in no way participates in being.

THEAETETUS: That was so.

STRANGER: Yes, but now this did come to light as participating in 'that which is', and hence perhaps he would no longer put up a fight on these lines; but perhaps he would assert that while some of the species do participate in 'that which is not', some do not, and precisely speech and opinion are among the nonparticipants, and

E hence he would persist in contending once more that the art of image-making and phantastics, in which we say he's engaged, altogether are not, since opinion and speech do not share in 'that which is not', for falsehood altogether is not, if this kind of sharing does not arise. It's for these reasons, then, that we first have to examine speech, opinion, and appearance, as to whatever they

261 are, in order that when they come to light we may catch sight of their sharing as well in 'that which is not', and once we do sight it prove that falsehood is, and once we've proved that, bind the sophist to it, if he is culpable, or maybe release him and seek him in a different genus.

THEAETETUS: Yes, but it seems, stranger, to be utterly true—it's what was said at the beginning about the sophist—that the genus is hard to hunt down. He really does appear to be full of defenses,[83] and whenever he sets up one of them in front of himself, it's necessary to fight through it first, before arriving at him himself. For now with difficulty we pierced through the defense that 'that

B which is not' is not, and he has to set up another, and we must now prove that there is falsehood of both speech and opinion, and after this perhaps there's another, and still a different one after that, and, it seems, that no limit will ever appear.

STRANGER: Whoever, Theaetetus, can always advance even to a slight extent must have confidence, for if one despairs while one's advancing, what would one do on different occasions, should one either be getting nowhere or maybe get pushed backwards again? Someone of that sort surely would hardly ever, as the proverbial saying goes, seize a city; but, as it is, my good fellow, since to use C
your expression, this has been pierced, we would already have taken, you know, the greatest wall, and all the rest from now on are easier and smaller.

THEAETETUS: You put it beautifully.

STRANGER: First, then, let's take speech and opinion, just as it was now said, in order that we may with greater vividness settle the account as to whether 'that which is not' cleaves to them, or both of them are altogether true, and neither is ever falsehood.

THEAETETUS: Right.

STRANGER: Come then, just as we were speaking about species and D
letters, let's likewise go on to examine again names, for that which is now being sought appears in this region hereabouts.

THEAETETUS: Just what is it exactly about names that I have to respond to?

STRANGER: Whether all of them fit together with each other or they don't at all, or whether some are willing and some not.

THEAETETUS: This much is clear, some are willing and some are not.

STRANGER: Perhaps you mean something of the following sort: some names, in being spoken in succession and making something plain, E
do fit together, and some, if they do not signify anything in their succession, do not fit.

THEAETETUS: How's that and what do you mean by this?

STRANGER: Just what I suspected you understood and were in agreement with. Surely there is a double genus for us of the indicators in sound of being.

THEAETETUS: How?

STRANGER: One is called names and one verbs. 262

THEAETETUS: Say what each of the two is.

STRANGER: While that which is an indicator for actions we surely speak of as a verb—

THEAETETUS: Yes.

STRANGER: That which is set in sound as a sign for those who are doing the actions (is) a name.

THEAETETUS: Yes, certainly.

STRANGER: Then isn't it the case that a speech is never composed out of only names spoken consecutively, nor in turn out of verbs said apart from names?

THEAETETUS: I don't understand this.

B STRANGER: That's plainly because you were looking at some other thing when you agreed just now, since I wanted to say this very thing, there is no speech if these are spoken consecutively in the following way.

THEAETETUS: How?

STRANGER: For example, "walks," "runs," "sleeps," and all the rest of the verbs that indicate actions, even if one speaks all of them successively, one does not any the more produce a speech.

THEAETETUS: Of course not.

STRANGER: And then again whenever "lion," "deer," "horse" are spoken, and all the names that are named for those who perform actions, in terms of this kind of connection too no speech is yet

C put together, for the things sounded do not make plain either in this way or in that way any action, inaction, or being of 'that which is' or of 'that which is not', before one mixes verbs with names. It's then that they come to fit, and straight off the first weaving together proves to be a speech, pretty nearly the first and smallest of the speeches.

THEAETETUS: Obviously you mean?

STRANGER: Whenever one says "(A) human being learns," do you say this to be the least and first speech?

D THEAETETUS: Yes, I for one do.

STRANGER: That's surely because it makes plain by then about the things which are, are becoming, have become, or are going to be, and it not only names but puts a limit on something, by weaving together the verbs with the names. It's for this reason that we said that it speaks and not only names, and the name we uttered for this plaiting was speech.

THEAETETUS: Right.

STRANGER: Then just as some things (*pragmata*) were agreed to fit one

E another and some not, so too it's the case about the signs of sound, some do not fit, and some of them in fitting produce a speech.

THEAETETUS: That's altogether so.

STRANGER: Still, here's a small point.

THEAETETUS: What sort?

STRANGER: It's necessary that a speech, whenever it is, be a speech of something, and it's impossible not to be of something.

THEAETETUS: That's so.

STRANGER: And must it also be of a certain sort?

THEAETETUS: Of course.

STRANGER: Let's then pay attention to ourselves.

THEAETETUS: We ought to at any rate.

STRANGER: Well, I'll tell you a speech by putting together a thing (*pragma*) with an action through name and verb, and you point out to me of whatever the speech is.

THEAETETUS: It shall be done to the best of my ability.   *263*

STRANGER: "Theaetetus sits." The speech isn't too long, is it?

THEAETETUS: No, it's the right length.

STRANGER: Then it's your task to point out about what and of what it is.

THEAETETUS: It's plainly about me and of me.

STRANGER: And what, in turn, of this speech?

THEAETETUS: What sort?

STRANGER: "Theaetetus, with whom I am now conversing, flies."

THEAETETUS: And about this one too, no one would say any differently, it's of me and about me.

STRANGER: Yes, and we say that it's necessary that each of the speeches be a certain sort.

THEAETETUS: Yes.   *B*

STRANGER: What sort must you say each of the two is?

THEAETETUS: One is surely false and one true.

STRANGER: And of them, while the true speech says the things which are, that they are about you—

THEAETETUS: Why certainly.

STRANGER: It's the false speech that says other things than the things which are.

THEAETETUS: Yes.

STRANGER: So it speaks the things which are not as the things which are.

THEAETETUS: Pretty nearly.

STRANGER: Yes, and they are the things which are other than the things which are about you. For surely we said there are many things which are about each thing, and many which are not.

THEAETETUS: Yes, certainly.

STRANGER: Now as to the later speech I have spoken about you, first *C* of all, out of which things we determined what a speech is, it's most necessary that it be one of the briefest.

THEAETETUS: We did at any rate come to an agreement just now along these lines.

STRANGER: Yes, and in the second place, it's most necessary that it be of something.

THEAETETUS: That's so.

STRANGER: And if it is not of you, it's not at least of anything else.

THEAETETUS: Of course.

STRANGER: But should a speech be of nothing, it would not be a speech altogether, for we showed that it was one of the impossibilities for there to be a speech and be a speech of nothing.

THEAETETUS: Most correctly.

D STRANGER: Although, then, the other things are spoken as the same and the things which are not as the things which are, they are still spoken about you, however, and it seems that a composition of this sort, which comes to be out of verbs and names, proves to be altogether in its being and truly a false speech.

THEAETETUS: Most truly, rather.

STRANGER: And what of this point? Thought, opinion, and appearance—isn't it plain by now that all these at least come to be in our souls both false and true?

THEAETETUS: How's that?

STRANGER: You'll know more easily in the following way—if you first take what ever they are and in what respect they severally differ

E from one another

THEAETETUS: Just make the offer.

STRANGER: Isn't it the case that thought and speech (are) the same? Except that whereas the conversation that comes to be within the soul before itself without sound is the very thing that in our view has this name, thought—[84]

THEAETETUS: Yes, of course.

STRANGER: Still the stream that proceeds away from it through the mouth with noise has been called speech?[85]

THEAETETUS: True.

STRANGER: And we furthermore know that there is in speeches—

THEAETETUS: What sort of thing?

STRANGER: Assertion and negation.

THEAETETUS: We know.

264 STRANGER: Whenever, then, this comes to be in soul according to thought with silence, do you know what to address it by except opinion?

THEAETETUS: How can I?

STRANGER: But whenever not in itself but through perception it is present to someone, is it possible to say correctly of an experience of the sort anything other than appearance?

THEAETETUS: No other.

STRANGER: Isn't it the case, then, inasmuch as speech was true and false, and of these the conversation of soul by itself before itself came to light as thought, and the completion of thought as opin-

B ion, and what we mean by "appears" is a mixing together of perception and thought, it's strictly a necessity that, since these things are in fact congeners to speech, some of them sometimes be false.

THEAETETUS: Of course.

STRANGER: Do you realize, then, that false opinion and speech were discovered sooner than in our anticipation we just now feared, that in seeking them we were setting upon ourselves an altogether unfinishable task?

THEAETETUS: I realize it.

STRANGER: Let's not then be in despair about the things remaining either. Now, since these things have come to light, let's recall *C* the previous divisions according to species.

THEAETETUS: What sorts exactly?

STRANGER: We divided the art of image-making into two species, one eikastics and one phantastics.

THEAETETUS: Yes.

STRANGER: And we said that we were perplexed as to into which one of the two we should set down the sophist.

THEAETETUS: That was so.

STRANGER: And when we were perplexed by this, a still greater dizziness got poured over us, when the speech came to light disputing with everything we mentioned that neither semblance nor image nor apparition was at all, on account of the fact that there never was falsehood anywhere in any way. *D*

THEAETETUS: What you say is true.

STRANGER: But now, since it has evidently appeared that there is false speech, and it has evidently appeared that there is false opinion, there's room for there to be imitations of 'the things which are' and a deceptive art come to be from this disposition (of false opinion).

THEAETETUS: There's room.

STRANGER: And in our previous remarks we had further agreed that the sophist was one of the two of these (a knower of eikastics or phantastics).

THEAETETUS: Yes.

STRANGER: Well, then, let's try once more, by splitting in two the *E* proposed genus, to proceed always toward the right-hand part of the section, keeping to that in which the sophist shares, until, once we strip away all things that he has in common and leave his own *265* nature, we may exhibit it, primarily to ourselves, and then to those who are by nature nearest in genus to a pursuit of this sort.[86]

THEAETETUS: Right.

STRANGER: Isn't it the case that while we then began by dividing the art of making and acquisition—

THEAETETUS: Yes.

STRANGER: And, in the case of the art of acquisition, he was showing us a series of apparitions in the art of hunting, competition, merchandising, and some species of the sort—

THEAETETUS: Yes, of course.

STRANGER: But now, since a mimetic art has encompassed him, it's
B   plainly the very art of making that must be first divided in two, for imitation is surely a kind of making, of images to be sure, we say, but not of the several things themselves. Isn't that so?

THEAETETUS: That's altogether so.

STRANGER: Let there first be, then, two parts of the art of making.

THEAETETUS: What sort of pair?

STRANGER: One divine and one human.

THEAETETUS: I've not yet understood.

STRANGER: If we remember what was said at the beginning, we said that every power, whichever became a cause for the things which previously were not to become subsequently, was a making.

THEAETETUS: We remember.

C STRANGER: All mortal animals as well as plants in general[87]—all that grow on earth out of seeds and roots no less than all soulless bodies that get put together in the earth, the fusible and the infusible—shall we really say of them that they are not previously but come to be subsequently when someone else than a god crafts them? Or are we to employ the opinion and the word of the many?[88]

THEAETETUS: What sort of word?

STRANGER: That nature generates them from some kind of spontaneous cause that grows them without thought, or is it with speech and divine science from a god that proves the cause?

D THEAETETUS: Well, I for one, perhaps on account of my age, have often been of both opinions about it in turn; yet now in looking at you and supposing you to believe that they come to be in conformity at least with a god, I myself now hold this too.

STRANGER: Beautifully, Theaetetus. And if we were convinced that you would be one of those who at a later time opine in a somewhat different way, then now, by means of speech with a compulsory persuasiveness, we would be trying to make you agree. But since I understand your nature, that it by itself will advance, even with-
E out the speeches from us, to the very position to which you claim you're now being dragged, I'll let it go, for time then would prove to be superfluous. Well, I'll set down that the things said (to be)

by nature are made by a divine art,[89] and the things put together by human beings out of these are made by a human art, and so in accordance with this speech I'll set down two genera of the art of making, one human and one divine.

THEAETETUS: Right.

STRANGER: And now that the two are, cut again each of the pair in two.

THEAETETUS: How?

STRANGER: Just as you were then cutting all of the art of making widthwise, now in turn do it lengthwise.   266

THEAETETUS: Let it have been so cut.

STRANGER: All its parts thus become four, two on our side of the cut, the human, and two in turn on the gods' side, the divine.

THEAETETUS: Yes.

STRANGER: And those that have undergone division in another way, one part from each section is the making of things themselves, and the pair left over would pretty nearly exactly be spoken of as the making of images, and in terms of this again the art of making gets divided in two.

THEAETETUS: Say once more at what point each of the two is divided.   B

STRANGER: Ourselves and all the other animals and those things out of which there are the things which are by nature—fire and water and their kindred—we surely know that not only all these severally have been produced as the offspring of a god, or how?

THEAETETUS: That's so.

STRANGER: But that the images of these several things themselves, they're not the things themselves, follow along in their train— these two have come to be by a more than human contrivance.

THEAETETUS: What sorts of things?

STRANGER: The apparitions on the occasions of sleeping as well as all those which occur in daylight and are spoken of as self-growing— a shadow whenever darkness occurs in the firelight—and whenever a double light, its own and that of another, come together   C into one in the region of shiny and smooth things, and by supplying a perception opposite to the customary vision in front produces a species.[90]

THEAETETUS: There are indeed these two works of divine making, (the work) itself and the image accompanying each.

STRANGER: And what of our own art? Shall we not say that it makes, by the art of house building, a house itself, and some other by the art of painting, produced as if it were a human dream for those awake?

THEAETETUS: Yes, of course.   D

STRANGER: Then all the rest too in this way are double works by twos of our own action of the art of making: one, we say, (is the work) itself, and one the image.

THEAETETUS: I understand better now, and I set down a pair of two species of making in a double way, a divine and human making according to the other cut, and, in turn, according to the other, one is of (the works) themselves, and one the offspring of certain similarities.

STRANGER: Well, then, let's recall that of the art of making images one was going to be the eikastic and one the phantastic genus, if falsehood was to come to light as being in its being a falsehood and by nature some one of the things which are.

THEAETETUS: Indeed it was.

STRANGER: And did it not come to light? And on account of this shall we now count the pair of them as themselves indisputably two species?

THEAETETUS: Yes.

STRANGER: Let's then divide again the phantastic kind in two.

THEAETETUS: At what point?

STRANGER: One comes to be through instruments, and one when, whoever is making the apparition, puts himself forward as the instrument.

THEAETETUS: How do you mean that?

STRANGER: Whenever, I suspect, someone uses his own body and makes your figure appear in a simulacrum (or by using his voice your voice), this (part) of phantastics has particularly been called imitation.

THEAETETUS: Yes.

STRANGER: Let's then assign exclusively to ourselves this (part) of the art and address it as mimetics, and let's go soft and dismiss all the rest, and leave it to another to bring it together into one and attribute to it some fitting name.

THEAETETUS: Let one assignment have been made, and, on the other hand, one dismissal.

STRANGER: And this too, Theaetetus, still deserves to be believed double. But consider for what reason.

THEAETETUS: Speak.

STRANGER: Of those who imitate, some do this while knowing that which they imitate, and some without knowing it. And yet, what greater division are we to set down than ignorance and cognition?

THEAETETUS: None.

STRANGER: Isn't it the case that the imitation just now mentioned was of those who know, for it would be because someone was familiar with you and your figure that he would do the imitation?

THEAETETUS: Of course.   C

STRANGER: But what of the figure of justice and of virtue in general? Don't many, though ignorant, still somehow opine and try to be extremely eager to make appear as if it were in them the opinion they have, imitating it as exactly as possible in deeds and speeches?

THEAETETUS: Yes, very many do indeed.

STRANGER: Is it the case, then, that all, if they are in no way just, fail to seem to be just, or is it entirely the contrary of this?

THEAETETUS: Entirely.

STRANGER: So I suspect that this imitator must be spoken of as other   D than that, the ignorant than the cognizant.

THEAETETUS: Yes.

STRANGER: What then is the source from which one will take a fitting name for each of the two of them? Or isn't it plain that it is difficult, because, it seems, there was some ancient and uncomprehending idleness among those earlier in regard to the division of the genera by species, so that no one even tried to divide. Accordingly, it's a necessity for there not to be a very great supply of names. But all the same, even if it's rather nervy for it to have been said, for the sake of discriminating them, let's address the imitation with   E opinion as opinion-mimetics and the one with science as a kind of historical imitation.[91]

THEAETETUS: Let them be.

STRANGER: We must then use the other, for the sophist was not among the knowers but precisely among the imitators.

THEAETETUS: Indeed he was.

STRANGER: Let's then examine the opinion-imitator just as if he were iron—is he sound, or does he still have in himself a kind of faulty weld?

THEAETETUS: Let's examine.

STRANGER: Well, he does have, and it's very extensive. One of them   268 is naive, believing he knows those things which he opines, but the figure of the other, on account of his knocking about among speeches, has much suspicion and fear that he's ignorant of those things which he has embodied in a figure before everyone else as if he knew.

THEAETETUS: Yes, of course, there is a genus of each of the two you've mentioned.

STRANGER: Are we then to set down one as some simple imitator and one as an ironic imitator?

THEAETETUS: It's likely at any rate.

STRANGER: And, in turn, are we to say that his genus is one or two?

THEAETETUS: You look.

STRANGER: I'm considering, and a pair of genera appears to me here. I'm catching sight of one who's capable of being ironical before multitudes in public and with long speeches, and one who in private and with brief speeches compels his interlocutor to contradict himself.

THEAETETUS: What you say is most correct.

STRANGER: Whom are we to declare the longer-speech-maker to be, a statesman or a public speaker?

THEAETETUS: A public speaker.

STRANGER: And what shall we say of the other? Wise or sophistic?

C THEAETETUS: It's surely impossible that he be of the wise, since we set him down as not knowing. But if he is an imitator of the wise he'll plainly get some derivative name of the wise, and now I've pretty nearly understood that he's the one whom we have to address truly as that very one who's altogether in his being the sophist.

STRANGER: Shall we then bind his name together, just as we did before, and weave it together from the end to the beginning?

THEAETETUS: Yes, of course.

STRANGER: The mimetic kind that the art of making contradictory speeches characterizes (it's the ironical part of the opinionative art), the proper part of the phantastic genus (it descends from
D the art of making images) that conjures in speeches, which distinctly set itself apart as not a divine but a human part of making—whoever says that the sophist in his being is "of this generation and blood,"[92] will say, it seems, what is the truest.

THEAETETUS: That's altogether so.

Sophist Commentary

I. MISTAKING
(216a1–218a3)

Theodorus, of whose scrupulousness in living up to his agreements we know, announces with his first words the decency of his coming. One could wonder whether he comes with any enthusiasm. He brings as well a stranger of a sort, who is from Elea, a comrade of Parmenides' and Zeno's followers and very much a philosopher. Theodorus neglects to tell Socrates the stranger's name. The day before, he had praised Theaetetus at much greater length without mentioning his name either; but Socrates shows his greater concern for Athens than for other places by not pressing for further details. He accepts the anonymity of the stranger and asks instead whether Theodorus has not made a mistake: might not Homer be right, and the stranger a god in disguise? Socrates combines two Homeric passages, in both of which he himself appears as a supreme criminal. The first is from a speech by Odysseus to the Cyclops Polyphemus, in terms of which Theodorus is, unknown to himself, Odysseus, Socrates is Polyphemus, and the stranger is Zeus. In the second passage, an anonymous suitor addresses Antinous, in terms of which the stranger is the disguised Odysseus, mistaken for a god, and Antinous is Socrates. According to Odysseus, Zeus invisibly accompanies respectful strangers. Socrates reminds Theodorus that he too, no less than the stranger, is a stranger;[1] but Theodorus does not acknowledge his own strangeness until he swears by his own god, Zeus Ammon.[2] According to the anonymous suitor, to whom Antinous does not bother to reply, the gods are invisibly present in another sense; they make themselves up to look like foreign strangers, even the lowest of the low, in order to survey in cities the law-abidingness and outrageous behavior of human beings.

Socrates, whom Meletus has just indicted for political criminality, suspects that his crime is philosophical as well. Has the stranger come to check up on Parmenides' prediction about Socrates' philosophic impulse? The stranger might be a sort of refutative god, come to punish Socrates for the poorness of his speeches. Socrates had made Theaetetus share in that poorness yesterday, for they shamelessly agreed that they must converse impurely, since they could not refrain from speaking of their knowing and understanding or their not knowing and not understanding while they examined what knowledge is.[3] If the stranger is a god, he is still a stranger, for as a god, he was either present yesterday as Zeus the god of strangers, or is now an anonymous god in a human disguise. Theodorus could then be guilty of bringing into Athens a new god, but a god of whom Athens would have to approve, since Socrates, in letting Theaetetus in on his secret, had inadvertently declared that he was a god. Socrates' philosophical crime, which combined an impure dialectics with himself as the infallible measure of truth and falsehood, is inseparable from his political crimes, according to which he has corrupted Theaetetus and, with his god-given art of maieutics, introduced a god in whom the city does not believe.

Theodorus, who knows his Homer,[4] takes all of this literally. With his usual rudeness, he tacitly agrees that Socrates is poor in speeches, but Socrates is mistaken about the stranger: "This is not the way, Socrates, of the stranger." He echoes the words of Socrates—"This is not the way of Theodorus"—when he denied that Theodorus' praise of Theaetetus was spoken in jest. We have come to doubt Theodorus' competence in such matters, but experience has convinced him that the stranger does not compel the stiff and unliquid Theodorus to engage in bare speeches against his will. The stranger is not another Socrates, whose "love of naked exercise in speeches" lets no one get away from him without first rendering an account of himself.[5] He is milder than those who engage in strife and contention. Socrates, then, is going to be punished. The stranger will show him how a proper conversation is conducted, but it will not be as much an ordeal for Socrates as Theodorus underwent at Socrates' hands. Socrates' misunderstanding of the stranger's way led him into a more serious error. Since Theodorus is more certain of the stranger's gentleness than of his not being a god, Theodorus implies that, even if the stranger were a god, the gods are not necessarily as punitive as Socrates believes. They do not care enough for human beings, we might suppose, to exact the full penalty for their transgressions.

The stranger is emphatically a man and not a god (cf. 216a4); he is, however, divine, for Theodorus addresses all the philosophers as of this sort. It is as certain as anything can be that Theodorus believes Socrates is not divine (cf. *Theaetetus,* 173c7); Antaeus, with whom Theodorus had compared Socrates, was a giant. Theodorus, in any case, knows what it is to be divine, but we do not know whether he would only call philosophers divine or whether he would say some poets, for example, deserve the appellation.[6] He surely does not see that Socrates' designation of the gods as "the Mightier" has already put into question the distinction between "god" and "divine." Is the stranger to some degree a god? Is "divine" a word of essence, so that the stranger is truly a god as Socrates said, or a word of likeness, so that the stranger, like the philosophers, has the look of a god, and Socrates has been taken in by an appearance? Theodorus' "of this sort" turns out to be the problematic word of the *Sophist.*

Socrates admits and does not admit his error. In praising Theodorus for his way of addressing philosophers, he calls him a friend. The stranger, if not a god, is at least not a friend. Socrates has no reason to expect that the stranger will benefit him. Perhaps Socrates was counting on the stranger as a god to be benevolent toward him, for no god, he told Theaetetus, is ill-disposed to human beings. Socrates then doubts whether the stranger is a philosopher either. This time he quotes three words of Homer, but without citing him, from the same speech of the anonymous suitor. All that a Homeric character had said about the gods, Socrates adopts as his own view of the philosophers. All the appearances and illusions, which Socrates in his "theology" had once proposed to strip from Homer's gods, are now applicable to the philosophers.[7] They are the truth of Homer's lies. Those who are really or in their being philosophers, as opposed to the feigned and spurious, look down "from on high" (*hypsothen*)—a poetic word—on the life of those below. Philosophers apparently neither punish nor benefit, for they have nothing but contempt for the life of nonphilosophers. Through the ignorance of others, they show themselves as all sorts of apparitions, from which some opine that they are worth nothing, while others opine they are worth everything.

If "divine" is a word of essence, Theodorus believes they are everything; if "divine" is a word of likeness, he believes they are nothing. At one time the apparition of the philosopher is a statesman, at another a sophist, and there are occasions when he gives the impression that he is altogether crazy. Some of the crazy, said Theaetetus, believe they are gods. If the stranger is a philosopher, Theodorus has penetrated his unwilled disguise and is not ignorant like the others. But if the stranger is not a philosopher, Theodorus mistook a deliberately fabricated appearance for the real thing. Socrates called Theodorus wise and described him as a high-flying theoretical man;[8] he never called him a philosopher.

Socrates is not being very friendly; he seems to be asking the stranger to prove his credentials, which by the very nature of the philosopher cannot but look counterfeit. If Socrates is right about philosophers, and the stranger is one of them, he is going to present apparitions of himself as sophist and statesman. He will define the sophist and the statesman while appearing to be them. The stranger is either now aware or becomes aware of Socrates' peculiar challenge. Theaetetus, he is afraid, will get the impression that he is crazy (242a10–b1).

The philosophers appear as nonphilosophers. Being, in this case at least, appears as not being or illusion. Perspectival distortion is an unavoidable concomitant of the philosopher's being, but this is not the first perplexity for us. Alongside the true philosopher's apparitions, there appear artful apparitions of the philosopher, which will look either like the philosopher's apparitions—sophist, statesman, or madman—or like the philosopher himself. The philosopher himself always looks like the sophist, statesman, or madman, and never as himself. It would be very easy to discern the false philosopher if only he proclaimed himself to be a philosopher. Since Socrates could not help but agree, or so we might hope, that some apparent madmen are really mad, those who are really sophists and statesmen would compound the confusion if they appeared together with the apparitional sophists and statesmen, some of whom would be really philosophers, others false philosophers, and still others apparitions of true sophists and statesmen. Odysseus, whom Athena disguised, looks as much a beggar as the real beggar Arnaeus, whose nickname Irus gives him the appearance of the gods' messenger.[9]

Socrates, however, would not be posing so great a riddle if he meant that sophists and statesmen are at best nothing but the apparitions of the true philosopher, and we did not have to discriminate his apparitions from those who are really sophists and statesmen, though even so there might be apparitions of sophists and statesmen which were not the apparitions of either the true or the false philosopher. The ward-heeler, after all, even if a spurious politician, does not look like a false philosopher. The manifold appearances, behind and above which the philosopher stands, hardly seem more susceptible of precise discrimination than the Protean apparitions of the gods. It can only be the impropriety of asking a god, if the stranger is a god, to prove that he is a god, that makes Socrates adopt Theodorus' point of view.

Socrates would be pleased to learn from the stranger "what those of the region there were accustomed to believe and name these things."

Socrates could not have phrased his question more obscurely. Is "the region there" the stranger's birthplace, or the place from which the true philosophers look down?[10] Out of politeness, the stranger must be as silent and remote as an oracle until his mouthpiece Theodorus understands enough of Socrates' question to answer on his behalf. Socrates explains what "these things" are, "sophist, statesman, philosopher." Theodorus now understands Socrates' expression but not the intention of his question. Socrates imitates in speech before a Parmenidean his own bafflement about Parmenides. He had excused himself from examining Parmenides on the grounds that he was afraid he did not understand what Parmenides said and trailed far behind what Parmenides intended. Parmenides' obscurity consists for Socrates in his apparent failure to discriminate among the apparitions of not being. The difference between a true and a false philosopher would not necessarily show up in speech.

Socrates utters three words, whose successive utterance cannot constitute, according to the stranger, a speech. The first two of these words are titles of Platonic dialogues, and the third the title of an unwritten dialogue, *Philosopher*, whose subtitle might well have been, "On a certain kind of madness." The stranger accepts Socrates' series as the proper order of discussion, but we do not know how Socrates' series is to be read. If sophist, statesman, philosopher are like one, two, three, we should gather up, in counting the *Statesman*, the *Sophist*, and in counting the *Philosopher* both. Each would be one and complete in itself, nor would each lose anything of itself in any larger collection. The order of exposition, then, would have nothing to do with the order of being, and Theodorus would be in principle correct when he later suggests that the stranger could just as well discuss the philosopher as the statesman after the sophist.[11] If, however, the stranger agrees with Socrates, that the sophist and the statesman are to the philosopher as appearance is to being, any counting of them as three, or two, or one would be misleading. Two apparitions do not add up to one being, nor can one being simply split into two apparitions. If we then suppose that Socrates' utterance is to be read as one Aristophanic word (*philosophistopolitikos*), Plato, in giving us only two of its parts, would not have given us parts, and *Sophist* and *Statesman* are, apart from the whole to which they properly belong, as different as god (*theos*) and gift (*dôron*) by themselves differ from their union in the proper name Theodorus.

We are not forced to construe Socrates in this way. We could alternatively suppose that sophist, statesman, and philosopher are each the name of a letter, and either two of them are consonants and one a vowel, or two of them form a diphthong while one is a consonant.

Sophist and statesman could name M and D respectively, and philosopher U, or sophist and statesman could name I and A respectively, and philosopher M. The first possibility would imply that the *Sophist* and the *Statesman* are only audible because vowels alien to them have been distributed among them, and the second would imply that while the *Sophist* and the *Statesman* are audible by themselves, they only get limited when the essentially silent *Philosopher* has been properly placed with them. Despite Socrates' *logos,* which we could simply read as saying that sophist, statesman, and philosopher are one class with two aspects, Socrates offers the stranger in a series of words several other ways of interpreting him. If the place from which the stranger is to speak is above the apparitions, the stranger would speak as a stranger, and the apparitions would not look the same to him as they do to us below.

Socrates wants to know whether the Parmenideans hold that sophist, statesman, philosopher are one, two, or just like their names three, and whether in dividing their classes in three, they attached one name to each. To count them truly is to count the classes, and to determine the genus is to determine the being. There are seven possibilities. The first would be the stranger's report on the Parmenidean view: there are three genera. But if the genera are two, there are three ways of associating and dividing them. (1) Sophist and statesman are really one, and the philosopher is other; (2) sophist and philosopher are really one, and the statesman is other; (3) statesman and philosopher are really one—the apparent view of the *Republic*—and the sophist is other. But if the genus is one, two of the named things must be illusory: (1) the statesman and philosopher are apparitions of the sophist; (2) the sophist and philosopher are apparitions of the statesman; (3) the sophist and the statesman (according to Socrates' proposal) are apparitions of the philosopher. Socrates seems to exclude an eighth possibility: there is the class of the wise or omniscient, which comprehends the other three. Such a class would be that of the gods. The stranger cannot, as Protagoras did, set the gods outside his argument; indeed, he concludes the *Sophist* with a distinction between divine and human making, and he begins the *Statesman* with the difference between gods and men as rulers. In the very name of philosophy there is incompleteness. If the real philosopher has his own class, must it not be a fragment of wisdom's, and therefore as apparitional as his own apparitions, the sophist and the statesman? Theaetetus comes to believe that the sophist impersonates or imitates the wise (268c1), but how would such an imitation differ from the philosopher's, who, according to Socrates, tries to assimilate himself to a god?[12] Socrates is guilty of asking the stranger somewhat the same question he has asked Theodorus. He has not, at least, exaggerated the difference in the degree of difficulty between determining the class of the god and the class of the philosopher.

If the stranger's answer "three" implies that they are all equal, it would seem to follow, in light of his practice of division by twos, that one of two schemes will be open to him. Either the philosopher will be divided off from the sophist or statesman in one cut, and the sophist and statesman from each other in another, or in the second cut, the sophist (statesman) will be divided from an unknown fourth class. In the first case, the redundancy of either sophist or statesman would pose a problem, inasmuch as there would be then two nonequivalent definitions of the same thing. And, in the second case, Socrates' question would have been formulated incorrectly, and the missing fourth would need to be accounted for, and particularly what there is about it that made Socrates overlook it. Since Socrates had assigned to the philosophers the same apparitional power as Homer gave to the gods, the possible redundancy or the possible discovery of a fourth could be the class of the gods. That the gods should be lying in wait on the stranger's way is in any event not implausible. The stranger comes to the problem of being through not being. The two most obvious cases in which not being is problematic are death and the gods. How and that 'that which is' ceases to be, and how and that 'that which is said to be' either is or is not are equally perplexing, but whereas Plato satisfied us through the *Phaedo* about the first question, he did not as openly satisfy us about the second. The missing *Philosopher* seems to be truly a desideratum.

The stranger, according to his spokesman Theodorus, will not begrudge Socrates a thorough answer to his question, but he distinguishes between the ungrudging short answer and the long and difficult task of plainly articulating what each of them is. The long answer turns out to be too long for Plato to have written out. He compromised between the single word—three—and the excessive length of the *Philosopher*, with the two dialogues, *Sophist* and *Statesman* (217e4).[13] Had not Socrates warned us against applying geometrical ratios to certain things, we might believe that Plato decided not to write the dialogue simply because the number of its words would have been on the order of 10^{10}. Plato's compromise, at any rate, recalls Socrates' in the *Theaetetus*. Somewhere between the urgency of the unimportant and the importance of the nonurgent was Theaetetus' soul, but Theaetetus' soul somehow yielded to the problem of false opinion, which proved to be Socrates' way of delineating his own wisdom. Socratic wisdom could be treated more adequately in a digression than the problem of being which Parmenides had first posed. And yet the stranger, though hardly unaware that Socrates has surrogated him to expound Parmenides' Rest (cf. 217b4–8), chooses to put being in a digression and subordinate it to the phantoms of the sophist. There seems to be no suitable occasion, let alone enough time, to discuss being in an adequate manner. Finite though being must be, if anything is to be even partly intelligible, and though something less a side-issue for philosophy cannot easily be imagined, being seems always to recede into the background, or threaten, if brought forward, to prolong any speech about it to infinity. Perhaps we only begin to understand what being is when we realize the necessity for it to submit to compromise of one sort or the other.

We do not know whether the stranger's short answer has already satisfied Socrates, but by a stroke of luck Socrates' question is just like that which the mathematicians had previously put to the stranger. They can now all beg him together to report what he had heard thoroughly and not forgotten; the only open question is how the stranger is to speak. There are, according to Socrates, only two possible ways. Either the stranger is more accustomed to go through on his own in a long speech whatever he wants to indicate to another, or to do it through questions, as Socrates once heard Parmenides go through very beautiful speeches. In principle, the stranger has no objection to one long speech, either by himself or before another, but as a stranger he is somewhat ashamed to make a display. A long speech would surely have been shorter than the *Sophist* and the *Statesman* combined, for the stranger would not have had to train Theaetetus on a simple example or clear up the misunderstandings of young Socrates. The stranger's shame, which is perhaps not altogether just, forces him to resort to Parmenides' way.

Parmenides' way differs from Socrates' in this respect. The purpose of a Parmenidean conversation is ostensibly for a bystander's benefit and not necessarily but only incidentally for the interlocutor's. Socrates had been the beneficiary when he heard Parmenides put Aristoteles through the exercise of hypothesis, and now again he seems to be the chief beneficiary of the stranger. It is, after all, Socrates' question that Theaetetus and young Socrates are to share in answering in the two later dialogues, and neither seems to show much interest in it. Theaetetus swore constantly throughout the *Theaetetus;* only the stranger swears in the *Sophist* and *Statesman.* Socrates himself seems to have adopted the Parmenidean way at least once—when he exhibited in Meno's slave what he wished Meno himself to understand. Socrates did not wish to teach either the slave or Meno something of geometry. Does the stranger, then, wish to teach Socrates something, for which the sophist and the statesman are each a *corpus vile?* We cannot answer this question before we know whether the stranger's single long speech could have been the same as the two dialogues he conducts. The unpredictable errors of Theaetetus and young Socrates might modify incorrigibly the stranger's way.

II. ANGLING
(218a4–221c4)

The stranger easily goes through a sixfold definition of the sophist; he surprisingly concludes that the sophist has eluded them. We should have supposed that a single definition could, without introducing any other element, comprehend all six separate speeches: The sophist is a hunter of rich young men, either at home or abroad, for the sake of selling them soul-goods, either his own or another's, which consist in all virtue, and which in turn cannot be acquired apart from the sophist's exercising the art of disputation, and in doing so cleansing those opinions which stand in the way of learning. Theaetetus does not suggest such a complex speech, and the stranger seems to preclude it. A definition can only make use of "vertical" elements (those of a wider range in the same line of descent) and not of any "horizontal" elements (those which belong to collateral branches of what is ultimately the same family or tribe). The stranger demands that a *logos* be pure, not hybrid, and amoebalike self-generated. He does not explain the reason for such stringent requirements, nor how he knows that the sophist, even if other things do, conforms to this type of speech. Theaetetus has never seen a sophist, and his pliancy, which subjects him to the stranger's whim, prevents him from ever asking what the stranger is up to. However, the stranger's own paradigm, the art of the angler, is not pure. Its nine elements break down into three groups of three elements each, with only the most tenuous link between any two groups. The first three elements give the way or *methodos* of the angler (acquisitive mastery performed in secret), the next three give the subject or the being which the angler pursues (an animal that dwells in water), and the last three give the instruments he employs (the hook and line).

An art is defined by the way, the being, and the means: how, what, and with what. Our proposed definition of the sophist adds one element to these three: the purpose or end for the sake of which the art is practiced. The stranger is altogether silent on ends. Ends lie outside the cognitive content of any art. The angler would be no less an angler if he threw back all the fish he caught. Would the sophist, then, still be a sophist if he gave away soul-goods for free? The sophist could then be a sort of lover, whose lure is virtue, with which he hooks the young. However spurious his soul-goods might be, the sophist would nonetheless be practicing an art. We should not care to say, I think, that only he who catches the wiliest of fish is an angler. Indeed, the more deceptive the fisherman's bait is, the more likely he is to succeed. We have thus drifted over, with the most elementary of considerations, to the art of imitation, to which the stranger finally attaches the sophist. If the stranger had not had a false modesty and had just given the long speech he knows, he could have quickly come to where the problem of being lurks, and we should not have had to wade through his spurious science of dichotomy. As it is, we are confronted with the riddle of a pseudoscience in pursuit of the pseudoscience of the sophist.

Theaetetus and the stranger are to replace the name they now have in common, sophist, with a speech which they are to arrive at in common through speeches. The matter itself or the deed is to be a jointly held agreement or common speech (*sunômologêsthai*). The stranger opposes the name apart from speech to the thing itself through speeches. Through speeches the name is transformed into the thing. The stranger seems to identify the sophist with that speech about the sophist which is arrived at dialogically. In the stranger's speech, the tribe of the sophist is the sophist, and to comprehend (*sullabein*) the sophist is to grasp together (*sullabein*) the sophist. The stranger speaks both literally and metaphorically. From the sophist's point of view, the stranger's speech is itself sophistic, for it conjures into being that which it is seeking to discover; but the stranger seems to imply that his sophistry is only an illusion, for its reality is the joint action of Theaetetus and himself. This implication cannot but seem spurious. The stranger invokes a proverb to ease the pursuit of their quarry. Not only does the proverb have to do with making and not acquiring, but it assumes that what they practice on is of the same kind as that which they wish to know. Only if their "method" is omnicompetent would the difference between a fish and a sophist be irrelevant. The stranger will in fact proclaim that their method is infallible, even as he denies that omniscience is available to human beings. The stranger looks like another Socrates.

The *logos* of the angler with which Theaetetus and the stranger end up is identical with the true opinion they had at the start about the meaning of the name. Indeed, the name contains by a spurious etymology the *logos* itself (221c1–2). The angler has the art of catching fish, but "art" remains unanalyzed. The stranger separates the angler from other artisans without giving the angler any specific knowledge. He does certain things, we are told, but we are not told what he must know in order to do them. The dichotomies reveal the deed but not the art which makes the deed possible. They are not exhaustive but exclusive definitions: So-and-so is not a farmer. We see a man seated by a river bank with a pole, from which a string dangles in the stream; he suddenly gives a jerk to the line and pulls up a fish on a hook. Have we seen the angler's art in practice? The stranger's speech could serve only two possible functions. First, if we were legislators and wanted to prohibit or condemn certain kinds of fishing and hunting but allow or praise others, the stranger's divisions would be a useful way of codifying our intentions.[14] The signs he gives would help the police to determine at once whether this or that hunter was breaking the law. So the paradigm behind the paradigm of angling would be the law (*Statesman*), and the stranger would be prosecuting the sophist for a crime he is not yet certain has been committed. Second, if we were painters and wanted a recipe to follow in order to make a picture of an angler, the stranger gives us enough material to fool anyone but the angler himself.[15] So the paradigm behind the paradigm of angling would be imitation (*Sophist*), and the stranger would be guilty of prosecuting the sophist for his own crime. The stranger's way confirms the sophist's existence. Only if we attend to what the stranger does, can we grasp what the sophist is. The sophist lives a double life. He is both a wild beast that Theaetetus and the stranger pursue and a hunter of tame animals like Theaetetus and the stranger (cf. 218a1). They seem to be more the stalked than the stalkers.

Of all arts there are just about two kinds. The stranger warns Theaetetus that the starting point lacks distinctness (cf. 220e6). One kind would most justly be called poetics, the other would most fittingly be called an acquisitive art. The art of making includes farming, every sort of caring for the whole mortal body, that which pertains to the composite and fabricated, and mimetics. Its character is to bring into being whatever is not. Since Socrates had likened his own maieutics to farming,[16] the stranger implies that it is a kind of making, even though Socrates' whole effort had been to distinguish himself from Protagoras on just this point. The stranger thinks it unimportant to distinguish between an art that helps to bring something into being and an art that makes something which could never come to be without the art. He does exclude, however, piety, which Euthyphro had tried to define as a caring of the gods. We also do not know how he would classify the art of killing and destruction—that which brings into nonbeing whatever is. We cannot put it with hunting and competition because the stranger does not now mention killing as an essential part of these arts.

In acquisition there is the whole class of learning and familiarization, moneymaking, competition, and hunting. None of these makes anything, but each either masters the beings already present by speeches and actions, or keeps others from gaining mastery of them. The stranger thinks it unimportant to distinguish between arts which acquire something which no one else can then possess and arts that in no way involve exclusive possession. We do not know where he would put the art of teaching—that which makes someone else acquire knowledge. More strangely, he says nothing about the use to which one's acquisitions are to be put. If the angler works for the money-maker, he only possesses in a sense what he catches. If we consider use, the art as a whole would be the art of acquiring goods. The class would be impressed with a greater unity than poetics, because no one wants to acquire spurious goods, whether they be counterfeit money or spurious sciences, whereas poetics is shot through with the spurious, whether it be the phantoms that Socrates' art brings forth or the images of poetry and painting.

Acquisition seems to be more self-regarding than poetics, for the practice of a poetic art does not affect or involve the artisan. No one, moreover, could be a maker if he never made anything,[17] but a boxer would not cease to be a boxer even if he lost every fight. It is unclear, to be sure, whether a hunter who never caught any game would still be a hunter—for example, in the *Theaetetus*, the apparently empty dovecote of Socrates. We can, in any case, suppose that some human being possessed, or that all human beings wanted to possess, the art of acquiring the human goods. The stranger seems to be thinking of justice or a part of justice when he speaks of arts that do not allow others to gain mastery,[18] but we cannot even imagine that the art of making as a whole could ever be a human art. The stranger does not speak of either whole or part in bringing under one head the art of making. The stranger, then, begins with a latent distinction between human and divine knowledge. His solution to the problem of the sophist requires that a god make everything out of which human beings make other things.

Theaetetus accepts without difficulty the distinction between a class of exchange, where both sides are willing participants, and a class of mastery, where one side resists the other, and he accepts again the distinction between open competition and secret hunting. But he wonders whether the dual hunting of lifeless and living things 'is'. The stranger admits that few parts of the hunting of lifeless quarry have names, and the one example he cites—sponge diving—is doubtful, for not only could sponges be thought alive, but there seems to be no need, if they are lifeless, to pursue them in secret. Theft would be a much better example, but the anonymous class as a whole would still be less well defined than the hunting of animals. If, however, we consider the single image which dominates the entire *Sophist,* the hunting of the sophist, the anonymous class is none other than philosophy, the hidden hunting of the hidden beings or kinds.[19] It is because Theaetetus and the stranger are hunters that they can proceed on the basis of the sophist's name alone without verifying his existence. The more they become aware of what they themselves are doing, the more acute becomes the problem of distinguishing between a genuine and a spurious hunting of the beings. Every mistake they make forces us to reflect on the grounds of their mistake and thus bring to light as the unavoidable companion of the philosopher, the sophist.

We hardly exaggerate if we say that no distinction the stranger proposes in either the *Sophist* or the *Statesman* is self-evident. The difference, for example, between the voluntary and the involuntary, which grounds here the distinction between exchange and mastery, becomes subject to a radical critique in the *Statesman,* and no sooner does the stranger classify warfare as a kind of hunting than he rediscovers fighting under open competition. But perhaps the most obvious and strangest sign of the instability of kinds is this: in every enumeration after the paradigm of fishing, someone—the stranger, Theaetetus, or young Socrates—either falsely distinguishes a fourth class from a third, or introduces a confusion between them. It is always here that the same is mistaken for the other or the other for the same, the avoidance of which double error the stranger assigns to dialectics. Theaetetus, for example, lists a fourth kind of sophist, when he is helping to summarize their definitions, contrary to the stranger's explicit denial that the kind deserves an independent status (cf. 225e4). The third and fourth divisions, on the other hand, are always in danger of collapsing into one another. So here Theaetetus questions whether the stranger's fourth division exists. He does not realize that, if it goes, the joint action in which he and the stranger are engaged, as well as the possibility of philosophy itself, vanishes along with it. Theaetetus forgets that his own sciences must belong to the hunting of lifeless things if they belong at all to the art of acquisition. He forgets Socrates' definition of arithmetic as the hunting of the knowledges of every odd and even number.[20]

The stranger omits the one indispensable element of angling in which all of its artfulness consists. He says nothing about the bait the angler must put on his hook, or the lure he must attach to his line (cf. 222e6). Had he done so, not only would the distinction between mastery and exchange have become questionable—a gift (*dôron*) is also a bribe—but also a part of the mimetic art would have been introduced into a branch of acquisition. But the stranger could argue that though the angler can make his own lures, he can just as well buy them from another or order them to be made to his own specifications. All of making, therefore, would seem to be in principle subordinate to acquisition: the farmer does not possess by his art the fruits he cultivates.[21] And this, in turn, would imply that the stranger, in shifting the sophist out of the class to which the philosopher belongs and into the art of making, puts him under the philosopher's control. The variety of acquisitive arts which the sophist practices would be due to his failure to be the perfect acquisitor, but as the possibly perfect maker, the sophist then threatens the philosopher's claim, for he denies that any of the distinctions the philosopher draws among the beings truly is. He makes everything the philosopher masters. The servant refuses to acknowledge his own servitude. We do not know as yet how making liberates itself from acquiring, or more generally how the arts, which are not self-regarding, dispute the evident superiority of the arts which concern the good; but the stranger cannot avoid the problem of ruling if he wants to put the sophist in his place. The *Statesman* must be part of the *Sophist*'s argument.

The anastrophic form in which the stranger casts his summary of the angler's art, so that it looks like a Homeric genealogy (cf. 268d2–3), does not readily lend itself to interpretation. Could he be satirizing Socrates' maieutics, according to which, if Theaetetus had delivered a fruitful offspring, he would have been able to generate a family of truths? "It is not the soul, Socrates," the stranger would be saying, "that generates true offspring with the help of a maieutic omphalotomy, but the careful dissection of kinds." This dissection necessarily ends up with an indivisible, that is, a barren, kind, but the kind is not false because it is barren but quite the contrary. It is an ultimate form, a letter, as it were, in the alphabet of knowledge. As a letter, it cannot be read by itself but requires the other letters to be properly spelled out. So far, however, the letter, angling, has been disentangled from only one other letter—spearfishing. All the other classes are still syllabic or polysyllabic (cf. 220a8–9), of which the biggest is art or knowledge itself. Art, one might say, is a confused noise, which we hear at a distance, rather than a clearly enunciated sound.

But if the stranger has now discovered the suffix of acquisition in angling, has he not also discovered another suffix, spearfishing, at the same time? Neither is the true reading to the exclusion of the other, and since, despite what the stranger says, the blow struck in spearfishing is not the opposite of angling's, the two kinds do not belong to a higher, single art. Should we ever, then, succeed in discerning every atomic bit of knowledge, we would never be able to put them together, for the atomic glue is not knowledge but true opinion. The dichotomy gives the illusion of order only because the rest of the atoms have not yet been discovered. The clarity and distinctness that angling has necessarily depend on the unclarity and indistinctness of everything else. The elements of knowledge fall apart once all the elements are known.

The stranger uses the word "other" twice, and both times of the class he subdivides further (220a9, d1). Indeed, not until the merchant of body-goods comes up is "other" used of a rejected class (223e6). Angling, as the last remaining other (220e6), is wholly parasitic on all we do not know. The light of day, without which the art of angling cannot be practiced, gets dropped in the name "barbed," of which the fishhook is one type. Openness and secrecy "are" by themselves and do not get established by the arts which need them. Openness is the bond between the art of friendly rivalry and the art of hostile fighting, but neither apart nor together do they constitute knowledge of openness. To exploit is not to know. The stranger, then, must genealogize his classification in order to conceal its inherent atomicity. The genealogy is his way of inserting into the dichotomies the order of his finding. He thus makes it appear that the order of finding is the order of being. The mating of finding with being produces a specious becoming (cf. 222d5–6). It is not very different from the union of Protagoras' measure and Heraclitean motion in Theaetetus' definition of knowledge as perception in the *Theaetetus*. "We see," says the stranger, "the winged tribe." Only here does he permit in his *logos* a word of knowing.

III. HUNTING
(221c5–223b8)

Theaetetus and the stranger are to find what the sophist is according to the paradigm of the angler. The point of contact is solely the fact that the *logos* of the sophist could consist in a series of divisions, regardless of whether the sophist were with or without an art. But two things bring the paradigm closer to the sophist; both are due as much to Theaetetus as to the stranger. He asks Theaetetus whether they are to put the sophist down as "altogether truly a sophist."[22] At this point, Theaetetus decisively intervenes. They have, to be sure, excluded Socrates' definition of sophistry in terms of experience and "flair" without *logos*,[23] for Theaetetus has forgotten that originally the stranger offered a threefold possibility with regard to the angler—an artisan, artless, or with some other kind of power. But if to be truly a sophist is to be an artisan, it is not possible to ask, as Theaetetus does, what kind of art the artisan has. Theaetetus first admits that anyone who has an art is a sophist, and then proposes to consider which art is sophistry. He asks for the seemingly impossible: a one which is many and yet one of the many. He innocently asks after their own doing. What is this art by which they track down the sophist or any other artisan, which every other would-be art must use in constituting itself as an art, and which appears in its own articulation of art as one art among many?

At the moment that both sophist and angler come to light as hunters, the paradigm ceases to be simply an example of a "method" and becomes something in its own right—the source of an image. The sophist, we say, is only metaphorically an angler. Theaetetus does not question or notice the metaphor, though the stranger goes out of his way to call his attention to it: "The sophist turns to land and some other kind of rivers, the generous meadows, as it were, of wealthy youth." The stranger pretends that the hunter-sophist is his own insight, but the insight is into the sophist's own art of disguise. The sophist is on the way of the stranger's inquiry. He is doing what the stranger himself is doing. He has made himself into a hunter (cf. 265a8). The stranger has not discovered anything about the sophist which the sophist himself has not set before him. It was not the angler who made him see a resemblance in the sophist, but the sophist who made him see a resemblance in the angler. The sophist has the power to make his own not being—whatever he is not—come to light. He is forever anticipating the stranger's next discovery. While the stranger was looking away from the sophist to the angler, the sophist was following the stranger's recipe for looking the angler's part. To trap the sophist is like trying to look straight into a mirror without seeing oneself. It is, more precisely, the problem of the soul's asking and answering its own questions. It is the problem of thinking.

The sophist and the angler are indistinguishable insofar as they are both acquisitors, subduers, and hunters; they diverge as to the element—earth or water—in which they hunt down their quarry. In order to get over the difficulty of bisecting the manifold of land animals (cf. 220a3), the stranger proposes that they be divided into tame and savage animals. Theaetetus is surprised: "Is there then any hunting of the tame?" He is surprised because the very word hunting (*thêra*) implies its restriction to wild beasts (*thêria*). The stranger offers Theaetetus several possibilities; these possibilities replace the natural manifold of land animals with a seemingly man-made distinction. If, however, a man-made distinction is applicable to man himself, man may have tamed himself while taming beasts. The distinction, in any case, between tame and savage looks the same as that between domesticated by man and not, and Theaetetus can hardly respond in any other way than he does: "I believe, stranger, we are a tame animal, and I say there is a hunting of men." The issue of bestiality makes Theaetetus self-conscious. He makes a double division at once—the hunting of tame animals and the hunting of men—which is properly recorded as two in the stranger's summary, but not clearly discerned as two by Theaetetus. Tame, tamed, and tameable are all the same to him. He has not remembered what Socrates said about his becoming tamer as a result of Socrates' maieutics, nor what the stranger himself implied in saying that his own refusal of Socrates' request would be unfriendly and savage. He has also forgotten Socrates' image of the sciences as birds in the *Theaetetus*, the capture of which entails their quasi-domestication, as does the mistaking of a tame for a wild dove. Theaetetus should surely have considered why fish and birds were not likewise differentiated. He is unaware of the connection between the political and civilization, or the dual potential in human nature, which in the *Statesman* the stranger takes such pains to get the young Socrates to acknowledge.

Theaetetus' obliviousness to the city is identical with the sophist's, for the sophist's quarry is not man but merely a tame animal. Sophistry is based on an overestimation of the power it has through speech.[24] That the human beings it ensnares are young, wealthy, and of high estimation in the city is a fact but not an element of their art. It differs in this respect from Socrates' maieutics, which can only handle the young, noble, and beautiful.[25] Theaetetus' choice here shows for the first time that he and not young Socrates is the proper interlocutor for the examination of the sophist. The stranger never corrects any of Theaetetus' errors. If Theaetetus had chosen any of the three other possibilities, the stranger would have been compelled to instruct him in the need for force and the character of law, and the *Sophist* would have become the *Statesman*. The *Statesman* is only temporally posterior to the *Sophist*.

The following four divisions are all suspect. Forcible hunting, to which the arts of piracy, enslavement, tyranny, and warfare belong, is a hunting by tame animals of tame animals through force; it seems rather to be a hunting by savages of savages, for otherwise one could entice by gifts and speeches the tame into one's net, as indeed some tyrants have done. Were it not for warfare, we could save the class by redefining it as the class of unlawful hunting, and thus oppose it to lawful hunting within the city; but the stranger is pointing to the force in law itself,[26] and the impossibility of distinguishing between force and persuasion if man is simply tame. He therefore drops it in his summary. The class paired with it, to which the sophist belongs, is already contaminated, as its name brings out—the art of conviction-producing (*pithanourgikē*)—with the art of making. And since it thereby is presented as independent of the acquisition of those persuaded, it too has to be dropped in the summary. His next distinction, between private and public hunting—and not, we should note, between private and public persuasion—is inadequate for another reason. Does the art of wooing the electorate with promises differ from the speeches of private erotics? Plato devotes an entire dialogue to clarifying that difference, but Theaetetus knows as little about *erôs* as about the city. His innocence is part of his tameness. It allows the stranger to suggest in passing the subject of a potential or actual Platonic dialogue, sometimes obscurely, sometimes obviously, as when the *Gorgias* and the *Phaedrus* are hinted at. Each of the species he discovers through speeches or dialectically is the seed of a dialogue. While his species look like parodies of the "ideas," they are in fact compressed formulas for dialogues. They raise the question of how we should classify the dialogues—whether they can all be deduced from a single principle with perfect clarity, or whether they are as riddling as the sophist, who jumps unconscionably from class to class. Plato's own imitation of conversing is as much the subject of the *Sophist* as is the problem of silent conversing or thinking.

For the first time Theaetetus does not understand a distinction; the stranger assumes that the wage-earning class of private hunting is self-explanatory, and he has only to explain gift bringing (cf. 223e5–6). Theaetetus has not yet paid attention to the hunting of lovers. Theodorus has nothing to worry about: no one would take Theaetetus as his beloved. The stranger distinguishes between prostitution, which would fall under the art of mutually voluntary exchange, and love, in which the lover presumably has to persuade the beloved of his "rights." The stranger isolates the lover's gift from both pleasing lures of the flatterer and the sophist's promise of virtue, and thereby lets us see the unanalyzed doubleness he attributes to both the flatterer and the sophist. In giving the purpose behind the flatterer's graciousness and the sophist's promise, he runs together two different arts, for if the sophist does not get paid or the flatterer fed, each still has the art, strictly understood, of giving virtue or pleasure. The stranger therefore presents this last division in his summary as two arts—selling for cash and education in improving one's "image." They do, however, belong together, for convention stamps its approval no less on "image" than on currency.

The erotic art, in contrast, which is so just that it exaggerates the merits of neither the beloved nor the lover, must be Socrates', who used to profess that it was his sole knowledge. Socrates appears in the descent of the sophist. They differ with respect to opinion and self-interest, which the stranger comprehends as one and contrasts with the gift. That a gift ceases to be a gift if it is an investment and given in calculation of its potential return, is far more intelligible than that something freely given can be subject to an art, and an art whose very name—erotics—points to the very opposite of *erôs*. In the *Symposium*, only Socrates and the doctor Eryximachus, whose avowed aim is to praise his own art, speak of "the erotic things." The difference, then, between Socrates and a sophist turns on the difference between the Socratic assertion—there is a science of love—and the sophistic, that virtue can be taught. But this difference turns on the sameness of erotics and dialectics, whose sole resemblance to one another seems so far to be the metaphorical class of hunting, to which they are both assigned. It is much easier to understand that eristics and the teachability of virtue go together.

The stranger's summary expresses the elusiveness of the sophist rather than his fixity. Certain classes which Theaetetus had regarded as one are now two. Some of these splittings were implicit in the argument, others seem arbitrary in the extreme—the distinction, for example, between appropriation and acquisition—until one reflects on the necessity that the sophist look two ways at once, to what he himself is and what he does, the plainest example of which is the last pair, the good he sells and the good he gets. It is the sophist's own incapacity to keep together this duality that ultimately justifies the stranger's dichotomies and leads to the definition of sophistry as itself the art of duality or image making.

IV. Selling
(223c1–224e5)

Socrates once defined the sophist as a merchant or retailer of wares from which the soul is nourished,[27] and the stranger, at much greater length, proposes the same as his second and third definitions. He offers no other excuse for a second definition than his observing that there has already been in what they have said an apparition of the sophist's class as some other, and this turns out to be most literally the sophist's class—some other (cf. 221e1). The sophist shows his true colors in only appearing the second time as his ordinary self. But if the sameness of the sophist is always to be another, the stranger's way cannot capture anything but one illusion after another, without ever discovering what an illusion is. The stranger could apparently have avoided this if he had first defined the philosopher and then measured off against this benchmark his spurious shadow. He seems to have made the same mistake as Socrates did in the *Theaetetus*, when he digressed on false opinion without first determining what knowledge was, but Socrates' mistake was merely a part of his conversation with Theaetetus, while the stranger seems committed to making a mistaken digression into a complete dialogue. The *Sophist* as a whole is the other of the sophist. The more faithful a "phenomenology" of the sophist it is, the more it becomes the sophist's own platform. The *Sophist* is not a dialogue "about" the sophist; it is the sophist—some other. Theaetetus and the stranger inadvertently fall at least twice into philosophy (231a1–b2, 253c6–9), for they already are in philosophy. The monologue, which the stranger implied he only had to repeat as hearsay, turns as a dialogue into his own confession that he has for a long time been in an endless perplexity, and not even the refutation of Parmenides is enough to remove it.

The stranger begins his second definition with a mistake. He coordinates the hunting part of acquisition with exchange (*allaktikon*), whereas another name for exchange (*metablêtikon*) had originally been split off from mastery (*kheirôtikon*), which in turn had disappeared in the summary of the sophist as hunter. This interchange of counters implies that the art of exchange can be understood as a sort of mastery, the art of buying cheap and selling dear. The sophist-exchanger is a one-for-another seller, and as such he would sell either self-made wares or others', and either from one city to another or at home. But though the stranger makes it a matter of indifference whether the retailer sells his own wares or not, he does not allow the merchant to be a maker. To be a professional foreigner, as it were, is to be unoriginal (cf. 224a3). The stranger seems to be thinking of himself; he undoubtedly wishes to postpone as long as possible the linkage of making and acquiring, which such a term as *autopôlikê* implies. *Autopôlikê* is the first name the stranger has coined whose formation does not convey its meaning; it compounds the *auto-* of *autourgos* (he who makes with his own hands) with *pôlikê* (the art of selling). It is therefore a double art in a single name.

Could it be a single art? Can there be an art which uses the same means for selling as for making, so that that by which it makes is that by which it sells? The advertiser's art can certainly advertise advertising, but only accidentally, as when a doctor heals himself. The line of patter which accompanies the sale must be due to the art by which one makes the product. If the product were food for the soul, the food for the soul would be manifest in the selling of "soul food." Let us suppose a soul food to be knowledge of soul; its seller would of necessity show this knowledge in his sales pitch. The stay-at-home Socrates would in this sense be an *autopôlês*. His speech in the *Theaetetus* on maieutics was itself a maieutic speech. The sophist-salesman, on the other hand, would remain double, for his experience in decking out his wares cannot be part of the virtue he sells. Spurious virtue cannot artfully manage its own campaign, but if knowledge of soul is virtue, it is most itself in being protreptic, though even in discouraging a sale it is still virtue. Socrates, then, would be the master sophist if his product were an artifact. But *autourgos* primarily refers to someone who cultivates his own land, and only in terms of the stranger's classification of farming under making, is Socrates in any danger of being taken for a sophist. It is Theaetetus who, in misconstruing the stranger's third class as two classes, puts the *autopôlês* in the center of the seven definitions of the sophist.

Merchants of a soul food sell entertainment, expertise, or virtue. The stranger does not explain why they are mutually exclusive; as the products of others, they could all be sold in books without requiring that the merchant know anything more about a Sophoclean play than about Protagoras' *Truth*. The stranger seems to assume that the merchant somehow represents his product: he has swallowed the merchandise and believes in his mission. Without this assumption, the merchant and retailer are being described in themselves divorced from any connection with sophistry. The merchant, for example, could have the art of holiness—unless the stranger had intended to put holiness with giftgiving—for it consists, according to Euthyphro, in exchanging prayers (speeches) and sacrifices (food and drink) for good things from the gods.[28]

V. Competing
(224e6–226a5)

The diversity of the sophist's arts has so far depended on, or better perhaps gone along with, the various ways in which the stranger has come to recognize him. He was a hunter because of his kinship with the angler, he was a merchant or retailer because of the apparition he gave of belonging among the exchangers, and he is a disputer because he resembles a competitor. The relation among these three signs by means of which the stranger and Theaetetus discover class membership can be said to be the theme of the *Sophist*.

Open acquisition divides into rivalry and battle. For the first time, the stranger makes a distinction which he does not explain, and for the first time, Theaetetus says that the two classes are (*estin*). In the past, he has immediately assented to the stranger's names for classes rather than to their being (219c1, 220a6, 223c11). His assent to the being of rivalry and battle seems to be due to their occurrence in the open, without any trace of obscurity as to their character. Rivalry embraces running and excludes boxing or wrestling, for one's rivals in running do not interfere with one's own activity; one does as well as one can, and not as much as others allow. Unrestrained by contact with another, one can fix one's own goal and better one's own record. To this class would belong learning. Its opposite falls into bodily or "logical" contention; the former the stranger calls forcible and the latter disputatious. Hoplite fighting, in which two armies meet head on in open country, would illustrate this kind of fighting, but the stranger thereby splits the art of war in two, the other part of which belongs to violent hunting along with the piratical and tyrannical arts. Since the stranger does not rank one type higher than the other, we cannot say that a "value" distinction has crept into the classification, but we cannot be sure that Theaetetus does not regard one as honorable and the other not. He certainly does not discern the possibility of violent disputation—the Thrasymachaean art of arousing anger with words[29]—nor is he puzzled that the judicial art is now both open and secret mastery. Theaetetus is much too tame to argue against the stranger.

At the fourth division something goes wrong. The stranger opposes lengthy speeches in public about the just and unjust to private questions and answers. Contradiction is not confined to the question of justice, for eristics, which is a part of it, disputes about justice itself and other things, in fact about everything (232e3). The stranger, moreover, assumes that there are no lengthy speeches in private, even though he had been prepared to deliver such a speech himself. If he had overcome his shame, or had not been a stranger, would the stranger have drawn up an indictment of Socrates, as Socrates had feared? Socrates, at any rate, can be grateful that the stranger is not an Athenian, and is therefore disqualified from making a public accusation. The dialogue has served to dilute the strength of his attack on Socrates (cf. 235b8). He has trapped Socrates in every family in which the sophist is found, and he does it again, for the last division is between the money-losing gossip who displeases many of his auditors while pleasing himself, and the sophist, who does not neglect his own profit while engaged in private disputations.[30] Socrates has been steadily approaching the sophist through the series of divisions, and though he was at first a rather distant kin of the sophist as the erotic hunter, he is now paired with him. Only money now separates them; but the stranger drops even that distinction when he summarizes this class as showing the sophist to be a prizefighter of eristic speeches (231e1). The "reality" of the sophist emerges in the silent contest between Socrates, whom the stranger has by indirection found out to be a sophist, and the stranger, whose prosecution of the sophist has taken on the coloring if not the substance of a sophist. The *Sophist* is a single speech with three unknowns—sophist, stranger, Socrates. Its action thus duplicates Socrates' question whether sophist, statesman, philosopher are one, two, or three.

The *logos*, says the stranger, has recognized as a distinct kind the artless disputation in private about contracts. On the face of it, this is impossible, for the stranger set out with the collection of all the arts, from which both artlessness and artless experience were excluded. There seems to be no reason, moreover, why haggling cannot be artfully conducted, unless the stranger wishes to imply that its injustice precludes its artfulness. Its insertion, however, shows the inconsequence of the sophist's moneymaking. Disputes about contracts are of necessity guided by the consideration of gain; no one willingly engages in them to the neglect of his own, for they are about one's own. Disputes, on the other hand, about the just itself are by nature theoretical, and the effect they have on one's own cannot solely be determined by the loss or gain of money. The sophist combines the haggling of the marketplace with philosophy. He puts together in a non-Socratic way the Socratic way, which goes through the marketplace on its way to what lies outside the city.

VI. Purifying
(226a6–231b8)

The sophist is a complex, wild beast, which cannot be captured casually or "with the left hand." Theaetetus proposes that they use all their might or "both hands." He seems to be calling for a way that overcomes the partiality or otherness of dichotomy; and the stranger does suppress somehow the distinction between making and acquiring. For the first and last time we are let into the stranger's workshop, so that we can see the coming-into-being of a class. The stranger first makes a collection of certain verbs, which he picked up from the language of servants. Although they belong to various arts, most of them are not arts themselves. Each denotes an action, which together with other interlocking actions characterizes a single art. In a sense, each of the prior definitions of the sophist was an isolated verb—hunts, sells (imports, retails), competes—to which the subsequent divisions in each case added object-nouns, adverbs, and adjectives; but the verbal core remained unaffected throughout its greater and greater specialization. We therefore could not help but get the impression that the fisherman, if he just took his net out of the water and hung it among the trees, would instantly become a fowler, and if each artisan were stripped of his special gear, and divorced from the object of his art, the artisan as such would appear. Now, however, the stranger looks first at the series of related actions and only afterward at the comprehensive art. If he had begun with the stroke of the spearfisherman, and then added to it the swordsman's lunge, the hoplite's thrust, and the boxer's jab, we would have seen at once that the art of giving a blow is in itself nonexistent. The stranger here cites filtering, sifting, winnowing, as one group, and carding, spinning, combing, as another, and before he reseparates them he calls them all divisive, and the single art manifest in them the art of discerning or diacritics. If someone knows how to card wool, he does not know how to filter wine of its impurities, and yet both he and the carder are practicing diacritics.

None of the individual verbs within the class of diacritics communicates with any other directly; they are only miscible through an art in which all of them partake but in which none is without qualification. There is only one simply diacritical art: the art which Theaetetus and the stranger have been practicing from the start. Diacritics is in itself an art even while being the comprehensive class characteristic of all the members of its class. Diacritics is never wholly itself when it is practical, for it then fragments into mutually exclusive actions; only in its apartness from everything else does it come into its own. Its own work is not restricted to wool or wine or wheat, for what it produces is the discrimination of the *eidê* themselves, and it itself is theoretical. We would only be guilty of imprecision but not of falsehood were we to speak of the discernment rather than the sifting of flour,[31] but our not ignoble imprecision would conceal from us that diacritics is one apart from the many, and is not simply a collective noun. The works and words of slaves are sometimes more revealing than the careless speech of free men.

All the discriminations up to now have been of like from like, for which the stranger has no name in general use, and not of better from worse, which all call "purification." However, at the end of this division they find Socrates' art, which the stranger wishes to keep apart, since it is "the sophistry noble in descent" and differs from the rest of sophistry as much as dog from wolf. Theaetetus sees only their resemblance. The stranger has been training him to discriminate among kinds without paying attention to which kind is better or worse, and he now brings out in the most emphatic manner the indifference of their way to the lowliness or pretentiousness of the arts. Their way therefore seems incapable of distinguishing between the genuine and the spurious if it can only note the likeness of one art to another, for the spurious can only be spurious if it looks genuine. The stranger seems headed for a crisis in his "methodology."

However, in a sense, there is no crisis. The stranger's way is indifferent to the general's reluctance to be classed with the lice killer, but the stranger does not observe that this resemblance is not due to an insight of his own diacritics but of generalship. Human beings are killed in war as if they are vermin, the most obvious sign of which are the names enemies call one another—"beasts," "rats," "scum," and the like. The art of war is as much a purification as it is a hunting,[32] even as lice killing is indifferently a part of hunting or of cleansing. The stranger's way does not control the source of the resemblances it finds. If it is not to be deceived, it must not only overlook the pretentiousness of an art but look into its pretentiousness. What is its boast, and how does it measure up to its claims? The art, however, of examining the spurious is the art he ends up defining here. The stranger must adopt the way of Socrates. The purification of soul is inseparable from dialectics and dialectics from the purification of soul.

In accordance with what we have learned from his conversation with Socrates, Theaetetus accepts the separation of cathartics into the purification of body, whether lifeless or living, and of soul by itself.[33] He does not ask whether soul too is to be distinguished into bodiless and embodied soul (cf. 248a10), to say nothing of living and lifeless nonbodies. He fails to notice that the stranger speaks of the purification of thought as well as of soul (227c4, cf. 229c6), and he takes it for granted that the soul is the human soul, even though the body is no more a man's than a pig's or a cloak's. The stranger indicates the difficulty of his division in several ways. Diacritics, in its attempt to see what is or is not akin in all the arts, puts medicine and gymnastics together with the arts of the bathman and fuller; but the stranger, in his attempt to distinguish two kinds of psychic purification, appeals to gymnastics and medicine as his model, both of which work on the insides of living bodies. Does the soul, then, have an inside too? And are there other arts which cleanse the outsides of soul? That which corresponds for soul to the cosmetic art for body would be, according to Socrates, the impersonations of gymnastics and medicine,[34] the names for which are sophistry and rhetoric. The stranger, then, either wishes to assign a place to the skin-deep arts, as indispensable in their way as clothes cleaning, or he implicitly distinguishes between the spurious and the genuine, even though his way cannot justify or acknowledge that distinction. Because Theaetetus did not recognize the difference between experience and art, which is of a piece with his acceptance of soul apart from ensouled body, the sophist must now show up with either a spurious art or, which is worse, a genuine art of the spurious.

We should furthermore ask whether gymnastics is adequately characterized as a purification. Is the beautiful the clean? Does the beautiful at which gymnastics aims come to be simply by the removal of what is worse from the body? Improvement in muscular tone does not only follow from a program of weight reduction. Exercise seems to be more comparable to the correct discrimination of like from like (symmetry) or the building-up (synthesis) of the body.

And finally there is a more general question. Does diacritics, in separating soul from ensouled body, merely mark a distinction already present? The most radical separation of soul from ensouled body is, again according to Socrates, none other than philosophy itself—the practice of dying and being dead. The stranger speaks of diacritics' indifference to the difference between the art of sponging and the drinking of drugs. It is indifferent to the difference between Socrates' bathing and his drinking hemlock. The stranger leaves no room for "religious" or ritual purification.

Theaetetus does not understand how the two kinds of vice or wickedness in soul correspond to illness and ugliness in body. "Perhaps you do not hold illness and stasis as the same?" Theaetetus, the stranger believes, understands the likeness of the ugly in soul but not of the sick; so in order to explain the likeness, he interposes between the illness of body and the illness of soul the stasis of the city. If Theaetetus, who does not even know the way to the marketplace, can see the sameness of stasis and illness, he can see the likeness of bodily illness in soul. For the second time in the dialogue the same (*tauton*) is mentioned (224b2). Why did not the stranger say "alike"? If illness and stasis were merely alike, the *logos* of their likeness would apply to both but be of neither, but the *logos* of stasis will be equally of illness if they are the same.[35] But to be the same, the two must be different, for otherwise they would be one. Their difference, however, must be inessential; their being or nature must be the same. Nature rides in on the coattails of the same. For the first time nature (*physis*) is mentioned. Stasis is "the variance or moving asunder of what is naturally akin that arises out of some sort of corruption." Theaetetus accepts the natural kinship of what is together in the city. He does not consider that stasis might be a necessary consequence of the unnatural togetherness of whatever is in the city, and therefore not comparable to bodily corruption.

The sameness of stasis and illness stands or falls with the naturalness of the city. Is the city a lifeless body, an ensouled body, or a soul? If it is an ensouled body, we should be able to speak, as Socrates does, of a healthy city.[36] Political faction (stasis) is unhealthy. It is the standing apart of the city's parts. It is a kind of inertia. It is not only the absence of motion but the presence of the wrong kind of motion,[37] motion that is directed away from the right goal. In stasis, the right goal lies unacknowledged, for the goal cannot be achieved by any one part by itself but only with the cooperation of other parts, all of which are equally recalcitrant to being harnessed together for the attainment of a goal beyond themselves. Stasis and illness arise from the stubborn refusal of parts to subordinate themselves to the common whole. This refusal to budge, each from its own position, is not due to inability but to the willfulness of invincible ignorance. Stasis reveals the natural propensity of parts when they do not recognize themselves as parts, toward unlimited aggrandizement at the expense of others. Stasis is blindness to the other. The same, therefore, first comes to light in a context in which there is no other. The same not only brings nature in its train but abstraction as well, of which the most obvious example is the asserted sameness of civil war and disease. It might be the task of dialectics to distinguish the sameness of abstraction from the sameness of nature.

The stranger assumes correctly that Theaetetus does not need any intermediary in order to understand the ugly, whether in body or soul. We do not know whether he wishes to deny that one can speak of the beautiful city.[38] The ugly is wherever there is the deformed class of disproportion. The class of the ugly is as ugly as ugly things are. The agreement of the naturally cognate is not in itself beautiful, for agreement is not commensuration. Disease, as either a falling-short or an overreaching, is not measurable by a standard built into the disease. To have a fever is to be too hot, but for the fever it is just so hot. It is a scalar quantity. Ugliness, on the other hand, carries within itself the measure of the beautiful; it is a vector with a built-in goal. It knows where it is going. The ugly comes from a motion which lays down for itself a target and then, in trying to hit it, misses and proves to be off course or a wandering away from the target.

Ugliness is to Illness as Motion is to Rest. Ugliness is an error or mistake, illness a conflict[39] or unresolved doubt. The beauty of Theaetetus no sooner appeared than he mistook the other (true opinion) for the same (knowledge), and the same (true opinion and true opinion with *logos*) for the other (knowledge). He was sick as long as he was caught in the grip of Protagorean self-contradiction. The failure of self-completion shows itself to be ugly, while the sick body or soul is as complete as its opposite;[40] what it needs is a ruler who is obeyed. In the *Theaetetus*, Socrates began to cure Theaetetus when he compelled him to submit to the illiberality of precise speech. The anarchy of illness consists of a manifold in disorder. The failure of ugliness consists of half-way measures. The commandment of health is, Nothing too much; the motto of beauty is, There is not enough. Health looks as if it is attainable, for everything is already there to be rearranged; beauty looks as if it is forever out of reach, for the impulse toward it is not unwilling but weak.

The stranger calls the illness or stasis of soul wickedness or moral vice, and the ugliness of soul ignorance. Wickedness results from a difference among things that are necessarily akin (228b6); the stranger does not say that they are naturally akin. Opinions, desires, anger, pleasures, *logos,* and pains seem to be akin solely through being together in soul. Moral vice seems to be closer to stasis than to illness, and the sameness of stasis and illness only a likeness. The stranger does not explain how these six elements of soul are related to one another. He and Theaetetus have merely perceived them in conflict. The stranger does not suggest that the soul has two, three, or more parts, for he still speaks of soul as if it were all of soul when he describes its derangement. Morality is the health, truth the beauty of soul. Morality would be the condition for the attainment of truth; but the soul is not unwillingly ignorant of morality. Wickedness is not a matter of ignorance. There is no impulse to courage, moderation, or justice, for each results from the proper relation between two elements, neither of which aims at that relation.

Theaetetus seems to interpret any conflict between opinions and desires, in which desire wins, as cowardice; between anger and pleasures, in which pleasure wins, as absence of self-control; and between *logos* and pains, in which pain wins, as injustice. He implies, for example, that opinions must prevail over desires in order for there to be courage and therefore that to stay at one's post, in the belief that one should, without at the same time desiring to live, is not courageous. If a dog retaliates for a beating it has received, there is no injustice, anymore than a man, who punishes another for an act which caused him no pain, can be just. The stranger mentioned only three of the possible fifteen conflicts between any two of his six elements, and Theaetetus might find it difficult to interpret all of them in moral terms. How does the overcoming of anger by desire differ from its overcoming by pain?[41] The stranger, moreover, does not exclude multiple conflicts, in which each of the elements disputes every other at the same time. Such complexities can be left to the poets of the moral life; intellectual virtue or vice seem to be simple, for there are no conflicts. Theaetetus and the stranger simply know that every soul is unwillingly ignorant of everything. Every soul, we might at once conclude, is ugly. But this would only follow if omniscience were humanly impossible, whereas the stranger's suggestion of a soul gymnastics might mean to Theaetetus that nothing but immorality stands in the way of the commensuration of the soul with truth.

The art of punishment, the stranger says, handles insolence, injustice, and cowardice, for of all arts it is most akin to Justice."It's likely, at any rate," Theaetetus says, "if one is to speak according to human opinion." A more precise speech, it seems, would not speak of punishment, for medicine cures and does not punish, though the sick soul would necessarily regard its cure as punishment. The cure, however, does not involve teaching; there is no reasoning with either disease or wickedness.

At this point, the argument becomes obscure. Contrary to the opinion of the many, the stranger and Theaetetus have agreed that ignorance is a vice even if it is only in soul and does not issue in action. All ignorance is ugly. The stranger now says that teaching must necessarily have two parts if ignorance has two. One kind of ignorance is what the stranger calls in his summary *doxosophia*, the believing and seeming to know what one does not know. The stranger calls it folly; he does not say what the other part of ignorance, which is equally ugly, should be called. Theaetetus says that instruction in the crafts or productive arts is one part of teaching, and education (*paideia*) is the Athenian name for the other. Despite the difficulty of separating folly as an *eidos* from all other parts of ignorance, the stranger now says that education (*paideia*) is the commonly accepted name among almost all Greeks for getting rid of folly. Theaetetus' first definition of knowledge had been the sum of all productive arts and what Socrates had called education—the sciences Theaetetus was learning from Theodorus.[42] Where, then, does Socrates' maieutics come in? The stranger finds room for it by splitting education still further. He does not split folly at the same time. It does not follow, apparently, that if the art of teaching is of two kinds, folly is of two kinds.

All education is in speeches: one way is rougher, the other smoother. One is the art of admonition, or more literally, the art of putting mind (*nous*) in someone. Fathers practice it on their sons whenever they make a mistake. Its speeches would seem to be these: "You think you're so smart"; "You don't know anything"; "When you are as old as I am, you'll see that I'm right." The admonitory art seems to be artless and not very effective. The other part of education is a more recent discovery; it has come about through reflection on the fact that all folly is unwilling and no one who believes himself to be wise is willing to learn anything. The unwillingness to be ignorant is not accompanied by the willingness to know. The stranger contradicts himself. He began with the ugliness of the unwillingly ignorant soul, regardless of what it did not know, but if Theaetetus correctly distinguished two kinds of education, to be ignorant of shoemaking makes the soul ugly. The stranger, however, has now restricted ugly ignorance to folly, the removal of which makes one most pure and beautiful. Theaetetus has made a far-reaching mistake. The Greek meaning of education is none other than education in folly; its true meaning is Socrates' maieutics, whose task, at least in part, is to correct Greek *paideia*.

The stranger has revised Theaetetus' division in such a way that instruction in the productive arts now includes instruction in the sciences as well, all of which necessarily induce the belief that one knows what one does not know. He has then divided the art of removing folly into the trivial part of admonition and the Socratic part of maieutics. His revision, however, leads to a new difficulty. He compares this noble sophistics, not to what gymnastic trainers do, but to what doctors do. It removes the impediments to the proper acquisition of knowledge; it makes the soul healthy and not beautiful. It differs from the art of punishment only because it induces self-punishment. By showing the contradictions in the opinions someone holds, it brings about a conflict between opinion and *logos*. Such a conflict was, according to the stranger, a disease, and its removal produces, according to Theaetetus, the best and most moderate of conditions. But moderation was the opposite of either intemperance or insolence (228e3, 229a3).

Noble sophistics is the art of taming. It is an indispensable condition for the beauty of omniscience, but it is not yet that beauty. Socrates, at any rate, does not know how to supply it. The confusion in the stranger's account, which led Theaetetus into his own confusion, began with his attempt to put everything under purification; for if there are genuine sciences to be learned, they cannot be themselves purifications. Purification begins with the induction of a disease. Prior to this induction, the disease looks like beauty; after the induction, it is recognized as a spurious beauty, or a real ugliness. The recognition of a real ugliness (*aiskhron*) establishes shame (*aiskhynê*). Shame brings about the beauty of self-knowledge, which in turn is embedded in ignorance, for one then truly knows the incommensuration of the soul's impulse with truth. Theaetetus has forgotten that no amount of gymnastics can make either Socrates or himself beautiful. The stranger as carefully conceals Theaetetus' ugliness from himself as Socrates had.

The gods know and never did not know; they have a cloistered knowledge, for they never experience false opinion. Does not, however, this experience of false opinion affect the philosopher's understanding, as much as the doctor's own illness alters his book-knowledge? Does he know something the gods cannot know?[43] The philosopher is not like a judge who has never committed a crime. He cannot punish the ignorant, but a god could punish him. Socrates was afraid that the stranger was a god of refutation come to punish his hubris, and he has now been shown that he did not properly cleanse Theaetetus. Theaetetus believes that the Socratic art is a version of Athenian education. He has reverted in less than a day to his very first definition of knowledge, according to which Socrates would be another Theodorus. Socrates' maieutics is a poor copy of the sophistic art noble by descent. He is no more successful than a father with his admonitions, for his dialectics is impure. The stranger indicts Socrates: Socrates is unjust. He induces his own illness in others in order to cure them, but he lacks the skill to cure whomever he has corrupted. Socrates is a noble failure.

The disproportion between Socrates' maieutics and the stranger's version of it condemns Socrates. But what of the stranger himself? He discovered that a part of the art of discernment—his own art— was Socrates' art idealized, but the discovery of Socrates' art was shared in by Theaetetus (227d2). His participation should have involved the stranger's practice of Socrates' art in the course of their joint discovering of Socrates' art. Socrates' art, however, was not discovered, for it was presented as identical with that which it itself declared to be the obstacle to learning. The diacritical art thus became impure as soon as it teamed up with an impure purification. The stranger vindicated Socrates—Socrates is wholly unsubversive—only by misrepresenting Socrates. Socrates came to light as an apparition of himself— the sophist—through the ignorance of another (Theaetetus) and the skill of the stranger. But this misrepresentation was also due to the mistaken diacritics of the stranger, who could not keep apart morality and intellectual virtue. His mistake was not incidental to his art. Socratic purification can only be practiced by those who have themselves been so purified. If there is not to be an infinite regression, it is necessary that the art of purification be applied to oneself while it is being applied to another. The art of purification therefore cannot be a perfected art. The practicing of this imperfect art is accordingly not commensurate with its goal. It is ugly. The art of beautification of soul is not itself beautiful. As a deformed (*duseides*) genus of disproportion it is not its own species (*eidos*).

VII. Appearing
(221b9–236c8)

The likeness which a perfect Socratic maieutics bears to sophistry is the same as the likeness a dog bears to a wolf, the most tame to the most savage. If, the stranger implies, the previous four or five definitions, which were of the ignoble sophist, were reworked, philosophy would come to light. Sophistry would seem to be degenerate philosophy. But if the sophist is the savage beast, he could be the philosopher's original, from whom the philosopher has slowly diverged through submission to training and discipline. A dog has a master. To what legislator could the future philosopher submit? A dog is not friendly to strangers. The stranger's image is a warning about the danger of likenesses, which because they are likenesses are always open to a double reading. A likeness requires that it be scanned in light of what is known. And if the known were the eminently knowable and not just what is known to us or the familiar, the perspective in which we discerned likenesses would be the natural perspective.

The stranger tries to warn Theaetetus that in the absence of the natural perspective, likeness is not a safe guide to the discrimination of kinds. He manages instead to induce in Theaetetus a perplexity before the many contradictory opinions he now holds, thanks to the stranger, about the sophist. His failure to be pure in either his diacritics or his purification has succeeded in bringing about the very first stage in the practice of sophistry noble by descent. Theaetetus is perplexed by the multiplicity of the sophist's appearance (*pephanthai*); he wants to know what speech would truly declare what the sophist is in his being (*ontôs*). He does not know that he is asking for the reality of the spurious or the genuine in the spurious. He does not connect the manifold of an appearance with a core of not being, but just the opposite, for Socrates too had proposed that the philosopher in his being (*ontôs*) gives forth a multiplicity of appearances.

The sophist was in turn a wage-earning hunter of rich, young men, a merchant and retailer of the soul's disciplines, a seller of his own "inventions" (Theaetetus' addition), a prizefighter of eristic speeches, and perhaps a purifier of opinions which are a hindrance to learning. The summary says nothing about virtue. If we cancel Theaetetus' addition, and combine the second and third (merchant and retailer), the sophist has four professions, in each of which he must show himself to possess at least the semblance of a different virtue. He would not even appear to be a hunter unless he showed courage, nor a seller unless he could present himself as a witness to the wisdom of his wares, nor a disputant about justice itself unless he looked just, nor finally a purifier of pseudowisdom unless he pretended to be moderate himself. To ask for the unity of the sophist is to inquire into the unity of virtue. Moderation and courage lie at opposite poles, with wisdom closer to courage and justice to moderation. The sophist's multiple appearance, then, resolves the apparent unity of virtue into its apparently conflicting parts. Appearance is not all of a piece. Virtue seems to be a single whole in everyday speech; on reflection, it frag-

ments into parts that seem to be at war with each other. The sophist
has the art to represent both seemings at once. His art therefore must
itself seem to be both one and many. His knowledge duplicates the
doubleness of knowledge. Is the sophist's knowledge, which looks like
knowledge, the same as the knowledge which looks both one and
many? The truth might be either that knowledge is really a many
which only looks one in sophistry, or that knowledge is really one
which only looks many in sophistry. Diagrammatically, the three possibilities are those outlined in figure 1.

At first, the stranger presents the problem in terms of the first
possibility (a): "Do you realize, then, that whenever someone appears
as the knower of many things, but is addressed with the name of one
art, this apparition is not sound, but plainly whoever experiences this
in regard to any art is not able to catch sight of that part of it, toward
which all these learnings look, and, accordingly, addresses him who
has them with many names instead of one?" The stranger allows that
an apparition of many could be sound. The sophist could then cast
over his many real knowledges a single appearance. This is our second
possibility (b); it recalls Parmenides' example of the sailcloth, with
which he showed the young Socrates the difficulty of separated "ideas":
the sailcloth hid the many under it. The stranger, moreover, phrases
the problem of the sophist's art in such a way that it is doing, he
suggests, double duty for the problem of being. If his conclusion were
rephrased in terms of being, it would go like this: "If there are many
phenomena but all are addressed as being, we have not found that
being, toward which all these phenomena look." This is our third
possibility (c); it is equivalent to the problem of Parmenides.

The sophist can contradict anyone about anything; and since he
teaches his pupils to do what he does—a sign of art—he must have
either the art he says he has or the art of convincing his pupils that
he has it. If the latter were true, the sophist's pupils, in believing they
have been instructed in a genuine art, would be far more persuasive
than he himself was, for they would not be pretending when they in
turn became teachers. One may question, however, the consistency
of the sophist's two arts. Is the kind of fakery involved in persuading
his potential pupils of his omniscience the same as that in his teaching
his fakery to them? The sophist's apparitional omniscience, precisely
because it has the result of giving him money and pupils, is plausibly
assumed to be willed and not solely due to the ignorance of others.
What he sells is that by which he sells. By contradicting the potential
pupil, the potential pupil comes to realize his need of what the sophist
offers; but what the sophist offers is the lure itself. The sophist therefore cannot afford to expose to the pupil the falseness of the "come-

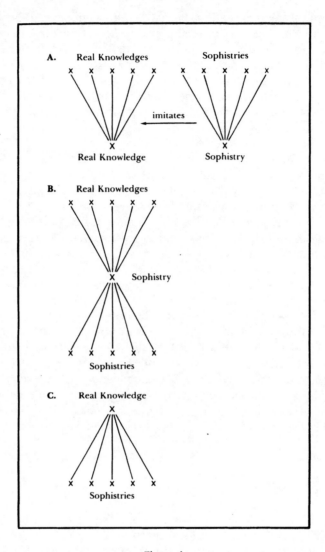

Figure 1

on." He cannot teach. But if he does teach, he cannot know what he is doing. He thus can only have an art if he lacks self-knowledge. He cannot be omniscient.

The stranger lists five topics in which the sophist offers instruction; Theaetetus believes that together they just about constitute omniscience: (1) all the divine things invisible to the many (arithmetic, geometry, and all that Euthyphro says he knows); (2) all the self-evident divine things like earth and sky (astronomy and physiology); (3) becoming and being; (4) laws and all political things; (5) each and every art. Between the divine things and the human—the stranger does not call the last two items the human—is becoming and being, which together comprehend the divine and the human and at the same time are the bond between them. If, however, the divine and the human are the two kinds of things most indicative of being and becoming and the core of both cosmology and the political is the soul, as the *Timaeus* and the *Republic* respectively assert, then psychology would be the one science of the sophist. But psychology is none other than sophistry noble by descent, and according to the stranger, it is, even if more solid than Socrates' maieutics, only preparatory to the sciences. The stranger assumes that these sciences are available; but if they are not within human capacity, the sophist's art of contradiction, grounded in psychology, would be the only defense against the pretensions of others, and Socrates would be the sophist. If, on the other hand, the sophist falsely laid claim to omniscience, and his art of contradiction was grounded in a pseudopsychology, the sophist would be the representative of sham wisdom, and accordingly, the most important patient of soul cathartics.

Theaetetus has no doubt that the sciences are all available; he believes that the human race would be blessed if a human being could know everything (cf. 230e3). Theaetetus knows that the human race is not blessed; he does not know whether an omniscient human being would suffice to make it happy. He does not consider the possibility of a community of human beings, who all together would know everything. The best city of the *Republic* looks like such a community. But even if it is not, actual cities certainly claim to know the most important things, and as such rival the sophist.[44] The sophist, however, is more elusive and playful than the city, for he is enlightened, and speaks from both within and without the city. He manifestly has opinionative knowledge about everything. Theaetetus believes they have no more to do; they have found the sophist. He does not see any difficulty in the juxtaposition of opinion and knowledge. Does "opinionative knowledge" mean a genuine knowledge of spurious beings, a spurious knowledge of spurious beings, or a spurious knowledge of genuine beings? If sophistry were the first, it would be a rational poetry—the knowledge of how to supply the soul with false opinions; if it were the second, it would seem to be the first; and if it were the third, it would simply be false opinion. Theaetetus has not yet realized that Socrates' question in the *Sophist* is the same as his question in the *Theaetetus*.

Theaetetus does not know what the problem is. It is not whether omniscience is possible, but whether omniscience by means of a single science is possible. The stranger has implied that knowledge of the divine things, invisible and visible, does not yield knowledge of the human things, and vice versa, but a science of being and becoming would seem to be just the required science of sophistry. To prove that a science of being and becoming is necessarily spurious would be tantamount to declaring all philosophers to be sophists, for if wisdom is not one, the love of wisdom is of a true many (cf. 235a3),[45] whose apparent unity would be due to the illusion of love. Every time the stranger has made a distinction he has posed the same problem, for the reality of any distinction seems to be inconsistent with the reality of the whole which is distinguished. It seems impossible to say that something is what it is because it has one factor which is uniquely true of it, and yet that it truly is a part of some larger whole. Not its uniqueness but its commonness would enroll it in the whole, and the whole would be characterized by a number of common factors, not one of which would belong to the whole exclusively. If, however, the whole of science is nothing but the sum of the sciences, Socrates' objection to Theaetetus' first answer holds. No science can determine what is unscientific about another science except by its own decree or an appeal to an extrascientific criterion. The wholeness of science thus first comes to light as the single apparition of the sophist's art, through whose power of likeness the differences among kinds are wiped out, and everything, starting with the sophist himself, slides from kind to kind.[46]

The sophist, then, seems to be refutable only at a price, for the restoration of differences, which are immune to the art of likening, must restamp the sum of the differences with the apparition of unity because there can be no knowledge of their differences. We are then confronted with the choice between Parmenides, who has to be refuted in order to let the sophist's art be something, and the result of the sophist's refutation, which readmits an illusion for which we cannot account. Neither a real one with an apparent many, nor a real many with an apparent one, is acceptable. A real one with a real many, of which the stranger's own dichotomies are a parody, seems to be necessarily a phantom.

Of the three paradigms which the stranger uses in succession—fisherman, verbs of separative action, and painter—the first seemed to impose upon the sophist a model with which he had to conform, the second led away from the sophist and toward Socrates, while the third, in accordance with its own power, seems to bring the sophist into being. If there is an art that can make everything in deed, Theaetetus can see no reason why there could not be another art that can make everything in speech. The dichotomy of deed and speech suffices to conjure up the sophist's art. As a straightforward deduction, it does not require that any deed confirm it; Theaetetus agrees to a conclusion the stranger draws from it, even though he admits he lacks the experience to lend any weight to his agreement. Theaetetus began by not even understanding the beginning of the stranger's speech. "Should anyone say, not that he knows how to say or contradict, but that he knows how to make and do all things together by one art—" "What do you mean by all?," is Theaetetus' interruption; the stranger, after all, had told him to pay very close attention. "All" means all individuals: Theaetetus, the stranger, the other animals and trees. Theaetetus now does not know what making means; he thinks of the farmer as a maker, even as the stranger had, but he does not think of the midwife as comparable to the farmer, even though Socrates had cited farming to justify the unity of his own art.[47]

If Socrates' maieutics, however, is an art that clears away the phantom growths of soul and thereby prepares its soil for the healthy seeds of knowledge, then the art of making everything, in the sense of helping to bring everything into the light and making it knowable and harvestable by men, would be the gymnastic cathartics of diacritics. Only when the stranger adds sea, earth, sky, gods, "and all the rest," and remarks on the speed with which each thing is made and the small amount for which it is sold, does Theaetetus at last understand that the stranger is speaking of a sort of amusement or play. He therefore does not ask now whether there is a divine making of everything, nor later, when the stranger proposes that a god makes everything, whether the god's knowledge is a universal farming. Such a knowledge would not be the know-how of creation, but an art of weeding out the sick and cultivating the sound beings. And if there are reasons which should have made Theaetetus hesitate to suppose that anything of the sort happens in deed, he should still have asked whether there is such a knowledge in speech.[48] Theaetetus does not attend closely enough. The stranger is always speaking over his head to Socrates.

The parallelism between omniscience in deed and omniscience in speech is not exact. The stranger replaces speaking with knowing everything and compares the speed of making each something with the short time needed to teach another everything. Here "everything" cannot mean all individuals—what would knowledge of the remotest stranger mean?—but the kinds of things the stranger had previously ascribed to the omniscience of the contradictor. The stranger then presents two pictures (fig. 2).

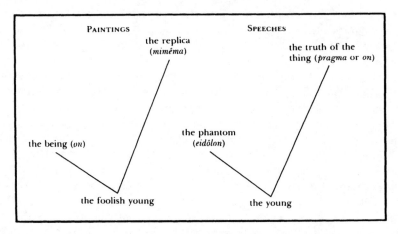

Figure 2

The stranger likens the distance of innocence to the distance of perspective. He likens the painter's duplication of reality to the sophist's replacement of reality. The painter images the beings the sophist makes. The young hear these phantoms of speech without experience; in time, many of them are compelled to encounter the beings nearer at hand and, in grasping them in all their vividness, abandon their earlier opinions, "so that the big or important things appear small, the easy hard, and all the apparitions in the speeches are turned topsy-turvy by the deeds which occur in their actions." The beings are, as we say, the tough or ugly facts of life, which force us to abandon our "ideals," but as the stranger makes plain, this inversion does not necessarily accompany an increase in understanding, for we encounter the beings and not the truth of the beings. Our later understanding is dictated by our experience, and our experience merely compels us to change a spoken apparition for a factual appearance. The stranger poses a dilemma. Either there is the distance of innocence (nothing but speeches) or the nearness of experience (nothing but suffering). We have seen the error of distance in the mathematician Theodorus, and we know of the error of experience from poetry. The stranger offers to try to move Theaetetus away from the phantoms of innocence and closer to the beings without inducing in him the delusions of experience. Is this possible? Socrates had tried in the *Theaetetus* to bring Theaetetus face to face with his ignorance; indeed, his maieutics had implied the most acute suffering on Theaetetus' part. But Theaetetus remained virginal to the end, and the stranger now tells Socrates that his effort was not only in vain but unnecessary. Theaetetus does not have to be corrupted in order to know.

If we consider the ugly and the beautiful in their relation to being, appearance, and phantom speeches, there are four possibilities for experience (fig. 3).

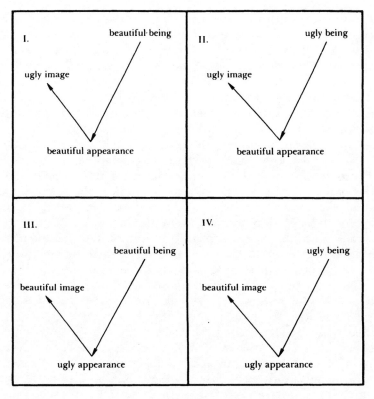

Figure 3

If the first or fourth were true, experience would be contrary to one's youthful convictions but in conformity with the truth, and if the second or third were true, one's youthful convictions would be true, only to be undermined by experience. The stranger says that the many come to believe in only the fourth possibility, and we can discount the first as not yet tried out in any city.[49] But it is not clear that the stranger wishes to handle Theaetetus as if the third possibility were true, so that he can, in bypassing the falseness of experience, move him directly from innocence to knowledge. There is a fifth possibility.

Being is neutral, neither ugly nor beautiful, but just as much one as the other. The stranger does not wish Theaetetus to experience it falsely as ugly, since in his innocence he is already much closer to it, whereas once his innocence were lost he could never be bent back toward the truth of the middle. The abstractness of the stranger's later speeches makes them look like a neutral version of a beautiful tale.

The stranger must now speak to Theaetetus and no longer to Socrates; they are to share in the common task of trapping the sophist (235a10, b7–8, d4), now that he has been driven into the class net of image making or mimetics. Once they have arrested the sophist, they are to turn him over to the royal speech, or speech of the king, for solely as hunters they do not know what to do with him.[50] The stranger implies that the *Sophist* is in the service of the *Statesman,* and he implies this at the very moment he and Theaetetus form a community of two. They are policemen acting under orders of an art which Theaetetus at least does not know. One of the most "metaphysical" discussions in Plato—its only rival is the central books of the *Republic*—occurs under political auspices. The political determines the discussion in a twofold way, one practical, the other "theoretical." Practically, Socrates is up on charges before the king-archon as the maker of gods;[51] theoretically, with the sophist's collapse as an acquisitor, whose acquisitions would be guided by his own knowledge of their use, the stranger's hunting too ceases to be independent. Theaetetus and the stranger are using instruments of division whose validity they have not tested, and on which the sophist, in his sliding from class to class, casts doubt. Their dialectics is as impure as Socrates'. The stranger gets them out of this difficulty. He distinguishes the sophist from themselves by declaring their own submission to the royal speech. The sophist is a beast of prey,[52] they are tame and law-abiding (cf. 216b3, 246c9, d6).

Now, if the sophist is a maker of the beings, and in particular of the greatest beings (the gods), they would have to show that the gods either are or are not, and that, no matter which, they are not what the sophist says they are. This they do not do. No being whatsoever is examined first hand, for the stranger says that he will not let Theaetetus experience any being. A hands-off account of the beings, then, must be attempted, but such an account seems impossible. What assurance do they have of their own ground if the evidence for it is not self-evident? Their assurance is not knowledge but the authority of the *Statesman.* Its authority is the substitute for the *Philosopher,* which the stranger slates third and which Plato does not write down. The stranger will soon tell Theaetetus that the sophist has always perplexed him; he as much as tells him that together they will not solve their problem. They establish the being of not being without knowing what being is, and the possibility of sophistry is proved prior to the possibility of philosophy, even though the sophist as imitator must be parasitic on the philosopher. And yet the *Sophist,* if it falls short of complete clarity, brings out into the open the problem of being. It is through the problem of not being that the problem of being gets known.

The stranger appears to catch sight of two kinds of mimetics; but the sought-for *idea,* that of the sophist, to which of the two it belongs, eludes him. He sees one to be eikastics; it assigns to each what is fitting according to the symmetries of the paradigm. Theaetetus believes all imitators try to do this. The stranger cites those who sculpt or paint any of the big deeds. "Should they give back the simply true proportions of the beautiful things, the upper segments, you know, would appear smaller than they should and the lower bigger, because we see the upper from a distance and the lower near at hand. Accordingly, they dismiss the truth, and work at producing in their images not the proportions that are but these that seem to be beautiful." The appearance looks like the beautiful because it is sighted from an unfair vantage point. But inasmuch as the appearance, if one had the ability to see it adequately, would not even look like what one says it looks like, it is an apparition or *phantasma,* and the art of making it is phantastics. Eikastics has nothing to do with the beautiful, for the paradigm can be either ugly or beautiful; it simply re-presents the paradigm. But phantastics necessarily involves the beautiful, for if perspectival distortion were left uncorrected, the parts of the copy would look ill-proportioned, and if the paradigm were itself ill-proportioned, the copy might then either re-present it in its ugliness or by chance present the ugly as beautiful, contrary to the intention of the artisan. Neither eikastics nor phantastics has the slightest trace in them of the spurious. Eikastics assumes knowledge of what is perceived, phantastics knowledge of the perceiver as well.

The stranger's dichotomy has let him down: sophistry cannot be either eikastics or phantastics in speech. In either case, it would be knowledge of what is, but with this difference: sophistry would display even deeper knowledge as phantastics than as eikastics, for it would include the knowledge of soul. The stranger already spoke of the perspective of innocence, by means of which the young swallow speeches that do not correspond to "what is," as later experience understands what is. The art of making these speeches is a poor sort of phantastics, for it does not forestall the disillusionment which comes with experience. Only a city which took elaborate precautions against experience, even to the point of banishing the images of experience, could rest content with this phantastics. But to present a series of images in speech, each set of which would correspond to stages of experience, is none other than the aim of elementary education, and particularly of moral education. The illusions of its images are an indispensable part of such an education, and if this is sophistry, every city and every father could only pray for its existence.

When the stranger returns to mimetics at the end of the dialogue, he assumes that it has been settled that sophistry is a kind of phantastics (cf. 239c9); he thereby avoids giving any example of eikastics in speech. A precisely drawn square or cube would illustrate eikastics in deed; but a poorly drawn geometric figure would much better serve to remind the pupil that geometry is not about that which the teacher draws in the sand. Indeed, a precisely drawn figure truly exemplifies phantastics, for it deceives the pupil into identifying the drawn with the intended figure and thus, in taking into account the pupil's need for clarity and distinctness, works against the difference between the aesthetic and the noetic straight line. The closer the image comes to the original, the more illusory would be the result.

This is perhaps a minor difficulty, but to which class of image making do Theaetetus' likenesses in the *Theaetetus* belong? It cannot be eikastics, for he gave to all dimensionless numbers two dimensions (cubes). Is it, then, phantastics? If we grant, for argument's sake, that a square and a rectangle are eikastic images respectively of nine and six, then the square, whose side is the square root of six, would be the *phantasma* of the oblong, for though it does not look like the oblong in its proportions, it looks as much like six as the oblong does. Perhaps, however, it would be safer to say that no art controls Theaetetus' image making. What, then, is eikastics in speech? Is eikastics in speech really possible? We should be back in our initial perplexity about the stranger's way if we said that the sophist as hunter is such an image. The sophist showed up as a hunter (221d13), but the stranger did not read it correctly as a sign of the sophist's art of image making but as an image of the sophist's art of enticing rich young men into his lair. He thought he was practicing eikastics in speech when in fact he was looking at one of the sophist's disguises. The stranger did not take into account the effect his own hunting of the sophist had on his understanding of the sophist, to say nothing of the resemblance Socrates' erotics bears to sophistry.

If something beautiful, which is to be imaged, is not in itself big, but an image bigger than "life-size" is to be made, then phantastics distorts the image in order that it appear true. But if something big were beautiful, an eikastic image of it would give a true picture of it which was false, since the image would not be corrected for perspective. The stranger, then, points to this principle and problem: the big by itself never comes to light as beautiful. Almost all good poets are makers of images and not of *phantasmata*, for they present what lies near at hand, the experiences of soul, just as they are in their nearness; but the experiences of soul thereby loom larger in the whole than they should. The most obvious sign of this distortion is the absence in tragedy of the representative of wisdom, for no one would say that the chorus of Sophocles' *Oedipus Tyrannus* is wise.

If the gods are big as well as beautiful, eikastics would present the gods as big and ugly; if the gods are big and ugly, eikastics might unwittingly present them as big and beautiful. If phantastics is employed, its *phantasma* of the gods could be of two kinds. If the gods are anthropomorphic, phantastics would make an image, like Phidias' Athena Parthenos, which if seen up close would be ugly, and if seen from the floor of the Parthenon would look as beautiful as she is. But if the gods are not anthropomorphic and yet beautiful, phantastics, in making an anthromorphic image of them, would indeed make them look as beautiful as they are, even though the proportions of the *phantasmata* would not be the proportions of the gods. Socrates once went so far as to declare that no living being is in itself beautiful, and only geometric figures are not relatively beautiful but always beautiful in themselves by nature.[53] So if a god were like a circle of infinite radius, his semblance could be a colossal statue of a beautiful animal, whose *phantasma* would have a beauty that was strangely true.

We are forced to bring this suggestion to bear on the *Sophist* itself. We are reading a work of imitation. Has Plato exercised the eikastic or the phantastic art? If it is eikastics and we are reading a dialogue between two wise men, we are not reading it correctly unless we too are wise. But the dialogue is not between two wise men—the stranger does not know the answer, Theaetetus does not know the question. The stranger, moreover, has just told Theaetetus that he will now speak to him—as if this had not been true from the start—from his perspective of innocence, for if he does not at least start from where Theaetetus stands, Theaetetus cannot join him in the hunting. All Platonic dialogues are *phantasmata*. They are images of what is and what is biggest, which are made ill-proportioned in themselves in order to appear perfectly proportioned. To whom, then, do they appear perfectly proportioned? The time spent on the angler is out of all proportion to his importance, but the time could be neither less nor more if Theaetetus were to understand anything. The stranger practices phantastics. If Plato wrote it down as it took place, do we read an eikastic speech? From the outside, before we reflect on what is being said, it is such an image, but as soon as we see it as a conversation between an ex-Parmenidean and a young mathematician, it becomes a *phantasma*—the difference between our own starting point and theirs. As we correct for their starting point, we correct for our own, and begin to rewrite the dialogue in its true proportions. What are its true proportions?

The *Sophist* is about the sophist, but the sophist, according to Socrates, is a *phantasma* of the philosopher. We stand, it seems, at the proper distance from the *Sophist* when its apparent beauty reflects the real beauty of philosophy. But is philosophy beautiful?[54] If it is not wisdom but forever incomplete, must it not necessarily be ugly, no matter how beautiful it is made to appear? This is only one perplexity. There is another. The stranger is perplexed before an art—phantastics—which Plato seems to have, but Plato cannot knowingly make a distorted image of what is, in order that what is can appear as what is, unless he knows what is. The *Sophist* is a riddle; if Plato knows the answer to the riddle, he can wrap it up as enigmatically as he wants. But if the *Sophist* is a riddle, to which Plato no more than the stranger knows the answer, can Plato have an art whose ground is ignorance? Platonic phantastics is the art of making thinking manifest and therefore immanifest, but thinking is the soul's silent conversation with itself as question and answer. To know how phantastics is possible is to know how thinking is possible, in which the soul is the same as itself when it is other and other when it is the same.

VIII. Lying
(236c9–239a12)

The truly wonder-working sophist fled to a class from which he cannot be extricated, for even prior to the problem of eikastics and phantastics is that of image making. There are two kinds of nonbeing: the nonbeing of image and the nonbeing of *phantasma*, which is of the nonbeing of image. The sophist can defend himself in two ways. The image cannot be distinguished from the being of which it is an image either because to be means to be like or because the *phantasma* is being, as Socrates had Theaetetus bring forth in the *Theaetetus*. If both of these defenses break down, the sophist is not helpless. His opponents must either allow not being to be or, following Parmenides, forbid it. In the first case, the sophist will say that, since they have shown that the imitations of the beings are beings, which are as much as the others, he must be a knower of beings; and in the second, his imitations are not, the art of imitation is not, and so he must know the beings, for if he knows nothing he cannot deceive (instruct) anyone.

The stranger might be thinking something of the sort when he reiterates his bafflement. Theaetetus says, "It looks like it (*eoiken*)." The stranger pounces on this *eoiken* (cf. 222a4): "Are you really then giving your consent because you recognize it, or did a kind of swing draw you along to a quick consent, now that you have grown accustomed to it by the *logos*?" Both Theaetetus and the stranger really are in a perplexity, and if Theaetetus had recognized it, he would not have said *eoiken*. Theaetetus knows from his first dialogue with Socrates the perplexity of false opinion, but he does not know the perplexity of image. His failure to know it makes him be the image of the perplexity of image. His *eoiken* is an expression of an artless image. Theaetetus is like someone who yawns in response to the yawn of another: he is not really as worn out (*apeirêkenai*) by the perplexity (*aporia*) as the stranger says he himself is (242a8).[55] His innocence makes him blessed.

Parmenides has long barred the way the stranger and Theaetetus already are on. He had drummed into the stranger from childhood that the nonbeings can never be. But unless nonbeing is, the stranger says, falsehood could never come to be a being. The stranger is in a dilemma. He will openly concede to Parmenides that total nonbeing is as impossible as total falsehood, but he does not make it as explicit that even if nonbeing partly is, falsehood does not automatically become possible. If the lie asserts what is not, and what-is-not is, the lie is true. The nonbeing of nonbeing would thus entail the impossibility of falsehood, and the being of nonbeing its truth. Obviously, the establishment of nonbeing's being cannot establish the truth of falsehood.[56]

The being of nonbeing cannot be understood atomistically, as if being and nonbeing were simply put together—for somewhere in the compound a nonbeing which wholly is not would be—anymore than falsehood can be understood as a juxtaposition of truth and falsehood. The penetration, therefore, of being into nonbeing must be total; every bit of nonbeing must be infected with being and vice versa. This interpenetration, however, of being and nonbeing not only seems to prevent any speech from being wholly true or wholly false, but to destroy the very possibility of division, as the stranger has so far practiced it. The sophist can only be caught at the price of losing the way to catch the sophist. The being of nonbeing in the Anaxagorean conglomerate of being and nonbeing cannot simultaneously be exhibited with the exhibition of the sophist. The sophist's being makes the sophist unknowable. Parmenides seems to have spoken truly.

Parmenides' argument against the being of nonbeing, as the stranger presents it, is in three parts, of which the last is more devastating than the second, and the second than the first. One, number, *logos* are successively the themes. Parmenides seems to have started with a distinction between being and human understanding. From the self-evident fact that the negative is exclusively human—not here, not now, not this—he drew the conclusion that it can have no part in being: a goddess informs Parmenides. The difference between being and not being comes to light in the stranger's first question and answer. The name "not being" is to be referred to what? It cannot be referred to being or what is. Whereas not being presents itself at once in speech as a name for which a "reality" must be found, being in speech is apparently not understood as belonging exclusively to speech: being is the only name that cannot solely be a name. There cannot be nothing. Being in speech shows itself as something and not as being: "We speak on each occasion this "something" for being, for to speak it (something) alone by itself, as if it were naked and isolated from all the beings, is impossible." In order for the name not being to enter into a speech, a something must first be found for it. But being is already present in speech as a something. Being always clothes "something"; being never leaves "something" destitute. Just as Socrates had implied that not to know is to be naked,[57] so the stranger implies that speech is never without being. There are no "bare speeches."

Now to speak something, which is to say something meaningful, must of necessity be to speak at least some one. The stranger then interprets Theaetetus' assent to this statement: "For you will declare that 'something' is the sign of one, 'somethings' (dual) of two, and 'some' (masculine or feminine plural) of many." The stranger does not place 'one' on the level of 'being' and 'something'; he does not ask whether 'one' is always among the beings,[58] and therefore whether 'something' must always refer to 'one'. The meaning of something is one, but its reference is being. Something is not the equivalent to one, but whatever else 'something' is a sign of, it must at least be a sign of one. A place is thus left open for nonbeing. If something is that by means of which one is made known, could not nothing be that by means of which being is made known? The best city of the *Republic* is in speech and not in deed, and yet it is in its nonbeing that by means of which and solely by means of which political things are made known. Accordingly, the beautiful *phantasma* of the colossal statue of Athena would be that by means of which and solely by means of which the beauty of Athena could be made known. We can therefore ask, Even if god is not, is he that by means of which and solely by means of which man can be made known? Socrates' question to Theodorus, whether he had unknowingly introduced a god into their gathering, was none other than this question.

That the being of nonbeing would entail that in speaking nothing or talking nonsense (*legein ouden*) one would still be speaking, even though speaking must always be speaking something, does not complete the perplexity of nonbeing's *logos*. The first and greatest perplexity involves the very principle of its own *logos*. It is one thing that nonbeing cannot enter speech in general, it is quite another that it cannot have its own speech. The stranger distinguishes between the minimal meaning of a speech (one) and its minimal structure (number). Any one of the beings might be added to being, but it is impossible that any of the beings be added to not being. Every being is in principle countable: it must be possible that it be one of a countable many. This is the most general condition of being. The converse is equally true. If there is a countable many, each of them is a being. The speech "nonbeing is," is thus impossible, for the stranger implies that speaking can never be apart from counting, and an account (*logos*) is at least two. Whenever we speak, therefore, we are either making a tally or assuming that a tally can be·made. "Nonbeings" cannot be told unless the not beings are countable, and only beings are countable. "Nonbeing is one" is as impossible as "nonbeing is." "Nonbeing is one" looks analytic: the one of nonbeing's form is declared to be one. The stranger, however, says that this can only hold if we can also say, "Being and nonbeing are two", but number is always of being.

The stranger, we might say, is confusing two different things. That $0 + 1 = 1$ means that the sum-operation cannot be carried through might be granted, but that '0' + '1' = 2 is false, where ' ' means the concept, does not follow. Nonbeing, however, is not a concept, for a concept has no plural. We would, moreover, be denying what the stranger and Theaetetus lay down: "All number is of the beings." If the premise is changed to read, "All beings are countable but not everything countable are beings," then the perplexity surely disappears. So deeply rooted among Theaetetus' convictions is the principle that only beings are countable, that the stranger can destroy Parmenides in the same way: 'being' and 'one' cannot be two names if there is nothing except one (244c8–10). The stranger assumes that *logos* is atomic; it is nothing but its parts without any bond between them. What *pros* means exactly, which the stranger compounds with several verbs to express addition or attachment, is now left unclarified: *prosgignesthai* (238a5, 7), *prospherein* (238b3), *prostithenai* (238c1, 239b9), *prosarmottein* (238c6), *prosaptein* (238e8, 239a3). The dialogue, in so far as it turns on the question of what *logos* is, moves toward replacing this *pros* with *syn: logos* is a weaving together (*symplokê*) rather than a juxtaposition of parts.

The stranger now gives the final twist to the argument. To say that nonbeing is irrational, is (1) contradictorily to declare it to be one both in itself and in the singular verb "is," (2) to attach "is" to it, and

(3) to make a speech before (*pros*) it as if it were one. No *logos*, then, can be uttered about nonbeing; there cannot even be the *logos* that no *logos* can be uttered about nonbeing. Nonbeing seems to be the Parmenidean way of speaking of the Heracliteans, for the stranger's conclusions have the same character as Socrates' refutation of total motion. And yet motion was established as soon as Socrates distinguished two kinds of motion: will not being cease to be irrational in the same way? Eikastics and phantastics seem to be either themselves the distinction or to point to the distinction required. Being would then belong to not being as *logos* to image and apparition.

The doubleness of any speech about an image—"Here is a picture" and "Here is Theaetetus" united in "Here is a picture of Theaetetus"—suggests that the speech about nonbeing might undergo a similar doubleness, of which the one which says that nonbeing is irrational would correspond to the recognition of a picture as a picture; while the other, which signifies the being of nonbeing, would correspond to the recognition of Theaetetus in the picture. Mistakenly, then, the stranger would be forcing nonbeing into the *eidos* of one to which it only seems to belong (cf. 239a10). If, however, not being is not one, it cannot be two in being double without being many. Double must be neither one nor many. To persuade a mathematician of this would not be easy.

He lied, the stranger says, in saying that the second and not the third argument was the greatest perplexity. The stranger takes back the *logos* of nonbeing, but not the fact of his lying. He speaks as if nonbeing deceived him and was the cause of his lying. He 'personifies' nonbeing thrice: (1) "Nonbeing puts its refuter in a perplexity"; (2) "In attaching 'is' (to nonbeing) were we not conversing with it as one?"; (3) "In saying it was irrational (*alogon*), unsayable (*arrêton*), and unutterable (*aphthenkton*), I was making my speech as if in the presence of (*pros*) one." The stranger does not now say that nonbeing is unthinkable (*adianoêton*, 238c10, cf. 238b7). He implies that nonbeing's resistance to speech does not entail that it has the power to annihilate thought, for otherwise it would not even have come to light as a perplexity. Nonbeing makes known the difference between silent conversing, which is thinking, and speaking out loud. The stranger's conversing with nonbeing as one is not the same as his thinking it through (*dianoeisthai*). To think is to question. To question is to be in a perplexity. Nonbeing causes perplexity for either its advocate or its prosecutor, but in allowing for neither its advocacy nor its prosecution, it causes one to doubt or be double (*distazein*) and recognize both sides (*amphignoein*). The principle of nonbeing is to be the cause of perplexity. It somehow is the ground of thinking itself.

IX. Imaging
(239b1–241b3)

The stranger mistook the bigger for the biggest perplexity about not being, but Theaetetus does not see it and asks the stranger to speak more plainly. "There's no need in my case," he says, "to look for what you call greater clarity," for the biggest perplexity is that not being cannot be presented as perplexing without perplexity. So even after he has made this perplexity more plain, the stranger confesses his own permanent defeat before it, and urges Theaetetus to strain with all the vigor of youth to utter something correct about not being (cf. 239d5). "I would in that case," Theaetetus answers, "have an overwhelmingly strange eagerness to try my hand at it, if when I see you undergoing this sort of thing I myself should try it." Theaetetus does not obey the stranger; he is brought closer to the beings without experience (cf. 234e5, 239c9). His perplexity is the same and not the same as the stranger's. It is the same because had they speeches to express it, their speeches would not differ, and not the same because Theaetetus discounts the proverb "learning by suffering" and accepts the stranger's experience as authoritative for his own. His is a 'yawn-perplexity'; it is an image of the stranger's. As a 'natural' imitation, we can read off everything from it which we could from the original and still be wholly mistaken: we would not know its being (236d9).

Theaetetus presents in himself both the problem of image and the *ad oculos* proof of the being of nonbeing. He is, we must keep in mind, Socrates' look-alike. Socrates' question had made it impossible for the stranger to give the speech he knew by heart. If both what the stranger and Socrates say is true, the *genos* of the sophist must be distinguished from the sophistic *phantasma* of the true philosopher. The artless *phantasma* of the philosopher must be separated from the *phantasmata* of the sophist, for with his art the sophist is going to look like the sophistic *phantasma* of the philosopher. In duplicating the philosopher's *phantasma*, the sophist produces a yawn that is phenomenally indistinguishable from the real yawn. To bring Theaetetus closer to the beings without experience is impossible. When therefore Theaetetus wishes to hold on to the being of a semblance, he says it really (*ontôs*) is a semblance. "Really" expresses a feeling about being; it is a sign of experience and not of knowledge.

Theaetetus, asked what an image is, answers: "Plainly, we shall say, the images in bodies of water and mirrors, as well as paintings and sculptures and all the rest that doubtless are other things of the sort (*toiauta hetera*)." The form of Theaetetus' answer recalls what he first had said knowledge was. Not only does an incomplete enumeration serve for a single *logos,* but both enumerations fall into two parts. Do the natural images in water and mirrors correspond to the theoretical sciences—geometry, astronomy, logistics—as the artificial images of painting and sculpture seem to correspond to the productive arts? Theaetetus himself had used images in order to comprehend the infinity of surds; and whatever art made them, it was not painting, for Theaetetus agreed that Theodorus was not a painter in being a geometrician, even though he spoke of a Theodoran proof as a drawing or painting (*egraphe*).[59] The stranger now tries to remind Theaetetus of those images which are primarily in speech: "You are manifest, Theaetetus, you have not seen a sophist." The sophist, then, whom the stranger has so far presented to Theaetetus is himself an example of a phantom in speech, the making of which is due to the sophist's own competence.

Theaetetus had spoken of his own hearsay knowledge of the sophist when it came to the sophist's knowledge of all the divine things not manifest to the many: "This is, at any rate, spoken of them" (232c3). The sophist pretends that he knows nothing of sight, mirrors, or water, for he wants an answer that does not appeal to anything outside of speech. If images were only visible, the sophist would be a blind man asking about color,[60] but Theaetetus has forgotten that the paradigm of the image maker in deed was a paradigm for the image maker in speech, who in turn was not a self-proclaimed sophist like Protagoras but a discovery of the stranger's own *logos* (cf. 234d1). The sophist, whom Theaetetus has not seen and who seems to have his eyes shut or is even without them, can never either be seen or see. He is a construction. His being is as puzzling as the paradigm in speech of the good city. "Do you believe," Socrates asked Glaucon, "he is any the less a good painter who painted the sort of paradigm the most beautiful human being would be, and though he gave the painting everything in an adequate manner, was not able to prove that a man of the sort could also come to be?"[61] The sophist, in his total lying, is a paradigm of the ugliest human being, which came to be in the dialogue because of the necessity that sophistry be one art. Theaetetus believes that the sophist they are hunting is "real"; he is blessedly ignorant that the stranger is asking him to track down themselves.

Theaetetus admits that his second characterization of image entails a very strange entanglement of being with nonbeing. To be really an image means that the image in its being is an image of another, whereas really to be means to be in its being a being, and not in any sense the property of another.[62] An image cannot be known as an image if that of which it is an image is unknown, but it looks as if we do not need to know whether that which really is, is wholly itself or not. The beings do not at once raise questions, images do: what makes the beings, of which the images are, not be images too? The answer to the question What is being? should lie in that which the being does not share with the image. Theaetetus, however, used "another of the sort" twice, once to express the sort of things that belong to the class (*eidos*) of images, and then to express the character of image itself. If the resemblance which qualifies images in mirrors to be classed as images is the same as the resemblance which an image has to a being, then (1) every class is constituted by an element in each member which is nonbeing, (2) the image belongs to the same class as that of which it is an image, and (3) the being of the simply true is not a qualification for its membership in the class. So if "another of the sort" were univocal, what causes X to be an image of Y, would cause Y to be of the same type as Z; and if the types, or *eidê*, were causes, there would be no images unless there were *eidê*, and no *eidê* unless there were images.

An image in deed most obviously separates the 'matter' from the 'form' of that of which it is an image. If this separation were the same as that which occurs when several things are put together in one class, the class would be the perfect image, and to be would mean to be like. The "another of the sort" of image, therefore, cannot be the same as the "another of the sort" of class inclusion. The difference, one might say, lies in the fact that in class inclusion, the "other of the sort" is not naturally posterior to that from which it is "other" and yet "of the sort." The temporal priority of the paradigm would seem to distinguish it from its image. But if every member of a class obtains its likeness to another through the class, and 'through the class' means nothing but a relation through likeness, then every member of the class is an image of the class, and the image-character of class membership would once more be the same as the being of image. The class of being would be solely constituted by nonbeings.

An image in deed separates 'matter' from 'form', but only to replace the matter of the paradigm with another matter, and even an image in speech has its own matter, the stream of sound that issues through the mouth and in which *logos* appears as the image of thought.[63] The *logos* of image is itself an image of a thought about the species of images. If the *logos* is true, it must be "another of the sort" of the thought which is, though an image, true. How is this possible? What is the matter of thought which speech replaces with sound? Or does thought have no matter, and *logos* arbitrarily have an audible component? But if thought is matterless, speech is always enigmatic. It can only be the concealing clothes of thought and never the truth, for inasmuch as sound in principle always accompanies *logos,* what is not sound in *logos* could not image thought. Even if thought were like the breadthless line of the geometers, and the 'movement' of thought comparable to the construction of a straight line between two points, thought would still need a ground that could keep its two 'points' apart. The form of these two points or moments is question and answer, which together are nothing other than thinking. The sophist, it would seem, has slipped into a place which indifferently serves for the making of images and the discovery of kinds.

Theaetetus' definition of image entails that not being somehow is; the stranger's definition of false opinion entails that things that in no way are (*ta mêdamôs onta*) somehow are. The parallelism between the arguments that come respectively from the two definitions extends even to the number of exchanges. Theaetetus, however, makes a mistake: instead of saying that one must opine that the nonbeings somehow are, he says that nonbeings must somehow be. He thus blurs the difference between a semblance (*eikôn*) and an illusion (*phantasma*). The true perplexity is that true opinion constitutes any class of beings by the same criterion it uses to recognize the nonbeing of an image, and the nonbeing of an image which is looks exactly like the false, and that is that which is not. But Theaetetus believes the perplexity to consist in the impossibility of our saying anything, not about that which is, but about that which is not. They are not the same perplexity.

It does not follow that if they can show that one can speak about nonbeing, they thereby separate false opinion from the being of image. To speak about nonbeing without contradiction is not to distinguish between the nonbeing which is really so and the nonbeing which only is in terms of opinion or speech. The way in which, "Theaetetus flies," is a false speech is not the way in which it is an image in speech of pre-Socratic philosophy. The rest of the *Sophist* is the stranger's exploitation of Theaetetus' failure to see the difference.

X. BEING
(241b4–250d4)

If the stranger and Theaetetus have gone through a small part of the almost endless perplexities the sophist hides behind, the sophist is coeval with the philosopher, and the completeness of the *Sophist* only apparent. And yet, despite the stranger's certainty that the sophist will elude them, Theaetetus agrees that they should not give up if they can by even a little increase their hold on the sophist (cf. 240e4). Partial clarity about a part will now content Theaetetus. This is the first of three concessions the stranger requests Theaetetus to make. The second is that he is not to suppose that the stranger is committing patricide. If Theaetetus has no qualms, he can kill Parmenides or his father's *logos* without committing a crime. A crime ceases to be a crime if its only witness does not denounce it. As his third request, the stranger asks Theaetetus not to believe him to be crazy if contrary to his own exhaustion before the problem of the sophist he renews his attack on the problem. Not even the refutation of Parmenides, the stranger implies, plus his own self-contradiction, are good for more than a partial solution.

The three concessions exactly parallel the three themes of the stranger's argument against the being of nonbeing. They were one, number, and *logos*. To the contradiction of a *logos* about that which has no *logos*, there corresponds the stranger's madness in contradicting himself; to the assertion that to be means to be countable and to be countable means to be, there corresponds the denial of Parmenides, whose understanding of being seems to preclude that assertion; and to the impossibility that nonbeing can be if it does not signify one and is not something, there corresponds the paradox that something can be known of a part if the whole to which it belongs is unknowable. The correspondence in the three cases is not of the same kind. The first and third of the stranger's requests contradict the first and third of his Parmenidean arguments, but the second request agrees with the convertibility of to be and to be countable. Theaetetus cannot share the reluctance of the stranger to kill Parmenides because as a mathematician he cannot have Parmenides as his father. The premise of his own science disposes of the oneness of being. That this premise is not in turn subject to doubt entails, as the stranger says, that they will have to force both not being to be in some respect and being not to be somehow. The assault on Parmenides is in a sense against the grain of being.

The first concession Theaetetus makes the stranger allows one to formulate the perplexity of being and nonbeing more exactly. The articulation of a kind requires the articulation of the whole. A part by itself is only partially knowable. Consequently, it cannot be represented strictly as a part but only as a part apart from the whole. Only by depriving the part of that which is essential to it as a part does it become partially intelligible. If, however, to be means to be a part, it is only by depriving something of its being that one understands partially. The apartness of a part is the part as nonbeing. Now the Parmenidean subsection found the commonality of being, as opposed to nonbeing, in number. Number tells us what things are together and not apart. Number therefore cannot be applicable to any part in its apartness. The speech of nonbeing cannot be arithmetical, for if its oneness and countability were the conditions for its being in a speech and not involving its refuter in contradiction, then these conditions, once met, would make it irrefutable, since these conditions are the criteria that the beings, and only the beings, now meet.

Theaetetus, who looked like the embodiment of moderation before Socrates showed up his madness, encourages the stranger to embark on an enterprise which the stranger knows is bound to fail. Instead of punishing Theaetetus for his hidden presumption, as Socrates tried to do in the *Theaetetus,* the stranger makes use of it. The image of hunting has had its effect. It has appealed to Theaetetus' latent madness while preserving his appearance of sobriety. The stranger has hit upon a mean between Socrates' and Theodorus' contrary interpretations of Theaetetus' nature, through which Theaetetus can approach the beings without ever losing his innocence (cf. 243c6). The stranger himself, however, has undergone the philosopher's equivalent to the disillusionment of the many. Parmenides' speeches, which included the paternal admonition to stay clear of nonbeing, gave him the illusion when young that he understood what he meant, but in time he discovered that he did not understand, for there were others who spoke of being as two, three, or many. The stranger's direct encounter with being and nonbeing resulted in a permanent condition of perplexity.

The stranger's condition is the philosophical counterpart to vulgar cynicism, but as a favor to Theaetetus (cf. 218a5), he will abandon his experience and adopt the innocence of Theaetetus. The perspective of innocence plus the *phantasma* of innocence are joined together to produce a partial solution. The stranger's condescension, which shows his inconsistency to be his moderation, seems to be the alternative to Socrates' maieutics, whose practice required that Theaetetus suffer in order that he become as barren as Socrates. But the know-nothing Socrates proved to be ironic: Theaetetus would not accept his knowledge as knowledge. How, then, do Socrates and the stranger differ? Is the stranger's concession to Theaetetus' mathematics any more than Socrates' discovery of Theaetetus' beauty? Neither is grounded through a *logos.* Theaetetus' defective understanding of soul is of a piece with his trust in the convertibility of being and number. Theaetetus, we can venture to guess, will no more with the stranger than he did with Socrates come to an understanding of wholes, but the stranger, unlike Socrates, will give him something that looks as if it can wholly take their place.

The stranger presents the problem of being in two parts. In the first, he reports and refutes the view of the myth-making philosophers, among whom he includes Parmenides, Heraclitus, and Empedocles; in the second, he himself reports on a mythical battle between giants and gods. He does not say about either the gods or giants that they tell myths; he implies that the first group's failure consists in their not taking part in their own myths. They set themselves far too high above the many, altogether indifferent, as they are, as to whether the many follow them or not, so that the ignorance of the many introduces a perspectival distortion into their words. Their words, the stranger implies, might be after all eikastic images of the truth. But since they do not correct for "us," they unwittingly give us *phantasmata*, which we can never know whether we are reading correctly (cf. 243b7).[64] All the philosophers are open to the jest of the Thracian slave-girl, for what is most at their feet is being. Regardless of the extraterrestrial station from which they finally spoke, they had to start from where we still are. The common starting point of "them" and "us" is betrayed by the language they use, which undergoes a surreptitious alteration in intention while it remains ostensibly the same. They speak of marriage, children and nurture, friendship, hatred and war, all of which indicate human, or more precisely, political things we believe we understand. But the beings, they say, and not men are the agents or patients of these events, and here we no longer can even believe we understand them.

The philosophers are artless sophists. They speak to us as if they were legislator-poets who expected that we receive as opinion what they themselves have as knowledge. The stranger speaks of "the Eleatic tribe *chez nous* (*para hêmin*)," as if his education in philosophy were the indoctrination every city imposes on its citizens from childhood (cf. 229d1–4). He tacitly contrasts himself with Socrates, of whom it could not be said that he belongs to the Attic tribe of philosophers,[65] as his imminent trial proves. The stranger, because he is now a stranger, can get away with patricide. His deliberate adoption of Theaetetus' innocence simultaneously liberates himself from dogma. His phantastics is closer to the true beginning of philosophy than any eikastics.

The stranger is at first very unfair to Parmenides, who, he pretends, said no more about being than Xenophanes and did not in fact first raise the problem of being. Parmenides was the first who realized that his predecessors were not speaking of that which they believed they were speaking of. "Water is," asserts that water is, but it does not say what makes water be water. Thales identified the subject without identifying the predicate, for had he done so, he would have had to say that water is because "is" is water. In all statements about the beings, being was neutral to and in no way involved with the beings. The being of the hot does not affect or get affected by the hot. Existence is neither heated nor chilled. If all things are composed of atoms, atoms alone are, and there are n atoms, then all things are n beings; but if atom$_p$ is and is nothing but being (*on*), and atom$_q$ is and is nothing but being, then atom$_p$ and atom$_q$ are one; whereas if atom$_p$ is so much being (the nth part of *on*), then *on* is not what atom$_p$ is, and *on* is again one. The pre-Parmenideans did not say that, for example, earth and water are what make the beings beings; they said that earth and water are the beings. But being is then neither earth nor water, nor earth and water. If, however, earth and water are causes of the beings, they would be in a way in which the beings are not, and the being of both the causes of the beings and of the beings themselves would be unintelligible in terms of either. Parmenides' being, therefore, is not as a noetic one on the same level as the beings of an aesthetic plurality. The stranger later acknowledges this, but he now begins from the standpoint of Theaetetus for whom the first question is always how many, and the impossibility of obtaining in a recounting the number which was originally counted—either one more or one less—suffices to destroy any understanding of the whole.

Of the five myths the stranger mentions, the first three are uninspired. The beings are three, two, or one. We are reminded that Socrates' question had also been numerical: Are sophist, statesman, philosopher one, two, or three? Are they the same question? The problem of being had originally been raised because the five or six appearances of the sophist must be due to one art, by means of which the sophist knew or seemed to know five different things: divine things immanifest to the many, divine and manifest things, being and becoming, political things, and all the arts. He who speaks of two beings points to the manifest pairs of moist and dry or hot and cold, whose betrothal and marriage are arranged by the speaker himself. The Eleatic tribe who say that all the so-called things are one would have to speak, as we have noted, of being and becoming. Of the two inspired myths, both take a safer course and say that what is is both one and many. The tauter strain of the Heracliteans maintains chaos and order simultaneously—"War is the king of all"—whereas the laxer muses of Empedocles, who let chaos and order alternate, show their affinity to the arts in Eryximachus' speech in the *Symposium*, with its simultaneous praise of Eros and medicine.

The stranger has put five very different myths into one class; they solely belong together because they speak of numbers, not because Heraclitus and Parmenides agree with each other about the one and the many. He seems to imply, however, that the sophist borrows from each philosophical myth its own peculiar language and then reapplies it to the things of which it seems to speak. The philosophers, in their contempt for us, neglect to clarify what they intend, but the sophist, in his desire to make money, takes what they say at face value and therefore looks omniscient. The philosophers lend themselves to this kind 'of abuse because their speeches are willy-nilly *phantasmata*. They are superior to the sophist only in intention. They therefore look like nonomniscient or defective sophists. Apart from what they say in private about being and becoming, the sophists sound as if they possess the political art, for not only would no one pay them unless they professed it, but the language in which the philosophers couched their thoughts was through and through political. Being (*ousia*) first meant property, and to be a cause to be guilty.[66]

When Protagoras said that man was the measure of all things (*khrê-mata*), he spoke, wittingly or not, the language of law, for man is the measure of all money and goods (*khrêmata*). The single art which ran through the first four or five arts in which the stranger successively trapped the sophist, was moneymaking. The sophist's unity consists in an art which knows how to turn everything into money, but the science without which there would be no money or moneymaking is the science of number. The science of number, therefore, looks as if it is the universal science, which would transform the stranger's class of philosophical myths, each of which speaks the precise language of number, into the true class of knowledge. But this science, when allied with the political language of the myths, emerges as moneymaking. The sophist's moneymaking unites in a monstrous *phantasma* the political and the theoretical elements of which the philosophical myths are composed. Protagoras' speech is the paradigm of the sophistic art.

The stranger pretends to speak directly to the myth-making philosophers seven times, and Theaetetus sometimes takes their part in answering and sometimes maintains his own. The stranger asks three questions of those who say that the beings are two, and three of those who say that being is only one. The central question, What does 'being' mean? though directed to the dualists, is equally applicable to the monists. The argument with the dualists is over as soon as the stranger presents the three possible ways of interpreting them; the argument with the monists takes much longer and seems much less cogent. Since the problem of being comes up because of the problem of nonbeing, the stranger seems to imply that nonbeing, if it could only be in some sense, would render the problem of being soluble. The dualists are first asked what they mean when they say that both and each are. Inasmuch as each is separately what they are together, and what they are together each is separately, there is no necessity that they be together. Neither is a part. It therefore follows that if each is being, the whole is a third, but if either is being, both are not in the same way, and there is only one; or if both are being, they are again one. The most obvious way out of this difficulty is the atomists': only body is, but nonbeing is another principle. The atomists were the first to distinguish between beings and principles, for body too must cease to be being and become a principle. Two principles, then, neither of which is a being, combine to produce the beings. But the necessary consequence of this is monism, for if we let O represent nonbeing or void, and N and Z two different atoms,[67] then one being, whose formula is NONON, and another, whose formula is ZOZ, will be separated by void, and both beings will be one being whose formula is NONONOZOZ.

Parmenidean being is subject to two different lines of argument; the first corresponds to the question the stranger had just raised about two beings, whether only one of them is; the second, which speaks of the whole but means the sum, corresponds to the question whether the two beings only are as both. Having shown that two beings necessarily reduce to one, the stranger asks into the meaning of this one. He asks whether being is a predicate like one. If it is, there are two predicates of something (*ti*); but it seems that there cannot be even one, for if either being or one is a predicate of and different from *ti*, then again there are two. And if neither being nor one is a predicate of *ti*, either must be the same as *ti*, and *ti* is either nothing, or it too is a predicate, and there is a predicate of a predicate. The possible range of the predicate must be shown to be exactly the same as *ti;* but the coincidence of their ranges makes the predicate no longer a predicate but at most a proper name.

To say that being is one is no more than to say that Athena is Minerva, whose reference is a goddess. Neither being nor one reveals anything by itself, but any showing on the Parmenideans' part that being or one is revealing and is not just a name will necessarily introduce plurality. They cannot, for example, distinguish between the being in "something is" and the being in "something is one," for if the first says that something exists, and the second that one is a property of this something, existence is not exhausted by being, since otherwise "one" would not be a property of something unless "existence" entailed "one." But it is something and not existence that entails one: even if something were not, it would still be one. The Parmenideans, therefore, must either admit nonbeing along with any distinction they make or confess that their speech about being is about nonbeing.[68]

The fragments of Parmenides' poem, as many have remarked, do not stress that to be means to be one: one is just one of the many things Parmenides has the goddess tell him about being.[69] Parmenides starts at a point prior to the stranger's argument, and he therefore remains to some extent unaffected by it. Men believe, or at least speak as if they believe, that "it is impossible" is not the same as "it is not," and likewise that "it is" is no more than the realization of "it is possible." But Parmenides saw that if to be means to be possible, it is a necessity that nonbeing be, for otherwise every possible being can be denied one by one until nothing would be left except nothing. However, since that is impossible if nothing comes from nothing, to be must mean to be necessary, and, again, since there is no aesthetic being which necessarily is, the being which is necessary is noetic. This being is the being to which the principle of noncontradiction points.[70] There is, however, a difficulty. The hypothetical denial of every contingent being assumes the being of every contingent being, none of which could have been brought into being by the one necessary being. The aesthetic must be if the noetic is to be discovered. Parmenides, therefore, would have to deny the movement of his own thought even as he was going on his journey, but his poem begins with his journey. We do not understand Parmenides.

The stranger first showed Theaetetus that the beings in their being are uncountable. If the hot and the cold are each a being, they are countable only if their difference is ignored—one apple and one orange are two fruits—so that in the counting neither the hot of the hot which is nor the cold of the cold which is can be counted. What one counts in each is the being (the "which is"). Being, then, is an abstraction from the "reality" of the hot, but it is absurd to regard being as an abstraction from being. The stranger then turned to the being which could in no sense lend itself to abstraction. This being, however, since it was only receptive to the label "being," suffered from the opposite of abstraction; its "reality" was too rich for being. But it is absurd to regard being as more than being. Being and precise speech are incompatible with one another. Their incompatibility arises from the double function of being, which cannot serve without equivocation for both the unit of counting and the counted.

From this point of view, Parmenides' move is all but inevitable, since precise speech seems necessary if being is one. Not only does precise speech turn out to be indistinguishable from arbitrary naming, but being cannot be a whole unless it is imprecisely spoken of. The stranger does not remark on it, but in the lines he quotes from Parmenides' poem, being is a whole because it resembles a sphere. Being, then, can be a whole if imprecisely understood, for to be affected by the one means to be one only in a sense. The whole, however, cannot be and yet be apart from being, for then being is not wholly itself; but if the whole is not, being cannot even come to be, let alone be, for that which has come to be (*to genomenon*) comes fully to term (*gegonen*) as a whole, and any definite many is a whole. In this last argument, the stranger casually introduces two principles which Theaetetus never challenges. The first, that sum and whole are the same, was due to Socrates' argument in the *Theaetetus;* the second, that becoming (*gig-nomenon* or *genesis*) and coming to be (*genomenon*) are the same, affects the course which the rest of the dialogue takes.[71]

The philosophers who speak mythically can say how many kinds of beings there are, but they cannot say what being is; whereas those who do not speak mythically can say what being is, but they cannot speak precisely; they cannot count the beings. Of this group the stranger himself speaks mythically, for he can count them as two kinds. He thereby implies that the problem of being is the apparent impossibility of combining a comprehensive account of being with a precise speaking of being.[72] To count is to speak mythically; to give an account is to speak imprecisely. The stranger's own myth puts together two unalterably opposed accounts of being; it therefore looks as if a reconciliation between the gods and the giants, in which each faction gives up something, would replace the myth with a *logos* about being that is simultaneously comprehensive and precise. That this does not happen, and yet the stranger solves the problem of nonbeing, is the riddle of the *Sophist.* The stranger shows not only that being is as perplexing as nonbeing, but apparently that it is the same kind of perplexity, for he says that there is hope that to whatever extent one of them comes to light the other will come to light. But if, as he also says, the sophist is hard to discern because he has run off to the darkness of nonbeing, while the philosopher is not easily seen because he resides in the region of being whose brilliance is blinding (253e8–254b2), then our being blinded by the light of being must be treated as if it were our blindness before nonbeing.

Because the resulting darkness is the same, though the reason is not, the stranger proposes to identify the absence of light with our incommensurability with the light. That which eludes us through its overwhelming us (being) is in its effect that which eludes us through our overwhelming it (nonbeing). The *logos,* which the stranger and Theaetetus are to push as decently as they can through the twin perplexity of being and nonbeing, seems to be an impossible compromise between their recent discovery that being 'involves' nonbeing if being is to be counted, and what they are about to discover, that nonbeing 'involves' being if being is to be known. On one hand, nonbeing brought the problem of being to light; nonbeing revealed number, for only with its help could the beings be numbered. Being, on the other hand, in its tension between body and "idea," will reveal soul (cf. 250b7). Number is the highest form that the eikastic can take; soul is the preserve of phantastics. The *Sophist* is a mixture of eikastics and phantastics, of innocence and experience, which itself represents the riddle of being.

In the *Theaetetus*, Socrates had presented the philosophical war as a battle between the armies of Heraclitus and Parmenides, between which Theodorus and himself were trapped; but the stranger presents a war between those who assert that to be means to be perceptible body and those who assert that to be means to be noetic "idea." Only after the stranger has refuted both does the issue become the unity of Motion and Rest. Insofar as the *Sophist* makes an advance over the *Theaetetus*, it is surely due to the stranger's introduction of the "friends of the ideas" and the giants, the first of whom Socrates did not mention, and the second Theaetetus found too repellent to consider. It strikes one at once that the gigantomachy does not involve as clear-cut an opposition as that between Motion and Rest, for the opposite of "to be means to be body," whether ensouled or not, is "to be means to be soul." That contrariety, at any rate, had been the stranger's own when he split the class of cathartics, and which Socrates had forced Theaetetus to accept in the *Theaetetus* the day before. Accordingly, though the giants are in themselves that which they say—being nothing but body they declare only body to be—the friends of the ideas, who would be the gods if the stranger's myth is to hold, are not identified, for they obviously cannot be what they say alone is.

That the gods are meant to be the friends of the ideas not only agrees in general with one's first impression about ideas—Eros is erotic, Justice is just—but it suits in particular the position of the *Sophist* in the heptad (the *Euthyphro* precedes it and raises just this question of the relation between ideas and gods) and brings Socrates' initial question to Theodorus back from its underground course. Socrates had questioned Theodorus' identification of the stranger and proposed instead that philosophers be treated as Homer's gods. They too were beings who were so far apart from their appearances as never to appear as they are in their being. The philosophers are above appearances. The stranger has now criticized one group of philosophers for our failure to understand them. He therefore is forced to make some of them appear in a way which is intelligible to us and especially to Theaetetus, and yet which is still in some conformity with their being. He cannot, however, do this if he does not employ phantastics, the very art he wishes to assign to the sophists. Since, in fact, the stranger has already proved Socrates' contention about the philosophers by looking exactly like the sophist he is looking for, it is inevitable that he end up by making a myth of his own. He too must cease to appear to be a hunter and become a maker.

The myth he makes differs from the eikastic myth of the precise philosophers. Theirs, to speak mythically, is generated unwittingly through their being above us, but the stranger's is contrived consciously and pulls Theaetetus into the picture. Theaetetus is pulled into the picture in order to put together two groups of philosophers who are in themselves apart. They are thus made into a whole that comprehends them. This comprehensive whole seems not to be subject to analysis, for it vanishes once the perspectival distortion that Theaetetus' presence adds is subtracted. Theaetetus' presence is simply a particular case of the presence of soul in the whole. The whole disappears if the soul is not taken into account, but the whole is elusive if the soul is accounted for. This is the problem of being.

The gigantomachy is obscure because while the giants drag everything down to earth out of the sky and the invisible, their opponents fight from somewhere above, from the vantage point of the invisible. The giants seem to be mistaken as to whom they are fighting, for the friends of the ideas have abandoned even the attempt at a cosmology if they do not defend the heavens with an interpretation of soul. There cannot be a war between a 'geology', which wants to be cosmology, and an 'ideology', which does not want to be an 'uranology'. In order to get the battle joined properly, the stranger would have to locate the one region which both sides claim for themselves. But the giants do not acknowledge becoming,[73] and though this is their opponents' name for body, the friends of the ideas neglect it. They apparently speak of bodiless kinds without ever looking at the embodied kinds they themselves call becoming. Whatever else these kinds are, they are not causes. One army, whose only weapon is brute force, stands opposed to another of speechmakers, who do not know they are on and of the earth. Socrates has surely not been for some time the captain of so self-ignorant an army, but Theaetetus and Theodorus are still enlisted in its ranks.

Theaetetus, who has met many of the giants, never even asks who their opponents are, or what they mean by noetic kinds. Presumably, he should understand them to mean being and nonbeing, likeness and unlikeness, the same and the other, one and number, the beautiful and the ugly, the good and bad—the very contraries, in short, which he himself told Socrates the soul without instruments examines by itself. The stranger, then, confronts Theaetetus with himself. He forces him to face up to the imprecision of the beautiful speech which Socrates, by appealing to the need for precise speech, had got him to utter the day before. Theaetetus is brought down to earth once more, but not entirely. He loses his "high" only to the point that the giants lose their terror for him. With the help of the stranger, he tames them in speech. They become law-abiding. The compromise of the

Sophist, by means of which the sophist can be put in his place, involves the law. Theaetetus believed that Socrates' cathartics was merely a more effective kind of Athenian education.

Theaetetus is the interpreter for both the giants and the gods (246e2–4, 248a4–6). He translates their several speeches in such a way that they cease to fight. He first has the giants agree that mortal animal is something and then that mortal animal is ensouled body. If adjective and noun correspond to adjective and noun, to be mortal means to have a soul, and to be an animal means to be a body; but since animal means a living being (*zôion*), to be mortal means to be a body and to be an animal to be ensouled. Either body makes animal mortal, or soul makes body mortal. Since to agree that mortal animal is does not need to entail more than the minimal speech "a body lives," in which the asserted modality of the body does not mean that the modality is a being by itself, Theaetetus should have had the giants assent to no more than that the soul is as life or mortality is. Theaetetus, in any case, now adds soul to number as one of the beings (cf. 238a10–b1). Its possible equivalence with mortality suggests that the soul as much as number points to nonbeing. The being of soul, however, marks only a stage in an argument which finally proposes a meaning of being other than the countable. The being of soul is a pretext for the stranger's letting becoming slip back in.

Without Theaetetus showing any awareness of it, the stranger moves from the being of the just and the unjust, and the prudent and the imprudent soul—they are not the same—to the becoming of each "by the having and presence of justice" and the like. The minimal condition, then, for something to be is the possibility that it become present to and become absent from something. The stranger implies that justice is not if it cannot become present to soul,[74] but he leaves it open whether justice is apart from every possible becoming or whether it only is when it becomes in soul. The giants, at any rate, have become better very quickly. Would not the just be if there can be just actions? The giants agree to the being of soul prior to their acceptance of the being of actions, and to the being of virtue and vice prior to that of the good and the bad.

The stranger next forces the giants to separate corporeality from visibility, for if they say that soul possesses a sort of body, they cannot say that it is visible. Air is one without being the other. Theaetetus, however, believes they would be ashamed to assert that either prudence is a body or is not one of the beings, but the stranger reminds him that those who are autochthonous have no shame and would admit to nothing which their hands would not squeeze. Inasmuch as not even white would pass this test, the stranger restricts the concession the giants have to make in order to become better to anything that is bodiless. Even number would suffice. Once they have agreed that something bodiless is, the stranger asks what do bodies and non-bodies have which as cognate with them both allows the giants to say that both are. He suggests the following: "I say that that which naturally possesses any power whatsoever either to do anything to another or to undergo anything even to the slightest extent by the most insignificant thing, even should this happen only once, all this really is. I lay it down as a definition that the beings are nothing else except power." We are reminded that Socrates' improvement in speech of Protagoras in the *Theaetetus* also consisted in defining being as power. It is the only definition of being which the stranger never refutes explicitly.

The immediate consequences of the stranger's definition are these: (1) there are only degrees of beings but not kinds of beings; (2) that which distinguishes a body from a nonbody has nothing to do with its being because the nature of something and the something as a being are entirely separate; (3) the minimal number of beings are two; (4) being only comes to light in a power relation; (5) the 'lowest' being would be one which was affected once and never affected anything else; (6) the 'highest' being would be one which affected everything else but was never itself affected; (7) all being is measurable. Being as power replaces the countability with the measurability of being. Continuity is more fundamental than discreteness. Theaetetus' powers—the roots of every number—now have an 'ontology'. They can measure every being, no matter how 'irrational'. The stranger, however, does not say what scale is to be used. He began with the being of mortal animal. What now makes mortal animal be? No longer because it is body but because soul affects it can we say that it is. Soul would be the paradigm of being as efficient cause (to be is to make something of another) and body of being as material cause (to be is to be made into something by another). But we cannot conclude that neither can be without the other, since the mutual effect of two bodies on one another also establishes their being (though not their being as bodies), and the effect of justice on soul could presumably occur without body. But even if body never did anything, and nothing ever affected soul, both would be if and only if they were in some causal relation to one another. Could we then distinguish body from soul? They would be simply two conventional names for the true being, animal. But since animal would not be unless it were in turn in some relation with another, all being would be one at the same time that it were two or more.

This difficulty is identical with that which Theaetetus confronted the day before when Socrates elicited from him the equation of knowledge with perception. The definition of being as power looks as if it speaks of potentiality even while it denies potentiality. It is such a powerful definition because, in pulling us away from our ordinary understanding, according to which there are rocks, trees, animals, and other things, it seems to preserve our ordinary understanding. It is a beautiful example of how easy it is to forget where we are. The stranger shows us what phantastics can do. Protagoras is a tame giant.[75]

Theaetetus does not interpret the friends of the ideas with the same assurance he had just shown before the Protagoreans (cf. 247c8, 248b7–8). He is more dependent on the stranger, even though he still has the final say. They begin with the distinction between becoming and being. The distinction is opposed to the conjunction "mortal animal" about which the giants were first asked. If "mortal" belongs to the class of becoming, perhaps "animal" belongs to the class of being. The giants' enemies are already in trouble. The stranger brings it home with his next question: "And that we share, on the one hand, in becoming by means of body through perception, and, on the other, by means of soul through calculation in being that really is, which you assert is always the same in all respects, while becoming varies from moment to moment?"

In accordance with the giants' identification of mortal animal with ensouled body, the stranger connects being with soul and becoming with body, but body must here mean ensouled body and not the body of which the unenlightened giants speak. The stranger's distinction is impossible. Not only do the gods of the gigantomachy say that body is becoming, so we must share in becoming (body) by becoming (body) through perception, but even if we were nothing but rocks we should still share in becoming. The stranger, moreover, employs the phrase "through perception" as if it does not entail that "our perceptions pertain to a single whole, either soul or whatever it should be called, by means of which we perceive all that is perceptible through the instruments, as it were, (of the eyes and ears)."[76] Soul is already implicated in perception, and the stranger's question, What is the sharing in both becoming and being? is merely an elaborate way to ask what is common to perceiving and knowing. The answer now should be "soul," which can be neither a body nor an "idea"; Theaetetus' answer when knowing and perceiving were identified, was *phantasia*.[77] As long as knowledge and perception are identified, the soul always has a tendency to appear as a *phantasma*. But even after knowledge and perception do get distinguished, soul gets no easier to understand. The doubleness of thinking is still not disentangled from the doubleness of image.

Being and becoming are apart. Had they always been apart in belief as well as in fact, the gods would not have had to separate them, but since they do not acknowledge this, the stranger grants them this and asks instead about their own recognition of both. Even if there were no other communion between being and becoming, our cognition of both establishes their communion. The common comes to light with soul, for nothing is in principle more shareable than knowledge. We thus have the paradox that nothing comprehends both being and becoming except comprehension: "Soul is somehow all things." Soul, then, is not all things. It cannot be both the 'place' of communion and the whole, for otherwise being would not be apart from becoming. Even before the stranger asks the gods about soul, we have to consider how soul fits in with what the gods and giants say. The stranger says that the power of affecting or being affected, if present to something, suffices to characterize being. He had formerly said that whatever is capable of being present and absent shows that it is. Could soul, then, have the power to be present to or come into the presence of being without affecting it? Could the soul's power be to be fitting to being and yet not be an agent or patient power?

As the stranger presents the problem, the gods must say that the soul is either an agent power, in which case the being when known is not the being as it is, or a patient power, in which case it would be a miracle that the soul's experience of a being be knowledge of the being itself. To say that the being reproduces itself exactly in the soul would be to deny once more any difference between being and becoming. The particular difficulty of a dialogue between Theaetetus, who without direct experience of the beings has only images to go on, and the stranger, whose experience of the beings prevents him from going on, exemplifies the general difficulty that the soul's communion with being must and cannot be either active or passive. Through his own assumption of Theaetetus' innocence, the stranger solved the particular difficulty. It would be strange if phantastics could solve the general difficulty too.

That the distinction between 'to know' (*gignôskein*) and 'to be known' (*gignôskesthai*) cannot be expressed with the two other most common verbs of knowing (*eidenai* and *epistasthai*), and that the stranger asks whether to know could be passive as well as active, show that grammatical forms are not dictating the problem. But the stranger considers 'to know' only as active and not as passive; he interrupts that consideration with an oath: "By Zeus! Shall we be easily persuaded that motion, life, soul, intelligence are truly not present to the perfect being, and it neither lives nor thinks, but awesome and holy without intellect, it is stationary and immobile?"[78] No sooner does the stranger present the ideas than he withdraws them in favor of the gods. He appeals to the friends of the ideas, whose being is threatened by the ideas they love, over against the ideas, which by their own nature are indifferent to the presence or absence of life, soul, and mind. Socrates, we recall, had had a dispute with Euthyphro the day before, shortly after he conversed with Theaetetus and Theodorus, about this question. He had then distinguished between the being of something and its affect—in this case, between what the holy is in itself and its being loved by the gods. Theaetetus, who has not yet paid attention to the hunting lovers do, accepts the stranger's argument that the soul in its cognitive doing must set the ideas in motion. But simply because something gets loved does not alter it, however much the lover might believe that the beloved is duty-bound to change. So the fact that the ideas are known would not involve their alteration, anymore than to be affected by the one which is strictly one means that the one itself becomes many.

The stranger avoids placing Theaetetus before the difficulties inherent in separated ideas, which Parmenides once showed the young Socrates; instead, he provokes Theaetetus' fear of such a *logos*. As interpreter of the giants, Theaetetus attributed to them his own shame of admitting that intelligence was body; as interpreter of the gods, he attributes to them his own fear of admitting that the beings could be nonliving, nonthinking kinds. His fear and shame, which he did not have before Socrates, but which Socrates had before Parmenides, unite to save him. The perfect being has intellect, life, soul, and since it is irrational for an ensouled being to be motionless and at rest, it must have motion. Motion is proved to be because soul is, soul is proved to be because life is, and life is because the perfect being has intellect. Life and soul are in between intellect and motion, which are themselves in between ideas and body. Theaetetus does not ask whether motion needs body. He does not ask the stranger to identify the animal they have deduced.

The upward movement of the giants and the downward movement of the gods are outlined in figure 4. For the giants, to be now means to be power; for the gods, to be perfectly means to be thinking (*noein*). If thinking is the greatest degree of the power to make, and body the lowest degree of the power to be affected, the tension between a comprehensive and a precise account of being would seem to be resolved. Being is on a sliding scale. The higher beings need the lower; the lowest in its total passivity needs at least one agent power. But the comprehensive definition of being as power does not allow any being to be something; so in order for a manifold of beings to be, the ideas are needed, each of which is a something. And yet the only kind of

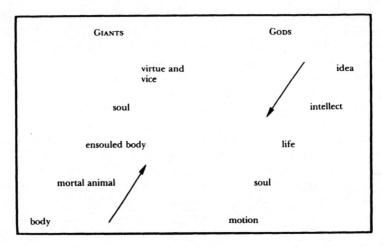

Figure 4

something which survives the stranger's criticism of the ideas is the ensouled being with intellect. There are at least two ways of under-standing this animal. Either each ensouled being is itself an. *eidos*— the class of the sophist is the sophist (218c5, 7, d4)—and the stranger's dichotomies are literally a genealogy, or the ensouled beings make the *eidê* immobile, awesome and holy, and the *eidê* are to their makers as images of the gods are to the gods. The *eidê* would be those things which are not to be moved, or the sacred. As either the images or the apparitions in speech of moving intelligences, they would be the sacred laws, which the beings themselves or false prophets (the sophists) promulgated.[79] The stranger has already indicated how difficult it would be to detect false prophets.

The stranger stops short of identifying the perfect being. If one says that it is God, one is saying no more than that, just as the sacred names the mode of being of the ideas (rest), so God names the mode of being of intelligent being (motion). Neither God nor the sacred is thereby known. Socrates rebuked Theodorus for thoughtlessly calling the stranger divine (216c2), for the adjective is indeterminate in mean-ing as long as we do not know what the stranger is. "Stranger" too is a modal word which grammatically looks like a "substance." The stranger, therefore, does not say anything more about the perfect being. He can hardly show that being is as perplexing as not being if he already knows what being is. The perfect being was an inspired means for showing that motion as well as rest must be. It points perhaps to the conclusion of the dialogue, where Theaetetus agrees that a divine intelligence makes everything come to be, but it is unnecessary to establish the being of motion. To admit, as the gods do, that our soul shares in being only through calculation and reflection is enough for that conclusion. But what the stranger's device does show is that nonbeing and being, even if equally perplexing, are not perplexing in the same way. The perplexity of nonbeing is initially that it must be; the perplexity of being cannot ever be about the that of its being. This is the minimal truth in the Parmenidean thesis: whatever being is it must be. The formal similarity between the being of nonbeing and the nonbeing of being is deceptive. It conceals the fact that the nonbeing of being is the being of nonbeing, and being itself does not alter.

Since intellect cannot belong to anything immobile and the total motion of everything equally precludes knowledge, prudence, or intellect, the philosopher is compelled to deny that the whole or the sum is either nothing but motion or nothing but rest. This denial does not entail anything more than that not all the beings undergo every sort of alteration and move locally in every respect all the time.[80] Both motion and rest must be. But whether there is any being of which there can be no knowledge whatever—Timaeus' "place," for example, or Aristotle's prime matter—or any being of which there can be complete knowledge because it is wholly at rest, and whether there is just one or many of these beings, no conclusion about any of these possibilities can be drawn from the necessary being of motion and rest. All that is, is either in motion or at rest. Motion and rest are contrary modalities of being; they say nothing about being insofar as to be means to be something. Being, therefore, cannot be exhausted in a speech which comprehends it as if it were nothing but the most comprehensive of contrary modalities. "We seem to divine truly," as Theaetetus says, "that being is something as a third whenever we say that motion and rest are." The stranger, however, argues against this divination, for he reasons that since being is a third it is neither at rest nor in motion according to its own nature. "If something is not in motion, how isn't it at rest? Or that which in no way is at rest, how isn't it, in turn, in motion?"

The stranger thus forces the comprehensive account to have recourse to number, and therefore to experience the same difficulty as the precise myth makers did. But the stranger assumes that one counts three beings in counting, for example, animal, soul, and justice as three, since animal, soul, and justice all are. He assumes that the that and the what of being are always the same. Justice is, as far as we know, solely because it can be absent from or present to soul as a condition, but Theaetetus does not acknowledge any difference between the being of justice and of soul. Being and countability are convertible; any 'it', regardless of whether it is a mode of something or the something, is as a 'that' a being. That a being has motion and that motion has being are to Theaetetus equivalent assertions (249b2). Arithmetic makes Theaetetus a natural believer in "ideas," even as it destroys the possibility that there are any ideas. The true class jumper is not his caricature—the moneymaking sophist—but Theaetetus the theoretical mathematician, the varying presence of whose art in every other art determines the cognitive status of each, while he himself practices his own art apart from all its applications. Theaetetus' art makes being as perplexing as nonbeing. Only if the stranger can show that the countability of the beings involves the nonbeing of the beings can he solve together the twin impossibilities of counting motion, rest, and being as three, on the one hand, and of saying anything about nonbeing, on the other (241b3, 250d4).

XI. Nonbeing
(250d5–259d8)

The stranger first showed that body can be communized with nonbody if being is defined as power, but he did not remark that such a definition leaves out of the range of being both the aspect of body and the aspect of nonbody which do not admit of communization. The stranger now has shown that motion and rest cannot be communized with one another even though both of them are. It therefore follows that the problem of being is to bring together noncommunicable being, which is motion or rest, with communicable being, which is power. The problem of being is the tension between conjunction and disjunction, between, if one speaks grammatically, "and" and "or." "And" and "or" are the two possible ways of understanding "two," which comes to be indifferently from the addition of one and one and from the division of one. Dichotomy begins with what is the same and finds the other; counting begins with what is other and finds the same. Dichotomy is the otherness of sameness, counting is the sameness of otherness. The stranger develops in what follows an argument somewhat along these lines, but before we turn to it, we have to ask whether he has now posed the question correctly.

Do motion and rest properly constitute the problem of noncommunicable being? Motion and rest characterize two kinds of being; they do not define the beings of either kind. The way in which a sacred law is wholly at rest is not the way in which the idea man, if there were a being of this sort, is wholly at rest. And the way in which seeing is a motion is not necessarily the way in which the sun is in motion, for to be a motion and to be in motion are not self-evidently the same. Motion and rest point simultaneously to the manifold of disjunctive being, which the stranger exemplifies with the class of consonantal letters, and to the manifold of conjunctive being, which the class of syllables exemplifies. The true problem of being is how to understand the relation of the sound IT—a moving thing—to the motionless and silent T. Is that which moves in IT that which is at rest as T? How can IT be a being if T is a being as well? The stranger does not raise these questions. Precisely because motion and rest came to be acknowledged as equally being by starting from those who initially claimed the exclusive being of one of them, motion and rest are now understood as wholly separate insofar as each of them is. It is the consequence of following an argument without following one's following of the argument.

Theaetetus is thus led to believe that motion and rest are like consonants, M and R respectively, and that they communicate with one another through being, O. So MO means "Motion is," and RO "Rest is." The stranger then asks what O could possibly be. Three mutually contradictory formulas resulted: MO→O, RO→O, M + R→O. But this impossible arithmetic merely images the real problem, in which MO must be replaced by a formula—IT, for example—that puts together a being which 'is' just because of what it is with a being which 'is' despite its not being just what it is. MO represents the kind of being which borrows from eidetic being (RO) its being something, while it itself seems to be in its own right. It is because the stranger has dropped this "seems to be" that the problem of being looks as if it were a problem in arithmetic. Self-evidential eikastics conceals the perplexity in phantastics.

The stranger first raised the question of sharing in connection with ourselves: we were the being which shared in both being and becoming through reasoning and perceiving. We are again the being which the stranger chooses to exemplify in what manner we address with many names the same this. Our cognitive partnership in being and becoming is most manifest in our speaking. We say that a human being is good, *et cetera, et cetera,* and we speak likewise of other things, despite the fact (or because of it) that we lay down each as one. If human being were nothing but human being, and the good nothing but good, it would be impossible that one could qualify the other; but since the human being called good is only hypothetically one, we seem to acknowledge, in calling him good, that he is not in fact one. Our speech corrects the falseness of our hypothesis without which we could not speak.

The stranger thus admits to the late-learning old men, one of whom may be Socrates, that our speaking contradicts its own foundation. The hypothetical singularity of the being seems to be at odds with the factual plurality of its predicates, but the very phrase "its predicates" requires that the hypothesis be true, for otherwise no predication would be possible. This problem is identical in character and possibly in substance with what the stranger said was the greatest perplexity of nonbeing. How is it possible to say that nonbeing is not susceptible to being spoken of if we have just spoken of it? Nonbeing can only enter speech if we lay it down as one, which is contrary to its being nonbeing, and thus ascribe being to it. The hypothetical ones of speech seem to be the nonbeings.

The stranger puts one question with three possible answers to all who ever said anything about being. He implies that since there is only one correct answer, it only lays down the minimal condition for discourse about being, and no more. Certain extreme positions are thereby excluded, but the stranger does not promise to settle the question as to whether this minimal condition entails a unique and sufficient condition as well. The three so-called biggest kinds he does discuss are only a sample (254c1–d2). The question all the philosophers are to answer is this: "Are we to attach neither being to motion nor rest nor anything else to anything else, but on the grounds that they are immiscible, and it's impossible for them to partake of one another, are we to set them down on this condition in the speeches we use? Or are we to bring them all together into the same on the grounds that they are capable of sharing in one another? Or some do and some don't?" The question of power returns, but not in the same way. Power was before a sign of being, now it means a possibility: the fact that something can share in something else does not mean that it ever does. A possible speech is not necessarily a speech that ever gets spoken, but something which never once exhibits the power to affect or be affected is not. To extend, moreover, the range of power in this way has one immediate advantage: false speech becomes possible. Theaetetus never has to fly in order for us to say "Theaetetus flies."

The difference between the two senses of power recalls the difference between, on the one hand, Socrates' question, whether the female human nature is capable of sharing in the nature of the male race in all deeds, or not even one, or it can in some and not others, and, on the other, Glaucon's question, whether the best city is capable of coming into being.[81] That the communized city could be brought into being does not prove that it is in accordance with human nature to be so communized, and likewise that it can be said that Theaetetus flies,does not prove that it is in accordance with his nature to fly. The best city after all is founded on a beautiful lie.

In the course of showing the impossibility of no communism, the stranger gives another list of the philosophers. Again, they are in groups, but almost everyone has been reassigned.

First List	Second list
1. The beings are three.	1. Everything is in motion.
2. The beings are two.	2. One being is at rest.
3. The being is one.	3. Many beings according to kinds are at rest.
4. Heraclitus	4. One and an infinite many alternately are.
5. Empedocles	5. One and a finite many alternately are.
6. Giants	6. One and an infinite many always are.
7. Gods	7. One and a finite many always are.

The stranger has, as it were, demythologized the philosophers. No longer does he speak of war, marriage, or Aphrodite; the battle between the gods and giants has disappeared. Has it been pure gain? The tension between the comprehensive and the precise has also disappeared, and along with that tension, the body, the soul, becoming, the noetic and the aesthetic cease to be evident. Parmenides' doctrine, it is true, now has greater content, and its noetic character is implied; but Heraclitus is split in two, and the gods' doctrine into three or four, for they would have to say not only that a limited number of eidetic beings are at rest, but also that infinitely many aesthetic beings somehow are in their continual motion. Greater clarity has been achieved at the expense of a philosopher's depth of thought.[82] Demythologization has the consequence that the discussion drops from the level of intention to the level of speech. To deny that anything has the power to share in anything looks equivalent to the denial that one thing can be addressed as another by a passive sharing in it. The minimal condition of coherence in speech about being leads to a concealment of the problem of being. "In reality" (ontôs) is no longer opposed to "in appearance" (252a9–10). When the stranger remarks on the self-contradiction in the speech which denies speech, and likens it to the ventriloquist Eurycles, Theaetetus says, "You say what is utterly similar and true." Theaetetus forgets that it was the difference between the similar and the true that first raised the problem of being.

The stranger's own language with which he expresses the conjunction (*synaptein*) of one thing with another is extraordinarily fluid and imprecise. He speaks of it at various times as "a sharing" (*koinônein*), "a participating" (*metekhein*), "a taking part" (*metalambanein*), "a commingling" (*symmeignysthai*), "a receiving" (*dekhesthai*), "a fitting together" (*synarmottein*), and several other variants of these. It recalls his list of verbs of separation, which he put together under the single class of diacritics before he split it into cathartics—the separation of the better from the worse—and an art of separating like from like. The stranger's dichotomies illustrated the theoretical practice of this nameless art; his analysis of the five classes seems to illustrate in turn the syncritical art at work. In its indifference to the difference in the kinds of classes which are combined—motion and rest similarly are (252a11)—the art corresponds to the art of separating like from like. Is there, then, another kind of syncritics which puts together the better and the worse? It remains for now nothing more than a possibility, but it seems to have something to do with the statesman's art, insofar as ruling necessarily involves such a union.[83]

The stranger calls the whole art of syncritics and diacritics, each with its two parts, dialectics. The unity of this art is as puzzling as the unity of the four virtues; it is plainly the philosophic parallel to the apparent unity and diversity of the sophist's art. Complete clarity about being and not being, the stranger suggests, will elude them; for the manner of their present inquiry precludes that they see sophistry in the light of philosophy. The boldness of their undertaking is due to their facing the derivative as if it were not derivative, or more precisely, as if it were enough to know that it is derivative without knowing perfectly the original from which it is derived. The *Sophist* is an image of that which it pretends to be.

The proof that partial sharing is necessary establishes the first principle of being and the science of being, but since the proof is a proof only if we wish to speak of being, the first principle is more like an axiom. Like an axiom, it is entirely silent as to how partial sharing does occur; it does not determine, for example, what the beings are which are at rest or in motion. It does not even say how partial the sharing is. The principle would be satisfied if only a point, as it were, resisted total communization. The stranger compares this as yet inchoate science with the grammatical and musical arts, but he also says that they would find other things of the same sort in the other arts and nonarts. The principle of partial sharing is the principle of all sciences, and not only of the science of being. What, then, are these "other things of the same sort?" If the grammarian knows that no letter combines with any other without the bond of a vowel, the dialectician must know which are the bonds and which not the bonds of all things. If the grammarian knows that the vowel letters in themselves are not bonds (for they can be sounded by themselves), the dialectician must know of some things which can act as bonds but can nevertheless be by themselves. If the grammarian knows distinctly the consonantal letters prior to their being sounded with any vowels, the dialectician must distinguish between the nature of an element and its being (255e5). Such a distinction, however, is intelligible in only one of two ways: either being means aesthetic, and nature noetic being, or nature means essence, and being existence. It is this latter distinction the stranger seems to mean and through which he points to a characteristic of the arts and sciences.

Every established science tends to wipe out the traces of its own origin, and this tendency is nowhere more conspicuous than in grammar. The speaker of a language says, for example, "king," "milk," "kiln," and so forth, but the inventor of its alphabet isolates the k-sound in such a way that it ceases to be a sound and yet does not cease to be. So extraordinary is this separation of the silent element from the sound that strict alphabetization is much less common than other kinds of writing. The syllabary is a revealing halfway house between the alphabet and the language as spoken. Now K in our example has a name, "kappa," which looks like any other word in the language and sounds like any other word with a k-sound. K is now so independent of its origin that the geometrician can use it to designate the point on the line, and the arithmetician a number. Within the grammatical art, then, K is the nature and kappa the being of the letter, and in both ways the letter takes precedence over the sounds of which it originally was the class characteristic—as if the K in "king" were somehow due to kappa.

The stranger offers Theaetetus a small sample from the alphabet of the science of being. As a would-be science, the stranger presents it in the same way as any established science and thus distorts or at least obscures that which the science intends to explain. Let us say that K is the class characteristic of all moving things, and S of all stationary things. No moving thing can be unless K is bonded to something else, I. The sounding of K is the being of KI. Now Socrates showed that total motion was impossible, and since KS cannot be (be sounded)—motion and rest are immiscible with one another—the minimal formula for any moving thing is KSI. But the stranger does not speak of moving things, only of motion, whose nature is K and whose being is kappa. Motion thus lends itself to being spoken of, while what it means drops out of sight. In order to understand the stranger's alphabet, then, we must look away from it and toward the things his alphabet has silenced. He gives Theaetetus the letters—

being, motion, rest—before he gives him the language: the phenomena are missing (cf. 253b8). The stranger's account is obscure primarily because he assumes the existence of a science which does not exist. He thus repeats the mistake of his dichotomies, which assumed that what was first by nature was first for us.

The Greek grammarian deals with twenty-four letters. In order to handle Homer he would have to add to them the digamma, and if he wished to become a grammarian of all languages, he would have to make further additions. Even these would only represent what was known and not what could possibly occur. Between Γ and Κ, for example, more than one consonant could be fitted in. At the point where the human ear could no longer discriminate, he might stop,[84] but the articulated sounds of human speech are embedded in a plenum of noises—the hiss of the snake, the grunt of the boar, the screech of the owl—and these in turn overlap the noises out of which the musical scales are formed. The class of sound, then, would fall under two arts, grammar and music, one of which would treat articulated, the other unarticulated sound, with a no-man's-land in between that both in part usurp.

The relation between a possible and an actual articulated sound in a given language—for example, between ΒΑΙ and ΒΑΕ—parallels the relation between possibly consonant and actually consonant notes in music. The musician will further separate the harmonious or beautiful from the ugly but still possible combinations of sounds, and the grammarian might likewise note the loathsome things that words beginning with ΒΑΕ in Greek denote. These loathsome things "are" as much as the beautiful things, and the stranger had insisted that their dichotomies were to ignore the difference between them. To ignore this difference means to attend more to the bonds than to the bonded. Ε is neutral with regard to the 'ugliness' of ΒΔΕΛΥΡΟΝ ("disgusting") and 'beauty' of ΒΕΛΤΙΟΝ ("better"). The stranger's alphabet, we can infer, will be more revealing about its vowels than its consonants. Being in its neutrality would seem to be the core of the stranger's science of communism.

Dialectics is the science of conjunction and disjunction. It examines which classes are consonant with which classes, and which do not receive one another. It examines, in particular, whether some classes are connecting elements through everything, and whether in the case of divisions there are other causes of division through wholes. The stranger suggests that there is a difference between wholes and non-wholes. He then reformulates this difference in a way which meets with Theaetetus's entire approval. If the philosopher, he says, can divide according to classes, and never believe the same kind to be other, or if other the same, then "he perceives adequately (A_1) one look stretched in every way through many, though each one of which is situated apart (from the rest), and (A_2) many looks other than one another comprehended on the outside by one look, and (B_1) one look, in turn, bound together into one through many wholes, and (B_2) many looks set apart and distinct in every way. And this is to know how to discern according to genus, in what way the genera are severally capable of sharing and in which not."

There are two kinds of one and two kinds of many, and as the stranger's language elsewhere seems to imply,[85] every *idea* of type A_1 is manifest as one *idea* among many other *ideai*, all of which are comprehended by another *idea* of type A_2. And every *idea* of type B_1 is manifest in manifold *ideai* of type B_2, which are not comprehended by another *idea*. The stranger's class of forcible hunting illustrates an *idea* of type A_1, for he discerned the forcible hunting of men in the arts of piracy, enslavement, tyranny, and warfare, each of which lies apart from the other. But the *idea* of forcible hunting is just one of many *ideai*, all of which are comprehended by the art of acquisition, which is "outside" them. It is outside because it cancels every difference among them: insofar as the hunter and the merchant both acquire, they are the same.

The second kind (B_1 and B_2), in contrast, finds no ready illustration in any one of the stranger's dichotomies, but it does appear somehow in the manifold arts to which the sophist lays claim. The sophist showed himself as many separated *ideai*, and the problem was to find the one *idea* that is joined in one through the many wholes. Since, however, they are now trying to stamp the sophist with the single *idea* of an art which will make his many separated *ideai* the illusory products of this art, the sophist does not exactly exemplify the second kind. We could wonder whether there are any kinds of types B_1 and B_2. We can, however, ask this question. To which kind does being belong? If being is exclusively of the first kind, it will be comprehensive, but there will be no manifold of truly separate beings or "ideas" which do not get lost in some larger class. But if being is exclusively of the second kind, it will show up as a manifold of "ideas," though it will not be comprehensive.

The stranger has already shown that being was problematic because it could not be accommodated into either kind. Being as the second kind was that which united the accurate mythmakers; being as the first kind was the issue between the gods and the giants. The accurate mythmakers were confronted with the difficulty that one became two, and two became three or one, and the gods and giants were confronted with the impossibility of their accounting for soul. The problem of being thus turned on the tension between number and soul. A number is the most obvious example of a single *idea* which stretches through many separate collections—five in five apples, five cows, five chairs, and so on—and which with all the other numbers is comprehended by number itself. Soul is the most obvious example of a kind which shows itself as both a whole and as many different types of wholes, each of which resists any inclusion into a more comprehensive whole. Theaetetus is not Theodorus; Theaetetus and Theodorus together do not make up anything; they are nonaddable wholes. Each is a unique type with many representatives.[86] The "many-headed sophist" represents this kind of being as much as he does the other, for he would not pose the problem of being as acutely as he does if he did not pretend to combine both.[87]

The stranger warns Theaetetus that the region of nonbeing, to which the sophist attaches himself by a knack and not by art, is murky and indistinct; so they must be careful that whatever light they cast on him does not distort his character. The region of nonbeing is largely arbitrary; one should not try to figure out patterns to cover everything one finds there. The division into kinds is bound to break down, and the sophist's class jumping is due not so much to his own perversity as to the necessity that everything there slide into everything else. It will be impossible, then, to keep apart the two kinds of one and two kinds of many to which the stranger has just referred. The five genera must be neutral to the difference between being and not being: same and other, motion and rest can equally apply to a shadow and that which casts a shadow. Neither the difference between number and soul nor that between image and that of which it is an image will be fully clarified by the stranger. There are five and not four classes because the other and being are not two names for a single class, but what these beings are which are by themselves and are not spoken of in relation to other beings is left unexplained. Only if we can make sense of this restriction on the other, which seems to be contrary to the drift of the stranger's argument, will we come to some understanding of the principle of partial sharing.

The stranger begins with three classes: being itself, motion, and rest. Motion and rest do not mix in one another, but being mixes with both. The three classes, then, are in relation to one another through two principles, miscibility and immiscibility. Immiscibility governs the relation between motion and rest, miscibility governs their relation to being. The stranger later says that motion and rest partake of being; they therefore do not partake of one another. Miscibility is the principle of participation; immiscibility is its opposite. But participation means that the participant in something is not entirely that something.

II.146

Participation, then, means partial sharing. Motion and rest partially share in being, and neither shares in the other. Not to share in one another means to be wholly other than one another. So the principle of nonsharing would be the other or the nature of the other, and the stranger says that each of the classes is other than the others because each participates in the *idea* of the other and not because of its own nature. Motion and rest, then, partially share in the principle of nonsharing. Since the principle of nonsharing does not preclude their partial sharing in this principle, this principle must be the principle of partial sharing. The nature of the other is the principle of participation. Were this not the case, the stranger could not say that motion is the same as itself because it participates in the same, for it is equally the same as itself because it only participates in the other and is not the other. Participation implies both same and other. The science of partial sharing is the science of the nature of the other.

Being, rest, and motion are three. The stranger concludes that each is other than the other two and the same as itself, for otherwise they could not be counted. Same and other are the principles of countability, and the first question he asks is whether the principles of countability are the same as the principles of being, motion, and rest. Motion and rest are not countable because they both share in being, but because they both share in same and other. They are two because of the mutual relation between them—same and other—that is independent of their relation to a third, being. To be and to be countable are no longer regarded as convertible. The stranger's third question, whether being and the same are one, is equivalent to asking whether there is no participation whatsoever, and his fourth question, whether being and the other are one, is equivalent to asking whether there is total participation.

They are in a sense the same question. On one hand, no participation meant that nothing could be said of another; so being could not be said of motion and rest unless they were the same. Total participation, on the other hand, would entail that everything could be said of another. "If being and the other were not very different," the stranger says, that is, if they were the same, "but the other participated in both kinds of beings (nonrelational and relational), there would be some one of the others that was not in relation to another." The other cannot participate in both kinds because it is the principle of partial sharing, and there would be no partial sharing if there were total participation. To say, however, that being does participate in both kinds of beings is to say that being is split into two kinds of beings. Participation, then, is division. But participation was the nature of the other. The nature of the other must be the single principle which governs both participation and division. Diacritics and syncritics belong to the same art.

The stranger's talk of five classes is misleading. It seems to imply that same and other are exactly like rest and motion, but the stranger never says that same partakes of other or other of same. The stranger blurs their difference on the model of the alphabet, in which the difference between vowels and consonants is suppressed in the sameness of their letter forms. Once a vowel and a consonant are each represented by a letter they are indistinguishable. The vowel sounds can be assigned names that are themselves the vowel sounds; the consonants are assigned names that cannot be the consonant sounds. The consonants need "images," the vowels do not; the consonants always appear as other, the vowels as the same. If rest is consonantal, it will always appear with a vowel. The vowel is of the nature of the other, which in its bond with the consonant of rest reveals the consonant as another, the syllable. Is, then, the other apart from its bonding with another? The stranger has denied its apartness, but a distinction would have to be drawn between its proper function as a bond and its illusory independence. The mathematical sciences are, according to Socrates, hypothetical, but they do not appear as hypothetical to their practitioners. And though they are meant to serve as the bonds, in the region of thinking, between the aesthetic and the noetic, they seem to be self-sufficient.

The other, moreover, can be deceptive in another way. In the stranger's divisions, "other" first occurs in the separation of the pedestrial class of animals from the swimming animal. It seems to be a fortuitous "other," dictated exclusively by the interest of the stranger to isolate fish, which he does not mention by name until the end of his divisions (220e9). Neither fish nor birds, both of which are included in this class, are other through their own nonshared nature; they are other solely because land animals are other than both of them. As the other animal, they are divided off and united with the land animal—divided because liquid (water or air) differs from solid as a medium of locomotion, united because both are animals. The label "other," however, does not indicate the extent to which the same holds of whatever is other. In the course of criticizing dichotomy as a way of classification, Aristotle says:

> It deserves inquiry why men did not address [the water and the winged animals] with one name, and comprehend both of them in a single higher class. For even these have certain attributes in common. However, the present nomenclature is correct. Classes that differ only in degree and the more and the less are

yoked under a single class; classes that have things in common by analogy are separated. For example, bird differs from bird by the more and the less (one is long-feathered, another short-feathered), but fish from bird by analogy; for what in one is feather, is in the other scale."[88]

The stranger implicitly questions Aristotle's distinction between disjunction by analogy and conjunction by degree. Perhaps birds and fish do truly belong together. Floating or liquid animal would thus be one and the same consonant for both birds and fish (T), and their difference would be only 'vocalic' (OT and ET). They would be aesthetically different and noetically the same. For Aristotle, on the other hand, birds and fish differ as much as the words that designate them do, and the "i" in both is insignificant apart from the individual word in which it is found. Aristotle therefore must accept the infima species as the being, with the attendant difficulty of accounting for its relation to an individual of that species, whereas the stranger hints at a much smaller number of kinds of beings, in light of which both birds and fish, contrary to appearances, would not be beings in themselves but beings only to be spoken of in relation to another.

To be the same and not the same is to be not other and other. No sooner does the stranger establish this than he drops any further mention of the same and introduces the equivalence of not being and other. The nature of the other is an agent-power; it affects every class and makes each not be. Not to be, then, means to be a patient-power, but since every class is both agent and patient, every class is and is not. The other dualizes every being, for it cannot bind unless it divides. A in CAT could not join C and T together unless it separated them, for C and T are not in CAT what they are in themselves. By themselves C and T are separate from each other, but they are not separate as parts. A makes C and T into parts. The other is the part maker. To be a part is to be dual. The stranger's first example is "the not big," which signifies the small and the equal. The negation of the big inserts the equal, which looks like a self-contained region, into a part which undercuts the contrariety of big and small. The equal does not cease to be itself in being of another.

The nature of the other, the stranger says, is as fragmented as knowledge. Although knowledge is one, the particular domain which each part of knowledge has is separated from it and gets a name peculiar to itself (cf. 236b1). The art of making shoes is both itself and a part of art. If this duality is expressed, "art" will appear twice: shoemaking is an art which is other than art. Accordingly, the shoemaking art looks to the shoemaker as art itself; in his eyes, it does not need another art to complete it, for it is the paradigm of what art is.[89] Every art tends toward an imperialism of assimilation, either 'subjectively', as in the case of the shoemaker, or 'objectively', as in the case of the more comprehensive arts like mathematics, whose progress is characterized by the mathematicization of the seemingly nonmathematicizable, and of which 'Pythagoreanism' is the symbol.[90] No art or science ever considers itself in its partiality, for this would be to look at itself from outside itself, which it could only do if it employed its principles outside the domain to which they are applicable. But since it cannot acknowledge scientifically, that is, in terms of itself as a science, the limitations of its domain, it necessarily enlarges its domain whenever it pretends to examine itself.

The stranger here offers Theaetetus a way to justify his very first answer to Socrates' question, What is knowledge? Socrates had criticized his list of the arts and sciences on the grounds that whoever does not know what knowledge is does not understand "the knowledge of shoes."[91] This would be sound, the stranger replies, if each part of knowledge resulted from a deductive articulation of knowledge, but because we live in the derivative, we do not see it as derivative, and the parts do not come to light as parts.

Parts appear to us as parts only negatively. Each part is restricted not through its own nature but through the restriction imposed upon it by other parts, all of which would extend themselves indefinitely were they not in fact restricted in turn. Parts therefore look like rival powers, whose factual localization is contrary to their inherent universality. We have chosen this political language not only because it is in keeping with the stranger's denial to the nature of each class any self-imposed limitation, but because it points to the most obvious examples of the other as nonbeing. The stranger, in accordance with the neutrality of his partial science of sharing, does not inform Theaetetus of the most obvious examples. Only in the *Statesman,* when young Socrates makes the mistake of separating the care of human beings from the care of beasts (*thêria*), does the stranger indicate the ambiguity in the nature of the other itself. Young Socrates' mistake is as "if someone tried to divide the human race in two as many here distribute it: they remove the Hellenic as one apart and away from all, and all the other genera, which are infinite, immiscible, and not consonant with one another, they address with the single designation "barbarian," and because of this designation, they expect it too to be a single genus."[92] "Barbarian" simply means non-Greek, but because it is a name, it conceals its negation and therefore does not look as if it is constituted solely by the other. The negation, moreover, works backward on the Greeks who perform the negation, so that they do not appear to themselves as a part but as a kind.[93]

Every kind, the stranger says, is a part, but not every part is a kind. The nature of the other, however, can negotiate between the regions of being and not being because the part is true of both. The region of not being is the region of "thats," the region of being the region of "whats." They are linked through the nature of the other, for everything that is, is a part, regardless of whether it is because its territory is here and not elsewhere, or because it always is what it is everywhere. The other permeates every being, whether it be by nature, by art, by chance, or by law. When Socrates asked Theodorus whether he had not inadvertently brought a god and not a stranger, he was asking whether "stranger" meant a part or a kind. "Stranger" is the most universal of all words that designate the other (217e6): the Spartans call the barbarians strangers.[94] If the stranger is a god he is a kind; if he is a man he is only a part. As a man, the stranger would be not "us," an "us" which blankets the disparate Socrates, Theodorus, Theaetetus, and young Socrates with a single name.

The stranger chooses to illustrate how the nature of the other undergoes the same fragmentation as knowledge with the part of the other which is opposed to the beautiful or the nature of the beautiful. This part is and has a name, the not beautiful. The not beautiful is a certain sort of opposition of being to being (*ontos pros on*). This expression, which seems to make the not beautiful something besides a being in relation to a being, is due to the doubleness of and the hidden redundancy in "the not beautiful" (cf. 258e2–3). Inasmuch as it is a part of not being, it is not being; insofar as it is set in opposition to the beautiful, it is the not beautiful. It is whatever is not in being not beautiful. It thus has the same doubleness which every art and science has, as itself and as a part. As a part, it is not being and in relation to the beautiful. As itself, it is something that is no less than the beautiful. What, then, is it as itself?

The stranger had distinguished between the beauty and the health of soul. The health of soul was moral virtue or justice, the beauty of soul omniscience; while, in contrast, the ugliness of soul was the failure of soul to hit the target which it had set for itself, and the sickness of soul the conflict among cognate things which were blind to any common goal. Beauty showed up as the commensuration of a motion with its goal, health as the forced agreement of contraries. Health, then, is a part of the not beautiful: moral or political virtue is a part which as itself looks like the whole of virtue. It does not know, any more than the city does, that it is a being to be spoken of only in relation to another. If moral virtue is properly understood, that is, as a part, it is the bond between ignorance and omniscience, but since in fact omniscience is impossible, partial knowledge looks as if it belongs to and completes moral virtue, even though in terms of its own standard it is a vice. Socrates' cathartics, therefore, was first presented as the gymnastics of soul, but it then proved to be a kind of medicine, for it seemingly could do no more than cleanse the soul of spurious wisdom and prepare it to receive the complete knowledge it itself could not supply. Socratic cathartics brings about a state of moderation that seems in its self-control and lack of insolence indistinguishable from the moderation of moral virtue. The friends of the ideas are law-abiding.

Despite Theaetetus' "Most plainly" (258b4) in response to the stranger's formulation of the being of not being, it is safe to say that Theaetetus does not understand the stranger's intention, for the duality of the beautiful is the culminating theme of the *Statesman* (306a8–c9). He certainly does not understand why the big, the beautiful, and the just should here be singled out. These three classes refer to the complex relation that the soul, philosophy, and the city have to one another. Perspectival distortion revealed the incompatibility of the big and the beautiful, and the shifting character of soul cathartics revealed the difficulty of separating the just from the beautiful.[95] The beautiful and the not beautiful are the link between these two problems. In the *Theaetetus*, its double role was foreshadowed in Socrates' initial questioning of Theodorus' competence to pass on Theaetetus' ugliness. Theaetetus follows the stranger now to just about the same extent that he understood his own beautiful answer to Socrates the day before, that the soul through itself examines being and not being.

The stranger began with the contrariety of motion and rest, in terms of which being was a third. He then replaced contrariety with otherness, of which the key example was the being of the not beautiful. The not beautiful links the health and the beauty of soul; it thereby constitutes the wholeness of soul, a wholeness which the contrary modalities of motion and rest deny, for it was in terms of motion and rest (or sedition) that the stranger had originally distinguished between two kinds of vice in soul. Modal *diaeresis* precludes the possibility of understanding the soul as a whole, for the overcoming of "rest" in soul, which is the health of soul, does not entail the beauty of soul; indeed, the soul's ugliness only becomes fully manifest once the obstacles to its motion toward the goal of omniscience begin to be overcome. Socrates had hinted at this when he called his own fearful love of naked exercise in speeches a disease.[96] But *diaeresis* according to the nature of the other does restore wholeness to soul, but only with an attendant loss of distinctness of its parts, for the parts of soul, like the parts of knowledge, could only be fully known as parts if the whole were known. Every part, insofar as it is not fully determined as a kind, is a mixed kind, for in sharing its border with another, it always is in dispute with the other and makes incursions into its domain (cf. 231a6–b1). The stranger had hinted at this when he called purification that which casts out the bad and leaves the other, for in ordinary usage "the other" is a euphemism for the bad (227d6). Socrates, we recall, had said that it was a necessity for something to be forever contrary to the good. Philosophy is always impure (cf. 253e5).

Being and the other go through everything and one another, but because their mutual pervasiveness is due to participation, neither ceases to be the other in exchanging their separate characters. Every being is not being itself, for in its being other than being itself, it is a not being or a part. This is as true of the not beautiful as of the beautiful, for the beautiful is included in the not ugly, and the stranger gives no reason why the deficient should not be negated as well. Truth (*alêtheia*) after all is a privative term.[97] But if with every determination being becomes not being, it would seem that the full determination of not being would make being vanish. What possible remainder could there be? If, however, not being is unlimited in its range (256e6), and therefore not wholly determinable, being is just that which escapes determination.

Being is the name for what we do not know.[98] It is in the strictest sense that which is always sought, but it could not be sought unless it in some way confronted us and already disclosed itself to us. The name for a being in its partial disclosure is "the stranger." The stranger's compliance with Socrates' request proved that he was not a stranger (*axenos*) while being a stranger (217e6). Being, then, is a question that looks like an answer. To say that being is something is not to give a complete answer but to pose the further question as to what something is. The form of the question "What is?" is always the same, but Parmenides, who first discovered the question, seems to have mistaken this sameness of form for the answer, about which nothing further could be said. If there was total communism, Parmenides would be right, but then no question could be asked, let alone answered. Partial communism, which entails a manifold of beings, is already implicit in our asking questions. So the question of being in both the *Theaetetus* and the *Sophist* was bound up with and came to light with the question of soul, for to raise the question of being is to raise the question of questioning: What is that which makes questioning possible?

Of the five classes that the stranger examines, there is only one which he discovers anything about, and that is the nature of the other. This discovery is itself the discovery of what he discovers. The nature of the other is the primary tool of discovery. Its dialectical function is to assault everything that appears to us as being exactly what it appears to be. It was for this reason that "the same" disappeared as soon as the stranger tried to establish the equivalence of not being and other. The sophist's slide from class to class showed the way to force the seemingly independent into its true dependent relation. The sophist was the guide to the discovery of the partiality of apartness. The sophist thus looks like the philosopher because he is the philosopher's own tool. His being is the philosopher's way to the beings.

XII. Speaking
(259d9–264d9)

Contrary to the all but unavoidable impression that the other is merely the name for negation in speech, the stranger treats speech as a sixth class in his alphabet of beings, and the kind of web which speech displays as different from the sharing which, as he has just shown, his first five classes undergo (260a5–6). "It is on account of the weaving together of the kinds that the speech has come to be for us." The article with "speech" can either be general or demonstrative. If it is demonstrative, the speech that has come to be through a weaving together of kinds must be their own speech. Its most obvious reference would be to the various divisions they have performed. Let us make a model of a typical set of divisions (fig. 5). In this model, B and C are together because of A and not because of B and C, which makes them apart; and the same holds for the togetherness of D and E, which is due to B; and that of F and G, which is due to D. The speech of F would consist in the separation of D and E and their union through B, and the separation of B and C and their union through

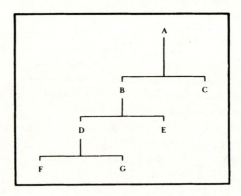

Figure 5

A. The speech of F therefore is exclusively neither of that which is apart nor of that which is together, but of both. This is the weaving together of kinds (cf. 268c6). It is obvious that this kind of speech partakes of nonbeing (without necessarily partaking of falsehood), for half the speech of F is constituted by nonbeing, inasmuch as C, E, and G are each the other of some other. The web of the speech of F is thus nonarithmetical. For if it were arithmetical, F would be D minus G; D would be B minus E; and B, A minus C; and by substitution F would be F, since D equals F plus G. The late learners would be right.

The parts of nonbeing "are" prior to our saying anything about them, for many of them enter speech under forms that disguise their true character. A single example makes the difference between the *eidê* section and the *logos* section clear. The stranger has been concerned so far with neither the utterance "The barbarians are coming!" nor the equivalent "The non-Greeks are coming!", let alone with its truth or falsehood, but with the question whether or not "Greekness" is truly a kind about which there can be knowledge and not mere opinion. No speech, therefore, that the stranger has given so far has been truly a weaving together of kinds, for the stranger, in keeping Theaetetus away from the experience of the beings, has kept him together with all the nonbeings of his innocence. Opinion is opinion and not knowledge because parts do not appear as parts but as self-subsisting wholes. In the cave, the difference between male and female looks exactly the same as the difference between Dorians and Ionians.[99] The stranger is guilty of gross deception in letting Theaetetus believe that falsehood and deception solely operate on the level of predicative speech and are not the very character of the beings which stand before us. "The things which are intelligible and first for each of us are often hardly intelligible, and have little or no being."[100]

The stranger's deception is an adoption of the deception of the sophist, who will refuse to acknowledge falsehood except in speech. The sophist pretended to have no eyes and not to know what a mirror was when Theaetetus gave the most evident examples of images. No longer the stranger but Theaetetus is disheartened by the apparently limitless defenses the sophist can draw up around himself. He believes that the problem of speech is not only more difficult than "the wall" they have already pulled down, but that there are other obstacles—he knows not what—beyond it. Theaetetus is discouraged by what he does not know; he is afraid of the unknown. His moderation, which consists in his believing to know only what he does know, is not accompanied by any awareness of what he does not know. The stranger was as incapable as Socrates of instilling in Theaetetus more than a semblance of courage. Theaetetus does not want to be as perplexed as the stranger confessed he himself was. His nature is of the sort always to want shortcuts to understanding. He prefers to be beautiful rather than to suffer. In the rest of the dialogue, the stranger satisfies that preference perfectly.

The stranger proposes that they consider whether words are like letters and kinds; do all, none, or some possibly fit with one another? Theaetetus says that some do and some do not, but when the stranger asks whether he means that some words spoken one after the other fit together if they make something plain, whereas others in their connectivity signify nothing, Theaetetus does not follow, and the stranger says, "Just what I believed you supposed in your agreement." What, then, was Theaetetus thinking of? Even after the stranger distinguishes between nouns and verbs, and says that neither nouns nor verbs by themselves, if spoken one after the other, ever constitute a speech, Theaetetus still does not understand, and the stranger remarks that plainly he must have been looking at something else when he agreed.

Theaetetus is surely right to be puzzled. At first, he probably took "fitting together" to mean truth and "not fitting together" to mean falsehood, for on such an assumption he would believe it difficult if not impossible to have not being share in speech. Nonbeing would thus be the mark of a nonspeech, and the sophist could only be charged with uttering sounds that looked like speech. But later, when the stranger assigned nouns to actors and doers, and verbs to their actions, Theaetetus could only be more puzzled to hear that the so-called nominal sentence "Lion (is) an animal," or "Seeing (is) perceiving," is not a speech. Is not the truth "Lion (is) neither deer nor horse" a speech? Since the stranger cannot want Theaetetus to deny something so absurd, we have to consider what he intends by restricting speech in the way he does.

If words are like the letters of the alphabet, it would seem plausible to assign to "is" and "becomes" the role of vowels, which allow some consonantal beings to be put together and which forbid the joining of others. "The child becomes a man" and "God is Zeus" would be permissible; "Zeus becomes a swan" and "Men are pigs" would not. The stranger, however, implies that these speeches are, despite their brevity, far from being simple; he also implies that the copulative "is" has nothing to do with the problem of being, for in Greek it is always eliminable. If, however, nouns and verbs are elements or letters of speech, which are the vowels and which the consonants? Since neither "lion" and "horse" nor "walks" and "sleeps" can be put together, nouns and verbs must both be consonants, and there are no vocalic elements of speech. A verb is a revealer for actions; a noun is a sign for those who perform actions. Each by itself does reveal something; but the juxtaposition of two nouns or two verbs ceases to be revealing of what is. Their separate revelatory power is cancelled through the juxtaposition.

Speech, in contrast, crosses a noun and a verb in order to delimit the unlimited significance of an actor and an action. Its own significance lies only at the intersection of noun and verb; it reveals what is through the bonding of noun and verb. The speech as speech signifies something other than its parts. "Man learns" carries with it the separate assertions that there are men and there is learning; but strictly as a speech its truth or falsity depends on the being it alone points to, and which would not come to light without it. So apparently simple a speech as "Man is a rational animal" would, accordingly, be the complex product of two separate, simple speeches: "Man lives" and "Man speaks," or perhaps "Man counts." The stranger thereby warns us that to go, as Theaetetus did, from the being of mortal animal to the being of soul through the being of ensouled body requires much more reflection than Theaetetus gave to the sequence. He also agrees with Aristotle's point, at least as a sound beginning, that "man" and "being man" are the same.[101] And, finally, he indicates that the relation which obtains between naming and counting is no more simple than that between soul and animal. In saying that "lion deer horse" do not make a speech, he implies that we cannot say they are three animals before we know, just as in the case of Socrates' utterance, "sophist statesman philosopher," whether they are one, two, or three classes, for if we say at once that they are three, we cannot be sure that we are counting beings and not names.[102] Fish and birds might be truly countable only as one.

To say "Theaetetus sits" or "Theaetetus flies" is to say something of Theaetetus and not of sitting or flying. If we imagine the noun to be a straight line of indeterminate length and the verb to be a transverse line by means of which a point can be marked on the nominal line, their intersection is the speech. This speech point can be either true or false. "Theaetetus flies" is false solely because it says that which is other than what is, "Theaetetus sits." It is not false because it is impossible for Theaetetus to fly: if Theaetetus dreams that he is flying, the speech that reports this is true. As the stranger puts it: "Theaetetus, with whom I am now conversing, flies." "Theaetetus flies" is just one of infinitely many false speeches, all of which would be equally false insofar as they state that Theaetetus is in local motion. "Theaetetus flies" is no more false than "Theaetetus walks" or "Theaetetus runs." That "Theaetetus sits" is more precise than "Theaetetus is locally at rest" is not at issue. "Theaetetus moves" and "Theaetetus rests" are both true, for Theaetetus could not be alive if he were wholly at rest, nor could he be Theaetetus if he were wholly in motion.

The kind of rest which "Theaetetus sits" determines, determines the kind of motion which it would be false to state of Theaetetus. Thus the falsehood of "Theaetetus sleeps" consists not in its being other than "Theaetetus sits"—they both can be true at the same time—but in its being other than "Theaetetus is awake." The stranger does not give this example because it would raise once more the question of how to tell apart the stranger as a figment of Theaetetus' dreaming from the stranger whom Theodorus believes to be really a stranger. The stranger, in any case, now gives definitions of thought and opinion which Theaetetus had heard the day before from Socrates, but the stranger shows none of Socrates' hesitation: Socrates had spoken as one who did not know and only reported on an image.[103]

Once the stranger shows that opinion and *phantasia* are cognate with speech, it is necessary that falsehood be miscible with them, and his case against the sophist is complete. But we can only be amazed at the ease with which he settles the problem of appearance. Apparently, in his eagerness to free Theaetetus of his fear that the sophist's defenses are not yet exhausted, the stranger simplifies the problem which phantastics raised to such a point that it no longer is the same problem. Phantastics as the art which corrects for perspectival distortion vanishes; it is replaced by something which turns out to be not an art at all. How does the stranger manage to conjure away the true problem? He first says that thought (*dianoia*) and speech (*logos*) are the same; he then says that thought is a dialogue (*dialogos*) within the soul before (*pros*) itself without voice (*phônê*) or sound (*phthongos*). Speech, then, doubles for both voiced thinking, which is conversing (*dialegesthai*), and voiced opining, which is speaking (*legein*). The stranger, however, never says what the nonsilent equivalent to opinion is. He seems to imply that it is a kind of appearing, for a heard utterance, which affirms or denies something, certainly mixes an opinion with a perception. "Theaetetus sits" is present to Theaetetus through perception; it is an affect which carries with it an opinion, for opinion is the conclusion of thinking.

The stranger belatedly points out that the speech "Theaetetus sits" does not necessarily express an opinion; it could be a question. If the stranger asks himself this question without sound, he is thinking; if he affirms it, again without sound, he is opining; but if the stranger asks it of Theaetetus, he is conversing, and if he affirms it before Theaetetus, he is speaking. What, then, is Theaetetus doing on these occasions? On the first occasion, if Theaetetus answers and says, "Yes" or "Theaetetus sits," he is both conversing and speaking. On the second occasion, he might be silent and thus appear to opine, but since the stranger's opinion is then present to him through hearing, he has only a *phantasma*. It would cease to be a *phantasma* and become his own opinion only when he removed from what he heard the fact that he had heard it and asked himself the question on his own. But if, instead, he accepted the *phantasma* as if it were not a *phantasma*, he would, if he spoke out and said "Yes" or "Theaetetus sits," be repeating the stranger's speech as his own. It would be indistinguishable from his own opinion as the conclusion of his own thinking. The stranger now explains how Theaetetus could so emphatically approve of what the stranger said the dialectician does (253d1–e3). Theaetetus' approval was the echo, that is, the phantastic confirmation, of the stranger's own opinion. The stranger, then, has not so much done away with the problem of appearance as alluded to it in his highly condensed account of appearance. Plato's dialogues are full of such echoes that look exactly like the expressions of genuine thought.

The initial difficulty that Theaetetus had in following the stranger's account of speech was due not only to the lack of parallelism between letters and words but also to the stranger's prior characterization of speech as the weaving together of kinds. The web of kinds fits what they have been doing; the web of noun and verb does not. The stranger deepened the difficulty by further characterizing speech as dialogue and the same as thought. Speech, then, is the weaving together of kinds, the weaving together of noun and verb, and conversation. Socrates, too, had proposed in the *Theaetetus* a triple characterization of speech: the image of thought in sound, the way through the elements, and the distinguishing mark of a being. If the first of Socrates' list corresponds more or less to the third of the stranger's and his second and third to the stranger's first, the stranger's grammatical definition seems to be a fourth that can be fitted with neither Socrates' list nor the rest of his own. Its position, however, in his account suggests that it is designed to negotiate between the web of kinds and dialogue. It thus might be the bond between them: "Theaetetus, with whom I am now conversing, flies." Dialogue requires two agents, and the weaving of kinds is an action. The stranger states that there can be no speech without agents and actions. There can be no dialogue without diacritics and no diacritics without dialogue. "Not to cut the art of hunting," the stranger said at the beginning, "is *alogon*," and Theaetetus had replied, "Speak at what point." The union, then, of diacritics and dialogue is speech. It is exemplified by the *Sophist*.

The stranger's account of *phantasia* is misleading because it fails to consider that perception itself can be misleading. Nonbeing mixes with speech, opinion, and *phantasia* but not, apparently, with perception. The stranger disregards the fact that the true speech "Theaetetus sits" is due to perception, and the false speech "Theaetetus flies" is not something which anyone sensible would say while Theaetetus and the stranger were conversing with one another. Whenever perception is held to be certain, it usually does not get expressed. The stranger says, "Theaetetus sits," and not "I see Theaetetus seated." If, however, there is uncertainty in our sensing, we say, "Theaetetus appears to sit." "Appears" means that Theaetetus perhaps does not sit. "Appears" inserts the other into whatever is affirmed. It is not the balanced entertainment of two contrary speeches, for which the formula is "Theaetetus either sits or does not sit"; it is their perceptual entertainment with a bias in favor of that which is doubted. Phantastics would thus be the art which removes "appears" from where it belongs; it would be the art of making the other disappear. It would replace a question with an answer. But if the other has already disappeared, the art of phantastics would be necessary to restore it. It would be the art of bringing to light the other as other.

This art, the exercise of which is manifest on every page of a Platonic dialogue, is not discussed by the stranger. Instead, on returning to their point of departure (eikastics and phantastics), the stranger enlists Theaetetus' nature in the task of suppressing the nature of the other. The last time Theaetetus said "It appears" was just before the stranger began his survey of the myths which the philosophers in their contempt for us tell about being (241d8), but Theaetetus never stops saying "It seems likely" or "It is likely,"[104] despite the stranger's having once caught him out in an "it seems likely" which expressed nothing but his yawn perplexity.

XIII. MAKING
(264d10–268d5)

Dichotomy is a way of stripping away from the sophist everything which he shares with other kinds until he stands revealed with his own nature. For some reason, which the stranger does not explain, the part in which the sophist is to be found is always on the right; perhaps he means no more than that the sophist must not be left behind in the other, that is, the left, part (cf. 226a7). The stranger implies, at any rate, that the sophist is apt to be mistaken for one of his relations, among whom he is initially entangled, and that even after he has been disengaged from them he must be defined as much by his partiality as by his apartness. The sophist exhibits the same doubleness as everything else; in a certain sense, his significance consists solely in his exhibiting this doubleness more clearly than anything else. But perhaps one should go even further and say that the sophist is just this fact—each thing is a part—and, like the nature of the other, his nature is to be nothing but a part of something else. The nature of the other is to have no proper nature. That the sophist has a nature distinct from the other would thus be his last and greatest illusion, for the being of an image was to be another of the sort. But since the difference between image and illusion remains unexplained to the end, the sophist only gets caught because eikastics ceases to be a problem. The stranger evades the problem of image by introducing a new distinction into the art of making. The difference between divine and human poetics substitutes for the unresolved difference between eikastics and phantastics, for divine poetics settles at a stroke the problem of being. There are only makers and the things they make.

Socrates had suggested to Theodorus that the stranger was a god of refutation; the stranger now suggests that there is a god of production. The link between a god who punishes and a god who makes is supplied by the notion of efficient causation. The god who punishes comes in disguise and does not reveal himself as who he is; the god who makes likewise does not reveal himself but relies on his works to show us who he is. Could Socrates' need for refutation be based on his failure to recognize the god of production in his works? If so, Socrates, who could see through the disguise of the stranger, could not see through man to the god of production.

The stranger distinguishes between images and the individual things (*auta hekasta*) of which there are images; Theaetetus does not ask and the stranger does not bother to say in what sense *auta hekasta* is to be taken. If a god makes every animal, does he exercise his art on each occasion an animal is born? Or did he make two of every kind? Are the offspring of the union of male and female so many artifacts? Since there is no room in the stranger's initial division for artless making, sexual generation would seem to be the most deep-seated of all illusions. More surprisingly, the stranger does not say whether the art by which god makes fire is the same as that by which he makes water, and if it is the same, whether it suffices to make man as well. If man making and fire making were not the same, there might be in Olympian fashion as many gods as there are arts; but if they are the same, the difference between body and soul would not be as great as Theaetetus had seemed to assume. Perhaps he believes, as Timaeus suggests, that their difference is no greater than that between arithmetic and geometry. Even if, however, there is a single divine poetics, would the god who possessed it know everything?

The stranger had distinguished before between the man who pretends he knows how to make everything and the man who pretends he knows everything, and Theaetetus had agreed that omniscience, whether it was in deed or in speech, was a plaything. Is the 'world' God's plaything?[105] By what standards would one judge how deep God's knowledge was? If the stranger has precluded the possibility of a making *ex nihilo*, a god who makes fire with as much knowledge as a shoemaker needs for making shoes, could not be said to know in the fullest sense. If the beauty of the whole were a sufficient index of God's full knowledge, we should want to know whether God practiced phantastics in making the whole, for if he did not, we should necessarily look upon the whole as ugly in the disproportion of its parts. If, however, God did practice phantastics, and the whole therefore looks beautiful to us, we could not tell whether its beauty were just an illusion or not, for if the visible whole is not a semblance of an intelligible whole, the visible whole would be a *phantasma* of a plan which would not itself show through anywhere. A visit to the stars would disclose their ugliness but not God's intention in making them ugly. If God simply hid what he did not understand, we should be none the wiser. The number of questions which divine poetics raises seems endless (265e2). Theaetetus, then, correctly and incorrectly feared that the sophist was ultimately elusive, for though the sophist's first defense would be that there is no divine poetics, and his second just the questions we have raised, Theaetetus' nature breaks through both lines of defense at once. Theaetetus is not even aware of the sophist's second line of defense.

The choice Theaetetus is offered is not clear-cut. There is obviously more than one possibility between nature as a random cause and God as a rational maker of everything, but the stranger knows Theaetetus' nature so well that he knows that Theaetetus considers the question only in the light of these two possibilities. "Well, I for one," he says, "perhaps on account of my age, have often been of both opinions about it in turn. Yet now in looking at you and supposing you to believe that they come to be in conformity at least with a god, I myself now hold this too." Theaetetus believes that the stranger is less poker-faced than Socrates, for he could not tell whether Socrates was expounding his own views on perception or merely trying him out.[106]

Theaetetus' hesitancy exemplifies the meaning of "it appears," for in his saying "perhaps on account of my youth" he indicates that he is inclined toward the view he believes the stranger holds. Furthermore, Theaetetus' glance at the stranger brings about a mixture of perception—the look on the stranger's face as Theaetetus reads it—with the opinion which Theaetetus forms on his own. So the stranger, perhaps without art and certainly without speech, causes Theaetetus' double opinion to disappear and be replaced by a *phantasma* the truth or falsity of which we ourselves cannot make out.

If the stranger's face is set by art, it is an example of ironic impersonation—a claim to know what he does not—if artlessly, it is natural and yet indistinguishable from self-suspected ignorance. The stranger praises Theaetetus' choice in the same way as Socrates had praised him for saying that the soul through itself without instruments examines certain things.[107] The illiberal force of precise speech which Socrates had employed to get Theaetetus to express such an opinion has its counterpart in the force the stranger's face now exercises on Theaetetus. In both cases, Socrates and the stranger are saved a lot of time. The stranger says that, without any speeches from him and others, Theaetetus' nature will proceed on its own to the acceptance of what he now lays down, that the things spoken of as being by nature are made by a divine art. Did a god make Theaetetus' nature? Or is his nature in its automatic and irrational motion the truth of so-called nature? If a god made Theaetetus' nature, he also made the nature of the many who hold that nature is irrational, and whereas Theaetetus' nature is such that it will never need speeches, their nature needs either speeches or some kind of irrational punishment to counter their arguments. If, however, a god did not make the various natures of men, neither Theaetetus' nor anyone else's, divine poetics is restricted to the making of lifeless and ensouled bodies in their most general character (266b2), and what the stranger calls Theaetetus' nature is the product of human contrivance. The stranger mentions animals, plants, all earthy things, fire and water; he does not name either air or any heavenly thing (232c4–5, 234a3–4).

The stranger now gives Theaetetus an order; he thereby shows how thoroughly he knows Theaetetus' nature. He tells him to cut all of poetics lengthwise, just as he has done widthwise. Theaetetus announces that the cut has been made and agrees that there are now two parts on "our side," and two on the gods' side. Theaetetus carries out an order without knowing what the order means. He only asks afterward what parts his cutting has produced (cf. 266d5). Apparently because the stranger speaks *more geometrico*, Theaetetus obeys automatically. His nature combines with his knowledge to advance the argument without argument. We cannot help but be reminded of the way in which Socrates made Theaetetus agree that a prepositional phrase was more accurate than an instrumental dative, for the stranger has likewise replaced the less precise expression "on the right" with the scientific terms "by length" and "by breadth." He imposes on class division the two-dimensional model of a plane figure. He thus calls our attention to the fact that there are no divine images in three dimensions, and perforce there cannot be divine eikastics, which renders without distortion the proportions of the paradigm in length, width, and depth (235d6–e2). The stranger calls both shadows and mirror images *phantasmata* (266b9). He says that they all follow on the offspring of God by a demonic contrivance. Since, however, he does not say that God makes each shadow or dream, he implies that these are what the many call natural beings: they are the thoughtless and random attendants of divine beings. Theaetetus' "nature" is dreamlike. Socrates, we recall, was able to interpret Theaetetus' last definition of knowledge because he shared his dream.

If the individual bodies we perceive were natural—the products of neither art nor thought—human artifacts, whether bodies or the imitations of bodies, would stand on a higher level of rationality. As products of intelligence, it would be hard to put them among the not beings, since what they lose in 'reality' they more than compensate for in intelligibility. Natural beings, then, could not be explained in terms of *logos*, but the imitations of these natural beings, either in deed or in speech, would be due entirely to *logos*. The falsehood of sophistic images would thus consist in their rationality: the illusion they instill would be of the rationality of nature. The sophist would thus represent the philosopher, since philosophy stands and falls with the possibility of *logos*. The truth would be Heraclitean, the false would be Platonic. The sophist's art would have two different roots, human reason and thoughtless nature, and his task would be to give an image of thoughtless nature that satisfies human reason. This image would conceal the truth of nature while pretending to be its revelation. Now, however, the stranger has guaranteed that no imitation can have a greater degree of rationality than what it imitates.

But if there is divine poetics, what would human wisdom be? Would it be the knowledge of how to duplicate the results of divine poetics? Or are human beings limited to discovering the plan of divine making without discovering its rationale? We should then get to know the pattern of things but not know how the pattern was arrived at. Astronomy would only be a predictive science, and there would be no true physics. For if a true physics were in principle possible, its products would be indistinguishable from the bodies of divine poetics. Sophistry could then only produce ultimately unsuccessful illusions. It would be the same as philosophy as long as philosophy were not wisdom. One therefore could be tempted to draw the apparently Socratic moral that divine poetics was unsuitable for human beings to pursue and men should restrict themselves to the study of human contrivances, but since there are human beings who profess to understand more than human things, one would be compelled either to banish them by law or supply a proof that there is a divine poetics. How such a proof could be obtained without trespassing the limits one had imposed on oneself, the stranger neither explains nor has to explain, not only because Theaetetus takes the stranger's face for the stranger's proof, but because the stranger eliminates the original question, which did not concern imitation in deed but imitation in speech (cf. 266c5). When he turns to phantastics he discusses only vocalized speech and not *logos,* for divine poetics only produces bodies and their images. Divine poetics seems to be the farthest one can go if one starts from the principle that to be means to be body.

Dreams are immune to human art; art does not enter into the makeup of our dreams. Prior to the introduction of the arts, Aeschylus' Prometheus says, men lived "like unto the shapes of dreams."[108] The human counterpart to dreams are the imitations of art; they are our waking dreams. They come the closest to duplicating divine art, for the difference between a good painting of a house and mirror image of a house can be indiscernible. Up to this point, neither falsehood nor truth belongs to divine and human image making. They are pictures in their otherness and not their sameness. A painted house is now "some other" house; it is no longer "another of the same sort." Indeed, the word *toiouton* does not recur once the stranger mentions divine poetics (265a8). If the beings are bodies, no one will ever take the bodiless for a being. What kind of being God is, Theaetetus does not ask; he naturally accepts, one might say, Socrates' "theology," according to which God never deceives.

The stranger recalls his former distinction between eikastics and phantastics, and without argument he proceeds to divide phantastics, as if divine image making had settled the question as to which art sophistry belongs. Accordingly, phantastics and by implication eikastics now mean something different. A semblance is not an apparition because the speech which accompanies it declares it to be a semblance, and an apparition is false solely because it is labeled falsely. The stranger rejects out of hand the apparition that is made through instruments, wherein its maker is not himself the instrument of deception. All apparitions in speech, whether written or not, which do not depend for their efficacy on the speaker pretending to be what he says, are dismissed. Plato slips by them. Theaetetus' failure to acknowledge speech as the soul's instrument now proves to be the obstacle to solving the original question. The stranger does not even give a name to instrumental phantastics; he urges Theaetetus to be lax and let another bring it into one and assign it a suitable name.

The part he does examine he calls impersonation (*mimêtikon*), in which one makes one's own body or voice appear to be another's. He goes on to divide impersonation into those who know what they imitate and those who do not. He introduces an artless class among the arts (cf. 225b12–c6), and what is more perplexing, the example he had just used to characterize impersonation as a whole now exemplifies a part of impersonation, for no one could impersonate Theaetetus unless he knew him. This confusion brings out the corporeal character of all mimesis. "The figure of justice and of virtues as a whole" is more of the body than of the soul; it comes about through habituation and not knowledge. Socrates calls it popular or political virtue.[109] The opinion impersonator tries to embody in all that he says and does the opinion he has of justice, but his opinion of justice is the common opinion, for otherwise he would not succeed in passing himself off as just. Political virtue assumes the possibility of its own realization in an individual; it knows nothing of the imprecision of action, let alone of a virtue which never gets incorporated because it never becomes.[110]

The ancients did not distinguish the imitation of political virtue from informed or "historic" imitation, for they did not discriminate between opinion and knowledge. The knowledgeable impersonator is thus in a quandary. If he knows what justice is, he cannot imitate it in such a way that it appears to be in him, for then justice will appear not to be in him; but if he wishes to appear just, he will have to disguise his artful imitation of true justice and adopt the artless imitation of spurious justice. If he succeeds in artfully faking what others sincerely practice, he will be ironic. His irony, however, will not be, like the sophist's, based on suspicion but on knowledge. Socrates, however, has not been wholly successful in disguising himself; he is about to go on trial. What he wanted to imitate in deed has broken through appearances; but he still does not appear in his true form. Meletus will mistake him for Anaxogoras.[111]

The stranger compounds still further the confusion that his distinction between knowledge and ignorance has entailed. He has Theaetetus agree that the sophist is among the imitators and not among the knowers, as if imitation had meant imitation of true virtue and not of political virtue. He thus implies that opinion is the image of knowledge; it would appear to be the same as what he had formerly called the health of the soul. The public or private sophist suspects that morality is double and of another, but since he does not know what the other is of which it is the other, he cannot imitate it and must fall back in his imitation on what passes in opinion for knowledge. The sophist comes very close to being the poet, whose superiority to Antigone and Ismene shows in his ability to portray them both, and yet who cannot point to an alternative. The sophist differs from the poet only because the sophist displays himself through himself and not through others. While suspecting that he does not know, he has the air or figure of one who knows, for he forces his interlocutor to contradict himself; but since Socrates does the same, he too arouses the suspicion in others that he knows. Regardless of the difference in their private opinions, Socrates and the sophist are indistinguishable in appearance.

Although Theaetetus refuses to join the stranger in dividing the class of ironical imitators, he is certain that the public ironist is not the statesman or politician but the *dêmologikos*. To be an experienced public speaker is to be ironical. Since Theaetetus cannot mean that the statesman is not so experienced, he must choose the nonce word *dêmologikos* on the grounds that it more readily conveys its meaning, and not that the statesman is someone else—a naive and simple impersonator of virtue, for example. It would be astonishing, in any case, if he implied, as the stranger now does, that wisdom is to sophistry as statesmanship is to demagogery. Theaetetus must be very tired when he says that the sophist impersonates the wise, for this equally applies to the *dêmologikos*. He should not have let the stranger casually drop in the word "wise"; in the context, it can only mean the wise maker or imitator. If Theaetetus is hazily remembering the early part of the discussion, in which the sophist was said to convince his disciples of his perfect wisdom, he should also be remembering that omniscience was then held to be impossible. Does Theaetetus believe that the sophist impersonates the blessed gods? The stranger emphasizes in his summary that the sophist is only human. He quotes from the *Iliad* a line with which Glaucos ended a genealogical speech that assured Diomedes that he was not a god.

Notes

1. Elea is a town in Italy, the birthplace of Parmenides and Zeno.
2. Socrates aludes to two passages in the *Odyssey* (IX.269–71; XVII.485–87). The first is spoken by Odysseus to the Cyclops: "But show shame, most powerful, before the gods; we are your suppliants, and Zeus is the avenger of suppliants and strangers, (Zeus) the god of strangers, who accompanies reverend strangers." The second is spoken by an anonymous suitor to Antinous: "Also the gods resembling strangers from different people, assuming all sorts of shapes, wander from city to city looking over the insolence (outrage) and law-abidingness of human beings." XVII.485–86 are quoted at *Republic* 381D.
3. The Mightier are the gods; cf. *Euthydemus* 291A.
4. The same phrasing is at *Theaetetus* 145C.
5. "Unbecoming a stranger" translates *axenos*, "not a stranger," and hence what does not suit a stranger.
6. There is a proverb, quoted at *Gorgias* 514E and *Laches* 187B, "pottery on a jar," applied to those who fail to practice on the elementary things before turning to the big things.
7. There is a fragment of the comic poet Epicrates (fr. 11K) that parodies this kind of division in the Academy:

> A: What are Plato, Speusippus, and Menedemus now up to? What is their concern? What kind of argument is investigated at their establishment? By mother Earth, tell me it cunningly, if you know anything.
>
> B: I'm very well informed. I saw a herd of lads at the Panathenaia in the gymnasia of the Academy and heard there strange speeches. They were making distinctions in nature and were separating the life of animals, the nature of trees, and the genus of vegetables. And then they examined to which genus the melon (a recent import) belonged.

A: Well, what did they define the plant to be and of what genus? Say, if you know anything about it.

B: Well, first they all stood in silence, and with their heads bowed they reflected for a long time, and then all of a sudden while the lads were still stooped and searching, one of them said it was a spherical vegetable, another said it was grass, and another a tree. And a physician from Sicily gave a fart in their direction as if they were talking nonsense.

A: Then they surely got angry and shouted at his abuse, for to do that in discussions of this sort is unseemly?

B: No, the lads paid no attention. And Plato who was there very gently, without a trace of anger, ordered them once more to determine of what genus it was, and they proceeded to divide.

8. In this list only *mimêtikê* (mimetic) has the suffix that implies it is an art, but in the list of acquisitive arts, all but "familiarization" have such a suffix.

9. One feature of the stranger's way of arranging his paradigm deserves mention. He usually presents the result of a division as a class, but when a class submits to further division, it is presented as an art. The alternation is quite regular. First there are the *metablêtikon* (exchange) and *kheirôtikon* (mastery) kinds of the art of acquisition; then there is the question of how to cut *kheirôtikê* (art of master) in two. First the *agônistikon* (competition) and *thêreutikon* (hunting) come from it, then the cutting in two of *thêreutikê* (art of hunting); first the lifeless class and the living, then *zôothêrikê* (art of hunting animals); first *pezothêrikon* (pedestrial hunting) and *enugrothêrikon* (in-liquid-hunting), then *ornitheutikê* (art of fowling) and *halieutikê* (art of fishing). But though the stranger speaks of *herkothêrikon* (fence hunting), he says *plêktikê thêra* (strike hunting), which designates neither a class nor an art (cf. 220c7). The stranger, then, proposes that we consider at each stage whether there could in fact be an art that would comprehend all subsequent divisions, or the class which he pretends to divide was already split in two, and no one with a single art could, for example, be both a contestant and a hunter. The ultimate question, of course, would be whether knowledge is simply one, and it undergoes modifications when it turns from fowling to fishing but essentially remains the same. The knower with a net is a sort of fisherman, but with a gift he practices the art of exchange.

10. The stranger puns on *herkos* (fence) and *heirgo* (confine). *Herkos* in the sense of net is known from poetry.

11. "The lower section" refers simultaneously to the fact that water is below air in deed, and to some manner of representing the divisions in which the class water was placed below air; cf. a similar ambiguity at 243B.

12. The stranger puns on *aspalieutês* (angler) and *anaspatai* (draws up), which is here translated "angles."

13. "Pedestrial" is meant to convey the ambiguity of *pezon* as either walking

on dry land (used of infantry, for example) or equipped with feet. This ambiguity persists throughout the *Sophist* and *Statesman*.

14. The original division was as follows.

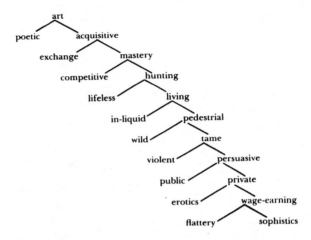

The summary departs radically from this, and several attempts have been made to bring it into line, none of them plausible. The key to its interpretation consists in seeing that the divisions are in pairs, with items dropped or rephrased to underline certain difficulties in the original divisions. Of the twelve arts, out of which the sophist's art is made, two are novel additions—appropriation and hunting on dry land—that seem to compensate for the omission of mastery and persuasion, of which the first cannot consist with the sophist's selling for cash, and the second would be repetitive after the hunting of human beings.

15. Exchanging (*allaktikon*) was originally called *metablêtikê* with no difference of sense (219D), but it then was opposed to mastery and not hunting. This confirms the elimination of mastery in the first summary. "Exchanging" *metablêtikê* will be used in note 16 for a division of marketing (223D).

16. The original division was

In the summary, it is assumed that one went directly from acquisition, but exchanging (*metablêtikê*) is restored and *allaktikê* dropped; the distinction between self-selling and exchanging others' goods is also dropped. The sophist as merchant or retailer can thus be inserted in the sophist's line of descent as hunter, but this undermines the paradigm of angler, for his art would now serve his avarice.

17. The summary restores self-selling as an alternative. One of Plato's techniques for indicating specious divisions is to use an "or" (*eite*) without a preceding "either" (*eite*); cf. 217E ("or maybe before another"); *Statesman* 283E ("or maybe in deeds").

18. The original division was

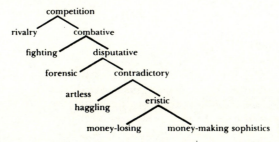

The summary assumes that the competitive art came directly off the acquisitive art, whereas it originally split away from mastery.

19. The other hand is the left hand; the saying corresponds to our "off-handedly"; "with both hands" means with all one's might.

20. The last verb seems to anticipate the characterization of the whole class, and various proposals have been made to replace it with some technical term for separation.

21. *Ponêria* ("wickedness") can characterize anything in a poor state, and morally it implies baseness more than viciousness. It is very close to *mokhthêria* (translated as "sorry state" at *Statesman* 302A), whose adjectival form is applied by Thucydides to Hyperbolus, who then goes on to say of him: "ostracized not because of fear of his power and rank, but because of the shame and *ponêria* of the city" (VIII.733).

22. "Sedition" (*stasis*) also means rest; it seems to have been a medical term for disease. It lurks behind *Theaetetus* 153A–D.

23. This is the reading of Galen. The manuscripts have, "anything else than the corruption (*diaphthora*) of that which is naturally akin out of some kind of variance (*diaphora*)." "Disruption" is used for the sake of the pun.

24. "Deficient measure" translates *ametria*, "without measure," and "deformed" *duseides*, "of ugly looks" or "of no looks (species)."

25. The stranger puns on "astray" (*paraphora*, "veering offcourse") and "distraction" (*paraphrosunê*, which has the root of *phrenes*, "wits").

26. The stranger alludes to the law-abiding man whose behavior does not correspond to the nature of his soul; cf. *Republic* 619B–C.

27. Cf. *Laws* 733 E.
28. Cf. *Gorgias* 464 B–466 A.
29. The parenthesis is meant to bring out the ambiguity of *dokei*, which is either the opinion one has of oneself or the opinion others have of you ("reputation"); cf. *Laws* 863 C; *Philebus* 49 A.
30. Cf. *Philebus* 55 D; *Laws* 643 D–644 A.
31. An allusion to Hesiod *Works and Days* 287–92: "Badness can be gathered by the handful with ease; the path is smooth and lies very near. But the immortal gods put sweat in front of virtue; the way to it is long and uphill, and rough at first, but when you come to the summit, it's easy thereafter, hard though it still may be."
32. Cf. *Symposium* 204 A.
33. Compare this account with Socrates' own of his maieutics, *Theaetetus* 149 A–151 D.
34. Cf. *Theaetetus* 210 C.
35. The great king is the king of Persia.
36. Cf. *Republic* 416 A.
37. The stranger puns on "noble" (*gennaios*) and "descent" (*genos*).
38. "Holds" is an addition to the text. It is not known what the feminine "all" referred to in the proverb; it could be, on the basis of 231 A, "hounds."
39. This phrase becomes the standard way in which Aristotle speaks of predication.
40. Cf. *Theaetetus* 178 E.
41. This could also be translated, but less plausibly, "what the craftsman himself must say in contradiction in the face of each controversial point."
42. *Makarie* is the vocative of *makarios* (blessed) as at 233 A, but there seems to be in Plato a suggestion of naivety. Theaetetus' innocence in this case refers to his unawareness that the law claims precisely the same things as sophistry: "others" is probably masculine.
43. Cf. *Republic* 595 C.
44. The Greek can also be translated by "and different things, plants"; Theaetetus certainly takes it this way (234 A).
45. The text is slightly corrupt here.
46. There is a scarcely concealed anapaestic-ionic rhythm to this sentence that the English tries to suggest.
47. A possible allusion to Sophocles *Oedipus at Colonus* 1022–24. Theseus is speaking of Creon's henchmen: "But if they prevail and escape, there's no need for us to toil; there are other pursuers, and they'll never boast to the gods to have avoided them and escaped from this land." At *Menexenus* 240 A–C and *Laws* 698 C–D, the story is told of the clean sweep of the Eretrians by Datis, a Persian general, ten years before Salamis: "His soldiers went up to the mountains of Eretrian territory and stationed themselves at intervals from sea to sea; they joined hands and

went through the entire country, so that they might tell the king that no one had escaped them."

48. Through a hyperbaton of "false things," the stranger makes it look as if it is the object of "say" and "opine"; (that) is meant to convey this ambiguity; cf. 241B. The form of the sentence is very like *Timaeus* 49B.

49. Parmenides fr. VII.1–2.

50. "A pair of somethings" translates a dual, and "someones" a masculine or feminine plural.

51. "Not even one thing" decomposes the elements of the word for nothing (*ouden* from *oude hen*).

52. A possible allusion to Sophocles fr. 662P: "Don't talk big yet before you see the end."

53. Socrates' criticism of Theaetetus' first answer to the question of knowledge is clearly alluded to (*Theaetetus* 146D–147C).

54. A variant and a series of words deleted by Madvig would permit this translation: "When it has been previously granted that the very terms of the admissions which have just been made are unutterable, unspeakable, irrational, and unthinkable" (L. Campbell, *The Sophistes and Politicus of Plato* (Oxford, 1867), p. 97).

55. The same hyperbaton explained in note 48.

56. Or possibly, "if we detach at any point even a slight bit of so mighty a speech and draw it over to our side."

57. Note how the proponents of the thesis become the arrangers of the elements of the things; cf. Aristotle *Metaphysics* 1000a5–15 for the stranger's criticism.

58. The strained Muse is Heraclitus, the relaxed Muse is Empedocles. The stranger quotes a fragment of Heraclitus (fr. 51) that is ridiculed by Eryximachus (*Symposium* 187A). The fragment quoted there reads "The one differing with itself agrees with itself, . . . just as the fitting together of a bow and of a lyre."

59. "In different places" refers both to parts of the universe and parts of the book; cf. note 11. A slight emendation would make this passage read very differently: "and whenever in turn someone else speaks of hot mixing with cold, positing disjunctions and conjunctions."

60. The transmitted text is probably corrupt; this seems the most plausible reconstruction. If one manuscript (B) is followed, the first half of the sentence would be "And the one being only the one of one . . ."

61. Parmenides fr. VIII.43–45.

62. The pun on "sky" (*ouranos*) and "invisible" (*aoratos*) also occurs at *Republic* 509D, *Timaeus* 36E. "Oaks and rocks" alludes to the proverb "not from oak nor rock," which characterizes those who have human origins; cf. *Apology of Socrates* 34D; *Republic* 544D; with a different sense *Phaedrus* 275B.

63. "Sweeping being" had been the phrase at *Theaetetus* 177C, 179D.

64. The "sown" (*spartoi*) usually refer to the armed men who sprang up

when Cadmus sowed the dragon's teeth at Thebes. Autochthony was the claim of many cities, particularly Athens and Thebes.

65. Aristotle calls attention to the similar defectiveness of this definition and Socrates' last definition of the beautiful in the *Hippias Major* at *Topics* 146a21–32; cf. *Theaetetus* 156A. The last clause of the stranger's speech would have to be translated, if the manuscript reading can be retained, as follows: "I'm proposing, in short, a definition (boundary-mark) to define (bound) the things which are, that they are, etc."

66. This is perhaps the most striking example in Plato of the omission of the first of two particles (*men-de*) that are meant to balance two clauses. Cf. 221E (a swimming part), 267B (Theaetetus' reply) and *Statesman* 291E (tyranny . . . kingship). Here it indicates the possibility that the friends of the species have made an improper division between becoming and being.

67. The word "august," which occurs several times in *Theaetetus, Sophist,* and *Statesman,* seems to convey in prose a specious air of self-importance (but cf. *Crito* 51A). In tragic poetry it usually does not; cf. Herodotus I.95.1; III.16.7. The Greek gods are not called holy precisely because they are alive.

68. Cf. *Philebus* 30C; *Timaeus* 30B.

69. It is rather obscurely phrased; another possible translation is "We shall push the speech at least through and away from both simultaneously." Cornford (*Plato's Theory of Knowledge* [London, 1935], p. 251, n. 1) understands *amphoin hama* as "with both hands," hence "with all our might" (cf. 226A).

70. Eurycles is referred to by Aristophanes as an image of himself in *Wasps* (1016–22): "The poet now desires to find fault with the spectators, for he says he was wronged first, though he had benefited them a lot, not openly but aiding other poets in secret—in imitation of the divination and thought of Eurycles—by slipping into the bellies of others he poured out many comic things, but afterward he courted danger openly and guided the tongue not of alien but of his own Muses."

71. A sentence difficult to interpret but not to translate; cf. in the first place, J. Stenzel, *Studien zur Entwicklung der Platonischen Dialektik von Sokrates zu Aristoteles*[2] (Leipzig, 1931), pp. 62–71.

72. "Same" and "other" are put in quotes in order to represent the double article of the Greek (*to tauton* and *to thateron*). It indicates that the "the same" and "the other" are being used as universals. The same device recurs at *Theaetetus* 185D.

73. It has been thought that there is a lacuna here, since Theaetetus does not answer the stranger's question directly, but Theaetetus understands the stranger to be appealing, by his contrary-to-fact question, to the principle of their argument.

74. "General and particular" is meant to convey, albeit inexactly, the difference between the two negatives in Greek, *ou* and *mê*. *Mê* is hypothetical and general, *ou* factual and particular.

75. A difficult sentence. It's clear from the words "again in turn" that the not beautiful is being characterized twice. But the sentence begins with *allo ti,* which can be an interrogative particle with no effect on the construction of the sentence, as in the text, with the consequence that the genitives that follow are those of belonging and exactly like "of the other" in the stranger's question above. It is also possible, but unlikely, to take it as follows: "something else of the things which are, in its isolation from a certain single genus." The common way of taking the first half of the sentence—*allo ti* interrogative and then "distinctly set apart . (isolated) from some one genus of the things which are"—would be a unique construction for Plato, who elsewhere does not have *aphoristhen* in this sense without a preposition of separation. Two manscripts have "part" for "genus."

76. Another difficult sentence, this time because of an hyperbaton and a possible ellipse. The crucial phrase could be read as "the antithesis of the nature of a proper part of the other," but the constancy of the phrase "the nature of the other" in this section seems to require the translation in the text (cf. 258D–E). There is a similar hyperbaton at *Statesman* 310A. The problem of the ellipse concerns the phrase "the nature of that which is," since, if the hyperbaton has some point, an ellipse of "proper part" could be assumed, and it would read, "the nature of a proper part of that which is." For parts of being, see *Parmenides* 144B.

77. "Likewise" fills in a lacuna in the text, which can also be supplemented this way: "the not big (is) not big and the not beautiful not beautiful."

78. "Distrust" and "disobeyed" are cognate (*apistia* and *apisteô*), and in another context the verb could be translated by "distrust."

79. An exact repetition of the lines quoted at 237A except that for the participle there ("searching"), a noun ("searching") is substituted.

80. This could also be translated as follows: "each proper part of the nature of the other in its opposition to that which is."

81. The stranger alludes to the proverb "The beautiful things are difficult."

82. The text after this reads "as possible." Since this seems impossible, various proposals have been made, none of them very persuasive.

83. "Defenses" could also be translated "problems" as at *Theaetetus* 180C.

84. Cf. *Theaetetus* 189E–190A. There is a pun here on "without" (*aneu*) and "thought" (*dianoia*); cf. *Republic* 494D.

85. Cf. *Theaetetus* 206D; *Philebus* 38B–E.

86. For the phrasing, cf. *Laches* 187E; *Hippias Major* 304D.

87. "Plants" (*phuta*) seems to be used to cover all natural things (*ta pephukota*); cf. 266B.

88. Cf. *Laws* 888E.

89. The supplement could also be "to be made" instead of "to be," but it is also possible that nothing is to be supplied.

90. Cf. *Theaetetus* 193C–D. Note that species (*eidos*) is used for image (*eidôlon*).

91. "Historical" as in "natural history." *Historia* is an Ionic word for inquiry.
92. *Iliad* VI.211. Half of this phrase is quoted at *Republic* 547A.

COMMENTARY

1. *Theaetetus* 145b8.
2. *Statesman* 257b5–6.
3. *Theaetetus* 196d2–197a5.
4. *Theaetetus* 170e1–2.
5. *Laches* 187e6–188a3.
6. *Republic* 331e6; *Meno* 99c7–d9.
7. *Republic* 381e4.
8. *Theaetetus* 146c2.
9. *Odyssey* 19.1–7.
10. *Theaetetus* 176b1.
11. *Statesman* 257b9–c1, 258b2–3.
12. *Theaetetus* 176b1–3.
13. *Statesman* 286e1 and context.
14. *Laws* 823b1–824a19.
15. *Ion* 538d1.
16. *Theaetetus* 149e1–8.
17. *Statesman* 258d8–e2.
18. *Laws* 730d2–7.
19. *Euthydemus* 290b1–8.
20. *Theaetetus* 198a7–8.
21. *Republic* 333a2–4.
22. *Theaetetus* 189c7.
23. *Gorgias* 463a6–b4.
24. Aristotle *Nicomachean Ethics* 1181a12–15; cf. *Gorgias* 456a7–8.
25. *Theaetetus* 210d1.
26. *Laws* 722b4–c2.
27. *Protagoras* 313c4–6.
28. *Euthyphro* 14c8–e8.
29. *Phaedrus* 267c7–d2.
30. *Parmenides* 135d3–5.
31. For this reason *diakrinein* is perhaps to be kept at 226b6.
32. *Laws* 735b1–e5.
33. 227c7–10; *Theaetetus* 185d7–e3.
34. *Gorgias* 464b2–465c7.
35. *Euthyphro* 5d1–5.
36. *Republic* 372e7.
37. *Theaetetus* 153c3–4; *Cratylus* 415b3–d6.
38. *Republic* 527c2.
39. *Theaetetus* 190a3.
40. *Timaeus* 89b4–c1.
41. *Republic* 439e6–440a7.
42. *Theaetetus* 145a7–8, 146c7–d2.
43. *Parmenides* 134d1–8.
44. *Republic* 492a5–e1.
45. *Theaetetus* 172c5.
46. *Phaedrus* 261d6–e4.
47. *Theaetetus* 149e1–5.
48. *Theaetetus* 176d5–6.
49. Xenophon *Cyropaedeia* I.6.31–33.
50. *Euthydemus* 290b1–d8.
51. *Euthyphro* 3a8–b4.
52. *Republic* 559d9.
53. *Philebus* 51c1–7.
54. *Erastae* 132b6–c3.
55. *Charmides* 169c3–6.
56. *Euthydemus* 283e7–284a8; *Parmenides* 161e4–162a1.
57. *Theaetetus* 197b9–10.
58. *Theaetetus* 188e7–9.
59. *Theaetetus* 147d3.
60. Aristotle *Physics* 193a3–9.
61. *Republic* 472d4–7.
62. *Laws* 668c7.
63. *Theaetetus* 208c5.
64. *Theaetetus* 184a1–3.
65. *Laws* 626d3–5.
66. *Theaetetus* 144d2, 169a4–5.
67. Aristotle *Metaphysics* 985b7–19.
68. Aristotle *Physics* 185b23–25.
69. Fr. 8, 1–6.
70. Aristotle *Metaphysics* 1007a20–b17.
71. *Parmenides* 141d7–e7; *Philebus* 27a1–2.
72. The Aristotelian equivalent to the tension between the precise and the comprehensive is found in the unstable counting of the principles of nature in Book I

of the *Physics*, and the 'dialectical' discovery of nature as found in Book II.

73. *Theaetetus* 155e5–6.
74. *Republic* 472b7–c3.
75. *Theaetetus* 171d1–3.
76. *Theaetetus* 184d2–5.
77. *Theaetetus* 152c1.
78. Isocrates *Busiris* (11) 25.
79. *Statesman* 290c3–291c6.
80. *Theaetetus* 181d8–e2.
81. *Republic* 453a1–3, 471c1–7.
82. *Theaetetus* 184a1.
83. *Laws* 627d11–628a3.
84. *Republic* 530e5–531b1.
85. *Statesman* 285b1–6.
86. *Phaedrus* 271c10–d7.
87. *Republic* 588c7.
88. *De partibus animalium* 644a12–22.
89. *Republic* 341d10–342b8.
90. *Statesman* 284e11–285a7.
91. *Theaetetus* 147b4–5.
92. *Statesman* 262c10–d6.
93. Thucydides I.3.3.
94. Herodotus IX.11.
95. *Laws* 859d3–860c3.
96. *Theaetetus* 169b5–c3.
97. Cf. J. Wackernagel, Vorlesungen über Syntax II (Basel, 1924), p. 294: "Auch ist beachtenswert, dass die Griechen bei der Namengebung, wo es ihnen doch auf Ausdrücke von gutem Omen ankam, Bildungen mit ἀ(ν)—gar nicht verschmähten. Waren die Griechen mehr als wir darauf eingestellt, das Schlimme als normal zu betrachten, und waren sie demgemäss öfter als wir veranlasst, das Fehlen von Schlimmem mit Vergnügen zu konstatieren?"
98. Aristotle *Metaphysics* 1028b2–4; *Cratylus* 421a7–b1.
99. Thucydides VI.79.2.
100. Aristotle *Metaphysics* 1029b8–10.
101. Aristotle *Metaphysics* 1003b27.
102. *Parmenides* 143a4–b8.
103. *Theaetetus* 189e6–190a7.
104. 236d4, 250c5, 254a7, 256e7, 268a8.
105. *Laws* 804b3.
106. *Theaetetus* 157c4–6.
107. *Theaetetus* 185d7–186a1.
108. Aeschylus *Prometheus Bound* 448–50.
109. *Republic* 430c3, 500d8, 518d9–e2.
110. *Republic* 472b7–473a4.
111. *Apology of Socrates* 26d1–e2.

STATESMAN

Statesman

SOCRATES

THEODORUS

STRANGER

YOUNG SOCRATES

SOCRATES: I really owe you a lot of gratitude, Theodorus, for my acquaintance with Theaetetus together with the stranger's as well.[1]

THEODORUS: But soon you'll owe triple this, Socrates, whenever they produce for you both the statesman and the philosopher.

SOCRATES: Well, well, are we to say, my dear Theodorus, that we've heard this stated thus by the mightiest in calculations and geometrical matters?

THEODORUS: How's that, Socrates?   B

SOCRATES: Because you set down each of the men as of equal worth, though in honor they stand further apart from one another than according to the proportions of your art.

THEODORUS: By our god Ammon, Socrates, that's a good and just point, or rather your rebuke of my mistake in calculation was a credit to your memory.[2] And I'll get you for it at a later time; but, stranger, don't weary of gratifying us, but in succession, whether you choose the statesman (the political man) first or the philosopher, make your choice and go through it.   C

STRANGER: It has to be done, Theodorus, since of course once we've undertaken it, we must not stand apart from it before we come to their completion. But what must I do about Theaetetus here?

THEODORUS: What about him?

III.3

STRANGER: Are we to give him a rest and have his fellow gymnast Socrates here take his turn? How do you advise?

THEODORUS: Just as you said, take his turn. A pair of youngsters if they rest awhile will put up with every kind of work more easily.

D SOCRATES: And there is the further point, stranger, that both of the pair probably have a kind of kinship with me from somewhere or other. One, you all say, appears similar to me, in accordance with the nature of his face, and one has his designation homonymous with our own, and the address makes for a kind of family relation; and we must always be eager to gain an acquaintance with our kinsmen through speeches. Now I myself associated with Theaetetus yesterday through speeches and I've now heard him answering, but neither's the case for Socrates, and one must examine him as well. Now let him answer me at a later time, but now you.

STRANGER: It shall be done. Socrates, do you hear Socrates?

YOUNG SOCRATES:[3] Yes.

STRANGER: Do you then go along with what he says?

SOCRATES: Yes, of course.

B STRANGER: It appears that nothing on your side's an obstacle, and perhaps still less should anything on mine be. But, more to the point, after the sophist, it's necessary, it appears to me, for the pair of us to seek for the statesman (the political man). Tell me. Must we set him down too as one of the knowers, or how?

SOCRATES: In this way.

STRANGER: Do we then have to take the sciences apart, just as when we were examining the former?

SOCRATES: Perhaps.

STRANGER: But, Socrates, it appears to me that their sectioning just isn't on the same terms.

SOCRATES: What else?

C STRANGER: It's on different terms.

SOCRATES: Yes, it seems likely.

STRANGER: In what direction, then, will one pick up and find the political straight-of-way? We have to find it and, once we've separated and removed it from everything else, stamp a single look (*idea*) on it, and by our putting the seal of a single different species upon all the rest of the turn-offs make our soul come to understand all the sciences as being two species.

SOCRATES: I suspect, stranger, that this now proves to be your work but not mine.

D STRANGER: Yes, but it still has to be yours as well, Socrates, whenever it becomes evident to us.

III.4

SOCRATES: You put it beautifully.

STRANGER: Aren't then arithmetic and some other arts akin to it stripped of actions and furnish only cognition?

SOCRATES: That is so.

STRANGER: Yes, but the arts of carpentry, in turn, and all manufacture, possess their science as if it naturally inheres in their actions, and E they bring to completion along with their actions the bodies that come to be through them and were not before.

SOCRATES: Why certainly.

STRANGER: Divide, then, all sciences in this way and address one as practical and one as only cognitive (gnostic).[4]

SOCRATES: You can have these as two species of one whole science.

STRANGER: Shall we, then, in addressing the statesman and king and slavemaster and, further, household-manager, set them all down as one, or are we to assert that there are as many arts as the names mentioned? Rather, though, follow me in this direction.

SOCRATES: Which?

STRANGER: The following. If someone, though himself in a private 259 station, is competent to advise one of the public physicians,[5] isn't it necessary for him to be addressed with the same name of the art as the one he advises has?

SOCRATES: Yes.

STRANGER: And what of this? Whoever is skilled enough, though himself private, to advise a man who is king of a land, shall we not say of him that he has the science which the ruler himself should have been in possession of?

SOCRATES: We shall assert it.

STRANGER: But yet it's the science of the simply true king that is the B royal science?

SOCRATES: Yes.

STRANGER: And so, whoever possesses it, regardless of whether he is in fact ruling or is private, won't he in any case be correctly addressed in strict conformity with the art itself as royal?

SOCRATES: It's just at any rate.

STRANGER: And, further, a household-manager and a slavemaster are the same?

SOCRATES: Why certainly.

STRANGER: And what of this? The figure of a large household or in turn the bulk of a small city—the pair of them won't at all differ in point of rule, will they?

SOCRATES: Not at all.

STRANGER: Then it's evident in that which we were just now examining C that there is one science that deals with all of these. And this science, whether one names it royal, political, or economic, let it not make for any difference between us.[6]

SOCRATES: No reason why it should.

STRANGER: Moreover, this is plain, that every king by means of his hands and all his body is capable of doing little for the maintenance of his rule in comparison with the intelligence and strength of his soul.[7]

SOCRATES: It's plain.

STRANGER: Do you want, then, for us to assert that the king is more at home with the gnostic rather than with the manual and practical art in general?

D

SOCRATES: Why certainly.

STRANGER: The political (science), then, and the statesman and the royal (science) and royalty—shall we put all these together into the same kind as one?

SOCRATES: It's plain.

STRANGER: Wouldn't we be proceeding in order if we should next determine the gnostic (science)?

SOCRATES: Certainly.

STRANGER: Pay attention. Are we to understand that there's after all a kind of natural joint in it?[8]

SOCRATES: What sort is it? Point it out.

E   STRANGER: The following sort. We agreed surely that there was an art of logistics.[9]

SOCRATES: Yes.

STRANGER: I suspect that it altogether belongs just to the gnostic arts.

SOCRATES: Of course.

STRANGER: Shall we grant, then, no more extensive work to logistics, with its cognition of the difference among numbers, than to discriminate the things cognized?

SOCRATES: Why certainly.

STRANGER: The reason is that every master-builder too is not himself engaged in work but is a ruler of workmen?

SOCRATES: Yes.

STRANGER: And it's surely because he furnishes cognition and not manual work?

SOCRATES: That's so.

260   STRANGER: Then he would justly be said to participate in the gnostic science.

SOCRATES: Certainly.

STRANGER: Yes, but it's appropriate for him, I suspect, once he's made a discrimination, not to be finished or to be quit of it, in the way the logistician was quit, but to charge each of the workmen with that which befits them until they've produced whatever's been charged to them.

SOCRATES: Right.

STRANGER: Isn't it the case, then, that though all (arts) of the sort and all that follow logistics are gnostic, still this pair of genera differs *B* from one another by the difference between discrimination and injunction?

SOCRATES: The pair does appear to.

STRANGER: Then in the case of all of gnostics together, if we should address in our division one part as injunctive (epitactic) and one as discriminative (critical), we would claim that it has been divided in a harmonious way?

SOCRATES: Yes, in my opinion at least.

STRANGER: And it's desirable for those who are doing anything in common to be unanimous.

SOCRATES: Of course.

STRANGER: Then as long as we alone share in this, we must dismiss the opinions of everyone else.

SOCRATES: Why certainly.

STRANGER: Come on then. In which of this pair of arts must we set *C* down royalty? Is it in the critical, just as if he were a kind of observer, or shall we set him down in the injunctive art as belonging to it, inasmuch as he is a master?

SOCRATES: Rather in the latter, of course.

STRANGER: One would then have to observe the epitactic art, whether it separates at some point. And it's my impression that it's in somewhat the following way: just as the art of retailers has been distinctly set apart from the art of self-sellers, so too the royal genus seems to have been distinctly set away from the genus of *D* heralds.

SOCRATES: How's that?

STRANGER: Surely retailers sell again a second time the previously sold works of others they receive.

SOCRATES: Yes, of course.

STRANGER: And the heraldic tribe too, in receiving the thoughts of others stated as injunctions, still a second time again on its own enjoins them on others.

SOCRATES: Most true.

STRANGER: What then? Shall we mix a royal (art) into the same kind as the art of the interpreter, the cox, the soothsayer, the herald, *E*

III.7

and many other arts akin to these, all of which do indeed enjoin? Or do you want, just as we were making a semblance just now, that we also make a name that parallels the semblance—since it's pretty nearly the case that the genus of self-injunctive arts is name-less—and do you want us to divide these in this way, to set down the genus of the kings into the self-injunctive (art) and neglect all the rest, and make way for someone other to set down a name for them? For our pursuit was for the sake of the ruler and not of his contrary.

SOCRATES: Yes, of course.

STRANGER: Since this now stands apart to a fair degree from those, distinct by the difference of whatever is another's in comparison with what is one's own, is it necessary in turn to divide again this very thing if we still have some kind of section that submits to the knife in it?

SOCRATES: Certainly.

STRANGER: And look, we do appear to have it. But follow along and join in the cutting.

SOCRATES: At what point?

STRANGER: Shall we not find that all rulers, as many as we think of as employing injunction, enjoin for the sake of some kind of coming-to-be?

SOCRATES: Of course.

STRANGER: And it is, moreover, not altogether difficut to take apart in two all the things which come into being.

SOCRATES: At what point?

STRANGER: Surely of all of them together some are soulless and some ensouled.

SOCRATES: Yes.

STRANGER: Yes, and if we want to cut the part of the gnostic kind which is injunctive, we'll cut it by these very things.

SOCRATES: In terms of what?

STRANGER: Ordering one kind of it to range over kinds of becoming of the soulless, and one over those of the ensouled. And everything will in this way be now divided in two.

SOCRATES: Altogether so.

STRANGER: Let's then leave aside one kind of them, and let's take up one. And once we've taken it up, let's part all of it into two.

SOCRATES: Which one of the pair of these are you saying has to be taken up?

STRANGER: There's no doubt about it; it's the injunctive kind that deals with animals. To supervise the soulless things, as if it were a master-builder's job, is never the characteristic of the royal science,

but it is nobler and grander, always in possession of its power in   *D*
the case of animals and about these very things.

SOCRATES: Right.

STRANGER: And as for the coming-into-being and nurture of the animals, anyone could see that there is single-animal nurture and
the common care of the nurslings in the herds.

SOCRATES: Right.

STRANGER: But we won't find the statesman at least to be a nurse-in-
private, like an oxdriver or a horse-groom, but with more of a
resemblance to a horse-feeder and cattle-feeder.

SOCRATES: Yes, now that it's said it does appear to be so.

STRANGER: Do we give, then, to the common nurture of many together,   *E*
which belongs to animal-nurture, the name of herd-nurture or a
kind of common-nurture?

SOCRATES: Whichever it turns out to be in the speech.

STRANGER: Beautiful, Socrates! And if you guard against taking names
seriously, you'll show up richer in point of intelligence as you
approach old age. But now, just as you urge, it must be done. Do
you notice at what point of the art of herd-nurture, by a showing
of its doubleness, one will make that which is now sought in the   *262*
doubles be sought from then on in the halves?

SOCRATES: I'll be eager. And it's my impression that there is some
other nurture of human beings, and in turn a different nurture
of beasts.

STRANGER: You've indeed made a division in an altogether most eager
and manly way. But still, as far as we can avoid it, let's not undergo
this at a later time.

SOCRATES: What sort of thing?

STRANGER: Let's not remove a single and small proper part over against
many and great parts, and let's not do it apart from species either,   *B*
but let the part have at the same time a species. For though it's
the most beautiful thing right at the start to separate apart and
away from anything else that which is being sought if it's correct—
just as you a little while ago, on the suspicion that you had the
division, urged forward the speech when you saw that it was proceeding toward human beings—but my dear, it's not safe to work
on so minute a scale, and it's safer to go cutting through the
middle; it's there rather that one might encounter looks (*ideai*).
This makes all the difference in inquiries.   *C*

SOCRATES: How do you mean this, stranger?

STRANGER: It's due to the goodwill that I have for your nature, Socrates, that I must try to point it out with still greater clarity, though
at the moment, in the present circumstances, it's impossible to

make it plain without falling short. But for the sake of clarity I must try to advance it forward a slight bit more.

SOCRATES: Just what sort of thing exactly are you pointing to? What were we not doing correctly just now in our dividing?

STRANGER: The following sort of thing. It's as if someone in an attempt
D to divide in two the human genus should divide as many here make the distribution—they remove apart from everyone the Hellenic genus as if it were one, and all the rest of the genera, which are infinite, immiscible, and not consonant with one another, they address with a single designation, "barbarian," and expect on account of this single designation that they also be one genus—or
E again if someone should hold that by dividing ten thousand away from all, as if he were separating apart one species, he was dividing number into two species, and then for all the remainder, by setting down one name, should claim that on account of the designation this genus too proves to be another one apart from that. But one would surely be dividing more beautifully in two and more in accordance with species if one should cut number by even and odd, and the genus of human beings in turn by male and female, and only then split off Lydians and Phrygians or any others and order them in opposition to everyone whenever one should be
263 perplexed as to how to find each of the splits as a genus and a part together.

SOCRATES: Most correctly. But as a matter of fact, stranger, this very thing—how would one come to recognize more vividly genus and part, that the pair of them is not the same but other than one another?

STRANGER: Best of men! It's no trivial matter, Socrates, that you impose, and though we even now have strayed further afield than we should have from the proposed speech, you are urging us to stray still more. So let's go back now, as it's fit and seemly, and
B we'll pursue these things as if we were trackers at a later time and at our leisure. But, however that may be, be altogether on your guard against this—don't ever get the impression that you've heard it from me as a vividly established distinction—

SOCRATES: What sort of thing?

STRANGER: That species and part are other than one another.

SOCRATES: What else?

STRANGER: That whenever there is a species of something, it's necessary that it also be a part of whatever thing (*pragma*) the species is said (to be) of, but there's no necessity that a part be a species. Always assert, Socrates, that I speak in this way rather than in the former.

SOCRATES: It shall be done.

STRANGER: Do, then, point out to me the next thing.   C

SOCRATES: What sort of thing?

STRANGER: The starting-point of our wandering off course, that which led us here. My own suspicion is that it was right around the point where you were asked where herd-nurture was to be divided, and you said very eagerly there were two genera of animals, the human, and, of all the rest together, another one of beasts.

SOCRATES: True.

STRANGER: And you then appeared to me, in removing a part, to believe you were in turn leaving behind the remainder as one genus of all, because you could attribute the same name to all of them with the designation beasts.   D

SOCRATES: This too was the way it was.

STRANGER: But the fact of the matter is—manliest of all!—that perhaps, if there is somewhere some other intelligent animal, such as the (genus) of cranes seems to be or anything else of the sort, which perhaps on the same terms as you separates by names, it sets up cranes as one genus in opposition to all the rest of the animals and on its own makes itself august and by comprehending all the rest along with human beings into the same kind addresses them as nothing else perhaps than beasts. Let us then try to take   E precautions against everything of the sort.

SOCRATES: How?

STRANGER: By not dividing the entire genus of animals, in order that we may be less subject to these errors.

SOCRATES: We mustn't be.

STRANGER: Yes, for there was at that time a further mistake at that point.

SOCRATES: What exactly?

STRANGER: All of our injunctive part of gnostics was surely agreed to be of the genus of animal-nurture, though it was, to be sure, of herd animals. Wasn't it?

SOCRATES: Yes.

STRANGER: Well, then, even at that time animal in its entirety had been   264 divided by the difference between the domesticated and the savage, for those animals that have a nature open to domestication have been addressed as tame, and those which are not willing to be domesticated as savage.

SOCRATES: Beautiful.

STRANGER: Yes, but the science we're hunting was and is engaged in the tame, but it has to be sought in the case of herd nurslings.

SOCRATES: Yes.

STRANGER: So let us not divide as we did then, when we fixed our gaze on all animals, nor with haste either, in order that we may not get too quickly to—of all things!—political (science), for it has

B made us even now experience the proverbial experience.

SOCRATES: What sort?

STRANGER: By not dividing well in our hastiness, it has made us accomplish it more slowly.

SOCRATES: Yes, though it has done beautifully by us too, stranger.

STRANGER: Let that be as it may. But regardless of this, let's try again from the beginning to divide the art of common-nurture, for perhaps the speech itself, on its being carried through to the end, will reveal to you even that for which you are eager more beautifully. Point out to me—

SOCRATES: What sort of thing exactly?

STRANGER: The following: whether you've heard of it after all perhaps

C from some, for I know that you yourself have never met up with the domestication of fish on the Nile and the lakes of the great king, though perhaps you might have noticed it in ponds.

SOCRATES: Yes, of course. I've observed the latter and heard of the former from many.

STRANGER: And there are besides the feeding ponds of geese and cranes. Even if you've not wandered in the Thessalian plains, you've at least heard of them and trust they are.

SOCRATES: Why certainly.

D STRANGER: Now it's for this reason, you see, that I asked all this, because there is an aqueous kind and there is as well a walking-on-dry-land kind of nurture of herd animals.

SOCRATES: Indeed there is.

STRANGER: Do you too, then, share my opinion that on these lines one must part in two the science of common-nurture and distribute each of the two parts of it to each of the two of these and name the other the liquid-nurture kind and the other the dry-nurture kind.

SOCRATES: Yes, I do.

E STRANGER: And if we do this, we'll not seek any further which of the two arts the royal kind belongs to, for it's plain to everyone.

SOCRATES: Of course.

STRANGER: Everyone certainly would divide the dry-nurture tribe of herd-nurture.

SOCRATES: How?

STRANGER: By a distinction between the feathered and pedestrial.

SOCRATES: Most true.

STRANGER: And what of this? Mustn't the political kind be sought in the pedestrial? Or don't you believe that just about even the stupidest holds this opinion?

SOCRATES: Yes, I do.

STRANGER: And one must show the (art) of pedestrial-grazing,[10] just as if it were an even number,[11] being cut in two.

SOCRATES: That's plain.

STRANGER: And right here and directed exactly toward that part for *265* which it has started out, our speech appears to catch sight of a pair of two extended roads. One is quicker, dividing itself into a small over against a big part, and one does have to a greater extent just that which we were talking about earlier, that one must cut down the middle as far as possible; it is, however, longer. So it is possible for us to make our way on whichever one we want.

SOCRATES: But why is that? Is it impossible to go both ways?

STRANGER: Yes, at least together it is—what a surprise you are! It's plainly possible, however, in turn.

SOCRATES: Well, in that case, I for one choose both in turn. *B*

STRANGER: It's easy, since the remainder's short. The demand, however, would have been hard for us at the beginning and while we were still in the middle of our journey, but now, since this is our resolve, let's go on the longer road first, for when we are fresher we'll traverse it more easily. Look then at the division.

SOCRATES: Speak.

STRANGER: The pedestrial of our tame animals, all that are herded, have undergone a natural division into two.

SOCRATES: By what?

STRANGER: By the fact that the coming-into-being of one is hornless and one is horn-bearing.

SOCRATES: It appears so. *C*

STRANGER: By the use of speech, then, divide the (art) of pedestrial-grazing and assign it to each of the two parts, for if you want to name them, you will have it more intricately woven than it should be.

SOCRATES: How then should I speak?

STRANGER: As follows. That once the science of pedestrial-grazing gets divided in two, the other proper part of it has been enjoined to range over the horn-bearing part of the herd, while the other over the part of the hornless herd.

SOCRATES: Let them be spoken of in this way, for it has in any case *D* been made plain adequately.

STRANGER: And it's evident to us besides that the king, at least, grazes some kind of herd docked of horns.

SOCRATES: Of course it's plain.

STRANGER: Let's then fragment the herd and try to assign to him that which he gets.

SOCRATES: Certainly.

STRANGER: Do you want then to divide it by the difference between the split and so-called single-hoofed, or by the difference between generation-in-common and generation-in-private? Surely you understand—

SOCRATES: What sort of thing?

E STRANGER: That whereas it's the natural characteristic of horses and donkeys to generate from one another[12]—

SOCRATES: Yes.

STRANGER: Still the remainder of the smooth herd of the tame does not mix by genus with one another.

SOCRATES: Of course not.

STRANGER: And what of this? Does the statesman appear to have a care of a common-genus nature or of some private-genus?

SOCRATES: Plainly his care's of the nonmixing nature.

STRANGER: We must, then, set this out in two, it seems, just as we did the previous kinds.

SOCRATES: We must indeed.

266 STRANGER: Now animal, all that's tame and in a herd, has been by now pretty nearly in its entirety chopped into bits except for a pair of two genera, for the genus of dogs does not deserve to be counted among herd nurslings.

SOCRATES: No, indeed it doesn't. But by what exactly do we divide the pair of two?

STRANGER: By the very means it's quite just for Theaetetus and you to distribute by, since the pair of you are involved in geometry.

SOCRATES: By what?

STRANGER: By the diameter, of course, and again by the diameter of the diameter.[13]

SOCRATES: How did you mean that?

B STRANGER: The nature that the genus of us human beings possesses— it isn't, is it, naturally geared in some different way for walking than as the diameter two foot in power is?

SOCRATES: No differently.

STRANGER: And the diameter of the remaining genus is, again in terms of power, the diameter of our power, if, that is, it's naturally twice two feet.

SOCRATES: Of course it is, that's it, and I pretty nearly understand what you want to make plain.

STRANGER: And besides these, Socrates, do we catch sight of some

other thing that has come to be, in what we have divided, which   C
might have earned us a fine reputation for provoking laughter?

SOCRATES: What sort of thing?

STRANGER: Our human genus has simultaneously got the same lot as
and run the course to a tie with the noblest and most accommodating genus of the things which are.

SOCRATES: I do catch sight of it, and it's a very strange result.

STRANGER: But what of this? Isn't it likely that the slowest things wind
up last?[14]

SOCRATES: Yes, in this case at any rate.

STRANGER: And do we realize this, that the king comes to light as still
more laughable in running along with his herd and having tra-   D
versed a joint course with the man who has, no less than his herd,
been best exercised for the commodious life?[15]

SOCRATES: That's altogether so.

STRANGER: You know, Socrates, that this is now more evident than
when it was stated at the time in the investigation of the sophist.

SOCRATES: What sort of thing's that?

STRANGER: That a pursuit of speeches of this sort no more cared for
the more august than for what was not, any more than it has denied
honor to the smaller in preference for the bigger, but it always
on its own terms gets on with the truest.

SOCRATES: It seems likely.

STRANGER: Am I then to proceed on my own for your sake to the next
point, in order that you may not get ahead of me and ask about   E
the shorter way, whatever it was that leads to the boundary-mark
(definition) of the king?

SOCRATES: Yes, exactly.

STRANGER: I say, then, that one must straight off at the start distribute
the pedestrial by the two-foot in relation to the four-foot genus
and—with the sighting of the human, that it still shares its lot with
only the winged—cut the two-footed herd again by the stripped
and wing-growing difference, and once it has been cut and the
human-grazing art has been by then made plain, carry forward
the statesman and the kingly and set him up over the herd as if
he were a charioteer, and hand over the reins of the city to him
on the grounds that they are his own and this is his science.

SOCRATES: That's beautiful, and like a debt you paid me back the   267
speech, and by the addition of the turnoff, as if it were interest,
you paid it back in full.[16]

STRANGER: Come then. Let's go back to the beginning and sew together
up to the end the speech of the name of the statesman's art.

SOCRATES: Yes, of course.

STRANGER: There was, then, at the beginning for us an injunctive part of the gnostic science; and the proper part of this, worked out by means of a semblance, was stated to be self-injunctive. And again

B   an art of animal-nurture was split off from the self-injunctive (art) as not the smallest of its genera; and there was a herd-nurturing species of the art of animal-nurture, and a pedestrial-grazing (species) in turn of herd-nurture; and of pedestrial-grazing there was cut off especially a nurturing art of the hornless nature. And if one wants to bring it together into one name, it's necessary in

C   turn to weave together the part of this in no less than a triple strand and address it as the grazing science of nonmixing becoming. And the cut after this, the only one still left—the human-grazing part assigned to the two-footed herd—this is then the very thing sought, the designation for which, royal and political, is simultaneously the same.[17]

SOCRATES: That's altogether so.

STRANGER: Has this really and truly, Socrates, been in fact done by us in just the way you have now spoken?

SOCRATES: What sort of thing exactly?

STRANGER: That the proposed topic has been said altogether ade-

D   quately? Or is this the very thing that the search most falls short of—though the speech has been said in a sense, it has not been altogether perfectly produced?

SOCRATES: How did you mean that?

STRANGER: I shall try to make still plainer to the pair of us just what it is I'm now thinking.

SOCRATES: You must speak.

STRANGER: Isn't it the case that of the many herding arts that just now came to light for us, the political was some single art and a care of some kind of single herd?

SOCRATES: Yes.

STRANGER: And the speech was determining this to be, not a nurse of horses or of different beasts either, but a common-nurturing science of human beings.

SOCRATES: That's so.

E   STRANGER: Let's then observe the difference between all the herdsmen and the kings.

SOCRATES: What sort of difference?

STRANGER: Whether someone, with the name of a different art, asserts and pretends to be a joint nurse of the herd in common with anyone of the rest of the herdsmen.

SOCRATES: How do you mean that?

STRANGER: For example, the merchants and farmers and all the food-makers, and besides them the trainers and the genus of physicians—do you know that all these would gang up on and altogether fight against the herdsmen of the human things, whom we called statesman, and insist in their speech that they take care *268* of human nurture, and not only of human beings in herds but also of the nurture of the rulers themselves?

SOCRATES: And wouldn't they be speaking correctly?

STRANGER: Perhaps. We'll go on to consider it, but we do know the following, that no one will dispute with a cowherd at any rate about any of this, but the cattleman is himself the nurse of the herd, himself the physician, himself as it were the marriage broker and in the case of the births and lyings-in that occur, the single knower of midwifery. And furthermore, to the extent that his *B* nurslings have partaken by nature in child's play and music, no one else is mightier than he to soothe them and by enchanting gentle them, both with instruments and by the mouth alone he handles best the music of his own herd.[18] And the same manner holds in general for all the rest of the herdsmen. Isn't that so?

SOCRATES: Most correctly.

STRANGER: How, then, will our speech about the king appear correct and unblemished, whenever we set him down as the only herdsman and nurse of a human herd and separate him out from the *C* rest of the thousands who dispute it?

SOCRATES: In no way.

STRANGER: Wasn't it correct, then, a little while ago for us to get scared when we suspected that we were in fact speaking of some kind of royal figure, but had not yet produced with precision the statesman, until we strip away those who have swamped him and who raise the counterclaim of a joint grazing with him, and once we've separated him away from them show him forth pure and alone?

SOCRATES: Most correctly, rather. *D*

STRANGER: Then we have to do this, Socrates, unless we intend to disgrace the speech at the end.

SOCRATES: But that's in no way to be done.

STRANGER: So we have to proceed again from a different beginning on some other way.

SOCRATES: What sort exactly?

STRANGER: By a mixture pretty near to child's play, for we have to make use of a large part of a big myth, and then afterwards, just *E* as before, by continually removing part from part come at the summit to that which is being sought. Mustn't we?

SOCRATES: Yes, of course.

STRANGER: Well, then, pay very close attention to my myth, just as children do. It is in any case not many years since you've fled from child's play.

SOCRATES: You must speak.

STRANGER: Well, then, of ancient stories, there was, among many different ones which occurred and will recur, the particular case of the portent in the storied strife between Atreus and Thyestes.[19] You've surely heard of it and remember what they say occurred at the time.

SOCRATES: Perhaps you're pointing at the sign about the golden ram.

269 STRANGER: No, not at all, mine pertains to the change in the setting and rising of the sun and the rest of the stars—the place, the story goes, from which it now rises was at that time where it set, and it rose from the opposite side, and that was the time when the god testified for Atreus and changed it into its present scheme.[20]

SOCRATES: Yes, this too is indeed said.

STRANGER: And we've heard as well from many of the kingdom which Cronus ruled.[21]

B SOCRATES: From most, rather.

STRANGER: And what of this? That those before grew up earth-born and were not generated from one another?[22]

SOCRATES: Yes, this too is one of the ancient stories.

STRANGER: Well, all these together are from the same affect (and besides these there are thousands of others still more astonishing than these), but, on account of the length of time, some of them have been extinguished and some have undergone a dispersal and been spoken of severally apart from one another. But no one

C has stated the affect which is the cause for all these things, but it must at last be said, for once it's stated it will eminently fit in with the showing forth of the king.

SOCRATES: You put it most beautifully, and without omitting anything, speak.

STRANGER: You must listen. The god himself at times joins in conducting this all and making it circle as it goes along, and at times he just lets go, whenever the circuits have obtained the measure of the time appropriate to the all, and it then gets to turn around

D spontaneously in the contrary direction since it is an animal and has obtained as its lot intelligence from him who at the beginning fitted it together. This going in reverse has been of necessity native to it on account of the following.

SOCRATES: On account of what sort of thing exactly?

STRANGER: It's fitting for only the most divine things of all to be always the same and in the same state and in the same respects, and the nature of body (is) not of this ordering. And that to which we've

III.18

given the name of heaven and cosmos, though it has partaken of many blessed things from its generator, it still despite that has a share in body too. This is the origin of its incapacity to be exempt *E* from alteration through all time, however much it is the case that to the best of its capacity its motion is single, in the same place, and on the same terms. It has therefore obtained for its lot reverse revolution, the smallest possible deviation from its own motion. But it's pretty nearly impossible for anything by itself—except for that which is the leader of all moving things—to twist itself around forever, and it's not sanctioned for him to set in motion (anything) at one time in a different way, and again in the contrary way. So on the basis of all this, one has to assert that the cosmos does not always on its own twist itself around, and in turn does not as a whole get twisted around by a god in two contrary revolutions, *270* and again some pair of gods who think contrary things to each other do not always twist it around,²³ but what was just now stated and is alone left—it sometimes is joined for its guidance by a different divine cause; reacquiring life again and receiving an artificial immortality from the craftsman (demiurge), and sometimes, whenever it is just let go, goes by itself through itself, released at a moment of such a sort so as for it to go in reverse for many thousands of circuits. And this is precisely due to the fact that, though it is the largest thing, it is also the most equally balanced and goes on the smallest foot.²⁴

SOCRATES: It does appear at any rate that everything you've gone *B* through has been said in a very likely way.

STRANGER: On the basis, then, of the present remarks, let's figure out and get to understand the affect which, we said, was the cause of all the wonderful things. It is in fact this very thing.

SOCRATES: What sort?

STRANGER: The fact that the locomotion of the all was sometimes in the direction in which it now circles, and sometimes in the contrary.

SOCRATES: How's that exactly?

STRANGER: Of all the revolutions that occur in the heaven, one must believe that this alteration was the biggest and most complete revolution.

SOCRATES: It seems likely at least.

STRANGER: Well, then, one must also hold that the greatest alterations *C* occur for those of us who at the time are dwelling within it.

SOCRATES: This too's likely.

STRANGER: And don't we know after all that the nature of animals has a hard time of enduring the convergence of many great alterations of all sorts?

SOCRATES: Of course.

STRANGER: Accordingly, the greatest destructions of necessity then
D   result, not only of the rest of the animals, but in particular the
genus of human beings survives as a small remnant. And in their
case, many different circumstances, marvelous and strange, coincide, but here is the greatest one and a consequence of the
unwinding at that time of the all whenever it goes into the turn
that's contrary to the one which obtains at present.

SOCRATES: What sort?

STRANGER: First of all, the age, which each and every animal had, came
to a halt, and everything that was mortal stopped its advance
E   toward looking older, but, in altering, each genus grew back in
the contrary direction, younger as it were and suppler. And the
white hair of the elders was getting black, and the cheeks of those
with beards were, in growing smooth, becoming what they were
in their previous period of bloom, and the bodies of youths in
growing smooth and in becoming smaller day by day and night
by night were going back toward the nature of the new-born child,
getting to be similar to it both in terms of the soul and in terms
of the body. And from that point on they began to wither away
and vanish utterly and completely. And of those, in turn, who
271   died violently at that time, the body of the corpse, in being affected
with these same affects, quickly in a few days wasted away and
disappeared.

SOCRATES: But what exactly, stranger, was the genesis of animals then?
And in what manner did they generate from one another?

STRANGER: It's plain, Socrates, that the generation from one another
was not in their nature at that time, but the earth-born genus that
is reported to have once been was this one at that time when it
turned itself round once more out of the earth. And it was remembered by our first ancestors who were neighbors in the suc-
B   cessive period of time to the former revolution when it was ending
and were born at the beginning of this revolution, for they were
the heralds to us of these speeches, distrusted by many now but
incorrectly. What happened next, I suspect, one has to figure out.
The fact that the elders go into the nature of the child and, on
the other hand, it's from the dead, who lie in the earth, that they
get put together there once more and live again, the connection
between them is that they accompany the turn in the direction of
generation that occurs along with the reversal of circular motion.
C   And it's precisely in conformity with this speech that, in growing
of necessity earth-born, all of them, whom a god did not carry
off to a different fate, get this name and this story.

SOCRATES: Yes, this certainly does follow at least on the previous remarks. But, more to the point, that life which you say was at the
time of Cronus' power—was it in those revolutions or in these?
For it's plain that the alteration of the stars and sun coincides with
the occurrence of each of the two revolutions.

STRANGER: You've followed the speech beautifully. But the question *D*
you ask, when all things came to human beings spontaneously,
that does not in the least belong to the presently established revolution, but this too belonged to the earlier. At that time, the god
who has it in his care first ruled the circling itself as a whole,[25] and
likewise in region by region there was this same kind of rule, when
all the parts of the cosmos had been distributed under ruling
gods. And, in particular, gods (*daimones*) had like divine shepherds
distributed the animals by genera and herds, each one of whom
was by himself all-sufficing for each of the groups that he himself
grazed, and as a consequence there was neither anything savage *E*
nor any act of feeding on one another, and there was no war at
all or sedition either. In short, to tell of all the different things
that are consequences of an arrangement of this sort would be to
speak of thousands and thousands. But, in any case, the story
about the spontaneous livelihood (life) of human beings has been
said on account of something of the following sort. A god was
himself in charge and grazed them, just as human beings now,
being another more divine animal, graze different genera inferior
to themselves. But when the god was grazing there were no regimes or possessions of women and children either, for everyone *272*
came alive again from earth without any memory of those before,
but all things of the sort were absent. And they had abundant
fruits from trees and woodlands of many different sorts, which
did not grow by farming, but the earth sent them up spontaneously. And they were grazed much of the time outdoors, naked
and without bedding, for that which characterized their seasons
was a mixture that gave no pain, and they had soft beds when an
abundance of grass grew up from earth. You've heard, Socrates, *B*
of the life in the times of Cronus, but this present life, of which
the story is that it's in the time of Zeus, you have by your own
presence been aware of—would you then be capable and willing
to decide which of the pair was happier?

SOCRATES: In no way.

STRANGER: Do you wish then that I be the one to make the decision
for you in a sense?

SOCRATES: Yes, of course.

STRANGER: Well, then, if the nurslings of Cronus, when they thus had

C   a lot of leisure and power for not only associating with human beings but also with beasts through speeches, were employing all these advantages for philosophy, in their association with beasts and one another, and learning by inquiry from every nature whether each with its own kind of private capacity was aware of something different from all the rest for the gathering and collection of intelligence, then it's easy to decide that those then excelled these now in point of happiness by a thousandfold. But if filling themselves to satiety with foods and drinks, they conversed with one another and the beasts with just the sort of stories

D   that even now are spoken of them, then this too—at least if it is to be declared according to my own opinion—is very easily decidable. But all the same, however this may be, let's disregard it, until some competent informant comes to light for us and reveals in which of the two ways those then had their desires about the sciences and the use of speeches. But the purpose for which we awakened the myth, this has to be said, in order that we may get on with the next thing that still lies ahead. After the time of all

E   these things had been completed and there had to be an alteration and, in particular, after the entire earthly genus had already been used up, when each soul had rendered back all its generations (*geneseis*), once it had let fall into the earth as many seeds as had been prescribed for each,[26] it was precisely at that moment that the helmsman of the all, just as if he had let go of the handle of the rudder, stood apart and withdrew to his own surveying-post, and a fated and inborn desire reversed once more the cosmos. Then all the gods who were jointly ruling with the greatest god (*daimôn*) in their several regions, on the recognition of what was

273   then occurring, let go in turn of the parts of the cosmos that were in their own care. And the cosmos in twisting round and sustaining a shock, starts out with an impulse contrary to the beginning and end,[27] and in making a lot of quaking in itself produced once more a different destruction of all sorts of animals. After this, when sufficient time had passed, and the cosmos had by then come to the end of its disturbances and perturbation, it gained fair weather free of quakes and was proceeding, in its reordered state, into its own usual course, with its own care of and au-

B   thority over those things in itself as well as itself, remembering to the best of its ability the instruction of its craftsman and father. Now at the beginning, it performed in a more precise and finished way, but finally with less keenness. The cause of this was the corporeal form of its mixture—the innate character of its onetime former nature—because it used to partake of a lot of disorder prior to its arrival at the order (cosmos) it now has. For from its composer it possesses all beautiful things, but from its former C condition, everything that proves to be harsh and unjust in heaven—these are the things it itself has from that state and works up into the animals. Now when along with the helmsman it nourished the animals in itself, the worthless things it gave birth to were small and the good things great. But in getting separated from him, during the time that is ever nearest to the moment of release, it conducts everything most beautifully. But when time advances and forgetfulness more and more arises in itself, then the affect of the ancient disharmony dominates, and at the final D moment of time it bursts out into full bloom, and the good things are small, and by the increasing mixture of the contraries, it comes to risk destruction of both itself and the things in it. It is accordingly at precisely this moment that the god who made it a cosmos, on looking down on its being in perplexities in anxious concern that in being tempest-tossed by perturbation it be dissolved and sink into the sea, which is limitless, of dissimilarity, once more takes his seat at its rudder, and by a twisting round of the E things diseased and sprung in the former circuit by itself, he makes it a cosmos and in correcting it, works it up into something deathless and ageless. Now the end point of everything has been stated, and it's adequate for the showing forth of the king if we attach the speech to a remark previously made. When the cosmos was twisted again into its way that leads to the present kind of becoming, the ages once again halted and gave back novelties the contrary of those then. The animals that had by their smallness almost vanished began to increase, and the new-born bodies out of earth grew gray and in dying went down once more into earth. And everything else altered as well, in imitation and in consequence 274 of the affect of the all, and in particular the imitation of conception, generation, and nurture followed them all by necessity. For it was no longer possible in earth, through the composition of others, for an animal to grow, but just as the cosmos had been ordered to be an independent authority over its own movement, so too in exactly the same way the parts themselves were ordered to grow, generate, and nurse, to the extent that they could, through B themselves by a similar conduct. Now it's just here that we're at last at the point for the sake of which the whole speech set out. For about all the rest of the beasts, it would prove to be too much and too long to go through, from what and on account of what causes they have severally altered, but about human beings it's shorter and more appropriate. Upon their isolation from the care of the god (*daimôn*) who possesses and grazes us, many of the beasts in turn, all that were harsh in their natures, became savage, and since human beings had themselves become weak and unguarded they were torn apart by the beasts, and they were still without devices and without arts in those first times, because the spontaneous nurture had given out. And they did not yet know how to supply it for themselves on account of the fact that no need had previously compelled them. From all of this, they were in great and resourceless perplexities, and this is the source of the storied gifts of long ago, to the effect that they have been bestowed on us from gods along with the necessary (indispensable) instruction and education, fire from Prometheus, arts from Hephaestus and his coartisan [Athena], and in turn seeds and plants from different ones.[28] And everything, all that has arranged human life, has been from these, after that which characterized the care from gods, as was stated before, gave out for human beings, and they through themselves had to manage their way of life and their own care for themselves just as the cosmos as a whole, in joint imitation of which and following along with which we now live and grow in this way and sometimes in that. Now let the end point of the myth be here, but we shall make the myth useful for catching sight of how great our error was when in the previous speech we made a presentation of royalty and the statesman.

SOCRATES: How then do you mean this? And how great has the error been for us?

STRANGER: In one sense, the mistake was of less compass. But in a sense it was a very grand mistake and greater and more extensive by far than it was then stated to be.

SOCRATES: How's that?

STRANGER: In the sense that we were asked for the king and the statesman from the present revolution and becoming, and instead we spoke of the shepherd of the onetime human herd from the contrary circuit, and, what's more, of a god instead of a mortal, we went very far off course. But in the sense that we showed him forth as the ruler of the entire city, but did not articulate in what manner he ruled, the statement, though it was true, was not, however, wholly said or with clarity, and therefore we've made a mistake that is of briefer compass than the former one.

SOCRATES: True.

STRANGER: We must then, it seems, expect if we determine the manner of his rule of the city, to have spoken, once we've done this, of the statesman completely.

SOCRATES: Beautiful.

STRANGER: It's for this reason too that we set down the myth alongside *B*
him—in order that it might point out about herd-nurture not only
that everyone now disputes it with the one we're looking for, but
that we might see more vividly him too, for whom alone it is
suitable to have a care of human nurture in accordance with the
paradigm of shepherds and cowherds and be held alone deserving
of this kind of address.

SOCRATES: Right.

STRANGER: Yes, Socrates, and I suspect that this figure of the divine
shepherd is still too big to be in accordance with a king, and that *C*
those who are statesmen here and now are far more similar in
their natures to the ruled than the divine shepherd is and have
shared an education and nurture more nearly the same as theirs.

SOCRATES: No doubt about it.

STRANGER: And yet, if they are by nature in this way or in that, they
would not have to be sought either less or more for all of that.

SOCRATES: Of course not.

STRANGER: Let's then go back once more to this point. We said it was
a self-injunctive art for animals, not however with its care in pri- *D*
vate but in common, and we then addressed it straight off as herd-
nurturing. Do you remember?

SOCRATES: Yes.

STRANGER: Well, it's somewhere hereabouts that we were making our
mistake. We did not anywhere grasp the statesman or name him
either, but he gave us the slip and escaped by way of nomenclature.

SOCRATES: How's that?

STRANGER: All the rest of the shepherds surely are engaged partly in
the nurture of their several herds, and, though the statesman is *E*
not, we applied the name to him, when we should have applied
some name that's common to them all together.

SOCRATES: What you say is true, provided, that is, that there was a
name.

STRANGER: Of course there was. Surely the fact of tending, at least, is
common to all, without any distinct determination of nurture or
of any different business either? But we could have named it some
kind of herd-grooming or tending or even some caring art, and
on the grounds of its applicability to all, it was possible to envelop
the statesman along with everyone else, since the speech was indicating that we should have done it.

SOCRATES: Right. But the division after this, in what manner would it *276*
then be coming to be?

STRANGER: On just the same lines as those on which we were previously
dividing the art of herd-nurturing—by pedestrial and wingless,

and by nonmixing and hornless—it would surely be by these same differences that if we were dividing them we would have in the speech comprehended similarly both the present kingship and that in the time of Cronus.

SOCRATES: It appears so. But I'm now looking for what's the next point.

STRANGER: It's plain that once the name of herd-grooming had been stated in this fashion, we would never have had anyone disputing us that it is not at all a caring either, just as then it was justly disputed that there is no art among us that deserves this kind of address— nutritive—but if in any case there should be, there were many who had a prior claim to it and for whom it was more suitable than for any of the kings.

SOCRATES: Right.

STRANGER: Yes, but no other (art) would be willing to assert at least that it rather was a care of an entire human community and an art of ruling prior to the royal (art) and applicable to all human beings.

SOCRATES: What you say's right.

STRANGER: Yes, and after this, Socrates, do we realize that just at the very final point a large mistake was again made?

SOCRATES: What sort?

STRANGER: The following: even if, after all, we had come to understand as well as we could that there was some nutritive art of the human herd, we should no more be addressing it straight off as royal and political as if it were completely perfected.

SOCRATES: Why exactly?

STRANGER: First of all, the name by which we are to speak of it had to be refurbished and applied to care rather than nurture, and in the second place it had to be cut, for no longer would it have small sections.

SOCRATES: What sort of sections?

STRANGER: No less by that surely by which we would have divided apart the divine shepherd and the human caretaker—

SOCRATES: Right.

STRANGER: Than again it was necessary to cut in two the assigned art of caring—

SOCRATES: By what?

STRANGER: By the forcible and voluntary.

SOCRATES: Why exactly?

STRANGER: It's surely at this point in fact that we earlier made a mistake of a sort more naive than we ought to have done, when we put together into the same kind king and tyrant, who are themselves

III.26

most dissimilar, and the manner of the rule of each of the two is as well.

SOCRATES: True.

STRANGER: Yes, but now are we to go back and correct it and, just as I said, divide in two the (art of) human caretaking by the forcible and voluntary?

SOCRATES: Yes, of course.

STRANGER: And is it no doubt the case that we are to address as a tyrannical (art) the care of those who submit to force, and as a political (art) the voluntary herd-grooming of voluntary two-footed animals, and declare that he who has this as an art and care is in his being king and statesman?

SOCRATES: Yes, stranger, it's probable that the showing forth of the statesman would in this way be perfectly complete for us.   277

STRANGER: That would be beautiful for us, Socrates. But this must not be just your opinion alone, but I too must share it in common with you. But now, according to my opinion at least, the king does not yet appear to have for us a perfectly complete figure, but just as statue-makers on occasion in their untimely haste dash in more and bigger things than they should and slow down each of their   B
works, so now we too, in order that—of all things—we might make plain in a magnificent way (as well as quickly) the mistake of the previous explication, in the belief that it was fitting to make up for the king great paradigms, we raised up an amazing bulk of the myth and were compelled to make use of a greater part of it than we should have. It's for this reason that we've made our showing forth longer and did not in any case put a complete finish to the myth, but our speech simply (artlessly), like an animal   C
(painting), though it seems likely to have its external outline adequately, has not yet received the vividness as it were that's in pigments and the mixture of colors. And it's more fitting to make plain by means of speaking and speech every animal—to those capable of following it—than by painting and every kind of handicraft, but to all the rest who are incapable, to do it through handcrafted works.

SOCRATES: This is no doubt correct. But do make it plain at what point you assert it has not yet been adequately said by us.

STRANGER: It's hard—you extraordinary being!—without the use of   D
paradigms to indicate adequately any of the bigger things, for it's probable that each of us knows everything as if in a dream and then again is ignorant of everything as it is in waking.

SOCRATES: How did you mean this?

STRANGER: It's very strange, but it seems likely that I've at the moment stirred up the experience that we have in us about knowledge.

SOCRATES: Why exactly?

STRANGER: It's my fault that the example too—you blessed innocent!—has itself a need in turn of an example.

E SOCRATES: What then? Speak and, as far as I'm concerned, don't shy off.

STRANGER: I must speak, since you in fact are quite prepared to follow. Well, we surely know of boys, whenever they just get experienced in letters—

SOCRATES: What sort of thing?

STRANGER: That they perceive adequately each of the elements in the shortest and easiest of the syllables, and they prove capable of pointing out the truth about them.

278 SOCRATES: Of course.

STRANGER: But on being in doubt about these same elements in different syllables, they once more are deceived both in opinion and in speech.

SOCRATES: Yes, of course.

STRANGER: Isn't this then the easiest and most beautiful way to bring them to whatever elements are not yet recognized?

SOCRATES: How?

STRANGER: First, to bring them back to those in which they were opining these same elements correctly, and once we've brought

B them back, to place them beside whatever elements are not yet recognized, and by our bringing them alongside, point out that the same similarity and nature are in both weavings, until the elements that are truly opined may be shown being placed alongside all those not recognized, and, once they have been shown, become in this way paradigms and make each of all the elements in all the syllables always be addressed on the same terms as itself—

C the other as being other than the rest, and the same as the same.

SOCRATES: That's altogether so.

STRANGER: Have we then comprehended this adequately, that the coming-into-being of a paradigm is at just that time whenever in being the same in another pulled apart from it, it's rightly opined and, on comparison, completes a single true opinion about each of the two as about both together?

SOCRATES: It appears so.

STRANGER: Would we then be full of wonder if our soul has been

D affected by nature in this same way with regard to the elements of all things, and that sometimes by truth it gets to be consistent about each one in some things, and sometimes it is in turn distracted about everything in other things, and here and there among their mixtures it rightly opines some of them, but when they're rearranged and placed in the long and not easy syllables of things (*pragmata*) it once more fails to recognize these same elements?

SOCRATES: No, there's nothing wonderful in that.

STRANGER: For how else would one be capable, my dear, in beginning from a false opinion to arrive at even some small part of the truth and acquire intelligence?   *E*

SOCRATES: In no way, pretty nearly.

STRANGER: Isn't it the case, then, that if these things are naturally in this state, you and I would not be striking any false note if we should first try to see the nature of paradigm as a whole in a small, different, and partial paradigm, and after that, if we should apply from somewhere or other that which is the same species (though from lesser things) to the greatest species of the king and intend through a paradigm to try in turn to recognize by art the tending of the things throughout the city, in order that it may prove to be for us a waking state instead of a dream?

SOCRATES: Yes, of course it's right.

STRANGER: We have to resume once more, then, the previous speech,   *279* which stated that since thousands upon thousands dispute with the royal genus about the care of cities, one must separate all these apart and leave only him. And we said besides that we had need of some kind of paradigm for this purpose.

SOCRATES: Indeed we did.

STRANGER: What's the smallest paradigm, then, with the same business as the political, that one could set alongside it and find adequately that which is sought? Do you want, by Zeus, Socrates, if we don't   *B* have any other ready at hand—well, do you want at any rate that we choose the art of weaving?[29] And, if it's so resolved, not all of this either? Perhaps the weaving that deals with robes woven from wool will suffice, for perhaps even this part of it, should it be chosen, would testify to what we want.

SOCRATES: Well, why not?

STRANGER: Why don't we then, just as previously we were cutting parts of parts and dividing each kind, also now, in the case of weaving,   *C* do this same thing, and to the best of our ability traverse all of it briefly and quickly and then go back to that which is now useful?

SOCRATES: How do you mean this?

STRANGER: I'll make the explication itself an answer to you.

SOCRATES: You put it most beautifully.

STRANGER: Well, of all the things we have that we craft and acquire, some are for the sake of affecting (making) something, and some

are repellents for the sake of not being affected; and of repellents
some are protective drugs both divine and human, and some are
D   defenses; and of defenses some are armor for war and some are
obstructions; and of obstructions some are screens and some protectors against storms and heat-spells; and of protectors some are
shelters and some coverings; and of coverings spreads are different and others are envelopments; and of envelopments some
E   are seamless wholes and others composite; and of composites some
are perforated and some bound together without perforation;
and of the unperforated some are the sinewy (fibrous) elements
of plants from earth and some hairy; and of the hairy some are
matted by water and earth and some are bound together by themselves. And the name we give to those kinds of repellents and
coverings made out of these things that bind themselves together
280   by themselves is cloaks, but as for the art whose special care is of
cloaks—are we to address it now from the thing (*pragma*) itself,
just as we then said the caring art of the city is political (civil), as
the art of cloakmaking? But are we to assert that the art of weaving
too, to the extent that its largest proper part was agreed to be for
the making of cloaks, does not at all differ except in name from
this cloakmaking, just as in that case too we then said the royal
art did not differ from the political?

SOCRATES: Yes, most correctly.

STRANGER: Then let us reflect on the next point—the fact that one
B   would perhaps be of the opinion that, if the art of weaving cloaks
should thus be stated, it has been adequately stated, if one were
not capable of realizing that it has not yet been distinguished from
its close coefficients, though it is parted from many other congeners.

SOCRATES: What do you mean, "congeners"? Speak.

STRANGER: It's apparent that you did not follow what was said; so it
seems that I have to go back over it once more beginning from
the end. Not only did we now cut its kin off from it, if you understand the family relation, by separating the composition of
spreads by the difference between casting-round and casting-
under—

SOCRATES: I understand.

C   STRANGER: But we further removed the entire manufacture out of
flax, grasses, and all that we just now spoke of by analogy (*logos*)
as the sinews of plants, and we distinguished in turn and set aside
the art of making felt and the composition that employs perforation and stitching, of which the largest element is shoemaking.

SOCRATES: Yes of course.

STRANGER: And we removed, then, the skinmaking treatment of seamlessly whole coverings as well as all the arts of shelters, which have the capacity to keep out streams, housebuilding, carpentry as a whole, and different arts as well, and all the arts of obstructions *D* that supply works of prevention in the case of thefts and violent actions—they deal with the coming-into-being of lidmaking and the joiner's work on doors, assigned apart as the proper parts of the art of bolting—and we cut away the art of making armor, which is a slice of the large and omnifarious defense-making capacity; and finally, straight off at the beginning we distinguished *E* the entire magical art of protective drugs, and we would be of the opinion that we've left behind the very sought-for art of repelling winter-storms, productive of a woolen defense, which goes by the name of weaving.[30]

SOCRATES: It does indeed seem likely.

STRANGER: But this has not yet, my boy, been stated perfectly, for whoever handles at the beginning the making of cloaks appears to do the contrary of weaving. *281*

SOCRATES: How's that?

STRANGER: Whereas that which characterizes weaving is surely a certain kind of plaiting together—

SOCRATES: Yes.

STRANGER: Still that which characterizes the initial process is a resolution of things that have coalesced and been matted together.

SOCRATES: What sort is it exactly?

STRANGER: It's the work of the art of the carder. Or shall we have the nerve to call the art of carding weaving and the carder a weaver on the grounds that he is one?

SOCRATES: In no way.

STRANGER: And if, moreover, one addresses the art productive of warp and woof as the art of weaving, one speaks a name that's paradoxical and a lie. *B .*

SOCRATES: Of course.

STRANGER: And what of this? Are we to set down the entire art of fulling and the art of repairing to be not any care and treatment of a garment, or shall we speak of all of these as arts of weaving?

SOCRATES: In no way.

STRANGER: But rather, all these will dispute with the capacity of the art of weaving about the treatment and the coming-into-being of cloaks, granting it the biggest part but reserving for themselves big parts too.

SOCRATES: Certainly. *C*

STRANGER: Well, besides these, there are still the arts productive of

III.31

the tools through which the works of weaving are finished. They must seem to lay claim to being at least the cocauses of every web.

SOCRATES: Most correctly.

STRANGER: Will our speech, then, about the art of weaving—the part

D we chose—be distinguished adequately if we assign it after all the most beautiful and biggest of all the operations and cares that deal with the woolen garment? Or would we be saying something true but not however with clarity or perfectly complete either, until we strip away from it all these as well?

SOCRATES: Right.

STRANGER: Then must we do next what we're saying, so that our speech be in an orderly succession?

SOCRATES: Of course.

STRANGER: Well, then, let's first observe that there are two arts that deal with everything that is being done.

SOCRATES: What?

STRANGER: One is the cocause of becoming and one the cause itself.

SOCRATES: How?

E STRANGER: All that do not craft the thing (*pragma*) itself, but prepare the tools for the arts that do craft it, and in whose absence the thing ordered would never be done by each of the arts, these are the cocauses, but those that produce the thing (*pragma*) itself are the causes.

SOCRATES: It does at any rate make sense.

STRANGER: Are we then to say next that the arts that deal with spindles, combs, and all the rest of the tools that have a share in the coming-into-being of wrappings are all cocauses, while those that treat and craft them are causes?

SOCRATES: Most correctly.

282 STRANGER: Of the causes, then, the art of washing and repairing and all the treatment of these things—though the cosmetic art is extensive, it's particularly fit and seemly for us to comprehend the entire proper part of it in this case with the name of the fulling art.

SOCRATES: Beautiful.

STRANGER: And the art of carding, moreover, and of spinning, as well as all the parts that deal with the very making of the garment we're speaking of, are some single art that is one of those in general use and said by everyone, the art of woolworking.

SOCRATES: Of course.

B STRANGER: There are two paired sections of the art of woolworking, and each one of this pair is by nature simultaneously a natural part of a pair of two arts.

III.32

SOCRATES: How?

STRANGER: Carding and half of the art of combing and everything that sets apart from one another things which are put together,[31] all this, as far as it is to be declared one, surely belongs to both the art of woolworking itself—and there was for us as well in each and every case a pair of some two great arts, the art of combination (syncritics) and of discernment (diacritics)[32]—

SOCRATES: Yes.

STRANGER: Well, the art of carding and everything just now mentioned belong to diacritics, for the art of discernment that's engaged in C wools and warp-threads (it works in a different way by means of the comb from the other way it works by means of hands), gets all the names that were just now mentioned.

SOCRATES: Yes, of course.

STRANGER: Then let's take up once more a proper part of syncritics that proves to be simultaneously a part of woolworking and engaged in it, and let's dismiss all the elements that belonged in this case to diacritics and cut woolworking in two by a diacritical and a syncritical section.

SOCRATES: Let it have been so divided.

STRANGER: Then we must, Socrates, divide for you in turn simultaneously the syncritical and woolworking proper part, if we're going D to seize adequately the aforementioned art of weaving.

SOCRATES: Indeed we must.

STRANGER: Yes, we must. And so let's say of it that one is twisting and one is plaiting.

SOCRATES: Do I really understand? It's my impression that you're speaking of that which deals with the making of the warp as twisting.

STRANGER: Yes, but not only that, but also of the woof. Or shall we find some coming-into-being of it without twisting?

SOCRATES: In no way.

STRANGER: Distinguish, then, each one of this pair, for the distinction E perhaps might prove to be a timely one for you.

SOCRATES: At what point?

STRANGER: At this: of the works of carding, do we speak of something as a thread if it's lengthened out and has width?

SOCRATES: Yes.

STRANGER: Then of this, that which gets twisted by a spindle and becomes a solid thread, declare it a warp-thread, and the art that straightens it out the art of warp-threadmaking.

SOCRATES: Right.

STRANGER: But all, on the other hand, that takes the twisted mass loose

III.33

and fluffy, and relative to the drawing out of carding obtains its softness to a degree proportionate to its being plaited in the warp, let's assert that these spun threads are, after all, the woof, and the art put in charge of them that of woof-threadmaking.

283

SOCRATES: Most correctly.

STRANGER: And lo and behold—it's surely by now plain to everyone— the part of the weaving art we proposed. Whenever the proper part of the syncritical art engaged in woolworking produces a plaited web by a straight plaiting of woof and warp, we address the entire plaited thing as a woolen garment, and the art that supervises it as weaving.

SOCRATES: Most correctly.

B STRANGER: So far so good. Why ever then did we not answer straight off that weaving was a plaiting of woof and warp, but we went round in a circle distinguishing very many things in vain?

SOCRATES: It's my opinion at any rate, stranger, that none of the statements was stated in vain.

STRANGER: No, there's nothing wonderful in that. But perhaps, you blessed innocent, there might be such an opinion. So in light of an illness of this sort, if perhaps after all it recurs—there's nothing wonderful in that—listen to a kind of speech that's suitably spoken about everything of the sort.

C

SOCRATES: Just speak.

STRANGER: Well, let's look first at the entirety of excess and defect, in order that we may praise and blame in proportion (logos) the things that are said on each occasion in engagements of this sort at greater and shorter length than they should.

SOCRATES: Indeed we must.

STRANGER: So I suspect that if our speech should prove to be about these very things, it would prove to be correct.

SOCRATES: What things?

D STRANGER: About length and brevity and every excess and defect, for surely the art of measurement deals with all these things.

SOCRATES: Yes.

STRANGER: Let's divide it into two parts, for they're needed for what we're now striving for.

SOCRATES: You must speak at what point the division is.

STRANGER: At this: one is to be characterized in terms of the mutually relative sharing in bigness and smallness, and one in terms of the necessary (indispensable) being of becoming.

SOCRATES: How do you mean that?*

STRANGER: Isn't it your opinion that it's by nature that the greater

must be said to be greater than nothing other than the less, and
the less, in turn, to be less than the greater and nothing else?   *E*

SOCRATES: Yes, it is.

STRANGER: And what of this? That which exceeds the nature of the
mean and is exceeded by it, in speeches or maybe in deeds—shall
we not speak of it in turn as in its being a coming-into-being, in
which the bad and good ones among us have their most particular
differences?

SOCRATES: It appears so.

STRANGER: So, after all, it's these one must set down as the twofold
modes of being and judging of the big and the small,[33] and not
only, as we just now said, must it be the mutually relative measure,
but rather as it has now been said, the mutually relative measure
and the measure relative to the mean must be said. Would we
want to understand what the latter is for?

SOCRATES: Why certainly.

STRANGER: If one will allow the nature of the bigger to be relative   *284*
to nothing other than to the less, it will never be relative to the mean,
will it?

SOCRATES: That's so.

STRANGER: Then won't we destroy by this speech the arts themselves
as well as all their works, and in particular we'll make vanish both
the political art that's now being sought and the art of weaving
that's been described? For all arts of this sort surely keep a close
watch in their actions on the more and less of the mean, not on
the grounds that it is not but on the grounds that it is difficult.   *B*
And it's in exactly this way, by preserving the mean, that they
produce everything good and beautiful?

SOCRATES: Why certainly.

STRANGER: And if we make the political (art) vanish, won't our search
after this for the royal science be perplexed?

SOCRATES: Yes indeed.

STRANGER: Then, just as in the case of the sophist we compelled 'that
which is not' to be, when the speech slipped by us along this line,
so also now, in turn, mustn't the more and the less be compelled
to become measurable relative not only to one another but also   *C*
to the becoming of the mean? For it's really not possible for either
a statesman or anyone else to have been proved to be indisputably
a scientific knower of matters of action if this is not agreed upon.

SOCRATES: Then we must as best as we can do the same thing now as
well.

STRANGER: This work, Socrates, is still more extensive than that. And
yet we recall how great the length of that was too—but though

indeed it's very just to suppose the following sort of thing about them—

SOCRATES: What sort of thing?

D STRANGER: That at some time or other there'll be a need of the present statement for the showing forth of the precise itself, but that it is beautifully and adequately shown for the present—it's my impression that this speech of ours takes the field in a magnificent way, and says that we are to believe, after all, that in a similar way all the arts are, and that simultaneously greater and less are measured relative not only to one another but also to the becoming of the mean. For if this is, those are, and if those are, this is too, and if either one of the two is not, neither of them will ever be.

E SOCRATES: That's right, but what's the next point?

STRANGER: It's plain. We would divide the art of measurement, just as it was said, by cutting it in two along these lines, by our setting down one proper part of it to be all the arts that measure number, lengths, depths, widths, and speeds relative to their contraries, and setting down the other as all the arts that measure relative to the mean, the fitting, the opportune, and the needful, and everything settled toward the middle and away from the extremes.

SOCRATES: Yes, each of the two you speak of is a big section and far different from each other.

STRANGER: It's something, Socrates, that many of the clever, in the
285 sheer belief that they're pointing out something wise, say on occasion, "After all, there is an art of measurement about everything that becomes." And this is in fact the very thing stated now, for in a certain manner everything artful has partaken in measurement. But on account of their failure to make it a habit to examine and divide according to species, they straight off combine into the same—in the belief that they're similar—these things that are so greatly different. And they do in turn the contrary of this, by not dividing other things by parts, although, whenever one first
B perceives the sharing of the many, one should not stand apart and withdraw before one comes to see all the differences in it (as many as are situated in species), and in turn whenever omnifarious dissimilarities are seen in multitudes, one should be incapable of being discountenanced and stopping before one confines all the family kin within a single similarity and comprehends them with the being of some genus. Now let these things have been stated as adequate, both about these things and about defects and excesses, and let's only keep this, that two genera of the art of
C measurement of them have been found, and let's remember what we say they are.

SOCRATES: We'll remember.

STRANGER: Then after this speech, let's welcome another that's no less about the very things sought than about the entire engagement in speeches of this sort.

SOCRATES: What sort is it?

STRANGER: Should someone quiz us about the association of those who are learning letters, whenever one of them is asked about any name whatsoever of what letters it is, are we to assert that his search at that time occurs for the sake of the one problem set before him or rather for the sake of his becoming more skilled *D* in letters about every problem set before him?

SOCRATES: Plainly about every.

STRANGER: Then what about our search now for the statesman? Has it been set as a problem for its own sake or rather for the sake of our becoming more skilled in dialectics about everything?

SOCRATES: Plainly this too about everything.

STRANGER: Then it surely follows that no one with any wit would be willing to hunt down the speech of the weaving art for its own sake. But, I suspect, most have been unaware that for some of the things which are, certain perceptible similarities of them are naturally there for easy understanding, and they're not difficult *E* to make plain, whenever one wants to point them out easily, without trouble (*pragmata*) and apart from speech, to whoever is asking for a speech about any of them; but that, on the other hand, there *286* has been no image devised as plain as day for human beings in the case of the biggest and most honorable of the things which are, by the showing of which, whoever wants to fill up the soul of the inquirer, will adequately fill it up by fitting it to one of the senses. It's for this reason that one must practice to be able to give and receive an account (*logos*) of each thing, for the bodiless things, being the most beautiful and the greatest, are only shown with clarity by speech and nothing else. And it's for the sake of them that all the present remarks are said. In the case of anything, the practice in smaller things is easier than about bigger things.[34] *B*

SOCRATES: You put it most beautifully.

STRANGER: Then let's remind ourselves of that for the sake of which we have said all these things about them.

SOCRATES: Which?

STRANGER: It's not least for the sake of this very disagreeableness with which we accepted disagreeably the lengthiness of speech about the art of weaving, about the unwinding of the all, and, in the case of the sophist, about the being of 'that which is not', in realizing that they had got an excessive length. And we rebuked

C ourselves for all of this, out of fear that we were speaking super-
fluously as well as too lengthily. In order, then, that we may not
undergo anything of the sort at a later time, do say that the
previous remarks have been stated by the pair of us for the sake
of all of this.

SOCRATES: It shall be done. Just speak what's next in order.

STRANGER: Well, I'm saying that you and I ought to remember the
present remarks and make our blame and praise of brevity and
length about whatever we're speaking, not by judging their lengths
relative to one another, but in accordance with the part of the art

D of measurement that we said at that time we must remember,
relative to the fitting.

SOCRATES: Right.

STRANGER: Well, but not everything relative to this either, for we'll
have no need of any fitting length relative to pleasure, unless it's
a by-product. And in turn, the speech advises us to be content
with and cherish the length relative to the search of the problem
set down, however we might find it most easily and quickly, but
as a second and not primary consideration. But it advises us to
honor most of all and in first place the pursuit itself of the capacity

E to divide by species, and, in particular, regardless of whether a
very lengthy speech is spoken and makes the auditor more capable
of discovery, the speech advises us to be in earnest about it and
not to be at all distressed by its length; or if in turn the speech is
shorter, the same holds true. And further, besides this, whoever
blames the lengths of speeches in associations of this sort and does
not welcome their circular orbitings, the speech advises us that

287 we should not let go of someone of the sort so quickly and straight
away with only the utterance of the reproach "The remarks are
too long," but we must believe that he must prove in addition that
if they had been shorter they would be making the associates more
capable of dialectic and more capable of finding the way to make
plain in speech the things which are. And we must be unconcerned
with everything else of praise and blame that looks to anything
else, and we must make it seem that we're altogether deaf to
speeches of the sort. And enough of this, if you too share in this

B opinion. But let's go back once more to the statesman and apply
to him the paradigm of the previously stated art of weaving.

SOCRATES: You put it beautifully, and let's do what you say.

STRANGER: Isn't it the case that the king has been separated out and
apart from many arts that were in the same field, or rather from
all that deal with herds, but the remainder, we assert, those of

the cocauses and causes throughout the city itself—these are the first that must be divided from one another?

SOCRATES: Right.

STRANGER: Do you know that it's difficult to cut them in two? But the   C cause, I suspect, will be no less apparent to us as we advance.

SOCRATES: Then that's what we must do.

STRANGER: Well, then, let's divide them, as if it were a sacrificial victim, limb by limb, since we're incapable of doing it in two, for one must always cut into that number that's as near as possible to two.

SOCRATES: How then are we to do it now?

STRANGER: Just as before when we surely set down all the arts that were supplying tools for weaving as cocauses.

SOCRATES: Yes.

STRANGER: So also now we have to do this same thing, but still more extensively than then. All the arts that craft any tool, large or   D small, throughout a city—all of them must be set down as being cocauses, for without them a city would never come to be, or a political (art) either, though, on the other hand, we shall surely not set down any of them as the work of a royal art.

SOCRATES: No indeed.

STRANGER: And yet it's a hard thing we're trying to do in separating this genus apart from all the rest, for it is possible, if one says that anything whatsoever of 'the things which are' is, as it were, a tool of at least some one thing, to seem to have said something persuasive. But all the same, let's speak of this as another of the   E possessions in the city.

SOCRATES: What sort of thing?

STRANGER: Say that it is not with that capacity, for it's not compacted to serve the cause of coming-into-being, as a tool is, but for the sake of a safekeeping of the artifact.

SOCRATES: What sort of thing?

STRANGER: It's this, that omnifarious species made for dry or liquid things and for fire or not for fire, which we address with a single designation, "vessel." It's a very extensive species indeed and, I   *288* suspect, simply (artlessly) unrelated to the science that is being sought.

SOCRATES: Of course.

STRANGER: The third that has to be caught sight of is other than these and a very extensive species of possessions—it's pedestrial and in liquid, it roams far and wide and does not roam at all, it's honored and dishonored, but with one name, because all of it is for the sake of some kind of propping in its coming to be on each and every occasion as a seat for someone.

SOCRATES: What sort is it?

STRANGER: We surely speak of it as a support, scarcely the work of a political (art), but far more of the (art) of carpentry, pottery, and coppersmithing.[35]

SOCRATES: I understand.

B STRANGER: And what of a fourth? Must it be said to be other than these—that in which most of the things mentioned awhile ago are—every kind of garment, much of armor, and walls (all kinds of envelopments of earth and stone), and thousands of others? And since all of them are made for the sake of defense, it would as a whole be most justly addressed as defense, and it would far more rightly be held to be mostly the work of a housebuilding art and weaving rather than of a political (art).

SOCRATES: Yes, of course.

C STRANGER: And would we be willing to set down as a fifth that which deals with ornament (order), painting (writing), and everything that in employing it and music perfects imitations worked up for our pleasure only, and justly to be comprehended with one name?

SOCRATES: What sort?

STRANGER: Surely there's something spoken of as plaything.

SOCRATES: Why certainly.

STRANGER: Well, then, this will be one name that's eminently a fitting form of address for these, for none of them's done for the sake of a serious intent, but all for the sake of playfulness.

D SOCRATES: I pretty nearly understand this too.

STRANGER: And that which supplies bodies for all these, out of which and in which all the arts now mentioned work and exercise their craft, an omnifarious species that is the offspring of many other arts—shall we not set it down as sixth?

SOCRATES: What sort of species exactly do you mean?

STRANGER: Gold and silver, and everything mined, and everything that the art of woodcutting and every kind of shearing supply by cutting to carpentry and plaiting; and, further, the art of peeling plants and cutting leather, which strips away the skins of ensouled

E bodies, and all the arts that deal with things of this sort; and the arts productive of corks, papyrus, and bonds that offer for manufacture species put together out of noncomposite genera. We address it as one thing in its entirety, the first-born and uncomposite possession for human beings, and which is in no way the work of a royal science.

SOCRATES: Beautiful.

STRANGER: The acquisition of nurture, then, and all the parts of body that are designed for the body and commingled with their parts,

have obtained as their lot a certain capacity for tending. It's to be *289*
said seventh and given the name in its entirety of our nourishment, unless we can set down something else more beautiful, but
in positing it, we'll more correctly attribute it in its entirety to
farming, hunting, gymnastics, medicine, and cookery than to the
political (art).

SOCRATES: Of course.

STRANGER: Then I suspect that pretty nearly anything that pertains
to possession, except for the tame animals, has been stated in
these seven genera. Consider. The first-born species would have
been most justly placed at the beginning, and after it, tool, vessel,
support, defense, plaything, nourishment. And whatever we omit, *B*
unless something big has slipped by us, it can be fitted into some
one of these—for example, the look (*idea*) of coinage, of seals,
and of every kind of stamp—for among themselves they don't
have any big genus of the same field, but though they're no doubt
dragged there by force, some into the genus of ornament (order),
some into that of tools, still and all they will be consonant. And
as for the acquisition of tame animals, except slaves, the previously *C*
partitioned art of herd-nurturing will come to light as comprehensive of them all.

SOCRATES: Yes, of course.

STRANGER: But as for the remainder of slaves and all servants, it's
among them somewhere, I divine, that those who dispute with
the king about the web itself will become evident, just as we then
said that those who deal with spinning, carding, and all the rest
dispute with the weavers. And everyone else, if they're spoken of
as cocauses, has been exhausted along with their now-stated works *D*
and separated apart from a royal and political action.

SOCRATES: They do at least seem likely to have been.

STRANGER: Come then. Let's come nearer and examine the remaining
close at hand, in order that we may know them with greater
certainty.

SOCRATES: Indeed we must.

STRANGER: Now the greatest servants, if seen from this vantage-point,
we find, have a practice and experience the contrary to what we
suspected.

SOCRATES: Who?

STRANGER: Those who are bought and in this manner possessed, whom
we can say indisputably to be slaves, and do not have in the least *E*
any pretensions to a royal art.

SOCRATES: Of course.

STRANGER: And what of this? All of the free who willingly range themselves for service in the things stated just now, and who convey to one another the produce of farming and the works of all the rest of the arts, and who strike an equality among them,[36] some in marketplaces, some exchanging on sea and land from city to city, and exchanging coinage relative to different wares and relative to itself, those whom we've called silver-exchangers, merchants, owner-captains, and retailers—they won't, will they, dispute any of the political (art)?

290

SOCRATES: Well, perhaps, that which deals with commercial matters.

STRANGER: Well, still, we won't ever find those at least who we see are hired for wages and, in serving for pay, serve everyone most readily, laying a claim to a royal (art).

SOCRATES: How could we?

STRANGER: And what about, after all, those who serve us on each occasion in the following sorts of things?

SOCRATES: What sorts of things and whom do you mean?

B STRANGER: The tribe of heralds belongs to them, and all those who by frequent service become wise in letters, and there are some others who are omnicompetent in accomplishing many other jobs involved in the offices of ruling. What shall we say of these?

SOCRATES: What you said just now, servants, but not themselves rulers in the cities.

STRANGER: But I still suspect that I didn't see a dream when I said that it's somewhere hereabouts that those who particularly dispute the political (art) will come to light. And yet it might seem to be extremely strange to look for them in some subservient portion.

C

SOCRATES: Yes, utterly.

STRANGER: Let's approach still closer, then, those who have not yet submitted to the touchstone (torture). As there are some who deal with divination and have a proper part of some ministerial science—they're surely held to be interpreters from gods for human beings—

SOCRATES: Yes.

STRANGER: So, in turn, the genus of the priests too has the know-how, as the lawful says, to offer gifts through sacrifices from us to gods according to their liking, and to formulate a petition by means of prayers for the acquisition of good things from them to us. And both of these are surely proper parts of a ministerial art.

D

SOCRATES: They appear so at least.

STRANGER: Well, then, it's my impression that by now we're latching onto a kind of trail that leads to where we're going. The figure of the priests and that of the diviners get very much swelled up with pride and receive an august reputation on account of the magnitude of their undertakings, so that in Egypt it is not even possible for a king to rule without a hieratic (art), and if, after all, he does in fact first force his way in from a different genus, it's E necessary for him to be subsequently enrolled in this genus. And, further, in many places among the Greeks one would find that the greatest kinds of sacrifices that deal with matters of this sort are enjoined upon the greatest offices of rule to perform, and in particular here among you it's not least of all plain what I mean, for they say that whoever gets to be king here by lot has been assigned the most august and particularly ancestral (native) of the ancient sacrifices.[37]

SOCRATES: Yes indeed.

STRANGER: Well, then, one must examine these lottery kings, along 291 with priests and their servants, as well as some other very large crowd which has just now become evident to us with the separation of the previous groups.

SOCRATES: But just whom do you mean?

STRANGER: Some very strange ones.

SOCRATES: Why exactly?

STRANGER: Their genus is of every kind of tribe, as it appears on just now examining it. Many of the men bear a resemblance to lions, B centaurs, and others of this sort, and a very large number to satyrs and the weak and wily beasts, and they quickly exchange their looks (*ideai*) and capacity with one another. And yet for all of that, Socrates, it's my impression that I've come to an understanding of these men just now.

SOCRATES: You must speak, for it seems that you're catching sight of something strange.

STRANGER: Yes, for it's from a failure of recognition that everyone falls in with the strange, and in this particular case I myself was now affected in just this way. I suddenly got bewildered when I C caught sight of the chorus that deal with the affairs (*pragmata*) of the cities.

SOCRATES: Of what sort?

STRANGER: The greatest enchanter of all the sophists and most experienced in this art. He is very difficult to remove from those who are in their being statesmen and royalty, and yet he has to be removed if we're going to see as plain as day that which is sought.

SOCRATES: Well, if that's the case one must not let up.

STRANGER: Indeed we must not, in my opinion at any rate. And point out to me the following.

SOCRATES: What sort of thing?

D STRANGER: Is not monarchy one of the political kinds of rule for us?
SOCRATES: Yes.
STRANGER: And after monarchy one would say, I suspect, there's the power held by the few.
SOCRATES: Of course.
STRANGER: And isn't the rule of the multitude a third figure of regime, designated with the name of democracy?
SOCRATES: Yes indeed.
STRANGER: And though they are three, don't they become five in a certain way, when two give birth from themselves to different names besides their own?
SOCRATES: What sorts exactly?
E STRANGER: They surely now look exclusively toward the forcible and voluntary, poverty and wealth, and law and lawlessness, as they arise in them, and by dividing in two each doublet of the two, they address monarchy, on the grounds that it supplies two species, with two names, tyranny and, on the other hand, kingship.
SOCRATES: Why certainly.
STRANGER: Whereas they address the city dominated on any occasion by few with the names aristocracy and oligarchy.
SOCRATES: Yes indeed.
292 STRANGER: In the case of democracy, however, regardless of whether the multitude rules over those with substantial property forcibly or voluntarily, and regardless of whether it scrupulously maintains the laws or not, no one in any case is accustomed to alter its name.
SOCRATES: True.
STRANGER: What then? Do we believe any of these regimes to be the right regime if it gets bounded by these kinds of boundaries, by one, few, and many, by wealth and poverty, by the forcible and voluntary, and if it turns out to come to be with writings and without laws?
SOCRATES: Well, what stands in the way?
B STRANGER: Consider it with greater clarity by following along in this direction.
SOCRATES: Which?
STRANGER: Shall we abide by what we stated at first or shall we sound a dissonant note?
SOCRATES: What sort of thing do you mean exactly?
STRANGER: We said, I believe, that the royal rule is some one of the sciences.
SOCRATES: Yes.
STRANGER: And not of all these either, but we certainly chose and separated from the rest a certain critical and supervisory (science).

SOCRATES: Yes.

STRANGER: And of the supervisory, one was for lifeless works and one
for animals, and in accordance with this way, by continually part-   C
ing, we've advanced to this point, not forgetting science, but not
yet capable of being sufficiently precise as to what kind it is.

SOCRATES: What you say is right.

STRANGER: Well, then, do we realize this very point, that the distinctive
mark (boundary) about them should not be few or many, not the
voluntary or the involuntary, not poverty or wealth, but a kind
of science, if we'll follow what was stated before?

SOCRATES: Well, it's just impossible not to do this.   D

STRANGER: It's of necessity, then, that this issue must now be examined
in this way, in which of these does there turn out to arise a science
of the rule of human beings, pretty nearly the hardest and greatest
to acquire. We have to see it, in order that we may observe whom
we have to remove from the intelligent king, who pretend that
they are statesmen and persuade many but are not in any way.

SOCRATES: This indeed must be done, as the speech has declared to
us.

STRANGER: Well, a multitude in a city at least does not seem, does it,   E
to be capable of acquiring this science?

SOCRATES: How could it?

STRANGER: Well, in a city of a thousand men is it possible for some-
hundred or even fifty to acquire it adequately?

SOCRATES: But if that were the case, it would be the easiest of all the
arts, for we know that out of a thousand men there would never
prove to be as many tip-top draughts-players as that in comparison
to those among all the rest of the Greeks, let alone those of course
who are strictly kings, for whoever has the royal science, regardless
of whether he rules or not, must all the same, according to the
previous speech, be addressesd as royal.   293

STRANGER: You recalled it beautifully. And I suspect the consequence
of this is that just as the right rule, whenever it proves to be right,
must be sought as the rule of some one, two, or altogether few—

SOCRATES: Why certainly.

STRANGER: So these, whether they rule the willing or the unwilling,
whether in conformity with writings or without writings, and
whether they are rich or poor, must be held to be just like those
who we now believe are exercising a rule in conformity with art,
whatsoever rule it is. So we've steadfastly held physicians (to be)   B
physicians regardless of whether they cure us when we're willing
or unwilling, by surgery, cautery, or by the application of some
different pain, and whether in conformity with writings or apart

from writings. And regardless of whether they are poor or rich, we all the same assert they are physicians no less, as long as they supervise by art, and, by purging or slimming (us) in a different way, or maybe increasing (us), if only for the good of the bodies, by making them better from worse, those who severally handle treatments save the things treated. It's on this line, I suspect, and not on a different one, that we'll set down this as the only right, distinctive mark of medicine and any different rule whatsoever.

C

SOCRATES: Yes, certainly.

STRANGER: It's necessary, then, it seems, that this too be of regimes the outstandingly right regime, and the only regime in which one might find the rulers truly with know-how and not only seeming to have it, regardless of whether they rule in conformity with laws or without laws, and over willing or unwilling (subjects), and themselves poor or rich, for one must not calculate in terms of any correctness any of these things in any way as a factor.

D

SOCRATES: Beautiful.

STRANGER: And so regardless of whether they purge the city for the good by killing some or maybe exiling, or they make the city smaller by sending out colonies somewhere like swarms of bees, or they increase it by importing some different people from somewhere or other outside and making them citizens, as long as they are employing science and the just and, in keeping it safe, make it better from worse to the best of their ability, we must state that this then is the only right regime and in accordance with definitions (boundary-marks) of this sort. And all the rest we speak of, we must say of them that they are not genuine (legitimate) and in their being are not, but they have imitated this one, and some, which we speak of as with good laws, have done it with more beautiful results, and all the rest with uglier.

E

SOCRATES: It seems that everything else, stranger, has been said in a measured way, but the statement that one must rule even without laws is more difficult to take in.

STRANGER: Yes, Socrates, you just anticipated my question. I was about to ask you whether you accept all of this, or you're distressed by something in the remarks. But now it's evident that we'll want to go through this point about the correctness of rulers without laws.

294

SOCRATES: Of course.

STRANGER: Although it's plain enough that in a certain sense the legislative (art) belongs to the royal (art), the best thing is not for the laws but for a man—the king with intelligence—to have strength. Do you know in what way?

SOCRATES: What way do you mean exactly?

STRANGER: Because (a) law would never be capable of comprehending with precision for all simultaneously the best and the most just *B* and enjoining the best, for the dissimilarities of human beings and of their actions and the fact that almost none of the human things is ever at rest do not allow any art whatsoever to declare in any case anything simple about all and over the entire time. We surely concede this?

SOCRATES: Why certainly.

STRANGER: Yes, but we see the law strains pretty nearly with all its might for this very end, as if it were some self-willing and foolish *C* human being who allows no one to do anything contrary to his own order or even for anyone to ask a question, not even if it turns out that, after all, something new is better for someone contrary to the speech which he himself enjoined.

SOCRATES: True. The law now simply (artlessly) does just as you've said for each of us.

STRANGER: Isn't it impossible, then, for that which proves to be simple through all times to be in a good condition relative to things that are never simple?

SOCRATES: Probably.

STRANGER: Then on account of what exactly is it necessary to legislate, inasmuch as the law's not most correct? One has to discover the *D* cause of this.

SOCRATES: Why certainly.

STRANGER: Isn't it true that here among you all as well as elsewhere in different cities there are certain sorts of group exercises of human beings, either for running or something else, for the sake of rivalrous victory?

SOCRATES: Yes, there are very many.

STRANGER: Come now, let's recover again in memory the injunctions of those who in offices of rule of this sort drill by art.

SOCRATES: What sort of thing about them?

STRANGER: That they don't believe there's room to work in minute detail on each individual one by one, by ordering what is suitable for each body, but they believe they must in a coarser way, as it *E* is for the most part and for many, make their arrangement for the advantage of bodies.

SOCRATES: Beautiful.

STRANGER: It's precisely for this reason that they now assign equal toils to them in groups and start them out together and make them stop together from running, wrestling, and all the bodily toils.

SOCRATES: That is so.

STRANGER: Well, then, let's believe that the legislator too, who is to
295 supervise the herds about the just and their mutual contracts will
never become competent enough, in giving orders to all of them
collectively, to prescribe precisely what is suitable for each one.

SOCRATES: It's likely at any rate.

STRANGER: But, I suspect, he'll prescribe, in his writings and without
writings—when he legislates by way of ancestral usages—that which
is for the many and for the most part, and it's in just this way that
he'll set down the law for individuals in a somewhat coarser way.

SOCRATES: Right.

B STRANGER: Right enough. For how could anyone, Socrates, ever be so
competent as to be always sitting beside each one throughout his
life and order with precision the suitable? Since I suspect that
should anyone whatsoever of those who have grasped in its being
the royal science be capable of this, he would hardly ever put
impediments in his own way by writing these so-called laws.

SOCRATES: Not at least, stranger, on the basis of the present remarks.

STRANGER: But still more, my splendid fellow, on the basis of what's
going to be remarked.

SOCRATES: What exactly?

STRANGER: The following sort. Let's say just among ourselves that a
C physician or maybe some trainer is going to go abroad and will
be away from his patients, he suspects, for a longish time, and in
the belief that the gymnasts or the sick won't remember his orders,
would he be willing to write for them reminders, or how?

SOCRATES: That's so.

STRANGER: But what if, contrary to his opinion, he should stay abroad
for less time and come back? Would he not have the nerve to
suggest different things contrary to those writings, when different
conditions turn out to be better for the sick—it's on account of
D winds or maybe of something else that occurs contrary to expectation (one of those things from Zeus that are somehow other
than the usual)? Would he staunchly believe that neither he, by
ordering different things, must trespass the ancient things that
were once legislated, nor the sick must have the nerve to do other
things contrary to what is written, on the grounds that these writings are medically scientific and sound (productive of health), and
the things that occur in another way are unsound (productive of
E illness) and are not artful? Or wouldn't everything of the sort,
should it happen in science at least and true art, prove in any case
to be altogether the biggest laugh that legislation of this sort incurs?

SOCRATES: That's altogether so.

STRANGER: But whoever wrote, and legislated without writing, the just

and unjust, beautiful and ugly, good and bad things for the herds
of human beings—all that severally are grazed city by city in conformity with the laws of the onetime writers—if he who wrote
with art, or someone other similar to him, comes back, shall he
really not be allowed to order other things contrary to these?
Or would this prohibition too no less than the former appear in   *296*
truth laughable?

SOCRATES: Why certainly.

STRANGER: Do you know, then, the speech that issues from the many
in a case of this sort?

SOCRATES: No, I don't have it in mind, not at the moment at least.

STRANGER: And it's specious. If anyone, they say, is familiar with better
laws contrary to those of the past, each must legislate once he's
persuaded his own city, but not on any different condition.

SOCRATES: What then? Isn't it right?

STRANGER: Perhaps. But in any case, if someone does not persuade   *B*
but forces the better, answer, what will be the name of the force?
Don't however answer yet, but first about the prior cases.

SOCRATES: What sort of thing do you mean exactly?

STRANGER: If someone after all does not persuade the patient of the
physician, but has correctly the physician's art and compels a child
or some man or maybe woman to do the better contrary to the
writings, what will be the name of this kind of force? Isn't it
anything rather than the so-called unsound (disease-making) error that's contrary to the art? And isn't it permitted for him who
is forcibly treated in a case of this sort to speak correctly everything   *C*
except that he has undergone unsound (disease-making) and un-
artful things at the hands of the physicians who applied force?

SOCRATES: What you say is most true.

STRANGER: And what about in our case? That which is spoken of as
a mistake contrary to the political art? Isn't it the ugly, bad, and
unjust?

SOCRATES: Altogether so.

STRANGER: Then in the case of those who are forced, contrary to the
writings and ancestral practices, to do other things more just, and
better, and more beautiful than the previous—come, in regard to   *D*
the blame attached to force of this sort in things of this sort—
mustn't he say on each occasion that it happens, if he's not going
to be the most ridiculous of all, anything except that those who
are forced by the enforcers have undergone ugly, unjust, and bad
things?

SOCRATES: What you say is most true.

STRANGER: Well, what if the enforcer is rich, are the enforcements

just, and if he's poor, unjust? Or regardless of whether someone
persuades or does not persuade, is rich or poor, acts either in
conformity with writings or contrary to writings, if he does ad-
E   vantageous things, mustn't this in these cases too be at least the
simply truest distinctive mark of the right arrangement of a city—
that which the wise and good man will arrange as the advantage
of the ruled? And just as the captain always maintains the advan-
297   tage of the ship and sailors, not by laying down writings but by
supplying his art as law, and keeps his fellow sailors safe and
sound, so too, in accordance with this same manner, would a right
regime issue from those who are capable of ruling in this way,
supplying the strength of the art that's mightier than the laws?
And there is no mistake in everything intelligent rulers do, as long
B   as they maintain one big thing—as long as they always distribute
to those in the city that which with mind and art is most just, and
can keep them safe and make them better from worse as far as
possible.

SOCRATES: It is not possible to speak in contradiction at least of what
has now been said.

STRANGER: No, and one must not speak in contradiction of those things
either.

SOCRATES: What sort do you mean?

STRANGER: That a multitude of no matter whom would never be able
C   to get the science of this sort and manage a city with mind, but
that one right regime is to be sought in the vicinity of a few, small,
and the one, and the rest of the regimes, just as it was said a little
while ago, are to be set down as imitations, some imitating this
with more beautiful results, and some with uglier.

SOCRATES: What? How have you meant that? I certainly didn't understand just now the remark about the imitations.

STRANGER: And for all of that it's not a trivial remark either, if someone
sets this kind of speech in motion and then just casts it down here
and does not go through it and point out the mistake that now
D   occurs about it.

SOCRATES: What sort exactly?

STRANGER: It's the following sort of thing that one must examine, but
it's scarcely usual or easy to see, but all the same let's try to get
it. Come. If this regime, which we've mentioned, is the only right
one for us, do you know that all the rest must in using its writings
keep themselves safe on this condition, by doing what is now
praised although it is not the most correct?

SOCRATES: What sort?

E STRANGER: The prohibition against anyone having the nerve to do anything of the things in the city contrary to the laws, and for anyone who does have the nerve, the penalty is death and all the extreme punishments, and this is the most correct and most beautiful condition as second, whenever one sets aside that which was now stated as first. But in what manner this has occurred—that which we declare second—let's go through that. Are we to?

SOCRATES: Yes, of course.

STRANGER: Then let's go back to the semblances, which it's necessary always to make the royal rulers resemble.

SOCRATES: What sort are they?

STRANGER: The grand captain and the physician "equivalent to many others."[38] Let's work up for ourselves a kind of picture of them and cast a glance at it.

SOCRATES: What sort is it?

STRANGER: It's the following. What if we should all think about them *298* that we're suffering most dreadfully at their hands? Whichever one of us each of the two of them is willing to save, they similarly save, and whom they want to ruin, they ruin by cutting and burning them and by ordering them to bring the costs like tribute to themselves—a small sum of which or even none at all they expend on the sick patient, but they themselves and their domestics use all the rest—and then finally they accept money as wages either *B* from the patient's relatives or from some of his enemies and kill him. And the captains in turn do many other things of the same sort, and in their voyages on the basis of some kind of plot leave some deserted, and by arranging accidents on the high seas they throw them out into the sea and do other criminal things. So if we should think this about them and come to some kind of plan in the course of our deliberations, no longer to allow either one of these arts to rule on its own authority either slaves or free, but *C* to collect an assembly of ourselves (either the whole people or only the rich), and allow both laymen and all the rest of the craftsmen to contribute their opinions about sailing or about illnesses, on what terms we must apply drugs and medical tools to the sick, and likewise to employ ships themselves and naval tools for the use of ships, and about the risks run on the voyage itself *D* from winds and sea and from the encounters with pirates, and if, after all, the need somewhere arises to engage in a naval battle with long ships against others of the sort; but what the multitude resolve about these, whether some physicians and captains or else laymen contribute their advice, we write on some kind of *kurbeis* and pillars, and lay down for ourselves as well some unwritten *E* ancestral customs, it's to be in conformity with all of this from then on forward that voyages are to be made and the sick treated.[39]

SOCRATES: What you've said is utterly strange.

STRANGER: Yes, and every year we establish rulers of the multitude, either out of the rich or out of the whole people, whoever gets it as his lot. And once the rulers are in office they rule as captains of the ships and healers of the sick in conformity with the writings.

SOCRATES: This is still harder.

STRANGER: Then observe what follows next. Whenever the year is over for each of the rulers, we'll have to establish courts of men, either by a prior selection of the rich or from a lottery of the whole people, and haul before them those who are done with their rule and have them audited, and whoever wants to do so can lodge the accusation that it was not in conformity with the writings that he captained the ships during the year, nor in conformity with the ancient customs of their ancestors either. And these same prescriptions also hold for those who heal the sick, and whatever the condemnation is for, the courts assess what some of them must suffer or pay for.

SOCRATES: Anyone who then is willing, and it's left up to him in circumstances of this sort, to rule, would suffer and pay for anything whatsoever most justly.

STRANGER: Well, one would still have to lay down a law for all these cases. If it's evident that someone is seeking, contrary to the writings, an art of piloting and the nautical or the healthy and the truth of medicine about winds and the conditions of heat and cold, and he is sophistically devising anything whatsoever about things of this sort, first of all he must be named neither a skilled physician nor a skilled captain but a talker about highfalutin things, a kind of garrulous sophist,[40] and then, in the second place, on the grounds that he's corrupting different people younger than himself and convincing them to engage in piloting and medicine not in conformity with laws, but to rule with their own authority the ships and the sick, then anyone who wants can and is permitted to draw up an indictment and haul him before a—what do you call it?—court of justice. And if it's decided that he persuades either young or old contrary to the laws and what is written, to punish him with the extreme penalties, for he must in no way be wiser than the laws,[41] for no one is ignorant of that which characterizes the medical and the healthy and piloting and the nautical, for it's possible for anyone who wants to do so to learn what has been written and the established ancestral customs. So if this should occur, Socrates, in the way we're speaking of them, not only in the case of these sciences but also in the case of generalship and every kind of hunting whatsoever, of painting or any part whatsoever of the entire imitative (art), of carpentry and the whole of equipment-making of whatever sort, or maybe of farming and the whole art concerned with plants—or should we in turn observe some kind of feeding of horses occurring in conformity with writings or the entire grooming of herds, or divination or whatever entire part serving has comprehended, or draughts-playing or all   *E* of arithmetic, or whether it's bare or plane or involved in three dimensions or in speeds—whatever would come to light if all these things should be practiced in this way, in conformity with writings and not in conformity with art?

SOCRATES: It's plain: all the arts we have would completely perish, and they would never come to be at a later time on account of this law that forbids their search. And hence life, which even now is hard, would prove to be altogether unlivable throughout that time.

STRANGER: But what of the following? If we should compel each of   *300* the artisans mentioned, and the one elected by a show of hands or chance lottery to supervise our writings, to be in conformity with writings, but the latter doesn't have any regard for the writings, and either for the sake of profit or private whim tries to do other things contrary to them, though he's not familiar with anything about them, wouldn't this prove to be a still greater evil than the previous evil?

SOCRATES: Most true.

STRANGER: The reason is, I suspect, that whoever has the nerve to act   *B* contrary to these writings is acting contrary to the laws that have been laid down on the basis of much trial and error, when certain advisers gave several pieces of advice in a neat and elegant way and persuaded the multitude to set them down, and he multiplies a mistake many times itself and would overturn every action to a still greater extent than the writings.

SOCRATES: Of course he will.

STRANGER: It's for these reasons that for those who lay down laws and   *C* writings about anything whatsoever, the prohibition against either any one or any multitude ever doing anything whatsoever contrary to them is a second sailing.⁴²

SOCRATES: Right.

STRANGER: And though they would be imitations of the truth, those that have been severally transcribed, to the extent that it's possible, from the knowers—

SOCRATES: Of course.

STRANGER: Still and all the knower, we were saying, who is in his being the statesman, will, if we remember, do many things by his art, as far as his own action goes, without any regard for the writings, whenever he is of the opinion that, contrary to what has been

D   written by him and set over any from whom he is absent, different things are better.

SOCRATES: Yes, we were saying it.

STRANGER: Isn't it the case, then, that any man whatever or any multitude whatever, for whomsoever laws happen to be laid down, whatever they try to do contrary to them on the grounds that another thing is better, are doing to the best of their ability the same thing which that simply true one does?

SOCRATES: Yes, of course.

STRANGER: Well, then, if they should be without knowledge and do something of the sort, though they would be trying to imitate the

E   truth, they would still be imitating it all very badly; but if they're artful, this is no longer an imitation but that most true thing itself?

SOCRATES: No doubt about it.

STRANGER: And yet it's been our previously established agreement that no multitude is capable of getting any art whatsoever.

SOCRATES: It's indeed been established.

STRANGER: Isn't it the case then that if there is some royal art, the multitude of the rich and the entire people together would never get this political science?

SOCRATES: How would they?

STRANGER: So it seems that regimes of this sort, if they are going to

301   imitate beautifully to the best of their ability that simply true regime of the single one who rules with art, must never do anything contrary to the writings and ancestral customs of the laws that have been established for them.

SOCRATES: You've spoken most beautifully.

STRANGER: So whenever the rich imitate this, we then call a regime of this sort an aristocracy, but whenever they have no regard for the laws, an oligarchy.

SOCRATES: Probably.

STRANGER: And then again whenever just one rules in conformity with

B   laws, imitating the knower, we call him a king, without distinguishing by name between the one who rules alone with science from the one with opinion in conformity with laws.

SOCRATES: We probably do.

STRANGER: Isn't it the case then that if someone who is in his being a knower rules as one, he will in any case be addressed with the same name "king" and no other? It's precisely for this reason that the five names of what are now spoken of as regimes have proved to be only one.[43]

SOCRATES: It seems likely at any rate.

STRANGER: But what about when there's just one ruler and he acts neither in conformity with laws nor in conformity with usages, *C* and "After all," he pretends, just as if he were the knower, "at least the best has to be done contrary to what has been written," but there is a certain kind of desire and ignorance in charge of this imitation, mustn't each one of this sort be then called a tyrant?

SOCRATES: Why certainly.

STRANGER: It's in just this way, then, that we say a tyrant has come to be, and a king and oligarchy and aristocracy and democracy, when that one monarch rankles human beings, and they don't trust that anyone would ever prove to be worthy of a rule of that sort, so as to be willing and able as ruler with virtue and science to dis- *D* tribute correctly the just and holy things to all, but (they're convinced) he ruins, kills, and harms whichever one of us he wants to on each and every occasion, since if there should come to be the sort we're speaking of, he would be welcomed warmly and in piloting with precision would be the only one to manage with happiness the right regime.[44]

SOCRATES: Of course.

STRANGER: But as it is, since there is no king that comes to be in the cities, as we in point of fact assert, who's of the sort that naturally *E* arises in hives—one who's right from the start exceptional in his body and his soul—they must, it seems, once they've come together, write up writings while they run after the traces of the truest regime.

SOCRATES: Probably.

STRANGER: Are we then astonished, Socrates, in regimes of this sort at all the bad things that turn out to occur, and all that will turn out, when a foundation of this sort underlies them—to perform their actions without science in conformity with writings and usages—the use of which by another (science) would plainly in *302* the eyes of all destroy all the things it's responsible for? Or should we be more astonished as to how a city is something strong by nature? For though the cities have been undergoing things of this sort now for endless time, still and all some of them are stable and do not get overturned, though at times many do sink below like ships and perish and have perished and will still go on perishing on account of the sorry state of their captains and crews. They've taken in the greatest ignorance about the greatest things, *B* for though they recognize nearly nothing of the political things, they believe they've taken in nearly everything of this, of all sciences, with utmost clarity.

SOCRATES: Most true.

STRANGER: Which, then, of these not right regimes is the least difficult to live with, though they are all difficult, and which the most grievous? Ought we to cast a glance here, and although it is, in light of our previous proposal, spoken of as a by-product, still and all, on the whole, perhaps everything all of us do is for the sake of something of the sort.

SOCRATES: We ought to, of course.

C   STRANGER: Well, then, declare that while there are three, the same one proves to be exceptionally difficult and most easy.

SOCRATES: How do you mean that?

STRANGER: In no different way, but I say monarchy, the rule of a few, and of many, were the three we spoke of when at the start the present speech flooded in on us.

SOCRATES: Indeed they were.

STRANGER: Well, then, let's cut each one of these in two and make six, but separate apart from these the right regime as the seventh.

SOCRATES: How?

D   STRANGER: Out of monarchy, we said, there was a royal and a tyrannical regime, and in turn out of the nonmany there was an aristocracy (of auspicious name) and an oligarchy. And in turn out of the many, we then set it down as simple and named it a democracy, but now we have to set down this too as double.

SOCRATES: How's that exactly? And by what difference do we divide it?

STRANGER: By nothing that differs from the rest, not even if its name
E   from now on is double (ambiguous), but the possibility of rule in conformity with laws as well as unlawfully holds no less for this regime than for the rest.

SOCRATES: Indeed it does.

STRANGER: Well, at that time, when we were looking for the right regime, this cut was not useful, as we previously showed, but after we had removed that one, and we set down the rest as indispensable (necessary), then in these the unlawful and the lawful cut each of them in two.

SOCRATES: Now that this speech is stated it seems likely.

STRANGER: Monarchy, then, if it's yoked in with good writings, which we speak of as laws, is the best of all the six, but if that's without law it's hard and most grievous to live with.

303   SOCRATES: Probably.

STRANGER: Yes, and as for the regime of the nonmany, in just the way the few is the mean of one and a multitude, let's believe that in this way it's the mean to both. And the regime of the multitude, in turn, is in nearly everything weak and has no capacity for any great good or evil, in comparison, that is, to the rest of the regimes. It's due to the fact that the offices of rule in it have been distributed in small segments over many officeholders. Accordingly, though of all regimes that are lawful it has proved to be the worst, it's the best of all that are unlawful. And though to live in a democracy *B* wins out over all that are intemperate, of those that are in due order, one must live in this least of all. But it's by far the first and best to live in the first regime, except for the seventh, for one must of course separate that out from all the rest of the regimes as a god from human beings.

SOCRATES: This does seem to turn out and come to be in this way, and one must act in just the way you're saying.

STRANGER: Then does it also appear that the partners of all these regimes must be removed—except from the scientific regime— *C* on the grounds that they are not statesmen but seditionaries, and being the patrons of the greatest images they are themselves of the same sort, and being the greatest imitators and greatest enchanters, they prove to be the sophists of sophists.

SOCRATES: It's probable that this remark has been twisted round to focus on the so-called statesmen most correctly.

STRANGER: So far so good. Now this to be sure is simply (artlessly) like a drama for us, and, as was said just before, when a certain band *D* of centaurs and satyrs was sighted, it had to be separated from a political art, and now in this way with great difficulty it did get separated.

SOCRATES: It appears so.

STRANGER: Yes, but there's still another harder than it left behind. It's due as much to its kinship and greater nearness to the royal genus as to the greater resistance it puts up to being understood. And it appears to me that we've undergone an experience similar to those who purify gold.

SOCRATES: How?

STRANGER: It's earth surely and stones and many other things that those craftsmen also separate first. And next, left mingled to- *E* gether with it, are those honorable congeners of gold—removable only by fire—copper and silver (and there is sometimes adamant as well),[45] which, once with assays by means of boilings they're removed with difficulty, allow us to see the so-called uncontaminated gold all alone by itself.

SOCRATES: It is indeed spoken of as occurring in this way.

STRANGER: Well, then, it seems that, analogously (*kata logon*), we too have separated apart the things other than political science, everything alien and unfriendly to it, but its honorable congeners are left. And among them there is surely generalship, the judicial (art), and all of rhetoric that shares in a royal (art) and by persuading of the just joins in piloting the actions in the cities.[46] In what way, then, will one most easily set them apart and show him naked and alone by himself, the one who is sought by us?

304

SOCRATES: It's plain that we must try to do this somehow or other.

STRANGER: Well, then, as far as trying goes, he will come to light. But it's through music that the attempt to make him plain must be made. So tell me.

SOCRATES: What sort of thing?

B STRANGER: There is surely for us a learning of music, and in general of the sciences that deal with handicrafts?

SOCRATES: There is.

STRANGER: And what of this? The question as to whether or not we must learn any one of these, shall we say that here too there is a kind of science that deals with this very question, or how?

SOCRATES: In this way, we'll say there is.

STRANGER: Shall we agree then that this is other than those?

SOCRATES: Yes.

STRANGER: And what are we to say? That none must rule over any of them, or that those must rule this, or that this must be in charge and rule all the rest?

C

SOCRATES: This those.

STRANGER: Then you are declaring after all that the (science) of whether one must learn or not must be for us the ruler of the (science) that is being learnt and doing the teaching?

SOCRATES: Exactly.

STRANGER: And the (science) of whether one must after all persuade or not must rule over the (science) capable of persuading?

SOCRATES: Of course.

STRANGER: So far so good. To what science, then, shall we assign the capacity to persuade a multitude and a crowd through mythology but not through instruction?

D

SOCRATES: This too, I suspect, is evident; it must be given to rhetoric.

STRANGER: And what of the question of whether through persuasion or maybe through force of some kind one must act in anything whatever against some people or altogether hold off—to what sort of science shall we add this?

SOCRATES: To the (science) that rules the (science) of persuasion and speaking.

STRANGER: And it would be nothing else, I suspect, than the power of the statesman.

SOCRATES: You've spoken most beautifully.

STRANGER: Then it seems that while this rhetorical kind has been *E*
quickly separated from a political (art), on the grounds that it is another species, subservient, however, to this—

SOCRATES: Yes.

STRANGER: What are we to think of the following sort of power?

SOCRATES: What sort?

STRANGER: That which is involved with how we are to wage war against whomever we choose to wage war against severally—shall we say it's without art or artful?

SOCRATES: But how could we ever think of it as without art, inasmuch as it's that which generalship and all of warfare do?

STRANGER: But the (science) that can and knows how to deliberate the question as to whether one is to wage war or be reconciled through friendship—are we to assume that it's other than that or the same as that?

SOCRATES: It's necessarily, by the previous consequences, another.

STRANGER: Then we'll declare it the ruler of that, if, that is, we shall *305*
assume it to be similar to the former cases.

SOCRATES: I agree.

STRANGER: Whatever, then, shall we even try to declare to be the master of so dreadful and great an art as the entirety of warfare except that of course which is in its being a royal (art)?

SOCRATES: Nothing else.

STRANGER: So we'll not set down the science of the generals, inasmuch as it is subservient, as political (science).

SOCRATES: No, it's unlikely.

STRANGER: Come then, let's observe as well the power of those judges *B*
who judge rightly.

SOCRATES: Yes, of course.

STRANGER: Does it really have any wider capacity than, in the case of contracts, to judge the things ordained to be the just and unjust in light of all the lawful things that have been established, and which it inherited from a legislator king, by supplying its own private virtue—defeated by neither any bribes nor terrors nor fits of pity nor any different kind of enmity and friendship[47]—and *C*
refusing to decide in the case of mutual accusations contrary to the ordinance of the legislator?

SOCRATES: No, but what you've said is pretty nearly all the work of this power.

STRANGER: And so we find that the strength of the judges is not royal but a guardian of laws and its servant.

SOCRATES: Yes, it seems likely.

STRANGER: Once we look at all the sciences mentioned we must realize

D this, that not one of them at least came to light as political (science), for that which is in its being royal must not itself act but rule those who have the capacity to act, in its cognizance of the beginning and initial impulse of the greatest things in cities in regard to opportunity and lack of opportunity, and all the rest must do what is ordered.

SOCRATES: Right.

STRANGER: So it's for these reasons that those which we've just now gone through, in ruling neither one another nor themselves, but each, in being involved with its own private (peculiar) action, has justly obtained, in accordance with its peculiarity, the name peculiar to its actions.

E SOCRATES: They seem at any rate likely to have done so.

STRANGER: But that which rules over all of these and the laws, cares for all the things throughout a city, and weaves them all together most correctly—should we comprehend its power by the designation of the common, we would address it most justly, it seems, as political (science).

SOCRATES: That's altogether so.

STRANGER: And wouldn't we also want to go over it now, in accordance with the paradigm of weaving, when also all the genera throughout a city have now become plain to us?

SOCRATES: Yes, exactly so.

306 STRANGER: The royal plaiting, then, it seems, must be stated, what sort it is, in what manner it plaits together, and what sort of woven thing it hands us.

SOCRATES: Plainly.

STRANGER: So, it appears, it's really become necessary after all to point out a difficult matter (*pragma*)—

SOCRATES: And yet for all of that it must be said.

STRANGER: It's because of the fact that a part of virtue is in a certain sense at variance with a species of virtue and thus, in light of the opinions of the many, is very easily open to attack by those skilled in disputations about speeches.

SOCRATES: I don't understand.

STRANGER: Well, here it is once more. I suspect that you believe that

B manliness (courage) is for us one part of virtue.

SOCRATES: Certainly.

STRANGER: And that moderation is other than manliness, but, regardless of that, this too is a proper part of that of which manliness is too.

SOCRATES: Yes.

STRANGER: Then we must have the nerve to declare a somewhat amazing speech about them.

SOCRATES: What sort?

STRANGER: That the pair of them is in a certain sense with a well-founded enmity toward each other and admits of a sedition of contraries in many of the things which are.

SOCRATES: How do you mean that?

STRANGER: It's in no way a usual speech. All the proper parts of virtue at least are surely spoken of as friendly with one another? C

SOCRATES: Yes.

STRANGER: Let's then pay very close attention and examine whether it is so simple, or it's as certain as anything can be that something of them admits a difference with its congeners in some respect?

SOCRATES: Yes, you must speak at what point it must be examined.

STRANGER: In all things we have to look for everything which, though we speak of them as beautiful, we place in two species contrary to one another.

SOCRATES: Speak with still greater clarity.

STRANGER: Quickness and speed, whether it's in terms of bodies or in souls or in terms of the movement of sound, and whether it is D themselves or as they are in images—all the imitations that music and still more painting (writing) supply by imitation—have you yourself ever been a praiser of any of these or been where you've perceived someone else praising them?

SOCRATES: Why certainly.

STRANGER: Do you have any recollection as well as to the manner in which they do it in each of these cases?

SOCRATES: In no way.

STRANGER: Then would I be capable of showing it to you through speeches in just the way I'm thinking of it?

SOCRATES: Why not? E

STRANGER: You seem to believe that something of the sort is easy. Well anyway let's examine it in opposing genera. There are often many actions when we express our admiration for the speed, intensity, and quickness of thought and body, as well as of sound, in which we speak our praise of it by using the single address of manliness.

SOCRATES: How?

STRANGER: We say at first surely "quick and manly" and "swift and manly," and likewise "intense," and in every case, by applying the name I speak of in common to all these natures, we praise them.

SOCRATES: Yes.

307 STRANGER: And what of this? Have we not often praised in turn in many actions the species of quiet becoming?

SOCRATES: Yes, exactly.

STRANGER: Aren't we then saying the contrary of that which we utter about the former?

SOCRATES: How?

STRANGER: Since we surely say on each occasion "quiet" and "moderate," when we express our admiration with "slow" and "soft" ("mild") in the case of doings that involve thought no less than in terms of actions, and further still in the case of sounds there's "smooth" and "grave," and every rhythmic motion and a whole

B muse that opportunely employs slowness—we don't apply the name of manliness but that of orderliness to all these things.

SOCRATES: Most true.

STRANGER: And yet, on the other hand, whenever both these things prove to be for us inopportune, we change each of the two around and direct our reproaches to the contrary quarter by making a reassignment of them with our names.

SOCRATES: How?

STRANGER: If they prove to be quicker and faster and come to light

C as stiffer than the opportune, we speak of them as hubristic and manic, but if heavier, slower, and softer, we say they're craven and doltish. And it's pretty nearly and for the most part no less the case about these things than about the moderate nature and the manliness of its opponents—they are as it were looks (*ideai*) that divide between them a hostile stance (sedition)—that we find them to be not only not mingling with one another in actions that involve things of this sort, but also, we'll further see, that those, if we track them down, who have them in their souls are at odds with one another.

SOCRATES: Where do you mean exactly?

D STRANGER: In all these things we now spoke of and, it's likely, in many others as well. It's in accordance, I suspect, with their own kinship with either of the two that people praise some as of their own family, and blame some of the differences as alien, and thus settle into an extensive and mutual enmity about many things.

SOCRATES: They probably do.

STRANGER: Well, at least this kind of difference of these species is child's play. But in the case of the greatest things, an illness results for cities that proves to be the most hateful of all.

SOCRATES: What sort of thing exactly are you speaking of?

STRANGER: It's likely to be of the whole arrangement of life. Those *E*
who are exceptionally well-ordered are ever prepared to live the
quiet life, minding their own business alone by themselves, associating with everyone at home on these terms, and likewise, in
confronting cities on the outside, they are prepared on every issue
to be at peace in some sense. And on account of just this love
(*erôs*), which is more untimely than it ought to be, whenever they
do what they want, they themselves come into an unwarlike state
without being aware of it, and so condition their young in the
same way, and they are always the prey of aggressors. It's from
these circumstances that in not many years they themselves and
their children and the entire city, instead of being free, often
become without their being aware of it slaves.   *308*

SOCRATES: You speak of a hard and dreadful experience.

STRANGER: But what of those whose inclination is more toward manliness? Aren't they always tensing up their own cities for some
war, and on account of their desire—more vehement than it should
be—for a life of this sort, they settle into a hatred with many
powerful people, and either they altogether destroy them, or in
turn they hazard their own fatherlands to be slaves and subjects
to their enemies?

SOCRATES: This is so too.   *B*

STRANGER: How then are we to deny that in these matters both these
genera always conceive of the greatest and overwhelming mutual
enmity and sedition?

SOCRATES: It's in no way that we'll deny it.

STRANGER: Then we've found just that which we were examining at
the beginning, that proper parts of virtue, not small, are as a pair
at variance with one another by nature, and, in particular, act on
those who have them in this same way?

SOCRATES: The pair probably does.

STRANGER: Then let's take up the following.

SOCRATES: What sort of thing?

STRANGER: Whether any of the compounding sciences anywhere will-   *C*
ingly puts together anything (*pragma*) whatsoever of its works,
even if it's the most trifling thing, out of some poor and good
stuff, or does every science everywhere throw out as best it can
the poor stuff and accept the suitable and good, and from these
things, which are both similar and dissimilar, by bringing them
all together into one, craft some single power and look (*idea*)?

SOCRATES: Why certainly.

STRANGER: So the political (art) that is for us truly by nature will never, *D* of its own will, put together any city out of good and bad human beings. But it's perfectly plain that it will assay them first by child's play, and after the assay it will hand them over to those who are capable of educating them and serving this purpose, while it itself gives orders and supervises, just as weaving gives orders to and supervises while in close attendance the carders and those who

E first prepare everything else that goes into its plaiting and, by pointing out things of this sort to them severally, completes the works of whatever sort it believes to be suitable for its own interweaving.

SOCRATES: Yes, of course.

STRANGER: It appears to me that it's in just this same way that the royal (art), itself with the power of the supervisory (art), will not allow all the lawful educators and nurses to practice anything except that which they, in producing in light of its own mixing, will use to perfect a fitting character. But it's these things alone that the royal art urges them to use in education, and whoever are incapable of sharing in a manly and moderate character and everything else that pertains to virtue, but are perforce pushed off towards godlessness and insolence and injustice by a bad na-

309 ture, it throws them out and punishes them with executions, exiles, and the greatest dishonors.

SOCRATES: Something like this is said at any rate.

STRANGER: But whoever, in turn, wallow in folly and excessive humility, it yokes under the slave genus.

SOCRATES: Most correctly.

STRANGER: The remainder, accordingly, all those whose natures are

B able in obtaining an education to become settled in the noble and grand and to receive with art a mutual commingling, when some of them tend more toward manliness—the royal (art) holds the view that their solid character is like a warp growth—and some tend to the orderly and enjoy in accordance with the semblance a wooflike thread, rich and soft, and their natures are straining in contrary directions to one another, it (the royal art) tries to bind and plait them together in some sort of way like the following.

SOCRATES: What sort exactly?

C STRANGER: First of all, it makes fit together by a divine bond, in accordance with the kinship, that part of their soul that is eternal-in-genus, and after the divine it fits together in turn their animal-genus with human bonds.

SOCRATES: Once more, how did you mean this?

STRANGER: Whenever that which is in its being true opinion with steadfastness about the beautiful, just, and good things (and about their contraries) comes to be in souls, then I say that a divine (opinion) is coming to be in a more-than-human genus.

SOCRATES: Its fitting, in any case, that this be so.

STRANGER: And we know, don't we, that it's suitable only for the *D* statesman and the good legislator to be capable by the muse of the royal (art) to instill this very thing in those whose correct participation in education we were speaking of just now?

SOCRATES: It's likely at any rate.

STRANGER: Yes, but whoever is incapable, Socrates, of doing anything of the sort, let us never address him with the names that are now being sought.

SOCRATES: Most correctly.

STRANGER: What then? If a manly soul takes hold of the truth of its own sort, doesn't it get tamed, and would it not be most willing in *E* this way to share in the just things? But if it does not get a share in them, will it not more incline toward some kind of bestial nature?

SOCRATES: Of course.

STRANGER: But what of that which characterizes the orderly nature? Doesn't it, if it partakes of these opinions, become in its being moderate and intelligent, within the limits of a regime, but if it does not share in what we're speaking of, doesn't it receive most justly a certain kind of reproachful renown for naive simplicity?

SOCRATES: Yes, of course.

STRANGER: Are we to say then that a weaving together and this kind of bonding prove to be never stable for the bad with themselves and for the good with the bad, and that there's no science that would ever use in all seriousness a bond for people of this sort?

SOCRATES: Of course.

STRANGER: But those whose characters are at birth well-born and alone *310* have been nurtured through laws to grow by nature, then it's for just these that we're to say that this is a drug by art, and, as we said, this is the more divine binding together of the dissimilar and contrarily diverging parts of the nature of virtue.[48]

SOCRATES: Most true.

STRANGER: Now as for the remaining bonds, inasmuch as they are human, it's pretty easy when this divine bond is present either to understand it or once understood to perfect it.

SOCRATES: How exactly? And what bonds? *B*

STRANGER: The bonds of intermarriage and the exchange of children (between cities) and the bonds of private betrothals and marriages. The many in these matters do not correctly bind themselves for the purpose of the generation of their children.

SOCRATES: Why exactly?

STRANGER: Now for what reason would anyone who reproaches the pursuit of wealth and powers in matters of this sort be in earnest as if they deserve a speech?

SOCRATES: For none.

STRANGER: Yes, but it's just rather to speak about those whose concern
C   is for their families (genera), if they're doing anything untoward.

SOCRATES: Indeed, it's likely at any rate.

STRANGER: It's not even on the basis of one correct speech that they act, in pursuing immediate convenience and by the fact that they welcome those who are similar to themselves, and they're discontent with the dissimilar and assign a very large part to the distress they feel.

SOCRATES: How?

STRANGER: The orderly seek out surely their own character, and con-
D   tract marriages as best they can from these and send out again to them their own daughters for betrothal. And the genus of manliness acts in the same way, in close pursuit of its own nature, though both genera ought to be doing entirely the opposite of this.

SOCRATES: How, and for what reason?

STRANGER: Because it's no less natural for manliness if it gets generated over many generations without mixing with a moderate nature, to flourish at the beginning at a peak of strength, and in the end to burst out altogether in fits of madness—

SOCRATES: It's likely.

STRANGER: Than for the soul too full of shame and unmixed with a
E   manly daring, if it comes to be generated in this way over many generations, to grow too sluggish to respond to the timely and to end up finally altogether maimed.

SOCRATES: This too is likely to turn out this way.

STRANGER: So I was saying that once there is present for both genera a single opinion about the beautiful and good things, it's not at all difficult to bind these bonds together. The reason I said it was that this is the single and whole work of royal weaving, never to allow moderate characters to stand apart from the manly, but by tamping them down together by means of joint-opinions, honors, dishonors, reputations (opinions), and mutual betrothals of hostages, and bringing together out of them a smooth web with—as the saying goes—a good hand, always to entrust to these in com-
311   mon the offices of rule in cities.

SOCRATES: How?

STRANGER: Whenever a need arises for one ruler, by choosing as supervisor the one who has them both; but whenever there's need of several, by mixing together a part of each of the two. The reason is that the characters of moderate rulers are extremely cautious, just, and safeguarding, but they lack intensity and a certain kind of quick and active keenness.

SOCRATES: This does seem at any rate to be the case.

STRANGER: Yes, but the manly characters, on the other hand, are more   *B* deficient than the former in regard to the just and the cautious, but they have to an exceptional degree keenness in their actions. And it's impossible for all the things that involve cities to turn out beautifully in private and in public if the pair of both of these is not present.

SOCRATES: Of course.

STRANGER: Let's say, then, that this proves to be the completion of the web of political action: The character of manly and moderate human beings woven together by direct intertexture whenever the royal art brings together their life into a common one by unanimity and friendship and completes the best and most mag-   *C* nificent of all webs—to the extent that this can hold of a common web[49]—and by wrapping everyone else in the cities in it, slaves and free, holds them together by this plaiting, and to the extent that it's suitable for a city to become happy, by omitting nothing that in any way belongs to this, rules and supervises.

SOCRATES: You completed and perfected most beautifully again for us, stranger, the royal man and the statesman.[50]

Statesman Commentary

I. SOCRATES
(257a1–258a10)

The structure of the *Sophist* duplicates its teaching: the discussion of being and nonbeing is the bond between the sophist as acquisitor and the sophist as imitator. The *Statesman* likewise contains a central section on paradigm and measure which effects the passage between the statesman as shepherd and the statesman as weaver. The fact and nature of bonding, which the stranger discovers in the *Sophist,* are put to use in the *Statesman* as especially characteristic of the statesman. The *Statesman* thus looks like the practical application of the 'theoretical' *Sophist.* We may call this the Theodoran view of the *Statesman.* Socrates tells Theodorus that he owes him much gratitude for his joint acquaintance with Theaetetus and the stranger. Theaetetus has shown his ability to greater advantage in his conversation with the stranger, for all his errors and misunderstandings, than in conversing with Socrates the day before. Theodorus at once understands Socrates' gratitude to be dependent on if not identical with the joint exhibition of the sophist by Theaetetus and the stranger. He does not take it in a petty way, as if "acquaintance" meant to become familiar with an individual's bodily traits. "Soon, you'll owe triple this, Socrates, whenever they produce for you both the statesman and the philosopher." Theodorus makes a false prediction. Theaetetus will no longer be the stranger's partner, and Socrates implies that he himself and young Socrates should complete the series. This is Theodorus' second false prediction; he had confidently asserted yesterday that Socrates would discuss Parmenides with Theaetetus. He knew nothing then of Socrates' fear and shame; he knows nothing now of the limitations of Theaetetus.

Theodorus makes another error: he mishears Socrates, for otherwise he would not have said that Socrates would owe three times more than "much gratitude." In the word "much" all of the *Philebus* is contained, and with it Socrates points forward to the nonarithmetical measure of the stranger. Theodorus believes perhaps that any much is a many and in principle countable. Socrates, however, does not catch Theodorus out on either his false prediction or his mishearing. He implies instead that they have misheard Theodorus, whose excellence in calculation and geometry is incompatible with what he has just said. Beneath Socrates' ironical surprise at Theodorus' error, which is all but inevitable for a mathematician to make, there is no irony. To be excellent in mathematics means to know the limits of mathematics; it means to know that the varying worth of sophist, statesman, and philosopher cannot be calculated according to any mathematical proportion. Socrates would have equally disapproved had Theodorus said that his gratitude would be twenty times greater. He would, however, have let him get away with saying that he would owe much more gratitude.[1] Socrates seems to quibble. A science of gratitude, worth, and honor does look in its imprecision like the artless class of haggling which the stranger's *logos* had discovered, and in light of the central importance honor has for the city, such a science could well be the statesman's.

Socrates seems to assume that his gratitude for the exposition of each man will be in direct proportion to their several worths. The *logos* of each is the honor of each. A perfect speech about a spurious being cannot be higher in rank than the spurious being itself. Unlike the stranger, Socrates refuses to separate the way of understanding from what is understood, so that the question "What is it?" is always accompanied by the question "What good is it?"[2] The sophist is worth something, but his worth is in a sense not his own but the philosopher's, for he is in part an unwilled illusion of the philosopher. Socrates' gratitude is partly due to the partial uncovering of what a philosopher is. If we knew exactly how much Socrates' "much" was, we should know exactly to what extent the philosopher is disguised when disguised as a sophist, and a fortiori to what extent philosophy must be sophistic. Theodorus, however, believes that the sophist was fully presented; he believes the stranger has finished one of three projects, each of which is wholly independent of the other two. Socrates counters with a more complex suggestion (fig. 1).

The sophist and the statesman are each distorted projections of the philosopher. Theaetetus and the stranger have moved beyond the

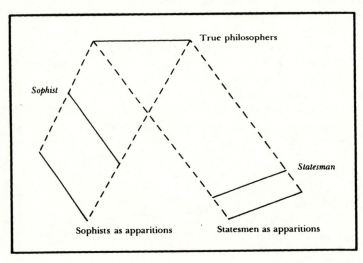

Figure 1

illusory sophist to a less distorted projection; it is necessarily at some nonmeasurable distance from the true philosopher. If the illusory statesman is of higher rank than the illusory sophist, even to go a smaller step beyond the illusion could call for more gratitude than a seemingly greater advance in the case of the sophist, for the true philosopher shows up in a less distorted way in the being of greater worth. Theodorus certainly acknowledges that the philosopher deserves more honor than the sophist: he calls all philosophers divine. But in what esteem does he hold the statesman? He once hoped that Protagoras could save him from the city's ridicule; he never expected that the city would honor him. The statesman, however, is not the city, and perhaps Theodorus agrees with Socrates that the philosopher whose body alone lies in the city does examine kingship and human happiness.[3]

Theodorus accepts, but not very gracefully, Socrates' correction. He understands it as a punishment for which he will pay Socrates back at another time.[4] He resents the correction; he believes no pupil has the right to correct a teacher, and therefore he is within his rights to punish Socrates in turn. It is perhaps for this reason that he invokes "our god," Zeus Ammon. He and Socrates are like two cities, for whom the only relation that can obtain between them is that of mutual retaliation. Theodorus had entered the lists with Socrates on behalf of his friend Protagoras as if he were submitting to fate,[5] and he had recommended the stranger on the grounds that he at least did not engage in the disagreeable contentiousness of eristics, but now he finds that no sooner does he utter a graceful remark than Socrates pounces on him again and delivers an unexpected blow. In the *Sophist,* Theodorus had himself corrected Socrates for supposing that the stranger was a god in disguise; in any case, the stranger had not come to punish Socrates for the poorness of his speeches.

Theodorus looks not to the stranger but to Zeus Ammon to take care of Socrates' carping. He could not have appealed to a god who would be less likely to back up his denial that the stranger is a god. Ammon is an Egyptian god, whose name was (and is) thought to mean "Concealed" or "Hidden," and who once revealed himself to Heracles in the shape of a ram.[6] The Greek stranger Theodorus swears by a strange barbarian god whose appearance suggests that Socrates was being too provincial when he restricted, by the authority of Homer, the apparitions of the gods to human shapes. If the sophist is a wild beast like the wolf, and the Socratic philosopher a most gentle dog— Socrates' favorite oath—then perhaps the gods are as polymorphic as the sophist or the philosopher. If Zeus wanted to rule unobtrusively a flock of sheep, a ram or a dog would be a most suitable disguise. We cannot help but remember that Odysseus, to whom Socrates had likened Theodorus when he cited Homer at the beginning of the *Sophist,* concealed himself in the fleece of the Cyclops' favorite ram in order to escape from the cave.

If the *Sophist* is somehow the punishment of Socrates, a punishment that the stranger has administered on behalf of the royal speech, the *Statesman* seems to be shaping up as Socrates' revenge. Socrates begins by attacking Theodorus for believing that everything is mathematicizable; he had initiated the problem of the *Sophist* by suggesting that the stranger was a god. Theodorus had evaded that suggestion with a thoughtless distinction between "god" and "divine." Socrates had then, without acknowledging the correctness of Theodorus' distinction, shifted the question from the class of the god to that of the philosophers, whose apparitions are almost as hard to interpret as the disguises of Homer's gods. Now, however, Socrates wins Theodorus' grudging admission of the incompetence of his own competence in a matter of honor and rank. We can therefore ask whether the limits Socrates has now imposed on mathematical proportion mark that boundary on the other side of which phantastics, as the science of perspectival distortion, has its home. For not only is mathematics as incompetent to determine the degree of illusion in a *phantasma* as the difference in honor between the sophist and the philosopher and statesman, but the tension between the big and the beautiful seems to be either the same as or at least like the recalcitrance honor shows to any kind of mathematicization, for honor is thought to be due to nothing but that which manifestly unites the big and the beautiful.

Theodorus' failure to recognize the limitations of his art would thus be the same as his incompetence to pronounce on whether the stranger was a god or a philosopher, an incompetence which Socrates had first hinted at when he questioned Theodorus' competence to assert that Theaetetus was ugly but gentle and courageous. Nothing better indicates the esteem in which Socrates holds Theodorus than his threefold assault, at the start of the *Theaetetus, Sophist,* and *Statesman,* on his art. The beauty of Theaetetus, the divinity of the stranger, and the gratitude of Socrates determine together the confines of mathematics. Inasmuch as Socrates only now makes explicit that the issue has always been mathematics, he seems to want to suggest that the *Statesman* has the edge in importance, however slight, over the *Sophist.*

Theodorus turns away from the contentious Socrates and, in asking the stranger to continue favoring them, offers him the choice of speaking on either the statesman or the philosopher. But the stranger believes it is not a matter of choice; since he plans to go on to the end, the statesman must of necessity be considered after the sophist. If the stranger does not mean that the statesman completes his project— the philosopher in his being is then to be inferred from his double apparition—Theodorus has just now confessed to one mistake and committed another. Are they the same mistake? Does the presumed commutability of statesman and philosopher rest on the same premise as the presumed equality of Socrates' gratitude for an account of sophist, statesman, or philosopher? The two presumptions would thus converge in the only error of Theodorus for which the stranger convicts him—his belief that Theaetetus is to be the interlocutor in the next two dialogues. Theodorus, who has something of Polonius about him,[7] agrees that Theaetetus should be given a rest and young Socrates assume the burden of the conversation. The indifference of the order in which statesman and philosopher are expounded seems to be of a piece with the interchangeability of Theaetetus and young Socrates.

Socrates confirms the choice of young Socrates for a different reason. He implies that his gratitude for knowing Theaetetus is as much due to his gaining knowledge of himself as to his learning the stranger's thoughts on the sophist. Perhaps Theaetetus impersonates Socrates to just about the same extent as the sophist does. In any case, Socrates coordinates self-knowledge with the knowledge of sophist, statesman, and philosopher. He reminds the stranger that the dialogues are primarily for his benefit. He recalls the beginning of the

Theaetetus, where the knowledge of Theaetetus consisted in the knowledge of his body and his name. The nature of Theaetetus' face, whose likeness to his own Socrates pretends to know by hearsay, if combined with the accidental homonymy of Theaetetus' fellow mathematician and himself, would yield a copy of the Socrates, who is about to go on trial, when he was young. The difference in the kind of kinship Theaetetus and young Socrates have to our Socrates would seem to reflect the difference in importance of the *Sophist* and the *Statesman.* Nature is to name as being is to law. But Theaetetus was beautiful. He first came to acknowledge, without speeches, that the soul by itself examines the beings, and then, again without speeches, that God makes the beings. Socrates' self-knowledge through knowledge of Theaetetus could therefore only occur if the beauty of Theaetetus' twofold insight were properly discounted in the speeches which Socrates and the stranger did not supply. If such a discounting were the action of the *Statesman,* the *Statesman* in itself would be equally defective, since it would still need the *Theaetetus* and the *Sophist* to compensate for its extravagance in debunking the unsupported insights of Theaetetus. Plato, moreover, saw fit to have us figure out young Socrates' kinship with Socrates by means of a single dialogue. The conversation between two Socrates', who would be as indistinguishable in a written dialogue as in a silent conversation Socrates conducted with himself, is missing.

The stranger had conversed with Theaetetus prior to enlisting him in the hunt for the sophist.[8] In accepting Socrates' recommendation, he hardly ran the risk of finding out too late that Theaetetus was an unsuitable partner. Young Socrates, however, is almost unknown to him; we, at least, know that he helped Theaetetus to discover the proper way of defining surds. All the stranger has to go on is Theaetetus' recommendation of his "fellow gymnast," from which he might have inferred that young Socrates was somewhat more resistant than Theaetetus to fatigue.[9] Is strength of soul, or whatever one should call such resistance, the prerequisite for the discovery of political science? Does the *Statesman* demand a special effort on our part not to grow tired? When Theaetetus was flagging, the stranger assured him that the sophist was almost caught,[10] and through Theaetetus' reading of the stranger's face the dialogue was soon concluded. The *Statesman,* on the other hand, seems to have no shortcuts; the stranger always seems to take the longest possible way (cf. 258c3). Indeed, so much is this the case that the stranger goes out of his way to lengthen the discussion with a defense of its already excessive length. Without a murmur, young Socrates takes everything the stranger dishes out. The punishment which Socrates had feared the stranger would inflict on him seems to be meted out to his namesake. Might not educative punishment, then, be the quasi-political action of the *Statesman*?

II. THEORY
(258b1–261d2)

Young Socrates' answer to the stranger's third question seems to show that he had failed to follow the discussion of the sophist. He agrees that the statesman too is to be placed among the knowers, but the stranger had concluded, with Theaetetus' assent, that the sophist, inasmuch as he was an imitator, was not a knower.[11] Young Socrates, however, could be thinking that the statesman must at first be posited as a knower even if he turns out in the end to have no greater claim to knowledge than the sophist. Socrates, moreover, had implied that the statesman outranks the sophist, and young Socrates might believe that only greater knowledge could entitle its possessor to greater honor and worth. Young Socrates, at any rate, did not answer thoughtlessly, for he is not as certain as the stranger is that the sciences now need to be redichotomized, though this would be merely to adopt the way in which the stranger examined the sophist. The statesman might already be lurking, young Socrates' hesitation implies, in one of the rejected classes of the *Sophist*. The art of punishment, which showed up in the discovery of the sophist noble by birth, or even some division of "historic mimetics"—either could have served as a starting point for the *Statesman*.

If they are to begin all over again, with a different initial cut of knowledge, either sophistry infected with its own spuriousness the split between making and acquisition, or, in accordance with the stranger's own teaching, the necessary intrusion of "the other" in every class entails the cross-classification of the arts and sciences. The way in which the sophist drifted out of the class of acquisition points to the first possibility, and the stranger himself seems now to stress the second by only speaking of "different" and not "other." He tells young Socrates that they must separate the political straight-of-way from all the different ones and seal it with a single look and, once they have imprinted a single different kind on the different runoffs, make their soul understand all the sciences as being two kinds.

The stranger identifies the way to political science with political science. The *Statesman* is the statesman. Every other science belongs to the same kind; political science stands alone. It has no congeners. The intrusive "other" would seem to be characteristic of every science except political science; its boundaries are fully fixed and do not admit of any alien element. The stranger presents political science as if it had borrowed from the city the city's exclusiveness: the *Menexenus* is the only Platonic dialogue in which the word "other" does not appear (cf. 245c6–d6). Political science rightly treats every other science as a stranger. But perhaps the statesman, through a sort of provincial self-importance, has incorrectly isolated himself, and his self-delusion has induced the stranger to find a place for him he does not deserve. In the course of the dialogue, the statesman's art drifts out of the class of theoretical knowledge into which the stranger first puts it (cf. 284c2, 289d1). It thus displays the same kind of class instability as the art of the sophist, which the stranger took to signify its spuriousness. Does statesmanship, then, have a doubleness of its own that parallels the doubleness of sophistry? The stranger implies, at least, that it can only come to light if all the other sciences are simultaneously grasped in their unity. The eidetic two of knowledge would thus be the broadest and deepest theme of the *Statesman* and political science.

Young Socrates believes that the task the stranger has proposed is not his but the stranger's, but he agrees that the task should be his as well whenever it becomes evident. It is not evident now. The stranger distinguishes "gnostics" from "practics." Arithmetic and arts akin to it are stripped of actions and supply only knowledge, whereas carpentry and every manufacturing art "possess their science as if it naturally inheres in their (several) actions, and along with their actions they bring to completion the bodies that come to be through them and are not before." Young Socrates then declares that the stranger has now the two kinds of the single whole of knowledge. He rashly assumes that the stranger has now made evident their common task. Since he can hardly believe that arithmetic is a branch of political science, he must suppose, not unreasonably, that political science is the queen of all the practical arts, and that just as carpentry becomes mostly guesswork at the moment it abandons its tools, which are nothing but embodied copies of the geometer's straightedge and compass,[12] so too political science is scientific only insofar as it is mathematical. Were this not the case, young Socrates could not have said, especially after having heard Socrates' conversation in the *Theaetetus* the day before, that knowledge is a single whole. Practical knowledge must look to him as if it were applied mathematics. He cannot suspect that the stranger wishes to place political science with arithmetic, and therefore that this initial division does not satisfy the stranger's demand that it be discovered in its distinctness from every other science.

At first glance, the stranger's contention is implausible. Carpentry as knowledge is inseparable from its actions; it shows what it is in the things it makes, and is coextensive with what it can do. It contains no unsolved problems, nothing comparable with Fermat's last theorem. All of these traits seem to be equally true of political science, for if it is not as complete as carpentry but subject, like mathematics, to revision in its foundations, the best possible regime would be merely an hypothesis. And if it is never manifest in actions, a politician of experience could always be mistaken—and rightly so—for the artful stateman. If, moreover, "action" here means what it does in the *Sophist,* that which verbs reveal (262a3–4), the stranger would, in stripping mathematics of verbs, be denying that mathematical construction was a part of mathematics. But, laughable though it is, mathematicians are compelled to speak "as if all their speechmaking was acting and for the sake of action."[13] Indeed, young Socrates' joint discovery with Theaetetus of the general definition of surds wholly depended on the actions of image making and squaring. The stranger could justifiably ignore here the problem which mathematical action poses if construction and model building did not pertain to political science, but he would then have to argue that the best city in speech, which Socrates presents in the *Republic,* was not a construction.

The stranger, accordingly, does not say whether numbers are and do not become, for if gnostics dealt solely with unchanging beings, political science could not possibly belong to it. Can the stranger wish to deny that the city is a kind of body, and that in its becoming (i.e., founding) political science can show itself? The sole point of contact between political science and arithmetic would seem to be this. Whether or not there is arithmetic, there are numbers, and whether or not there is political science, there are cities, for the city is "something strong by nature" and does not depend for its existence on knowledge (cf. 302a3). And, consequently, just as arithmetic stands apart from numbers, political science is not a part of politics. Things, however, can be counted without our knowing the difference between the odd and the even. Are cities likewise ruled in ignorance of something as elementary?

The stranger does not immediately assign political science to gnostics; instead, he raises another question, whether statesman, king, slavemaster, and household manager are to be addressed as one. But he does not let young Socrates answer that question either, but turns to a third consideration. This confusing procedure, which is a foretaste of the manner the stranger adopts throughout the dialogue, is dictated by the need to correct young Socrates' tacit assumption that the statesman's art is practical. The analogy, however, which the stranger now offers, compounds the confusion. If someone in private practice, he asks, is capable of advising a public physician, must he not be addressed with the same name of the art which the one he advises has?

But is medicine an art stripped of actions and only a supplier of knowledge?[14] Could not a carpenter, then, set himself up as a consultant to other carpenters and never touch a tool? And the lay physician, in the stranger's example, advises another physician. But since the king is not necessarily a genuine king, that is, in possession of the royal art, would not the private statesman, who can advise the nominal king of a country, need the art of persuading the king to take his advice? Would he not also have to want to give advice? Without these qualifications, which the stranger never mentions, the true king has a truly unique art. Inasmuch as he has no need ever to prove his competence in political affairs, he can live out his life and never once be known as a statesman. Socrates looks of necessity like a sophist; he does not look like a statesman.[15] How, then, can Socrates say that statesmen are sometimes the apparitions of true philosophers?

Young Socrates is more certain of the justice than of the correctness of calling the competent adviser to a king, who in deed neither rules nor advises, kingly (cf. 259a2, 260a1), but he accepts without question the identification of political science with royal science. A king might not be kingly. Would the incompetent ruler of a city not be a statesman (*politikos*) but a citizen (*politês*)? The stranger speaks of the king as king of a country or land. He owns the land. But Pericles did not own Athens. The stranger implies that whatever one can use correctly is one's own.[16] He thus can bring together the king and the private man, for the household manager and the slavemaster are primarily owners, one of his house and household goods, the other of slaves. Property unites Socrates and the Great King. Socrates' wife and children should have sufficed to instruct him in the art of ruling the Persian Empire.[17] That the rule over slaves, whether a few or an entire tribe, differs from the rule over one's own wife and children, and both in turn from the rule in a city over free men, each of whom has his own family and slaves, must seem unimportant to young Socrates,[18] but we should rather say that the stranger has made him oblivious of these differences. The stranger invites young Socrates to look at political science in terms of economics, the most mathematical or mathematicizable part of political science. Household and kingdom only differ in size, or, as the stranger puts it *more geometrico:* "The (plane) figure of a large household and the (three-dimensional) bulk of a small city won't at all differ in point of rule." The city is the family raised one power.

Because the stranger abstracts from political science everything which properly distinguishes political life from other kinds of living together, young Socrates comes to recognize the gnostic character of political science. Abstraction is the specious equivalent to theory. It here induces young Socrates to make the same mistake as Theodorus did, when he thought mathematical proportion an adequate way to express the degree of Socrates' future gratitude. Young Socrates' error is, however, more understandable. He would hardly know that the best regime requires the abolition of the family, and therefore that household and city must be more distinguishable than 2^2 and 2^3 are. If, moreover, the artful household manager has the kingly art, it would be superfluous to say that the competent adviser to a king, even if he never offers advice, is the true king, for he must in fact be practicing the kingly art within his own family. Young Socrates takes the identification of the private with the public, which is due to an illegitimate abstraction, as validating the identification of the knower of political things, even if he lives a private life, with the true king. He still does not know what makes political science gnostic and a part of philosophy.

Arithmetic counts, that is, knows things insofar as they are countable. Political science, then, should know things only insofar as they can be politicized, and the particular way in which some things are politicized are of no concern to it. Ruling would thus be one of many things whose absence from a given situation would not deprive that situation of its political character. The stranger does not argue in this way; Socrates does so when he presents, in the *Republic*, a city in which there are no rulers: Socrates calls it the true and healthy city. For the stranger, on the other hand, ruling is the primary human relation. Its presence in the city, house, or kingdom, regardless of every other difference, designates that situation as political. And since the seemingly least political of the terms for ruler which the stranger mentions is the slavemaster, we should have to say that the constitutive element of the political is the master-slave relation. Is this, then, the fact, as elementary as odd and even, of which all artless rulers are unaware? If so, tyranny might seem to be the regime that reveals most plainly the political. But the stranger speaks of the art of ruling, and the tyrant's unceasing need to employ force would indicate that he goes against the natural grain of political life, which political science, one might suppose, is best able to account for as well as take into account.

In the course of the dialogue, the stranger does explain the reasons for his strange beginning, in which more questions are raised than answered, but even now his procedure can be justified, albeit poorly. Contrary to the stranger's own insistence that nomenclature is of no importance, the very term *politikos*, like its common English translation, necessarily points to ruling, and the stranger had no choice, given the problem Socrates had set him, but to examine political science in its light. After all, to identify political science with the science of ruling would only put at the start what Socrates put at the end:

the necessary condition for the surcease of all political evils is the philosopher-king.

The king is "more at home" in gnostics than in handicraft and practics because intelligence and strength of soul are incomparably more capable of maintaining a king's rule than his own bodily strength. Even the tyrant cannot rely on force to control his own bodyguards. For the first time, the stranger makes an obvious point and ruins his case. What need does the out-of-office *politikos* have of strength of soul, if he has no rule to hold onto? Would he need it just in case he were to advise a king? The king would have to have wit enough to understand his adviser, and strength of soul to resist the lure of seductive but imprudent policies, but the adviser's character, like the arithmetician's, can have no bearing on his art. Strength of soul seems not to have an equivalent among the sciences (cf. 297a4–5). No sooner, then, does the stranger separate gnostics from practics than he begins to rejoin them. He thus acknowledges the presence of the intrusive other in political science. Political science is as alien from arithmetic as from carpentry. This becomes even plainer at the stranger's next division. His example of a gnostic art is now logistics: "Once logistics knows the difference among numbers, are we to grant it a larger task than to judge the things known?" To judge the things known and to know the difference among numbers seem to be the same, for the stranger denies that the master builder has appropriately finished his job once he has judged it. Discernment (*krisis*), then, would be cognition (*gnôsis*), and the proposed dichotomy of gnostics into critics and epitactics would be spurious. The stranger, at any rate, fails to mention gnostics when he later recalls his first division (292b9–11). On this reading, political epitactics would supplement political gnostics and not determine more narrowly its scope.

When, however, the stranger comes to place the true king in the proper class, he says he would be like a spectator if he had the art of judging. The logistician, then, both knows the difference among numbers and contemplates what he knows, while the statesman would presumably know without contemplating the difference among regimes.[19] This is not altogether satisfactory, for the stranger has allowed the masterbuilder to be something of a judge (cf. 260c5). Would it, then, be more exact to say that the statesman's knowledge of political things is inseparable from his judgment of political things, and their unity is the science of ruling, which knows what honor and worth are to be assigned to everything and everyone in the household, the city, and the kingdom? If the stranger has this in mind, he surely has not made it clear to young Socrates, who is made to look at political science in the light of an example which conceals as much as arithmetic did the uniqueness of political science. To this example we must now turn.

The master builder does not work with his hands but rules those who do. His right to rule follows at once upon his comprehensive knowledge, for none of the workmen under him needs to know anything more than the part of the project to which he is assigned. This comprehensive knowledge entitles the master builder to a place among the gnostic arts; but it can no longer be said of him that his knowledge is stripped of actions, and that if he merely drew up plans for splendid buildings he would still be a master builder, to say nothing of the difficulty involved in his act of drawing. The stranger has extended the meaning of gnostics. He seems to have forgotten all about the competent adviser who never advises. It is fitting, he remarks, for the master builder not to quit after he has judged but to see to it that each workman completes the orders he has been given. Is the stranger thinking of the statesman who leaves after he has laid down laws for his subjects? However this may be, the distinction between the arts of judging and ordering would be idle if epitactics did not mean the knowledge of how to give orders that will be carried out, the art, in short, of inducing obedience.

The stranger should at this point distinguish between arts in which, like the master builder's, everyone, from the hod-carrier on up, accepts his place, and those in which this or that subordination is not an evident necessity to the subordinated. But instead, the stranger appeals to the fact that the master builder should oversee the job from start to finish. To translate knowledge of political things into a given set of orders thus looks relatively easy: a glance at the paradigm of the best regime will inform the true king of what his day's orders should be. The denial of such translatability is one of the tenets of classical political philosophy, and it is as well no small part of the stranger's education of young Socrates, whose impulse to interpret political things mathematically the stranger judiciously both indulges and restrains.

On his being asked whether all of gnostics is fittingly divided into a judgmental and an injunctional part, young Socrates replies, "Yes, in my opinion at least." Those who are acting in common, the stranger then says, are to be content with their own agreement, and as long as they share a common ground, the opinions of others are to be dismissed. Two potential knowers of political science now form a community; if that community endures until they are political scientists, they will be the true rulers of any political community regardless of what its other members might opine. Young Socrates is no more aware of the stranger's pointing to the problem of obedience than of the import of their own common action, for if the way to the discovery of the statesman is the statesman, as the stranger had implied, their own action cannot be inconsistent with the gnostic character of political science. And yet, right after they agree that the true king is not like a spectator, the stranger asks where they should look for the split in the epitactical art. The stranger and young Socrates diverge from the statesman's own way at the very moment the stranger stresses their own action, which would seem to join them even more closely with the statesman, since he in turn has lost, through the example of the master builder, most of his original claim to a gnostic art. The spectator's detachment, which the nonpracticing statesman closely resembles, cannot be reconciled with the involvement of ruling. In the stranger's myth, the god contemplates when he does not rule, and he rules when he does not contemplate (cf. 272e5).

The stranger finds guidance for his third division in a third division of the *Sophist*, but he fails to remind young Socrates that Theaetetus on his own, and contrary to the stranger's own statement, had taken the distinction between retailer and manufacturer-retailer as a warrant for two separate definitions of the sophist.[20] Had young Socrates remembered, he might have realized the impossibility of the present dichotomy (cf. 292b9–10). To detach the class of heralds from that of kings is one thing, to make each a subclass of gnostics is another, for the herald's art neither demands intelligence and strength of soul nor includes knowledge of the reasons for the orders he receives.[21] The herald cannot take his orders from the ruler if both spring from the same class. Whatever the ruler commands are his own thoughts; he does not take his orders from anyone whatsoever. True statesmanship precludes revelation. Political science falls with the existence and stands with the nonexistence of commanding gods. The arts of divination and interpretation are not akin to the art of ruling. The stranger does not just anticipate here the teaching of the myth; he alludes to the incorrigible distortion the class of heralds could introduce in their transmission of the king's thoughts unless the king were his own herald. The king can have no spokesman; he must both make and give the orders. Absentee kingship is impossible. The stranger has now discarded the legislators along with the gods in his attempt to isolate the kingly art, but through a spurious division, the pretenders to that art have slipped into a place equal in rank to it. Dichotomy is no more able here than in the *Sophist* to cope with imitation.

For the fourth division—or, if our argument is sound, the third—the stranger orders young Socrates to join him in making the cut. With the exclusion of the gods from political science and its differentiation from mathematics, the stranger assumes that young Socrates is now clear about their task. The stranger seems at first to be mistaken, for young Socrates professes not to know that the kingly science orders living beings, but young Socrates is not to be blamed for the stranger's own lack of clarity. All rulers issue commands for the sake of some kind of *genesis*, and all things that come into being are easily divided into lifeless and living things. Even if *genesis* means the same as *praxis*, lifeless and living would not adequately divide all acts. A general can be said to be concerned with the *genesis* of victory in war, and the statesman with the *genesis* of virtue in the city, but neither victory nor virtue can be said to be, except poetically, alive,[22] and to call them lifeless is just as implausible. To distinguish all becomings into lifeless and living is perhaps theoretically exact—natural things could be so classified—but it seems irrelevant to the art of giving orders. Is the stranger's present order to young Socrates meant to generate a lifeless or a living cut (cf. 266a5)? If the master builder rules over workmen for the sake of producing lifeless buildings, does not the shepherd rule over sheep for the sake of producing lifeless wool, and the states-man over citizens for the sake of their producing, at least partly, the lifeless goods of exchange? Only through the vagueness of "in the case of animals and involved with them," does the stranger get young Socrates to agree that the greater nobility of the kingly science consists in its concern with the *genesis* of animals.

Let us even grant that breeding is all and not just a part of shep-herding. Does the shepherd's rule over his flock mean that he orders a ram to mate with a ewe? If political science is nothing but eugenics— the secret art of old Socrates' mother—the science of ruling would soon make itself redundant, for if its subjects can be made to order, they can be made self-regulating. Why should it settle for less than fully rational human beings? Is political science a poor substitute for the science of the "nuptial number"? The stranger has a reason for leading young Socrates toward so extravagant a suggestion. He wants to define the science of ruling in terms of that which is most recalcitrant to rule, what Glaucon calls "not geometric but erotic necessities."[23] Socrates' knowledge of *erôs* stands on the other side of the limits of political science. But the stranger's division not only points ahead to the city's human bonds and to the kind of intermarriage the statesman must encourage, it also serves a more immediate end—to make young Soc-rates consider the statesman on the model of the herdsman. Young Socrates was in danger of forgetting that men are not the only beings that are ruled. He did not object to the equation of household, city, and kingdom; he does not suspect that the stranger contemplates their equivalence to the bird farm, fishtank, and pigpen.

The first divisions of the *Statesman* surpass in difficulty any in the

Sophist. Until the stranger stated his own perplexity before the dichotomy of eikastics and phantastics, his intention at each cut could more or less clearly be made out. Here, however, the stranger seems to have encapsulated the entire *Statesman* in the first three or four divisions. At a comparable point in the *Sophist,* Theaetetus was hesitating over the existence of the hunting of lifeless things. But even though that was suggestive of the lifeless "ideas," on which the stranger later cast doubt, one could not then figure out the *Sophist's* argument. The *Statesman's* argument, on the other hand, is now complete; we now have the scheme the stranger will have to flesh out for the young Socrates. Even the question of the double measure has been alluded to: the class of heralds is said to stand apart to a fair degree from the class of kings (261a3; cf. 260b5).

The *Sophist* itself, no doubt, has helped the stranger to outline political science so quickly. Young Socrates did not need any practice-run on the angler. But even if we disregard the angler and count instead from the point where the hunter-sophist diverges from the angler, Theaetetus would be just accepting the distinction between the private and public arts of persuasion. Young Socrates seems to have denied any difference between the private and the public at the very start. In the *Sophist,* Theaetetus is asked to take, for the most part, very small steps, and with few exceptions the dichotomies codify commonly accepted classifications. The stranger's way seems to work fairly well but at the price of a certain triviality. In the *Statesman,* all this is changed. The way of dichotomy now outrages common sense at every turn, and the gain in novelty hardly compensates for the loss in plausibility. Indeed, the stranger could be charged with inverting the proper approach to each topic. He domesticates the sophist while making something exotic of political science. In the *Republic,* political things are examined in the light of justice, and in the *Laws,* of legislation, but in the *Statesman,* in the light of knowledge. Knowledge must be that which puts political things in so strange a perspective. Knowledge seems compelled, as the stranger presents it, to distort political things in order to grasp them, and a fortiori confesses its own incapacity to grasp them. Political science appears to be as much an oxymoron as the erotic science of Socrates.

III. PART AND KIND
(261d3–263b11)

As soon as the stranger turns to the next cut, political science ceases to be restricted to eugenics. He first adds nurture to *genesis,* and then, even more carelessly, speaks of the care of animals. Should he not, then, have distinguished from the start between those arts of ruling that care for their subordinates and those, like the master builder's, which do not? No artisan is of interest to the foreman when he is not on the job and at work. Caring and ruling seem to be somewhat at odds with one another. One pertains to the ruled, the other to an end the ruled serve and in which the ruled may or may not have a share. The shepherd's care of his flock is strictly geared to its usefulness for himself, and if this is the statesman's model, his subjects are there to be fleeced.[24]

Genesis tilted the art of ruling toward that of caring while keeping in view the purpose of ruling. But the apparent unity of the ends of caring and of ruling in generation cannot survive the stranger's distinction between the common care of animals in herds and the nurture of a single animal. Neither the many nor the one takes into account the two of mating. Even if the city or some part of it can be called a herd, does such a term apply to the family?[25] The shepherd can introduce each sheep into his herd separately, so that none has any prior relation to any other, and provided he has enough watchdogs and unlimited pasturage, his herd can in principle comprehend all sheep. Through the herd, the stranger raises the question of the universal state, whose cohesiveness would be solely due to its ruler, but in doing so he grants the possibility of a nonpolitical, gnostic, and commanding art which originates its own orders for the sake of some kind of *genesis* in an individual human being. We are inclined to locate this art in the neighborhood of the stranger's former discovery of a sophistry noble in descent. Perhaps we should even identify them.

The difference between the terms groom and oxdriver, on the one hand, and horse-feeder (*hippophorbos*) and cattle-feeder (*bouphorbos*), on the other, implies that, in contrast with the rule over any collective, individual care involves more than the alleviation of hunger. The city's survival, then, is the single end for whose realization all the statesman's ordinances are designed. Young Socrates fails to draw this consequence from the likeness of the *politikos* to *hippophorbos* and *bouphorbos*, let alone to notice that the true statesman may rule his herd in silence and with beatings. The rationality of statesmanship does not require that it issue rational commands. It thus stands farthest apart from the stranger's first characterization of sophistry: it knew nothing about men except that they were tame animals, open as such to the persuasion of speech. If young Socrates had attended to the stranger's likeness, he would have wondered how the stranger could now ask for a further dichotomy. The only distinction which would strictly follow would be not, as young Socrates supposes, of the ruled but of the rulers—the distinction, in short, between human rulers and more-than-human rulers of the human herd, or, to make it as general as possible, between those rulers who are of the same species as the herd they rule and those who are not. In the latter case, the ruler's manifest superiority to the ruled would dispense entirely with the need to distinguish between a command and the art of getting it executed. There would be, as it were, order (*taxis*) without ordering (*epitaxis*), and disobedience would not pose a serious problem (cf. 261b13). It is not surprising that young Socrates divides the art of common tendance incorrectly. What does call for an explanation is the roundabout way the stranger uses in order to correct him, for both the barnyard section and the myth were equally avoidable. The action of the dialogue is a large part of the dialogue's argument.

The stranger plays fair with young Socrates. He urges him to maintain his indifference to nomenclature just prior to young Socrates' assertion that the nurture of human beings is one thing (*hetera*), that of beasts is different (*allē*). Young Socrates is deceived by a name; he does not know that 'beast' is or can be a concealed negation of 'human being', no more revealing than the not-big, which comprehends both the small and the equal. The dominant image of the *Sophist* should have warned young Socrates: the sophist was a beast. And usage, after all, warrants the equation of the true king with the shepherd. At the very least, young Socrates would need an argument to show that the non-bestiality of man affects the art of ruling men.

The issue Theodorus unwittingly raised, when he corrected Socrates and called the stranger divine but not a god, now emerges from its underground passage through the *Sophist*, but only to reappear in another form. The issue is now the difference between 'human being' and 'human' (cf. 263c6). The stranger underlines the complexity of this issue even while bringing it to light. He addresses young Socrates as most manly for anticipating, with his distinction between human beings and beasts, the goal of their argument. According to the stranger himself, this address is a way of praising someone, and yet the stranger blames young Socrates for his haste. Young Socrates' manliness is that element of the human which most resembles something in the beastly; it either contradicts or qualifies his own distinction between men and beasts. Young Socrates did not understand why the stranger identified their way to the statesman with the statesman. Their approach must show statesmanlike caution.

It is most beautiful, the stranger admits, to hit upon at once the correct separation of whatever is sought from everything else, but as a rule it is safer to cut through the middle. Indeed, the stranger had warned young Socrates that he would have to show the art of tending herds to be twofold if they were to inquire in the half for what was now in the double. Not only does this mathematical formula not puzzle young Socrates, but, more surprisingly, it has no effect on the distinction he does make. Since the stranger devises as a correction a set of divisions which allow finally $\sqrt{2}$ and 2^2 to differentiate men from pigs, young Socrates would apparently not have been rebuked if he had designated men as two-footed and horses and cattle as four-footed animals. (His inexperience would have excused him from taking Thessalian aviaries and Egyptian fishtanks into account.) We witness in the barnyard section the laughable use of mathematics as an instrument of moderation. A young mathematician forgets for a moment his mathematics and relies instead on human pride; so the stranger goes out of his way to humiliate him (and, through him, man) as a token of his goodwill for his nature.

The difference between the *Statesman* and the *Sophist* is nowhere more manifest than here. Theaetetus was not altogether certain that a god made everything; but the stranger decided to dispense with any argument in its favor, since he divined that Theaetetus' nature would lead him to this conviction without argument. Now, however, when the cosmological issue of divine knowledge versus irrational nature has its counterpart in the self-evident opposition between the rationality of man and the irrationality of beasts, the stranger intervenes on behalf of the dumb animals in order to counteract the tendency of young Socrates' nature. His nature cannot be trusted to come to the desired understanding by itself. The lowness of man calls more urgently for a proof than the true cosmology. In the *Theaetetus*, we recall, Socrates had in the same speech proclaimed what God is and left it as a question what man is.

Just as the stranger excused himself in the *Sophist* from fully clarifying being and nonbeing, so now he pleads their present circumstances as a bar to a nondefective account of the relation between part and kind.[26] We have already given reasons for associating the two problems, but we could not then point to the paradox of political science. Political science more plainly reveals "the other," and accordingly must take it into account to a greater extent than any other science. And yet its own completeness does not depend on the complete solution to the problem of part and kind; rather, its own completeness would seem to be correlated with the unavailability of any but partial solutions to this problem. The stranger first connected this problem with political science when he proposed as their task the division of all sciences into two kinds, of which one was to be political science, and the other was to include every other science. Such a division looks very much like young Socrates' distinction between men and beasts and the vulgar Greek distinction between Greeks and barbarians, for in all three cases, a part seems to impose upon another part a spurious unity. How, then, can the stranger avoid giving a complete clarification of the difference between part and kind if political science itself cannot even be established without it? Must not political science continue to look spurious in the absence of such a complete clarification? Is this what Socrates meant when he said that true philosophers are sometimes apparitional statesmen?

We can put the difficulty in another way. The stranger has just distinguished between the caring of one animal and the caring of herds. But is a herd anything more than a part? If the stranger were dividing kinds of animals and not kinds of arts, would he not have distinguished between naturally gregarious and monadic animals, and thus have been forced to ask into which class man belongs? Horses, we would say, are gregarious by nature even though one can single one out of the herd and train him. So perhaps man is naturally monadic, and men are only together through their being ruled. We miss Aristotle's remark that man is naturally political, and whoever has no need for the city is either a beast or a god. If, as the stranger asserted, city, household, and a group of slaves are all ruled by the same art, it must be the case that either men are not naturally gregarious or that political science can be indifferent as to whether they are or not. Political science would simply attend to the fact that men live together. Its concern would be with human things and not human nature.

Although the stranger suggests that the distinction between male and female would be more eidetic than that between Greek and barbarian, he does not now introduce that distinction into the art of ruling; indeed, he bypassed it when he shifted from generation to feeding and caring as the proper end of ruling. The stranger, moreover, concedes that parts and kinds dominate political life. Each city, nation, or tribe is a part and apart from every other part of the human race. "Us" and "Them" is built into the name a people gives itself. All non-Lydians are strangers. The universal art of ruling the human herd will always show itself in fact as the art of ruling this or that particular herd of human beings. Young Socrates has to be taught the meaning of part even more than the meaning of kind. His mistake does not consist so much in his comprehending all nonhuman herds into one as in his deducing from the universality of political science (a universality characteristic of any art and distinguishing it from experience), the all-inclusiveness of the herd it rules. Young Socrates knows nothing as yet of the best city, which can only be of a limited size, and all of whose members cannot be understood as a herd. He has unwittingly defined political science as the art which the god exercised in the age of Cronus, when there were no cities and not even the beasts were strangers.

The barnyard section, then, rather than correcting young Socrates, prepares for the myth, and shows young Socrates the way in which his mistaken division could be maintained. The humiliation of man ultimately serves to establish the rule of the gods. Only the gods could consider all human beings as a single herd, and separate them from other animals by the criteria the stranger uses. But this divine perspective, from which young Socrates is persuaded to look down upon man,[27] is indispensable for the discovery of political science. The art of ruling finds it safer to regard men as beasts than as nonbeasts. Human beings are only potentially human.

Young Socrates is not satisfied with the stranger's examples of parts and kinds; he asks him how one would know more vividly that part and kind are not the same but different. The stranger would not even have digressed as far as he did if it were not for his goodwill toward young Socrates' nature. They have already wandered farther afield than the needful. To be diverted by young Socrates' nature is to lose track of the argument. There would be, then, according to the stranger, no connection whatever between the action and the argument of the dialogue, and the instruction of young Socrates would not pertain to the discovery of the statesman. The stranger publicly maintains this view until he reveals to young Socrates the existence of two kinds of measures. He then retracts it in favor of a different understanding of the needful, which retroactively makes all his former digressions indispensable elements of the argument. But until the nonmathematical measure is introduced, the argument is presented as if it were a theorem with just so many steps to its proof.

The problem of part and kind was therefore prefaced by the stranger's pseudomathematical problem: to find the half of political science in the double of the art of herding (cf. 264e12). In trying to solve that problem, young Socrates stumbled upon a true problem which is not always susceptible of mathematical treatment. The stranger will later criticize the Pythagoreans for correlating male and female with odd and even. At the moment, however, he thwarts young Socrates' natural desire for further enlightenment. He understands that desire as a command (263a5, 8). The full participation of young Socrates in the argument leads to the argument getting out of hand. The stranger's care for young Socrates is incompatible with his rule of young Socrates. It thus looks as if the tension between action and argument is the dialogic counterpart to the tension between caring and ruling in political science. The stranger, at any rate, once he has briefly formulated the difference between part and kind, reasserts his authority over young Socrates: he gives him an order (263c1; cf. 261e7–8).

IV. THE BARNYARD
(263c1–267c4)

The stranger had at first abstracted from the difference between slave and free, wife and children, city and family, city and kingdom, and he now has gone to great lengths to get young Socrates to abstract from the difference between men and other animals. Human pride, which men interpret as a consequence of their rationality, is merely due to their sexual exclusiveness. Nonmiscegenation passes among men as a title of superiority. Men forget that other animals are equally exclusive and would as justifiably object to their being lumped together as would all the human races which, despite their mutual immiscibility, the Greeks call barbarian.[28] That Greeks do not understand any other tongue than their own is no more significant than the unintelligibility to men of animal noises. But pride, particularly if it is false, is the engine of disobedience and presents the greatest obstacle to rule. Human pride, moreover, is inseparable from manliness, but we usually do not asssociate manliness with rationality and prudence. Rather, we believe there to be a virtual identity between prudence and moderation, and between moderation and obedience.[29]

So when the stranger says that the race of cranes, which is thought to be prudent (*phronimon*), might classify human beings along with all other animals as beasts, he is not only criticizing young Socrates for his anthropocentrism, but pointing to a recognized human excellence that is consonant with being ruled. That Thessalians exercise rule over cranes does not invalidate the stranger's argument; on the contrary, it confirms it. The cranes in their prudence sensibly acknowledge the superiority of certain men. But the stranger thereby weakens another part of his argument. The Thessalians are not noted for their wisdom, and the fact of rule has nothing to do with the right to rule. The stranger thus begins to weave in another strand of the problem of political science. If only the king with knowledge is the true king, but moderation, rationality, and obedience are not separable from one another, are we only to submit to the rule of the true king, and in his absence are moderation and obedience, if not rationality itself, to be discounted? Political science cannot recommend anarchy in the present while holding out the fantastic hope that some day a Socrates might put his knowledge at the service of the city.

In the *Sophist*, the stranger evaded the difficulty of offering a dichotomized classification of all land animals; he divided them into wild and tame, and on Theaetetus' questioning whether there was a hunting of tame animals, he let Theaetetus identify the tame animal with man. "We, I believe," Theaetetus says, "are a tame animal." This was the sixth cut in the arts. In the *Statesman*, however, the stranger's procedure is different. He admits that prior to young Socrates' mistake there was one of his own. The sixth cut of the sciences should not have been individual-herd but wild-tame, "for those animals which have the nature open to domestication have been addressed as tame, and those which do not as savage." So important does the stranger regard this correction that he qualifies almost every subsequent division with the word "tame" (264c2, 265b8, e4, 266a1). But since he omits this correction from his summary, he implies that it is built into the characterization of political science as an art of commanding animals.

The stranger would seem to deny to the leader of the wolf pack the art of ruling. Animals are tame by definition if they are ruled. But does not Homer say that each Cyclops rules his own family? The stranger, then, must mean that the ruler is of a different species from the ruled, for only in that case would the ruled necessarily be tame. Perhaps the ruler's possession of the art of ruling suffices to make him different. The stranger, in any case, speaks of their own hunting of the art: the ruler of the tame herd does not have to be tame himself. The stranger, moreover, leaves himself open to the charge that he has fallen into a version of the error young Socrates has just committed. Is not the distinction of tame and wild as anthropocentric as that of men and beasts, and only slightly less provincial than that of Greeks and barbarians? "Wild" seems to mean whatever man cannot subjugate, and the limit of human competence negatively determines the savagery of the wild. The stranger hints at his answer to this charge by speaking of animals with the nature to be domesticated. Tame also means tameable, and tameability is not solely a question of art; the art perfects the nature of tame animals. If this is the stranger's answer, the art of taming either precedes or always accompanies the art of ruling. But in either case its task would be to habituate the ruled to being ruled, and it would be inseparable from legislation. The Cyclopes have no laws (*themista*). "Tame," then, is a term that, in standing in for "law-abiding," conceals the problem of law; it allows the stranger to postpone that problem as long as possible. Indeed, the belated insertion of the term already adumbrates the tension between the lawgiver and the statesman.

The stranger does everything possible to delay as well the discovery of man in his dichotomies. He needs two cuts in order to separate birds from land animals; in the *Sophist* he did it in one. Birds and fish were there neatly combined into one class; here, birds are first put with pedestrial animals because they walk on dry land and then separated from them because they are feathered. So awkward is this distinction that the stranger neglects it both in his summary and in his shorter way ("pedestrial" then means terrestrial animals), even though he went to such trouble to introduce it in the first place. One can explain the awkwardness away, at least in part, by saying that geese and cranes are fed on the ground, and that even though birds might seem exempt from the rule of a nonbird, to control their source of food suffices to rule them completely. Aristotle reports that in Egypt priests had domesticated crocodiles through an abundant supply of food.[30] We cannot help thinking too of Euelpides and Pithetairos.

The stranger, however, has something more in mind than to anticipate the myth and the paradigm of the perfect shepherd. He knows that young Socrates has not seen Egyptian or Persian fish farms; but perhaps he has seen such enterprises on a smaller scale and has heard about the others; and even if he has not wandered in Thessaly, he at least has heard and trusts that feeding pens for geese and cranes exist there. Young Socrates is given a further lesson in moderation. He is made to defer to hearsay evidence. His own judgment is at a discount. Man is to be discovered in such a way that no one can question it. Universal consent is to replace the exclusive partnership of young Socrates and the stranger. The stranger had dismissed the opinions of everyone when young Socrates had agreed to the division of gnostics into critics and epitactics, but now they do not have to find out whether political science belongs to the art of subaqueous or terrene caring ("it is plain to everyone") or hesitate over whether it concerns flying or walking animals ("all but the stupidest" have the correct opinion).

The stranger seems to be saying that not even the goose can dispute these steps or any of those that follow, for in every case it is obvious where the king belongs (cf. 265d3–5, e9). The ruler cannot make any distinctions which are not intelligible to the meanest capacity of his subjects. The difference between part and kind must be blurred if not obliterated by the ruler. Ignorance must somehow color the presentation of his own understanding. The right of ignorance, which is suggested at the same time as the equation of ruling and feeding, is the first and last political fact the stranger teaches young Socrates. Here the way to political science most plainly is political science.

The stranger now offers young Socrates the choice of a longer or a shorter way. The shorter way violates the principle of cutting down the middle; the longer way keeps closer to it. Young Socrates has learned so well the waste in haste that he chooses to hear both in turn.

He is too chastened to ask for the significance of the alternative for political science. One might be tempted to say that the longer way is a "theoretical" exercise in holding part and kind together; the shorter way is good enough "for all practical purposes." That the longer way involves three absurdities in its final division, while the shorter way allows the stranger to adorn the statesman with a noble lineage (266e9–10), seems to confirm this. As Socrates tried to explain to Theodorus, theory is inseparable from the laughable and necessarily ugly. But if political science is theoretical, the longer way must be more akin to it than the shorter, for political science would of all sciences most run the risk of preening. The ruler of men needs to be immunized from the contagion of human pride. Young Socrates correctly regards the shorter way as interest paid on the principal of the longer way, but he would have been more correct to call it a consolation for the battering that the longer way gives to the dignity of political science. Man is no less contemptible as a plucked chicken than as a pig on two legs, but only the concurrence of the swineherd and the king makes the king look as swinish as his subjects. The longer way has the effect of making the ruler appear to be of the same species as the ruled (cf. 268a3, 275b8–c4).

The labels "feathered" and "pedestrial" (*pezon*) are deceptive, for they imply that birds are either footless or do not walk on dry land. *Pezon* only means not-fledged, just as barbarian only means not-Greek (cf. 276a4). The class to which man belongs is negatively determined. He is an animal that lacks wings, horns, and the ability to generate outside his own class; even his two feet result from the squaring of an irrational (*alogon*) magnitude. The stranger's pairs of terms are not complementary, as male-female and odd-even are; rather, they look at man in light of animal traits which he does not have. The human herd is defective (265d4; cf. 265e4, 266e7). It is as mindless as it is helpless. It surely needs someone to care for it, and to an even greater extent than any other herd animal. These divisions, however, still do not differentiate the rule of men from any other type of herd rule. The art of managing pedestrial animals does not split into two parts simply because there are two parts to the class of pedestrial animals (265c2–8). There is not one science of even numbers and another of odd. If the art of ruling were unlike arithmetic in this respect, the art of ruling herd animals with split hooves would differ from the art of ruling herd animals which do not breed outside their own class. Does the art of ruling ask why all pure-breeding, hornless, featherless, land-based herd animals have toes? And if such animals could also have solid hooves, would there be another art of ruling them?

The stranger later admits to young Socrates that they have failed here to divide the art of ruling while they divided the animals; but the stranger's sexual distinction between horses and asses, on the one hand, and pigs and men, on the other, is not altogether impertinent to the discovery of political science. First of all, this sexual distinction did not obtain during the age of Cronus, when all animals were earth-born, and there were no mules. The art of ruling mules is unknown to the gods, even as eugenics is. The divine art of ruling can have nothing to do with the *genesis* of animals. Erotics is not a divine science. In the second place, the horseman must know of the possibility of mules, for otherwise he could find himself the ruler of a mixed herd, some of whose members would have a nature different from that of horses. If we take the word of a writer who did not have the *Statesman* in mind, to say nothing of the *Theaetetus* and the *Sophist*, we can already discern in the mention of the mule the conclusion of its argument. The mule, he says, "possesses the sobriety, patience, endurance and surefootedness of the ass, and the vigor, strength, and courage of the horse."[31] And thirdly, since the mule is sterile, a herd of mules cannot perpetuate itself; so if the mule hints at the union of moderation and courage, the ultimate end of statesmanship cannot be the rule of such a herd. The stranger likewise does not count the dog among herd animals. We do not have to think of the doglike guardians of Socrates' best city in order to see the bearing of this exclusion; we need only remember the stranger's likeness of Socrates, the sophist noble in descent, to a tame dog, and that dogs in packs are wild.

The living subjects of the statesman are characterized in seven ways: they are tame (tamed, or tameable), in a herd, on dry land, without wings and horns, pure-breeding bipeds. Of these seven ways the last is discovered in the most laughable manner, but even more laughable is young Socrates himself who takes it straight. Even the dullest of the stranger's listeners must now realize the necessity of sobering up young Socrates if he believes it to be "just" that geometry be invoked to distinguish men from pigs. Young Socrates sees no difference between the nature of human locomotion and the square root of two feet. Not only are a pair of feet and two square feet the same, but the magnitude which is the incommensurable root of one is the nature of the other. The stranger seems to have been present in the *Theaetetus* when Socrates made mathematical operations of this sort the basis of a Protagorean physiology. Indeed, had not Socrates wondered then why Protagoras did not say that the pig and not man was the measure of all things? The irony of Socrates seems to be the true starting point of political science. In his own way, the stranger points to the city of pigs as the true city, but for young Socrates, unlike for Glaucon, this does not call for indignation. "Geometrical necessities" do, after all, have a political use.

V. THE MYTH
(267c5–277a2)

For all of young Socrates' impetuousness, the stranger's rigmarole did not tax his patience; he could wait it out because he assumed, and was in a way assured, that as soon as they found man among the herd animals the discovery of political science would be complete. Young Socrates is too much the Theodoran philosopher, whose body alone lies in the city while his thought geometrizes above the heavens and below the earth, for the absence of the city and the things of the city in their account of the science of the city to puzzle him. The city is a place, within as without, of rivalry, disputation, and conflict. The statesman differs from other herdsmen because others differ with the statesman about his competence. Merchants, farmers, bakers, gymnasts, and doctors, each with the name of a single art, would all contentiously insist that they take care of human nurture, "not only of human beings in herds but also of the nurture of the rulers themselves." The statesman's rivals are willing to divide among themselves the several aspects of nurture, but they leave no room for the statesman. Political science seems to have the same relation to the other arts within the city as philosophy appears to have to the various sciences. Either is at best a collective name for a group of well-defined specializations. The statesman looks like the sophist of the city.[32]

The stranger, however, does not come at once to the defense of the statesman and confute his challengers; instead, he whisks the statesman away from the city and there fashions him into a noncontroversial figure. He settles the dispute by removing everything that makes such disputations possible. He begins with the cowherd, who lives outside the city, and whose competence no one questions, despite the multiplicity of his pastoral tasks. The stranger mentions five. The cowherd is nurse, doctor, go-between, midwife, and musician, and he assumes these several roles as the occasion warrants without ever ceasing to be a cowherd. Theaetetus and the stranger sought in vain for the unity of the sophist as hunter, merchant, retailer, disputant, and purifier of souls. They could only conclude that sophistry had an apparitional unity which sophistry as an art contrives. It now seems as if they overlooked the herdsman, who would have supplied them with the paradigm of a genuine one refracted into a genuine many. The *Statesman* begins to overlap more and more with the *Sophist*. A simple consideration shows this. There is a striking lack of parallelism between the five rivals of the statesman and the five roles of the cowherd. What is uniquely the same in both lists is medicine; what uniquely holds for the human herd is gymnastics; what uniquely holds for cattle is eugenics (the art of go-between and midwife) and music. The stranger had likened the art of punishment to medicine, and sophistry noble in descent to gymnastics; and in the *Theaetetus* Socrates himself had compared his mother's art with his own. If we add that the stranger later likens statesmanship to medicine and legislation to gymnastics, we see that Socrates' music is intertwined as inextricably with political science as with sophistry.[33]

The stranger and young Socrates have given the royal outline or figure, but they have not yet accurately worked out the statesman. The king in his generality is not the same as the statesman in his precision. The paradigm for the first is the shepherd of woolbearing animals; the paradigm for the second turns out to be the weaver of wool. Since it seems absurd to suggest that the ruler shears his flock of their natural covering in order to clothe them again in a garment of his own making, the two paradigms stand apart from one another at least as much as the sophist-hunter did from the sophist-imitator. The stranger, at any rate, asserts their difference to be one of kind. God is the shepherd, man is the weaver. The myth discloses that the shepherd, for all his apparent modesty as a paradigm, is far too general to suit anyone but the maker and ruler of the visible whole. We are thus forcibly reminded of the tension between the comprehensive and the precise interpretations of being.

That tension now reappears in another form. The stranger had criticized the philosophers of the precise accounts for telling us myths as if we were children; but he now orders young Socrates to listen, as children do, to a myth, which seems to be the comprehensive account of political science. Do myths, then, hinder the understanding of being and help the understanding of political science? We have already remarked on how politically colored the myths about being were. Were these myths unintelligible because their makers lacked political science? Had they begun with the stranger's myth, perhaps they would not have needed to mythologize being. The stranger's comprehensive myth prepares the way for a precise account of political science which is altogether nonmythical. Whereas in the *Sophist*, the stranger could not settle the problem of the sophist before he gave Theaetetus to understand that the gods make everything, political science cannot be or be understood unless it is truly settled that the gods do not rule anything. Mythology, according to the stranger, is a subordinate branch of political science.

The myth is the unwieldy bulk of that of which the previous dichotomies were the frame. It is, as it were, the setting in motion of those dichotomies so that young Socrates can see them at work in place and in time. The place is the universe, the time the age of Cronus. The stranger's myth is composed of three mythical events whose original unity has been forgotten, for no myth records their single cause. Two of the events are still known as belonging together; the other has been displaced in time and reinterpreted as a miraculous sign of legitimacy for a mortal king. Young Socrates suspects that the stranger alludes to the golden lamb in Atreus' flock, but the stranger means the momentary reversal in the rising and setting of the sun and other stars which the god made bear witness to Atreus. In the stranger's myth, however, the reversal is a matter of necessity, lasts as long as the god rules, and alters entirely the conditions of life as we know them. With this interpretation, the stranger can make fragmentary events into a whole, a whole which reveals the necessity for political science by presenting the conditions which would have to be met in order for political science to be unnecessary. These conditions prove to be neither humanly desirable nor humanly feasible. The myth thereby debunks myth, for it disenchants us from the enchantment of the golden past and from the longing to see once more gods' rule on earth. Nowhere has divine providence been made to look less providential or paradise uglier. Milton's suggestion, if it is that, that it was better for man to have sinned, is trivial in comparison. If the stranger's myth is playful, it seems hardly suitable for children.

Before the stranger first comes to the point of the myth—he announces the coming to the point four times (272d5, 273e4, 274b1, 274e1)—the myth falls into seven parts: (1) the god alternately rules and does not rule (269c4–d3); (2) the cause of this alternation (269d5–270a8); (3) the difference between earthly and heavenly changes (270b3–d4); (4) the transition from the present to the former age (270d6–271a1); (5) *genesis* in the age of Cronus (271a4–c2); (6) life in the age of Cronus (271c8–272b4); (7) the judgment on happiness (272b8–d4). Each part raises questions of its own that go beyond the scope and competence of political science. For all its excessive length the myth is much too short. We do not know, for example, where the cosmos would fit in the scheme of the stranger's dichotomies. It is an animal endowed with intelligence, but is it one of a herd or alone? Timaeus granted that there might be five, a number perhaps not big enough to qualify it as a herd animal. And what kind of animal is it? It is as sterile as the mule, and as wingless and hornless as man, but it moves on a single foot around its pole (cf. 269c5, 270a3, 8). Had the stranger continued his divisions, would one cut be, as Aristophanes has it, Zeus' threatened punishment for man's hubris, and the other the cosmos? We are no less in doubt as to where we should place the god in the stranger's dichotomies. If the god is both the craftsman and the king of the cosmos, he possesses both a gnostic and a practical art. Are they the same? If he had never made the cosmos, or once it was made had never taken the helm, would he still possess the art of ruling? He surely does not lose it when he lets go. And yet the stranger said that it was not fitting for the master builder to let go; he was to make sure that his subordinates carried out his commands (cf. 274a5). But the god must let go; perfect rule is impossible, and unless one counts as part of its knowledge the knowledge that perfect rule is impossible, the royal art is not in the strict sense knowledge.

Body, according to the stranger, confronted the god with a problem he could not solve perfectly. The god's solution is wholly lacking in prudence, for prudence would dictate that the god continually correct the innate waywardness of the cosmos, rather than suppress its nature periodically. The god cannot rule unless he goes wholly against the grain of nature. This is the ordinary understanding of tyrannical rule. There is, however, a mitigating circumstance. Since only the most divine things never alter, and the god alternately rules and does not rule, the god partakes of the nature of the body, and in this respect does not differ from the animal or animals he rules. Men are as corporeal as sheep. We can wonder, then, whether the god does not need to rest from rule as much as the cosmos needs to be rewound by god, and the god goes against his own grain in going against the grain of nature. Socrates once remarked that the philosopher only rules under compulsion.[34]

The stranger lays down three principles from which it follows that the cosmos undergoes a periodic reversal of its motion. He accords, however, to each principle a different status. That the cosmos turns itself forever is impossible, that the efficient cause of all motion moves in contrary ways is not religiously sanctioned, and that two gods think contrary things is something one should not say. The stranger does not explain why two gods cannot be acting in concert if they cause contrary motions. Are thinking and moving the same for a god? Timaeus' compromise, which consisted in the union of two contrary motions he called the motion of the same and of the other, is precluded. The god thinks only in terms of opposites; "the other," which the stranger himself had discovered, and which broke down the opposition of opposites, is either unknown to the god or inapplicable to the governance of the visible whole.

Its inapplicability would seem to be due to the tension between whole and part. The god cannot provide for the least disturbance of the whole without causing the greatest disturbances for all animals on earth. The god could have, in other words, protected men from almost complete destruction, but only at the price of injuring the heavenly bodies. Particular and universal providence are incompatible with one another. The ambiguity in the word *kosmos* somewhat conceals this incompatibility. The stranger first speaks of heaven as equivalent to *kosmos* (269d7–8), but he later speaks of the parts of the *kosmos* (271d5, 272e8, 274a6), and at least once *kosmos* means the same as order (273b6).[35] Now the the tension between whole and part would seem to obtain regardless of the god's ruling or not, and one could therefore wonder whether the repulsiveness of the stranger's myth, insofar as it applies to man, does not chiefly serve to make that tension as vivid as possible. There can be no ordered corporeal whole unless some of its parts are ugly. Socrates himself might be a fair example of this cosmological theorem. Socrates had, at any rate, told Theodorus that something must be forever contrary to the good.

In order, however, for our cosmological theorem to explain all the details of the myth, it must be qualified. The most mythical part of the myth is that upon which the difference for all earthly animals between the age of Cronus and the age of Zeus rests—life goes backwards in time at the moment the cosmos reverses direction and continues to do so as long as the god rules. Only if the region where the sun appears to rise each day is still considered to be evening and later in time than dawn, can it follow that old age precedes youth, and the embryonic state heralds death. Otherwise, the change in the sun's direction could not possibly affect the sequence of zoological time. The stranger, moreover, says nothing about any inversion of the seasons, and he cannot want young Socrates to infer that winter precedes fall, and summer spring, for then plants would die before they withered, though it would be fully in accord with the myth if fruit were born ripe and then flowered. The sequence summer, spring, fall, winter would agree with the inverted ages of animals but not with a simple reversal of the year. The myth, then, is necessarily silent about the sun's motion on the ecliptic. Eternal summer reigns in the age of Cronus, there are no seasons, and the sun is no longer a cause of growth and decay. The earth generates spontaneously. Heaven and earth are wholly apart, linked solely through their joint rule, but otherwise going their separate ways. The god's cosmos is, to be sure, not chaos, but in an important sense it is not a whole (cf. 272e4, 274d6). Its lack of wholeness is chiefly due to the way in which—if not to the fact that—the god rules. The myth illustrates, in short, the thesis that no doctrine of divine providence can consist with a natural teleology. It is this thesis, more limited in scope than our cosmological theorem, which constitutes the element in the myth that contributes most to the understanding of political science.

Mushrooms are the model of growth in the age of Cronus. Every animal conforms with Theodorus' description of the Heracliteans, who without pupils or teachers sprout spontaneously.[36] The earth-born giants of myth are human beings under a god's rule. Does the stranger, then, wish to imply that if men then philosophized, they would necessarily hold that to be is to be body, and "the friends of the ideas" are only possible in the so-called age of Zeus? The necessary but not sufficient condition for the *genesis* of Socrates would be sexual generation. No Socrates without Phaenarete. And since the myth connects sexual generation with the existence of cities, the impossibility of Socrates without political science is likewise implied. The god does not alter the natures of things. Men and women are still sexually different in appearance, but either they lack the desire to perpetuate themselves, or they are segregated into two noncommunicating herds. That no animal then eats another, does not mean that all animals are naturally herbivorous. Carnivores are still carnivores, but again either their several herdsmen force them to ruminate, or meat grows on trees. The myth separates harshness from savagery (274b7; cf. 273c1); the first is natural, the second a consequence of anarchy and scarcity.

In the age of Cronus there are no beasts. And like the distinction between tame and wild, that between monadic and gregarious cannot then be drawn, for "by herd" and "by kind" are equivalent expressions (cf. 271d6). The god certainly could not have allowed the race of dogs to wander freely among the herds. Although in general farming is to herding as teaching is to ruling, and in the age of Cronus the ruling of animals hardly differs from the caring of plants, the stranger only speaks about teaching when the god ceases to rule (273b2, 274c6); so even if some kinds of animals or some individuals require by nature a treatment different from herd rule, the god and his subordinates disregard it. In this context, the issue of human happiness is raised. Not even the god, according to the stranger, can order philosophy into existence, for if he could, there would be no doubt that his subjects are happier than ourselves (cf. 271c2). Human beings, under his guidance, need to do nothing for themselves except eat and sleep, and though they can hardly be gluttons without the arts of luxury, the god cannot prevent them from being lazy and remaining satisfied with Aesopian homilies on moderation. The god can remove every possible occasion for fear, even to the point of arranging that death can occur when men are most thoughtless, but he cannot instill in them the desire to know. If the gods, as Diotima says, do not philosophize, perhaps their omniscience has a blind spot. They do not care whether men are happy or not because they cannot experience human happiness.

That the myth means by the rule of the god final cause, and by his absence the sway of efficient and mechanical causation, seems at first to be a plausible interpretation. But the stranger speaks of a "fated and innate desire" of the cosmos which aims at imitating the rule of the god even though it turns the cosmos in a direction contrary to the god's. To imitate the rule of the god does not consist in doing less well what the god does. The cosmos, at least at the beginning of its run, is a harmony of desire and intelligence. It achieves an order for itself without issuing orders, for the autonomy of the whole entails the autonomy of its parts, and on earth the animal equivalent to cosmic autonomy is sexual generation or *erôs*. *Erôs*, however, is exhaustible; when it is about to give out, the god takes over, and since he rules without it, it is apparently replenished during that time. The age of Cronus is the fallow time of *erôs*. Its gradual replenishment coincides with the gradual exhaustion of the seeds of each soul. It would not be misleading to call such souls, after Aristotle, vegetative; they are capable of germinating more perfect bodies than any known to us. But whether the vegetative soul suffices to sustain the pursuit of wisdom must be left an open question.

The god can only guarantee a life without bestiality of bestial contentment; the cosmos cannot make the life of philosophy possible without at the same time putting the philosopher's life in jeopardy. Socrates is about to go on trial. After leading a long nonpolitical life he has just appeared before the king archon, who holds the oldest and most sacred magistracy in Athens. The city has now decided that philosophy is subject to its rule. The stranger, who caught Socrates in his hunting down of the sophist, now seems to inform Socrates through the myth that his autonomy is at its end, for Socrates represents to a degree otherwise unknown to human memory precisely that cooperative union of desire and intelligence which characterizes the self-ruling cosmos,[37] and to which Socrates gave the name erotics. Now Socrates had suspected that the stranger might be Zeus in disguise, but the myth declares that Zeus is not. So if the stranger is nonetheless a god, he must be Cronus, come to advise Socrates of his imminent reassumption of divine rule. The exhaustion of Socrates' *erôs* would thus coincide with that of the cosmos', and the Athenians' punishment be in full agreement with the stranger's counsel. The stranger's myth is in a sense an Aesopian fable, for it too has a moral.

The myth brings out that the stranger and young Socrates erred in their divisions. They modeled the statesman on the misleading paradigm of the shepherd, whose comprehensive care of his flock dimly reflects the rule of the god. Shepherding is an unpolitical type of rule; it could only be paradigmatic in the marginal case of a human community in which no division of labor based on the arts had yet occurred, and consequently its members relied entirely on their ruler for everything. In such a paternal monarchy the subjects lack individually the competence, and a fortiori the vanity that competence breeds, to challenge the king. They are nothing but consumers, the king nothing but a jack-of-all-trades, who in the absence of competition has no need to refine any one art at the expense of another. Let the shepherd's pipe stand for the level of his competence in general.

The myth thus sketches a way of life which overcomes the opposition of Socrates' healthy city, each of whose members is granted citizenship solely because he knows one art perfectly, and Socrates' best city, in which these same artisans have a place solely because they form the class of moneymakers, which parallels in turn the desiring part of the soul. Once the citizens are free of any mutual responsibility for their own care, they simply become appetitive bodies whose needs their ruler, to whom all knowledge has been transferred, can easily satisfy. It is not so much, then, the statesman's inability to conform perfectly with the paradigm of the shepherd that makes the paradigm inappropriate (the statesman could still hold it to be his goal however unrealizable), as it is the impossibility of the city to conform with the paradigm of the herd. The city is the rejection of the pastoral life: the descendants of Cain founded the first city. The age of the city and the age of iron are coterminous.

That young Socrates did not know to which era the stranger assigned the life under Cronus (271c4–5), despite its obviousness, betrayed his concern that he does not live under the rule of the god. Man's pride, which young Socrates revealed in his distinction between men and beasts, only partly arises from man's belief in the superiority of his intelligence; it arises primarily from his belief in particular providence. The stranger indicates this in his correction of the dichotomies; he places the distinction between human and divine ruling after man has been distinguished from the other animals, even though the myth declares that the god rules either all animals or none. The humiliation of young Socrates, which the dichotomies accomplished, turns out to have another intention besides that of making him obedient to divine rule; it frees him from the vanity that necessarily accompanies such obedience when it is regarded as a privilege of man alone. To moderate young Socrates is to encourage him to philosophize, and in doing so it teaches him that political philosophy is the indispensable condition for philosophy itself.

The two errors which the myth was designed to show up are directly

related to this lesson in moderation and courage, for each error eliminated in its own way political science. The more generous error was
to magnify the ruler into a god, and hence to depress the ruled too
much, and the error on the side of briefness was to swamp the statesman with his rivals, so that he could no more be distinguished from
the baker than men from pigs. The stranger, then, asks how one can
delineate political science in such a way as to adjust the higher rank
which the ruler must have with the fact that he belongs in nature,
education, and nurture to the same class as the ruled. If, moreover,
the way to political science is political science, as the stranger stated
at the start, he implies that adjustments of this kind are the content
of political science itself. How difficult the problem he now sets is
comes out plainly when we later learn that the best regime is as separated from all other regimes "as a god from human beings" (303b4),
and that one of the bonds the true statesman employs is "divine"
(309c2). The movement of the argument from now on thus seems to
consist in restoring to the statesman the godlike status of which he
has just been deprived. If a non-Platonic expression may be used, we
can say that the dialogue's action represents the negation of a negation, which is in turn philosophical moderation at work. "The other
othered" describes the *Statesman* both in itself and in its relation to
the *Sophist*.

The stranger proposes to young Socrates two ways they can correct
the deficiency in their account of the statesman's manner of ruling.
The first is a change in nomenclature: the art of feeding is to be
replaced by the art of caring for the human herd. Young Socrates
does not notice that, since this change precedes the distinction between
the divine shepherd and the human caretaker, the artisans who formerly disputed with the statesman cease to do so only because they
cannot dispute with the god. They must perforce agree that they
cannot supply the total care of which the god is capable (sexual generation precludes it), but why they should abandon their joint assault
on the competence of the statesman is obscure. It seems as if the
magniloquence of "the royal art" is enough to cow them (cf. 277b1–
4), but all that the change of terms really does is to forestall the
statesman's immediate defeat at the hands of his rivals: they cannot
deny that "caring" envelops the art of ruling as well as their own arts.
The statesman now has at least the semblance of being the peer of
the doctor and the gymnast.

The second change is more fundamental; it prepares the ground
for the rest of the discussion. Since the tyrant and the king are to be
distinguished, the stranger now drops the identification of the king
and the slavemaster with which he began. Young Socrates fails again

to notice the significance of this concession to fact which the myth has forced them to admit. It raises once more the problem of taming and law. Are the willing subjects of the king merely the tamed, and the forced subjects of the tyrant those who have not yet been domesticated? Tyranny would then be either the indispensable precursor to kingship or the repository of terror which the king can invoke if his herd ever becomes unruly. Divine rule, on the other hand, does not have to be divided into tyranny and kingship; the consent of the governed follows at once from the godness of the god, and in this sense the distinction between constraint and consent repeats the distinction between human and divine rule. Disobedience can only trouble the human ruler; the god steps down before it can threaten his own rule. Contrary to Socrates' fear, there is no divine punishment.

VI. Paradigm
(277a3–278e11)

Young Socrates twice mistakes a pause for the conclusion of the stranger's argument—first in response to the stranger's summary of the dichotomies, and now again after the correction of those dichotomies. On the first occasion, the stranger took issue with young Socrates' use of a conversational idiom, "That's altogether so," and asked him whether they had "truly" done just that—an altogether perfect execution of the argument (cf. 295e1, 3). Such insistence that no expression be used, no matter how idiomatic, except in the most literal sense, recalls the stranger's catching Theaetetus out in a thoughtless use of "it seems likely" (*eoiken*). The stranger, however, handles each mathematician differently in this regard. He did not point out to Theaetetus that his *eoiken* lay in fact at the heart of his own perplexity about being and nonbeing. On reflection, the connection between *eoiken* and semblance (*eikôn*), and image and true being, was plain, but it is characteristic of the *Sophist* that the connection between its action and its argument is at the most allusive. It never becomes a thematic part of the dialogue. It seems to be just a coincidence, if we rely solely on explicit statements, that the angler, chosen as an example to illustrate the stranger's way, turns out to be the first model for the understanding of the sophist.

In the *Statesman*, on the other hand, the stranger almost obsessively harps on their own doing; the dialogue thus resembles the second half of the *Theaetetus*, where Socrates and Theaetetus became the recurrent examples of objects of knowledge. The need for self-knowledge is never far from the surface of the *Statesman*. The stranger told young Socrates that his manliness made him distinguish between men and beasts; he did not tell Theaetetus what in his nature would lead him to believe that a god made everything. Self-knowledge is indispensable for the statesman. His own nature, education, and nurture are similar to his subjects, but their belief, sanctioned by myth, in the equatability of shepherd and king cannot be his own. He must not be ·seduced, as Theaetetus and the stranger were, by spurious paradigms. A discussion of paradigm has been long overdue. That it turns out to be as inadequate as the discussion of part and kind comes as no surprise.

The stranger cannot perfect and complete political science unless he makes imperfect and incomplete digressions from political science. In the *Statesman* there are four: (1) part and kind; (2) the myth; (3) paradigm; (4) measure. The first two are linked to the statesman as shepherd, the third and fourth to the statesman as weaver. In shorthand jargon, the problems they severally raise can be titled as follows: (1) Ontology; (2) Cosmology; (3) Methodology; (4) Teleology. The first and third are as plainly to be paired together as the second and fourth, and each in turn is presented as a problem in doubleness: (1) part and kind; (2) god and nature; (3) paradigm and what it exemplifies; (4) number and the fitting. All four pairs culminate in the doubleness of the beautiful that is commonly called moderation and courage, the stranger's discussion of which falls into a playful (digressive) and a serious (relevant) part. The stranger thus comes to an interpretation of the beautiful in the ugliest manner possible. He makes a *kosmos,* which is the dialogue, that resembles the visible whole both as it is under the god's rule and as it is on its own. Its digressions are like the natures of things which the god renders wholly inoperative during his rule, but which the stranger for his part can neither suppress nor liberate entirely. The *Statesman* seems to be doing double duty, for itself and for the absent *Philosopher.* Perhaps the *Statesman,* then, comes closest to putting in writing what Plato chose not to put in writing.

The stranger admits that in correcting the mistake of the dichotomies he made another mistake; the myth showed up the mistake without making the statesman any more vivid and distinct. His rivals will dispute with him his right to rule (279a1–5); indeed, the myth strengthened the force of their arguments, since the statesman cannot now gloss over the arguments with any utopian promises. The myth, moreover, gave the impression that the stranger's mistake was glorious, as if cosmology were the indispensable setting for political science, which, if true, would preclude the possibility of the stranger's completing his account of political science. The difference between the *Statesman* and the *Sophist* on this point is clear. The stranger was not being altogether ironic when he forebade Theaetetus, in the name of the sophist, from giving examples of images and asked instead for an account of images that even a blind sophist would acknowledge. But now the stranger admits that we cannot dispense with examples (cf. 285d9–e4). Each of us has a dreamlike knowledge of everything and at the same time lacks all waking knowledge of anything. Examples are the drug of awakening, but the myth was soporific, for it could be construed as counseling us to abandon the attempt to discover political science.

The stranger's example, which he chooses to illustrate the character of examples, also helps to differentiate example from myth. Although we learn to read while we are still being told myths, writing is only possible in the age of Zeus, when the arts have already been highly developed in the city, and then learning to read is very likely to be our first experience of art itself, in which what we already know—the language we speak—appears in a form we do not recognize. To know how to speak is to the art of reading as the citizen's knowledge of political things is to political science. The paradigm of weaving is designed to be the transition from the first to the second kind of knowledge, but there are several obstacles that have to be removed before that paradigm can function properly, the chief of which is this: young Socrates does not realize, precisely because he is still dreaming, that he has a citizen's knowledge of political things. The original assimilation of political science to arithmetic has virtually concealed his own knowledge from him. The *Statesman* has now reached a stage comparable with that in the *Sophist* when the stranger presented Theaetetus with part of the alphabet of kinds. But just at this point, where the two dialogues converge, they once more diverge. The stranger never informed Theaetetus of the language, the phenomena, from which he derived the letters being, motion, rest, same and other. Whereas now he uses the example of letters in order to remind young Socrates of what he must know before he can learn the elements of political science. The movement of the *Statesman* is perverse. It is one long descent into the cave.

The example of an example is somewhat misleading. It describes a situation in which a child can read the letters A, H, M, N, T in the words MAT, HAT, and ANT but fails to recognize them in MANHATTAN. One could therefore conclude erroneously that the elements in weaving are the same as those in political science, however differently arranged. But were this the case, the warp of the weaver would be the warp of the statesman, and not, as it is, an image of courage. The stranger seems to treat paradigm apart from image. No one would say that HAT partially images MANHATTAN. In order, then, for the example of example to bear directly on the example of weaving, the elements of weaving would have to be reidentified, so that it would not be the spindle or the comb which showed up in political science, but rather the fact that both arts employ tools. So if we let "T" stand for tool, we can grant that "T" is easier to discern in weaving than in political science.

However, the stranger does more than use weaving to pick out such elements in political science; he also appeals to the weaver's operations as the statesman's model. Each art binds one thing to another. But a characteristic of letters which was so important in the *Sophist*—some are vowels, others consonants—cannot help us here, for no vowels seem to bind together the warp and the woof in either art, and it would be highly arbitrary to declare the woof to be a vowel and the warp a consonant (or vice versa). Not even the Pythagoreans dared to put vowel and consonant in their table of opposites. Weaving and political science, moreover, have something in common for which there cannot be a parallel in letters. They are poetic arts, grammatics is not. The whole which letters make up is all the words in the language, but the elements of weaving do not make a "word" which antedates its own making. Indeed, if tool is a letter of weaving, it is never present in any of its works. Grammatics, in short, no longer constitutes the single paradigm with which all knowledge has to conform. Its relegation to an example of an example proves it. It does illustrate our experiencing of the same as the other and of the other as the same and how these twin mistakes are corrigible, but it does not lay down any further conditions for knowledge. Weaving and political science are much more complex arts than grammatics.

The weaver is not the same kind of example as the angler or the shepherd was. Angler and sophist exhibited divergent structures; weaver and statesman are parallel throughout. Up to a certain point, the angler and the sophist were each samples of artisans who were engaged in the acquisition, mastery, and hunting of animals; afterward, the angler became distinct from the sophist through the addition of qualifiers that did not pertain to the sophist. To look for a comprehensive class to which the upward jerk of the fishing line and some action of the sophist equally belong would be vain. It is not revealing to say that the sophist too hooks his quarry, for it is no less accurate to say that he nets his prey. The weaver, on the other hand, emerges from a tenfold classification of arts into which the stranger makes no attempt to fit the statesman. The kinship (*syngeneia*) which the weaver, shoemaker, and hatter have does not include the statesman; rather, it is meant to suggest to the stranger and young Socrates that they consider the arts of their first division as those to which political science is likewise akin (287b4–8), just as the coefficients (*synerga*) of weaving lead to the discovery of the comparable coefficients of political science.

Weaving is a syllabic whole whose articulation casts light on the wholeness of political science. Its analysis begins where that of angling ended. Angling was a part of acquisition whose apparent wholeness resulted from its atomicity, but indivisibility and wholeness are not interchangeable, for something is a whole if and only if none of its parts is missing. Angling is not architectonic. The arts of acquisition were put together into a class without any consideration of their rank within the class; none was subordinate to any other. The stranger was wholly silent on the ultimate end of acquisition, and how the several goods these arts acquire form a complete good. But as he indicated in the myth, political science is inseparable from a comprehensive reflection on human happiness (cf. 311c5). It is surely not accidental that the life of hunting is as far removed from the city as the shepherd's. The shepherd ends up by killing and eating the sheep he cares for.

VII. Weaving
(279a1–283a9)

The stranger chooses weaving because it is in the same business as political science, but its business is susceptible of two interpretations, of which the stranger considers only one, and that the less obvious. Weaving is to be exemplary not because it makes something which protects the body, but because it cares for cloaks (279e6), an expression that stretches the ordinary meaning of care to an unwarranted extent, and which seems all the more inappropriate if it is to serve as the basis for establishing a science. We should, however, first consider the more obvious, the imagistic, interpretation of the business of weaving.

The winter cloak of wool, to the making of which the stranger restricts weaving, clothes an individual human body between the head and the feet; it is incapable of protecting the human herd as such, nor does it readily lend itself, as a house might, to exemplifying such protection.[38] Of the three basic human needs, food, clothing, and shelter, the model of the shepherd, insofar as he was a human being, failed to be adequate for the first, and the stranger only hinted at the third when he distinguished critics from epitactics with the examples of the logistician and the master builder. The model of weaving is taken from the age of Zeus, when men can no longer go naked. And nakedness reminds us that the need for clothing is inseparable from sexual shame, which in the absence of sexual generation had no place in the golden age. The stranger's confusing omission of screens in his explanation of the congeners of weaving—it is part of the fourth dichotomy—calls attention to this other purpose of clothing, especially since the human bond of political science turns out to be marriage in a noncommunist city. Clothing is part of the language of concealment, as weaving is of deception, and we cannot help thinking of Socrates' "dread love of naked exercise in speeches" as well as of Theodorus' shame of being stripped and ridiculed in the *Theaetetus*. Socrates the midwife and Socrates the true statesman seem to be in possession of complementary sciences, as if Socrates could not lay bare the soul unless he first knew how it should be properly covered. That political science, at any rate, has to do more with necessary than with sufficient conditions is confirmed not only by the myth but by the classification of cloaks.

Of all the things we make or acquire, cloaks belong to protective devices designed to ward off suffering; they are not meant to do or make anything. If this distinction is as truly comprehensive as the stranger pretends, we shall have to interpret it rather generously. Some artifacts are directed to the enhancement of life, others to the avoidance of death, either individually (self-preservation) or collectively. Political science, then, would be more concerned with the preservation than with the actualization of potential, more with our fears than with our hopes. It is primarily a defensive art, and as such to be negatively determined. Just as man as a herd animal was defined by his hornlessness, so now cloaks are placed among coverings that are put together without holes.

The classification of weaving further implies that all the rejected arts of defense are less suitable paradigms of political science. Neither divine nor human drugs—neither religion nor medicine—would be revealing, the first because of the stranger's distinction between autepitactics and epitactics, the second because of the likeness of medicine to the art of punishment. Political science must take its example from a means of prevention against an external threat, but warfare is not exemplary either, though theft-proof safes are closer to the desired model. Criminality, however, seems not to be that against which political science arms the city; its enemy is more comparable to summer heat and winter cold, which only mythically can be called acts of injustice (cf. 273c1). The weather is a mixture of seasonal regularity and daily randomness; it would seem to be the proper model for bringing out the mixture of order and contingency in political things, which the stranger expresses as the tension between the legislator and the statesman.

III.108

We have learned by now not to take the stranger's word for it whenever he asserts that a difference in nomenclature makes no difference to the argument. He now says that the art of making cloaks (*himatiourgikê*) and the art of weaving (*hyphantikê*) no more differ from one another than the political art of the city (*hê tês poleôs politikê*) does from the kingly art (*basilikê*). But were we not so instructed we might be inclined to believe that *himatiourgikê* comprehends better than *hyphantikê* all the operations which go into the making of a cloak, and at the same time declares what the art makes. *Hyphantikê,* on the other hand, refers only to the final operation in *himatiourgikê* and is silent about the kind of web it makes. If, then, *himatiourgikê* is to *hyphantikê* as *politikê* is to *basilikê,* can we not say that *basilikê* is not political enough, silent as it is as to what kind of community the king rules, so that it suits the god rather than any man (cf. 268c5–8)? We can even wonder whether *basilikê* refers to political things at all, or is rather the name for the queen of the sciences, philosophy (cf. 284b4–5). However this may be, the stranger prefers the term *hyphantikê.* He thereby lets the final operation in cloakmaking do double duty: it designates both a part and the whole of the art. It simultaneously distinguishes an art from all its congeners, and one of the coefficients from all the others in the art itself.

Young Socrates does not understand the difference between coefficient and congener. Since the stranger has to go over again what he has just done, his attempt at brevity has once more slowed him down. But in fact he never expected to get away with it (286a8–b3), for he gave the summary before he gave the account. Young Socrates can no more follow the summary without the examples in the account than Theaetetus could follow Socrates' list of all the possible cases of true and false opinion before he heard their exemplification in Socrates, Theodorus, and himself. Young Socrates is given another example of dreamlike knowledge. Even the example of political science is not known at first with clarity; young Socrates is truly a beginner, who does not yet understand the difference between the shepherd and the weaver as models. All the previous divisions in both the *Sophist* and the *Statesman* would have led him to expect that the art of weaving has now been perfectly defined, for the stranger never went beyond a presentation of the congeners of either the sophist or the ruler of the human herd. To put it as generally as possible, the same and the other no longer suffice; part and whole must supplement them as tools of analysis. Parts are now considered as the coefficient arts in the constitution of a whole and perfect science.

Before, however, we turn to the coefficients of weaving, we should reexamine, as the stranger does, its congeners. The stranger begins again from the sixth division (spreads/envelopments), which he calls the end, of his tenfold classification. He then jumps to the ninth (fibrous/hairy), adds the tenth and the eighth (perforated/unperforated), and pauses for young Socrates' assent. He then starts from the seventh (seamless wholes/composites), which he combines with the fifth (shelters/coverings), exemplifies the rejected parts of the fifth and the third (shelters and armor), and ends with a partial characterization of the second dichotomy (protective drugs/defenses). The stranger certainly shows off in this way the advantages of dichotomy and illustrates as well the difference between the jumble of experience and the order of knowledge, but his procedure also has a more particular purpose. In calling the sixth pair the end, he underlines the fact that the last four pairs do not characterize functions but materials and modes of making; hats, shoes, and cloaks are all protective envelopes, and only an analysis in terms of the human body and its parts would distinguish them functionally. We doubt whether such an analysis could even be forced into a series of dichotomies; it would not, in any case, dispense with the need to distinguish the modes and materials of making protective envelopes for the human trunk. We therefore have to ask this question: Are there other sciences besides political science whose function is the same as political science, but whose modes and materials are different? The stranger now distinguishes weaving from religion, but he no longer mentions the drugs of medicine.

Although the stranger consistently puts the coefficients of weaving into pairs, he makes no effort to present them as a deductive system. Perhaps the failure of young Socrates to follow his tenfold classification prevents him. It would not be the only case where the systematization of discovery is less revealing than the way of discovery (fig. 2).

The stranger gives two accounts of the coefficients of weaving. The first with five coefficients is meant to show the inadequacy of labeling every procedure in weaving "weaving" (280e6–281d4); the second with seven is meant to place every procedure in weaving in its most general class (281d5–283a9), so that political science can be examined in the light of these classes rather than in terms of weaving itself. Weaving only becomes paradigmatic through the second account. The first, however, discloses the need to replace honorific terms like big and beautiful with more precise determinations. The carder, the fuller, and the shuttle maker cannot be called weavers. And while they grant that the greatest and most beautiful part of the caring for a wool garment is the weaver's, they assign large shares of it to themselves.

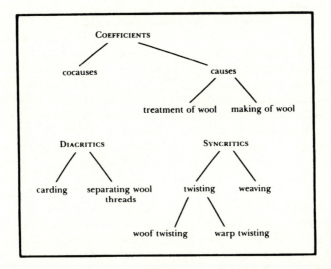

Figure 2

The stranger speaks as if the coefficients of weaving were independent of weaving itself, and their consent is necessary before weaving could assume its proper place. Their subordination is somehow at odds with their own competence. It shows in the vagueness of "big" and "beautiful," terms they would never admit into the vocabulary of their own special skills. The second account adopts a different perspective from the first. It looks at the coefficients of weaving "theoretically" (cf. 281d9), a vantage point which is far closer to the weaver's than to the carder's. The carder looks up, as it were, at the weaver, the weaver looks down at the carder; so only the weaver can say precisely what kind of contribution his cohelpers make to his own job. They know they are necessary but not sufficient; they do not know or are apt to forget that they owe their being to the weaver.

Two kinds of arts make up weaving, cocauses (toolmaking) and causes. And of causes some are therapeutic (washing, fulling, repairing), others demiurgic and deal directly with the making of the garment. This threefold articulation is disturbing, for the stranger had, in correcting the model of the shepherd, adopted therapeutics as the comprehensive name of the class to which political science belongs (275e5), but now he splits it away from that part of weaving which best exemplifies political science. The difficulty which young Socrates had of identifying political science with an art that commands the *genesis* of animals returns (cf. 281b8, 282a7). Political science still seems to hover between therapeutics and demiurgics. It is both a corrective and a productive art. Therapeutics itself, moreover, is not all of a piece. It includes the arts which remove the grease from the fresh-shorn wool, clean the cloak after it has been worn, and repair it when it has partly unraveled. Therapeutics is a part of cosmetics (282a3), and as such it is one part of cathartics, the art of separating the worse from the better among the lifeless and living bodies.[39] To this part of cathartics, we recall, belonged medicine and gymnastics; to the other part, the sophistry noble in descent. Cathartics as a whole was a part of diacritics, to which the stranger now appeals, along with its congener syncritics, to make a fourfold distinction in woolworking. Political science, then, shares in at least three of the four parts of diacritics and syncritics: the separation of like from like, the union of like with like, and the separation of worse from better. We shall not be surprised if it turns out to share as well in the union of better and worse and thus reveals itself as the most complete and possibly the only paradigm of dialectical knowledge.

Young Socrates has no trouble in following the stranger's use of syncritics and diacritics to articulate woolworking until he erroneously identifies the art of twisting thread with the making of the warp. He seems to forget the woof (cf. 281a12), or rather to believe that since the woof is made by hand without the spindle, the woof does not differ from the thread which the carder makes by hand (cf. 282c2, e4). The stranger takes great pains to set him straight; he suggests that the elaborate distinction between warp and woof is particularly suitable for young Socrates (282e2, cf. 282c10). The stranger's language at this point assumes a quasi-mathematical tone. He defines thread as if it were a plane figure, and the warp as if it were a solid generated by revolving a thread around its vertical axis. The woof, in contrast, is a thread of an open or fluffy texture, whose softness is properly proportioned to its being interwoven with the warp. If we consider how the stranger uses weaving at the end, we can draw now some tentative conclusions.

Since the warp, or vertical threads, which is kept distinct on the loom, stands to the woof, or horizontal threads, which must be packed tightly together, as courage to moderation, the stranger seems to imply that moderation must be adapted to courage and not vice versa. It is easier to make young Socrates moderate than Theaetetus courageous. The measure of the fitting characterizes moderation, the arithmetical measure courage. The stranger, moreover, speaks of the warp in the singular and the woof in the neuter plural, and the art of warpmaking he calls a directing or ruling art, but the art of woofmaking is set over the woof threads. Moderation, then, would primarily be the result of the carrying out of orders, and courage the activity of the ruler in himself. Moderation is somehow the apparition of courage. The woof is the herd, the warp the ruler, and this interweaving of commandment and obedience is the web of political science as the art of caring for the whole city. We can go one step further. If solidity describes the warp, and openness the woof, each should also fit respectively courage and moderation, but "solid" (*stereon*), when applied to character, implies hardness and cruelty, and "open" or "fluffy" (*khaunon*) conceit.[40] The dialogue so far has not prepared us for the latter implication, for the stranger connected young Socrates' courage with man's pride in his rationality. Could the stranger have been ironic when he blamed young Socrates? We have to go back to the *Sophist* and *Theaetetus*, and the joint uncovering by Socrates and the stranger of Theaetetus' nature, in order to see how vanity accompanies unphilosophical moderation no less than unphilosophical courage. It is an insight which Theodorus especially would be reluctant to acknowledge.

VIII. METRICS
(283b1–287b3)

The stranger's discussion about part and kind was too brief, his myth too long. His discussion of paradigm was again too brief, and he now asks why he and young Socrates went so far out of their way in defining weaving, instead of simply saying that it is the plaiting of warp and woof. The stranger has been far more explicit about excessive length than excessive brevity. He even called the discussion of part and kind too long, though he admitted its inadequacy (263a6). Young Socrates, in contrast, has never objected to the stranger's digressions, and now he gives his own opinion that the account of weaving was not spoken in vain. It is the first time he has not gone along with the stranger; but the disagreement does not surprise the stranger (cf. 278d7). Every example is necessarily a compromise between its two functions: it must illuminate that which is not yet known and enlighten him who does not yet know.[41] The more it is self-evident to the nonknower, the more it is likely to obscure and distort the unknown. Paradigm, like image, must carry with it a residue of the inapplicable.[42] There cannot be a perfect paradigm, something which for all men in all situations is a catalytic means of knowledge (cf. 277c3–6). If weaving is right for young Socrates, it cannot be right for Theaetetus, let alone for Glaucon and Adeimantus. The stranger has not yet admitted this; indeed, he begins his discussion with a self-contradictory proposal: "Let us look at the entirety of excess and deficiency, in order that we may praise or blame in proportion the things that are said on each occasion in engagements of this sort at greater and shorter length than they should." If we duly praise a speech, it cannot be either long or short, for otherwise we can duly blame a speech for its being the proper length (cf. 283e8–11).

The human herd as object of political science was arrived at in three ways: (1) young Socrates separated men from beasts; (2) the stranger separated men from pigs; (3) the stranger separated men from birds. After the stranger rebuked young Socrates for going too quickly, young Socrates praised the stranger for giving him both the longer and the shorter ways. But if the shorter way adequately accomplishes what the longer way did, it is the way of the proper length, and the longer way is too long; if not, the shorter way is too short, and its addition to the longer way made the discussion too long. The stranger had urged young Socrates to cut through the middle (*mesotomein*). This meant "Do not go too fast"; it should have meant "Go at the proper speed." *Mesotomein* expressed a confusion of both metrics, for it turned out to be the quasi-mathematical mean between young Socrates' answer and the exhaustive pairing of man with every other animal in turn. The stranger had suggested such a pairing in the myth: if men are happy in the golden age, they benefit from conversing with the beasts (*sic*), "inquiring from every nature, whether each with its kind of private capacity was aware of something different from all the rest for the gathering and collection of intelligence" (272c2–4). The deficiency in young Socrates' answer did not lie in its brevity but in its assumption that man as a rational animal was relevant to political science if the model of ruling was the divine shepherd. And the stranger's longer way was not long at all, since his intention was to humiliate man and the human ruler. But his shorter way was too long, for it hardly contributed anything to either the argument or the action of the dialogue. It comes the closest of any Platonic passage to being superfluous, but in this sense it ceases to be superfluous.

The stranger reminds young Socrates of his patricide, in defense of which he had argued that unless he and Theaetetus could force nonbeing somehow to be, no speech about false speech or false opinion, phantoms, images, imitations, or their apparitions, as well as the arts which handle these things, could possibly avoid contradiction.[43] He now declares that they are likewise compelled to have the more and less, whether in deed or in speech, become measurable not only against one another but also against the *genesis* of the mean (*to metrion*), for otherwise the arts themselves and their works, and in particular political science, will lack their evidence. The being of nonbeing is to nonbeing as the measure of the mean is to the arithmetical measure. "The other," then, does not suffice for the understanding of all the arts and sciences, for it does not comprehend action and what the stranger calls "the indispensable being of becoming." The other of the big is the small and the equal, and the equal is between the big and the small. But the equal is not necessarily the measure of the fitting (cf. 284e7). Even though the phrase "to cut in two" does not mean "to cut in two equal pieces," all the stranger's talk about dichotomy has suggested their equivalence. And he certainly never advised either Theaetetus or young Socrates to distinguish them; indeed, he once spoke about doubles and halves of classes (262a1–2). On the one occasion he said that a class stood properly (*metriôs*) apart from one another, this rejected class of heralds, soothsayers, and interpreters was not a part of his dichotomies (261a3).

The stranger has let two mathematicians assimilate his procedure to a geometer's bisection of a line or figure, for he has let each of them believe that the dialogue in which they took part was not an action and did not involve becoming. Young Socrates is made to realize this at the same time that the stranger says that the statesman's knowledge pertains to actions. Nongnostic political science, the science of nonarithmetical measures, and the science of division are linked together through the stranger's attempt to get young Socrates to acknowledge the partial knowability of becoming. And insofar as the nature of the mean measures excess and defect in becoming, it gives becoming its being (283e5, cf. e8). The more and less of mathematics, however, has a secondary role in actions and becoming, somewhat similar to the place the legislator has to the statesman. The statesman might rule that drunken outrage is to be more severely punished than a *crime passionel*, and the legislator accordingly might double the length of imprisonment for the former.

Such a translation, however, of one measure into the other is not always possible, nor does it, when possible, always preserve the meaning of the ruling measure. That the statesman has a higher rank that the sophist is seemingly contradicted by the fact that the *Sophist* is longer than the *Statesman* (284c6–7). No one, however, would assert that the ratio of eight to one corresponds to the importance political science has relative to the making and plaiting of warp and woof, though that ratio does obtain between the number of exchanges the stranger devotes to each. In order to estimate the relative weight of the two metrics, one should rather consider young Socrates' omission of the woof from the art of twisting thread. The solid warp and the fluffy woof are in the same ratio as the two metrics are to one another, and weaving exemplifies political science primarily because it makes so distinct a use of both metrics. But young Socrates' error and the stranger's correction of it are even more revealing than the paradigm in itself. That action is the true paradigm of political science.

The sciences of relative measure are logistics, plane and solid geometry, and the still undiscovered science of solid bodies in motion, of which astronomy is an imperfect copy.[44] The stranger does not say whether the nature of the mean is likewise handled by several sciences. All the arts of making, insofar as they use the criteria of the fitting, the opportune, and the needful, presuppose the nature of the mean, but whether they would acknowledge that there are general sciences of the mean is more doubtful (cf. 284b10, d4). Is there one science of the opportune, and another of the needful? The stranger seems to imply that the one comprehensive science of the mean would include all the mathematical sciences as well, for he says that the present discussion of the mean will be needed for "the demonstration of the precise itself." The precise itself looks like another name for the idea of the good or the good itself, which gives both being and intelligibility to everything. But the nature of the mean, though it determines the good and the bad among ourselves (283e5–6), does not extend beyond the range of becoming, and even within becoming it is more evident in the arts of making than in, for example, human eugenics, with which the stranger first identified political science.

That the stranger has shifted from a living to a lifeless paradigm (from herding to weaving) is a sign of this difficulty. The nature of the mean, moreover, is introduced as the digressional counterpart of the nature of the other, and we have already observed that political science is necessarily more aware of the other, or of the difference between part and kind, than any other science. Is it likewise more aware of the nature of the mean? Every poetic art makes use of the mean for itself, but none understands its relation to all the other poetic arts in its light. Since, however, political science regulates the arts in the city according to their appropriateness to the city—it decides, for example, whether or not music is to be learned—the measure of the mean cannot be applied to itself without simultaneously being applied to its relations with all other arts. The measure of the mean, in its most general form, is political science, but political science does not demonstrate the precise itself. It therefore can only be paradigmatic for such a demonstration, which must be concerned with being and not becoming.

The ontological equivalent to the genetic measure of the mean is the science of part and whole. This science would unite the nature of the other with the nature of the mean and thereby show in their togetherness the congeners and the coefficients of the intelligible whole. This science is unavailable, for a teleology of the whole is plainly at odds with an eidetic analysis of the whole.[45] The separation of beings into kinds does not consist with the conjunction of beings into subordinate and supraordinate causes. The awkwardness of combining the political science which was revealed among its congeners (a theoretical science) with the political science which emerges in the articulation of its coefficients (a practical science) represents a first approximation to the true inconsistency. Even the final account of the two ultimate strands of political science does not indicate any way of resolving the ontological problem. As the distinctness of moderation and courage increases, the possibility of their cooperation decreases; just as the less they severally tend toward the contrariety of mutual annihilation, the more each seems to vanish as itself into prudence or wisdom. Both moderation and courage are apparitions of prudence, but the apparitional duality of a true one was Socrates' original question and not an answer.

Of all the dichotomies the stranger makes, he seems to hold that the division of measurement into two arts is the most important. It prompts him to criticize the Pythagoreans for passing off their cleverness for wisdom, since they failed to distinguish between the metrics of good and evil, on the one hand, and the metrics of odd and even, on the other. Their unfamiliarity with eidetic division led them to draw from a true proposition (wherever art is possible measurement is possible) a false conclusion (mathematics is the one and only art of measurement). This error exemplifies the taking of the other for the same, and the opposite error—the taking of the same for the other— they likewise made, when, for instance, they separated right from left in terms of better and worse, though this has no greater evidence than the vulgar Greek distinction between Greek and barbarian that it is by nature.[46] The stranger thus hints at the double ground for the Pythagoreans' double error. The first was due to an unwarranted application of the arithmetical measure, and the second to an equally unwarranted application, however unwitting, of the measure of the mean.

Just as the arithmetical measure by itself cannot but understand every apparent other as noetically the same, so the measure of the mean is apt to accept every apparent other as noetically other. Theaetetus' identification of knowledge with true opinion in the *Theaetetus*, we recall, was essentially a mathematician's error, but he could not maintain that true opinion with *logos* was knowledge without asserting the nonmathematical proposition that "whole" and "all" were not the same. That a difference in nomenclature makes a difference is the crudest form this second error takes, whereas the first error first shows itself in its utter indifference to terminology. The *Sophist* and the *Statesman* are filled with examples of both errors, not all of which are explicitly corrected. If, however, each kind of measure must rescue the other from its natural tendency to intrude into the other's domain, the measure of the mean must be the ruling measure of both, for it alone measures excess and thereby limits both itself and the other measure. Self-knowledge is inseparable from the measure of the mean.

The stranger chose the art of weaving to exemplify political science; but its account became so lengthy, at least in the stranger's view, that he turned aside to discuss the doubleness in metrics in order to justify its length. The justification is somewhat distressing. Since political science is itself an example of dialectics, the art of weaving is not the quickest and easiest way for young Socrates to come to an understanding of political science. It is a compromise between such a paradigm and that which would, without the interposition of political science, exemplify dialectical knowledge. This compromise puts a great strain on both the art of weaving and political science, a strain that shows up in the very need to discuss the appropriateness of a long speech on weaving. It leads the stranger to say that the measure of the mean is not to be used, except incidentally, to determine how much pleasure a discussion should give.

The *Statesman* is certainly designed to affect us unpleasantly, for its parts seem not to be in proportion to one another. Its ugliness arises from the stranger's refusal to make use of phantastics, the art of making the big appear beautiful. He has instead brought young Socrates right into his own workshop, where he can see up close, without the corrective of perspective, the disproportionate colossus of the statesman (cf. 277a4–b7). No sensible man, the stranger says, would ever give an account of weaving for its own sake, but he does not say whether or not a sensible man would give an account of political science for its own sake. Aristotle's *Politics* would seem to be such an account; Plato's *Statesman* is not. It shows rather the necessity for the ugliness of political science if political science is to serve as a paradigm for dialectics, which examines the greatest and most beautiful beings that are bodiless. No phantom image can be made to show these beings; only speech can reveal them. The stranger, however, had implied that the statesman, like any other living being, could be shown, albeit inadequately, in a painting or sculpture (277c3–6).

A speech about the statesman in himself would have to take into account that the statesman neither is a bodiless being nor deals with bodiless beings, whereas to give a speech about the statesman as if he were the dialectician is to distort the statesman. The *Statesman* puts together and side by side both kinds of speeches; side by side, for example, in the shift from political science as theoretical to political science as practical, and, in turn, together, when the stranger, in discussing political science as practical, asks: "And if we make the political (art) vanish, won't our search after this for the royal science be perplexed (284b4–5)?" This paradoxical question brings us up against the ultimate riddle of the *Statesman*.

The stranger admits that the art of weaving is not indispensable for the understanding of political science; other paradigms would have served as well or better. But he does not say whether political science is an indispensable or the unique paradigm for dialectics. That some paradigm is necessary he even admitted at the beginning of the *Sophist* (218c7–d2), but political science is the only paradigm he completes and does not renounce. Let us grant, then, that it is indispensable; the very fact that Socrates in starting with the city reaches the idea of the good supports this supposition. But does political science so perfectly exemplify all of the dialectics which can be exemplified that no other paradigm must supplement it? Were this the case, the *Sophist* would have to be understood as essentially either derivative from or in preparation for the *Statesman*, but in no sense independent of it. We have already been given several indications that this is indeed so, but the proof only comes in the course of the stranger's attempt to articulate the coefficients of political science. Strangely enough, the proof comes as a great shock to the stranger.

IX. The City
(287b4–292a4)

In order to place weaving properly among its congeners, the stranger had classified all the things we make or acquire into ten pairs. In order to determine the causes and the cocauses of political science, he now restricts himself to all the possessions in the city and says that it is hard or impossible to dichotomize them. The discussion of the double metrics seems to have had two effects. It has finally brought the stranger to the city itself (now that the city is no longer in the misleading disguise of the artless human herd) and forced him to abandon the methodological tyranny of dichotomy. The things of the city are peculiarly resistant to dichotomy, for the several ends that the seven kinds of things the stranger lists serve do not come in pairs of larger or smaller extent. They are, somewhat plausibly, all classifiable as tools, but such a class does not admit of continual dichotomy. The diversity of the needs they fulfill recalls the various definitions of the sophist which Theaetetus could not bring together into one in the *Sophist*. Just as the sophist, if a hunter, was not a merchant, so the class of nutritive goods is not the class of vehicles. These two classes, however, can belong together on a given occasion if, for example, the merchant ships food from one country to another. The seven classes of possessions, then, are in terms of dichotomy no less an uncombinable many than an indivisible one.

For this reason the stranger likens them to a sacrificial animal, which is as a whole a means to propitiate the gods, and whose several parts, insofar as they are functionally definable, do not form an instrumental cluster of pairs. The seven classes form a whole which is not hierarchically arranged but, like the parts of an animal body, are mutually useful and dependent. The stranger, then, suggests two things about the city which is the object of political science. First it is a city of artisans, which is completely self-sufficient and hence resentful of the intrusion of the ruling art, for it surely will not acknowledge itself to be a means like a sacrificial animal; and, second, it is a city in which the division of labor has advanced so far that toolmakers are a specialized class. Such specialization is necessary under two conditions— if a great number of things of the same kind are to be made, and if these things have to meet very high standards.[47] Accordingly, political science is only possible when the city is least favorable to the rule of political science, for it must prove itself to be needed where every need, from food to entertainment, has been satisfied, and to be as precise in its knowledge as is the art of making the carpenter's straight-edge. It cannot, however, prove its own precision in terms of the arithmetical measure, although that is the only measure of precision all the artisans of the city accept unreservedly. No matter whether he competes against the divine shepherd or the human artisan, the statesman seems bound to lose.

The stranger repeatedly asks young Socrates the same question, whether political science belongs in turn to the class of tools, containers, vehicles, defenses, materials, or nourishment, but he does not ask whether it is to be found in the class of playthings, which are solely made for our pleasure. It is too obvious, one might say, that political science, unlike sophistry, is not an amusement.[48] And yet Plato's Athenian stranger has grave doubts about its status,[49] and the Eleatic stranger has thought it proper to indulge in the childishness of a myth (268d8–e6). Political science itself would not countenance the stranger's playfulness. But political science here is a paradigm of dialectics, and therefore serious only to the degree to which it is such a tool of understanding. To witness, at any rate, the stranger's adaptation of it to this purpose has been painful. His next series of questions seems to repeat the point he had made before, when he contrasted the omnicompetent herdsman with the artisans who would dispute with the statesman his right to the title of caretaker of the human herd. Does the stranger now go beyond that? Since all the herdsman is said to do fits comfortably into two classes, nourishment and playthings, the argument has been altered by the addition of five classes: tools, containers, vehicles, defenses, and materials. These five classes distinguish the city from any herd. They criticize implicitly the definition of man as a herd animal on the ground that he was then negatively determined, whereas he should have been defined in terms of his possessions which make up for his bodily defectiveness. Although he walks by nature on dry land, he has managed by art to travel on water (288a4). Everything he can put his hands on he has turned to his own use. Man is an acquisitive being whose artfulness recognizes no limits. When the stranger denies, for example, that the statesman's job is to make defenses, despite the fact that the paradigm of weaving is a part of that class, he means that these defensive arts are indifferent to the political suitability of their artifacts. They could never decide to be idle, even if it were better that the city not be walled, or its citizens go naked. The statesman, then, now has artisans less as rivals, who rightly insist that they can do what he cannot, than as contradictors, who resist any infringement on the unlimited exercise of their self-evident competence. Their resistance shows itself in their joint demand to make as much money as they can, a demand which entails politically the infinite expansion of the city, or imperialism. The city of arts is a city at war or on the brink of war.[50] The stranger, however, barely hints at this consequence; he merely remarks that money can only be fitted by force into his list of the city's possessions.

The basis of the city is its inanimate possessions, which the stranger has now divided into several parts; he next adds to the city six living classes: herd animals, slaves, merchants-retailers, heralds-secretaries, soothsayers, and priests. These six classes might in fact be only five, for the stranger leaves it open whether slaves are to be classed with tame animals (289a7–8, b8), which would imply that political science as a kind of herding cannot be of free men and hence is the same as the slavemaster's art. The stranger, moreover, does not say whether or not slaves exercise the instrumental arts which produce the seven inanimate possessions of the city. The city of art would then be a city of slaves, with their owners a superfluous part of such a city. The difficulty of placing properly the class of herd animals in the city makes this problem even more acute.

In terms of their function, all herd animals belong either to the class of materials or of nourishment (cf. 288d8–e1). They do not contribute anything to the city apart from these ends. Draft animals, to be sure, would belong to the class of tools, and horses to that of vehicles. But neither are herd animals (261d8), and the stranger does not mention the art of caring for nonherd animals. Are only herd animals tame? Watchdogs would belong to the class of defenses, but watch-dogs are not altogether tame. And it would be a foolish master who believed that his slaves were tame. The stranger only speaks of purchased slaves, for those acquired in war could not be called slaves unambiguously (289d10–e2).[51] We can draw two conclusions from all of this. The stranger wishes to show the basic city to be almost wholly artificial and without any traces of life in its possessions, and he wishes, in the second place, to raise the problem of freedom in as radical a manner as possible. That the city of arts is also the city of free men is more of a paradox than it seems.

The stranger divines that the statesman's chief rivals belong to the class of slaves and servants. His waking divination is his way of pointing to the difference between caring and ruling. Servants are under two potentially contradictory constraints. They are to see to their masters' best interest while they obey them. And yet their obedience is not a product of their knowledge, for their knowledge could conceivably enjoin them to disobey their masters. Socrates had raised this difficulty with Thrasymachus, who had defined the just to be the lawful or the advantage of the stronger. Through a consideration of servants, the stranger likewise begins to delineate the conflict between knowledge and law-abidingness. Servants are of three kinds: economic, civil, and religious. They belong together because they all are concerned with exchange or communication. They have a social role; or, to put it in a way which brings out their rivalry with the weaver-statesman, they establish and care for the bonds of the city (cf. 289c5).

Young Socrates suggests that political science might have something to do with the city's economic bonds,[52] but the stranger objects that, inasmuch as they are for hire, merchants and shippers cannot even pretend to the art of ruling. It is not their art which disqualifies them, it is themselves. The true ruler cannot be bought; the city does not write his contract, for it is not his client. The only kind of servants of the city whom the city seems not to hire or fire at its discretion are the soothsayers and the priests. The law declares them to be servants of the gods as well as of men. But no sooner does the stranger establish their title to rule than he demolishes it. He could have done so by reminding young Socrates either of the myth, which precluded the possibility of a genuine priesthood, or of his distinction between epitactics and autepitactics, when he classed soothsayers with heralds and interpreters since they too do not originate, as statesmen must, the commands they convey. Instead, the stranger chooses to appeal to facts—the present position of priests in Egypt and Athens (cf. 291c1).

No one can be king in Egypt if he is not a priest, and if someone chances to usurp the throne he must be enrolled into the priesthood. And in Athens the king archon, who is elected by lot, oversees the most solemn and ancestral of sacrifices. In the distant past the king and the priest were the same, but since political science is not possible unless the city has fully developed the arts, and in Greece at least this development is recent, the ancient kings lacked the kingly art. That chance alone decides who is to be the king archon testifies to the Athenians' own acknowledgment of and apparent indifference to the speciousness of priestly knowledge. The city of art is the nonsacred city. Despite his name, the king archon holds the least important office in Athens, but though a survival from the distant past, he is not yet wholly unimportant. Socrates appeared before him the day before. So the stranger, who hauled the sophist Socrates before the royal argument, now hauls the king archon before Socrates (cf. 291b4). The king archon must answer for his ignorance.

The stranger moves from the city of art to the city of law by reflecting on priestcraft. It reminds him of the most elementary of political facts, which his argument so far has checked him from acknowledging. It is not artisans or even shepherds but those who are masters of illusion and self-delusion who dispute most forcefully with the statesman. The stranger's keenness in tracking down political science has made him forget all the unscientific titles to rule. He has stayed so long in the light of knowledge that he now blinks in the darkness of the cave. His opponents look monstrous to him, though they are his neighbors. He should have recognized them at once, for they are the greatest sophists of the sophists (303c4–5) and should have been the main subject of his conversation with Theaetetus, not shunted aside with the title of public speakers, or left to lurk in the class of doxomimetics. They are more sophistic than the "sophists" not only because they sincerely believe that the lawful is the just, and no irony accompanies their several attempts to embody it, but because the "sophists," in desiring to appear wise, agree that wisdom is the greatest good. But political sophists deny it and do not consider even the appearance worth having. They do, however, agree with the true kings on one important point: the priest-kings have no right to rule. They have been dethroned not by philosophy but by chance.

Aristotle says that the office of polemarch was introduced when some of the kings proved to be too soft militarily.[53] Once the priesthood is relegated to a subordinate place in the city,[54] the authority of the ancestral is diminished (though not eliminated), and a contest soon arises as to what kind of regime should replace it.[55] If the traditional kings had not shown themselves to be incompetent, or if the true statesmen could have got their credentials accepted, such a contest would not have been possible. The political struggle occurs within these two poles, and it will always so occur as long as the city remains caught between the sacred, which is the city's dim recollection of the rule of the gods, and wisdom, of which the city is no less dimly aware through the arts (cf. 290b1–2). The shepherd and the weaver mark out between them the two boundaries within which all politicians move.

The criteria that the stranger used to distinguish the human herd from others were laughable, particularly because they were such an affront to human dignity. The single criterion that we ordinarily use for distinguishing regimes is also laughable, for it is, though speciously scientific, so crude. The three chief types are the rule of one, of few, and of many. We thereby make a double error, for this triple distinction not only fails to keep part and kind together, but it employs the measure of relative size in an inappropriate way. Were a city fortunate enough to have at the same time several statesmen, it would not be an oligarchy (cf. 293a2–4). Athens, after all, has just recovered from the rule of the thirty tyrants. These numerical differences, however, are modified by three pairs of opposites: violence/willingness, wealth/poverty, law/lawlessness. We likewise do not use these differences with sufficient discrimination. We are inclined, for example, to label the usurper of a throne a tyrant regardless of whether he rules thereafter according to the laws (cf. 290d9–e3), or even whether he rules with the willingness of his subjects.[56]

The stranger himself does not consider the possible varieties within tyranny and other regimes; instead, he accepts the ordinary view with one exception. Despite the fact that his three pairs of opposites yield six regimes there are only names for five: kingship, tyranny, aristocracy, oligarchy, and democracy. No one holds that the rule of the many over the rich deserved two names, one for violent and lawless rule, and another if the many scrupulously guard the laws and the few acquiesce. The rich, one might conclude, are never willing to be ruled by the many, or alternatively, the distinction between lawful and unlawful rule is hard to draw when the people can lawfully alter daily the fundamental laws. But whatever the reason, democracy in its undivided form offers the best possible way to understand the city.[57] Monarchy, for example, is not too revealing about the economics of the city, and oligarchy obscures somewhat the opposition between force and willingness, and even that between law and lawlessness. The stranger's argument requires that law be understood as law devised and written down by men; it cannot include either custom or divine law. Only written law is compatible with conscious change of the law, and democracy is the only regime that cannot survive without writing, for in its absence the rule of the city would devolve on those who were held to remember the laws best. To attack, then, the written law is to attack democracy, and though the stranger's argument is somewhat applicable to unwritten laws (or, as the stranger calls them, "ancestral customs"), it does not treat them adequately. They have been, as it were, condemned in advance along with the priest-kings (cf. 301d2).

X. LAW
(292a5–302b4)

That the correctness of political rule cannot be estimated by numbers, wealth, poverty, force, or willingness, young Socrates has no trouble in accepting, but he draws the line at the stranger's abandonment of legality. Only then does young Socrates wake up to a recognition of his own prescientific knowledge of political things—of the language which must precede his learning of its alphabet. Young Socrates falls short of the Theodoran philosopher, who, according to Socrates, does not know when young the way to the marketplace, and neither sees nor hears (i.e., obeys) the city's spoken and written laws and decrees.[58] Such innocent disobedience is not young Socrates', nor would it be desirable in the pupil of statesmanship, who must especially learn that the knowledge he wants cannot be the common bond of the city. Young Socrates therefore rightly objects to the stranger's failure to discriminate between law and the other criteria which distinguish regimes.

To be law-abiding certainly seems to be different from being the partisan advocate of monarchy or democracy. The stranger, however, is not altogether mistaken, for law cannot be separated from the regime which dictates its content. Law does not precede but follows the regime, though the power of the law resides to a great extent in its apparent inversion of this principle. Once young Socrates has boldly conceded that knowledge and not numbers, wealth, poverty, force, or willingness is the criterion for determining the correct regime, he has already conceded that law does not count either. But that he balks at this consequence shows that his courage has already been moderated. Paradoxically, however, in freeing young Socrates from the law, the stranger perfects the moderation of young Socrates.

In order to prove the irrelevance or defectiveness of the usual political criteria, the stranger goes back to the beginning of their discussion, when young Socrates agreed that the statesman was no less a knower than the sophist. But neither the stranger nor young Socrates recalls exactly the argument. They thus seem to give an unintended praise of writing, for if they were reading from scripts their inexactness would be neither tolerated nor possible. Are we then to conclude that their inexactness, which is inseparable from action,[59] does more for the argument than a literal recording could? Young Socrates does not quarrel with the following statement of the stranger: "We asserted, I believe, that kingly rule was one of the sciences." One could of course interpret this to be literally true of philosophy, or alternatively, a compendious way of saying that the true king rules by science, but at first glance it combines the action of the king with his knowledge, even though the stranger had assigned political science to gnostics because it was not necessarily manifest in action (cf. 293c3). The stranger then compounds his error: "It was not, however, of all these sciences, but we surely selected it from the rest as a kind of critical and supervisory science." Young Socrates again concurs. But political science had originally been placed in the noncritical part of the gnostic sciences.

So the stranger seems to imply that political knowledge must be theoretical or at least have theoretical implications even when it is practical. Political wisdom and political science go together. We are familiar with an image of this thought in the dialogue itself, for that which guides the action of the *Statesman* is that which guides its argument, but the stranger only now begins to show that the same holds true for the statesman. The true statesman knows what is fitting for any occasion because he knows the precise itself—the one and only correct regime—which is never or hardly ever fitting. How a measure, which finds nothing up to its own standard, can yet determine the measures appropriate for everything not up to its own standard, and do this without attempting to realize its own standard, is the question which the stranger now raises. The law is plainly the antithesis of such a measure.

The longest speech young Socrates ever makes confirms the stranger's assertion that neither the many in the city nor fifty in a city of a thousand possess political science. The oligarchical prejudices embedded in language,[60] of which one seems to be the equation of lawless with lawful democracy, dimly reflect the truth that only a few can be true statesmen. The oligarchical few is in fact too many (cf. 300e8), and the monarchical one is a shade too grudging; but the democratic many is a wholly incorrect measure. Young Socrates' example brings this out very well: "We know that out of a thousand men there would never prove to be as many tip-top draughts-players as that in comparison to those among all the rest of the Greeks." A city will have fewer qualified rulers in its population than players of a game capable of competing against the best strangers. Young Socrates recognizes that the true statesman might be a stranger and hence never be in a position to rule the city which needs him (cf. 301d8–e4). The city is at least as arbitrary a part in which to find one statesman as a thousand is to find therein one Capablanca.

Young Socrates' example of draughts playing is suggestive in another way, for the placing of draughts is not unlike the positing of laws,[61] even to the point of there being a line on the draughts board called the sacred line. There are at least three kinds of rules. Arithmetic exemplifies one kind, for its rules are presumably nonarbitrary and consistent; chess exemplifies another, for its rules are consistent and arbitrary. The legislator lays down some rules which are as arbitrary and consistent as those for chess (traffic regulations, for example) and others which might be nonarbitrary though possibly inconsistent, like the two which Euthyphro finds impossible to reconcile: "Do not prosecute your own father," and "Prosecute anyone guilty of unholiness." Instructed by Euthyphro, we might say that nonarbitrary and inconsistent rules are likely to be found among sacred laws or those which a city holds in the highest honor. Now the stranger will undercut all legislation by making it a principle of political science that no rule whatsoever can ever be entirely consistent with the nonarbitrary end of statesmanship. This principle is no more in accordance with art than it is with law, but it just might square with philosophy. It is, in any case, a principle which uniquely characterizes statesmanship among all the sciences.

The stranger makes medicine into an elaborate analogue of statesmanship as outlined below. But as we have learned from his criticism of the shepherd-statesman, he thereby runs the risk of putting statesmanship into an alien light. It is safe to say that medicine is as illuminating and as misleading as shepherding.

293a9–c3	293d4–e5
A. Whether we are cured willingly or unwillingly,	So it is necessary that this be the only correct regime, in which one would find the ruler to be truly a knower and not only seem to be,
B. by surgery, cautery, or the application of any other pain, we no less hold them to be doctors;	
C. and whether in accordance with writings or apart from writings,	C'. regardless of whether they rule in accordance with law or without law,
D. and whether they are poor or rich, we do not hesitate to pronounce them doctors,	A'. and whether over willing or unwilling subjects,
E. as long as they are in charge by art,	D'. and whether they are poor or rich none of these things must be taken into consideration. . . .

F. and in purifying us

G. either by slimming us down or increasing our weight,

H. if only they act for the good of our bodies,

I. and in making them better from worse

J. they severally preserve the bodies they care for;

K. in this way and no other, I believe, we shall lay down the only correct criterion for medicine and any other rule.

B'. And whether by death or exile

F'. they purify the city

H'. for the good,

G'. either by sending out colonies elsewhere like swarms of bees they make the city smaller, or by importing from somewhere outside other citizens they increase it,

E'. as long as they, in employing science and the just,

I'. make the city better from worse as much as possible,

J'. and preserve it,

K'. we must declare this to be the only correct regime according to these criteria.

The two columns speak for themselves. The stranger implies that the city is a kind of body which cannot maintain its health without the aid of political science.[62] There is nothing natural or self-regulating about the city's well-being. To rule scientifically is to heal, but to kill is not to heal. If the patient dies under the surgeon's knife, his death is not necessarily the surgeon's fault. Could the statesman wipe out the city by art, on the ground that it is too far gone to be saved (cf. 302a2–3)? If, however, the doctor cannot inflict pain for the whole life of the patient, the statesman's cures cannot be too prolonged, even if this entails that no cure is permanent. The statesman cannot exile everyone over ten, as Socrates once proposed.

We usually know by symptoms whether we are well or ill.[63] Must the city realize that it is in poor shape before the statesman can act? In that case, the city would voluntarily consult the statesman, though it would no doubt want a second opinion if the recommended remedy was too unpleasant. Does the city know who the true statesmen are as well as we know who the quack doctors are? There are many political sophists. No matter how unwilling we are to submit to surgery, the doctor does not cease to be a doctor. But since the doctor cannot compel us to submit, or even by his own art persuade us,[64] the statesman's art would be equally ineffective. The true statesman does not have to hold office; his advice can be as ruthless as the circumstances require as long as he does not have to see to it that it is carried out. The stranger's analogy so blurs the distinction between gnostics and practics that the one correct regime seems to be both the best city in speech and any city in which the rulers act by art. A one-armed man is defective even if he is healthy; he is certainly better off than when his arm was gangrened. And the statesman likewise might have to cut so deep into the city in order to save it that he has to dispense with some element of the city which would have, under other conditions,

III.128

contributed to the perfection of the city. Regeneration does not always follow surgery, and grafting has its own problems.

The true statesman employs "science and the just." If the phrase is not an hendiadys—"the justice of science"—the stranger admits that there is a difference between medicine and statesmanship. The surgery of the statesman looks like a punishment to the city, but if there is no law, how can the city tell whether it is a just punishment or not? If the statesman orders someone's betrothed to be killed, does her fiancé recognize that the city will benefit? The city is not like a single body unless the members of the city have a comparable sense of community, and if they do, they will suffer all the more from the statesman's art and at times prefer to perish with their own rather than survive without them.

Young Socrates is innocent or bold enough to find nothing objectionable in the statesman's killing of citizens, but he is rather repelled to hear that the statesman does not have to do it "by the book." His repugnance is partly due to a theoretical mistake which the language induces him to make. "Lawless" is taken to be the opposite of "lawful," but in fact it is merely the other of "lawful," comprehending both the scientific and the unjust ways of ruling. It does not differ in its ambiguity from "nonbarbarian," which means both Greek and civilized. Young Socrates' repugnance is further due to his unawareness that law is of necessity opinion, even if true opinion, and never knowledge. The stranger, in opposing law and knowledge, denies to knowledge the possibility of its ever appearing publicly (cf. 285e4–286a4). It must seem odd to a mathematician that if he writes down a theorem it ceases to be knowledge. How, then, can the truths of political science never be embodied in law? The mathematician, moreover, stands apart from mathematics; he does no more than discover and contemplate its truths. But we are inclined to laugh if a fat doctor advises us to go on a diet, and if a rich statesman ordered us to cut our profits, we should become indignant. Socrates is merely ridiculous when he tells the Athenians that wealth comes from virtue while living himself in ten-thousand-fold poverty.[65] So the statesman is necessarily visible as ruler and invisible as knower. Only a god could get away with such doubleness; in a human being it would look like duplicity.

The stranger did not anticipate young Socrates' objection to lawless rule, although he had expected that he would find something hard to take. Young Socrates believes that lawful killing redeems killing itself, as if the death of Socrates will not conform perfectly with Athenian law. Clinias would surely have thought of law as a way of bringing harmony to the city, not as a way of dismembering it,[66] and Glaucon would have asked what is the good for the sake of which the statesman purifies the city. Young Socrates is more certain than Glaucon of the goodness of justice, and he is less reluctant than Clinias to entertain the possibility of lawless rule. The discussion of law is the proper mean between the theme of the *Republic* and that of the *Laws*. It is, however, in a sense as much a digression as the myth, for everything that is not a genuine part of a science is a digression, and the legislative art is only "in a way" part of the royal science.

To judge from the number of digressions in the *Statesman,* much the largest part of political science concerns the spurious interpretations of political things, either because like the law they fall short of a true understanding of political things, or because like the paradigm of weaving they go beyond political science in the direction of philosophy. In the perspective of political science proper, both kinds of interpretations appear to be digressions. If a discussion of law seems to be more pertinent than a protracted account of weaving, it is only because it is the more common, that is, the more political error. False opinions almost constitute political things. "All the rest we speak of, we must say of them that they are not genuine (legitimate), and in their being are not, but they have imitated this (the one correct regime), and if with more beautiful results we say they are law-abiding (with good laws), while the rest are uglier imitations (293e2–5)." Lawless rule distresses young Socrates too much to notice at first the stranger's more startling proposition: Political science is grounded in the science of being. The *Sophist*'s proper place is both before and after the *Statesman*.

The stranger undertakes to prove that, though law cannot be the best simply, law is indispensable. The statesman must legislate. He must have an art that is of necessity spurious, for no art which propounds the simple can be an art of what is never simple. Neither human beings nor human actions are comparable with one another, and human things are almost without rest. The political event is unprecedented, but the law declares that it itself is the precedent in light of which the unprecedented is to be judged. Young Socrates does not notice the defect in the stranger's argument. Granted that the law cannot be both comprehensive and precise, the stranger would still have to show that the dissimilarities among human beings are significant and that the inconstancy in human things needs to be taken into account politically. Perhaps the law roughly estimates that which cannot and should not be estimated precisely. The crudeness of the law could thus be in agreement with the crudeness of things. "Rough justice" is just.

Young Socrates, however, does not raise this objection, for two disparate reasons. He is a mathematician, and therefore precision, despite or because of what the stranger said about the doubleness of metrics, is still the standard for every art. And again, despite the stranger's equation of herd and city, young Socrates is aware that every human being considers himself an exception from one rule or another (294c6). Individual self-importance coincides in the city of art with the knowledge each citizen has from his own art of what precision is. The law then becomes most irritating, for it must seem uneducated in comparison with the arts and a relic of primitive conditions. It claims for itself a certainty which could only obtain if men were more like the stars in their courses than they are.

The law thus seems willful, since it mistakes what it wants for what is. The pattern it claims to discern in human things is of its own devising, but if its injunctions are obeyed strictly, it comes to validate its own claim. The law, however, needs interpreters; it turns out to be in practice not as simple as it is on paper. The law itself seems to recognize fully the dissimilarities among men and their actions. Criminal actions are graded by the law in one list according to their seriousness. But criminals are graded in another list according to the degree of their culpability, and no law can lay down a rule for matching the two lists perfectly. The law thus acknowledges the superiority of prudence within the limits of the law, but it does not acknowledge the possibility that prudence could dictate a judgment in violation of the law. The law cannot contain within itself a clause which allows for its own suspension.[67] The lawgiver knows enough to leave some things at the discretion of future jurists; he knows he cannot include in the law even all the cases he can imagine without making the law unworkable and unintelligible to those who are to obey it. But the lawgiver cannot translate into law prudential rules, for even those of an Aesopian simplicity tend to come in contradictory pairs: He who hesitates is lost; Look before you leap. Since the tension between courage and moderation, which these two proverbs illustrate respectively, cannot be legally represented, moderation and courage must be misrepresented by the law. The law is incapable of instilling true virtue.

No sooner has the stranger attacked the law than he comes to its defense. Boldness and sobriety have never alternated more rapidly, nor has the proper mean ever been more succinctly or silently conveyed. Only the foolish would hold that the stranger, in upholding the law he has just demoted, speaks eristically. His example, in light of which he shows the law's necessity, is even more important than usual, for gymnastics—coming as it does after medicine has been used against the primacy of the law—reminds us of the likeness the stranger had drawn between Socratic cathartics and gymnastics on the one hand, and political punishment and medicine on the other. Since gymnastics tries to remove ugliness, and medicine illness, it seems inconsistent for the stranger now to present the correct regime in terms of health (justice), and the spurious though lawful regimes in terms of beauty (knowledge). The stranger thus implies that the city, if properly understood, cannot rise higher than morality, while all law-abiding cities err because they aim too high.

The law cannot bother to heal in its zeal to beautify. It fosters injustice as it pretends to final knowledge. It is too general to handle the individual case individually and too partial to distinguish between part and kind (cf. 262b5, 294d10). The law, in generalizing the individual, mistakes the same for the other. The balance it strikes looks like the measure of the mean, but it is only the average. The average suits everybody and fits nobody. The law and gymnastic exercises have this much in common. Neither knowingly enjoins anything of advantage to one which is not of advantage to all. And yet gymnasts do not train together for their mutual advantage, for only one wins the race, but the law makes contracts possible in which no one is meant to gain at another's expense. Perhaps, however, the law prescribes our behavior in order to open up for us a way to compete for honors within the city. The social bonding of the law would thus serve to discover the individual or individuals most worthy of the city's recognition. Equalization through the law would be the law's devious way to ensure inequality of reward. For all the apparent unity it imposes, the law is ultimately divisive. The correct regime is likened to a single body, the lawful regime to a collection of bodies in training.

To read a training manual will not make one fit; to hear the law is not to obey it. One must be habituated to do what it says. Accordingly, the stranger now mentions ancestral habits and customs, though strictly speaking they could never have been legislated as habits. (We can exclude the legislator who innovates under the guise of reviving the old ways.) The written law can want nothing better than to pass for unwritten.[68] Even a democracy will invent for its laws the authority of a monarchical past. Theseus is an ancient example, Washington, the father of his country, is a modern. So we can now distribute among seven regimes the seven principles according to which they are principally governed. (1) Tyranny: violence; (2) Oligarchy: wealth; (3) Democracy without law: poverty; (4) Democracy under law: freedom; (5) Aristocracy: written law; (6) Kingship: unwritten law; (7) Correct regime: knowledge. The statesman's knowledge is no more effective in itself than any recently passed law. He therefore cannot dispense with habituation, but he cannot habituate the city to obey one command without diminishing the city's willingness to obey another which contradicts it. And it seems impossible to habituate the city of art, unlike small children or a flock of sheep, to obey simply and not set it in its ways. A city without bias is as imaginary as an athlete as well-trained for running as for wrestling. The true statesman will often have to diverge prudently from the most prudent course. The captain of a relief expedition might be compelled, just because he leads a relief expedition, to engage the enemy against his better judgment. He would then look as if he were following orders. It is not the case, then, as the stranger says, that someone who was capable of giving to each throughout his life the most appropriate injunction would not hinder his own freedom of action by writing laws. The true statesman can never exercise such a capacity as ruler, however much he has it as adviser. He cannot be, like the poet, always at the side of his subjects without being, like the poet, their maker. He must dilute what he knows. And the prudential dilution of prudence can be at times indistinguishable from the law.

The stranger asks young Socrates to picture the following. A doctor or trainer before going abroad leaves written instructions for his patients in the belief that they will not remember them otherwise, but when he returns sooner than expected and finds that circumstances have changed for the better or worse, he does not hesitate to cancel his former prescriptions and devise new ones. The stranger, however, cannot quite make this picture into a paradigm for the statesman-legislator. If he lays down unwritten laws, he does not write up others because he fears the city will forget them. And if the doctor cannot stay away longer than the lifetime of his patients, the statesman cannot do any good on his return if his laws have already become second nature to his subjects. If the time lapse between the first legislator and another of like ability is greater than two or three generations, the second could alter even less. A different regimen may or may not be more pleasant, but a change in laws, no matter how beneficial, cannot but seem an act of violence. The very success of the lawgiver is an obstacle to the statesman's; indeed, the law can undo the city it was meant to save, not only because it might preclude the only way out of a crisis, but because the prudence which even the law acknowledges to be necessary cannot be taught by the law. The most law-abiding do not make the best statesmen. Aristides was not Themistocles' equal.

exeat aula
qui volt esse pius.

The city at times must have recourse to a wisdom alien to its own ways. The true statesman, even if bred within the city, is always a stranger. In the eyes of the city, the good, the just, and the beautiful proclaimed by law look as if they are themselves the permanent goals of the city, but for the statesman-legislator, they are merely the changeable ingredients of his remedies (cf. 309c5–8). The lawful is a means which seems to be an end, but the law would not be as effective as it is unless it gave this illusion. "In truth," the stranger says, to prohibit the true statesman from overturning established laws is laughable; we scarcely have to add that only in truth is it laughable.

The possibility for the statesman on his return to change his own laws or as a stranger those of another seems to be so slight that one is forced to wonder whether the stranger is not thinking here of something other than written laws in the ordinary sense. He often calls them, after all, just writings. His reference to unexpected alterations for the better from Zeus (295c9–d2) suggests, in light of the myth according to which Zeus is nothing but a spoken phantom, that the stranger has in mind fundamental alterations in religion as those changes in circumstances for better or worse that would require a different presentation of the teaching of the *Statesman* (cf. 297d6). Plato could thus be hinting at the limit of intelligibility to be assigned to his own writings, so that even if they survived such upheavals they would need to be redone, either by their translation or in some other form more suitable to the times. The stranger, then, would not only be announcing through the myth the end of Socrates, but through his interpretation of the law the no less certain end of Plato.

The more the stranger details the deficiencies in the law, the more the necessity for the law becomes clear, for the law's deficiencies are part of the beliefs of the law-abiding. The many believe that if one knows of better laws, one should persuade one's own city to adopt them. The many cannot conceive of something better than the present law which is not itself a law. It is to the law's credit that they would not allow a law to be suspended without its being superseded by another law. The many always wish to make the exception into the rule. And yet the difficulty the stranger again has in paralleling the doctor and the statesman shows the many's objection to be not wholly specious. They, after all, will have to undergo the violent though artful treatment of the statesman.

The stranger fails to distinguish between two kinds of medical force, one, as in the setting of a broken bone, which hurts regardless of one's willingness, another which makes the patient do something in itself painless against his will (as when he refuses to swallow a pill). Are, then, the violent actions of statesmanship unavoidable, or do they only occur when the city balks? The stranger is perhaps thinking as much of the former as of the latter, for the feeling of their being forced would still accompany the many even if they were persuaded to abandon their habits. They would therefore associate the better regimen—the more just and more beautiful—with pain. The many, moreover, do not expeience the legislator's artfulness as artfulness. It is for them the experience of the good, the just, and the beautiful; so they cannot help but experience the legislator's new laws as bad, unjust, and ugly. It does not occur to them to blame their suffering on the legislator's lack of skill. If the many admitted the possibility of a political art they would never have chosen regimes based on wealth or poverty, law or freedom, and political sophistry would have been recognized for what it is. Once, however, the true statesman turns to legislation, he too must become sophistic, for law can hardly be framed according to any other principles than wealth or poverty, law or freedom. To decree that only those who use their wealth properly should retain it would be equivalent to the sanctioning of permanent revolution, even if one could avoid the twin plagues of informers and litigants. Prudence is always contingent, law can never be. The stranger now likens the statesman to the captain of a ship.

The statesman speaks of knowledge, the law of obedience. The statesman speaks of error, the law of transgressions and crimes. In the face of error, the statesman corrects; in the face of crime, the law punishes. If the true statesman who does not rule breaks the law in correcting an error, the law will punish him with death or other extreme penalties. The law must pretend to know that death is an unqualified evil; it cannot know that the unexamined life is not worth living. The law's simplicity is perhaps ultimately due to the necessity that it grade evils on a single scale. The law's simplicity makes the law innocent, for it is ignorant of its own ignorance. But this makes the knowledge of ignorance in the eyes of the law into guilt. Now, more than at any other time, the stranger, in attacking the law, speaks to young Socrates on behalf of old Socrates (cf. 299d2). How, then, can the stranger speak of all regimes as imitations of the one correct regime? Is mistaking the original of which sinning is the copy? The imitation is, as we should say, purely formal. The tyrant uses the same "line" as the true statesman: whatever is best cannot be done unless the written laws are violated. Since the true statesman would have to agree with this, he would have to persuade—he cannot teach—the many that the tyrant does not "really" know what he is saying. The many may be pardoned if they find it impossible to tell the two of them apart. How would the many know that the cancerous growth that the true statesman cut out of the city was truly cancerous? Political science looks like willfulness. No one, therefore, is more exposed to the charge of corruption than the true statesman. For him to prove that he was not bribed to kill a citizen would be as impossible as for Socrates to prove that he never seduced Charmides. Appearances are against them both. It is not too difficult to imagine a situation in which the true statesman acts in such a way that his friends make a killing on the market and his enemies are wiped out.

The second way in which there is imitation of the one correct regime only applies to the law-abiding regimes. They lay it down that no one should violate the law. The unchangeableness which this prohibition tries to maintain on the level of action corresponds to the constant goal of political science. It therefore is an imitation of that goal, for on the level of action the true statesman is always altering his course. The imitation, however, is even more plain at the moment a city abandons its law, for then it too must say that something is better than the law. We will not exaggerate by much if we say that most partisan political proposals will issue from the lips of the true statesman at one time or another.[69]

Young Socrates is most dismayed by the stranger's picture of the stagnation which would follow if the arts were forbidden to advance on their own. He believes all the arts would utterly vanish never to re-emerge, and "life, which even now is hard, would at that time be completely unlivable." Young Socrates' doubt as to when the golden age was is now explained (271c4–5). He cannot conceive of life without the arts. The law, however, is necessarily old-fashioned. It is as non-innovating as the shepherd's traditional ways, although the shepherd was the false paradigm of the human statesman and the true paradigm of divine rule. The law, then, is the human equivalent of divine rule, but when the god rules there are no cities. The law unwittingly wills the dissolution of the city, for the law cannot guarantee the conditions which alone would make it perfectly adequate. The law understands the city as a fall from the golden age. It does not care whether philosophy was then possible. The law, however, in its inability to go along with the progressive character of the arts, stands closer to political science than the arts do. If political science were like the arts, it too would be progressive, but political science cannot be unfinishable without ceasing to be competent to rule. The other arts and sciences do not now know what they will discover; political science does not now know what the statesman will face. The unpredictable is embedded in the present knowledge of the other arts and sciences. The unpredictable, with which it deals, stands outside the present completeness of political science. The law, however, refuses to acknowledge either kind of contingency; it does not see that technical innovation brings along with it political changes.

In order to show the connection between the arts and the different regimes, the stranger asks young Socrates what effect the law would have on seven pairs of arts. In each pair, the first is an example of the second comprehensive class. (1) generalship: hunting; (2) painting: imitation; (3) carpentry: manufacturing; (4) farming: plant care; (5) horsefeeding: herding; (6) prophecy: services; (7) draughts: mathematics.[70] We do not need the *Sophist* to relate the first to tyranny (222c5–8); nor is it hard to find oligarchical regimes well-disposed to the fostering of the imitative arts. Lawless democracy is an urban democracy, in which all the manufacturing arts flourish, while democracy in accordance with the law is agrarian. Aristocracy, or the rule of the law-abiding few, is the regime of knights, and traditional monarchy, as the stranger has remarked, identifies the king with the priest. That the stranger, however, identifies the correct regime with mathematics, which might remind one of the *Republic*, indicates the extent to which his disparagement of the law needs correction. He mentions both solid geometry and the science of solid bodies in motion, the first of which was first worked out by an older Theaetetus, while the second was only Socrates' dream. Political science must be immune from the undiscovered truths of mathematics, but the measure of the mean must be fully disclosed to it.

The law's defectiveness consists in its imprecision, the law's excellence in its comprehensiveness. If everyone is prohibited from acting contrary to the law, and all but a few are incapable of having political science, the law is only slightly mistaken in its view that it has no equal in wisdom. The laws which arise from the experiences—the trial and error—of many generations and the particular insights of several counselors almost duplicate the prudence of the true king (cf. 294a8). The stranger casually points to the fact that the best laws violate in their origin their own prohibition against their own violation. They do not spring fully grown from the head of Zeus. But since they cannot admit that change is the necessary precondition for their own unchangeableness, they are wholly lacking in self-knowledge. They do not know that they are a "second sailing" (300c2); they are blind to the necessity of their own ugliness. The *Statesman* has its chief purpose in bringing into the light that necessity. It therefore could not help but appear as ugly as the law is. It thus imitates the law in the element of self-knowledge. Young Socrates is made to experience the trial and error from which the best laws come to be while learning through trial and error the science of statesmanship. The *Statesman's* argument is its action.

XI. REGIMES
(302b5–303d3)

The number of common names for the kinds of regimes—tyranny, oligarchy, democracy, aristocracy, and kingship—is equal to the number of disguises in which the sophist showed up in the stranger's divisions in the *Sophist*. The parallel extends even farther. Not only is the one name of a regime (kingship) the only possible name for the correct regime, just as Socrates' cathartics is the one sophistry noble in descent, but the double form of democracy, which hides under a single name, is exactly parallel to Theaetetus' mistaking the double form of the stranger's third division for the third and fourth. Theaetetus had been puzzled as to how the sophist's many appearances could be unified; the stranger proposed that all be considered the apparitions of the imitation sophistry itself. This proposal led to endless perplexities from which the stranger extricated Theaetetus without extricating himself. Theaetetus was brought as near as possible to the beings while keeping his innocence. The stranger has taken another tack with young Socrates. He has been made to experience an argument to a degree not matched by any other Platonic character. The consequence of this experience has been the discovery that all past, present, and future regimes are the sophistic imitations of the one correct regime (cf. 302e6). Young Socrates learns that the city is the natural locus of all sophistry. It is the concrete unity of the apparitional manifold of the sophist. The sophist was ironic; the city can never be. The sophist of the *Sophist*, in contrast, was not the sophist. The sophist was and was not the philosopher. But didn't Socrates suggest that, inasmuch as the statesman was an occasional apparition of the philosopher, the same held true for the statesman?

The statesman, however, is the paradigm of the philosopher. His art is in itself genuine; it is not, like the sophistry of the *Sophist*, an artless art, or philosophy without self-knowledge. Theodorus more than Protagoras was its representative. Political science has its origin in the philosopher's reflection on the conditions for philosophy. It is grounded in the distinction between opinion and knowledge. The *Statesman* therefore fully reveals the city in the light of knowledge and philosophy, while the *Sophist*, insofar as it forgets the city, partly conceals philosophy in the shadows of the city. The discussion of nonbeing was a digression in the *Sophist;* the discussion of which kind of city is most tolerable to live in is declared to be a digression in the *Statesman*'s argument. Despite the fact that, as the stranger implies, all of us do everything on the whole for the sake of living as comfortably as we can (cf. 286d6), young Socrates and the stranger cannot be bothered with what is for them an academic question. Young Socrates is wholly free of any political ambitions (299a7–b1); he does not intend to display his rudimentary knowledge of statesmanship in the affairs of the city. The stranger has seen to that.

It seems, then, a tremendous paradox to instruct young Socrates in a political wisdom he will never use. But if Athens is about to kill Socrates in his sixty-ninth year, it is not altogether idle for young Socrates to know that he would have fared worse in an oligarchy. Socrates' death is not a great evil (303a4–7). Young Socrates knows that life at the present time (and considering that he has not traveled abroad, that means life in Athens) is hard (cf. 264c1, 7). But he does not know that all possible regimes are more or less hard for philosophy. He believes, moreover, that the arts alone in their free development make life tolerable. But though he himself does not hanker after luxury, he does not realize that he favors such a life because of his own interest in mathematics, which is more likely to flourish where the arts have attained a high degree of precision. The stranger's ranking of regimes is meant, on the one hand, to correct the selfishness that young Socrates betrays in this belief, and on the other, to concede the correctness of this belief insofar as it points to philosophy. The stranger's ranking is prudential; he would not have spoken in just this way to everyone. He balances the interests of the many, for whom the law is more important than the arts, against the interests of the few, which a city like Athens unwittingly serves. The stranger thus offers an example of political prudence most fit for the unpolitical young Socrates to hear.

XII. OFFICES
(303d4–305e7)

Weaving had suggested to the stranger that he distinguish between the congeners and the coefficients of political science. He has long turned away from its congeners to its coefficients, or causes and co-causes (287b4–8). But before he could get through the cocauses, the twin obstacles of law and political sophistry diverted him, and now, though they are presumably out of his way, they prevent him from resuming his former argument. The judicial, military, and propaganda ministries are not, as we would expect, spoken of as the coefficients but as the congeners of the kingly race. The stranger will prove that all three are subordinate to political science, but he cannot prove that two of them can ever work together with political science. The stranger's own image of their experience in discovering the true statesman first points to the difficulty. The impurities of rock and earth in gold ore are a fair likeness of the false statesman. But if bronze, silver, and adamant are then like the respectable kin of the statesman, they do not cooperate with the statesman once the statesman is made into pure gold. Perhaps the analysis even dissolved their kinship with the statesman, for, if the image holds, they are only found together in their unrefined states. Only if young Socrates and the stranger do not isolate the statesman but keep him alloyed with his servants will the servants do what they are told, and yet as part of an alloy the statesman might be worth less than the others combined. The statesman might be the standard according to which the other officers of the city are weighed, although he may be absent from the city itself. The stranger runs the risk of refining the statesman out of a job.

Young Socrates readily agrees that no science is competent to judge whether or not it is to be learned but that there is a science which is competent to make such a judgment about all practical sciences. He does not ask, and is not told, whether its competence extends to itself, and whether the statesman knows when not to be a statesman. Young Socrates further agrees that the science which knows if another science is to be learned is the same as the science which knows if another science is to be used. No science ever ceases to be *in statu pupillari*. The rhetorician can persuade; he cannot know by rhetoric whether he is to persuade, use force, or do nothing. But if the statesman alone knows that a situation calls for a rhetorican, can the rhetorican know what the situation calls for? The competence of the statesman must reach very far into rhetoric, at least as far as Socrates' does in the second and third books of the *Republic*. The stranger does not mention another problem. Since the rhetorician cannot know by rhetoric when and where he is to persuade, but will necessarily believe as a rhetorician that rhetoric is unlimited in its scope, he cannot know by rhetoric that he is to obey the statesman.

Does the statesman use a mythology of his own invention to persuade the rhetorician? He surely could not ask the rhetorician to write up a myth about his own inferiority. The statesman could, of course, force the rhetorician to obey, but even if the statesman knows when force is to be used, he does not have the force in his own art (cf. 297a4–5). If the justice which the rhetorician is to persuade the many of is the justice of the statesman, he would have to persuade them of the justice of a justice which is indifferent as to whether it is persuasive or not, and which is careless of its agreement with the law. But since this is an impossible assignment, for it leaves the law without support, the rhetorician must speak on behalf of the law against the statesman. This is no less impossible. The rhetorician, then, if he is to consist

with the statesman, must know how to make the justice of the statesman look like the justice of the law even if they are in conflict with
one another. A law-abiding rhetorician could not fulfill this delicate
task; a lawless rhetorician would not. The statesman seems to be in
need of the *dêmologikos,* the public version of the ironic sophist, who
would suspect that the law does not know what it pretends to know.
It would be difficult to say whether the tragic or the comic poet is
more ironical, and which would better serve the statesman's interests.

The statesman can show himself to be more independent of the
law in his conduct of the city's foreign affairs. The law has much less
to say about them than about things closer to home. Indeed, the law
has built into itself a bias which works for the statesman. It must
distinguish between citizen and stranger, and it grants the stranger
no rights, only revocable privileges. Whether there is to be war or
peace with the stranger is not the province of the general, whose art
only begins once war has been decided on. The stranger means that
the statesman could equally start a war which the general knows the
city must lose and call off a war which needs one more battle to win.
Although it is no less doubtful whether there is a rhetorical art, the
stranger only casts doubt on the artfulness of the martial powers,
which young Socrates believes all martial action proves to be the case.
Warfare, one might have supposed, proves just the opposite; art then
takes a backseat to chance. The art of war must have a very narrow
range, sandwiched in as it is between what it cannot and what it should
not control. This puts the general on campaign in an awkward spot.
If his opponent offers to surrender the night before a battle, must
he wait until the absent statesman gives him the word? The stranger,
moreover, does not call young Socrates' attention to the fact that a
general rules an army and hence more nearly duplicates the statesman's work than either judge or rhetorician. The general, if a sophist,
is the tyrant. He poses the greatest threat to the statesman, for they
necessarily agree that art is not incompatible with force. A city, after
all, is most like a herd when it has been marshalled into troops. Homer
calls Agamemnon the shepherd of men.

The judiciary, or the third branch of the statesman's government,
cannot consist with the statesman's governance. It decides cases solely
on the basis of the laws of the legislator-king, and the stranger does
not even mention that it is incompetent to decide whether a case is
to be judged according to the law. The judges' virtue is their law-
abidingness (305b7–c3); the stranger does not say that they have any
knowledge. The law, of course, could make an exception of the king—
"the king can do no wrong"—but it cannot be so framed as to make

an exception of the true king and no one else. The true king does not act, he rules, for he rules even when he does not rule.

Young Socrates could not be more indifferent to the feasibility of the stranger's proposals, though, in a sense, the stranger has made none. Neither the structure of the city nor the education of its citizens has been alluded to, whereas the very nature of the statesman's wisdom precludes its description (cf. 306a5–7, d9–10). His wisdom can only be shown in action, but the true king does not act. This is the paradox under which the *Statesman* has been laboring from the start. Political science can alone ground the judgment of the most experienced politician about what should be done today, but it can only ground his judgment in a way most alien to the city and its politicians. Political science knows the city without being of the city; its roots are elsewhere. The city is a whole whose parts the statesman knows how to weave together, but no weaver has ever been an element of his own web.

XIII. Virtue
(305e8–307d5)

The *Statesman* is more profound than the *Sophist*. Nothing shows it more plainly than the analysis of virtue in each. In the *Sophist*, the moral vices are likened to disease by way of the sameness of disease and civil faction or stasis. Though nothing is said about it, the likeness assumes that the restoration of health in one respect will not interfere with its restoration in another. In the *Statesman*, however, the stranger can only bring out the statesman's own work, which cannot be delegated, by revealing the hatred and faction which obtain between courage and moderation as they are popularly understood. The cure the art of punishment effects is merely a more refined disease. Virtue consists in the fraternal strife of the beautiful with the beautiful. Young Socrates no more understands this than Theaetetus understood that of the two vices in soul one is like disease and the other like ugliness in body. He certainly does not notice that the beautiful has crossed lines and replaced health as the standard of morality. The stranger remarks that the sophists, or those whose imitation of virtue is not without a certain doubleness, find the supposed simplicity of virtue easily assailable. A part of virtue is somewhat at variance with a kind of virtue.

Not surprisingly, young Socrates does not catch the stranger's allusion to his earlier reproof of young Socrates, when he took him to task for mistaking every part for a kind. Even when the stranger asks him whether he recalls how keenness and speed are praised, young

Socrates still does not get it—that the stranger praised him for his division of herd animals into men and beasts as showing his surpassing courage. But young Socrates can be forgiven; the stranger did not sound as if he were then uttering praise. And if it were praise, it was praise of human pride, to which the distinction between men and beasts is ultimately due. Manliness, however, if carried to an extreme, is indistinguishable from bestiality, and of bestiality only men are capable. Through the willful absolutization of the relative "other," men come to recognize themselves. Human pride is both blindness and insight. It pretends to have overcome the bestial and thus acknowledges the necessity that the bestial be overcome. It is this tacit acknowledgment which permits one to conclude that the stranger's rebuke of young Socrates for his courage was ironical.

In contrast, the stranger's praise of Theaetetus in the *Sophist* for his having accepted the existence of a divine maker is much more straightforward. Theaetetus did not need to be humiliated in order to put man in his place. Courage discovers the distinction between man and beast, moderation acknowledges at a glance the distinction between man and god. These two virtues indeterminately fix between them the human. Moderation without courage must lapse into self-contempt, for pig and man are equally god's artifacts or god's subjects; but courage without moderation must lapse into atheism, for nothing would be higher for it than man. Man, then, is in his excellence the representative of the other. He is simultaneously other than god and other than beast. So the stranger, when called upon to expound his answer to Socrates' initial question, adopted a position midway between shamelessness and savagery, and therefore neither delivered a monologue nor kept silent.[71] Dialectics, it seems, is the practice of resolving the strife between moderation and courage. In order, however, for this practice to become manifest to others, there must of necessity be two dialogues, as the action of each moves each toward the other in a direction contrary to the other's, and away from the boundary definition of man which it itself presupposes and the other initially denies. The *Sophist* and the *Statesman* are only one in their interweaving. They constitute the *logos* which is the plaiting of kinds.

The stranger was able to reduce justice to wisdom through an argument that eliminated the lawful from any place in the strict definition of the just. But when confronted with moderation and courage, he does not even attempt to show that any course of action which is popularly labeled moderate or courageous should strictly be called wise. Apparently because hardly anyone would take either of these virtues to be separately the whole of virtue—an ascription not at all implausible for justice—the stranger does not invoke the standard of the wise man's judgment. And yet if praise of a noble action is based on the recognition of what the given circumstances properly call for, moderation and courage must together be the measure of the mean. The measure of the mean, then, must be in practice double, and only single in speech. Any given, whether it be a field for action or for thought, must be so infected with the nature of the other that it is impossible for us simply to start with the mean and then to realize it. Nature might herself be neutral, but her apparitions are always skewed and cluster around either one of two partial kinds. Male and female are the plainest examples of this duality, just as moderation and courage, as the very name in the latter case indicates (manliness), are in common opinion their disjoint perfections. Despite the fact that no motion, force, or weight, no matter how great, can be considered to be entirely apart from any other, no matter how small, a middle stretch of no merit whatever separates praiseworthy quickness from praiseworthy inertia, praiseworthy intensity from praiseworthy laxness, and praiseworthy heaviness from praiseworthy levity. This middle stretch, which has something in common with an arithmetical mean, is the negative standard in light of which moderation and courage are discerned, and in whose absence not only would neither appear beautiful but moderation and courage would be wholly disjoint and without any influence on one another.

It is against the grain of moderation for moderation to be praised, for the praise of safety and caution is itself immoderate, since it necessarily borrows its intensity and vehemence (*sphodrotês*), without which it would cease to be praise and become instead a back-handed compliment, from the class to which moderation is opposed.[72] When the stranger asks whether we do not often praise the class of gradual becoming, young Socrates' assent has a trace of manly vigor (*kai sphodra ge*).[73] Moderation thereby shows its inadequacy in isolation, to say nothing of the need for courage to hold it back from sliding into excessive softness. To picture, then, moderation and courage as the endpoints of a linear magnitude would be misleading, for the magnitude extends beyond each point into vice, from which each virtue is only checked by the other (fig. 3). This picture, however, is in turn misleading, for it does not bring out that on any occasion when one of the virtues is praised, the other virtue is necessarily swallowed up in the class of the "other," even though cowardice (*anandreia*) is not moderation,[74] nor immoderation (*akolasia*) courage (fig. 4).

The bond between moderation and courage consists in the indifferent continua out of which they both arise. These continua are made known to us through the relative measures of mathematics, in terms

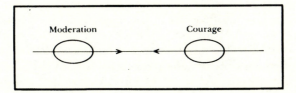

Figure 3

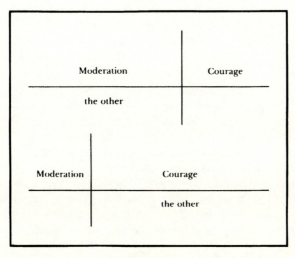

Figure 4

of which moderation and courage seem to be in some definite ratio to one another. But since more than one property of bodies in motion shows up in either virtue, the mutual coherence of these properties in a kind lies outside the scope of any arithmetic to determine. Motion, force, and weight are in themselves independent variables; they can only become dependent if the class characteristic of either virtue is in principle not arithmetical, however easy it might always be to fix numerical values, which will not always be spuriously Pythagorean, to every manifestation of courage and moderation. The measure of the mean, indeed, cannot dispense with the arithmetical measure. There is, after all, some connection between the beautiful and mathematical proportion. The "matter" of the virtues is a reminder that the soul, even in its completion, is not all things. Moderation and courage in their apartness point to the partiality of the soul's experiences. They are the joint measure of our ignorance. Their apparent duality is a sign of the true duality in the science of metrics, whose unity, the stranger implied, lies in the science of the precise itself. If we correctly identified the precise itself with the idea of the good, then the ultimate problem is the unresolved tension between the doubleness of the beautiful and the oneness of the good.[75]

The beautiful is double in a twofold way—for the soul, in the opposition of two kinds of virtue, and for knowledge, in the opposition of two kinds of metrics. The relation between them is again determined by the nature of the other, for the arithmetical measure is for knowledge one of two kinds, while for soul it binds and separates two kinds of virtue from which it is itself excluded. So were we to use the paradigm of letters, the mathematicals would be a vowel between two consonants in the case of soul, but in the case of knowledge, a consonant. The soul can thus be whole while knowledge for us cannot, for the philosopher's dialectic practice keeps together that which in speech stands apart. Virtue is and is not knowledge. One contradiction Socrates told Theaetetus he would experience if he laid down the sameness of knowledge and perception, namely, that one could then know the same thing intensely or slightly, now turns out to be the fundamental opposition within virtue.[76]

Theaetetus and young Socrates are united in their knowledge and separate in their natures. The stranger's practice consisted in the attempt to unite them in virtue. In the *Sophist,* he worked against the bias of Theaetetus' moderate nature, which made him take for granted man's tameness, by encouraging him to track down the elusive beast, the sophist. In the *Statesman,* he worked against the bias of young Socrates' courageous nature, which made him take for granted man's rationality, by forcing him to submit to the ordeal of a descent to the cave. Theaetetus' moderation had to be enlivened by scepticism, young Socrates' courage had to be disciplined by authority. The stranger's homeopathic medicine, however, is not an unqualified success. Theaetetus' nature finally reasserts itself in his belief in a divine maker, and it would not be surprising if young Socrates, after a single lesson, likewise reverted. Perhaps we would need the *Philosopher* to know for sure, but the consequences of excessive moderation certainly appall young Socrates more than the consequences of excessive courage (308a3, b1).

XIV. BONDS
(307d6–311c8)

The friendship between Theaetetus and young Socrates does not impress the stranger. It is not as if they had first to overcome the enmity to which their different natures would naturally provoke them before they joined together in solving a geometrical problem. They were not even aware of the possibility of conflict, and the stranger wisely conversed with them separately lest the difference between what each would praise or blame should ever distract either from his proper education.[77] They only participated in the same *logos* through the mediation of the stranger. As mathematicians their difference was not serious, for it could never lead to anything more than mock warfare, but politically, their difference is equivalent to the difference between a martial and a peace-loving people. A city of Theaetetuses minds its own business and is inclined to treat other cities as it treats its own citizens. It ignores the otherness of the stranger, for it easily loses sight of its own partiality as a part. Moved by the spirit of accommodation, such a city ends up enslaved, its unwilled and inadvertent cowardice hardly separable from its stupidity. A city of young Socrateses, in contrast, looks at every other city as its enemy. It knows nothing of the difference between a potential and an actual enemy. Its insight is too keen. The otherness of the stranger is for it so absolute that it must be constantly engaged in war, until it brings upon itself either its enslavement or destruction. The stranger disregards the possibility that such a city might never fail and thus achieve a universal empire. But apart from the difficulty that it would then be forced to turn against itself if it were not to give up its own nature, the myth has taught us that God alone is capable of universal rule, and even he is periodically forced to abandon control. Excessive moderation, then, is more a danger to the city than the hubris of courage. The nature of things is more disposed to check the tyranny of a part over the whole than the enslavement of a part to a part. We perhaps might believe that the stranger in this regard is a shade too hopeful.

Every science of composition is necessarily a kind of cathartics, for it rejects as far as it can everything that is base and worthless.[78] Hardly does the stranger apply this rule to "our truly natural political science" than he seems to contradict it. The city which the royal art puts together does execute, exile, or disgrace those natures which are forcibly pushed toward atheism, hubris, and injustice; but those who wallow in excessive ignorance and humility, it enslaves. The city cannot afford excessive courage; it cannot dispense with excessive moderation. Slaves, however, are not part of the cloak which the statesman weaves, even though such a cloak is designed to clothe everyone in the city, both slave and free (311c3–4). The city enjoys the result of the statesman's weaving, but it itself is not the statesman's web. The stranger distinguishes between the life in which the moderate and courageous share and the bonding of the entire city. Moderation alone, in the form of obedience, binds the city together, and therefore the city, as a whole, cannot strictly be said to be happy.[79] But not even the ruling part of the city is a seamless whole. The self-binding of moderation and courage, which the paradigm of weaving implies, cannot be accomplished politically. The stranger replaces self-binding with a double bond (*desmos*), true opinion and marriage.

The lawful education of moderate and courageous natures does not alter the nature of either, anymore than the recommended type of their intermarriage guarantees that their offspring will exhibit the proper mixture of moderation and courage. The ruling part of the city is always in need of a ruler, for in his absence there can only be a harmony of opposing families. Intermarriage and common opinion cannot eliminate but can only soften the brutal resolution of conflicting interests which would otherwise occur. The stranger's solution, then, really amounts to this: the true king assigns the members of courageous families to the city's army, and the members of moderate families to its lawcourts.[80] The army has been tamed enough so as not to turn against its fellow citizens, and the judges are by law restricted to the internal affairs of the city. But the stranger does not even hint at which families are to supply the rhetoricians of the city.

The double bond of the city's ruling families originates in soul. The stranger calls one the eternal, the other the animal-born part of the soul. We can call the first pure mind, the second *erôs*. The stranger assures young Socrates that once the law has instilled the same true opinions about the beautiful, good, and just things in both kinds of families, the human bonds of marriage are easily conceived and effected. But he makes it much clearer what the obstacles are to intermarriage than how the statesman is to overcome them. Since he assumes that like attracts and unlike repels, he argues that each kind follows the path of least resistance, seeking out its own nature and rejecting with loathing that nature which in the long run would save itself from either madness, if it is courageous, or imbecility, if it is moderate. The statesman can of course arrange the most suitable marriages, but he cannot make the partners love one another, however much each couple might be convinced that their marriage is good for the city and their own families. Insofar as *erôs* is love of the beautiful, and not identical with sexual desire, these most suitable marriages are against the grain of *erôs*. And, likewise, since the divine bond of the city consists of opinions about the beautiful, just, and good, which are for the wise statesman nothing but prescriptions for the health of the city, the city through the law incorporates in its ruling families as little satisfaction of the requirements of pure mind as of the needs of *erôs*.

The law, said the stranger, is like a stupid and willful human being.

We now know what this means. The law combines the vice of moderation with the vice of courage and thus passes itself off as the perfect weaving into the web of justice of the beautiful with the beautiful. But the true synergy of mind and *erôs* in soul was the impure dialectics of Socrates, and Socrates is about to go on trial.

Notes

1. "Acquaintance" (*gnôrisis*) also occurred in the list of acquisitive arts at *Sophist* 219C ("familiarization").

2. Theodorus seems to be correcting himself, and crediting Socrates' memory rather than his justice; for a possible explanation see the commentary. But *panu men oun* remains difficult; see Denniston, *Greek Particles*² (Oxford 1954), p. 480; des Places, *Études sur quelques particules de liaison chez Platon* (Paris, 1929), p. 118.

3. After his first speech, the young Socrates is identified throughout as Socrates.

4. For a discussion of this distinction, see *Gorgias* 450B–E.

5. It is not clear whether the stranger alludes to physicians employed by a city or simply to practicing physicians; cf. *Gorgias* 514D–E.

6. At the beginning of Aristotle's *Politics* (1252a7–16), there is the following comment on this passage: "All who believe anyone competent as statesman, king, household-manager, and slavemaster to be the same, do not speak beautifully (for they hold that they differ by multitude and fewness, and not that each of them differs by species. But if one rules a few, he's a slavemaster, if more, a household-manager, and if still more, a statesman or king. And a statesman and a king differ by this, whenever he's on his own while in charge, he's a king, but whenever he rules and is ruled in turn according to the rules of such a science, he's a statesman. But these things are not true.)"

7. "Strength of soul" is not a common expression; cf. Xenophon *Memorabilia* IV.viii.1.

8. "Natural joint" (*diaphuê*) designates at *Phaedo* 98C the separation of bones from one another which are linked together by the sinews. Although it looks as if it here means a separation, it turns out to mean no less a bonding, as all words with *dia* (either "through" or "apart") tend

III.150

to do. "A natural conjoint disjoint joint" would thus be a more precise translation.

9. Logistics is distinguished from arithmetic in the *Gorgias* (451B–C) by the fact that, though both deal with odd and even, "logistics examines the odd and even with regard to their multitude, how they (the even and the odd) are in relation to themselves and one another." For a fuller discussion, see J. Klein, *Greek Mathematical Thought and the Origins of Algebra* (Cambridge, 1968), pp. 17–25.

10. "Grazing" is meant to bring out the root in the second half of the compound *pezonomikê* (**nem*), which means to distribute in a regular fashion and referred primarily to grazing lands, but it was extended to the management of herds. A herdsman is a *nomeus*. The words for law (*nomos*) and coinage (*nomisma*) are cognates.

11. This translates the text; Burnet reads with Ast "as just now number."

12. For mules, see *Apology of Socrates* 27C–E.

13. The diagonal of the unit square is called its diameter; the square built on the diagonal, whose "power" is the square root of two, yields a two-foot square. And if the diagonal of that square, which equals two feet, is used to form another square, its area is four square feet. The slave in the *Meno* has this explained to him by Socrates.

14. The word for "last" (*hustaton*) puns on the word for "pig" (*hus*); "things wind" is intended to reproduce this.

15. Odysseus' faithful swineherd Eumaeus, whom Homer calls "lord of men," should be kept in mind, as well as Circe's transformation of Odysseus' men into pigs, "though their mind remained intact." Cf. *Republic* 535E.

16. For the language, cf. *Republic* 507A.

17. The original division is shown in the figure on page 152. The summary does not acknowledge the distinction between footed and dry land, but uses pedestrial to cover both, just as in the shorter way. Cf. *Sophist* 223B.

18. For the language, cf. *Theaetetus* 149A–151D; *Sophist* 267A.

19. The word "portent" was translated as "hallucination" at *Theaetetus* 155A. In the dispute over the succession to the kingdom of the Pelopidae, Hermes is said to have put a golden ram among Atreus' flock, but Thyestes pesuaded Atreus' wife to give it to him; so Zeus reversed the course of the sun to confirm Atreus' right. The story is summarized in a choral ode of Euripides' *Orestes* (988–1006) and at greater length in his *Electra* (699–745).

20. Herodotus refers to an Egyptian story about the exchange of east and west for the rising and setting of the sun; it is said to have occurred four times, but without any effect on life (II.142.4; cf. 26.2).

21. The age of Cronus, whom his son Zeus bound, is the golden age; cf. Hesiod *Works and Days* 111–22. The age of Zeus corresponds to the iron age, the fifth of Hesiod's ages. Hesiod implies that there is a cycle

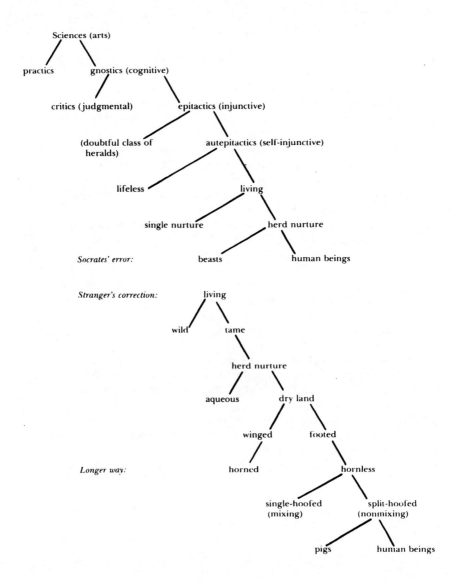

Sciences (arts)

practics   gnostics (cognitive)

critics (judgmental)   epitactics (injunctive)

(doubtful class of heralds)   autepitactics (self-injunctive)

lifeless   living

single nurture   herd nurture

Socrates' error: beasts   human beings

Stranger's correction: living

wild   tame

herd nurture

aqueous   dry land

winged   footed

Longer way: horned   hornless

single-hoofed (mixing)   split-hoofed (nonmixing)

pigs   human beings

Shorter way: footed

four feet   two feet

winged   wingless

of ages; cf. *Republic* 546E–547A; *Laws* 713C–714A (cf. especially 713D with 271E here).

22. The earth-born are usually identified with the giants, as in the stranger's gigantomachy (*Sophist* 248C). See further *Symposium* 190B.
23. An almost perfect tragic trimeter is in the words "pair of gods . . . round"; cf. *Phaedo* 60C for an embedded hexameter in a mythical passage.
24. The "foot" refers presumably to the central axis of the universe or to the center of the sphere.
25. This is Burnet's text; the manuscripts have "as now" after "whole," but nothing for "and likewise."
26. Either the text is corrupt or Plato has extended the intransitive verb "fall" to take some kind of internal accusative, as in the translation.
27. If something reverses its circular motion, the point of reversal is the end of its former motion and the beginning and end of its present motion.
28. The stranger alludes primarily to Demeter and Dionysus.
29. In Aristophanes' *Lysistrata* (565–86), Lysistrata argues for the competence of women in ruling the city as follows.

> MAGISTRATE: How are all you women capable of putting a stop to so many disturbed matters among countries and disentangling them?
>
> LYSISTRATA: It's quite trivial.
>
> M: How? Show me.
>
> L: Just like a ball of wool, when we've tangled it all up, we handle it this way: by means of spindles we carry it out hither and yon, so too we'll loosen the war, if no one interferes, by dispersing it through embassies hither and yon.
>
> M: From wool, and balls, and spindles, you believe, you idiots, you'll put a stop to terrible things?
>
> L: Yes, and what's more, if you had any sense, everything political would be managed on the basis of wool.
>
> M: How's that? Let me see how.
>
> L: First off, you should, just as you would with newly shorn fleece, wash out the sheep dung from the city in the washroom, stretch the rascals on a bed and scourge them, pick off the burrs, and card thoroughly those matted coalitions which aim at rule and pluck their head-clumps. Secondly, gather into a basket the shared good will of all, mixing together the metics, any friendly stranger, and anyone who solely owes money to the treasury; and, by Zeus, the cities, those which are your colonies, adjudicate with discernment, because they now severally lie apart like flock. And then from all of them take a great clew, and out of this weave a cloak for the people.

30. The recapitulation does not keep to the original differentiation, for seamlessly whole envelopments came after coverings, which in turn were distinguished from shelters.
31. It is half the art of combing because the comb is also used to force the

woof threads together. Here its purpose is to disentangle warp and woof threads; cf. *Cratylus* 388A–B.

32. The "was" seems to be an allusion to *Sophist* 226C. The dashes after "woolworking itself" and "(diacritics)" indicate that the stranger breaks off the correlative to "both" before completing the thought in a different way in his next speech.

33. "Modes of being and judging" translates the plural *ousiai* (beings) and *kriseis. Ousia* in the plural (except in the meaning "property"), though common in Aristotle, occurs only once elsewhere in Plato (*Parmenides* 149E).

34. Cf. *Phaedrus* 250B–C.

35. The function of pottery in artifacts of this class is obscure; it possibly may refer to baby commodes and thus explain "dishonored."

36. Cf. *Laws* 918B.

37. The king archon was in charge of the mysteries and the Lenaean Dionysia; he also arranged all torch races, "and to exaggerate a little he manages all the ancestral sacrifices" (Aristotle *Constitution of the Athenians* 57). A sign of the antiquity of the office, to which Aristotle refers, is the marriage of the king archon's wife with Dionysus (3). Cf. Xenophon *Constitution of the Spartans* 15.5.

38. *Iliad* XI.514. Homer has *allôn* ("different") instead of "others" (*heterôn*); it is quoted correctly at *Symposium* 214B.

39. *Kurbeis* were wooden pillars on which Solon's laws were originally inscribed. It is chosen, along with the phrase "long ships" (the old-fashioned warship prior to the trireme), in order to indicate the consequences for technical advance if the stranger's proposal was adopted; cf. Thucydides I.14.

40. Cf. *Cratylus* 401B; *Phaedrus* 269E; *Parmendies* 135D; *Republic* 488E; *Lovers* 132B.

41. Cf. Thucydides I.84.3; III.37.3–4.

42. A second sailing is to use oars instead of wind; it is proverbial for those who are thwarted in their first choice. Cf. *Phaedo* 99C; *Philebus* 19C.

43. Diès reads, "that the names of what are now spoken of as regimes have proved to be only five," arguing that "one" (*hen*) is a misreading of the letter sign for five (*epsilon*).

44. An alternative translation would be, "would manage with happiness the only right regime."

45. "Adamant" may be diamond, but cf. *Timaeus* 59B.

46. "Rhetoric" is here *rhêtoreia* (not elsewhere in Plato) rather than the expected *rhêtorikê;* the difference is not clear, unless the stranger wishes to imply that it is not an art. A more common pair of quasi synonyms is *manteia* and *mantikê* ("divination"); cf. *Symposium* 202E.

47. The last clause could be translated without "different," if enmity and friendship were thought not to include the previous items.

48. The hyperbaton of "nature" recalls that at *Sophist* 258A–B. But unlike that one it cannot be translated without admitting hyperbaton; so if hy-

perbaton is disallowed, it would have to be emended to read "parts of virtue dissimilar by nature."

49. The phrase is deleted by those editors who do not accept a slight correction by Campbell.

50. Editors have often assigned this last speech to (old) Socrates, but a comparison of the stranger's remark and young Socrates' reply at 275A shows this to be unnecessary (cf. 277A).

COMMENTARY

1. *Theaetetus* 155d9–e2; cf. *Protagoras* 310a5–7.
2. *Charmides* 169a7–b5.
3. *Theaetetus* 175c5.
4. *Republic* 529c4–5. *Metienai* as to exact vengeance is not uncommon in tragic poetry.
5. *Theaetetus* 169c5.
6. Herodotus 2.42.3–4; Jacoby on Hecataeus of Abdera, fr. 4, p. 45 in *Die Fragmente der griechischen Historiker* (Leiden, 1964), Dritter Teil a, Kommentar zu Nr. 262–91.
7. *Theaetetus* 146b4–6.
8. *Sophist* 218a2.
9. *Sophist* 218b1–4.
10. *Sophist* 261b5–c4.
11. *Sophist* 267e4–6, 268b11–12.
12. *Philebus* 56b4–c3.
13. *Republic* 527a1–b2.
14. *Symposium* 186c5–d5.
15. *Gorgias* 521d6–8.
16. *Lysis* 210a9–c5.
17. Xenophon *Symposium* ii.9–10.
18. Aristotle *Politics* 1252a6–16.
19. Contemplation (*thea*) and judgment (*krisis*) are linked in a not dissimilar context at *Republic* 545c6–7.
20. *Sophist* 231d9–10.
21. This perhaps explains why the stranger uses *diestêken* ("separates") and *aphestêken* ("stands away from") at 260c7 and

261a3, terms that do not occur in the *Sophist* for divisions.
22. *Symposium* 197c3–6; *Republic* 395c1.
23. *Republic* 458d5.
24. *Republic* 343b1–c1.
25. *Republic* 451c8.
26. *Sophist* 254c7–8.
27. *Sophist* 216c6.
28. Herodotus II.181.
29. Thucydides I.84.3.
30. *Historia animalium* 608b29–609a2.
31. *Encyclopedia Britannica* (11th ed.), art. Mule, p. 959.
32. *Sophist* 268b7–9.
33. Cf. 268b1–5 with *Symposium* 215b8–d1.
34. *Republic* 499b5.
35. *Philebus* 28c6–e6.
36. *Theaetetus* 180c1.
37. *Republic* 496c3–5.
38. *Philebus* 62b5–9, 61a7–b3.
39. *Sophist* 226e8–227c9.
40. *Theaetetus* 175b3; *Sophist* 227b6; *Lysis* 210e4; *Laws* 728e4, *Epistle* 7, 341e5.
41. *Sophist* 237b4–6.
42. *Cratylus* 432b1–d3.
43. *Sophist* 241d5–e5.
44. *Republic* 528a9–b5.
45. *Phaedo* 99c6–d2.
46. *Laws* 794d5–e4.
47. *Republic* 370c8–9.
48. *Sophist* 234b1–2.

49. *Laws* 804b3–c1.
50. *Republic* 373d4–e8.
51. *Sophist* 222b6–c8.
52. *Republic* 371e12–372a4.
53. *Constitution of Athens* 3.2.
54. *Laches* 198e2–199a5; Aristotle *Politics* 1328b11–12.
55. Herodotus III.79.3–80.1.
56. *Symposium* 182c7–d2.
57. *Republic* 561e3–7.
58. *Theaetetus* 173c8–d4.
59. *Republic* 473a1–4.
60. *Republic* 556d7–e1.
61. *Republic* 333a10–b10.
62. *Republic* 341e2–6.
63. *Gorgias* 464a3–b1.
64. *Gorgias* 456b1–5.
65. *Apology of Socrates* 30b3.
66. *Laws* 627d11–628a5.
67. Herodotus III.31.
68. Cf. *Mishnah*, Sanhedrin 16.3 (tr. H. Danby [London, 1933], p. 400): "Greater stringency applies to [the observance of] the words of the Scribes than to [the observance of] the words of the [written] laws."
69. *Laws* 709e6.
70. *Laws* 820d1–2.
71. *Sophist* 217d8–218a3.
72. Thucydides II.45.2.
73. *Philebus* 24b9–c6.
74. *Republic* 560d3.
75. The first of Aristotle's perplexities in *Metaphysics* B concerns the unity of wisdom, a unity which first seems implausible because of the tension between the beautiful (rest) and the good (motion), and then because of the tension between the good and being (996a21–996b1; 996b10–26; cf. 1078a31–b5).
76. *Theaetetus* 165d5.
77. Socrates could converse with Glaucon and Adeimantus, who correspond somewhat to young Socrates and Theaetetus respectively, partly because they were brothers.
78. *Sophist* 227d6–7.
79. *Republic* 420b4–8.
80. Perhaps one could consider the use Hyrcanus made of the Sadducees and the Pharisees as an example of this arrangement. For the vices inherent in courage and moderation when apart, see Tacitus' presentation of Drusus and Germanicus in the first book of the *Annals*.

Selected Bibliography

BIBLIOGRAPHIES

Brisson, L. "Platon, 1958–75." *Lustrum* 20. Göttingen, 1977.
Cherniss, H. "Platon, 1950–57." *Lustrum* 4, 5. Göttingen, 1959–60.
McKirahan, R. D. *Plato and Socrates: A Comprehensive Bibliography, 1958–1973*. New York, 1978.

EDITIONS, TRANSLATIONS, COMMENTARIES

Allen, R. E. *Studies in Plato's Metaphysics*. New York, 1965.
Apelt, O. *Platonis Sophista*. Leipzig, 1897.
————. *Platons Dialog Politikos oder vom Staatsman²*. Leipzig, 1922.
Bluck, R. S. *Plato's Sophist: A Commentary*, ed. G. C. Neal. Manchester, 1975.
Burnet, J. *Platonis Opera I–V*. Oxford, 1901.
Campbell, L. *The Sophistes and Politicus of Plato*, with a revised text and English notes. Oxford, 1867.
————. *The Theaetetus of Plato*, with a revised text and English notes. Oxford, 1871.
Cornford, F. M. *Plato's Theory of Knowledge: The Theaetetus and the Sophist of Plato*, translated with a running commentary. London, 1935.
Diès, A. *Théétète*. Vol. 8, part 2 of *Platon oeuvres completes*. Paris, 1924.
————. *Le Sophiste*. Vol. 8, part 3 of *Platon oeuvres completes*. Paris, 1925.
————. *Le Politique*. Vol. 9 of *Platon oeuvres completes*. Paris, 1935.
Klein, J. *Plato's Trilogy*. Chicago, 1977.
McDowell, J. *Plato's Theaetetus*. Oxford, 1973.
Manasse, E. M. *Platons Sophistes und Politikos: Das Problem der Wahrheit*. Berlin, 1937.
Miller, M. H. *The Philosopher in Plato's Statesman*. The Hague, 1980.
Skemp, J. B. *Plato's Statesman*. New Haven, 1952.
Taylor, A. E. *The Sophist and the Statesman*, ed. R. Klibansky and E. Anscombe. Edinburgh, 1961.

Vlastos, G. *Plato: A Collection of Critical Essays.* Vol. 1: *Metaphysics.* Notre Dame, 1971.

ARTICLES

The items are keyed to the sections of the *Theaetetus* and *Sophist* in the commentary.

Theaetetus

146c7–147c6

Bierman, A. K. "Socratic Humour: Understanding the Most Important Philosophical Argument." *Apeiron* 5 (1971): 23–42.

151d7–157a7

Bluck, R. S., "The Puzzles of Size and Number in Plato's *Theaetetus*," *Proceedings of the Cambridge Philological Society,* n.s. 7 (1961): 7–9.

162b8–171e9

Lee, E. M. "Hoist with His Own Petard: Ironic and Comic Elements in Plato's Critique of Protagoras (*Tht.* 161–171)." *Phronesis Supplement* 1 (1973): 225–61.

183c5–187c6

Bondeson, W. B. "Perception, True Opinion, and Knowledge in Plato's *Theaetetus*." *Phronesis* 14 (1969): 111–22.

Burnyeat, M. F. "Plato on the Grammar of Perceiving." *Classical Quarterly* 26 (1976): 29–51.

Cooper, J. M. "Plato on Sense-Perception and Knowledge (*Theaetetus* 184–186)." *Phronesis* 15 (1970): 123–46.

187c7–190e4

Ackrill, J. "Plato on False Belief (*Theaetetus* 187–200)." *Monist* 50 (1966): 383–402.

Fine, G. J. "False Belief in the *Theaetetus*." *Phronesis* 24 (1979): 70–80.

90e5–196c3

Deicke, W., "*Theaetetus* 192c10." *Phronesis* 9 (1964): 136–42.

196c4–210c7

Lee, H. D. P. "The Aviary Simile in the *Theaetetus*." *Classical Quarterly* 33 (1939): 208–11.

200c8–206b12

Burnyeat, M. F. "The Material and Source of Plato's Dream." *Phronesis* 15 (1970) 101–22.

Hicken, W. F. "Knowledge and Forms in Plato's *Theaetetus*." *Journal of Hellenic Studies* 77 (1957): 48–53.

Meyerhoff, H. "Socrates' Dream in the *Theaetetus*." *Classical Quarterly,* n.s. 8 (1958): 131–38.

Rorty, A. O. "A Speculative Note on Some Dramatic Elements in the *Theaetetus.*" *Phronesis* 17 (1972): 227–38.

206c1–206b10

Bondeson, W. B. "The Dream of Socrates and the Conclusion of the *Theaetetus.*" *Apeiron* 3 (1969): 1–13.

Fine, G. J. "Knowledge and Logos in the *Theaetetus.*" *Philosophical Review* 88 (1979): 366–97.

Sophist

226a6–231b8

Booth, N. B. "Plato *Sophist* 231a, etc." *Classical Quarterly*, n.s. 6 (1956): 89–90.

Gooch, P. W. "Vice Is Ignorance: The Interpretation of *Sophist* 226A–231B." *Phoenix* 25 (1971): 124–33.

Kerferd, G. B. "Plato's Noble Art of Sophistry." *Classical Quarterly*, n.s. 4 (1954): 84–90.

Skemp, J. B. "Plato *Sophistes* 230e–231b." *Proceedings of the Cambridge Philological Society*, n.s. 2 (1952–53): 8–9.

231b9–236c8

Bondeson, W. "Plato's *Sophist:* Falsehoods and Images." *Apeiron* 6 (1972): 1–6.

239b1–241b4

Kohnke, F. W. "Plato's Conception of *to ouk ontôs ouk on.*" *Phronesis* 2 (1957): 32–40.

Peck, A. L. "Plato and the Megista Gene of the *Sophist:* A Reinterpretation." *Classical Quarterly*, n.s. 2 (1952): 32–56.

250d5–259d8

Ackrill, J. L. "Plato and the Copula: *Sophist* 215–259." *Journal of Hellenic Studies* 77 (1957): 1–6.

Gomez-Lobo, A. "Plato's Description of Dialectic in the *Sophist* 253D1–E2." *Phronesis* 22 (1977): 29–47.

Lee, E. N. "Plato on Negation and Not-being in the *Sophist.*" *Philosophical Review* 81 (1972): 267–304.

Waletzki, W. "Platons Ideenlehre und Dialektik im *Sophistes* 253d." *Phronesis* 24 (1979): 241–52.

259d9–264d9

Bluck, R. S. "False Statement in the *Sophist.*" *Journal of Hellenic Studies* 77 (1957): 181–86.

Lorenz, K., and Mittelstrass, J. "Theaetetos fliegt: Zur Theorie wahre und falscher Sätze bei Platon (*Soph.* 251d–263d)." *Archiv für Geschichte der Philosophie* 47 (1966): 133–52.

Statesman

Rosen, S. "Plato's Myth of the Reversed Cosmos." *Review of Metaphysics* 33 (1979): 59–85.

Schuhl, P. M. "Sur le mythe du Politique." *Revue de Metaphysique et Morale* 39 (1932): 47–58.

Strauss, L. "Plato." In *History of Political Philosophy*, ed. L. Strauss and J. Cropsey, 2d ed., pp. 42–51. Chicago, 1972.

Index

Achilles, xxi, xxxviii–xxxix
Acquisitive art, II.79–83, 84, 88, 89, 91, III.107
Addition, and *logos*, I.189, II.115
Adimantus, xxiii, III.113
Admonition, art of, II.97–98
Aeschylus, II.165
Agamemnon, III.141
Alcibiades, xxiv, I.85, 90
Allo, xiii–xiv
Alphabet. *See* Letters
Anaxagoras, xxviii, II.113, 166
Angling, as paradigm, II.77–83, 84, 89, 91, 104, 111, III.83, 103, 106–7
Antaeus, II.71
Antinous, II.69
Anytus, I.150
Aphrodite, xxviii, xlii, II.141
Apollo, xlii
Apology of Socrates (Plato), xvi
Aristides, III.133
Aristocracy, III.124, 132, 137, 138
Aristophanes, xxx–xxxi, xliii, II.73, III.96–97
Aristoteles, I.160, II.76
Aristotle, xiv, xlix–l, I.145, II.137, 157, III.87, 91, 100, 123; on beauty, xxv, xxix; on dichotomy, II.148–49; *Politics*, of, III.118
Arithmetic, I.165, II.81, 102–3, 138, 161, III.75, 76, 77, 78, 79–80, 92, 105, 127. *See also* Mathematics and number
Arnaeus, II.72
Art(s): competence in, I.91; dichotomy of making and acquisitive, II.77, 79–83; duality of, II.149–50; and law, III.136–37; measure of the mean in,

III.116; midwifery as, I.99; progress in, and wisdom, xxi–xxiii, xxvii, xxxiii; and sciences, as knowledge, I.93–96, 104, 180, II.97, 150; sophistry as, II.83–84
Artemis, I.99–100
Artisan, as rival of statesman, III.102, 120–21
Astronomy, I.93, 122, 131, 136, 149, 180, II.103, 118, 164, III.116
Atekhnôs, xiv
Athena Parthenos, xxxi, II.72, 126; statue of, xxii, xxvii, xxviii–xxix, xxxv, II.111, 114
Athens, xxi, xviii, xxx, xxxiii, I.87, 88–89, 117, II.70; education in, II.97, 99, 131; regime in, I.129, III.77, 123, 124, 129, 139
Atomicity, I.115, 169, II.83, 113–15, 125–26
Atreus, III.96
Aural pleasure, as beauty, xl–xlvi
Autepitactics, III.108, 122–23
Autopôlikê, II.88–89
Aviary, paradigm of, I.149, 153, 155–56, 162–69, II.85

Barbarian and Greek, II.150–51, 155, III.86–87, 89, 90, 117, 129
Battle, II.89–90. *See also* Warfare
Beast and human, III.85–88, 90, 99, 100, 103–4, 114, 143
Beauty (the beautiful), xv, xix–xx, I.94; agreement compelled by, xxiii–xxiv, xxxvi; and bigness, xxix, xxxv, xxxix, II.109, 110–11, 152, III.71–72; burial as, xxii–xxxii; as cause, I.146; for cities, I.121; duality of, xxvi, xxvii,

531